THE CASE FOR THE EN1

CW00537788

The Case for the Enlightenment is an important and ambitious comparative study of the emergence of Enlightenment in Scotland and in Naples. Challenging the recent tendency to fragment the Enlightenment in eighteenth-century Europe into multiple Enlightenments, John Robertson demonstrates the extent to which thinkers in two societies at the opposite ends of Europe shared common intellectual preoccupations. Before 1700, Scotland and Naples faced a bleak future as backward, provincial kingdoms in a Europe of aggressive commercial states. Yet by 1760, Scottish and Neapolitan thinkers, led by David Hume and Antonio Genovesi, were in the van of those advocating the cause of Enlightenment by means of political economy. By study of the social and institutional contexts of intellectual life in the two countries, and the currents of thought promoted within them, *The Case for the Enlightenment* explains this transformation. At its centre is an examination of Giambattista Vico's *New Science* and David Hume's *Treatise of Human Nature* and *Natural History of Religion* as works informed by a similar, Epicurean moral philosophy, and as responses to the notorious argument of Pierre Bayle that a society of atheists was as plausible as a society of idolaters. Unexpected contemporaries, Vico and Hume illuminate the common intellectual foundations of Enlightenment in the two countries, in which Epicurean philosophy was the midwife of political economy.

JOHN ROBERTSON is University Lecturer in Modern History and a Fellow of St Hugh's College, Oxford.

IDEAS IN CONTEXT 73

The Case for the Enlightenment

IDEAS IN CONTEXT

Edited by Quentin Skinner and James Tully

The books in this series will discuss the emergence of intellectual traditions and of related new disciplines. The procedures, aims and vocabularies that were generated will be set in the context of the alternatives available within the contemporary frameworks of ideas and institutions. Through detailed studies of the evolution of such traditions, and their modification by different audiences, it is hoped that a new picture will form of the development of ideas in their concrete contexts. By this means, artificial distinctions between the history of philosophy, of the various sciences, of society and politics, and of literature may be seen to dissolve.

The series is published with the support of the Exxon Foundation.

A list of books in the series will be found at the end of the volume.

THE CASE FOR THE ENLIGHTENMENT

Scotland and Naples 1680–1760

JOHN ROBERTSON

CAMBRIDGE
UNIVERSITY PRESS

CAMBRIDGE UNIVERSITY PRESS
Cambridge, New York, Melbourne, Madrid, Cape Town, Singapore, São Paulo

Cambridge University Press
The Edinburgh Building, Cambridge CB2 8RU, UK

Published in the United States of America by Cambridge University Press, New York

www.cambridge.org
Information on this title: www.cambridge.org/9780521847872

First published 2005
Reprinted 2006
This digitally printed version (with corrections) 2007

A catalogue record for this publication is available from the British Library

ISBN 978-0-521-84787-2 hardback
ISBN 978-0-521-03572-9 paperback

Contents

Preface

The idea of this book had two origins: a remark by Arnaldo Momigliano that Edinburgh and Naples were good places from which to observe the legacy of feudalism in the eighteenth century, and a journey in 1978 through southern Italy in the company of my wife Maxine, my late brother Mark, and Norman Douglas's *Old Calabria*.[1] The latter's tales of flying monks and the pleasures of 'reposing at Castrovillari' were happily confirmed by observation and experience; but gradually I also appreciated the deeper affinity which Douglas felt as a Scot for the Italian south. Waiting the obligatory hours for the bus connection between the railway station for Matera and the city, itself still many miles distant, I was struck by a resemblance between the landscapes of Basilicata and the Scottish Highlands. In colour and natural aspect, of course, they could hardly be more different: by late September the hills of Basilicata are bleached white, turning lunar in appearance. Yet there was a historical, human reality in common: this too was a land once occupied by many more inhabitants, who had laboured for their lords until modern commercial agriculture had made the way of life redundant. In the event, neither feudalism nor the Highlands were to play more than a very small part in the book, and the truth of Momigliano's remark (to which I return only in the conclusion) remains to be properly investigated. Instead I became fascinated by why and how the Enlightenment should have come to two such distant and unpromising countries in the first place. The original intuition of a comparable social experience is still present in what follows, in the importance attached to political economy as a common interest of both the Scots and the Neapolitans. But the stimulus of others' scholarship has helped to enlarge the ambition of my enquiry, leading me to investigate the cultural resources and intellectual inspirations available to the two sets of philosophers, and particularly to attempt to understand the achievements of the most original of these, Giambattista Vico and David Hume.

[1] Norman Douglas, *Old Calabria* (1915; Harmondsworth, 1962).

ix

The idea of the book has in turn been given focus by its argument, which is with the now widespread conviction that it is impossible, or redundant, to think and write of 'the' Enlightenment as one coherent intellectual movement. No one has made this claim more cogently than John Pocock, and the title of this book is deliberately chosen to maintain a unitary conception of Enlightenment, in contradistinction to Pocock's preference for plural 'Enlightenments'. To argue with John Pocock, however, is more instructive than any agreement; this book is indebted alike to the inspiration of his scholarship and to the personal courtesy with which he has responded to my attempted challenge.

In preparing and writing a book so long in the gestation, I have inevitably acquired many other debts, institutional and personal. First among the former are my debts to St Hugh's College and to the Modern History Faculty at Oxford, which together have granted me the periods of sabbatical and other leave essential to research and writing. Within these are individuals whose willingness to shoulder extra burdens has been the necessary corollary of my freedom: the late Colin Matthew, George Garnett, and Senia Paseta at St Hugh's, and in the Faculty, Joanna Innes and Laurence Brockliss. The Bodleian, the National Library, and the National Archives of Scotland are wonderful places in which to work; once again I am grateful to their staff for their assistance, expertise, and courtesy. I also acknowledge with gratitude the award of a Senior Research Fellowship by the British Academy in 1996–97, and of four months of research leave by the Arts and Humanities Research Board in 2003. The former provided the opportunity to embed myself in the scholarship already devoted to Naples in the period, as well as to work in the city's libraries and archives; the latter enabled me to complete the writing of the principal chapters.

Those with whom I have discussed the project are legion, and to all I owe thanks. Special mention should be made of those who have studied 'The Science of Society 1650–1800' with me at Oxford since 1990, since it was with them that I gradually learned to understand Vico in the company of his contemporaries. Audiences at seminars and conferences in Oxford, Edinburgh, Naples, Dublin, London, Reading, Leicester, Venice, Budapest, Tel Aviv, Chicago, and Vancouver have given me the opportunity to try out my arguments, and to test the strength of their foundations. Over the years, certain individuals have formed a core group of fellow scholars of the Scottish Enlightenment, with whom I have discussed issues general and particular: in alphabetical order, Roger Emerson, Istvan Hont, Colin Kidd, Ned Landsman, Jim Moore, David Norton, Fania Oz-Salzberger, Nicholas Phillipson, Isabel Rivers, Richard Sher, Silvia Sebastiani, Sandy Stewart, and Paul Wood. I am particularly grateful to those who have also read and commented on draft chapters: Dena Goodman, Steve Pincus, Istvan Hont, and Jim Moore. The last two have been the kind of readers whose different, conflicting, occasionally mischievous suggestions have made it imperative to think again. The chapter on Vico was also read to Hugh Trevor-Roper, whose aversion to theology was no barrier to intelligent listening and helpful criticism. My debt to him is the oldest of all; the clarity of his intelligence and warmth of his encouragement never dimmed. Once it had been submitted, the book was read again for the Press; to both of its readers I am indebted for comments shrewd, constructive, and encouraging.

The opportunity to work in Naples has added another dimension to the pleasure of preparing this book. I am indebted first of all to those who have made my visits possible by their hospitality and friendship – and by their very practical help in finding me accommodation. Barbara Dawes and her husband Franco Clemente have fulfilled all these roles from the beginning; they have since been joined by Mark Weir, Nick Robinson, and Roberta Invernizzi. For the past ten years Lidia and Giovanni Porrini have been the kindest of hosts in Viale Fornelli. My gratitude to Enrico and Cinzia Nuzzo is of another order. When I began research in Naples in 1987 I travelled down to Salerno to consult Enrico Nuzzo as a Vico scholar; I have returned ever since, for the pleasure of a friendship which has enriched my life immeasurably.

Neapolitan historians have been as welcoming personally as they have been helpful intellectually. John Davis was one of the first to encourage my interest, and provided many introductions. Ever hospitable, Anna Maria Rao has been a generous source of suggestions and references; with Girolamo Imbruglia, to whom I have similar debts, she exemplifies a commitment to studying Neapolitan history in a cosmopolitan perspective. Among the older generation, whose scholarship provided the foundation of so much of this book, I have cause to be grateful to Giuseppe Galasso, to Raffaele Ajello (generous with suggestions when I began); and, at a distance, to Giuseppe Giarrizzo. In Naples I have also incurred many institutional debts: to the Istituto per gli Studi Filosofici (and to its secretary Antonio Gargano); to the older Istituto per gli Studi Storici and its staff, and to the librarians and archivists of the Biblioteca Nazionale, the Società Napoletana per la Storia Patria, the Biblioteca dei Girolamini, and the Archivio di Stato. From the other great capital of Italian Enlightenment scholarship, Turin, I have received encouragement from Giuseppe Ricuperati, Vincenzo Ferrone, Maria Luisa Pesante, and Patrizia Delpiano. Torinese by scholarly association, Robert Oresko is also justly mentioned in this context, even if he is of a different mind on the Enlightenment. Behind all these was Franco Venturi, whose intellectual inspiration was enhanced by personal kindness, in Oxford and at Vico Equense, when this project was in its infancy.

At the Press, the editors of the series, headed by Quentin Skinner, have been loyally encouraging; Richard Fisher, to me as to so many others in the field of intellectual history, has been the most supportive of publishers.

It is right as well as conventional to end these acknowledgements with my family. My mother was a constant supporter and reader of my work, and it is my greatest regret that she could not live to see the book. But I hope that my father will, and will accept the thanks that I owe to both of them. I owe most of all to Maxine Berg and our daughters, Frances, Gabriel, and Jessie. Maxine has lived with the idea and eventually the slowly growing reality of this book since our journey south of Naples in 1978, which is to say for almost all of our marriage. Even as she was writing her own books, she has constantly made more time for mine; and she has read the entire book. For this, and for much happiness throughout these years, I am profoundly grateful.

CHAPTER I

The case for the Enlightenment

By the end of the twentieth century, the Enlightenment was beleaguered. In the eyes of many philosophers as well as of a wider, educated public this eighteenth-century movement of ideas was still regarded as having laid the intellectual foundations of the modern world. By its confidence in the power of human reason, its commitment to individual freedom of expression against clerical or royal tyranny, and its optimistic assumption that these were the values that would improve the human condition everywhere, it was believed to have inspired and justified the nineteenth- and twentieth-century achievements of industrialisation, liberalism, and democracy. But this lay-philosophical view of the Enlightenment easily acquired another, darker face. For the Enlightenment was also charged with fostering ideals, of rationalism, universalism, and human perfectibility, to which could be traced the modern world's greatest evils. The charge was pressed particularly by those who held the Enlightenment responsible for the violence of the French Revolution, which followed so quickly upon it. In this perspective it was argued that Nazi genocide, Western imperialism, and Soviet communism all had their intellectual origins in the Enlightenment. Not surprisingly, it became increasingly fashionable to conclude that if this was where the Enlightenment had led the modern world, it was time to repudiate it, and to create a postmodern world on new intellectual foundations. The Enlightenment stood condemned as a misguided 'project' to establish a single, universal, rational standard of morality.[1] Against it, postmodernists argued that different cultures should be left to determine their own ends, and refused to discriminate morally or politically between them. At best the Enlightenment had been one of those cultures, peculiar to

---

[1] The concept of an 'Enlightenment project' appears to have been coined by Alasdair Macintyre, in *After Virtue: a Study in Moral Theory* (London, 1981), esp. chs. 4–6. Macintyre's definition of the 'project' was strictly philosophical, as 'the project of an independent rational justification of morality' (p. 38); subsequent usages have often been much more expansive.

eighteenth-century Europe; it was a terrible mistake ever to have accepted its claims to universal significance.

The crisis of the Enlightenment was compounded by the shifting interests of scholars themselves. As criticism of the 'Enlightenment project' gathered force, it seemed that scholars were less and less able to say what the Enlightenment had been. Thirty years earlier, they too had understood it in straightforward terms. The Enlightenment was identified principally with a group of French philosophers, the *philosophes*, who, along with a few curious foreign visitors, gathered in Paris in the middle decades of the eighteenth century to talk and to write about ways of improving the world. While the subjects which the *philosophes* discussed were many and varied, they shared and expounded a common set of intellectual values, prominent among which were reason, humanity, liberty, and tolerance. The Enlightenment, in other words, had existed in a certain time and place, was identified with a particular group of men, and was characterised by specific ideas. Since the 1960s, however, virtually all of these assumptions have been questioned. The Enlightenment has been extended far beyond France, and has been associated with a wider range of intellectual interests than those which formed the staple of the Paris *salons*. Still more scholarly energy has been devoted to writing its social history, enlarging our knowledge of its institutional and cultural contexts, doing justice to the contribution of women, and giving credit to the part played by its publishers and booksellers.

Not surprisingly, the result of all this activity was to open an ever-widening gulf between the public idea of the Enlightenment and that of the scholars. The clichés of the former had come to seem seriously misleading, and sometimes downright false. But instead of simply correcting popular error, the scholars themselves suffered a crisis of confidence. Faced with the mounting complication of their accounts of the Enlightenment, and the disagreements which ensued, many were inclined to conclude that a single, cohesive account of the Enlightenment could no longer be written. The loss of confidence was especially marked in English-language scholarship. The last major synthesis in English was Peter Gay's *The Enlightenment: an Interpretation*, published in two volumes in 1966 and 1969.[2] Even though it sought to combine a social with an intellectual history of the Enlightenment, Gay's work was immediately found wanting by Robert Darnton.[3]

---

[2] Peter Gay, *The Enlightenment: an Interpretation*, 2 vols. I: *The Rise of Modern Paganism*; II: *The Science of Freedom* (New York, 1966–9).

[3] Robert Darnton, 'In search of the Enlightenment: recent attempts to create a social history of ideas', *Journal of Modern History*, 43 (1971), 113–32.

Very soon Gay's insistence on the unities of the Enlightenment had come to seem either irrelevant or untenable in the face of a new emphasis on its diversity. The demands of textbook publishing did eventually ensure that short, single-volume studies of the Enlightenment reappeared in the 1990s. But if their authors still wrote of 'the' Enlightenment, they now did so in a loose and inclusive way, characterising it as a series of debates and concerns, rather than as a unified intellectual movement.[4] More ambitious but even more accurately reflective of the fragmented state of Enlightenment studies has been the series of dictionaries and encyclopaedias devoted to the subject. These now exist in English, German, French, and Italian, the largest as well as the most recent being the four-volume *Encyclopedia of the Enlightenment* (2003).[5] With scholars from all over the world contributing their specialist expertise to entries in these volumes, it seems that pluralism has triumphed. The monolithic edifice which the lay-philosophic view holds responsible for modernity has crumbled; but in its place scholars have refashioned Enlightenment as a postmodern kaleidoscope of diversity and difference. *The* Enlightenment is dead; but many Enlightenment*s* may yet flourish.

By far the most powerful scholarly exponent of this position has been John Pocock. Pocock first made the case for a distinct 'conservative Enlightenment' in the early 1980s, referring particularly to eighteenth-century England, but extending its reach to include the moderate Protestant

---

4 Dorinda Outram's *The Enlightenment* (Cambridge, 1995) was apparently the first textbook on the subject written in English for almost thirty years, since Norman Hampson's *The Enlightenment* (Harmondsworth, 1968). (It was narrowly preceded by Ulrich Im Hof, *The Enlightenment* (Oxford, 1994), but this was translated from German.) Outram has been followed by Thomas Munck, *The Enlightenment: a Comparative Social History 1721–1794* (London, 2000), where the Enlightenment is defined as 'an attitude of mind, rather than a coherent system of beliefs' (p. 7). But as the subtitle indicates, Munck is not attempting to give an intellectual history of the Enlightenment; and he resists its fragmentation more than most. Two shorter, pamphlet-length introductions are Roy Porter, *The Enlightenment* (London, 1990; second edn 2001), and Margaret C. Jacob, *The Enlightenment: A Brief History with Documents* (Boston and New York, 2001). Porter was an early and always enthusiastic proponent of diversity. A thoughtful contrast to these, which continues to take the ideas of the Enlightenment seriously while recognising that a comprehensive textbook is now impossible to write, is Edoardo Tortarolo, *L'Illuminismo. Ragioni e dubbi della modernità* (Rome, 1999).

5 Beginning with J. W. Yolton and others (eds.), *The Blackwell Companion to the Enlightenment* (Oxford, 1991), and continuing through W. Schneiders (ed.), *Lexikon der Aufklärung* (Munich, 1995), to Vincenzo Ferrone and Daniel Roche (eds.), *L'Illuminismo. Dizionario storico* (Rome and Bari, 1997), French translation: *Le Monde des Lumières* (Paris, 1999), and M. Delon (ed.), *Dictionnaire européen des lumières* (Paris, 1997), before culminating (for the moment), in A. C. Kors (ed.), *Encyclopedia of the Enlightenment*, 4 vols. (New York and Oxford, 2003). For comment on the significance of the phenomenon: Tortarolo, *L'Illuminismo*, p. 12, and Fania Oz-Salzberger, 'New approaches towards a history of the Enlightenment: can disparate perspectives make a general picture?', *Tel Aviver Jahrbuch für deutsche Geschichte*, 29 (2000), pp. 171–6.

philosophers of contemporary Scotland and north Germany.[6] A preoccupation with the difference of England continues to drive Pocock's enquiries;[7]
but his most recent and eloquent statement of his case, in *The Enlightenments of Edward Gibbon*, ranges much further. Here not only is English
Enlightenment set off against that of the French *philosophes*; other major
contexts for the intellectual formation of Gibbon are identified in a Socinian
Enlightenment, itself with English and Swiss variants, and in the 'Utrecht
Enlightenment', whose adherents took their cue from the peace settlement of 1713 to defend a conception of Europe as a 'system of states' regulated by commercial interest rather than confessional allegiance. Pocock
acknowledges that there was 'a process of Enlightenment' (in the singular)
at work across the multiple Enlightenments with which he is concerned;
but he insists that a process must be grounded in specific historical contexts, national or other, and that accordingly it is only in the plural that
Enlightenments can be understood by the historian. There can no longer
be any question of studying 'the Enlightenment', with the definite article.[8]

   To some observers, the new pluralism of the scholars is itself a sufficient
response to those who have equated the Enlightenment with a single doc-
trinaire 'project'. Historians, they point out, have shown that there was no
such thing.[9] Taking the point, some of the Enlightenment's critics have
been willing to temper their hostility and draw distinctions. Richard Rorty
believes that the Enlightenment philosophical project, which he defines as
the search for a comprehensive worldview which would replace God with
nature and reason, must be discarded for good. But its political project, 'a
world without caste, class or cruelty', remains valid, and ought still to be

---

[6] John G. A. Pocock, 'Clergy and commerce: the conservative Enlightenment in England', in Raffaele
Ajello and others, *L'età dei lumi. Studi storici sul Settecento europeo in onore di Franco Venturi*,
2 vols. (Naples, 1985), pp. 523–62.

[7] For example, his contribution, 'Gran Bretagna' to Ferrone and Roche, *L'Illuminismo*, pp. 478–92.

[8] John G. A. Pocock, *Barbarism and Religion*, 3 vols., to date (Cambridge, 1999–2003): I: *The Enlightenments of Edward Gibbon, 1737–1764*, p. 13: 'it is a premise of this book that we can no longer write
satisfactorily of "the Enlightenment" as a unified and universal intellectual movement'; also pp. 5–10,
292–308. See also, most recently, 'The re-description of Enlightenment', Isaiah Berlin lecture, *Proceedings of the British Academy*, forthcoming. For comment, John Robertson, 'The Enlightenments
of J. G. A. Pocock', *Storia della storiografia – History of Historiography*, 39 (2001), 140–51.
   Another to object to the definite article has been P. N. Furbank, in *Diderot: a Critical Biography*
(London, 1992), pp. 450–1. Furbank's standpoint is that of the literary critic, for whom invocation of
'the Enlightenment' draws attention only to the commonplace themes of the period, at the expense
of what was particular to an individual text. His concern is with the interpretation of individual texts,
not with the existence of plural Enlightenments.

[9] Most notably, James Schmidt, 'What Enlightenment project?', *Political Theory*, 28 (2000), 734–57,
quoting Outram and Pocock with approval on p. 737; followed by an exchange with Christian
Delacampagne in *Political Theory*, 29 (2001), 80–90.

pursued.[10] Other observers believe that the compromise with postmodern pluralism has gone much too far. As one working mainly on the twentieth century, David Hollinger argues that if intellectual history is to be of any use in trying to understand where we are today, 'the Enlightenment is extremely difficult to avoid'. In his view its historians have done remarkably little, at least in 'venues which count', to resist the proliferation of 'cardboard-character representations of the Enlightenment mind'. Intellectual historians studying the seventeenth and eighteenth centuries should by no means abandon the attempt to provide their more modern colleagues with 'a sound and stable sense of the Enlightenment to work with'.[11]

Among Enlightenment scholars themselves, one or two voices have already been raised in defiance of the retreat into pluralism. Perhaps unexpectedly, one of these was Robert Darnton's. In an essay for the *New York Review of Books* (which may, perhaps, qualify as 'a venue which counts') in 1997, the one-time scourge of Peter Gay upheld the existence of the Enlightenment as 'a movement, a cause, a campaign to change minds and reform institutions'. Throughout he characterised it in the singular. The Enlightenment was 'a concerted campaign on the part of a self-conscious group of intellectuals' to advance certain *idées-forces*, including liberty, happiness, nature, and nature's laws. As such the Enlightenment was not guilty of the charges now being levelled against it: of cultural imperialism on behalf of the West, of racism, of moral nihilism, or of an excessive faith in reason. It championed, rather, respect for the individual, for liberty, and for all the rights of man; it stood, in short, for progress with a small 'p', in an age when the pain of toothache was one of life's most constant, pervasive blights.[12]

Refreshing – and well placed – as Darnton's essay was, it has not convinced fellow scholars. There is puzzlement at the apparently very traditional terms of its argument, which seem to slight the social-historical approach to the Enlightenment of which Darnton himself has been such a distinguished exponent. It is also clear that Darnton's is an Enlightenment

---

[10] Richard Rorty, 'The continuity between the Enlightenment and "Postmodernism"', in K. M. Baker and P. H. Reill (eds.), *What's Left of Enlightenment? A Postmodern Question* (Stanford, 2001), pp. 19–36.

[11] David A. Hollinger, 'The Enlightenment and the genealogy of cultural conflict in the United States', in Baker and Reill, *What's Left of Enlightenment?*, pp. 17–18.

[12] Robert Darnton, 'George Washington's false teeth', originally in *The New York Review of Books* (27 March 1997), pp. 34–8; reprinted as 'The case for the Enlightenment: George Washington's false teeth', in the author's collection of essays, *George Washington's False Teeth: an Unconventional Guide to the Eighteenth Century* (New York and London, 2003), pp. 3–24.

closely linked to the American and French revolutions, which he regards, in their better parts, as its fulfilment. His is not, therefore, an Enlightenment which stands or falls on its own independent merits.

A second, much more substantial restatement of the case for the Enlightenment as a coherent intellectual movement is Jonathan Israel's 800-page *Radical Enlightenment* (2001). As its subtitle, *Philosophy and the Making of Modernity*, would indicate, Israel's claims for the Enlightenment in shaping the modern world are as high as if not higher than those of Darnton. But here the case is specifically for a 'radical' Enlightenment, occurring in the period 1650–1750, before the Enlightenment as it is conventionally thought of, which is associated with the period after 1750. In Israel's view, historians need to put much more emphasis on what was happening in the hundred years before 1750. The subsequent, so-called 'High' Enlightenment cannot compare with its radical predecessor in its impact – in the depth and extent of the changes it brought about; by the end of the 1740s, he writes, 'the real business was over'.[13] The importance of the early Enlightenment has been missed, according to Israel, because its most powerful and provocative intellectual force has been overlooked. This was the philosophy of Benedict Spinoza. Spinoza's ideas were already notorious by the time of his death in 1677, but their impact, Israel argues, was greatly magnified by the publication immediately afterwards, in Latin and Dutch, of his *Opera Posthuma* (1677–8), and by the debates which they provoked among his Dutch contemporaries. From the United Provinces his ideas spread outwards, through the writings of Pierre Bayle and Bernard de Fontenelle, to be discussed in France, England, Germany, and Italy. Israel does not deny the simultaneous existence of a 'moderate mainstream', whose leading spokesmen included Isaac Newton and John Locke, Newton's Dutch popularisers, and the German philosopher Christian Thomasius. But lacking the radical edge of the Spinozists, their impact, it is implied, was rather less than we have been taught to suppose.[14]

Israel's emphasis on the early or radical Enlightenment is not without good precedent. The classic discussion of that period's seminal significance was Paul Hazard's *La crise de la conscience européenne* (1935), in which the moment of decisive intellectual upheaval was located in the three and a half decades following 1680.[15] Israel acknowledges Hazard's insight, but

---

[13] Jonathan I. Israel, *Radical Enlightenment: Philosophy and the Making of Modernity 1650–1750* (Oxford, 2001), pp. 6–7.
[14] Israel, *Radical Enlightenment*, *passim*.
[15] English translation: Paul Hazard, *The European Mind 1680–1715* (1953; Harmondsworth, 1964).

relocates the period of the crisis to the three decades before 1680.[16] At the same time, Israel builds on the work of scholars who have studied free-thinking, *libertinage érudit*, and irreligion in the late seventeenth and early eighteenth centuries: Ira O. Wade and J. S. Spink in France, Margaret Jacob and Justin Champion in the Netherlands and England, Franco Venturi, Giuseppe Ricuperati, Vincenzo Ferrone, and Sivia Berti in Italy.[17] None of these, however, had directed the spotlight quite so emphatically on to Spinoza and his Dutch followers. Jacob had earlier made large claims for the Newtonians; Venturi had emphasised the importance of the English republicans, not all of whom were Spinozists.[18] Most striking, however, is the extent to which Israel's focus on Spinoza obliges him to play down the significance of Hobbes and of Bayle. Besides being an absolutist in his politics, Hobbes was 'philosophically less bold and comprehensive' than Spinoza: therefore he could not have had the latter's radical, intellectually transforming impact.[19] Yet Hobbes's work, as Noel Malcolm points out, was both more widely available and more generally discussed, within the mainstream as well as by radicals.[20] Bayle, meanwhile, is reduced to following in Spinoza's slipstream, a secret Spinozist – despite being the author of what was generally regarded as the most critical discussion of his philosophy.[21] In diminishing the intellectual contribution of Bayle, Israel also places less weight than he might have wished to do on the innovations by which Bayle transformed the Republic of Letters, not least

---

[16] Israel, *Radical Enlightenment*, pp. 14–22.

[17] See the commentary by Giuseppe Ricuperati, 'In margine al *Radical Enlightenment* di Jonathan I. Israel', *Rivista Storica Italiana*, 115 (1) (2003), 285–329. The works of Israel's predecessors include Ira O. Wade, *The Clandestine Organisation and Diffusion of Philosophic Ideas in France from 1700 to 1750* (Princeton, 1938); J. S. Spink, *French Free-thought from Gassendi to Voltaire* (London, 1960); Margaret C. Jacob, *The Radical Enlightenment: Pantheists, Freemasons, and Republicans* (London, 1981); Justin Champion, *The Pillars of Priestcraft Shaken: the Church of England and its Enemies 1660–1730* (Cambridge, 1992); Franco Venturi, *Saggi sull'Europa illuminista. I: Alberto Radicati di Passerano* (Turin, 1954); Giuseppe Ricuperati, *L'esperienza civile e religiosa di Pietro Giannone* (Milan and Naples, 1970); Vincenzo Ferrone, *Scienza natura religione. Mondo Newtoniano e cultura italiana nel primo Settecento* (Naples, 1982), transl., *The Intellectual Roots of the Italian Enlightenment: Natural Science, Religion, and Politics in the Early Eighteenth Century* (Atlantic Highlands, N.J., 1995); Silvia Berti (ed.), *Trattato de tre impostori. La vita e lo spirito del signor Benedetto Spinoza* (Turin, 1994).

[18] Margaret C. Jacob, *The Newtonians and the English Revolution 1689–1720* (Hassocks, 1976); Franco Venturi, *Utopia and Reform in the Enlightenment* (Cambridge, 1971).

[19] Israel, *Radical Enlightenment*, pp. 159, 602.

[20] Noel Malcolm, 'Hobbes and the European Republic of Letters', in the same author's *Aspects of Hobbes* (Oxford, 2002), pp. 457–545, discussing Israel's treatment of Hobbes on pp. 535–7.

[21] Israel, *Radical Enlightenment*, pp. 331–41. Bayle discussed Spinoza in his article 'Spinoza' in the *Dictionnaire historique et critique* (Rotterdam, 1697; second edn 1702), translated in part by Richard H. Popkin, in Pierre Bayle, *Historical and Critical Dictionary: Selections* (Indianapolis, New York and Kansas City, 1965), pp. 288–338. Israel, however, proposes to return to the relation between Spinoza and Bayle in a sequel to *Radical Enlightenment*.

his pioneering of the literary review in the *Nouvelles de la République des Lettres* (1684–7), and his subsequent use of its successors for controversial purposes.[22]

Yet when these features of *Radical Enlightenment* have been noted, there is no denying that Israel's is a case for the Enlightenment to be reckoned with. In mounting another case for the Enlightenment in this book, I will also be reckoning with Israel's. Here too, much attention will be given to the period before 1750: this book shares the conviction that developments between 1680 and 1740 hold the key to the intellectual history of the Enlightenment which followed. But there are also critical differences between our arguments. The most important should perhaps be indicated at the outset.

In the first place, 'the Enlightenment' as it is understood in this book remains the movement which began in the 1740s and ended in the 1790s. There is no need to go so far as to eliminate use of the terms 'pre', 'early' or even 'radical' Enlightenment to distinguish the period between 1680 and 1740; but by no means do I accept Israel's view that 'the real business was over' by the 1740s. What was over by then, in all but a few privileged enclaves, was the radical assault on the foundations of the Christian religion; it was over because the authorities, Protestant as well as Catholic, had effectively suppressed it, or at least curtailed its expression. Instead, what characterised the Enlightenment from the 1740s onwards was a new focus on betterment in this world, without regard for the existence or non-existence of the next. For such betterment to be achieved, it was indeed important that those who claimed to exercise authority in this world on the basis of their knowledge of the next should be removed to the sidelines. But intellectual effort was now concentrated on understanding the means of progress in human society, not on demolishing belief in a divine counterpart.

Underpinning this different understanding of the Enlightenment is a different assessment of its intellectual history, and of the relation it sought to develop between thought and society. It is not Spinozism which will be at the centre of this study, but the convergence between Augustinian and Epicurean currents of thinking about the nature of man and the possibility of society which occurred after 1680. This is an intellectual

---

[22] Israel surveys the learned journals, *Radical Enlightenment*, pp. 142–55, underlining the necessarily limited opportunities for the expression of radical ideas in their pages. He misses the way in which Bayle used them to develop the art of controversy, providing readers many decades later with a rich source for his arguments. See below, ch. 6, 'Hume, after Bayle and Mandeville', pp. 303–4 for an example.

history in which Hobbes, Gassendi, and especially Bayle will feature more strongly; but the frameworks in which Augustinian and Epicurean ideas were combined and developed were various, and claims on behalf of individual influence are not my primary concern. It will also be suggested that the Enlightenment's conception of the progress of society was intimately connected to a novel view of how men of letters should seek influence over it, by appealing to public opinion rather than to rulers and their ministers.

Finally, the present case for the Enlightenment differs from Israel's in being comparative rather than universal in scope. In Israel's *Radical Enlightenment* it is as if ideas were free to fly at will across international borders, before coming down to land more or less directly in individual minds. By contrast, this study seeks to ground the Enlightenment in specific historical contexts, the better to establish whether we can indeed still speak of one Enlightenment. Two contexts are singled out, for an explicitly comparative study: Scotland and Naples, both historically subordinate or 'provincial' kingdoms on the margins of Europe, which between them produced some of the most original thinking about man and society of the entire period from 1680 to 1790. Pocock appears to suggest that even if a process of Enlightenment can be observed in two places, the differences of context would lead to the emergence of distinct Enlightenments; by contrast, it will be the contention of this book that while Scotland and Naples were two contexts, there was only one Enlightenment.[23]

Before explaining the choice of contexts to study, however, I shall review in more detail the development of Enlightenment studies since they became a major scholarly preoccupation in the mid-twentieth century. It is important to see why the Enlightenment has come to seem so fragmented before an attempt is made to reconstitute it. Having offered a fresh account – or model – of the Enlightenment, I shall then outline why Scotland and Naples have been chosen to test it, and what I hope to achieve by the comparison.

[23] *The Case for the Enlightenment* is thus, in one of its meanings, the case that there was one Enlightenment, not several Enlightenments. I will not, however, labour the case by always placing the definite article before Enlightenment: 'Enlightenment' and 'the Enlightenment' will hereafter be used to denote the same European-wide intellectual movement. An argument that there was one Enlightenment permits but does not require use of the definite article, and I do not wish to reduce the issues involved in discussing the unity and coherence of Enlightenment thinking across different countries to a dispute over that article. A further meaning of 'the case for the Enlightenment', referring to the terms in which eighteenth-century Scots and Neapolitans framed their argument for betterment in this world, will be clarified in due course.

THE ENLIGHTENMENT OF LITERARY AND
PHILOSOPHICAL SCHOLARSHIP

'The Enlightenment' was never simply a scholarly abstraction. It existed in the eighteenth century in three languages, as *les lumières* or *i lumi*, and as *Aufklärung*. In both its French and German denominations it was a fiercely contested concept for most of the nineteenth century, the animosities created by the French Revolution ensuring that any historical investigation of its character was bound to have an ideological charge. By contrast, it was not until the late nineteenth century that 'Enlightenment' came into use in English as a translation for *Aufklärung*; *l'Illuminismo* followed in the early twentieth century. In both cases the translation reflected the spread of interest in German idealist philosophy.[24] Gradually, this diffusion of the concept seems to have dissipated the ideological charge which it had carried, even in its original languages; as several have recently remarked, any ideological intention was muted (or at least well hidden) in Ernst Cassirer's classic account of Enlightenment philosophy, *Die Philosophie der Aufklärung*, published in 1932.[25]

The Second World War was the turning point. Its immediate outcome, it is true, was a revival of the philosophical concept of *Aufklärung*, made the subject of a fierce new critique by Max Horkheimer and Theodor Adorno in *Die Dialektik der Aufklärung* (1947). Later this work would be an inspiration to the postmodern critique of Enlightenment; at the time, however, its impact was blunted by a quite different response to war and the horrors of Nazism – a turn, even a rush, to scholarship. Though not without ideological motivation, nor, in important individual cases, without roots in work begun before the war, the new turn in Enlightenment studies put scholarship first. The underlying object might be to demonstrate that France, Germany, and Italy possessed an intellectual heritage older, stronger, and utterly antagonistic to the ideals of Nazism and Fascism; but the means

---

[24] On the introduction of the term in English, see James Schmidt, 'Inventing the Enlightenment: Anti-Jacobins, British Hegelians, and the *Oxford English Dictionary*', *Journal of the History of Ideas*, 64 (2003), 421–3 – an object lesson in the dangers of relying on a dictionary for a definition of a concept.

[25] For an account of the Enlightenment as a concept and subject of study (as well as a prospectus for its future), Daniel Roche and Vincenzo Ferrone, 'Postfazione' to their *L'Illuminismo*, pp. 513–92; separately published as Vincenzo Ferrone and Daniel Roche, *L'Illuminismo nella cultura contemporanea. Storie e storiografie* (Rome and Bari, 2002). Likewise, though with most emphasis on the ideological uses of Enlightenment: Lynn Hunt with Margaret C. Jacob, 'Enlightenment Studies', in Kors, *Encyclopedia of the Enlightenment*.

On Cassirer, the informative article by Johnson Kent Wright, '"A bright clear mirror": Cassirer's *Philosophy of the Enlightenment*', in Baker and Reill, *What's Left of Enlightenment?*, pp. 71–101; and Fania Oz-Salzberger, 'Cassirer's Enlightenment and its recent critics: is Reason out of season?', in Jeffrey Barash (ed.), *Ernst Cassirer: Symbol, Science, and Culture* (Madison, Wis.: forthcoming).

chosen to demonstrate this were those of research and scholarship. Initially two approaches were dominant: the literary and the philosophical. Together they had established the existence and the reputation of the Enlightenment as a subject of historical study by the 1960s; at the beginning of the twenty-first century, both are still very much alive.[26]

The literary historians identified the Enlightenment almost exclusively with *les lumières*, and thus with a small circle of *philosophes* and their supporters in France. They were content, in short, to take *les lumières* at their literary face value. On this understanding the Enlightenment had consisted of a number of writers, who had made their way to Paris between the 1730s and 1780s, were admitted to the *salons* of free-thinking but well-connected women to discuss their ideas, and then or later made these ideas public in an array of books and pamphlets. Since the *salon* conversations were not recorded, it was the *philosophes'* books which were taken as defining the intellectual content of the Enlightenment. The dates of their publication also served to determine the Enlightenment's chronology. Thus the founding fathers were Montesquieu, whose *Lettres persanes* appeared in 1721, and Voltaire, whose *Lettres philosophiques* of 1734 inaugurated a stream of publications ended only by his death in 1778. The appearance of Montesquieu's masterpiece, *De l'esprit des lois* (1748) narrowly preceded the earliest works of the second, central generation of *philosophes*: the great, collaborative *Encyclopédie*, edited by Diderot and D'Alembert, whose publication began in 1751, and the early *Discourses* of the profoundly original if rebellious political philosopher Jean-Jacques Rousseau. Between the 1750s and the 1780s there followed successive volumes of the *Encyclopédie* (the last, of illustrations, in 1772) as well as Rousseau's most famous books, *Du Contrat Social* (1761) and *Emile* (1762). These were accompanied by the works of the philosophers Condillac, Helvétius, and D'Holbach, the last two unusual in expressing an increasingly aggressive hostility to revealed religion, and of the political economists Mirabeau, Quesnay, and Turgot, who would have the free market imposed on French agriculture. The end came in the 1790s, with the posthumous publication in 1797 of Condorcet's statement of faith in humanity's capacity for progress, the *Esquisse d'un tableau historique des progrès de l'esprit humain*, Condorcet himself having died three years earlier, horrified by the Terror.

The scholars who adhered to this view of *les lumières* were aware of the need for nuance. It was acknowledged that many *philosophes* spent

---

[26] Though raging against almost everything that had happened in Enlightenment studies up to the time of writing, John Lough, 'Reflections on "Enlightenment" and "Lumières"', in Ajello and others, *L'età dei lumi*, I, pp. 33–56 (also in *British Journal for Eighteenth-Century Studies*, 8 (1985), 1–15), confirms that scholarly development of the subject only took off in the 1950s.

more time out of Paris than in it. After 1755 Voltaire was safely resident near the Swiss border, at Les Délices and later at Ferney; Montesquieu did his work at La Brède, his chateau outside Bordeaux; Rousseau was soon alienated by the *salons*, and took to wandering within and beyond France. Nor was this Enlightenment ever entirely a French preserve. Visitors from as far afield as Scotland and Naples were drawn to Paris and admitted to the *salons*, where a David Hume or a Ferdinando Galiani was welcome to contribute to the conversations. The *philosophes'* discussions, moreover, were by no means always harmonious: a common set of values did not preclude sharp disagreement on specific issues. Rousseau's differences with D'Alembert, Diderot, and Hume became so many and bitter that it was hard to think of him as remaining within the Enlightenment at all; but disputes could arise between its securest adherents, as when Galiani, supported by Diderot, unexpectedly attacked the physiocrats in 1770. Even when these qualifications have been entered, however, the Enlightenment of the literary scholars has remained focused on the thoughts of a limited number of writers, and on France.[27]

A second line of scholarly enquiry was pursued by scholars trained in the history of philosophy. For many of these, especially in the United States, the starting point was the translation of Cassirer's pre-war study, *The Philosophy of the Enlightenment* (1951). It was also assumed that Kant's philosophy could be regarded as a systematic summation of the entire intellectual project of the Enlightenment, and thus used as a framework in which to place and assess the contributions of other thinkers across a range of fields, including metaphysics, aesthetics, morals, and politics. Cassirer himself had not gone so far. He did not treat Kant directly in his book, and he implied that Kant's philosophy had been both the climax and the definitive critique of the philosophy of the Enlightenment.[28] Nevertheless, his own allegiance to Kantianism as well as Kant's enduring reputation ensured that the history of Enlightenment philosophy was generally written in a Kantian perspective. There was an obvious difficulty in combining this perspective with the francocentric focus of the literary scholars: Kant lived and taught in Königsberg (now Kaliningrad), on the Baltic coast in East Prussia, and never once visited Paris. But the philosophic historians of the Enlightenment were prepared to concede that its works were otherwise overwhelmingly French: the point of their approach was that it enabled the thought of Montesquieu, Voltaire, Rousseau, and others to be discussed

---

[27] Alphonse Dupront, *Qu'est-ce que les lumières?* (Paris, 1996) – but written as lectures in the 1960s – is a classic statement of *Les lumières* as a French literary phenomenon.

[28] Ernst Cassirer, *The Philosophy of the Enlightenment* (Princeton, 1951); on the place of Kant in its argument: Wright, "'A bright clear mirror'", pp. 81–96.

systematically, and their values of reason, liberty, and tolerance to be given philosophical substance.

Despite the awkwardness of Kant's geographical dislocation, the combination of literary and philosophical approaches was successful in giving the Enlightenment a clear historical identity. It had an accepted name, as *les lumières* and *Aufklärung* came to be treated as virtual equivalents, and both were translated as 'the Enlightenment' or *l'Illuminismo*. It had been placed chronologically and geographically, and the texts containing its thought had been established and accommodated within a philosophical framework.[29] With such recognition came a danger of relegation: the Enlightenment could safely be regarded by most historians as a subject best left to specialists in the history of literature and philosophy. But once they were confident that they knew what it was and what, in general terms, it thought, ordinary historians could also proceed to determine the Enlightenment's relation to other important developments in the eighteenth century. One obvious question concerned the Enlightenment's influence on contemporary European rulers, a question too quickly reduced to the problem of so-called 'enlightened despotism', and now better understood as that of enlightened absolutism.[30] Another, still more important, concerned the relation between the Enlightenment and the French Revolution. Attempts to answer the question still lay under the shadow of the contemporary accusation, first heard in the 1790s, that the Revolution had been the result of a *philosophe* conspiracy (an accusation which continues to resonate in the postmodern charge that the Enlightenment was responsible for the disasters of the twentieth century). But given a secure definition of the Enlightenment, historians could in principle be confident that the question was answerable by determining whether or not there was positive evidence of the influence of Enlightenment ideas on those who criticised the *ancien régime*, or who joined in designing the revolutionary constitutions.[31]

---

[29] Intellectually, this was the point reached by Peter Gay in his two-volume study *The Enlightenment*, although he also anticipated several of the lines of enquiry which the social historians of the Enlightenment were later to champion.

[30] H. M. Scott (ed.), *Enlightened Absolutism: Reform and Reformers in Later Eighteenth-century Europe* (Basingstoke and London, 1990): the editor's 'Introduction: the problem of enlightened absolutism', pp. 1–35, traces the shift from 'despotism' to 'absolutism'.

[31] A classic example, measuring the influence of the *philosophes* as less than that of Locke, was Alfred Cobban, 'The Enlightenment and the French Revolution', in his *Aspects of the French Revolution* (London, 1968); another was Norman Hampson, *Will and Circumstance: Montesquieu, Rousseau, and the French Revolution* (London, 1983). By contrast Gay suggested that the Enlightenment had already been implemented by the American Revolution, and thus prudently avoided entangling it in the French Revolution: *The Enlightenment*, II: *The Science of Freedom*: 'Finale: the programme in practice'.

NEW DIRECTIONS IN ENLIGHTENMENT SCHOLARSHIP

The ground had begun to shift under Enlightenment scholarship by the 1960s. Enlightenment studies then began to move in several new directions, which were pursued with increasing enthusiasm through the last three decades of the century. Although the divisions between them are not hard and fast, the new directions can be grouped under three headings – intellectual, social, and national. Each of these has led to a better understanding of the Enlightenment; but they have also been taken to lengths which have made it very difficult to maintain a coherent view of the Enlightenment as a whole.

The first of these new directions has been towards a much more complex appreciation of Enlightenment thought. Most fundamental, the old shibboleth that the Enlightenment was the 'Age of Reason' has long since been abandoned by historians of philosophy. If anything, it is now suggested, Kant was attempting to rehabilitate the concept of reason in response to the criticism to which it had been subjected by other Enlightenment philosophers. The idea that reason was humanity's key to knowledge of the external world and of moral value was after all a commonplace of Christian Aristotelianism; dissatisfied with this, almost all serious philosophers since the seventeenth century, from Descartes, Gassendi, and Hobbes to Locke, Berkeley, and Hume, had insisted on the need to accept the challenge of scepticism. As sceptics, they conceded that knowledge of the external world was acquired through the senses, and that the passions dominated human nature. If reason still counted, it was within these limits.[32] Attempts were certainly made, by Descartes and his followers, by natural jurists, and by rational theologians, to place reason's role on a more secure foundation. But the devastating intervention of Bayle at the turn of the century ensured that scepticism's inroads would be impossible to reverse. This was especially clear in moral philosophy, where 'the passions and the interests', in Albert Hirschman's phrase, became the starting point for enquiries in this and the related fields of political economy and historical theory.[33] Even Kant had to start from there: while insisting that reason was conceivable *a priori*, and even attainable by men, he acknowledged that it was interest,

---

[32] Richard H. Popkin, *The History of Scepticism from Erasmus to Spinoza* (Berkeley, 1979, but first published in 1960 as *The History of Scepticism from Erasmus to Descartes*); and the same author's *The High Road to Pyrrhonism*, edited by R. E. Watson and J. E. Force (1980; repr. Indianapolis, 1993), carrying the story of scepticism into the eighteenth century.

[33] Albert O. Hirschman, *The Passions and the Interests: Political Arguments for Capitalism before its Triumph* (Princeton, N.J., 1977).

'the crooked timber of humanity',[34] which shaped their behaviour in the existing world.

As the simple equation of the Enlightenment with a philosophy of reason was discarded, it became apparent that no single philosophical system had given intellectual unity to Enlightenment thinking. It also became clearer that the relation between Enlightenment thought and religion was not simply adversarial. The challenge of scepticism might be unavoidable, but scepticism did not necessarily lead to disbelief. As Israel has reminded us, the currents of radical heterodoxy and irreligion flowed fast and variously; but heterodoxy was not incompatible with faith. Even Pierre Bayle emerged from the magisterial researches of Elizabeth Labrousse a serious believer.[35] Unbelievers there were at the heart of the Enlightenment: David Hume and, more aggressively, Baron d'Holbach and his coterie. But they were a small minority.[36] Many more Enlightenment thinkers retained some religious beliefs, even if they were unorthodox, and many remained comfortably in clerical orders, both Protestant and Catholic. To explain this, what Hugh Trevor-Roper called 'the religious origins of the Enlightenment' have increasingly been recognised. On the Protestant side his suggestion that those origins were to be found in the 'liberal' traditions of Arminianism and Socinianism has been widely accepted – if not yet intensively researched. On the Catholic, his (briefer) remarks on the contribution of the Oratory have been supplemented by attention to the other great Catholic dissidents of the late seventeenth century, the Jansenists of Port Royal.[37] Encouraged by the identification of such antecedents, historians have been further inclined to divide the Enlightenment along confessional lines, into distinct Protestant and Catholic Enlightenments.[38] Some would even challenge the traditional depiction of the Enlightenment as a

---

[34] Isaiah Berlin's translation of a phrase in Kant's *Idea for a Universal History with a Cosmopolitan Purpose* (1784), Sixth Proposition: Isaiah Berlin, *The Crooked Timber of Humanity: Chapters in the History of Ideas* (London, 1991) with the passage from Kant cited on p. [v].

[35] Elisabeth Labrousse, *Pierre Bayle*, 2 vols. (The Hague, 1963–4).

[36] A. C. Kors, 'The atheism of D'Holbach and Naigeon', in Michael Hunter and David Wootton (eds.), *Atheism from the Reformation to the Enlightenment* (Oxford, 1992). Visiting Paris in 1763, the young Edward Gibbon was shocked to find d'Holbach and his coterie ridiculing the timidity of Hume's unbelief: *The Autobiographies of Edward Gibbon*, ed. John Murray (London, 1896), p. 204.

[37] H. R. Trevor-Roper, 'The religious origins of the Enlightenment', in his *Religion, the Reformation and Social Change* (London, 1967; second edn 1972). Socinian origins of Enlightenment have been pursued by Pocock, in *The Enlightenments of Edward Gibbon*.

[38] On the Protestant side, John G. A. Pocock, 'Settecento protestante? L'Illuminismo riconsiderato', *Quaderni storici*, 94 (1997), 315–37: the argument is closely connected with its author's case for an English Enlightenment. On the Catholic side, Mario Rosa, 'Introduzione all'Aufklärung cattolica in Italia', in Mario Rosa (ed.), *Cattolicesimo e lumi nel Settecento italiano*, Italia Sacra, Studi e documenti di storia ecclesiastica 33 (Rome, 1981), 1–47.

secularising force, maintaining that 'the religious Enlightenment' should be taken as seriously as any other Enlightenment.[39]

The loss of an overarching philosophical framework, together with a new appreciation of the complexity of the Enlightenment's relation to religion, have made possible a much more credible account of Enlightenment intellectual activity. But they have also created an unprecedented uncertainty over what should count as Enlightenment thinking. For one thing, intellectual historians are liable to wonder where the Enlightenment is supposed to begin and end. Given the extent to which eighteenth-century philosophers continued to engage with the works of seventeenth-century predecessors, should it not be taken to start by 1650? Since political economy developed continuously after Adam Smith, should we not think of the Enlightenment as carrying over into the early nineteenth century? On these extended time-scales, 'the Enlightenment' may remain a handy periodisation, but its historical particularity is much attenuated. On the other hand, scholars whose subjects have not hitherto been regarded as central to the Enlightenment have scented an opportunity. If no single philosophy characterises Enlightenment thinking, they ask, why should any area of intellectual activity be excluded? Not content with the seventeenth-century 'scientific revolution', historians of science have been especially keen to see their subject raised to a central place in the Enlightenment as well. Literary scholars, especially in the anglophone world, have likewise pressed the claims of a much wider range of writers who seem to share Enlightenment values. Ultimately it becomes impossible to exclude any not obviously reactionary form of thought from the Enlightenment's liberal embrace. But there is a price to pay: an Enlightenment so inclusive is in danger of losing any coherent, distinctive, intellectual identity.

For Enlightenment scholarship, the price has been high. Many intellectual historians have found that they have less and less stake in the Enlightenment as such. Important studies of individual thinkers and of their contexts continue to be written, but the question of their contribution to the Enlightenment has become secondary. It is hardly surprising that many intellectual historians have left the field to their colleagues working in social and cultural history, allowing these to refashion the Enlightenment in their own images, to the detriment of its once primary intellectual character.

When Robert Darnton repudiated the approach to the Enlightenment embodied in the work of Peter Gay, he did so in the name of a new,

---

[39] David Sorkin, '*A wise, enlightened and reliable piety*': *The Religious Enlightenment in Central and Western Europe, 1689–1789*, University of Southampton, Parkes Institute Pamphlet, 1 (2002). Sorkin takes his cue from Pocock's endorsement of plural Enlightenments.

social-historical approach, which quickly established itself as the second major new departure in Enlightenment studies. First in the field was the French *Annaliste* historian Daniel Roche and his *équipe* of researchers. Making full use of statistical methods, Roche explored first the problem of literacy and the readership of books, and then the membership of provincial French academies.[40] Since 1980 Roche has persistently championed study of the Enlightenment as the social history of culture, potentially extending its reach to include every social practice, every material object, in which ideas may be seen to be represented.[41]

Darnton himself took a different – and more dramatic – approach. Discovery of the riches of the archive of the Société typographique de Neuchâtel made possible a comprehensive reconstruction of the publishing history of the *Encyclopédie* in the 1770s and 1780s. Chronicling an extraordinary tale of entrepreneurial collaboration and rivalry between the editors, publishers, smugglers, and sellers of the quarto and octavo editions of the *Encyclopédie*, he demonstrated that while its price remained beyond the labouring poor, it came within reach of many of the middle and professional ranks.[42] But Darnton became best known for his thesis that by the last quarter of the century a divide had opened up between the 'high' Enlightenment and the 'low' life of literary journalism. The first was the Enlightenment of the *philosophes* and their immediate associates: despite their struggles with the censors, Darnton argued, these had eventually secured their position in society, gaining recognition and remuneration in the official royal academies. Just as this 'high' Enlightenment settled complacently into a niche in the *ancien régime*, however, it was challenged by those it now excluded, who were left to eke out a living as Grub-Street journalists. It was these, Darnton suggested, who would shortly turn the ideals of the 'high' Enlightenment into the simplified slogans which would drive the Revolution.[43] In subsequent work on the 'forbidden literature' of pre-revolutionary France

[40] Daniel Roche and others, *Livre et société dans la France du XVIIIe siècle*, 2 vols. (Paris and The Hague, 1965–70); Daniel Roche, *Le siècle des lumières en province. Académies et académiciens provinciaux 1680–1789* (Paris and The Hague, 1978).

[41] Daniel Roche, *France in the Enlightenment*, transl. Arthur Goldhammer (Cambridge, Mass. and London, 1998; original French edn, 1993), part III, and many other works. A recent programmatic statement is 'Dell'Illuminismo. Per una storia sociale della cultura', *Rivista Storica Italiana*, 113 (2001), 86–106: the message is as oracular as could be expected from an inaugural lecture to the Collège de France.

[42] Robert Darnton, *The Business of the Enlightenment: a Publishing History of the Encyclopédie* (Cambridge, Mass., 1979).

[43] Robert Darnton, 'The high Enlightenment and the low-life of literature in pre-Revolutionary France', *Past and Present*, 51 (1971), 81–115. Note that the distinction is between the 'high' Enlightenment and the 'low-life' of literature: Darnton was not being inconsistent when in 'George Washington's false teeth' he restricted the Enlightenment to a high intellectual movement of *philosophes*.

Darnton has continued to illuminate the interconnections between high and low culture, between the mechanistic philosophy of D'Holbach and the mechanistic pornography of *Thérèse Philosophe*.[44] More recently he has pursued the low life of literature further back, through the archives of the Paris police, into the world of newsvendors and songwriters who were spreading reports damaging to the crown, the court, and royal ministers well before 1750.[45]

Much of this, as Darnton would certainly admit, has very little to do with Enlightenment. Another reference point takes precedence: the Revolution. There is a fundamental respect in which Darnton's concerns, like those of Roger Chartier, remain those of Daniel Mornet, whose *Les origines intellectuelles de la Révolution française* (1933) had sought to give a scholarly answer to Tocqueville's question about whether ideas were responsible for the Revolution. Neither Darnton nor Chartier believes that this can any longer be reduced to a question of the influence of the Enlightenment. In asking 'Do books make revolutions?', and exploring a French equivalent of Grub Street, Darnton is deliberately casting the net much wider.[46] But the danger, as several critics have pointed out, is that in the process the Enlightenment itself is diminished, being reduced to a small and discrete role in the lead up to revolution.[47]

Not surprisingly, a younger generation of Enlightenment historians is now contesting Darnton's approach. Adapting the suggestion of the German philosopher Jürgen Habermas that the Enlightenment marked the emergence of a new 'public sphere', in which literate men and women could engage in independent public discussion, these historians argue that Darnton has missed the connection between the Enlightenment and the emergence of a new 'public', practising a broad-based culture of 'sociability'. This 'public' was made up of middle, professional, and even noble classes who wished to live their lives independently, without constantly deferring to standards set for them by courts, churches, and officials. They adopted sociability as a culture which valued 'politeness' in conversation, correspondence, and literary exchange, and which deprecated religious or

---

[44] Robert Darnton, *The Forbidden Best-Sellers of Pre-Revolutionary France* (London, 1996), esp. ch. 3, 'Philosophical pornography'.

[45] Robert Darnton, 'The news in Paris: an early information society', in *George Washington's False Teeth*, pp. 25–75.

[46] Darnton, *The Forbidden Best-Sellers*, part III, 'Do books cause revolutions?'; cf. Roger Chartier, *The Cultural Origins of the French Revolution* (Durham, N.C. and London, 1991), chs. 4, 'Do books make revolutions?' and 8 'Do revolutions have cultural origins?'

[47] Haydn T. Mason (ed.), *The Darnton Debate: Books and Revolution in the Eighteenth Century* (Voltaire Foundation, Oxford, 1999), gives the critics their opportunity; especially vigorous were Jeremy Popkin, Daniel Gordon, and Elizabeth Eisenstein. But Darnton was accorded space to reply, in 'Two paths through the social history of ideas', and gave at least as good as he got.

political partisanship. First articulated in the widely admired and frequently copied English journals *The Spectator* and *The Tatler*, this was a culture which could be practised in any forum in which men and women were free to meet of their own accord, unregulated by any authority higher than themselves. In a novel way sociability was a culture of citizenship, but a citizenship by no means narrowly republican or revolutionary.[48]

Two phenomena often associated with Enlightenment seem particularly amenable to explanation in terms of this culture of sociability. One is freemasonry. As a self-conscious creed and set of rituals this had originated in later sixteenth- and seventeenth-century Scotland, and had migrated to England in the early eighteenth century; thence it spread rapidly across the continent, offering its 'lodges' a variety of rites. By no means every adherent of Enlightenment was a freemason. But in many parts of Europe, and particularly in the 1770s and 1780s, membership was common, with strong concentrations in France, the German-speaking lands, and Naples. Quite why such a secretive, ritualistic creed should have appealed to men (and a few women) who were otherwise committed to the free, public discussion of ideas remains a puzzle: but it is at least plausible to suggest that its internal egalitarianism was in accord with the new ideals of sociability, while its secrecy asserted (if it did not always secure) its autonomy from religious and governmental authorities. Whether its sociability also embodied the modern political values of liberty or equality, or whether it was apolitical, and hence dangerously utopian, are questions which continue to divide historians. But those who have doubted its significance for the Enlightenment are now in a distinct minority.[49]

---

[48] Jürgen Habermas, *The Structural Transformation of the Public Sphere: an Inquiry into a Category of Bourgeois Society* (Cambridge, Mass., 1989; first published in German in 1962). US scholars have been among the most enthusiastic: Dena Goodman, 'Public sphere and private life: towards a synthesis of current historiographical approaches to the Old Regime', *History and Theory*, 31 (1992), 1–20; Margaret C. Jacob, 'The mental landscape of the public sphere: a European perspective', *Eighteenth-Century Studies*, 28 (1994), 95–113; Daniel Gordon, *Citizens without Sovereignty: Equality and Sociability in French Thought 1670–1789* (Princeton, 1994). But Germans preceded them: Ulrich Im Hof, *Das gesellige Jahrhundert. Gesellschaft und Gesellschaften im Zeitalter der Aufklärung* (Munich, 1982); Richard van Dülmen, *The Society of Enlightenment: the Rise of the Middle Class and Enlightenment Culture in Germany* (Cambridge and Oxford, 1992; first published in German in 1986). An excellent new synthesis, by a US scholar who has worked in Germany, is James van Horn Melton, *The Rise of the Public in Enlightenment Europe* (Cambridge, 2001).

[49] Margaret C. Jacob, *Living the Enlightenment: Freemasonry and Politics in Eighteenth-century Europe* (Oxford, 1991), emphasises the political implications of Enlightenment freemasonry. The accusation that freemasonry fostered a dangerously apolitical utopianism was advanced earlier by Reinhart Koselleck, *Critique and Crisis: Enlightenment and the Pathogenesis of Modern Society* (Oxford, New York and Hamburg, 1988; originally in German, 1959). The most substantial recent account treats freemasonry and the Enlightenment as distinct but interrelated manifestations of eighteenth-century culture: Giuseppe Giarrizzo, *Massoneria e illuminismo nell'Europa del Settecento* (Venice, 1994). Van Horn Melton, *The Rise of the Public*, pp. 252–72, provides an up-to-date conspectus.

The Paris *salons* offer a second example of Enlightenment sociability. In a thought-provoking study, Dena Goodman has argued that the *salonnières* were not mere hostesses, but the directors and arbiters of a distinctive Enlightenment culture, enforcing the rules of polite conversation and mediating epistolary exchange. Here sociability was female centred, the Enlightenment gendered as feminine. Unfortunately, Goodman suggests, it was a culture which men were to undermine when they insisted on taking their disagreements into print, and then devised new institutions which excluded women. Typically these were the *musées*, the literary clubs of the 1780s, from which a direct line can be traced through to the *Cercle Social* and the Jacobin clubs of the 1790s.[50] Superficially, this argument may seem analogous to Darnton's: the polite Enlightenment of the *salons* challenged by the rougher, more radical assemblies of ideologically motivated young men. But Goodman's argument avoids tying the question of Enlightenment directly to that of revolution, offering instead an analysis of the place of the *salons* in the development of the Republic of Letters during the Enlightenment. No longer, she argues, were men of letters content simply to address each other, confining themselves to the existing of the Republic of Letters. Instead the *philosophes* sought to engage with a much wider 'public' of readers and consumers of ideas. The long-running collaborative enterprise of the *Encyclopédie* was one means of doing so, the *salons* were another. When the *salons* broke up and were superseded by the *musées*, it was because the character and orientation of the Republic of Letters had changed. By the 1780s political, revolutionary objectives were substituted for the meliorist goals of the Enlightenment, and access to the increasingly politicised Republic of Letters was redefined and, at least for women, narrowed. So arguing, Goodman can distinguish what she calls the 'culture' of the Enlightenment from the revolutionary culture which followed, without suggesting that there was any necessary, causal relation between them.[51]

For all their differences, the work of scholars such as Roche, Darnton, and Goodman is widely regarded as among the most exciting in recent Enlightenment studies. There is still much to be done to apply its insights beyond France: publishing and the role of censorship in Enlightenment Italy, for example, are subjects only beginning to be explored. Nor are these scholars necessarily hostile to or dismissive of the Enlightenment. Darnton, as we have seen, is happy to make the case for a very traditional version of the

---

[50] Dena Goodman, *The Republic of Letters: a Cultural History of the French Enlightenment* (Ithaca and London, 1994).

[51] The relation between Enlightenment and the Republic of Letters is discussed at greater length below, pp. 38–41.

Enlightenment; Goodman's cultural history of the French Enlightenment is intended to provide a strong defence of its unity and significance. But a defence of the Enlightenment on the terms offered by these historians carries a price. In setting out to write a 'cultural' rather than an intellectual history of Enlightenment, they have encouraged a view that the ideas themselves were of secondary importance. As it is, many less sophisticated exponents of the social historian's approach to the Enlightenment barely disguise their opinion that a focus on ideas is unacceptably elitist. Yet it is as a movement of thought that the Enlightenment possesses historical significance, for good or ill: to marginalise study of its intellectual content, as its social and cultural historians tend to do, is to lose an indispensable dimension of the subject.

The third new direction in Enlightenment studies has been towards writing its history in national context. The traditional account of *les lumières* was of course concentrated on one nation, France. But this, to its proponents, was precisely what made the Enlightenment universal, not national. The first to question such an assumption was the Italian historian, the late Franco Venturi. In Paris in exile during the 1930s, Venturi began by writing on the young Diderot and the *Encyclopédie*; and he never denied the centrality of France to the Enlightenment. But from the first he was also alert to the existence of thinkers with similar ideas in his native Piedmont and elsewhere in eighteenth-century Italy.[52] This realisation was transformed after the war into a full-scale programme of research, as Venturi called for a new account of the relation between the eighteenth century and the Risorgimento. The programme soon yielded several volumes of selections from the writings of individual Italian *illuministi*, with biographical introductions, and culminated in his own multi-volume narrative of Enlightenment activity in Italy, *Settecento riformatore* (in five volumes, 1969–90).[53]

---

[52] Franco Venturi, *Jeunesse de Diderot (1713 à 1753)* (Paris, 1939), closely followed by a thesis on the Piedmontese reformer *Dalmazzo Francesco Vasco (1732–1794)* (Paris, 1940). On Venturi's intellectual formation, Edoardo Tortarolo, 'La rivolta e le riforme. Appunti per una biografia intellettuale di Franco Venturi (1914–1994)', *Studi settecenteschi*, 15 (1995), 9–42.

[53] The programme was announced in 1953, and published as 'La circolazione delle idee', *Rassegna storica del Risorgimento*, 41 (1954), 203–22. Venturi himself edited two volumes of *Illuministi italiani*. III: *Riformatori lombardi, piemontesi e toscani* (Milan and Naples, 1958), and V: *Riformatori napoletani* (Milan and Naples, 1962); and he contributed with Giuseppe Giarrizzo and Gianfranco Torcellan to a third, VII: *Riformatori delle antiche repubbliche, dei ducati, dello Stato Pontificio e delle isole* (Milan and Naples, 1965).

The five volumes of *Settecento riformatore*, all published by Einaudi in Turin, appeared as I: *Da Muratori a Beccaria 1730–1764* (1969); II: *La chiesa e la repubblica dentro i loro limiti 1758–1774* (1976); III: *La prima crisi dell'Antico Regime 1768–1776* (1979); IV: *La caduta dell'Antico Regime 1776–1789*, in two parts, 1. *I grandi stati dell'Occidente*, and 2. *Il patriottismo repubblicano e gli imperi dell'Est*

Venturi's point of departure was the realisation that the traditional account of the Enlightenment, which treated Italians such as Ferdinando Galiani and Cesare Beccaria as 'visiting members' by virtue of their stays in Paris and reception in the *salons*, had overlooked the extent of their activities and connections in their own country. In Milan Beccaria had formed the *Il caffè* group along with the brothers Pietro and Alessandro Verri; in Naples Galiani had been the contemporary of Antonio Genovesi, holder of the first chair of political economy in Europe, and the teacher of a school of younger reformers headed by Gaetano Filangieri and Francesco Mario Pagano. Similar groups of *illuministi* were to be found in Piedmont, Venice, Tuscany, and even the Papal States. All did indeed look to Paris for inspiration; but their thinking also had indigenous roots, in the works of an earlier generation of reformers headed by Ludovico Muratori, and they forged their own bilateral connections with reformers elsewhere in Europe, from Spain to Germany, and even Russia. In charting the course of Enlightenment in Italy Venturi was always appreciative of the variety imposed by the political division of the peninsula, and particularly sympathetic towards the radical and embattled Neapolitans. But while this enhanced the political focus of his work, it did not compromise the integrative, national character of his treatment of the Enlightenment in Italy. *Settecento riformatore* is a work of Italian history, in which less weight is attached to the intellectual contributions of the *illuministi* than to their practical, reforming ambitions. As such, its perspective shaped and inspired scholarship devoted to Enlightenment in Italy over the second half of the twentieth century.[54]

The perspective is not without its critics. Their quarrel, however, has been with what they regard as the prematurely 'Italian' scope of Venturi's Enlightenment. The proper subjects of study, Mario Mirri insisted, were rather the

---

(1984); v: *L'Italia dei lumi 1764–1790*, again in two parts, *1. La rivoluzione di Corsica; Le grande carestie degli anni sessanta; la Lombardia delle riforme* (1987), and *2. La repubblica di Venezia 1761–1797* (1990). Even then, the work was unfinished when Venturi died in 1994; what he had written has been published posthumously as *Saggi preparatori per Settecento riformatore. L'Italia dei lumi: La repubblica di Genova (1761–1797)* (Accademia Nazionale dei Lincei, Rome, 2002). Volumes III and IV (both parts) of *Settecento riformatore* have been translated into English in three volumes by R. Burr Litchfield, as *The End of the Old Regime in Europe 1768–1776: the First Crisis* (Princeton 1989), and *The End of the Old Regime in Europe 1776–1789*, 2 vols. (Princeton 1991), the translation a heroic enterprise in itself. For reviews of these volumes and guides to Venturi's great enterprise: John Robertson, 'Franco Venturi's Enlightenment', *Past and Present*, 137 (1992), 183–206 and Giuseppe Ricuperati, 'The historiographical legacy of Franco Venturi (1914–1994)', *Journal of Modern Italian Studies*, 2 (1997), 67–88.

[54] For accounts in English: D. Carpanetto and G. Ricuperati, *Italy in the Age of Reason 1685–1789* (London, 1987); and the excellent chapter by Anna Maria Rao, 'Enlightenment and reform', in John A. Marino (ed.), *Early Modern Italy*, in the series Short Oxford History of Italy (Oxford, 2002), pp. 229–52.

'ancient Italian states' – the individual kingdoms, principalities, duchies, and republics into which the peninsula was still divided. For these critics, in short, Venturi's focus was not specific enough: in eighteenth-century Italy the true national contexts were Tuscan, Milanese, Neapolitan, and many others even lesser in scale.[55] Even scholars close to Venturi have begun to emphasise the peculiarities of Enlightenment in different Italian contexts. In the case of Naples, for example, Giuseppe Galasso has drawn attention to the extent to which the kingdom's 'original characteristics' provided a distinctive setting for the reception and development of Enlightenment thinking.[56]

Post-war German historians were understandably less inclined to study the Enlightenment in a specifically national perspective. They have been much more inclined to take their cue from Habermas and the *Annales* school in exploring the Enlightenment's social underpinnings. Nevertheless, the attractions of adopting an approach similar to that developed in Italy have become increasingly clear. The political structure of eighteenth-century Germany most closely resembled that of Italy: it too was fragmented into a variety of principalities and even smaller states, whose courts and administrations provided openings for the educated and reforming. Out in Königsberg Kant may have remained aloof from political entanglements, confining himself to writing in oblique praise of his king, Frederick II; but Frederick's capital Berlin was a centre of debate over issues of tolerance, freedom of the press, and economic reform. Other, smaller German courts facilitated a greater or lesser degree of discussion of these and other issues among officials and university teachers. In Hanover, whose prince was also the king of Great Britain, the professors at the new university of Göttingen were in the forefront of developments in the *Staatswissenschaften* or 'state sciences' and in philosophical history. In the Catholic south, Enlightenment ideas (and freemasonry) entered the principality of Bavaria both from

---

[55] Mario Mirri, 'Della storia dei "Lumi" e delle "riforme" alla storia degli "antichi stati italiani"', in M. Verga and A. Fratoianni (eds.), *Pompeo Neri* (Castelfiorentino, 1992), pp. 401–540. The merits of this perspective are discussed with particular reference to Tuscany and Milan by Till Wahnbaeck, *Luxury and Public Happiness: Political Economy in the Italian Enlightenment* (Oxford, 2004).

[56] Giuseppe Galasso, *La filosofia in soccorso de' governi. La cultura napoletana del Settecento* (Naples, 1989), pp. 15–66: ch. 1: 'Iluminismo napoletano e Illuminismo europeo'. A useful and representative recent collection in English of contributions by younger Italian scholars is Girolamo Imbruglia (ed.), *Naples in the Eighteenth Century: the Birth and Death of a Nation State* (Cambridge, 2000). Imbruglia's own contribution, 'Enlightenment in eighteenth-century Naples', pp. 70–94, tests Venturi's categories against the Neapolitan evidence. Among those writing in English, Melissa Calaresu has pointed to the potential of a national context approach to the Neapolitan Enlightenment: see e.g. 'Images of ancient Rome in late eighteenth-century Neapolitan historiography', *Journal of the History of Ideas*, 58 (1997), 641–61.

France and, more congenially, from Italy. German *Aufklärer*, indeed, were political in a sense different from that associated with the Italian *illuministi*: more willingly employed by their princes, their thinking tended in return to be more practical and less critical.[57] It has been argued too that the 'national' character of the Enlightenment in Germany was evident in the translation and reception of foreign books: concepts which in other, more open, political cultures denoted participatory activism were rendered into German equivalents associated with individual striving and political acquiescence.[58]

But the most wholehearted in their adoption of the national approach to Enlightenment have been English-speaking scholars, British and North American. The presence and nature of Enlightenment in North America became the subject of intensive discussion among historians in the later 1970s.[59] At the centre of their discussions lay, unavoidably, the relation between Enlightenment and the revolution which began in 1776. It was clear that many of those who rebelled against British rule did so believing themselves to be members of a wider Enlightenment Republic of Letters; and subsequent French enthusiasm for their cause only strengthened the conviction. When Benjamin Franklin and later Thomas Jefferson took up residence in Paris as the American minister, they were more fêted by the *philosophes* than any visiting Scot or Italian. But the sense of belonging to the European world was offset by the force of local circumstance. Political necessity, and the remarkable intellectual inventiveness which was its offspring, combined to give American Enlightenment thinking a quite distinctive character. What that character was, whether it was republican or liberal, and how it related to colonial religious traditions, continues to be a subject of fierce dispute among historians; but the value of a national approach to the Enlightenment in America is unquestioned.

Still greater, however, has been the enthusiasm with which Enlightenment has been discovered and studied in eighteenth-century Scotland. Before 1960 it was scarcely recognised at all. Few remembered even that David Hume and Adam Smith were Scottish; that their contemporaries included Francis Hutcheson, Adam Ferguson, William Robertson, Thomas Reid, Lord Kames, and John Millar was long forgotten by all except a

---

[57] For recent guides in English: Johan van der Zande, 'Prussia and the Enlightenment', in Philip G. Dwyer (ed.), *The Rise of Prussia 1700–1830* (Harlow and London, 2000), pp. 89–107; on states other than Prussia, Charles Ingrao, 'The smaller German states', in Scott, *Enlightened Absolutism*, pp. 221–43.

[58] Fania Oz-Salzberger, *Translating the Enlightenment: Scottish Civic Discourse in Eighteenth-century Germany* (Oxford, 1995).

[59] Notably Donald H. Meyer, *The Democratic Enlightenment* (New York, 1976), and, perhaps the most influential, Henry F. May, *The Enlightenment in America* (New York, 1976).

handful of specialists. In very different contributions, Duncan Forbes and Hugh Trevor-Roper then brought 'the Scottish Enlightenment' to scholarly attention. Though they disputed priority in use of the term – mistakenly, because it had been coined by W. R. Scott in 1900 – they agreed in giving it a definite intellectual content, focusing on the Scottish thinkers' intense preoccupation with what they called 'the progress of society'.[60] Their explanations for the phenomenon were by no means confined to Scotland, emphasising rather the renewal early in the eighteenth century of Scottish connections with continental European thinking. By the 1980s, however, an approach to the Scottish Enlightenment in more strictly national context had become popular. Nicholas Phillipson led the way, the better to write a social history of ideas after the French model.[61] Quickly the scope of enquiry widened to include the social milieu of the philosophers, the universities and voluntary societies which provided them with careers and an appreciative audience for their ideas.[62] The extent to which Aberdeen and Glasgow were centres of intellectual activity alongside Edinburgh has increasingly been emphasised, underlining the 'national' character of this Enlightenment.[63] By 1990s, the grinding of patriotic, even 'nationalist' axes was becoming audible in the determination of some scholars to give priority to national origins of a national achievement.[64] Given that the Scots had accepted the loss of their Parliament at the Union with England in 1707, their Enlightenment could not have had the political focus provided by the independent states of Italy and Germany, or by the rebellion in the North American colonies. But the intensity of the Scots' discussions of moral philosophy, political economy, and history may have reflected an attempt to come to terms with their new political situation, and even to

[60] H. R. Trevor-Roper, 'The Scottish Enlightenment', *Studies on Voltaire and the Eighteenth Century*, 68 (1967), 1635–58. Duncan Forbes's major published contribution was *Hume's Philosophical Politics* (Cambridge, 1975). But before that he had drawn the attention of a generation of young scholars to its significance through his Cambridge history special subject, 'Hume, Smith and the Scottish Enlightenment', which ran during the 1960s; its takers included Quentin Skinner and Nicholas Phillipson.

[61] Nicholas T. Phillipson, 'Culture and society in the eighteenth-century province: the case of Edinburgh and the Scottish Enlightenment', in Lawrence Stone (ed.), *The University in Society*, 2 vols. (Princeton, 1974), II, pp. 407–48, and 'The Scottish Enlightenment', in Roy Porter and Mikulas Teich (eds.), *The Enlightenment in National Context* (Cambridge, 1981), pp. 19–40.

[62] Richard B. Sher, *Church and University in the Scottish Enlightenment: the Moderate Literati of Edinburgh* (Edinburgh and Princeton, 1985) being the outstanding study, complete with a comprehensive bibliography of the subject to that date.

[63] J. J. Carter and J. H. Pittock (eds.), *Aberdeen and the Enlightenment* (Aberdeen, 1987); Andrew Hook and Richard B. Sher (eds.), *The Glasgow Enlightenment* (East Linton, 1995).

[64] Alexander Broadie, *The Tradition of Scottish Philosophy* (Edinburgh, 1990); David Allan, *Virtue, Learning and the Scottish Enlightenment: Ideas of Scholarship in Early Modern History* (Edinburgh, 1993).

contribute to the creation of a new, British political identity.[65] If Enlight-enment in Scotland was only indirectly political, this was itself a function of its national setting.

By 2000, however, the Scottish Enlightenment was in some danger of being eclipsed – or (worse) subsumed – by a surge of interest in Enlighten-ment in England. Before the 1980s English historians had been inclined to accept Tocqueville's view that the Enlightenment was something England had not needed, since its public life was already open to the participation of men of letters. England had been spared that unhealthy separation of speculative thinking from the realities and responsibilities of active pol-itics which was so characteristic of the Enlightenment in *ancien régime* France. But with the waning of English historical isolationism, there was a new interest in finding common ground with the continent. If eighteenth-century England were itself to be regarded as an *ancien régime* society, as one historian forcibly argued it should,[66] there ought at least to be the com-pensation of discovering that it also had an Enlightenment. The most likely candidates for membership of such an English Enlightenment seemed to be the dissenters, especially the rational dissenters who took up the cause of religious liberty and the rights of the colonists in the last quarter of the century.[67] But a powerful alternative case has also been mounted, by John Pocock and Brian Young, for the development over the century as a whole of a distinctively conservative, anglican Enlightenment. This Pocock would treat as the English variant of the Protestant Enlightenment, comparable with similar Enlightenments in Scotland, North Germany, and Switzerland in its Erastian and Socinian tendency.[68] Even more enthusiasm for the cause was displayed by the late Roy Porter. Having first announced that there was Enlightenment in England in an essay published in 1981, Porter finally set out his case in full in *Enlightenment: Britain and the Creation of the Modern World* in 2000. As his title indicated, Porter's premise was the opposite of Pocock's: eighteenth-century England (and, by osmosis, Britain) was a modern, not an *ancien régime* society. Since it was modern, it followed that it must have had an Enlightenment to articulate its modernity. This

---

[65] Phillipson, 'Culture and society'; Colin Kidd, *Subverting Scotland's Past: Scottish Whig Historians and the Creation of an Anglo-British identity 1689–c.1830* (Cambridge, 1993).

[66] J. C. D. Clark, *English Society 1688–1832* (Cambridge, 1985).

[67] The dissenting Enlightenment is reviewed from various points of view in Knud Haakonssen (ed.), *Enlightenment and Religion: Rational Dissent in Eighteenth-century Britain* (Cambridge, 1996).

[68] John G. A. Pocock, in 'Clergy and commerce: the conservative Enlightenment in England'; 'Sette-cento Protestante?' and *The Enlightenments of Edward Gibbon*. By contrast, Brian W. Young, *Religion and Enlightenment in Eighteenth-century England: Theological Debate from Locke to Burke* (Oxford, 1998), has little time for Pocock's disquieting suggestion that the Anglican mainstream was Erastian and Socinian.

simple proposition asserted, Porter was free to include in his account of the British Enlightenment any and every aspect of eighteenth-century British intellectual and cultural life which took his expansive and inclusive fancy.[69]

Whatever the merits of his case for Enlightenment in England, it is Porter, along with his Cambridge colleague Mikulas Teich, who deserves the credit for spotting the potential of the national approach to the Enlightenment. It was their collaborative volume *The Enlightenment in National Context* (1981) which gave the approach a name and a focus. As a collection of articles devoted to Enlightenment in England, Scotland, and North America, as well as in the Netherlands, Sweden, Switzerland, Austria, Bohemia, and Russia, the volume quickly proved its usefulness for teaching (where its success made it the model for a whole series of thematic collections 'in national context'). But it also marked a turning point in Enlightenment scholarship. Although its title still acknowledged one Enlightenment, its implication was that each national Enlightenment could be studied as a separate phenomenon. In his opening plea for the recognition of Enlightenment in England, Porter himself confidently pronounced that the unity of the Enlightenment was a 'hallucination': the enquiry into Enlightenment in its national contexts should not be constrained by the belief that there must be common features in every case.[70] Although the editors left open the question of what counted as a 'nation', the tendency to divide the Enlightenment along political and confessional grounds was more or less explicitly endorsed.

That the national turn in Enlightenment studies has been enormously fruitful is beyond doubt. It has enlarged our understanding of the extent of Enlightenment activity across Europe, burying for ever the assumption that it was simply a movement of French *philosophes*, afforced by the occasional foreign visitor to Paris and the distant genius of Kant. The importance of Italian, German, and Scottish contributions to Enlightenment is now clearly established, and the contributions themselves are much better understood. As a result, a much more thoroughly historical account of Enlightenment across Europe can now be written, one which not only relates ideas to their political and social contexts, but which is sensitive to the various pre-existing settings in which ideas were received and developed in particular regions and states. The once clear division of labour between those who studied the Enlightenment's thinking through literature and philosophy and those who explored the ideas' application by absolutist rulers and their

---

[69] Roy Porter, 'The Enlightenment in England', in Porter and Teich, *The Enlightenment in National Context*; and *Enlightenment: Britain and the Creation of the Modern World* (London, 2000).

[70] Porter, 'The Enlightenment in England', pp. 4–5.

revolutionary antagonists has long since dissolved. But the consolidation of
the approach under the rubric of 'the Enlightenment in national context'
has also clarified its dangers. Its natural tendency has been to fragment
the Enlightenment into a series of more or less distinct Enlightenments,
each defined as best suits national historiography. Given that intellectual
historians are no longer certain what counts as Enlightenment thought,
while the social historians seek Enlightenment wherever they can identify
a sociable, 'public' culture, it seems prudent to concede national variety;
conversely, it seems unreasonable to deny Enlightenment to any individual nation, even to England. It is not the outcome which Venturi had in
mind when he pointed to the importance of the Enlightenment for Italy;
indeed he regarded England as proof that Enlightenment was not to be
found everywhere, remarking that 'in England the rhythm was different'.[71]
But as we shall see, Venturi never imagined that Enlightenment could be
understood in national context alone.

The volume and richness of the scholarship which has resulted from
the new directions in study of the Enlightenment since the 1960s plainly
make any return to a simple, traditional account of it impossible. But
if the implications of this work are to deprive the Enlightenment of a
coherent intellectual identity, to reduce its ideas to the discursive practices
of sociability, and to fragment it into separate, national units, is there
any prospect of restoring to it the character of a connected intellectual
movement?

RECONSTITUTING THE ENLIGHTENMENT

If a case for the Enlightenment is to be made at all, it must begin with
ideas. It is clear that an account of Enlightenment thought can no longer
be based simply on the contents of the *philosophes*' books, and given a
greater or lesser degree of philosophic coherence by reference to Kant. But
the intellectual coherence of the Enlightenment may still be found, I will
contend, in the commitment to understanding, and hence to advancing,
the causes and conditions of human betterment in this world. The first
part of this formula is as important as the second: the Enlightenment was
committed to understanding, that is to analysis on the basis of good argument, leading to reasoned conclusions. There was a core of original thinking
to the Enlightenment: it was not simply a matter of common aspirations

---

[71] Venturi, *Utopia and Reform*, p. 132.

and values. Within that core the understanding of human betterment was pursued across a number of interdependent lines of enquiry.

For many the starting point was human nature itself – the connected study of the understanding, the passions, and the process of moral judgement which David Hume christened 'the science of man'. In systematic study of the understanding and the passions, as, still more, in the sceptical subordination of reason to the passions, eighteenth-century philosophers were of course the heirs of several predecessors in the seventeenth century. The Enlightenment philosophers were original, however, in the deliberate attempt to join mental and moral philosophy in a single science, in which the framework for the investigation of individual behaviour was provided by human society rather than divine authority.

A second line of enquiry was into the conditions specifically of material betterment, the subject matter of political economy. Sophisticated writing on economic affairs of course predated the Enlightenment, being increasingly widespread from the later seventeenth century. But from the 1740s there can be seen a conscious attempt on the part of French, Italian, German, and Scottish thinkers to render political economy a distinct, systematic field of investigation. No longer concerned with the aggrandisement of governments at each other's expense, this was a political economy whose goals were the wealth of nations (in the plural) and the improvement of the condition of all of society's members. Understood in these terms, political economy was the key to what the Enlightenment explicitly thought of as 'the progress of society'.

But the progress of society was not simply a matter of material improvement. Accompanying the enquiry into political economy was a third, more general concern to investigate the structure and manners of societies at the various stages of their development, to trace and explain the historical process as a passage from 'barbarism' to 'refinement' or 'civilisation'. The scope of this enquiry was potentially wide, ranging across manners in all their variety, the rise and refinement of the arts and sciences, moral relations, including those between the sexes, forms of property-holding, including the exercise of property rights over the labour of others, and the means and ends of punishment. In turn many of these were closely related to the question of which forms of government were associated with different stages of development. Given a capacity on the part of humanity to 'polish' or even (as many followed Rousseau in supposing) to 'perfect' its nature, it was widely believed that the progress of society should culminate in the achievement of a new state of civilisation. But given too that the progress of many actual societies had by no means been uninterrupted, few thought they had good reason to suppose that progress would end in a state of perfection; like Rousseau, many continued to doubt whether civilisation could ever be made fully secure against 'corruption' or 'degeneration'.

Together these three lines of enquiry converged upon the concept of 'sociability'. In the study of human nature, the starting point was the question so dramatically put by Hobbes, whether sociability was natural to man, or his artificial construction. Political economy was founded on the premise that self-interested exchange, based on a division of labour, was the first and most essential social activity. On these foundations, the critical question for those who studied the progress of society was whether that progress (or its reverse) was the product of human design, or the outcome of unintended consequences. Across the three spheres of enquiry, in short, the objective was to establish the material and moral conditions and mechanisms of sociability, the better to clear the path for human betterment, and to assess the prospects of its realisation. If sociability was also a culture, as the social historians of Enlightenment would suggest, it was as a contested idea that it concentrated the minds of Enlightenment thinkers.

A case for the Enlightenment's intellectual originality in these terms requires a number of qualifications. To identify the integrated study of human nature, of political economy, and of the progress and refinement of society as the connecting threads of the Enlightenment's commitment to understanding human betterment is not to suggest that they constituted a single, seamless intellectual project, pursued by all the Enlightenment's adherents. Few thinkers were equally interested, let alone competent, in each of the fields of enquiry. At the same time, few confined their interests to these fields. Many Enlightenment thinkers were also students of the natural world; others were passionately interested in music. It was a matter of priorities; what characterised the Enlightenment was the new primacy accorded to human betterment, to the possibility – not the inevitability – of progress in the present world. Even then there remained wide scope for disagreement over the means to achieve progress, as well as over the definition and compatibility of its ends. Philosophers continued to argue over the powers of the mind, its capacity to apprehend the external world and to establish moral truths. Political economists differed over whether agricultural and commercial societies should follow distinct paths of development. Strongest of all, perhaps, were the disagreements among those concerned with manners and culture, between those who heeded and those who rejected Rousseau's warnings that refinement would lead to corruption, and that progress must end in decline. Yet even those most fearful of decline accepted a central proposition: societies are subject to change, and humans can better their condition. Enlightenment enquiries, moreover, adapted and developed in response to fresh intellectual stimuli: the debates of the 1770s and 1780s were often markedly different in their concerns from those of the 1750s.

It is also important to emphasise that the intellectual coherence of the Enlightenment was not predicated upon a complete denial of the possibility of revealed religion. It is here, as I have already indicated, that the perspective of this book differs from that of Israel's *Radical Enlightenment*. The boldness with which Spinoza, Toland, and Giannone had criticised the authority of Scripture continued to be an inspiration to many well after 1750. But Spinoza's materialism did not exhaust the philosophical resources available to Enlightenment thinkers; a far more common reference point was the works of Bayle, whose scepticism seemed, at least, to stop short of revelation, leaving it to his readers to decide what weight they wished to place on it. In Catholic Europe the notorious fate of Giannone, kidnapped, imprisoned, and suffering the confiscation of his writings, was an exemplary warning that open irreligion would not be tolerated. Even in Protestant countries there were boundaries which could not be crossed with impunity. Radicals like Toland and Radicati were marginalised and isolated, while the ecclesiastical and civil authorities in both the United Kingdom and the United Provinces remained vigilant against overt manifestations of Socinianism, still regarded, with its elder cousin Arianism, as the most dangerous of heresies. By the 1740s, therefore, it was clear that radical heterodoxy and open irreligion – Israel's 'radical Enlightenment' – had failed to break down the barriers which the authorities had erected against them, and could not expect to dictate the intellectual agenda.

This is not to say that Enlightenment criticisms of organised religion were of marginal significance. As an institution in this world, the church – any church – was all too likely to be the target of criticism for the intolerance of its clergy towards the beliefs of those who disagreed or dissented. Additional criticism was levelled at the Roman Catholic church for the scale and nature of its property-holding, widely perceived as an obstacle to economic development in the backward regions of Europe. Any pretension to exercise power over the affairs of this world on the basis of an authority derived from the next had become unacceptable. But such criticism did not automatically touch revelation itself: a focus on betterment in this world carried no necessary implication about the existence of the next. A small number of sceptical Enlightenment philosophers did indeed openly question its existence; but many more retained their faith. What the latter did have to concede was the inadequacy, indeed inhumanity, of the doctrine which held out the pleasures of the next world as consolation for the hardships of the present. Whatever might be awaiting the redeemed in the world to come, improvement of the human lot was possible in this world, here and now.

Equally, to claim that the intellectual originality of the Enlightenment lay in its commitment to the study of human betterment does not entail that its choice of intellectual interests was unprecedented, without roots in the concerns of later seventeenth- and early eighteenth-century thinkers. The conviction that it should be possible systematically to investigate human social and economic relations and the course of their historical development clearly owed much to the example of the revolution wrought in the study of the natural world over the seventeenth century. The confidence of Galileo and Newton that nature was governed by observable laws was transferred to the study of society, along with the Baconian aspiration to apply this knowledge to the benefit of mankind. This did not mean that the investigation of nature itself remained central to the Enlightenment, or that Enlightenment thinkers can be characterised simply as 'Baconian' or 'Newtonian' in their methods. Nevertheless the ideal of scientific method continued to be a source of inspiration, its potential perhaps most fully realised in the *science sociale* projected by one of the last of the *philosophes*, Condorcet.[72]

In this book, it is other ideas inherited from the seventeenth and early eighteenth centuries which receive most attention as inspiration of Enlightenment enquiries. Prominent among these will be found to have been the encounter between the Augustinian rigorism of Pascal and Port Royal and the revived, supposedly Christianised Epicureanism championed by Gassendi and his followers. From this encounter developed the realisation, articulated most provocatively by Bayle, that a society of self-interested men, driven by their passions rather than their reason, could nevertheless survive and meet its needs with no external assistance from divine providence and only limited intervention by government. Together with the growing corpus of economic writings and the increasingly historical cast of the natural jurists' accounts of the formation of society, the development of this Augustinian–Epicurean understanding of man goes far to explain why the Enlightenment thinkers focused their interests in the way they did. But it does not mean that their enquiries should simply be assimilated to those which went before. In their systematic ambition as well as in their

[72] Keith M. Baker, *Condorcet: from Natural Philosophy to Social Mathematics* (Chicago and London, 1975).

scope, the Enlightenment's enquiries into human nature, political economy, and the progress of society were a profoundly original contribution to the development of European thought.

A renewed emphasis on the primacy of ideas to the Enlightenment does not mean that the questions raised by its social historians can simply be set aside. Its adherents had to live in the world as well as think about it, and needed careers and recognition, along with outlets for their writings. Outwith France there are still many countries where the material and cultural infrastructure of the Enlightenment remains little studied. But the social history of Enlightenment cannot simply be left to its 'social historians'. A case for the Enlightenment which restores the primacy of its intellectual contribution also needs to reconsider the perspective in which its social history is written. It is too often assumed that the integrity of ideas will be compromised by any evidence of material or institutional dependence on the part of a writer.[73] But Enlightenment thinkers were by no means hostage to their careers and institutional backgrounds. On the contrary, it may be argued, their distinguishing social characteristic was their claim to an independent status in society, by virtue of their intellectual leadership.

It is true that no single term quite captures the status to which the Enlightenment thinkers aspired. It was most confidently assumed by the *philosophes*, whose success as authors, often underpinned by private means and a sympathetic female patron, enabled them to assert their independence from the ecclesiastical, university, and academic authorities. But the term *philosophe* had too many connotations specific to its Parisian origins to be used of all the Enlightenment's adherents: David Hume, though he knew the *philosophes* well, and shared many of their interests, would not have welcomed that appellation. To get round the problem, it has been suggested, notably by Venturi and Darnton, that the *philosophes* were prototypical 'intellectuals', and that this term may be extended to their counterparts elsewhere. Venturi may well have borrowed the term from the nineteenth-century Russian intelligentsia, the focus of his study of Russian populism;[74] but there appears to be no such proximate rationale for Darnton's bald statement that 'the *philosophe* was a new social type, known to us today as the intellectual'.[75] Pocock has justifiably objected to this retrospective

---

[73] The issue has dogged Darnton and his critics, notably Daniel Gordon: see the latter's contribution, 'The great Enlightenment massacre', in Mason, *The Darnton Debate*, esp. pp. 138–45; and Darnton's reply. 'Two paths', esp. pp. 267–72.

[74] Franco Venturi, *Roots of Revolution: a History of the Populist and Socialist Movements in Nineteenth-century Russia*, transl. F. H. Haskell (London, 1960); originally published in Italian in 1952.

[75] Darnton, 'George Washington's false teeth', p. 5.

conceptualisation, with its connotation of alienation from the states and societies in which Enlightenment thinkers lived. In his view, we must accept the much looser contemporary designation 'men of letters', and admit that men of letters played different Enlightenment roles in different contexts.[76] But the usage of a term which was both older than the Enlightenment and adopted by many with quite different interests did not prevent adherents of Enlightenment from asserting an independent identity within and beyond their respective societies. They might not be able to declare themselves a single, unified corps; but they made very similar claims to recognition from their societies, claims founded on the authority of their ideas, rather than on that of the established institutions.[77]

Many men of letters, especially in Protestant countries, also enjoyed careers in clerical orders or in the universities. The universities in particular continued to offer one of the securest and most congenial employments any man of letters could hope for. But it does not follow that the Enlightenment in those countries should be treated as an academic, university phenomenon.[78] That there was a difference between universities and Enlightenment was the point made by Kant, himself the finest ornament of the Prussian university system, when he addressed the question *Was ist Aufklärung?* in 1784. In their 'private' capacity as clergymen or professors, he conceded, individuals were bound to accept the restrictions on their freedom to speak which the institutions they served might impose. It was in their 'public' capacity, as members of society at large, that they should expect to advance the goals of Enlightenment.[79] In practice the point had been made forty years earlier, when David Hume was denied the chair of moral philosophy at Edinburgh in 1745, at least partly because of the suspicion that he would refuse to accept that his teaching must endorse certain theological propositions. But it was not simply a matter of religious restrictions: both Adam Smith and Adam Ferguson, who conformed to the religious requirements of teaching moral philosophy, seem to have chafed at the intellectual restrictions which their chairs imposed. Dominated as they were by natural and civil jurisprudence, the lecture courses of Protestant as

---

[76] Pocock, *The Enlightenments of Edward Gibbon*, pp. 6–7, 299.

[77] For a characterisation of the Enlightenment man of letters: Roger Chartier, 'The Man of Letters', in M. Vovelle (ed.), *Enlightenment Portraits* (Chicago and London, 1997), pp. 142–89.

[78] As suggested, for example, by Pocock, 'Settecento protestante?', pp. 328–9.

[79] James Schmidt (ed.), *What is Enlightenment? Eighteenth-Century Answers and Twentieth-Century Questions* (Berkeley, Los Angeles and London, 1996), pp. 58–64: Immanuel Kant, 'An answer to the question: What is Enlightenment?' (1784). The volume includes other contributions to the debate which had been instigated by the *Berliner Monatsschrift*, and an excellent commentary by John Christian Laursen, 'The subversive Kant: the vocabulary of "public" and "publicity"', pp. 253–69.

well as Catholic universities were not necessarily well adapted to the sorts of enquiry in which Enlightenment thinkers were engaged, or to the forms in which they wished to publish their conclusions.[80]

Instead of the churches and universities, the source of authority to which the Enlightenment thinkers most frequently appealed was 'public opinion'. The phenomenon of public opinion has been the subject of intensive recent discussion by historians, particularly those of France. Following Keith Baker, many now believe that it holds the key to explaining how ideas became a political force, and hence offers a new opportunity to re-assess the cultural and ideological causes of the Revolution.[81] But the phenomenon has also attracted the attention of historians of the Enlightenment in France. These historians have asked the prior question of the way in which Enlightenment thinkers themselves understood and sought to use public opinion in support of their claim to intellectual leadership.[82]

Exactly what constituted 'the public' and its 'opinion', and how it should be addressed, were most thoroughly discussed in France. The advantage to writers of addressing 'the public' rather than a more specific audience was clear: it enabled them to retain the intellectual initiative, setting the terms on which they engaged with their readers. Through the *Encyclopédie* and in their individual works, the *philosophes* made inventive use of literary form as well as intellectual content in the effort to encourage readers to respond critically to what they were reading. That this response might not be the one expected was disconcerting and sometimes frustrating, but the fact of the response itself was confirmation that the public recognised the writers' intellectual leadership.[83] What could compromise their position, however, was too close an association with politics. On specific issues of injustice,

---

[80] For a study of teaching in Catholic universities, in a state whose civil rulers were anxious to control education without alienating the ecclesiastical hierarchy, Patrizia Delpiano, *Il trono e la cattedra. Istruzione e formazione dell'élite nel Piemonte del Settecento* (Turin, 1997).

[81] Keith M. Baker, 'Public opinion as political invention', in his *Inventing the French Revolution: Essays on French Political Culture in the Eighteenth Century* (Cambridge, 1990), pp. 167–99. See also Mona Ozouf, '"Public Opinion" at the end of the Old Regime', *Journal of Modern History*, 60 (1988), supplement, 1–21; Chartier, *Cultural Origins*, pp. 20–37; Darnton, *Forbidden Best-Sellers*, pp. 232–46. For an assessment of Darnton's use of the concept: Thomas E. Kaiser, 'Enlightenment, public opinion and politics in the work of Robert Darnton', in Mason, *The Darnton Debate*, pp. 189–206. Van Horn Melton, *The Rise of the Public*, ch. 2, 'Opacity and transparency: French political culture in the eighteenth century' is an excellent recent overview of the subject.

[82] Gordon, *Citizens without Sovereignty*, pp. 199–208; Goodman, *The Republic of Letters*, pp. 118–19, 235–42.

[83] See the earlier study by Dena Goodman, *Criticism in Action: Enlightenment Experiments in Political Writing* (Ithaca and London, 1989); also, on a specific case where public opinion was invoked, and gave an unexpected response, 'The Hume–Rousseau affair: from private *Querelle* to public *Procès*', *Eighteenth-Century Studies*, 25 (1991–92), 171–201.

such as the great judicial *causes célèbres* of Jean Calas and the Chevalier de la Barre, public opinion might be invoked as a court of appeal. But the fate of Turgot's carefully orchestrated campaign to mobilise opinion on behalf of a liberalisation of the grain trade, a measure whose failure brought down his ministry, was a warning against tying intellectual authority too closely to a particular political cause.

Elsewhere, the scope for treating public opinion as an independent tribunal of intellectual authority was often much less. It was perhaps least in England, the country in which, as the French acknowledged, the idea of public opinion had originated, for the reason that there it was already politicised. Hume's attempts to use the essay as a vehicle for raising the level of public discussion of economic and political subjects met with limited success in London, where he was initially received as another opposition partisan.[84] Fortunately, there was more scope for such discussion in Scotland, where the loss of the Scottish Parliament in 1707 had removed the focus of politics, and made it easier for men of letters to claim independent standing. In Germany and Italy, by contrast, the problem was the opposite: many rulers were reluctant to allow public debate beyond the confines of the court and the administration. They might be more or less willing to offer men of letters the opportunity to exercise a direct influence on policy through government office. But office could not be a substitute for public opinion as a source of intellectual authority, and was all too likely to lead to the obscuring of the Enlightenment's larger objectives in the struggle to enact specific reforms. In the kingdom of Naples, as we shall see, it was a conviction that effective reforms were far more likely to follow the raising of public expectations of economic and social change which inspired Antonio Genovesi's remarkable attempt to create a public opinion independent of the court and the administrative tribunals.

Even if the public opinion to which Enlightenment men of letters appealed was sometimes little more than a figment of their imagination, a point was still made by invoking it. For it signalled a deliberate breaking with the traditional, humanist model of the philosopher as the private counsellor of kings and ministers, whose advice was given in secret. By choosing instead to address an educated 'public', Enlightenment men of letters took an independent intellectual initiative, and broadened the scope of debate.

---

[84] M. M. Goldsmith, 'Faction detected: ideological consequences of Robert Walpole's decline and fall', *History*, 64 (1979), pp. 14–19.

This was not simply self-promotion: the Enlightenment thinkers had good intellectual reason to value public opinion above direct political influence. For implicit in their commitment to the study of the laws of political economy and of the progress of society was a recognition of the limits which they set upon politics. In a world in which commerce was becoming ever more widespread and important, decisions which affected the lives and well-being of many were being taken by individual economic agents out of a prevailing motive of self-interest, with little or no regard for what rulers wished to happen.[85] When the Enlightenment thinkers set themselves to identify the regularities in the patterns of men's commercial activities, or in the historical relations between forms of property-holding and stages of social organisation, they were explaining why the powers of politicians and statesmen over society were by no means as great as they supposed. By failing to appreciate this, moreover, the politicians were far more likely to obstruct than to facilitate the workings of society. These conclusions did not lead Enlightenment thinkers to discount the possibility of reform; the Enlightenment was by no means apolitical. Even the most sceptical of Enlightenment thinkers left room at least for remedial political action. But the purpose of reform should be the removal of obstacles to the optimal course of development, not the imposition of ambitious schemes of the politician's own devising. Enlightenment thinking thus ran counter to the traditional doctrine of 'reason of state', by which rulers and their advisers had claimed to know what was good for their subjects, and had presumed to manipulate their affairs accordingly. Instead the point of appealing to 'public opinion' was to exert an external, constraining influence on governments. By invoking 'the public' as their tribunal, the Enlightenment thinkers could hope simultaneously to establish their own credentials as an independent source of intellectual authority, and to educate government and society at large in the forces which were shaping the modern world. By the end of the 1780s, writers in several parts of the continent were confident enough to address their rulers directly, and not merely through public opinion. But they did so with the confidence that they now spoke *for*, not simply to, 'the public', and were thus entitled to expect rulers to heed their opinions.

---

[85] On this fundamental theme, Istvan Hont, 'Free trade and the economic limits to national politics: neo-Machiavellian political economy reconsidered', in John Dunn (ed.), *The Economic Limits to Modern Politics* (Cambridge, 1990), pp. 41–120; reprinted in Istvan Hont, *Jealousy of Trade: International Competition and the Nation State in Historical Perspective* (Cambridge, Mass., 2005).

Without recourse to the anachronism of calling them 'intellectuals', therefore, it is possible to regard Enlightenment men of letters as having engaged with their societies from a position of independence, an independence earned by intellectual standing and expressed by addressing a public opinion distinct from the policy of rulers and their ministers. But if their energies were devoted to their publics, does this not suggest that Enlightenment men of letters were indeed, as Pocock maintains, bound closely to their national or state contexts? Can we speak of one Enlightenment in the absence of a common European 'public'? Plainly there can be no going back to the traditional view of an Enlightenment cosmopolitan simply by virtue of being French. A formula which would encompass both the unity and the variety of the Enlightenment was, however, suggested some time ago by Franco Venturi, the pioneer of the 'national' approach. To Venturi the point of the Enlightenment lay in its successful combination of the cosmopolitan with the patriotic. Adherents of the Enlightenment were cosmopolitan in their awareness of the similarity of their intellectual interests and goals, and in taking it for granted that they should communicate these across frontiers and language barriers. But they were equally patriotic in their commitment to harnessing the common stock of ideas to the improvement of their own individual societies.[86] Of itself, Venturi's formula was generic; but it clearly informed his own work on the Italians, and it will be one of the purposes of this study to give it renewed substance.

An infrastructure of intellectual cosmopolitanism was already in existence, in the institutions and practices of the Republic of Letters. By 1700 the term *respublica literaria* was three centuries old; what it and its direct vernacular equivalents represented has been the subject of increasingly intensive investigation by historians.[87] What is still a topic for debate is the extent to which the Enlightenment marked a fresh phase in its development.

While the term itself has been found in use in 1417, a Europe-wide Republic of Letters was effectively the creation of Erasmus a century later. The key to its character as a network for correspondence and the exchange of books, manuscripts, antiquities, and specimens was its independence of the church. The Republic of Letters was from its inception a lay institution, not in the sense that it excluded clergymen, but in that it was designed to operate outwith the structures of the church, preventing the ecclesiastical hierarchy from dictating the terms of intellectual exchange.

---

[86] Franco Venturi, *Italy and the Enlightenment: Studies in a Cosmopolitan Century*, ed. Stuart Woolf (London, 1972), preface.

[87] On both the term and what it respresented: Françoise Waquet, 'Qu'est-ce que la République des Lettres? Essai de sémantique historique', *Bibliothèque de l'École des chartes*, 147 (1989), 473–502.

When, within decades, the Western church broke up as a result of Reformation and Counter-Reformation, the Republic of Letters survived as the only genuinely international framework for intellectual communication. Rising above confessional polarisation, the Republic continued to grow and develop in the seventeenth century. The first phase of expansion came with the emergence of individuals, most famously Nicolas-Claude Fabri de Peiresc and Marin Mersenne, who were prepared to act as focal correspondents, connecting others across Europe; later their heroic labours were taken over by the secretaries of learned academies, keen to establish connections with each other.[88] But the most dramatic phase in the Republic's development came in the late seventeenth and early eighteenth centuries, when enterprising minds in the Huguenot exile community in the United Provinces pioneered new means for the dissemination of knowledge. One was the journal of book reviews (usually containing substantial extracts from the book under review as well as critical comment). Bayle's *Nouvelles de la République des Lettres* (1684–7) led the way; even more assiduous was Jean le Clerc, whose *Bibliothèque Universelle* (1686–93) was succeeded by two more ventures.[89] Bayle, meanwhile, had turned aside to transform another instrument for the dissemination of knowledge by his *Dictionnaire historique et critique* (1697, with a second edition in 1702). Underpinning these new forms of publication lay a growing infrastructure of printers, publishers, authors' agents, and booksellers, whose living depended on the Republic's existence and continued development.[90]

What is less clear is the extent to which the Republic of Letters had come to embody a distinct set of values. Its operation certainly depended on a set of conventions, to which letters of introduction and a willingness to accept reciprocity in the exchange of books and objects were fundamental. For many, perhaps the majority, of the Republic's members, this was all: the pursuit of scholarly, erudite interests required an etiquette, not an ideology.[91] But the leading role taken in the Republic's transformation from the 1680s onwards by the Huguenot exile community invested the idea of the *république des lettres* with a greater significance. For many of its members it became, self-consciously, a refuge, even a bastion, of intellectual and religious tolerance. In their communications members of the

---

[88] Maarten Ultee, 'The Republic of Letters: learned correspondence 1680–1720', *The Seventeenth Century*, 2 (1987), 95–112.

[89] Israel, *Radical Enlightenment*, pp. 142–55: 'The Learned Journals'.

[90] Anne Goldgar, *Impolite Learning: Conduct and Community in the Republic of Letters, 1680–1750* (New Haven and London, 1995).

[91] One point on which Goldgar, *Impolite Learning*, is in broad agreement with Laurence Brockliss, *Calvet's Web: Enlightenment and the Republic of Letters in Eighteenth-century France* (Oxford, 2002).

Republic expected each other to rise above confessional differences, and in their foreign correspondence to step outside of whatever constraints their local rulers might place them under. In this there may have been an echo of the universalism of the *respublica christiana* – though tolerance would require that the content of that potentially aggressive ideal was not examined too closely.[92] Strongly as these cosmopolitan values were felt, however, the autonomy they asserted remained inward looking. The Republic of Letters existed to facilitate the exchanges of its members, but it was not – yet – a platform from which to address a wider 'public'.

This, it may be suggested, was what the Enlightenment added to the Republic of Letters later in the eighteenth century. Determined to address a wider public as well as each other, Enlightenment men of letters took advantage of an increasingly adaptable publishing industry to achieve their ends. By collaborating with enterprising publishers, they were able to realise the project of the *Encyclopédie*, to make available many more translations into and out of French, and to reach different levels of reader and different sizes of pocket by reissuing books in cheaper formats. Improvement and reform, rather than erudition for its own sake, were the watchwords.[93] None of these developments would make it possible to override all differences of inherited religious or national intellectual culture. Even the process of translation was liable to modify meaning, sometimes substantially.[94] Nevertheless, it is clear that the Republic of Letters now gave Enlightenment men of letters access to an unprecedented range of means of communication, enabling them to set themselves a common intellectual agenda directed towards human betterment, at the same time as they educated their publics on the means to its achievement. Intellectual cosmopolitanism could be combined with an outward-looking, public-conscious patriotism.

Laurence Brockliss has gone so far as to suggest that the Enlightenment and the Republic of Letters may be regarded as one. But as he acknowledges

---

[92] Waquet, 'Qu'est-ce que la République des Lettres?', pp. 494–500, offers a relatively generous assessment of the Republic's ideals; Lorraine Daston, 'The ideal and reality of the Republic of Letters in the Enlightenment', *Science in Context*, 4 (1991), pp. 370–5, emphasises the new 'gregarious sociability' of 'intellectuals' from the later seventeenth century onwards. A more cautious note is struck by Malcolm, 'Hobbes and the European Republic of Letters', pp. 539–41.

[93] Goodman, *The Republic of Letters*, pp. 12–52, charts the transformation of the Republic of Letters in relation to the new public sphere; Goldgar, *Impolite Learning*, pp. 219–50, contends that the Enlightenment Republic of Letters represented a sad decline after its scholarly predecessor, substituting polite manners – 'talking about nothing' – for erudition.

[94] On 'the hazards of translation', Oz-Salzberger, *Translating the Enlightenment*, pp. 77–85, 138–66; more recently (and more positively), her article on 'Translation', in the *Encyclopedia of the Enlightenment*. For another, subtly stated case: László Kontler, 'William Robertson and his German audience on European and pan-European civilisations', *Scottish Historical Review*, 80 (2001), 63–89.

in his study of Esprit Calvet, an assiduous Provençal member of the Republic in the later eighteenth century, it was perfectly possible to participate in the Republic of Letters as a correspondent, antiquary, natural historian, and bibliophile – and remain contentedly ignorant of Enlightenment thinking.[95] It seems better to think of the eighteenth-century Republic of Letters as being adapted, not absorbed, by the Enlightenment. Adherents of Enlightenment worked within it, the better to use it for their own distinctive intellectual and public purposes.

An Enlightenment reconstituted on the terms I have suggested does not include everything which many recent scholars have wished to associate with it. There were limits, first of all, to its intellectual range. Although individual Enlightenment thinkers had a variety of interests, the focus of their enquiries, and subject of their most original contributions, was human society and the physical and moral well-being of individuals in this world. As such, Enlightenment by no means encompassed every area of intellectual activity in the period, and it excluded or marginalised several other original lines of thought. To limit the intellectual range of Enlightenment in this way is also to narrow its possible chronological extent: though beginning at different times in different places, it was broadly between the 1740s and the 1790s that the investigation of the progress of society and the accompanying confidence in the prospects of its betterment were concentrated. It bears repeating that to set Enlightenment within chronological limits is not to imply that it was cut off from the intellectual worlds which preceded and followed it: both the form and the content of its enquiries were profoundly shaped by several currents in late seventeenth- and early eighteenth-century thought, and in turn shaped the intellectual culture of the nineteenth century. What is being suggested, however, is that the Enlightenment should be understood as a distinct episode in European intellectual history. At the same time, the Enlightenment as it has been reconstituted here was also confined geographically to the European world (which still included colonial America). If historians find it convenient to speak of 'Enlightenments' in other civilisations, they were not extensions of the European original. Even within Europe, the reach of the Enlightenment was uneven. There were areas in which individuals bravely pursued the intellectual commitments of the Enlightenment, but were too isolated to be active participants in the wider movement. Greece and the Balkans, whose connections with the Enlightenment

---

[95] Brockliss, *Calvet's Web, passim.* Calvet knew of Voltaire and Rousseau by reputation, but owned only one small pamphlet by Voltaire, and nothing by Rousseau, Diderot, d'Holbach, or Helvétius.

have been studied by Paschalis Kitromilides, appear to have been such a region.[96]

At the other end of the spectrum was the case of England. As it has been characterised here, the Enlightenment did not have a significant presence in England. The ideas of the early eighteenth-century English deists and anti-trinitarians, Collins, Clarke, and (by association) Toland, reinforced by the anti-clerical writings of the neo-republicans Walter Moyle and John Trenchard, were indeed an inspiration to heterodoxy among continental Catholics as much as Protestants. More generally, the works of the great philosophers of the late seventeenth and early eighteenth centuries, Newton, Locke, and Shaftesbury, would contribute much to the intellectual formation of Enlightenment thinkers across Europe. Yet the commitments which were central to the Enlightenment itself, the development of the sciences of man and of political economy, the historical investigation of the progress of society, and the critical application of ideas for human betterment to the existing social and political order – these were not at the forefront of English intellectual life between 1740 and 1780. Each of these fields of enquiry had its devotees; but they were not in England, as they were in France, Germany, Italy, and Scotland, the focus of concerted, systematic attention among the country's leading minds. The one Englishman whose Enlightenment interests led to a major work, the historian Edward Gibbon, looked to Scotland for recognition, and retreated to Switzerland to write. Nor did English men and women of letters lay claim to a position of intellectual leadership comparable with that assumed by their continental or even their Scottish counterparts. Instead they had to compete with writers and journalists of every level of talent and none in the great literary marketplace of London. To adapt Roy Porter's terms, there is a sense in which in England modernity pre-empted Enlightenment. Most English men of letters were already confident of their liberty, and of enjoying the benefits of commerce; they evidently felt no pressing need to study them systematically. If there was an English contribution to the Enlightenment, it may be found among the radical and unitarian minority who doubted whether liberty and the gains of commerce were quite what they seemed. These came to the fore between the 1770s and 1790s, and included Richard Price, Joseph Priestley, Jeremy Bentham, Mary Wollstonecraft, and William Godwin. Alert to developments in the rest of Europe, early supporters and anguished observers of the Revolution in France, they may

---

[96] Paschalis M. Kitromilides, *The Enlightenment as Social Criticism: Iosipos Moisiodax and Greek Culture in the Eighteenth Century* (Princeton, 1992).

well be regarded as belonging in the late Enlightenment whose leaders were Condorcet and Gaetano Filangieri. But their very radicalism excluded them from a central role in English public life; they could not make up for the absence of Enlightenment thinkers in the previous four decades. It was an absence which left a lasting gap in the history of English intellectual and public life.

The Enlightenment depicted here was limited in one further respect. It was, unavoidably, a movement of an intellectual elite. Its adherents were indeed committed to the wider dissemination of their ideas; they were keen to engage 'the public' in discussion. But their priorities remained intellectual, and they looked to public opinion to confirm their intellectual authority. As an intellectual movement, in short, the Enlightenment was not equivalent to a culture of sociability, however it may have encouraged one to develop.

To insist on these limits to the Enlightenment is to set aside much that recent scholarship has suggested is of great interest. (It is not, of course, to suggest that what is set aside should not be studied in its own right.) But it is equally the case that the unrestricted definition of Enlightenment, or its alternative, the admission that there were multiple Enlightenments, has rendered the subject so blurred and indeterminate that it is impossible to reach any assessment of its historical significance. Even if this is an effective response to those who imagined that there was a clear-cut 'Enlightenment project', it is a response close to conceding that the Enlightenment is no longer worth arguing over. By contrast, the Enlightenment for which I have made a case here is one whose significance it is possible to assess as a historical phenomenon rather than as an arbitrary philosophical construct. It is an Enlightenment which took root in very different intellectual, social, and political settings across eighteenth-century Europe (and North America), and whose adherents thus addressed themselves to a wide variety of economic and social conditions. It is not an Enlightenment whose horizons extended beyond the world of the *ancien régime*; if many of its younger adherents found themselves taking responsibility for its ideas in the revolutionary decade of the 1790s, that responsibility does not extend, in any direct way, far into the nineteenth let alone the twentieth centuries. Far too much history lies in between for it to make sense to hold the Enlightenment accountable for the horrors, any more than the advances, of the twentieth century. But as a specific intellectual movement of the eighteenth century, the Enlightenment can be matched against the conditions which faced it in its own time. Its contribution to the modern world may then be judged on the intellectual interest of its reflection on the societies it observed, and on the cogency of its recommendations for the improvement of the human condition as it found it. It is as a small step towards making such an assessment possible that this book proposes to undertake a comparative study of the Enlightenment in Scotland and Naples.

A COMPARATIVE STUDY: ENLIGHTENMENT IN SCOTLAND AND NAPLES

Why a comparative study? In his pioneering discussion 'For a comparative history of European societies', Marc Bloch observed that historical comparison presupposes both common ground and difference between the subjects to be studied. There must be a certain similarity between the facts observed, and a certain dissimilarity between the milieus in which the facts occurred. The similarities are likely to be stronger between neighbouring or contemporary societies, which can mutually influence each other; but actual connections are not essential to establish similar facts. The possible objectives of comparative study of the facts are various: among them Bloch himself included the discovery of unexpected similar facts, the identification of the general causes underlying similarities, and the establishment of hitherto unnoticed differences.[97] With some rephrasing, each of Bloch's objectives may be adapted to the present case.

First, the discovery of unexpected similar facts in dissimilar milieus. For the purposes of this study, it is not so much a matter of discovering facts which are unexpected as of testing their existence where they are disputed. What is to be explored is the extent to which a similar Enlightenment – Enlightenment in the singular, with or without the definite article – was present in the separate and dissimilar milieus of eighteenth-century Scotland and Naples (by the latter being indicated the kingdom as well as the city). Prima facie, there is evidence of the presence of Enlightenment in the two societies. In both Scotland and Naples we can find major thinkers interested in the study of human nature, political economy, and the progress of society, and committed to the betterment of life on earth regardless of the next. Scotland was perhaps especially fortunate to have two thinkers of the stature of David Hume and Adam Smith. But Enlightenment could not have been of their making alone (any more than it could be of Gibbon's in England). The contributions of Francis Hutcheson, Lord Kames, Adam Ferguson, William Robertson, Thomas Reid, John Millar,

---

[97] Marc Bloch, 'Pour une histoire comparée des sociétés européennes', in his *Mélanges Historiques*, 2 vols. (Paris, 1963), I, pp. 16–40.

and several others were substantial in their own right, broadening the scope of intellectual enquiry beyond the interests of Hume and Smith. In Naples the two most powerful minds of the century, Pietro Giannone and Giambattista Vico, were active before the Enlightenment, but their works provided the generation of the Enlightenment with a rich intellectual base. Antonio Genovesi and Ferdinando Galiani, Giuseppe Maria Galanti, Gaetano Filangieri, and Francesco Mario Pagano were no less absorbed than the Scots by the questions which were exercising their Enlightenment contemporaries across Europe. In both cases, moreover, thinkers may be seen to have participated actively in the affairs of their societies, setting themselves to address and influence a wider 'public' than those actually wielding power.

It was Bloch's observation that similarities are likely to be more evident between neighbouring or contemporary societies where there was scope for mutual influence. The societies considered here were contemporary, if hardly neighbouring. Yet we shall encounter very little evidence of connection, let alone influence, between them in the period with which this study is chiefly concerned. Later in the eighteenth century the Neapolitans did begin to read their Scottish contemporaries, but the Scots barely returned the favour. What follows will not, therefore, be other than incidentally a study of connections and influences; it is a straightforward comparison. The absence of connection may well reflect the distance which separated the two countries; it certainly reinforces the impression that the apparent similarity between the interests of their thinkers occurred in quite dissimilar milieus.

The dissimilarities of milieu are indeed striking. These were two countries at opposite ends of Europe, differing in their natural resources, economic and social structures, political arrangements, confessional allegiances, and intellectual traditions. Given such differences, the need to give due weight to national context in any study of Enlightenment in either Scotland or Naples is undeniable; indeed it might reasonably be anticipated that the subjects of study would be distinct Scottish and Neapolitan Enlightenments, in the plural, rather than one common Enlightenment. Such, as we have seen, has been the tendency of much recent scholarship devoted to Enlightenment in Scotland. The tendency has been less marked among students of Enlightenment in Naples, whose agenda remains broadly that set by Venturi; but here too there has been a recognition that specific, 'national' features of the Neapolitan situation should be given more weight. The first and most important objective of the present comparative study, therefore, is to determine whether it is still possible to identify the existence of a similar Enlightenment, understood as a single, coherent intellectual movement, in two such different 'national' contexts.[98]

Bloch's second objective for comparative history was the identification of general causes underlying similarities. In the present case two such general causes may be observed. One derives from the apparent similarity of social and political predicament in which the two kingdoms were placed at the beginning of the eighteenth century. In the two decades either side of 1700, the kingdoms of Scotland and Naples found themselves independently facing the prospect of a radical adjustment of their position within the larger composite monarchies to which they had hitherto belonged. Faced with this predicament, which in both kingdoms was characterised as that of a dependent 'province', Scottish and Neapolitan thinkers can be seen to have sought explanations for it in the political and economic developments which they observed in Europe around them. In the debates which ensued, thinkers in both countries may be observed to focus on the causes of their perceived economic backwardness, and on the possibilities for escaping from it, by testing for themselves the concepts available for the purpose.

The second general cause to be observed concerns the intellectual resources available to Scottish and Neapolitan thinkers. First in Naples, and later in Scotland, concepts deriving from the encounter between Augustinian moral rigorism and a revitalised Epicureanism would seem to have been particularly helpful in the investigation of human nature, the conditions of sociability, political economy, and the possibility of 'progress' in the history of societies. In both cases, it appears, access to the legacy of late seventeenth-century francophone philosophy was crucial in enabling Neapolitan and Scottish thinkers to move beyond investigation of their countries' initial predicament, to explore what would be the central questions of Enlightenment intellectual enquiry.

Bloch complicated his prospectus for comparative history, however, when he insisted, as his third objective, that the comparative historian remain alert to the discovery of hitherto unnoticed differences. The identification of similar developments in dissimilar milieus may be explained by

---

[98] I have previously commented on the issues in three articles: 'The Enlightenment above national context: political economy in eighteenth-century Scotland and Naples', *The Historical Journal*, 40 (1997), 667–97, esp. 667–75; 'The Scottish contribution to the Enlightenment', in Paul Wood (ed.), *The Scottish Enlightenment: Essays in Reinterpretation* (Rochester, N.Y. and Woodbridge, Suffolk, 2000), pp. 37–62 (a revised version of 'The Scottish Enlightenment', *Rivista Storica Italiana*, 108 (1996), 792–829); and 'The case for the Enlightenment: a comparative approach', in Joseph Mali and Robert Wokler (eds.), *Isaiah Berlin's Counter-Enlightenment*, published as *Transactions of the American Philosophical Society*, vol. 93, part 5 (Philadelphia, 2003), pp. 73–90.

the observation of general causes at work in both; but these causes are unlikely to have been identical in their operation. In the present case significant differences are indeed observable when the similarities of economic and political predicament and of sources of intellectual inspiration are subjected to closer scrutiny. On the one hand, the apparently similar predicaments of the two kingdoms in 1700 were belied by an underlying divergence in their economic prospects – a divergence which became more and more marked as their political status changed in the following decades. By 1750 development of the economy of the newly independent kingdom of Naples seemed to require a very different approach from that appropriate to Scotland, which had earlier renounced its pretension to independence, and agreed to join England in a single united kingdom. On the other hand, the Scots' access to the resources of Augustinian–Epicurean moral thinking was significantly delayed. Widely available and discussed in Naples by 1700, such thinking was effectively excluded (perhaps by design) from Scotland until the 1720s. It may not be quite true to say that the absence of this line of thought from Scotland before then has gone unnoticed; but the contrast with its active presence in Neapolitan intellectual culture is striking in its implications. Specifically, the comparison has the effect of returning the spotlight to David Hume, suggesting that his was the crucial initiative in bringing Enlightenment to Scotland.

The outcome of the comparison, therefore, is intended to be the demonstration of similarity amid difference: the presence of a common Enlightenment in the two very different 'national' contexts of Scotland and Naples. To use comparison to demonstrate the unity of the Enlightenment across Europe is not to devalue difference. On the contrary, the value – and, for me at least, the fascination – of the comparison lies precisely in the extent and depth of the differences of context. What I hope to achieve by the comparison is a richer, 'thicker' historical description of Enlightenment in both places. But in so doing I also wish to vindicate the existence of Enlightenment as a coherent, unified intellectual movement of the eighteenth century, whose adherents engaged in original enquiry into the fundamentals of human sociability, and were committed to the cause of bettering the human condition in this world without regard for the next. The case for the Enlightenment as a single intellectual movement, in other words, is argued on the basis of the case for Enlightenment made by Scottish and Neapolitan contemporaries, for whom the means to better man's condition on earth was an improved understanding of economy and society.

Whether this will be enough to give historians of more recent periods a 'sound and stable sense of the Enlightenment to work with'[99] is not, perhaps, for a historian of the eighteenth century to judge. By drawing particular attention to two of the eighteenth-century settings in which Enlightenment flourished, this study may well be read as emphasising the distance which separates the Enlightenment in its own contexts from its intellectual legacy as that was understood and developed in much later periods and settings. If Enlightenment is to be equated with 'modernity', then we will need to recognise that its vision of modernity has been stretched and shaped to fit very different circumstances, in its own time as well as since. We may also need to admit that its 'fit' to different contexts was neither uniform nor equally convincing, even in its own century. Given the very different fortunes of the two countries as they emerged from the eighteenth century, one at the forefront of industrial revolution, the other apparently locked into economic backwardness by its reliance on latifundist agriculture and the export of primary commodities, it might even be asked whether Enlightenment 'succeeded' in Scotland but 'failed' in Naples. This is not a question which this book will attempt to answer, and perhaps not a question a historian should ever expect to be able to answer. What is to be explored here is simply the extent to which the movement of ideas known as the Enlightenment did take hold in two such dissimilar contexts. But by observing how Enlightenment came to be established in both Scotland and Naples, we may at least be better placed to understand the appeal of its ideas, the nature of its intellectual achievement, and, perhaps, why it should continue to be taken seriously.

In the chapters which follow, the comparison will move from contexts to ideas, culminating in the moment when a distinct set of ideas was applied to the two contexts to make the case for Enlightenment. The contexts will be reconstructed from the bottom up, beginning in ch. 2 with an account of the political and social settings from which the intellectual movement of Enlightenment would emerge. The focus of this chapter will be political, social, and economic: ideas themselves will rarely be mentioned. It is included because a grasp of the political circumstances, social structures, and economic potential of the two kingdoms is essential to understanding the concerns of Scots and Neapolitans as they sought to explain and find ways of bettering their condition from 1700 onwards. More than this, the chapter reflects the conviction that a comparative, contextual approach to

---

[99] The formulation of David Hollinger, 'The Enlightenment and cultural conflict', p. 18. See above p. 5.

intellectual history presupposes the 'grounding' of ideas in specific political and social settings. Without an appreciation of these settings, the study of the ideas themselves is liable to become divorced not only from the experience of their own time, but from the concerns of other historians seeking to understand different aspects of the two societies in the same period.

Reconstruction of the political, economic, and social contexts of intellectual life in the two countries will be followed in ch. 3 by closer examination of the intellectual worlds of Scotland and Naples at the end of the seventeenth century. Here the focus will be on the immediate settings of intellectual life: on universities and academies, on libraries and their contents, on publishing and bookselling. The critical questions concern the availability of ideas in the two countries, and the facility with which they could be communicated. Of vital importance were the connections of Neapolitan and Scottish men of letters to the wider European Republic of Letters, through access to the new review journals as well as by personal correspondence and visits. The ideas which were communicated will be considered here in broad rather than specific terms: we need to identify the intellectual currents available to Scots and Neapolitans before we can explore their treatment in particular texts by individual authors. As we shall see, the existence of certain currents of thought in Europe at the time was no guarantee that they were equally available in both contexts: fundamental to the comparative analysis is an assessment of the extent to which Scots and Neapolitans did have access to the same ideas.

Ideas, or more accurately arguments, are the subject of the remaining four chapters. In two of these, chs. 4 and 7, the ideas are directly related to the contexts reconstructed previously, and specifically to the political and economic contexts discussed in ch. 2. The subject of ch. 4 is the debates which occurred contemporaneously in the two kingdoms in response to the succession crises within the Spanish and British monarchies in the years immediately before and after 1700. In both Scotland and Naples commentators sought to come to terms with the political and economic predicaments of their kingdoms; as they did so, they tested the terms then available to them, exploring their limitations as instruments for the analysis of the modern, commercial world. This chapter in turn provides the starting point for ch. 7, in which the introduction of political economy will be seen to transform the analysis of the economies of Scotland and Naples, by setting them in a much broader analytical framework.

Between chs. 4 and 7 are two whose subject matter is at a higher level of intellectual abstraction, and which take off from the intellectual contexts set out in ch. 3. Chapter 5 is devoted to the *New Science* of Giambattista Vico, in both its first and in its third editions, and ch. 6 to the philosophy of David Hume, as set out in the *Treatise of Human Nature* and related later works. In these chapters the reader may well experience a change of gear, and find her- or himself on a much steeper intellectual gradient. For the chapters differ in two important respects from the others. In the first place the Neapolitan and the Scottish thinkers are considered separately: where in other chapters comparison is developed within the individual chapter, in these the subjects are treated apart, and the threads of comparison are explicitly picked up only at the end of ch. 6. Second, each of these chapters includes an enlargement of the intellectual context appropriate to its principal subject. Where ch. 3 was concerned to identify the main currents of thought in the two kingdoms, and to establish the broad intellectual agenda of Scottish and Neapolitan philosophers in the decades before and after 1700, the focus of chs. 5 and 6 is on the specific arguments of Vico and Hume, and on their relation to the arguments of particular predecessors. In Vico's case the predecessors who will receive closer attention are Hobbes, Spinoza, and especially Bayle; in Hume's they are Mandeville (himself read in the light of Bayle) and, to a lesser extent, Warburton and Hutcheson. Consideration of these predecessors, it is contended, is crucial to understanding how Vico and Hume received and responded to the intellectual agenda identified in ch. 3. Space is therefore devoted early in each of chs. 5 and 6 to an exposition of the arguments of the selected predecessors, as a basis for the close textual analysis of the works of Vico and of Hume which follows. Given the difficulty of Vico's and Hume's principal works, the frequently gnomic propositions of Vico's *New Science* being set off by the technical refinement of Hume's *Treatise*, the demands on the reader will not be light. But intellectual history which spares its readers the complexity of its subjects' arguments cannot expect to do justice to their achievements. However much they owed to the institutions which educated and supported them, to the libraries, publishers, and booksellers where they found the books they needed, the thinkers themselves put ideas first. They wrote for the sake of their arguments, and it is these arguments which are the primary focus of the two chapters.

In subject matter ch. 7 takes up where ch. 4 left off, with the renewal of debate over the economic and social condition of the two countries in the three decades between 1730 and 1760. But this phase of debate was markedly different, for it rested on the intellectual foundations explored in the intervening two chapters. In political economy the Scots and the Neapolitans found a conceptual resource which allowed them to bring to bear on their own countries lessons from Europe's most successful commercial societies, as well as a body of argument which could be addressed to a 'public' far wider than the ministerial circles previously concerned with such matters. But more than that, they found a set of ideas itself grounded in the most powerful currents in contemporary philosophy, currents whose potential to illuminate the operation of human sociability Vico and Hume, in their contrasting ways, had done so much to clarify. For this reason political economy had an intellectual authority lacking in the arguments which the previous generation of political and economic commentators had used in the debates of 1690–1710. This intellectual authority was not diminished by the presence of sharp disagreement between the Neapolitans and the Scots over the appropriate model for their economies – disagreement which reflected the increasingly divergent political and economic experience of the two kingdoms. For the disagreement also highlighted a commitment in common: the choice of political economy as the primary intellectual discourse with which to address a wider 'public' among their fellow countrymen, because it held the key to understanding the conditions of betterment in this world. It was the decision of leading Scottish and Neapolitan thinkers in the early 1750s to take up political economy and to publicise its lessons which marked the advent of Enlightenment in the two countries. In this way, it will be argued, out of two very different 'national' contexts came one Enlightenment.

CHAPTER 2

Scotland and Naples in 1700

If the primary purpose of this book is to make the case for the Enlightenment as a coherent, Europe-wide intellectual movement, its substance derives from studying Enlightenment's emergence in two distinct, contrasting contexts, the kingdoms of Scotland and Naples. These contexts now need to be evoked and set before the reader. Accordingly the aim of this and the following chapter is to establish the framework from which Enlightenment thinking was subsequently to emerge in the two places. In the present chapter, the focus will be on the political, economic, and social circumstances of the two kingdoms at the turn of the seventeenth and eighteenth centuries; in the next, it will be on the structures of intellectual life. Following Bloch's guidelines for comparative history, these chapters will be studies in dissimilarity, highlighting the many, often marked differences between the two countries' political systems, economic condition, and intellectual culture. At the same time, it will be seen that the dissimilarities were not so great as to prevent the historian from observing patterns of convergence in both the political and economic situations and the intellectual interests of the Scots and the Neapolitans. In neither case was the convergence straightforward or exact; but it was sufficient to establish a common ground of experience between the two countries, while enabling thinkers in both to draw on the same intellectual resources. It is this common ground, both political-economic and intellectual, which makes it possible to pursue the comparison between two such apparently contrasting milieus as Scotland and Naples, and thereby, as I shall argue, to explain why Enlightenment flourished so brightly in both.

The present chapter compares the positions in which the kingdoms of Scotland and Naples found themselves by 1700, in political, economic, and social terms. Uniquely in this book, the chapter is not concerned with ideas. Its purpose is the preliminary but necessary one of enabling the reader to grasp the settings in which thinking was done in the two places, and to appreciate the problems on which the thinkers were to reflect. The need for such a chapter is both general and particular. Without this preliminary account of the material context of thought, the reader will be missing the sense of place which is as necessary to historical understanding – even to the understanding of ideas – as the sense of time. Comparison of Enlightenment in Scotland and in Naples will be pointless if the two countries remain no more than abstractions in readers' minds. But the chapter also serves a particular purpose in the argument of the book. As will be shown in ch. 4, the Scots and the Neapolitans began their attempts to understand their countries' positions in the modern world in the years immediately before and after 1700, before the advent of Enlightenment. Why they should have done so will be much easier to appreciate if the reader has been made aware of the political and economic predicament confronting each kingdom in the years around 1700. In important structural respects, it will be argued in this chapter, those predicaments were remarkably similar; and in ch. 4, it will be argued that there were likewise significant similarities in the terms in which Scots and Neapolitans discussed their situations, despite their different pasts and political cultures. Connecting the two, by interpreting those debates in the light of the comparable challenges facing the two kingdoms in 1700, is the key to establishing the argument which will then run through this book – that similar causes at work in the apparently very dissimilar milieus of Scotland and Naples explain why Enlightenment should have taken root and flowered in both.

The chapter begins with a brief outline of the political position of the two countries during the seventeenth century, when they were formally independent but, in the absence of their kings, subordinate kingdoms within larger composite monarchies. A short description of the system of governance in each is followed by an account of the crises which engulfed them in the middle decades of the century, when both were the setting for major revolts. In each case, it will be suggested, revolt was provoked by structural problems in the kingdom's relations with the larger monarchy of which it was a part; and the outcome of the revolt determined the scope which the kingdom's ruling elite would have to respond to pressures for change. The final sections of the chapter are devoted to a closer analysis of the economy and social structure of each kingdom. In the course of this, it will be seen that even if the Scots were more open to change than their Neapolitan counterparts, their economy remained acutely vulnerable to both harvest failure and commercial rivalry. By 1700 it was clear in both cases that only by a transformation of its political situation and economic opportunities could a poor, subordinate kingdom hope to overcome the disadvantages it faced in relation to richer, more developed neighbours. If therefore an opportunity to escape from dependency were to arise – as it would do, in both countries, simultaneously, in 1700–1 – the Scots and the Neapolitans had every incentive to take it.

KINGDOMS WITHIN COMPOSITE MONARCHIES

By the seventeenth century, Scotland and Naples were historically well-established kingdoms, defined territorially and by formal title. The kingdom of Scotland consisted of the lands and islands between the line from Berwick-upon-Tweed to the Solway in the south and the Shetland Islands in the north. Even if the exact location of the southern border with England had long been contested, its existence, and hence the formal independence of the kingdom, was not in doubt; its ruler's title was simply and unequivocally, 'king of Scotland'. The territories of the kingdom of Naples were similarly well defined, stretching from the border with the Papal States in the centre of the Italian peninsula to its southern coastline. Within it were the regions of the Abruzzo, the Molise, and the Terra di Lavoro (the hinterland of Naples and Salerno) in its northern part, Puglia, Basilicata, and Calabria in the south. Less straightforward, however, was the formal title of the kingdom's ruler, which was not king of Naples. Instead the historic title was 'king of the Sicilies', a title which covered both the *Regnum Siciliae citra farum* – the kingdom of Siciliy on this side of the lighthouse (of Messina) – and the *Regnum Siciliae ultra farum* – the kingdom of Sicily beyond the lighthouse. The former designated the kingdom of Naples as already defined (and the phrase 'kingdom of Naples' was used even though the title 'king of Naples' was not); the latter applied to the island of Sicily, likewise known as the kingdom of Sicily. The shared title notwithstanding, the two kingdoms were independent of each other, and ruled separately, even when the king was the same person in both.[1] Here it is only the kingdom of Naples with which we are concerned, and developments in Sicily, political or intellectual, will not be discussed other than incidentally in what follows.

In their formal independence, the kingdoms of Scotland and Naples were equivalent to the several other territories of Europe whose rulers were recognised to have a royal title.[2] They were also alike, and also by no

---

[1] When the Bourbons were restored to their Neapolitan and Sicilian thrones in 1816 following the ten years of French rule, they adopted the title 'kingdom of the Two Sicilies' to enhance the impression of a unity in its parts. The title should not, however, be used retrospectively.

[2] There were, as yet, only three such kingdoms in the territories of Italy: Naples, Sicily, and Sardinia. The dukes of Savoy did not acquire a royal title until the Peace of Utrecht in 1713, and then only by virtue of being awarded the kingdom of Sicily, which they swapped in 1720 for the kingdom of Sardinia.

means unusual in their time, in happening to have as their kings men who simultaneously held several royal titles, and who now resided elsewhere. The kingdom of Naples had been in this position for a century longer than Scotland. Ever since its recapture from the French by the royal house of Aragon in 1504, Naples had been ruled in tandem with the kingdom of Aragon; and because the dynasties of Aragon and Castile had earlier united through the marriage of Ferdinand and Isabella in 1469, the Aragonese kingdoms (which also numbered Sicily and Sardinia) had in turn to share their monarch with the kingdoms of Castile, Leon, Navarre, Granada, Valencia, and the several other territories historically associated with them. From 1517 until 1700, the common ruler of all these kingdoms was always a Habsburg. It is true that he (the ruler was always male) was often referred to as 'king of Spain', but the title had no formal status. Naples was ruled by the king of the Sicilies, just as Castile was by the king of Castile. The principle was that enunciated by the Castilian jurist Solórzano Pereira: each of these kingdoms was to be ruled *aeque principaliter*, 'as if the king who holds them all together were king only of each one of them'. (By contrast, the kingdoms of Mexico and Peru were subordinate to, and incorporated within, the kingdom of Castile alone.)[3] The one serious potential qualification to this picture, as Solórzano acknowledged, concerned the kingdom of Naples (but not Sicily): in its case the papacy had a claim to homage from its king, on the grounds that the kingdom had originally been established, in 1130, as a papal fief.[4] But although the claim was a source of embarrassment to any ruler of Naples, and gave the papacy an unusually strong hand in the affairs of the Neapolitan church, it did not challenge the king's title, or deprive the kingdom of its independence.

Scotland had kept its king to itself until 1603, when the Scottish royal house of Stewart succeeded by inheritance to the neighbouring kingdoms of England and Ireland following the death of their last Tudor sovereign, Elizabeth I. In doing so, James VI of Scotland not only became James I of England and Ireland; he moved his court south to London, and for a while actively encouraged proposals for a closer, fully incorporating union of the two kingdoms. But nothing came of these, and the Scots certainly did not allow the loss of a resident court to lead to any diminution of the kingdom's status in relation to England. Like England's, the Scottish was an 'imperial' crown, which was worn closed over its wearer's head to indicate that its holder acknowledged no superior in this world; and the

[3] Juan de Solórzano Pereira, *Politica Indiana* (1647; repr. Madrid, 1972), bk IV, ch. xix, para. 37, quoted in J. H. Elliott, 'A Europe of composite monarchies', *Past and Present*, 137 (1992), pp. 52–3.
[4] Juan de Solórzano Pereira, *De Indiarum Iure* (Madrid, 1629), bk III, ch. 67.

Scots vigorously contested any English claim that their kings had once acknowledged English overlordship.[5] With the critical exception of the years 1654–60 (to which I shall return), the formal independence of the kingdom of Scotland was secure until 1707.

In both cases, however, formal independence belied a more complex and less satisfactory reality. The kingdoms which made up the composite monarchies of early modern Europe were rarely equal in weight; and in several critical respects the two kingdoms of Naples and Scotland were no more than junior partners within the larger monarchies to which they belonged. The most obvious mark of this subordinate status was the absence of a resident monarch and an accompanying court. In the intensely dynastic world of early modern monarchy this was an absence sorely felt: without a court, a kingdom's nobility was deprived of a stage on which to assert and display its own status, and lacked a convenient, direct means of access to patronage and influence. Without a court and a king or queen, moreover, it was much more difficult to affirm a kingdom's independent identity: however ample their fortunes, private patrons were no substitute for a court in offering employment to artists, and could not easily commission works or buildings on behalf of the kingdom as a whole. The absence of a royal court did not of course mean that there was no royal government. In both Naples and Scotland the apparatus of government continued to grow across the early modern period. But there could be no disguising the threat to these kingdoms' status entailed by the absence of their kings.

In the kingdom of Naples there was an explicit substitute for the king, in the person of his viceroy. Usually chosen from the ranks of the highest nobility in Castile or (more rarely) another Spanish territory, the viceroy represented the person of the king, enjoyed the simulacrum of royal status, and held a court. In making their ceremonial entries to the city of Naples on taking office, and on the occasions of a king's death, when they were responsible for the obsequies, the viceroys made a very public statement on behalf of the kingdom's formal independence. But precisely because the viceroy was a substitute for the person of the king, his power was carefully circumscribed: there were obvious limits to which the viceroy could be allowed to assert the actual independence of the kingdom. Most viceroys held office for a few years only; at the first sign of trouble with the locals

[5] Roger A. Mason, '*Regnum et Imperium*: humanism and the political culture of early Renaissance Scotland', in his, *Kingship and Commonweal: Political Thought in Renaissance and Reformation Scotland* (East Linton, 1998) pp. 126–37; David Armitage, 'Making the Empire British: Scotland in the Atlantic World 1542–1707', *Past and Present*, 155 (1997), pp. 38–9.

they were liable to be moved, in order to ensure that criticism was not reflected on to the king himself.[6] There were also continuous institutional constraints on their power.

These constraints came from above, alongside, and below the viceroy. From above the viceroy was overseen by the councils at the centre of the Spanish monarchy, the Council of State and the Council of Italy. The Council of State appointed the viceroys, and decided matters of policy and strategy covering the interests of the monarchy as a whole; the Council of Italy, which drew its members from the several states ruled by the Spanish Habsburgs in Italy, was more specifically concerned with their internal affairs. Viceroys were required to be in regular correspondence with both of these councils, and to receive and act on their instructions. At the same time, the viceroy needed to maintain informal connections with the royal court in Madrid or at the Escorial, to ensure that he continued to enjoy the political backing of the king and his principal advisers.[7] A further limitation on viceregal independence was placed, literally, alongside him in Naples, in the form of the Collateral Council (*Consiglio Collaterale*), whose membership was divided between Spaniards and Neapolitans, and which constituted the highest governmental authority in the kingdom.

Within the kingdom of Naples the viceroy was even more constrained from below, by the noble and legal elites, and by the institutions through which they traditionally governed the city and the kingdom. For the feudal nobility, the important institutions were the *eletti*, the highest offices in the city of Naples, and, until it ceased to be summoned after 1642, the *Parlamento* of the kingdom. The legal elite, known as the *ceto civile* or, at its highest level, as the *togati* (a term whose closest equivalent was the French *noblesse de robe*), exercised their authority in the complex structure of tribunals which met in the city and oversaw the affairs of the kingdom. Under the Collateral Council the highest court was the *Sacro Regio Consiglio*, while the *Camera della Sommaria* presided over the kingdom's finances; beneath them an untidy hierarchy of other councils continued and extended this division of functions. All of these councils were constituted as tribunals, combining administrative with judicial functions, and between them conflicts of jurisdiction were endemic. The result was to create a dense, intractably contradictory network of interests, which divided

---

[6] The pioneering account of the nature and limits of viceregal power in the Spanish monarchy was that of H. G. Koenigsberger, *The Government of Sicily under Philip II of Spain: a Study in the Practice of Empire* (London and New York, 1951). There is no comparable study of the Neapolitan viceroyalty.

[7] J. H. Elliott, *Imperial Spain 1469–1716* (Harmondsworth, 1970), pp. 170–81, gives a lucid account of the system of councils and viceroys in the monarchy.

and yet bound together the elites in defending their spheres of author-ity within the kingdom.[8] Rarely did the viceroy act on his own initia-tive to threaten their authority, and for most of the period of Spanish Habsburg rule the Neapolitan elites were perfectly content to collabo-rate with the agents of the monarchy in return for confirmation of their local privileges and the power they conferred over the rest of Neapolitan society.

What the monarchy took in its turn, however, underlined those elites' acceptance of the kingdom's dependence. For what the monarchy wanted above all was taxation to finance its power and reputation wherever these needed to be upheld: viewed from Madrid, the entrenchment of the priv-ileges of the Neapolitan nobility and legal elite was of little account if it facilitated the increase of the monarchy's disposable revenue. And the increase was inexorable, taxes rising across the sixteenth century and even more steeply in the first half of the seventeenth, while the city of Naples developed into a financial centre of considerable sophistication.[9]

In seventeenth-century Scotland, by contrast, government without a resident king was a much less formal affair. There was no viceroy, and hence not even a viceregal court. Initially, under James VI, the loss of a court was offset by his policy of keeping large numbers of Scots with him at his court in London. But the Scots early made it clear that they would regard the imposition of a viceroy as a sign that they were being treated as 'a conquered and slavish province'; and James VI agreed, telling the English Parliament that he had no intention of ruling Scotland in the same manner as the Spaniards ruled Naples.[10] The Scottish nobility were far happier to treat the situation in the manner of a regency, a shift to which they had often been put in the past by royal minorities. As the royal absence was prolonged, the crown found it prudent to rely on one noble to take the lead in managing Scottish politics; but there was no Scottish equivalent even of the office of Lord Deputy by which royal authority was upheld in Ireland. Nor was the conciliar system anything like as developed in the British as in the Spanish monarchy. The English Privy Council acted as, in effect,

---

[8] Rosario Villari, *The Revolt of Naples*, transl. James Newell (Cambridge, 1993), pp. 10–18, for an account of the institutions of government in the kingdom, and the respective roles of nobility and lawyers. See especially the table of councils on pp. 12–13.

[9] Antonio Calabria, *The Cost of Empire: the Finances of the Kingdom of Naples in the Time of Spanish Rule* (Cambridge, 1991).

[10] James I, 'A Speach to both the Houses of Parliament, the last day of March 1607', in C. H. McIlwain (ed.), *The Political Works of James I* (Cambridge, Mass., 1918; repr. New York, 1965), pp. 290–305; letter of the Scottish Estates to James VI, August 1607, *Register of the Privy Council of Scotland*: Vol. VII, *1604–1607* (Edinburgh, 1885), pp. 535–6.

a council for the monarchy as a whole, and usually had a small number of Scottish members. But the internal affairs of Scotland were left to the Scottish Privy Council, on which there was no significant English presence. Constituted in three estates, the Scottish Parliament also continued to meet throughout the century. Until 1688 it was more or less firmly controlled by the Privy Council through a Council-appointed steering committee, the Lords of the Articles; but since Scottish taxation was not expected to do more than cover the costs of government, the Parliament's dependence did not have adverse consequences for Scottish autonomy.[11] For most of the century, the most visible mark of the kingdom's secondary status was the king's absence and the consequent loss of a court and all that it might have offered to the nobility and the city of Edinburgh.

The two kingdoms' political and (in the Neapolitan case) fiscal subordination to the more powerful centre of their monarchies was compounded by their commercial weakness. By 1600 it was clear that commerce had become, as David Hume would later put it, 'an affair of state':[12] the wealth it was now capable of generating had made it a source of a state's power in a way it had not been (except in the cities of northern Italy) even a hundred years earlier. First the Venetians and the Genoese, the latter virtually as agents of the Spanish monarchy, then the Dutch, the English, and the French had grasped the potential of advances in ship design, navigation, and gunnery, and committed substantial resources to the construction of shipping and the funding of trade. On the assumption that trade between nations was a zero sum, governments encouraged their merchants to establish monopolies wherever possible; there was no question of encouraging latecomers or lesser powers to take up trade on their own behalf.

Both Naples and Scotland were in the latter position. With no mercantile elite to match that of the north Italian cities, Naples had allowed the Genoese to fill the vacuum, making the city's commerce virtually a branch of that of Genoa. Along the Adriatic coast of the kingdom, the Venetians had established an equal dominance. As Spanish power in the Mediterranean weakened in the course of the seventeenth century, the French, the Dutch, and the English stepped in to challenge the older Italian maritime cities. The Mediterranean became particularly important to English shipping, which used the free port of Livorno (Leghorn to the English) in Tuscany as an entrepôt. Coastal craft from Naples and other southern Italian ports carried

---

[11] Keith M. Brown, *Kingdom or Province? Scotland and the Regal Union 1603–1715* (Basingstoke and London, 1992), pp. 6–32.

[12] David Hume, 'Of Civil Liberty' (1741), in David Hume, *Essays Moral, Political, and Literary* (1741–1777), ed. Eugene F. Miller (Indianapolis, 1985), p. 88.

goods thence to Livorno; but there was no attempt to extend Neapolitan trade further afield, and the coastal trade itself remained acutely vulnerable to North African or Barbary pirates. With few galleys of its own, and with only infrequent assistance from the Spanish, the kingdom was powerless to check the pirates, let alone to challenge the northern Europeans.[13]

The Scots in the seventeenth century enjoyed a more extensive trade, their merchant ships travelling regularly to the Baltic, the Netherlands, France, Spain, and Portugal as well as to Ireland and England. The volume of trade with England in particular grew under the Union of the Crowns. But the Union also placed limitations on the Scots' freedom of manoeuvre. Partly because they contributed so much to the Plantation of Ulster early in the seventeenth century, the Scots were unable to play more than a minor role in the colonisation of North America. After 1660 the English Parliament imposed tariffs and the provisions of the Navigation Acts on trade with Scotland. The latter did not prevent trade between the two kingdoms, but effectively obstructed Scottish shipping, impeding trade with North America. Attempts by the Scottish Privy Council to protect Scottish trade could not be enforced: at its strongest, during the early 1690s, the Scottish navy consisted of three warships, and was still unable to prevent English seizures of Scottish merchantmen.[14] Even if the Scots were not as completely beholden to foreign merchants and their ships as the Neapolitans, it was clear that they could not hope to establish themselves as an independent commercial power without taking very radical steps, and great risks.

THE 'GENERAL CRISIS' IN NAPLES AND SCOTLAND

So far, the circumstances of the kingdoms of Naples and Scotland have been described in relatively static terms, as if they were constant throughout the seventeenth century. But in the mid-century both kingdoms found themselves caught up in revolts which threw the existing order into question, and whose outcome would define the terms under which they were ruled until the end of the century. In each case the revolts had features in common with events elsewhere in Europe at the same time, and particularly in the wider Spanish and British monarchies, forming a pattern

[13] Gigliola Pagano de Divitiis, *Mercanti inglesi nell'Italia del seicento. Navi, traffici, egemonie* (Venice, 1990), and, 'Il porto di Livorno fra Inghilterra e Oriente', *Nuovi Studi Livornesi*, 1 (1993), 43–87.

[14] T. C. Smout, *Scottish Trade on the Eve of the Union 1660–1707* (Edinburgh and London, 1963), esp. pp. 2–29, 195–6; Eric J. Graham, 'In defence of the Scottish maritime interest, 1681–1713', *Scottish Historical Review*, 71 (1992), 88–109.

which Hugh Trevor-Roper christened the 'general crisis of the seventeenth century'.[15] Revolt broke out in Scotland in 1638, beginning a cycle of war and revolution from which the Scots were not to emerge and be restored to something like their initial position until 1660. In Naples the revolutionary events were much shorter lasting, being over in nine months between 1647 and 1648; but they were at least as spectacular in their form. As the scholars who responded to Trevor-Roper's essay discovered, the thesis that these contemporaneous revolts constituted a 'general crisis' is difficult to sustain in detail: the differences of circumstances were many. But the suggestion remains revealing for the two kingdoms under examination here: in both cases revolt was provoked by escalating pressure on the subordinate kingdoms from the centre of their monarchies.

In Naples the pressure was overwhelmingly fiscal. As the Spanish monarchy struggled to hold its own in war with France and the Protestant powers, its demands upon outlying kingdoms increased sharply. Naples in particular was expected to send ever larger amounts out of the kingdom, along with recruits and military supplies. By 1636 the public debt had reached 40 million ducats, and the interest alone exceeded ordinary income. Pressing for still more, the crown granted a virtual monopoly over the entire financial system to one Neapolitan financier, Bartolomeo d'Aquino, who with his associates raised a further 36 million ducats between 1637 and 1644. Because the financiers were granted commissions of over 50 per cent on the taxes they farmed, however, the actual revenues of the crown fell sharply. The result was yet more taxes, both direct and excises, at a time of severe economic contraction.[16] Not surprisingly, the pressure provoked acute social tension. Among the teeming population of the city of Naples as well as in the isolated, subsistence-farming countryside there was real desperation. As the authorities were well aware, the inhabitants of Naples had a tradition of violent rioting over high bread prices, most notoriously in 1585, when the *eletto* of the people (who was actually chosen by the viceroy) had been ritually executed by a crowd chanting 'Death to bad government' (*malgoverno*). In the countryside desperation was habitually expressed in banditry, likewise a marked feature of the late sixteenth century, and once again widespread in the 1630s and 1640s.[17]

At moments like these, moreover, the upper classes were likely to exploit the tension to assert their own interests. Among the lawyers there was a tradition of civic constitutionalism, which recalled that Naples had been

---

[15] H. R. Trevor-Roper, 'The general crisis of the seventeenth century', in his *Religion, the Reformation and Social Change* (second edn London and Basingstoke, 1972).
[16] Villari, *The Revolt of Naples*, pp. 74–97.   [17] Ibid., pp. 19–55.

founded as a colony of Athens, independently of ancient Rome, and which asserted the rights of the *popolo* against the nobility. Articulated in the *Historia della città e regno di Napoli* (1601–2) of Giovanni Antonio Summonte, the tradition had been refined in the first half of the seventeenth century by the members of the Accademia degli Oziosi.[18] The nobility were no less restive. There were protests against new taxes in the Parliament from leading members of the nobility in 1640, and a succession of noble conspiracies at intervals in the 1630s and early 1640s. Of these much the most significant was on behalf of Prince Tommaso of Savoy, whose potential as a king of Naples was deliberately cultivated by Cardinal Mazarin in the French interest.[19] Finally there was the church. The messianic, insurrectionary utopianism of Tommaso Campanella and the radical Dominicans had been crushed in the 1590s; but the hierarchy itself, under the Cardinal Archbishop Filomarino, was unlikely to waste an opportunity to strengthen its position at the expense of the secular government.[20] All of these interests were agitated by the financial crisis, and by the general crisis of Spanish authority which it brought on. One more tax, an excise on fruit, and the desperation of the people fused with the contradictory ambitions of their superiors to explode in open revolt.

The revolt of Naples in 1647–8 made an impression on the rest of Europe second only to the public trial and execution a year later of the king of England. The initial impact of the revolt owed almost everything to the image – and the organising ability – of its first leader, a mere fish-seller, Tommaso Masaniello. For nine days, from 7 to 16 July 1647, Masaniello inspired and held together a coalition of the city's poorest inhabitants and their immediate superiors, the corporations of artisans and traders, in violent defiance of the new taxes. Pouring out from the poor quarter of the Mercato, the crowds harassed tax collectors, assailed the palaces of prominent nobility, and invaded the royal palace itself, once again crying 'Death to bad government'. Later the Spanish authorities would pretend that this was the only real revolt, a deception in which they have been supported by modern historians for whom popular revolt is only truly interesting as anthropological spectacle.[21] In fact the revolt had only just begun, and was

---

[18] In addition to Villari, *Revolt of Naples*, pp. 32–3, 65–73; see Aurelio Musi, 'Non pigra quies. Il linguaggio politico degli Accademici Oziosi e la rivolta napoletana del 1647–48', in Eluggero Pii (ed.), *I linguaggi politici delle rivoluzioni in Europa xvii–xix secolo* (Florence, 1992), pp. 85–104.

[19] Villari, *The Revolt of Naples*, pp. 123–35; Aurelio Musi, *La rivolta di Masaniello nella scena politica barocca* (Naples, 1989), pp. 72–95.

[20] Villari, *The Revolt of Naples*, pp. 60–3.

[21] Peter Burke, 'The Virgin of the Carmine and the revolt of Masaniello', *Past and Present*, 99 (1983), 3–21; in response, Rosario Villari, 'Masaniello: contemporary and recent interpretations', *Past and Present*, 108 (1985), 117–32, repr. in *The Revolt of Naples*, Afterword One, pp. 153–70.

to continue for another nine months, following a course as complex as the interests involved in it.[22] Masaniello's murder brought the first phase to an end, and after a period of uncertainty leadership of the revolt passed to a group drawn from the legal and ministerial elite, the *togati*, headed by Vincenzo d'Andrea. Their programme reflected the constitutionalist ideals of the Accademia degli Oziosi, and culminated in the virtual declaration of a republic at the end of October. But unity of purpose still proved elusive. There was no agreement on the form of a republic: d'Andrea favoured a senatorial model, while the leaders of the city militias wanted to exclude the nobility altogether. Support was sought from the church, but the cardinal archbishop was consistently ambivalent. The French crown had early decided not to intervene directly, which allowed Henry of Lorraine, duke of Guise, to seek to take advantage on his own account. Like so many 'sovereign princes' with pretensions to a throne of their own, Guise almost certainly hoped to take the kingdom for himself. But when he arrived in the city from Rome in mid-November his impact was wholly disruptive: he divided the leadership of the revolt and offended the nobility whose support he had particularly hoped to attract. The viceroy, meanwhile, was never physically displaced from Naples, remaining secure in the Castelnuovo. A Spanish attempt to send him reinforcements in October was repelled after a bombardment of the city; but the best the revolt could achieve was a military and political stand-off.

A more fundamental cause of the revolt's eventual failure, however, was the lack of coordination between the leadership in the city of Naples and rebels in the rest of the kingdom. Although the history of the rural revolt remains to be written in full, it is clear that many communities seized the opportunity to challenge the powers of the feudal lord. In some areas, notably Basilicata, there was fierce fighting between peasant armies and bands put out by the barons. But gradually the barons recovered, and by the spring of 1648 repression was under way. In Naples itself negotiations between d'Andrea, the duke of Arcos, and his replacement as viceroy, the count of Oñate, had reached a conclusion. On 5 April the Spanish reclaimed military control of the city, and in a set of 'Graces' the crown effectively conceded what had been demanded in September: the withdrawal of extraordinary taxes, the reservation of offices for Neapolitans, and equality for the popular vote in the city's government.

[22] The following account of its course derives from Musi, *La rivolta di Masaniello*, and Pier Luigi Rovito, 'La rivoluzione costituzionale di Napoli 1647–48', *Rivista Storica Italiana*, 98 (1986), 367–462. The public declarations of the 'constitutional' phase of the revolt are printed in Vittorio Conti, *Le leggi di una rivoluzione. I bandi della repubblica napoletana dall'ottobre 1647 all'aprile 1648* (Naples, 1983).

Although over in less than a year, the revolt not only makes a remarkable story; over its full course it is extremely revealing of the complex and contradictory structure of Neapolitan society. The same combination of interests which sustained the revolt was also responsible for undermining it; and the outcome, while certainly to the advantage of individual interests, was to block the further development of the kingdom. For the crown the viceroy was able to recover his authority, and to keep the kingdom within the Spanish monarchy. But the price was high: never again could the crown tax Naples as heavily and relentlessly as it had in the 1630s and early 1640s. Successor viceroys would have to accept the relative autonomy of the kingdom, and respect the privileges of its noble and legal elites. The ambitions of viceregal governments would be limited to keeping disorder at more or less tolerable levels, on the streets of the capital and in the countryside. For their part, both the feudal nobility and the *togati* gained enormously from their renewed acquiescence in Spanish rule. The nobility were confirmed in the fiefs, jurisdictions, and offices which they had purchased from the crown, and their power over their inferiors, especially in the countryside, was less inhibited than ever. The legal elite strengthened its grip on the tribunals through which both the city and the kingdom were administered. The church, meanwhile, kept its independence, successive archbishops upholding clerical privilege and the authority of Rome whatever their own background.

In effect, it was as if the revolt of 1647–8 had mobilised the various elements of the Neapolitan political community into staging a dramatic act of defiance, only to immobilise them all the more securely in its aftermath. If the outcome of the revolt was a compromise, it was also deeply compromising for all involved. No political interest had any incentive to take the initiative after 1650; and in the absence of meetings of the discredited *Parlamento*, there was no forum in which to come together to articulate demands for change. Whether there were forces for change within the society and economy of the city and the kingdom we shall examine shortly; but even if there were, the outcome of the events of 1647–8 left little political scope for their expression. Spectacular as it was, the revolt of Masaniello, his associates, and successors had succeeded in doing no more than relaxing the kingdom's subordination to the Spanish monarchy; it had not opened new political horizons.

The pattern of events in Scotland differed in several obvious respects. Not only did the revolt which began in 1638 disrupt Scottish politics and society for far longer, the pressures which provoked and sustained it were religious rather than fiscal. Charles I (1625–49) was never as attentive to

Scottish interests as his father, and early aroused hostility by declaring an intention to reclaim former church lands from the laity. He was equally high-handed in his personal relations with the senior Scottish nobility, who enjoyed far less favour at his court. But the greatest provocation was his attempt to impose episcopal government on the church in Scotland, along with a Prayer Book modelled on that used in England. Attachment to the presbyterian form of church government was already deep rooted among the majority of Scottish clergy, as among a significant proportion of the lairds, or lesser nobility, and the people; if the highest nobility were less convinced, they resented the power which Charles gave the bishops on the Scottish Privy Council.[23]

Opposition to the new Prayer Book was first signalled by small-scale popular riots in Glasgow and Edinburgh in 1637. But there was no question of allowing a Scottish Masaniello to set the pace of resistance. By February 1638 a broad coalition of great nobles, lairds, and ministers had subscribed to the National Covenant, which demanded the abolition of episcopacy and an end to arbitrary, prerogative rule from London. This was followed up by military pressure on the north of England, the unilateral reorganisation of the church on presbyterian lines, and a meeting of the Scottish Parliament in 1640–1 which passed a series of Acts asserting its control over its own agenda and the appointment of officers of state. Under growing pressure from his opponents in England, Charles I acceded to these demands in August 1641. It was a decisive concession. However untrustworthy Charles subsequently proved himself, the Scots never afterwards voluntarily abandoned their allegiance to their king.[24]

Made confident by their success, the Scots extended their ambitions to the rest of the British monarchy. By the Solemn League and Covenant of 1643 they agreed to give military support to the English Parliament in return for its acceptance of presbyterian church government. But there they over-reached themselves, the more so as by 1645 it was clear that the English parliamentary armies could defeat the king's forces without Scottish support. Anxious to protect what they had won, the Scots negotiated separately

[23] David Stevenson, *The Scottish Revolution 1637–1644: the Triumph of the Covenanters* (Newton Abbot, 1973), pp. 15–55; Maurice Lee Jr, *The Road to Revolution: Scotland under Charles I 1625–1637* (Urbana and Chicago, 1985).

[24] Stevenson, *The Scottish Revolution*, pp. 56–242, provides a narrative; for further comment, Roger A. Mason, 'The aristocracy, episcopacy, and the revolution of 1638', in Terry Brotherstone (ed.), *Covenant, Charter and Party: Traditions of Revolt and Protest in Modern Scottish History* (Aberdeen, 1989), pp. 7–24; John Morrill (ed.), *The Scottish National Covenant in its British Context 1638–1651* (Edinburgh, 1990); and William Ferguson, *Scotland's Relations with England: a Survey to 1707* (Edinburgh, 1977), pp. 117–23.

with the king, agreeing the 'Engagement' with him in December 1647. This not only brought the Scots into open conflict with the now much superior English parliamentary army; it opened up serious divisions among the Scots themselves. For the first time the authority of the nobility was questioned, as militant presbyterian ministers collaborated with fellow radicals among the lairds and tenant farmers between 1649 and 1651 to overthrow lay patronage in the appointment of ministers and to curb the powers of feudal landowners. It was the closest the Scots came to social revolution, and in the short term disastrously undermined their ability to resist the English.[25]

Even at its most radical, the Scottish revolution never renounced the monarchy. No sooner had the English executed Charles I and abolished kingship in England and Ireland than the Scots proclaimed his son, Charles II, king of Scotland, England, and Ireland. If the English regicides had been prepared to leave Scotland out of their proceedings, the Scots had wilfully failed to take the hint. Further conflict was unavoidable, and in 1650 and 1651 Oliver Cromwell inflicted decisive defeats on the Scottish armies. Occupied by an English army, Scotland was declared to be 'incorporated into one Commonwealth with England'.[26] With union came not only representation in Parliament at Westminster and free trade across the border, but measures of genuine reform in Scottish society, including the abolition of the hereditary jurisdictions of the Scottish nobility. These benefits of union were not afterwards forgotten, but a union by conquest was never likely to be lasting if there was a prospect of reversing it; with the death of Cromwell in 1658, and the collapse of the republican regime in London, that prospect was realised in 1660.[27]

On the face of it, Scotland had returned in 1660 to a condition very like that of Naples in 1648: both were kingdoms the terms of whose subordination to the larger monarchies of which they were parts had been noticeably relaxed. But there was a critical difference. Accepted without negotiation, the restoration of Charles II was not a compromise, and the various interests in the Scottish political community were far less compromised by it. After 1660 Charles II might be an absentee monarch with an uncertain

[25] Walter Makey, *The Church of the Covenant 1637–1651: Revolution and Social Change in Scotland* (Edinburgh, 1979).

[26] 'An Ordinance by the Protector for the Union of England and Scotland, 12 April 1654', in S. R. Gardiner (ed.), *The Constitutional Documents of the Puritan Revolution 1625–1660* (Oxford, 1936), p. 418.

[27] H. R. Trevor-Roper, 'Scotland and the Puritan Revolution', in his *Religion, the Reformation and Social Change*, pp. 411–44; David Stevenson, 'Cromwell, Scotland and Ireland', in John Morrill (ed.), *Oliver Cromwell and the English Revolution* (London and New York, 1990), pp. 149–80.

touch in Scottish affairs; the bullying nobleman to whom he entrusted the kingdom's management, the earl, later duke, of Lauderdale, was widely resented. But Charles was not wilfully provocative in the manner of his father, and in 1679 he pulled off an inadvertent masterstroke. Embarrassed by the presence in London of his brother and heir, James, duke of York, when Whig Parliaments were seeking his exclusion from the succession, Charles sent him up to Edinburgh. There James, under his Scottish title of the duke of Albany, set up a princely court at Holyrood, complete with the appurtenances of assemblies for the nobility and patronage for artists and men of letters.[28] Although he had left by 1682, and never visited Scotland when he became its king as James VII in 1685, the idea of a Scottish royal court had been revived, and a firm basis laid for the subsequent allegiance of so many Scottish nobles to the Jacobite cause after 1689.

The Scottish nobility, meanwhile, had reclaimed their place at the head of government within the kingdom. The powers of jurisdiction which had made them so formidable in the localities were restored to them, and they still exercised considerable military clout, raising the Scottish militia in 1668.[29] But in the actual process of government it is clear that the great nobility now needed the support of two other groups. In the shires it was the lairds who filled the increasingly important office of Commissioner of Supply and who predominated among the heritors in the parishes. At the centre, in Edinburgh, both nobles and lairds relied on the expertise of the legal profession, writers, and advocates, a high proportion of whom were themselves of landed origin.[30] The senior members of the profession, men like Sir James Dalrymple, Lord Stair, his sons Sir John and David Dalrymple, and the Lockharts, Sir George and Sir William, were needed by any administration, and formed a small ministerial elite. But they were not a putative *noblesse de robe*, insisting on their privileges: what distinguished the Scottish political elite in the later seventeenth century was its cohesiveness, not its divisions.

For this the clergy were largely responsible. The important fault-line in Scottish society after 1660 was that between the landowning laity and the committed presbyterians, both ministers and their congregations. The reimposition of bishops on the Church of Scotland at the Restoration was

---

[28] Hugh Ouston, 'York in Edinburgh: James VII and the patronage of learning in Scotland 1679–1688', in John Dwyer, Roger A. Mason, and Alexander Murdoch (eds.), *New Perspectives on the Politics and Culture of Early Modern Scotland* (Edinburgh [1982]), pp. 133–55.

[29] Bruce Lenman, 'Militia, Fencible men and home defence, 1660–1797', in Norman Macdougall (ed.), *Scotland and War AD 79–1918* (Edinburgh, 1991), pp. 170–92.

[30] Nicholas T. Phillipson, 'Lawyers, landowners, and the civic leadership of post-Union Scotland', *Juridical Review*, New Series 21 (1976), pp. 100–2.

unpopular in many areas, and ejected ministers were an articulate focus of resistance to episcopacy and the crown. But the experience of clerical power between 1649 and 1651 had cost the presbyterians the support of lairds and nobility. Whatever their formal allegiance, these were increasingly Erastian in their attitude to church government, determined to keep bishop and presbyter alike in their place.[31] In the later 1660s and 1670s the more radical presbyterians resorted to illegal conventicling, and even to arms, which the authorities met with superior and increasingly repressive force, driving dissident clergy and some laity into exile in the Netherlands.[32] But the government's most effective response was to exploit the embarrassment of moderate presbyterians at the sectarianism of the covenanters, and thereby to encourage a drift towards (implicit) Erastianism among presbyterians themselves.[33]

The equilibrium of Scottish politics was temporarily broken by James VII. Having created such a favourable impression on his visit, James did his best to lose it by pursuing a policy of catholicisation no less unwelcome to episcopalians than to presbyterians. The Scottish elite struggled to maintain their autonomy by acquiescence, and a significant number of ejected or exiled presbyterian ministers were even willing to accept James's offer of an Indulgence in 1687.[34] A year later the Scots were passive observers when the English obliged James to abdicate by welcoming the invading army of William of Orange. When the Revolution was brought to Scotland in 1689 there was no change in the status of the kingdom within the monarchy, and little indication of a new direction in its affairs. Episcopacy was finally discarded in favour of presbyterianism in the church (encouraging persecuted episcopalians to become Jacobites); but the strength of lay Erastianism prevented any recovery by the clergy of the power they had enjoyed

---

[31] Julia Buckroyd, *Church and State in Scotland 1660–1681* (Edinburgh, 1980), is the fundamental discussion of the assertion of lay power in Scottish ecclesiastical politics. See also her 'Anticlericalism in Scotland during the Restoration', in Norman Macdougall (ed.), *Church, Politics and Society: Scotland 1408–1929* (Edinburgh, 1983), pp. 167–85, on the emergence of a self-conscious lay Erastianism. There is further evidence to this effect in J. C. L. Jackson, *Restoration Scotland, 1660–1690: Royalist Politics, Religion and Ideas* (Woodbridge, 2003), ch. 5, 'The politics of religion', recording (on p. 115) an incident in which Sir Robert Moray and the earl of Tweeddale received a letter from Archbishop Sharp, and 'laughd till wee was weary at the letter of the Bishops . . . what a silly company of people they are'.

[32] Ginny Gardner, *The Scottish Exile Community in the Netherlands 1660–1690* (East Linton, 2004).

[33] Ian B. Cowan, *The Scottish Covenanters 1660–88* (London, 1976); and Colin Kidd, 'Religious realignment between the Restoration and Union', in John Robertson (ed.), *A Union for Empire: Political Thought and the British Union of 1707* (Cambridge, 1995), pp. 145–63, on the different strands of presbyterianism.

[34] On the willingness of presbyterian exiles to return to Scotland in response to the second indulgence in particular: Gardner, *The Scottish Exile Community*, ch. 6, 'James VII and II's Indulgences, 1687'.

between 1649 and 1651. Government continued to be in the hands of the nobility, the lairds, and the lawyers. In one important respect the lairds in particular gained a new freedom: with the abolition of the Lords of the Articles the crown lost control over Parliament's agenda. This irritated the king's ministers in London, who found Scottish affairs more difficult to control; but it created a new opportunity for Scots to take the initiative in their own affairs.[35]

Like the Neapolitan, the Scottish experience of the 'general crisis' of government in the middle years of the seventeenth century was highly revealing, both of the kingdom's place within the larger monarchy to which it belonged, and of the fissures in Scottish society. But the outcomes of the crisis in the two kingdoms were significantly different. While events in Scotland were much less dramatic than those in Naples, and took longer to unfold, they had certain decisive consequences. The revolt of Naples was over so quickly because none of the various protagonists was sufficiently powerful on its own to impose an outcome, and because external involvement was limited to the ineffectual intervention of Guise, an individual dynastic adventurer. The resulting compromise between the Spanish and the Neapolitan elites so entrenched the power and privileges of the latter that the kingdom was politically immobilised for the remainder of Spanish Habsburg rule. By contrast, the Scottish revolt was much less easy to settle, because its outcome became dependent on the course of the simultaneous civil war in England. But when the monarchy was restored in 1660 it was too late to check the process of social realignment which the revolt had initiated. Increasingly the greater nobility and lairds came together with their relatives in the legal profession to form a single, landed, ruling elite, in which differences of rank and authority, though still important, took second place to their common interest in governing the kingdom. This willingness to make common cause almost certainly owed most to a determination not to let the clergy assume the power they had exercised at the height of the revolt, a determination which held fast in 1689. After the revolt as before, Scotland might remain, like Naples, a subordinate kingdom within a composite monarchy; it was still dependent politically and economically on a crown beholden to the interests of the more powerful kingdom in which it had its court. But a cohesive Scottish ruling elite now possessed a freedom of political manoeuvre which its Neapolitan

---

[35] Ferguson, *Scotland's Relations with England*, pp. 166–79; Bruce Lenman, 'The Scottish nobility and the Revolution of 1688–90', in Robert Beddard (ed.), *The Revolutions of 1688* (Oxford, 1991), pp. 137–62.

counterparts did not, along with an incentive to think of the kingdom's future in terms of secular priorities.

ECONOMY AND SOCIETY IN THE KINGDOM OF NAPLES

Having followed the political development of the two kingdoms from the revolts of the mid-seventeenth century, we need now to look at the underlying structures of economy and society, in order to reach a fuller assessment of the kingdoms' prospects by the century's end. Outside the city of Naples, the Neapolitan economy was overwhelmingly agrarian, and still at the mercy of the kingdom's geography. Along the coasts areas of plain were interrupted by mountains or hills reaching down to the sea; in the interior the Apennines stretched from the Abruzzo in the north to Calabria in the south, a virtually unbroken chain of mountains and isolated valleys. Through the kingdom ran a geological fault-line, creating a constant danger of earthquakes, of which there were five serious instances between 1659 and 1694. Except in the Terra di Lavoro, around Naples, or in Puglia, on the eastern coast, the plains were poorly drained and endemically malarial; they were also very exposed to North African raiders and slave-traders. As a result, settlements tended to be on hill-tops, forcing peasants to travel great distances to reach cultivable lands. In the absence of irrigation, water supplies in the hills were irregular, the heaviest winter rains draining away uselessly, and the available pasture was unable to support cattle in any quantity. Since cattle (and oxen) were draught animals as well as sources of fertiliser, their absence created a need for more human labour, while adversely affecting fertility: it thus severely restricted the scope for productivity gains.[36] The principal crop was grain, whose yields ranged from 2.6 to 5.4 per measure of grain sown in the mountainous Abruzzo to 7.5 per measure of grain sown in Puglia.[37] Other crops included olives, vines, and silk. At the same time there was a substantial pastoral economy in sheep. In the north and east this was organised by the *Dogana* of Foggia, which functioned as a Neapolitan equivalent of the Spanish *Mesta*, regulating the seasonal pattern of grazing and transhumance between Puglia and the Abruzzo.[38]

One reason geography remained so important was that overland communications were everywhere poor. The only roads capable of taking wheeled

---

[36] Gérard Delille, 'Agricultural systems and demographic structures in the kingdom of Naples', in A. Calabria and J. A. Marino (eds.), *Good Government in Spanish Naples* (New York, 1990).

[37] Aurelio Lepre, *Feudi e masserie. Problemi della società meridionale nel' 600 e nel' 700* (Naples, 1973), pp. 54, 119–22.

[38] John A. Marino, *Pastoral Economics in the Kingdom of Naples* (Baltimore and London, 1988).

transport led out of Naples, and stopped well short of their intended destinations. Roads between towns in the provinces were non-existent until the end of the eighteenth century. Goods had to go by mule, which meant that it was uneconomic to carry large amounts of bulky agricultural produce. Traffic was subject to frequent tolls, most of which were levied by the nobility rather than the government; by 1690 there were some 800 tolls in the kingdom. But virtually no protection was offered against banditry, which was often abetted by the nobility. Given such obstacles to land transport, almost all goods went by sea. Grain and oil were shipped round to Naples from a number of ports in Puglia, Basilicata, and Calabria. Ports on the east coast, including Gallipoli and Taranto, also traded directly with Venice and Trieste. But shipping too, as we have seen, was vulnerable to piracy, and port facilities were often primitive and unsuitable for ships of any size.[39]

Dependence on the environment was reinforced by the priority given to subsistence. The great majority of rural producers sought no more than to survive, to feed their families, and to pay their rents and taxes. Since rents were generally collected in kind, most small producers had little or no contact with the market; those who did found that the market in all the main products was controlled to their disadvantage by the system of the *contratto alla voce*, by which the price paid to producers was publicly determined early in the season, while the merchant profited from any subsequent rise. (In effect the *contratto alla voce* functioned as a system of credit, by which the merchant paid in advance to the producer and received interest, at a high rate, in his subsequent profit.)[40] A dramatic fall in the kingdom's population after the plague of 1656 appears to have ensured that the subsistence sector of the economy was in rough equilibrium in the second half of the seventeenth century. Although population recovered (perhaps from a little over 2 million to 3 million at the beginning of the eighteenth century), a trend of low grain prices until well into the eighteenth century would seem to indicate that the supply was normally sufficient.[41]

[39] Luigi de Rosa, 'Land and sea transport and economic depression in the kingdom of Naples from the fourteenth to the eighteenth century', *Journal of European Economic History*, 25 (1996), pp. 339–68.

[40] S. R. Epstein, 'The peasantries of Italy 1350–1750', in Tom Scott (ed.), *The Peasantries of Europe from the Fourteenth to the Eighteenth Centuries* (Harlow, 1998), p. 99. There are lucid accounts of the working of the *contratto alla voce* in the eighteenth century by Parick Chorley, *Oil, Silk, and Enlightenment: Economic Problems in xviiith-century Naples* (Naples, 1965), pp. 83–98, and Paolo Macry, *Mercato e società nel Regno di Napoli. Commercio del grano e politica economica nel Settecento* (Naples, 1974), pp. 15–27.

[41] The rate of recovery of the population is discussed by Augusto Placanica, 'Tra Spagnoli ed Austriaci', in G. Galasso and R. Romeo (eds.), *Storia del Mezzogiorno*, 11 vols. (Rome, 1986–91), iv: *Il Regno dagli Angioini ai Borboni*, pp. 313–15. Rough population estimates are tabulated by Gérard Delille,

There is no evidence, however, that the much smaller commercial sector of the rural economy recovered the buoyancy it seems to have enjoyed in the sixteenth century. The markets for grain, olives, wool, and silk had all contracted at the beginning of the seventeenth century. Such as they were, moreover, they were either in Naples or abroad: there was almost no rural industry to take advantage of the kingdom's raw materials. There was certainly no equivalent in the south of the technologically sophisticated rural wool and silk manufactures which developed in the Veneto, Lombardy, and Tuscany in the seventeenth century to offset the decline of the old urban industries.[42] Without such specialisation the rural economy of the kingdom lacked a potentially critical incentive to improve and overcome the limitations of geography and transport; instead, its commercial sector remained locked into dependence on one great city, Naples itself.[43]

The primacy of the city in the economy of the kingdom was a function, in the first instance, of its population. In 1600, when its population was in the region of 280,000, Naples was the largest city in Europe; and it almost certainly continued to grow in the first half of the seventeenth century, rising perhaps to around 400,000. The devastating plague of 1656 may have reduced the city's population by as much as two-thirds, to 150,000. But it quickly demonstrated remarkable resilience, climbing back to over 200,000 and perhaps closer to 300,000 by the early eighteenth century. Such powers of growth contrasted with the stagnation of the major cities of northern Italy, and kept Naples in the company of a select few of Europe's greatest cities; in 1700 it was still Europe's third city, after London and Paris.[44] But the basis on which it achieved this ranking was quite different from that of its northern counterparts. The great cities of London, Paris,

---

in his article 'Demografia', in vol. VIII of *Storia del Mezzogiorno: Aspetti e problemi del medioevo e dell'età moderna*, p. 22.

[42] Domenico Sella, *Crisis and Continuity: the Economy of Spanish Lombardy in the Seventeenth Century* (Cambridge, Mass., 1979). With few opportunities of seasonal by-employment in industrial activities, southern peasants did not even have the flexibility which helped those of the Valpolicella to survive hard times: on these, Peter Musgrave, *Land and Economy in Baroque Italy: Valpolicella 1630–1797* (Leicester and London, 1992).

[43] For a sketch of the relation between the subsistence and commercial sectors of the rural economy, see Chorley, *Oil, Silk, and Enlightenment*, pp. 11–16. There are suggestive remarks on the relative lack of market integration in the kingdom of Naples (as compared with Sicily) in the seventeenth century in S. R. Epstein, *An Island for Itself: Economic Development and Social Change in Late Medieval Sicily* (Cambridge, 1992), pp. 402–12.

[44] Estimates of the city's population are provided by Delille, 'Demografia', *Storia del Mezzogiorno*, VIII, p. 25; and by Jan de Vries, *European Urbanization 1500–1800* (London, 1984), p. 277, with comparative figures for other Italian and European cities given on pp. 270–8. See also Claudia Petraccone, *Napoli dal'500 all'800. Problemi di storia demografica e sociale* (Naples, 1974), pp. 35–53 on the impact of the plague in 1656.

and Amsterdam each stood at the head of a more or less even pyramid
of cities and towns within their countries; and together these hierarchies
of cities formed what was effectively an 'urban system' stretching across
the north-west of Europe.[45] Such a level of urbanisation could only be
achieved through economic integration, and a high degree of commercialisation. Naples, by contrast, stood alone in the kingdom, no other city
having more than 20,000 inhabitants.[46] It was sustained, not by integration into an urban system, or by an extensively commercialised economy,
but by constant transfers of resources from the country to the city, in the
form of rents, interest payments disguised as profits, taxes, and legal fees.
Unevenly redistributed down through the population, these paid for the
city's provisioning, the services it offered, and the goods it produced or
imported.

The city made the country pay for its provisioning twice over. Income
from the country (rather than income generated by productive enterprise
within the city) paid for the grain which the city needed, while its price
was determined by the authorities in Naples, in the interests of the city's
merchants. The provisioning system, known as the *annona*, was supervised
by the *Tribunale di San Lorenzo* and the *Camera della Sommaria*, respectively
the highest tribunal in city government and the senior financial court in the
kingdom. It ensured that producers received a fixed price, determined *alla
voce*, before the grain came to market. This was effectively a 'political' price,
reflecting the power of the nobility and the merchants over producers, and
it gave the merchants who made up the *partito* supplying Naples a virtual
monopoly, and a near guarantee of substantial profits. At times of shortage
the city authorities might lower the selling price or open more ovens, but city
funds would be used to compensate the merchants.[47] Such a provisioning
system was not itself unusual in Italy: similar *annona* operated in Rome
and many other cities.[48] But the mechanism by which it was imposed in
the southern kingdom, by the price fixed *alla voce*, made transparent the
rural economy's dependence on the city, and the city's reluctance to permit
the development of a properly commercial economy in grain.

---

[45] These terms and their application to the cities of early modern Europe are discussed by de Vries,
European Urbanization, pp. 81–172.

[46] Bari, with 15–20,000 inhabitants, was the second city in the kingdom.

[47] The operation of the *annona* is described by Macry, *Mercato e società*, part 1. The prices fixed do
indicate changes in the supply and demand for grain in the long term; but not being market prices,
they do not do so in the short or medium term.

[48] Volker Reinhardt, *Überleben in der frühneuzeitlichen Stadt. Annona und Getreideversorgung in Rom
1563–1797* (Tübingen, 1991).

Income from the country likewise paid for the services which Naples provided and for the goods it manufactured or imported. The services provided were legal, religious, and domestic, and the city was famous for containing unusually large numbers of lawyers, clergy, musicians, and domestic servants.[49] By the same token, however, Naples did not have a reputation as an important manufacturing centre. A range of luxury goods was produced for the upper classes, from fine clothing to musical instruments, even if their quality was not thought to match that of the luxuries of the northern Italian cities. Basic clothes and implements must also have been made or recycled for the lower classes. The impression, nevertheless, is of relatively limited manufacturing activity. The silk industry, vigorous in the sixteenth century, was in decline from early in the seventeenth; and even building suffered after 1656, though it seems to have recovered by the end of the century.[50] There was apparently very little production for export, or even for sale to the rest of the kingdom. Although the produce of the commercial sector of the rural economy (grain, olives, wool, and silk) tended to be brought to Naples, only a small portion was used for manufacturing, the greater part being exported from the kingdom, usually through Livorno. In return the city imported fine manufactures and luxury goods, along with salted fish and those primary commodities (such as wood and lead) which were in short supply in the kingdom.[51] The fact that few of these imports were passed on to the rest of the kingdom (the ships which brought goods to Naples from the provinces often returning empty) only confirmed the lack of an internal market in the wider kingdom, and the concentration of consumption in the city. In a very real sense, Naples was a city parasitic on the rural economy of the kingdom, with a high propensity to consume rather than to invest in the development of manufacturing and the commercial sector of the economy.[52] As such it was the opposite of the great northern cities, London and Amsterdam, which stimulated the economies around them, enlarging the market for both agricultural and manufactured

---

[49] Petraccone, *Napoli dal'500 all'800*, pp. 55–66, for some observations on the socio-professional structure of the seventeenth-century population, including the proportion in service; on the clergy, G. Brancaccio, 'La geografia ecclesiastica', in *Storia del Mezzogiorno*, IX, p. 258, for figures which suggest they numbered 3–4 per cent of the urban population.

[50] Ruggiero Romano, *Napoli: dal Viceregno al Regno. Storia economica* (Turin, 1976), pp. 12–21, 48–63.

[51] In 1689 the English consul in Naples named cloth (including various types of 'new drapery'), lead, and cured foods as the principal goods brought to the city by English merchants; they exported oil, wine, grain, and silk. A few luxury goods, including soap and aromatics, were also occasionally exported. See Gigliola Pagano de Divitiis (ed.), *Il commercio inglese nel Mediterraneo dal cinquecento al settecento* (Naples, 1984), pp. 6–14.

[52] Chorley, *Oil, Silk, and Enlightenment*, pp. 14–16.

goods, encouraging specialisation and facilitating investment.[53] If, as economic historians argue, these were the features of the emerging modern economy, the economy presided over by the great city of Naples was still firmly pre-modern.

Were there, nevertheless, pressures for change from within Neapolitan society, from classes or groups whose interest lay in the promotion rather than obstruction of economic development? If we look first at the traditional nobility, we shall find little sign of such an orientation, for this was a class whose priorities were security and survival. By the end of the seventeenth century, the traditional nobility, the nobility of the sword, was composed of some 2,500 families, making up about 1–2 per cent of the total population (a relatively low proportion by European standards). Of these, just under one thousand families (937 by 1675) were 'feudal' nobility, in the sense that they owned feudal communities or fiefs, with the extensive rights which such ownership brought. The numbers of these had risen sharply since the late sixteenth century, the increase fuelled by a vigorous market in fiefs and regular sales of rights by the crown. At the same time, there was an inflation of titles, and particularly of the higher titles, so that the ranks of the titled baronage swelled from just over 100 in 1590 to nearly 450 by 1675.[54] Within this nobility there was, as elsewhere, a marked hierarchy. At the top were just six great noble houses, including the Carafa, the Caracciolo, the Sanseverino, Avalos d'Aquino, the Pignatelli, and the Orsini, whose branches owned fiefs throughout the kingdom; at the bottom was a much more numerous poor provincial baronage.[55] The important distinction, however, was between those who did, and those who did not, combine the possession of rural fiefs with membership of one of the noble *seggi* in the city.

The ultimate source of the nobility's wealth and power was its ownership of fiefs in the countryside. Ownership of a fief did not indicate absolute

[53] E. A. Wrigley, 'A simple model of London's importance in changing English society and economy 1650–1750', and 'Urban growth and agricultural change: England and the Continent', in E. A. Wrigley, *People, Cities and Wealth* (Oxford, 1987); Jan de Vries and Ad van der Woude, *The First Modern Economy: Success, Failure and Perseverance of the Dutch Economy 1500–1815* (Cambridge, 1997), pp. 687–99.

[54] Villari, *The Revolt of Naples*, pp. 98–102, 118–22.

[55] Maria Antonietta Visceglia, 'Un groupe social ambigu. Organisation, stratégies et représentations de la noblesse napolitaine xvie–xviiie siècles', *Annales ESC*, 48(4) (1993), 819–51; Claudio Donati, 'The Italian nobilities in the seventeenth and eighteenth centuries', in H. M. Scott (ed.), *The European Nobilities in the Seventeenth and Eighteenth Centuries*. I: *Western Europe* (London and New York, 1995), pp. 248–9. For comparisons of size between different European nobilities: J. P. Cooper, 'General introduction' to *The New Cambridge Modern History*. IV: *The Decline of Spain and the Thirty Years War 1609–1648/59* (Cambridge, 1970), pp. 17–18.

ownership of the land it contained. Rather, a fief consisted of a set of rights over the land and over those who lived within the fief and worked on the land, who were the 'vassals' of the lord. Feudal rights included extensive powers of jurisdiction, with the right to try and punish in a wide range of cases; the right to claim *terragio*, a levy of, usually, 10 per cent of the harvest from land within the feudal domain; various economic monopolies, over mills, ovens, inns, and hunting and fishing rights within the fief; levies on such occasions as the marriage of a female member of the lord's family; and fees for exercising powers on behalf of the crown, such as collecting tolls and taxes.[56] Altogether the feudal nobility exercised these powers over between 70 per cent and 80 per cent of the total population of the kingdom. The leading seventeen families alone accounted for 199 fiefs, covering 190,000 households, and over half of the population within fiefs, while the next thirty-nine families possessed 136 fiefs between them. Below these the average holding of fiefs fell to between one and two, and most nobles still possessed no more than a single, sometimes quite small fief.[57] Fiefs existed across the kingdom, and only in two regions, the coastal plain of Puglia and the hinterland of Naples, was feudal authority significantly qualified by the requirements of commercial farming.

But numbers alone cannot adequately convey the extraordinary power of this feudal nobility. A leap of imagination, to grasp the setting in which they exercised their rights, is also needed. Perched on hill-tops, remote and isolated by the lack of communications, the communities subject to feudal ownership knew no authority to match that of their lord. The resulting concentration of power in the hands of the baron was far greater than if he had simply been the owner of private property; and the concentration was compounded by the tendency of those with more than one fief to hold them in a single area (only the very greatest possessing fiefs throughout the kingdom). The Caracciolo of Brienza, studied by Tommaso Astarita, offer an excellent example: their four contiguous fiefs of Brienza, Pietrafesa, Sasso, and Atena were located deep in the interior of the kingdom, on the borderlands of Principato Citra and Basilicata. Of these, the first three were all in the mountains; only Atena, in the marshy Vallo di Diano, was close to a – very poor – road.[58] The pattern would appear to have been similar throughout the mountainous interior. A feudal nobility with a vengeance,

---

[56] Tommaso Astarita, *The Continuity of Feudal Power: the Caracciolo of Brienza in Spanish Naples* (Cambridge, 1992), pp. 37–40, for a clear and convenient summary of feudal powers.
[57] Visceglia, 'Un groupe social ambigu', pp. 832–43.
[58] Astarita, *Continuity of Feudal Power*, pp. 37–56, for a description of the four Caracciolo fiefs.

the Neapolitan baronage wielded awesomely arbitrary powers over entire communities.

There were periods in which the power of the feudal lords was contested by the rural communities, or *università*. The *università* had an independent legal status, and traditionally enjoyed a measure of self-government, allowing members of the community to determine the division of the community's 'demesne' land and pasture. In the last quarter of the sixteenth century there was a movement by *università* to rent the lord's feudal rights en bloc, paying him a fixed sum in return for the right to collect the dues. But the initiative was undermined by the crisis years of the 1590s, and by the economic depression which followed, which left many *università* heavily in debt. Over the first half of the century the lords re-established their feudal powers to the extent that the period has been characterised as one of 'refeudalisation'. At the same time the vigorous sixteenth-century market in fiefs dried up, and noble families consolidated their holdings by the widespread use of entails. The rural revolts of 1647–8 may be seen as a final, violent spasm of protest against this process; once they had been suppressed, the nobility encountered no further obstacles to the exercise of their rights, least of all from the monarchy.[59] Despite the sharp fall in the population after 1656, evidence from different branches of the Caracciolo clan suggests that the nobility's feudal income declined hardly at all in the late seventeenth century.[60] But it was how this was achieved which was critical. There was, it seems, no question of investment to increase productivity; rather the nobility concentrated on maintaining income by enforcement of their rights, while keeping management costs to a minimum. Some *università* fought on, doggedly pursuing cases against their lords in the royal courts. But these were typically not resolved until well into the eighteenth century (under the new, independent monarchy); in the meantime, individual vassals were usually powerless against lords who were uninhibited in their use of violence and imprisonment in their hill-top strongholds to subdue the recalcitrant. Since the Neapolitan nobility was not permanently absentee, but tended to live in their fiefs for parts of the year, or even for periods of years, the harshness of the regime may have been softened by a measure of paternalism. But even a family commended by its modern historian for its relative benevolence, the Caracciolo of Brienza,

---

[59] Rosario Villari, *Mezzogiorno e contadini nell'età moderna* (Bari, 1961), pp. 118–42. Much of Villari's evidence was drawn from the same four fiefs belonging to the Caracciolo of Brienza, since studied by Astarita, *Continuity of Feudal Power*, pp. 102–5, 146–51.

[60] Lepre, *Feudi e masserie*, pp. 36–59, on the fiefs of the Caracciolo of Santobuono and of Villa in the Abruzzi; on the Caracciolo of Brienza, Astarita, *Continuity of Feudal Power*, pp. 77–81.

did not hesitate to employ violence against those who stood up to it.[61] On such evidence, it seems unduly mild to describe the nobility's commitment to upholding their feudal power simply as 'continuous'; it was positively intransigent.

For a significant portion of the nobility, the defence of feudal power was complemented by the assertion of their status in the capital of the kingdom, the city of Naples. Here the key to status was membership of one of the five *seggi*, for which some 130 families were qualified by 1700. The *seggi* were groupings of noble families, associated with a particular quarter of the city, not unlike the *alberghi* of Genoa. Of the five, those of Capuana and Nido claimed a certain precedence over Montagna, Portanova, and Porto, and hence a right to a larger portion of the offices and honours of the kingdom. Families had traditional associations with particular *seggi*, the various Caracciolo families, for instance, all belonging to the *seggio di Capuana*. Membership was exclusive, since the admission of new families was technically barred after 1553, though claims could be made under a pretext of 'resuming' the status. Each *seggio* appointed an *eletto* (the Montagna exceptionally appointed two) to the *Tribunale di San Lorenzo*, the governing council of the city; since there was only one *eletto* of the people, the council was in principle dominated by the nobility. Membership of the *seggi* was also a route to royal office, and to a share in the financial spoils of a monarchy heavily dependent on credit.[62]

A presence in Naples, however, was important for more than access to political power. It was in the city that the nobility secured their families' future, arranging the marriages of their offspring, and agreeing their marriage settlements. In addition to investing in the family's future, the nobility also spent money in the city in displaying their status. Since they did not live permanently in the city, families did not necessarily own a palace, but rented for the period; and those who did tended to embellish them piecemeal. Fine entrances and inner courtyards with architecturally inventive staircases were a feature of Neapolitan palaces, the more so as narrow streets and the requirements of street-level security limited the scope for elaborate façades. The interiors were decorated with movables, furniture, hangings, and pictures. Few of the nobility had reputations as collectors of art; but they did commission sculptors and painters to decorate family chapels in churches with

---

[61] Astarita, *Continuity of Feudal Power*, pp. 119–31, 156–7; Villari, *Mezzogiorno e contadini*, pp. 140, 149–51, on an incident of baronial violence as late as 1747–8, the subject of a defensive footnote by Astarita, *Continuity of Feudal Power*, p. 138n.

[62] Visceglia, 'Un groupe social ambigu', pp. 822–8; Astarita, *Continuity of Feudal Power*, pp. 24–5.

which they wished to be associated.[63] If there were thus many ways for the nobility to spend their feudal incomes, however, what they did not do, in the city any more than in the country, was invest in productive, manufacturing activity. In the past the nobility had invested in the financial market created to service the monarchy's fiscal demands; such speculation was probably the most important factor in the turnover and expansion of the noble class before 1650. But opportunities for this were much reduced in the second half of the century, and the nobility do not seem actively to have sought alternatives.

The social and economic interest closest to that of the nobility, in both the country and the city, was that of the church. The visiting Scottish cleric Gilbert Burnet may have exaggerated when he suggested that the church possessed above half of the land in the kingdom in 1685;[64] but the religious orders were major landowners in virtually every province. Moreover, as a result of the institution of mortmain, a kind of ecclesiastical entail, land once lost to the church was almost impossible to recover. The religious orders were responsible for many of the churches, the more so as the provision of parish churches in many rural areas was highly uneven. They did therefore tend to spend a greater portion of their income than the nobility within the countryside. But once churches had been established in a community, they tended to acquire or be left property locally, adding piecemeal to their holdings. There was certainly no shortage of clergy; gaps were quickly filled after the plague, and the numbers of clergy probably grew faster than the general population in the later seventeenth century.[65] Even in the remote community of Brienza, for example, there were seven churches (including two parish churches) in 1659, with another six outside the village; they were served by fifty-four priests and deacons.[66] In such communities the church did make a definite economic contribution, providing small loans to the peasantry. But these tended rather to perpetuate the existing division of cultivable land into small plots, and could not act as a catalyst for agrarian change.[67] Elsewhere, on the grain-growing plains of Puglia, the Jesuits were substantial owners of *masserie*, or large farms, which they had bought during the boom of the late sixteenth century. Failing to sell when recession had

---

[63] On these forms of aristocratic 'investment', Gérard Labrot, 'Le comportement collectif de l'aristocratie napolitaine du seizième au dix-huitième siècle', *Revue Historique*, 258 (1977), 45–71; Gérard Labrot and Renato Ruotolo, 'Pour une étude historique de la commande aristocratique dans le royaume de Naples espagnol', *Revue Historique*, 264 (1980), 25–48.

[64] Gilbert Burnet, *Some Letters containing an Account of what seemed most remarkable in Switzerland, Italy &c.* (Amsterdam, 1686): 'The Fourth Letter, from Rome 8 December 1685', p. 192.

[65] Brancaccio, 'La geografia ecclesiastica', p. 259.   [66] Astarita, *Continuity of Feudal Power*, p. 132.

[67] Villari, *Mezzogiorno e contadini*, pp. 27–32; Astarita, *Continuity of Feudal Power*, pp. 135–6.

struck in the 1600s, they hung on to profit again from a gradual increase in prices from the later seventeenth century.[68] But there is little indication that this was earned by investment. When its leadership was supposed to make its priority the struggle to replace the obdurate superstitions of the peasantry with Counter-Reformation piety, and the rank-and-file clergy simply struggled to survive, the church was not likely to be a source of economic initiative.

It was the same in the city. Here too numbers of clergy seem to have recovered quickly after the plague, more quickly even than the population (suggesting that the standards for entry were not set high). Thirty-seven parishes (rising to thirty-nine by 1734) were served by 1,900 diocesan clergy; to these must be added nearly 5,000 members of religious orders, distributed across about a hundred houses, and another 3,000 nuns, in thirty to forty convents. The numbers, of religious and of buildings, dazzled and scandalised every visitor: in the words of an envoy from Savoy, Naples was 'the new Oxyrinchus'.[69] The list of regular orders was headed by the Franciscans (in their several rules) and the Dominicans; but almost every Counter-Reformation order was represented, along with others more specifically Neapolitan. Their houses occupied an increasing amount of urban space, as they exercised rights to acquire contiguous properties; the most spectacular capture was the palace of the Sanseverino, transformed by the Jesuits into a basilica, the Gesù Nuovo, but retaining the defensive stonework of the original palace façade. The religious orders as well as individual churches were also lavish patrons of the arts, providing more employment for painters, sculptors, and musicians than the nobility.[70] Other of the clergy's pleasures were less durable: Burnet was shocked (but clearly impressed) by the size of the Jesuits' wine cellars.[71] A further expenditure was the provision of charity to various categories of poor and deserving: like the nobility, the clergy gave priority to the provision of marriage funds, as an antidote to prostitution.[72] As in the countryside,

---

[68] Lepre, *Feudi e masserie*, pp. 83–123.

[69] Romeo de Maio, *Società e vita religiosa a Napoli nell'età moderna* (Naples, 1971), pp. 14–20, 40–2. Oxyrinchus was a city in Roman Egypt famed for the unparalleled size of its population of monks and nuns, and the number of its religious buildings. De Maio observes that while its reputed religious population exceeded that of seventeenth-century Naples, the latter was superior in numbers of buildings.

[70] Francis Haskell, 'The patronage of painting in seicento Naples', in C. Whitfield and J. Martineau (eds.), *Painting in Naples from Caravaggio to Giordano* (London, 1982), pp. 60–2; Haskell observes that it was from the 1630s that Neapolitan (rather than Roman or Bolognese) artists began to be commissioned for major works.

[71] Burnet, *Some Letters*, p. 194. He suggests, however, that the Jesuits also traded in wine.

[72] De Maio, *Società e vita religiosa*, pp. 133–40.

however, such expenditure reinforced rather than challenged existing economic structures. In a city of consumers, the clergy were the most avid of
them all.

Was any more to be expected from the other great service class of the capital, the legal profession? Although the lawyers' political importance has been
much emphasised in recent historiography, there has been no systematic
study of their character as a social class.[73] Even reliable estimates of their
numbers are hard to come by: as a whole, including lawyers, office-holders,
university professors, and other 'professionals', the *ceto civile* may have constituted between 5 and 10 per cent of the population of the city.[74] But there
were clear and perhaps growing differences within the *ceto civile*, between
the 'ministerial', office-holding elite, the judges of the supreme courts and
members of governing councils, who presented themselves as a *nobiltà di
toga*, or nobility of the robe, and the larger numbers of practising advocates, notaries, and professors.[75] The nobility of the *seggi* certainly regarded
the *togati* as rivals to their power. Since the consolidation of Spanish rule
in the mid-sixteenth century, the *togati* had insisted on their precedence
in all decisions involving matters of law: though nobles might sit on the
governing councils, it was not for *idioti* (as they were expressly termed) to
question the decisions of *dottori* learned in law. Early in the seventeenth
century it seemed that the latter's monopoly of expertise might be challenged by nobles willing to acquire a legal training; but after the revolt of
1647–8 the nobility were back on the defensive, and the stand-off between
them and the *togati* within the administration was renewed.[76]

It is far from clear, however, that this rivalry can be translated into
radically different visions of the future of Neapolitan society. The institutionalised hostility between sword and robe belied a considerable area of
common interest. Nobles and *togati* continued to share the government of
city and kingdom. Within the wider *ceto civile*, the advocates owed much
of their bread-and-butter litigation to the nobility. Moreover, the aspirations of the successful members of this class seem to have mimicked those

---

[73] The political significance of the lawyers has been championed with signal energy by Raffaele Ajello
and his pupils. A recent statement of Ajello's argument is 'Alle origini del problema meridionale
nell'età moderna', the introduction to his *Una società anomala. Il programma e la sconfitta della
nobiltà napoletana in due memoriali cinquecenteschi* (Naples, 1996), pp. 9–260. See also Pier Luigi
Rovito, *Respublica dei togati. Giuristi e società nella Napoli del Seicento*. Vol. 1: *Le garanzie giuridiche*
(Naples, 1981).

[74] Petraccone, *Napoli dal'500 all'800*, pp. 59–61, and Donati, 'The Italian nobilities', p. 249, offer some
estimates.

[75] On this division, Giuseppe Galasso, *Napoli Spagnola dopo Masaniello*, 2 vols. (Florence, 1982), I,
pp. 252–6, 312–17.

[76] Ajello, *Una società anomala*, pp. 193–207.

of the nobility. Those who accumulated the necessary wealth sought to transform it into the most enduring expression of noble status, ownership of a fief. A few even sought admission to a *seggio*. Other outlets for their wealth were financial speculation and patronage of the arts; if they differed from the nobility it was likely to be in their willingness to invest in books and antiquities as well as decorations. But no more than the nobility, it seems, were the *ceto civile* likely to seek out opportunities for productive investment.

As we shall see in the following chapter, by 1700 a number of leading members of the *ceto civile* had identified themselves with the new intellectual culture of Cartesian and Epicurean natural and moral philosophy, and with criticism of the privileges and intellectual authority of the church. Among their concerns was Naples' inability to benefit from the expansion of European commerce. But before 1700 only one of their number, Francesco d'Andrea, was in any position to act on this concern; and his efforts to do so, in 1690–1, were quickly stalled. There is no indication that he was expressing the aspirations of the *ceto civile* as a whole.[77]

The *ceto civile* would in any case have needed the support of an active and ambitious class of merchants. If little is known about the *ceto civile* as a socio-economic group, however, even less appears to be known about the Neapolitan merchant community in the later seventeenth century. The presence of Genoese and other foreign merchants was well established by the first half of the century. But in the present state of knowledge it is impossible to say whether there were later equivalents of figures such as the Fleming Gaspar Roomer, the most important individual patron and collector of fine art in seventeenth-century Naples, or Bartolomeo d'Aquino, the financier who took on the burden of meeting the monarchy's fiscal demands in the early 1640s. Even if there were, it is likely that they put their wealth to the same uses as those predecessors, buying fiefs and pictures rather than ploughing it into productive enterprises.[78] The zeal with which the merchants involved in the supply of grain to the city defended their monopoly privileges does not suggest a class actively looking for new economic opportunities.

One final potential interest in economic change remains to be considered: the better-off members of the rural communities. As we have seen, the *università* possessed a corporate legal identity which gave them some

---

[77] Ibid., pp. 213–15.

[78] On d'Aquino and Roomer, Villari, *The Revolt of Naples*, pp. 76–97; on Roomer as a collector, Francis Haskell, *Patrons and painters: A Study in the Relations between Italian Art and Society in the Age of the Baroque* (London, 1963), pp. 205–8. Roomer's dominance as a patron lasted until his death in 1674.

institutional autonomy from their feudal lords. Formally self-governing, they decided important economic matters, including the division of the community's demesne lands. In practice the direction of a community was often in the hands of an oligarchy of the better-off. But the scope for these to pursue an independent economic interest was limited at almost every turn. Not only were they subject to the rights and monopolies held by the feudal lord, but traditional, communal customs governing the distribution of cultivable land and pasture made it impossible to achieve any consolidation of holdings. When they had a surplus to dispose of, they would find their market limited to the immediate neighbourhood by the absence of communications further afield. Not until the second half of the eighteenth century would differentiation within rural communities reach the point at which real pressures for change emerged, and the attempt could be made by reformers within government to harness these pressures to replace communal with commercial agriculture.[79]

It has become fashionable to suggest that the economy of the Mezzogiorno in the early modern period had a distinct rationality, and that the adoption by the nobility of a strategy of survival and continuity was no more than rational self-interest.[80] If there is validity to such a suggestion, however, it is far better applied to those lower on the social scale, the peasants and herdsmen of the interior, the artisans and the underemployed poor, the notorious *lazzaroni*, of the city. They *had* to adopt strategies of survival in an economy relentlessly controlled in the interests of the feudal lords and the urban elites. But when even elsewhere in Italy, let alone in northern Europe, there were landowners and merchants looking for new economic opportunities, it is the almost total lack of interest shown by their Neapolitan counterparts which is striking. Not only was this an economy with a high propensity to consume; no social class of economic consequence had indicated more than the most fleeting aspiration to change that priority.

ECONOMY AND SOCIETY IN SCOTLAND

In its principal features the economic geography of Scotland was not unlike that of Naples. There was the same mixture of lowland and highland, with a long coastline west and east. But the distribution, agricultural potential,

---

[79] Villari, *Mezzogiorno e contadini*, pp. 56–9, 142–57.
[80] Marino, *Pastoral Economics in the Kingdom of Naples*, esp. the introduction; see also his 'Economic idylls and pastoral realities: the "trickster" economy in the kingdom of Naples', *Comparative Studies in Society and History*, 24 (1982), 210–34. A defence of the nobility in these terms is central to Astarita, *Continuity of Feudal Power*, pp. 68–71.

and accessibility of the land were all different. The Scottish lowlands were concentrated in the centre of the country, and the land itself was good for farming, both arable and pastoral. Grain, predominantly oats and barley, formed the principal crop, but flax was also grown in several areas, while there was grazing for cattle and sheep. The highlands to the north and the border hills to the south formed, it is true, a large area of which only a small part was cultivable; but ample rainfall ensured that they contained a plentiful supply of rough pasture for animals, cattle as well as sheep.

The forms of settlement also differed in Scotland. Across the lowlands the traditional settlement was the separate farm, or fermtoun. Before 1700 this was often held by two or more families in a multiple tenancy, with the lands divided between tenants under a customary system known as 'runrig'. But while runrig, like any such customary system, gave priority to the pursuit of subsistence, the separation of farms ensured that the interests involved in the distribution of land were never as many or as complex as those on the communal demesnes of the Italian south. Moreover the farms were rarely distant from a village or small town, and between these settlements there was an established though poorly maintained network of communications. The lowland Scottish peasantry, therefore, were at once more independent in their farming practices and a good deal less isolated from the rest of the kingdom than their Neapolitan counterparts. In the highlands, by contrast, settlements tended to be gathered in the glens and straths, to be close to what little cultivable land there was, as well as to the sea for fishing. There subsistence was the priority for most, and while the clan chiefs behaved increasingly as landlords, tenurial relations were still qualified by the mutual obligations of kinship. Isolation, and reliance on the sea for communications, was naturally greater; but it was at least diminished by the existence of the drove-roads along which the cattle and sheep travelled southwards, into the lowlands and beyond.[81]

At around 1.2 million, the population of Scotland in the second half of the seventeenth century was under half that of the kingdom of Naples. Plague had struck in 1644–9, but with less devastating effect than in Naples in 1656, even if Edinburgh lost perhaps a third or a quarter of its inhabitants. Though rates of mortality fluctuated thereafter, a sustained fall in grain prices after 1653 suggests that population was more or less in equilibrium with the food

---

[81] Robert A. Dodgshon, *Land and Society in Early Scotland* (Oxford, 1981); Ian Whyte, *Agriculture and Society in Seventeenth-Century Scotland* (Edinburgh, 1979).

supply.[82] If this condition of equilibrium resembled that found in the kingdom of Naples, however, there was an important difference. The Scottish rural economy was more open to the market. Although the Scottish burghs sought to regulate the price of grain, its supply was not distorted by the requirements of an official provisioning system like the Neapolitan *annona*. The demand from Edinburgh may even have encouraged the emergence of a national market in grain, evident in the convergence of regional prices which had begun by 1700. In good years grain was exported.[83] Production for the market also involved more of the rural population, as rents traditionally paid in kind began to be raised in money. This was reinforced by the first indications of a shift from multiple- to single-tenant farms, encouraging the disuse of runrig.[84] Livestock production was also commercialised, as both cattle and sheep passed south from the highlands and southern uplands for export to England in tens of thousands per annum by the 1680s.[85] The effects of this trade were particularly marked in the highlands, drawing these too into the market economy.

The commercialisation of the rural economy was reinforced by the pattern of urban development. The capital and largest city, Edinburgh, had no more than 40–45,000 inhabitants in 1700, or some 4–5 per cent of the country's population (as compared with Naples' 10 per cent of the population of the kingdom). The hierarchy beneath Edinburgh was also more even: Glasgow (growing rapidly up to 18,000), Dundee, and Aberdeen (both static at 5–10,000) were substantial centres. At least as significant were the much more numerous smaller towns of 1–2,000 inhabitants which offered urban facilities, above all by holding fairs or markets. Over 300 markets and fairs were authorised between 1660 and 1707, dramatically increasing the scope for market integration.[86] The main centres also supported a range of manufacturing industries, the most important of which,

---

[82] Michael Flinn and others, *Scottish Population History from the 17th century to the 1930s* (Cambridge, 1977), pp. 133–64. A. J. S. Gibson and T. C. Smout, *Prices, Food and Wages in Scotland 1550–1780* (Cambridge, 1990), pp. 165–7.

[83] Rosalind Mitchison, 'The movements of Scottish corn prices in the seventeenth and eighteenth centuries', *Economic History Review*, Second Series 18 (1965), pp. 281–3; Whyte, *Agriculture and Society*, pp. 222–34; Gibson and Smout, *Prices, Food and Wages*, pp. 136–7.

[84] Whyte, *Agriculture and Society*, pp. 141–5, 151–3; qualified by Dodgshon, *Land and Society*, pp. 241–65, and T. M. Devine, *The Transformation of Rural Scotland: Social Change and the Agrarian Economy 1660–1815* (Edinburgh, 1994), pp. 1–16.

[85] Donald Woodward, 'A comparative study of the Irish and Scottish livestock trades in the seventeenth century', in L. M. Cullen and T. C. Smout (eds.), *Comparative Aspects of Scottish and Irish Economic and Social History* (Edinburgh, 1977), pp. 147–64.

[86] De Vries, *European Urbanization*, p. 271; Whyte, *Agriculture and Society*, pp. 183–92; Christopher A. Whatley, *Scottish Society 1707–1830: beyond Jacobitism, towards Industrialisation* (Manchester, 2000), pp. 19–23.

in linen and wool, were located in the countryside but organised from the towns. Except in Edinburgh there were few luxury trades, although Dundee was noted for its decorated arms; but the linen and wool industries were clearly producing for the market, within Scotland and beyond. As we have seen, Scottish merchants traded across the North Sea to the Baltic, the Netherlands, and France as well as to England; and in the west Glasgow merchants were opening up the trade with the North American colonies.[87]

The scale of this economic activity was by no means such as to make Scotland a rich country by 1700.[88] Not only was it poor relative to England; by comparison with Naples, there was far less wealth available in Edinburgh for conspicuous consumption. Nevertheless, the small Scottish economy already possessed an advantage over the Neapolitan. With a higher degree of market integration, it was more diversified. At the same time, the propensity to consume at the expense of investment was less marked. Why this should have been so may become clearer if we also look at changes within Scottish social structure.

At the head of Scottish rural society were some 1,500 substantial landowners, of whom 130–150 were titled nobility. Formally the system of landholding in Scotland was even more feudal than that in the kingdom of Naples, since all land in Scotland (other than church land) was held ultimately of the king in feudal tenure. Only those who were, in feudal terms, tenants-in-chief of the king, or feudal 'superiors', counted as 'freeholders' proper. In practice, however, the importance of feudal tenure was limited. The implications for landownership itself had been diluted by subinfeudation, by which many who were technically vassals had come to possess land in *dominium utile*, which gave effective ownership. Aside from various irritating 'casualties' by which the vassal might forfeit the fee to the superior, the one feudal power which continued to count was that of jurisdiction.

The 'heritable jurisdictions', as they were called, had been restored after 1660, and ranged from the regality courts of the greatest nobility, which could try major crimes and authorise capital punishment, to the lesser barony courts, which confined themselves to petty crime and the obligations of tenants. The importance which the great nobility attached to their jurisdictions was underlined by their insistence on their confirmation in

[87] Whatley, *Scottish Society*, pp. 23–6.

[88] T. C. Smout, 'Where had the Scottish economy got to by the third quarter of the eighteenth century?', in Istvan Hont and Michael Ignatieff (eds.), *Wealth and Virtue: the Shaping of Political Economy in the Scottish Enlightenment* (Cambridge, 1983), pp. 45–8, for a balance-sheet of developments up to 1707.

1689. Even so, regality courts were never possessed by all the nobility, and in the lowlands were less and less likely to exercise their jurisdiction in capital crimes. They remained important for longer in the highlands, no family being more jealous of its jurisdiction than the Campbell earls of Argyll. But the nobility's new willingness to send its sons to learn and practise the law in Edinburgh, and to take their own disputes to the crown courts, were clear indications of an increasing acceptance of the primacy of royal justice. Barony courts remained in active use by lairds as well as nobles, but as an adjunct to the powers which all landowners already held over their tenants, who enjoyed little protection from common or customary law.[89]

Another traditional source of power in Scottish rural society was kinship. In the highlands kinship, whether indicated by possession of the same patronymic or by adoption of the clan name, remained the principal basis of membership of a clan and allegiance to its chief.[90] Even in the lowlands the recognition of ties of kinship remained an essential element of effective lordship into the late seventeenth century and beyond. Yet here too the power of the great nobility appears to have weakened by 1700. A crucial test was their ability to raise men for military service on the strength of family and local connections. These connections were certainly still invoked, for example to raise forces to counter the covenanters in the 1670s; but the men were now being recruited for the newly established militia, or for the king's regiments, in both of which the nobility themselves were increasingly keen to serve as officers.[91] The great nobility were no longer an autonomous military power. A similar tendency was evident in the legal profession. The presence of increasing numbers of sons of nobles among the advocates and judges may actually have created a new field of influence for kinship connections; but they worked through the institutions of the crown.[92]

---

[89] There has yet to be a proper study of the hereditary jurisdictions and barony courts. For some remarks: Rosalind Mitchison, *Lordship to Patronage: Scotland 1603–1745* (London, 1983), pp. 80–1, 85–6; and on the barony courts, Ian Whyte, 'The emergence of the new estate structure', in M. L. Parry and T. R. Slater (eds.), *The Making of the Scottish Countryside* (London, 1980), pp. 118–21. A recent, brave attempt at a Marxist interpretation of Scottish society in the period highlights the continuing importance of the jurisdictions in maintaining a feudal order: Neil Davidson, *Discovering the Scottish Revolution 1692–1746* (London, 2003), pp. 19–21; but the suggestion that the opposition of the Edinburgh legal profession to these jurisdictions set them at odds with the nobility seems to me misleading.

[90] Robert A. Dodgshon, '"Pretense of blude" and "place of thair duelling": the nature of highland clans 1500–1745', in R. A. Houston and I. D. Whyte (eds.), *Scottish Society 1500–1800* (Cambridge, 1989).

[91] Lenman, 'Militia, Fencible men and home defence', pp. 176–84; Keith M. Brown, 'From Scottish lords to British officers: state building, elite integration and the army in the seventeenth century', in Macdougall *Scotland and War*, pp. 133–48.

[92] Phillipson, 'Lawyers, landowners and civic leadership', pp. 100–6.

Here, as in central and local government, the nobility now ruled along-side the untitled lairds and barons, who had replaced the clergy as the second estate in Parliament. As we have seen, this collaboration overrode differences of status: there was no Scottish equivalent of the division found in Naples between the feudal nobility and the *togati*. While rank still mattered to the Scots nobility, it was not protected by a carapace of privilege. The collaboration of nobility and lairds in government, moreover, was underpinned by a common interest in landownership – and by the first indications of a common commitment to developing the rural economy. In Scotland as in Naples there was a notable concentration of landownership, almost 50 per cent of landed wealth in 1690 being in the hands of between 300 and 350 owners, including most of the titled nobility.[93] The scope for such concentration was reinforced when in 1685 the Parliament authorised the creation of entails to protect the family inheritance. But the presence of as many untitled lairds among the larger landowners was equally significant; and there appears to have been no rush to take up the opportunity to entail lands. Landowners were not yet self-conscious improvers; but both great nobles and lairds were involved in the introduction of single tenancies and the transformation of rents in kind into money rents. During a period of stable prices the returns on such changes were likely to be limited, and tenants themselves were understandably cautious, while the ending of multiple tenancies may have exacerbated the problem of poor relief in years of bad harvests. But landowners seem to have been willing to take the risk, and to introduce changes while taking some responsibility as parish heritors for funding and administering poor relief.[94] It was an attitude in marked contrast with that of the Neapolitan nobility.

The Scottish nobility and lairds also differed in their relation with their capital city. The absence of a court in Edinburgh was clearly a matter for regret, all the more so after James, duke of Albany had reminded them of what they were missing during his visits between 1679 and 1682; the lack encouraged those with means and political ambition to move on to London. But even without a court the nobility and many lairds were drawn to Edinburgh for meetings of Parliament and the business of the law courts. While there they resided for the most part in lodgings in the great tenements of the old town; only a few owned town houses, and there were no

[93] Loretta Timperley, 'Landownership in Scotland in the eighteenth century', University of Edinburgh doctoral thesis (1977), p. 199.
[94] Rosalind Mitchison, 'North and South: the development of the gulf in Poor Law practice', in Houston and Whyte, *Scottish Society*, esp. pp. 207–14.

palaces other than the royal palace of Holyrood.[95] Naturally they spent on services, which by the 1690s included those of a resident portrait painter, Sir John Medina, and on luxuries, including fine furniture, Delft ware, and high quality textiles, all imported. But there were few examples of the sort of conspicuous consumption which embellished the palaces and family chapels of the Neapolitan nobility. What was wholly missing in Edinburgh, moreover, was the reciprocal relation between status and power accorded by the *seggi* of Naples. The nobility had no formal, institutionalised status within the city, which, like all the Scottish royal burghs, was ruled exclusively by a council of leading townsmen, chosen from the members of the merchant and trades corporations.

These burgh councils wielded considerable power within their communities, regulating economic life, providing for the poor and (in Edinburgh, Glasgow, Aberdeen, and St Andrews) governing the universities. Collectively they possessed in the Convention of Royal Burghs an effective voice for their economic interests, and the individual councils were also directly represented, as a separate estate, in the Parliament, where they likewise felt free to take the initiative on economic matters. In outlook, especially in economic policy, the councils were inclined to be cautious; but they did not simply protect existing privileges.[96] This probably reflected the traditional, and perhaps growing, importance of merchants in the councils. By the later seventeenth century recruits to their ranks came from a variety of backgrounds, including the sons of landowners.[97] The most successful merchants might themselves buy land, but they did not do so in order to withdraw from productive enterprise. The Glasgow merchants who opened up the Atlantic trade invested in both land and local manufactures; Edinburgh merchants were behind the most ambitious single industrial project of the period, the cloth manufactory at Newmills in East Lothian. No individual Glasgow or Edinburgh merchant was anything like as wealthy as Gaspar Roomer – and none is known to have been a patron and collector of art: by these standards Scottish merchants, and the burgh communities they led, would have seemed far inferior to their Neapolitan contemporaries.

[95] R. A. Houston, *Social Change in the Age of Enlightenment: Edinburgh 1660–1760* (Oxford, 1994), pp. 70–4.

[96] Michael Lynch, 'Continuity and change in urban society, 1500–1700', in Houston and Whyte, *Scottish Society*, pp. 85–114; discussing Edinburgh in particular, Houston, *Social Change in the Age of the Enlightenment*, pp. 343–73, puts more emphasis on the conservatism of the council.

[97] T. M. Devine, 'The Scottish merchant community 1680–1740', in R. H. Campbell and A. S. Skinner (eds.), *The Origins and Nature of the Scottish Enlightenment* (Edinburgh, 1982), pp. 26–41; and 'The social composition of the business class in the larger Scottish towns 1680–1740', in T. M. Devine and David Dickson (eds.), *Ireland and Scotland 1600–1850: Parallels and Contrasts in Economic and Social Development* (Edinburgh 1983).

Nevertheless, this Scottish urban elite was alert to economic opportunities in a way that the privileged, protected merchants of Naples apparently were not.

There is therefore little doubt which of the two societies, Neapolitan and Scottish, was more open to change by 1700. In Naples the priority of the nobilities, both feudal and robe, was the perpetuation of their traditional privileges, and the satisfaction of their propensity to consume in order to maintain their status. The ruling elites of Scotland, by contrast, were ready to respond to economic opportunity, both within Scotland and in the world around them. This willingness collectively to promote economic activity is evident in the increasing attention devoted to matters of trade and agricultural improvement by the Privy Council, which had its own Committee of Trade, and by the Scottish Parliament. A series of Council decrees and parliamentary Acts to this effect culminated in the Acts of Parliament of 1695 which authorised the division of common lands and the unification of open fields at the instigation of the landowner alone, instituted the Bank of Scotland, and established 'a Company trading to Africa and the Indies', intended as the Scottish answer to the English and Dutch East India Companies.[98]

But the best evidence of a commitment to change was the willingness of both merchants and landowners to invest. The development of the Newmills cloth manufactory in the 1680s, for example, required an initial investment of £5,000 by the twenty-three merchants who participated, and a further £4,000 was raised by a new group in 1694.[99] Opening its books a year later, the Bank of Scotland raised over £60,000 in subscriptions. Much the largest Scottish investment, however, was that required by the company instituted by the Act of 1695, the Company of Scotland, whose great project was the Darien venture of 1698–1700. Towards this the Scots were asked to raise £300,000, later increased to £400,000, which has been estimated as equivalent to half the total capital available in Scotland at that time. The sum was subscribed within six months in 1696, and the first 25 per cent paid when called for; recent analysis has shown just how broad based subscription was. The nobility made a point of identifying with the cause: the first to sign was Anne, duchess of Hamilton, and there was a

[98] On the legislation concerning the division of lands: Whyte, *Agriculture and Society*, pp. 105–10. For measures to encourage manufactures and trade: George Pratt Insh, *The Company of Scotland Trading to Africa and the Indies* (London and New York, 1932), pp. 17–35; and Smout, *Scottish Trade on the Eve of Union*, pp. 20–3.

[99] Gordon Marshall, *Presbyteries and Profits: Calvinism and the Development of Capitalism in Scotland 1560–1707* (Oxford, 1980), pp. 142–55.

small rush to pledge contributions in the few days before publication of the printed list of subscribers. From among the lairds, Andrew Fletcher of Saltoun subscribed £1,000 on the opening day, and several prominent Edinburgh and Glasgow merchants matched or bettered that figure. But subscriptions came from throughout Scotland (only one county was not represented) and from the middling as well as the upper classes; if the landed classes contributed some 45 per cent of the nominal capital, the share of merchants and officials was 37 per cent, that of craftsmen and professionals a further 6 per cent. In relation to Edinburgh, Glasgow's contribution was in proportion to its population.[100] There could hardly be clearer evidence that those with means in Scottish society were prepared to invest in the country's development.

Willingness to invest, however, was no guarantee of success. Instead the 1690s saw the Scottish economy suffer one disaster after another, in the midst of which the Darien scheme takes on the appearance of a more or less desperate, speculative remedy.[101] It was already clear that Scotland's overseas trade had been hard hit by William III's war with France. The French had barred Scottish salt and herrings, for the second of which they were Scotland's main market. Markets for salt and coal were also being lost in the Netherlands. But instead of easing the difficulties of their ally, the English had tightened the provisions of the Navigation Act which impeded direct Scottish trade with the North American colonies.[102] Commercial crisis was then compounded by its agricultural counterpart, as the country suffered a sequence of harvest failures between 1695 and 1698. The consequence was severe shortage in most areas and famine in some: population loss (by death and emigration) has been estimated at between 5 and 15 per cent, but 20 per cent in Aberdeenshire. Neither the provisioning trade nor the poor relief system could cope, and the sharply increased numbers of vagrants – 'vagabonds' to contemporaries – were a cause for alarm.[103] The final blow was the rapid disintegration of the Darien venture itself. In 1698

---

[100] Insh, *The Company of Scotland*, pp. 65–8; and now, in much more revealing detail, W. Douglas Jones, '"The Bold Adventurers": a quantitative analysis of the Darien subscription list (1696)', *Scottish Economic and Social History*, 21 (2001), 22–42. The list of subscribers was printed as an appendix to *The Darien Papers*, edited for the Bannatyne Club by J. H. Burton (Edinburgh, 1849); p. 373 for 26 February 1696, the day the book opened, with Andrew Fletcher's subscription.

[101] The reality of the economic setbacks of the 1690s, and the extent to which they should qualify favourable assessments of the state of the Scottish economy, have recently been re-emphasised by Whatley, *Scottish Society*, pp. 32–41; another to highlight the significance of the decade has been Davidson, *Discovering the Scottish Revolution*, ch. 2, 'Three dimensions of socio-economic crisis (the 1690s)'.

[102] Smout, *Scottish Trade on the Eve of Union*, pp. 245–56.

[103] Flinn, *Scottish Population History*, pp. 164–85; Gibson and Smout, *Prices, Food and Wages*, pp. 170–1.

and again in 1699 expeditions set out from Leith to plant a colony on the Darien isthmus in Panama, in the hope of establishing an entrepôt for Atlantic and in due course Pacific trade. But it was clear by 1700 that the venture had failed. An unfamiliar climate, determined Spanish opposition, England's refusal to assist, but above all the inability of the Scots to support the colony logistically or militarily were to blame.[104] Despite the best efforts of both landowners and merchants, therefore, it seemed that the Scottish economy remained irredeemably weak, vulnerable both to natural misfortunes and to the exclusive commercial policies of its richer and more powerful neighbours.

The latter, commercial weakness of the Scots also drove home the point that their problem was not simply or even primarily one of economics. The political problem of subordination within a composite monarchy still existed: all the Scots' loyalty to their kings over the seventeenth century had not brought any substantial, structural improvement in their relations with the most powerful kingdom within the regal union, the neighbouring kingdom of England. By 1700, therefore, the Scottish elite had every reason to feel frustrated, both economically and politically. Openness to change and a willingness to invest in it had yielded no tangible rewards.

By comparison, the final decade of the seventeenth century does not seem to have been markedly worse for the Neapolitan economy than any other since the 1650s. Even so, the adverse trends only became more apparent over time. The Neapolitan silk industry continued to decline, a depression measurable in a further fall in the numbers qualifying to enter the trade.[105] Within the merchant community, the numbers of resident French and English continued to rise, and Naples became more markedly an outpost of Livorno. Since Neapolitan economic expectations, at least as measured by willingness to invest, were lower than those of the Scots, there was perhaps less reason for frustration. Nevertheless there are signs, among the more internationally aware in the civil and administrative elite, of a growing exasperation over the prolonged demise of the Spanish Habsburg monarchy, and of hopes that a change of dynasty would bring an opportunity for a government which would pay more attention to the kingdom's economic needs. In Naples too, in other words, the predicament of a subordinate kingdom within a composite monarchy was increasingly felt.

Finally, in 1700, Charles II of Castile died. The long-awaited crisis of the Spanish succession was unleashed, and the kingdom of Naples found

---

[104] Insh, *The Company of Scotland*, pp. 109–242: bk. II, 'America', tells the tale.
[105] Galasso, *Napoli Spagnola dopo Masaniello*, II, p. 739, showing a continued drop in the numbers qualifying for the trade between 1659–60 and 1706.

itself caught between the competing claims of the French Bourbons and the Austrian Habsburgs. Just a year later, the Scots also found themselves facing a succession crisis, when it became clear that William's heir, the future Queen Anne, was herself unlikely to have children, and the English Parliament proceeded to choose her successor without reference to Scotland. In each case, as we shall see in ch. 4, the crisis would provide an opportunity for intensive discussion by contemporaries themselves of the predicament of their kingdoms, and in particular of their economic prospects. As they grappled with the problems identified in this chapter, there can be observed the first expressions of the concerns which were to be at the centre of Enlightenment enquiries into human betterment. Before turning to these discussions, however, we need to take a closer look at the intellectual settings in which they took place. The next chapter, therefore, will explore the nature and extent of the differences between the intellectual cultures of Naples and Scotland at the end of the seventeenth and the beginning of the eighteenth centuries. In this sphere, we shall find, it was the Neapolitans who held the advantage in 1700.

CHAPTER 3

The intellectual worlds of Naples and Scotland 1680–c.1725

'ATHEISTS' ON TRIAL

There were trials of 'atheists' in both Scotland and Naples at the end of the seventeenth century. As so often in such prosecutions, the victims in the two cases were young men. In other respects the trials were markedly different. In Naples the case was complex, protracted, and inconclusive. It began in 1688, when the twenty-one-year-old Francesco Paolo Manuzzi denounced two slightly older acquaintances, Basilio Giannelli and Giacinto Cristofaro, to the Inquisition. By 1690 Manuzzi himself had been arrested, and in 1692, as others were implicated, Giannelli was persuaded to turn his evidence against Cristofaro. Even then the case did not reach a conclusion, since the civil authorities succeeded in taking their objections to Rome; and though the accused suffered varying periods of imprisonment, they were all released by the end of the decade. In Scotland, by contrast, the case was straightforward, the trial and its aftermath mercilessly short. Thomas Aikenhead was charged on 10 November 1696, tried on 23 December, sentenced the following day, and hanged on 8 January 1697, two months short of his twenty-first birthday.[1]

What were the charges against these unfortunate young men? Since in both cases the key witnesses were themselves vulnerable as associates of those on trial, it is all too likely that they said what they thought the respective authorities wanted to hear, rather than accurately reporting the opinions of the accused. Precisely because of this, however, the charge-sheets may tell us something interesting about the intellectual climate in

---

[1] For the ensuing analysis of the two trials I have drawn on the following studies: for Naples, Vittor Ivo Comparato, *Giuseppe Valletta. Un intellettuale napoletano della fine del Seicento* (Naples, 1970), chs. iv–v; Luciano Osbat, *L'Inquisizione a Napoli. Il processo agli ateisti 1688–97* (Rome, 1974); and Giuseppe Galasso, *Napoli Spagnola dopo Masaniello*, 2 vols. (Florence, 1982), pp. 443–73. For Scotland, the admirable article by Michael Hunter, '"Aikenhead the atheist": the context and consequences of articulate irreligion in the late seventeenth century', in Michael Hunter and David Wootton (eds.), *Atheism from the Reformation to the Enlightenment* (Oxford, 1992), pp. 221–54.

the two countries. What Manuzzi reportedly told the Inquisitor in Naples was that he had heard Giannelli and Cristofaro saying that Christ was not God, but a mere man; that there were men in the world before Adam, and that they were composed of atoms like the animals; and that Christ was an impostor, from which it followed that the pope had neither spiritual nor temporal authority. When Giannelli himself confessed to the archbishop of Naples, Giacomo Cantelmo, in 1692, he confirmed these opinions, adding the belief that the soul was mortal, and acknowledged that their source had been the ancient philosophers Democritus, Epicurus, and Lucretius. Still not satisfied, the archbishop had obtained further confessions from lesser figures, yielding an even longer charge-sheet of truly dreadful heresies. The accused were supposed to believe that God neither created nor governed the world, which was formed by chance out of atoms, and existed as a self-governing machine; that there were other worlds; that it was impossible Christ was born of a virgin, he was but a man, a leader of a sect; that there were no greater pleasures in the world than those of the flesh; that there was no hell, purgatory, or paradise; and even that there were no miracles. Since this entailed denying not only the resurrection but also the great miracle of Naples, the twice-yearly liquefying of the blood of San Gennaro, the city's patron saint, the archbishop regarded it as the worst charge of all.[2]

Aikenhead too faced a bundle of accusations, derived from the testimony of his fellow student and perhaps former friend, Mungo Craig. The charges against him included ridiculing theology and scoffing at the Scriptures (which he had reportedly described as 'Ezra's fables'); holding Christ an impostor and denying the doctrine of the Trinity; questioning the compatibility of revelation and providence; and suggesting that God, the world, and nature were one, and that the world was eternal. Though the charges did not identify the sources of these errors, Craig later suggested that Aikenhead had been familiar with Epicurus and Descartes, Hobbes and Spinoza.[3]

If each set of charges was a composite, there were differences of emphasis. In Naples it is clear that the prosecutors were much concerned by non-Christian accounts of the origin and development of the world, and particularly by ideas associated with Epicureanism. In Scotland, by contrast, heterodox ideas about nature and the eternity of the world were secondary in importance to disrespect for Scripture and denial of the Trinity. Given what we know of the prevailing concerns of churchmen in the two countries, the difference is perhaps not surprising. In Naples, as everywhere else in Catholic Italy, the papal condemnation of Galileo in 1633 had thrown a

---

[2] Comparato, *Valletta*, pp. 143–9.   [3] Hunter, '"Aikenhead the atheist"', pp. 224–6, 248.

pall of suspicion over new thinking in natural philosophy. More recently, in 1671, Rome had specifically warned the archbishop of Naples to be on his guard against 'a certain Renato Descartes', whose works had revived 'ancient Greek opinions concerning atoms'.[4] Just before it began proceedings against the 'atheists' the Inquisition had also acted against quietism in Naples, condemning Miguel Molinos, the Spanish-born author of a *Guida spirituale* (1675), on sixty-eight counts in November 1687, and charging Antonio Torres with the same heresy. Torres was not strictly a follower of Molinos, but was clearly regarded as suspect because he enjoyed considerable respect among men of letters for his moral asceticism and disdain for popular superstition.[5] Scotland too had its quietists and moral ascetics, notably Henry Scougal and George Garden, but these gave the church authorities no major cause for alarm. Their current preoccupation was with anti-trinitarianism or Socinianism, a heresy of acute concern to the Protestant churches in both Scotland and England in the late seventeenth and early eighteenth centuries. Although it may have been Aikenhead's sheer brazenness which caused most offence, the prominence of the charge of denying the Trinity is unsurprising.

In neither case, of course, were the trials simply about alleged doctrinal error. The course and outcome of each were critically dependent on the personal circumstances of the accused, and on the relation between the ecclesiastical and civil authorities in the two countries. In Naples the proceedings were complicated and prolonged by the numbers involved, a product of the archbishop's desire to implicate as many as possible, and by the influential family connections of Cristofaro in particular. By contrast, Aikenhead was tried alone: an orphan since the age of nine, he had no protection whatever.

The decisive complication in Naples, however, lay in the antagonism which the trial aroused between church and state. Proceedings began in the Holy Office or Inquisition, which in Naples was the Roman rather than the Spanish institution (the Spanish one having been rejected in an uprising in 1547). Coming so soon after the condemnation of Molinos, the action of the Inquisitor seemed to represent a deliberate assertion of an external ecclesiastical authority. Even after the Inquisitor had been expelled by the viceroy in 1690, and the case had transferred to the city's archbishop, there was clearly no diminution in the church's determination to assert its right to jurisdiction. It was a contest which for much of the century the Spanish

---

[4] Comparato, *Valletta*, p. 140; Osbat, *L'Inquisizione a Napoli*, pp. 11–12.
[5] On this similarly complex affair: Romeo de Maio, 'Il problema del Quietismo napoletano', *Rivista Storica Italiana*, 81 (1969), 721–44.

monarchy and its viceroys had been careful not to join; the whole issue of the kingdom's relation to the papacy, which had a historic claim to be its feudal overlord, had recently been dormant. But the new challenge was one which the incumbent viceroy, the count of Santo Stefano, was unable to evade, for he was put under intense pressure to act by the two long-standing rivals of the clergy, the nobility and the *ceto civile*. Of these the nobility of the *seggi* were the most militant, their *eletti* pressing for the expulsion of the Inquisitor; but if anything the *ceto civile* had more to lose in such a matter of jurisdiction. Eventually a compromise was reached, the viceroy nominating a delegation to put the kingdom's case in Rome, where the issue would then be lost in the Vatican's endless corridors. But the civil authorities were clearly powerful and determined enough to prevent the accused suffering a worse fate than imprisonment.[6]

Very different was the balance of forces facing Aikenhead. Here the church was not extra-territorial, but legally constituted by the Revolution of 1689 as the Church of Scotland. With only a few, half-hearted exceptions its ministers were set upon enforcement of the law against blasphemy, which had been strengthened in 1695. Their gossip embroidered the accusations against Aikenhead: the Reverend Robert Wylie claimed to have heard that Aikenhead supposed Christ to have learned his magic in Egypt. The trial itself took place before the Privy Council, a tribunal in which the accused might have been expected to benefit from the well-established anti-clericalism of the laity. In the event Aikenhead came within one vote of being reprieved, but the Council was swayed by leading members who had reason to stay in with the church – none more so than the Lord Advocate, Sir James Steuart, the one-time covenanting radical who in 1687 had come out in support of James VII, and thus had ground to make up.[7] Along with the Lord Chancellor, Sir Patrick Hume of Polwarth, once a fellow exile in the Netherlands, Steuart insisted that the state should enforce orthodoxy as declared by the church: Aikenhead had to suffer just as did the witches whom the Council was simultaneously busy persecuting in Renfrew.[8]

There was more to the outcomes of the trials, however, than the fates of the individuals accused. In Naples the later stages of the affair were accompanied by a vigorous semi-public debate over its implications, a debate which carried on into the early 1700s. Discussion was 'semi-public' in that

---

[6] Osbat, *L'Inquisizione a Napoli*; Galasso, *Napoli Spagnola*, pp. 450–69.

[7] In Macaulay's withering words, Steuart 'had been so often a Whig, and so often a Jacobite that it is difficult to keep an account of his apostasies. He was now a Whig for the third, if not for the fourth, time': T. B. Macaulay, *History of England* (Albany edition: London, 1897), ch. 22, p. 257.

[8] Hunter, '"Aikenhead the atheist"', pp. 235–9.

few contributions were printed and formally published, but the number of manuscript copies in which they survive suggests that they circulated extensively among those most concerned. The initial focus of the debate was the jurisdiction of the Inquisition and the justice of its special procedures. The case against the Inquisition was led by the *togato* Serafino Biscardi, in a series of exchanges with a group of cardinals in Rome over the historical precedents.[9] But the fullest development of this argument was the work of the lawyer and acknowledged leader of Neapolitan intellectual life in the 1680s and 1690s, Giuseppe Valletta. In his letter 'Al nostro Santissimo Padre Innocentio XII' (1693), Valletta arraigned the extraordinary jurisdiction of the Holy Office, and in particular its secrecy, demonstrating their injustice by the light of natural law. Both up to date and careful in his choice of authorities, Valletta supported his arguments by invoking Grotius but also Aquinas, Cicero as well as the French *politique* jurist Pierre Ayrault.[10]

But this was only the first round in the debate, which quickly moved on to the philosophical issues underlying the charges against the accused. It had been clear to all concerned from the outset that the Inquisitor and the archbishop meant also to implicate the teachers of the accused, who included, besides Valletta, the surviving leaders of the Accademia degli Investiganti, Leonardo di Capua, Luc'Antonio Porzio, and Francesco d'Andrea. These were now assailed directly by the prefect of the Jesuit school in Naples, Giovan Battista de Benedictis, in the *Lettere apologetiche in difesa della teologia scolastica e della filosofia peripatetica* (1694), and in the still more polemical, anonymous *Turris fortitudinis propugnata a filiis lucis adversus filiis tenebrarum* (1695). Here the connection between scepticism, Descartes, atomism, and Epicureanism was plainly asserted, and the contrary truths of scholasticism reaffirmed; at the same time de Benedictis defended the Jesuits from the charges of laxity levelled at them by the Jansenists.[11]

Both Valletta and d'Andrea replied to these attacks in lengthy manuscript works. D'Andrea's two 'Responses to the apologetical letters of Father de Benedictis in defence of Leonardo di Capua' (1697–8) were the more sharply focused. He defended atomism as the best basis for understanding nature, and with it the Cartesian theory of matter as extension. But he did not endorse Descartes' metaphysics, upholding di Capua's reliance on

---

[9] Comparato, *Valletta*, pp. 153–65.   [10] Ibid., pp. 165–94.

[11] On de Benedictis (or Benedetti), who used the pseudonym Benedetto Aletino: Comparato, *Valletta*, pp. 196–200; Harold Samuel Stone, *Vico's Cultural History: the Publication and Transmission of Ideas in Naples 1685–1750* (Leiden, New York, and Cologne, 1997), pp. 46–52; and Paolo Rossi, *Le sterminate antichità e nuovi saggi vichiani* (Florence, 1999), pp. 485–9: 'Sulle *Lettere apologetiche* di Benedetto Aletino'. The authorship of the *Turris Fortitudinis* is uncertain, though de Benedictis was clearly associated with it.

experiment and the 'certainty' achievable by observation. At the same time d'Andrea defended Epicurean morals, contrasting their restraint with the laxity permitted by scholasticism.[12]

More comprehensive, and perhaps less compelling, was Valletta's defence of modern philosophy in a further letter addressed to Innocent XII, and most fully in an 'Istoria filosofica' (completed by 1704). Invoking the French philosopher Pierre Gassendi, Valletta argued that the atomism of Democritus and Epicurus was not incompatible with the divine creation of the world. In the belief that a good genealogy was a sign of philosophic merit, he also traced the doctrines of Epicurus back through Plato to Pythagoras, through whom the wisdom of Egypt was supposed to have passed, first to Italy and thence to Greece. At the same time Valletta defended the opinions of Descartes as in accord with those of Augustine, citing in his support the many French Catholic (and Augustinian) philosophers who were Descartes' followers, including Mersenne, Arnauld, Nicole, and Malebranche. Far from these moderns being proponents of heresy, Valletta contended, it was Aristotle who was the source of all the great heresies, from the Arian to the Socinian; it was his ideas which had led the Renaissance philosophers Cremonini and Cesalpino towards atheism, and which had inspired the three 'great impostors' of recent times, Herbert of Cherbury, Hobbes, and Spinoza. As for the scholastics (from whom Valletta carefully distinguished Aquinas) they had compounded the damage by their insistence on the unity of philosophy and theology. They had confused spheres of knowledge which should be kept separate, to the corruption of both. In the case of nature, the *libertà filosofica*, the freedom to philosophise, was the essential condition of advances in understanding. But Valletta, like d'Andrea, was careful not to suggest that the same methods should apply to morals as to nature: the freedom to experiment should not extend to moral laxity.[13]

The contrast presented by the aftermath of Aikenhead's trial could not be sharper. In Scotland there was no debate at all. After an interval of more than fifteen years the case was resurrected by Thomas Halyburton, the pious professor of divinity at St Andrews, the better to display the perils of atheism. As George Davie pointed out, Halyburton's autobiography

---

[12] Comparato, *Valletta*, pp. 219–24; Stone, *Vico's Cultural History*, pp. 54–6.

[13] Comparato, *Valletta*, pp. 200–17, 225–43, gives a full account of the development of Valletta's arguments. Both the 'Lettera in difesa della moderna filosofia e de' cultivatori di essa' (1691–97), and the 'Istoria filosofica' (1697–1704) are included in Giuseppe Valletta, *Opere filosofiche*, ed. Michele Rak (Florence, 1975); for the references to the French Catholic philosophers, pp. 136–7 ('Lettera'), and to the 'impostors', pp. 142 ('Lettera'), 325–6, 330 ('Istoria').

shows him to have been troubled by doubts very similar to Aikenhead's during the 1690s; but he had conquered them by the simple expedient of suspending all critical judgement in the name of faith.[14] Almost certainly others held opinions not far removed from Aikenhead's. He himself claimed that several of his contemporaries were Socinians; and at the time of his trial the authorities were holding another young man, John Frazer, on similar charges. As Halyburton testified at the time, students were being exposed to disturbing new ideas by lecturers who had by now read Descartes and sometimes Newton.[15] Among their elders the Jacobite and Newtonian physician Archibald Pitcairne was a notorious deist, while the republican-leaning landowner Andrew Fletcher had written to John Locke in 1695 that he was engaged in tracing priestcraft to its origin in Egypt, 'wheir I find lickways many other monsters but none so abominable'.[16] Another of Locke's correspondents, probably James Johnstoun, expressed doubts specifically about Aikenhead's trial and conviction.[17] But if Aikenhead was not alone in his views, no one offered publicly to defend him. It is hard to believe that the case did not seem shameful to the laity, but perhaps it was not felt to raise larger philosophical issues. Certainly, there was no cry that philosophic freedom was at stake.

The significance of the two trials would therefore seem to have been very different. In Naples the affair was a turning point, in at least two major respects. It raised anew the question of the authority of the Church of Rome within the kingdom – at a time when, as we shall see, the kingdom's leaders were increasingly conscious that it might soon be free of the Spanish monarchy. At the same time, the trial and its aftermath brought out the extent to which Neapolitan intellectual life was absorbed by discussion of a variety of ideas – Epicurean, Cartesian, and Augustinian – which were generating acute philosophical and theological tensions for their adherents. The 'affair of the atheists', in short, may be taken as a testimony to the vigour of Neapolitan intellectual life in the late seventeenth century, to its sense of new philosophical opportunities and its willingness to

[14] George Elder Davie, *The Scottish Enlightenment* (Edinburgh, 1991), pp. 8–10; Halyburton had sought to refute Aikenhead's views (and those of Herbert of Cherbury) in *Natural Religion Insufficient; and Reveal'd Religion Necessary to Man's Happiness in his Present State* (1714). On Halyburton see also M. A. Stewart, 'Religion and natural theology', in Alexander Broadie (ed.), *The Cambridge Companion to the Scottish Enlightenment* (Cambridge, 2003), pp. 33–4.

[15] Hunter, '"Aikenhead the atheist"', pp. 240–2, 245–9.

[16] On Pitcairne, Douglas Duncan, *Thomas Ruddiman: a Study in Scottish scholarship of the Early Eighteenth Century* (Edinburgh, 1965), pp. 15–20. Andrew Fletcher to John Locke, 22 February 1695, in *The Correspondence of John Locke*, ed. E. S. De Beer, vol. v (Oxford, 1979), no. 1851, p. 275.

[17] [James Johnstoun?] to [Locke], London, 27 February 1697, *John Locke: Selected Correspondence*, ed. Mark Goldie (Oxford, 2002), no. 2207, pp. 241–2.

take on the ecclesiastical authorities. In Aikenhead's case, by contrast, it is the silence surrounding his fate which is so striking. No doubt there was embarrassment; but the silence suggests a reluctance to debate theological orthodoxy and, perhaps, a less active intellectual culture.

We now need to test these impressions, by examining in more detail the structures of intellectual life in the two kingdoms, and the currents of thought running through them. In doing this, the chapter is intended to establish the second, intellectual dimension of the contexts out of which Enlightenment would emerge in Naples and Scotland. Here, as in the previous chapter, dissimilarities will be many and evident; at the same time, we shall observe another pattern of convergence, this time in access to one of the most lively currents of contemporary thinking about man and society. In this case, however, the convergence took longer to complete: while the presence of Epicurean-Augustinian ideas was causing intellectual ferment in Naples by 1700, those ideas were absent, perhaps deliberately excluded, from Scotland until the 1720s. As we shall see, the discrepancy did not mean that Enlightenment came earlier to Naples; but it does help to explain why it was in Naples, in 1725, that there appeared the first major reckoning with the implications of Epicurean ideas for the study of man, his sociability, and his history.

STRUCTURES OF INTELLECTUAL LIFE IN NAPLES

The oldest institution of learning in Naples was its university. Restored in 1688 to its original home in the convent of San Domenico Maggiore, the *studio* was the responsibility of the crown. It was not, as in other Italian cities, an independent corporation, with its own statutes and privileges. Its rector, the *Capellano Maggiore*, and the professors were appointed by the viceroy, who also set its rules. In return, the crown protected the university by refusing to recognise any others in the kingdom, or the qualifications of those educated elsewhere. What the university could not control, however, was the awarding of degrees, which was the responsibility of independent 'colleges'. This division of functions created the opportunity for private teaching by the professors and others, which flourished despite official attempts to prevent it: it was possible to take a degree from one of the colleges without having studied at the university itself.[18]

---

[18] There is a dearth of modern scholarly work on the university of Naples. This and the following paragraph are drawn from Nino Cortese, 'L'età spagnuola', in Aa. Vv., *Storia della Università di Napoli* (Naples, 1924), pp. 201–431.

Only occasionally did the crown show a serious interest in reform. In the 1610s the viceroy Count Lemos had sought to remodel the university after the example of Salamanca, with partial success. By the end of Spanish rule the *studio* was widely perceived to be in decline, and the last viceroy, the marquis of Villena (1703–7) responded with proposals to institute genuine competitions for appointments, and to re-organise the faculties – proposals which the incoming Austrian government promptly abrogated. Even then, reform was directed towards the improved delivery of teaching; the university was not an institution in which new thinking was expected, let alone encouraged for its own sake. But proponents of new thinking had not been excluded from university chairs: the natural philosopher Tommaso Cornelio had been appointed to one in mathematics in 1653, and Leonardo di Capua later obtained one in medicine. There was vitality too in the teaching of law: writing his autobiography, the *Vita scritta da lui medesimo*, forty years later while imprisoned in Savoy, Pietro Giannone paid warm tribute to the stimulus he had received from Domenico Aulisio, one of the professors of civil law. As they made their way through the crowded streets of Naples after lectures, Giannone recalled, Aulisio had patiently directed his first studies in civil and ecclesiastical law.[19]

Institutions which were intended to foster intellectual innovation were the academies. Two in particular made a significant impact on Neapolitan intellectual culture, the Accademia degli Investiganti (1663–70) and the Accademia Medina Coeli (1698–1700). The Investiganti was founded on the initiative of Tommaso Cornelio, who as a young man had travelled in northern Italy, making the acquaintance of several of Galileo's pupils; he himself was the author of works of physics and mathematics. In forming the academy he was joined by the physician Leonardo di Capua, by the anatomist Luc'Antonio Porzio, and by the jurist Francesco d'Andrea. The academy's patron was the marquis of Arena, in whose apartments the meetings were held, and who purchased instruments for its work. Under a motto adapted from Lucretius, *Vestigis lustrat*, the members discussed a range of topics in mechanics, optics, the properties of bodies, and animal life. Correspondence was established with Michelangelo Ricci in Rome, and through him with the Accademia del Cimento in Florence (which flourished between 1657 and 1667, and was perhaps the closest Italian equivalent to the Neapolitan academy). The Investiganti was also visited by Borelli, to repeat experiments he had conducted in the Cimento, and by several

---

[19] Pietro Giannone, *Vita scritta da lui medesimo* (composed 1736–7), in *Opere di Pietro Giannone*, ed. Sergio Bertelli and Giuseppe Ricuperati (Milan and Naples, 1971), pp. 19–32.

members of the Royal Society of London, including Sir John Finch, Thomas Baines, Francis Willoughby, and John Ray. It did not avoid public controversy, in particular with city medical officials, and this eventually led to its formal disbandment by the authorities in 1670. But the academy's influence continued to be felt through publication and the continued presence in the city of its leading members (with the exception of Porzio, who left to spend eighteen years in Rome). Cornelio's *Progymnasmata physica* was published in Venice, but under the aegis of the Investiganti, in 1663, and again in an enlarged Neapolitan edition in 1688, shortly after Cornelio's death in 1684. Di Capua's major work on medicine, the *Parere*, was published in Naples in 1681; and correspondence with Queen Christina of Sweden, of whose academy in Rome Porzio had become a member, encouraged him to expand it for further editions in 1689 and 1695.[20] But the clearest indication of the academy's continued influence was the trial of the 'atheists': in their determination to prosecute, the ecclesiastical authorities effectively admitted that the suppression of the Investiganti had failed to check the dissemination of its members' ideas.

The Accademia Medina Coeli was named directly after its patron, Luis de la Cerda, ninth duke of Medina Coeli, viceroy from 1695 until 1702, and a notable patron of the arts.[21] Its origins lay in occasional meetings in 1696 and 1697 in which selected men of letters had celebrated royal events with recitations of poetry; and poetry reading continued to play a part in proceedings after the academy had been formalised in 1698. As an academy, however, its principal purpose was to hear papers, or *lezioni*, prepared by its members. These have survived in manuscript copies.[22] The majority of papers (some 70 out of a total of 127) were on historical topics: most of these were on Roman history, especially from the period of the emperors, but there was also a series on Persian history, and latterly the viceroy appears to have encouraged members to write on the alleged papal investiture of the kingdom of Naples itself. Papers on philosophical subjects were fewer (about thirty) but, as we shall see, in at least two cases of considerable significance. Among the twenty-five or twenty-six members who gave papers, two were

[20] M. H. Fisch, 'The Academy of the Investigators', in E. A. Underwood (ed.), *Science, Medicine and History: Essays in Honour of Charles Singer*, 2 vols. (London, 1953), I, pp. 521–46. On Cornelio: Paolo Cristofolini, 'Tommaso Cornelio et l'histoire du matérialisme', in Sylvia Murr (ed.), *Gassendi et l'Europe (1592–1792)* (Paris, 1997), pp. 335–46.

[21] Vicente Lleó Cañal, 'The art collection of the ninth Duke of Medinaceli', *The Burlington Magazine*, 131 (1989), 108–16.

[22] The best being that in the Biblioteca Nazionale of Naples: 'Delle Lezioni Accademiche de' diversi valentuomini de' nostri tempi recitate avanti l'Eccmo. Sig. Duca di Medina Coeli Vice-Re, che fu del Regno di Napoli', parte I, libri i–iii, II, III, 'copiate dall'originale, che si conservava presso il Sig D. Niccolo Sersale', BNN Mss XIII.B.69–73.

nobles *di seggio*, and a further three from the nobility *fuori piazza*; but most were from the *ceto civile*, being lawyers and professors. Relatively few were from the older generation, though both Valletta and Porzio were members. The most numerous and active, including Gregorio Caloprese, Paolo Mattia Doria, and Niccolò Sersale, were in middle age, while the younger members included Niccolò Capasso, Niccolò Cirillo, and Giambattista Vico.[23] The academy did not include all those then active in the city's intellectual life: among those who were not members were Domenico Aulisio, Serafino Biscardi, Matteo Egizio, and Costantino Grimaldi, while Pietro Giannone was missing from the younger generation.

The absence of these men, and the fact that the Medina Coeli did not attract foreign visitors, has been held to cast doubt on its importance.[24] But the terms in which Giannone discussed it in his *Vita* suggest that the stimulus of the academy could reach well beyond its invited membership. Still in his early twenties, Giannone was simply too young to have been considered for membership; the youngest member, Capasso, was five years older. But he was soon to become the close friend of both Capasso and Cirillo, who introduced him to the works of Descartes, and to that 'learned and acute book of Malebranche, *De inquirenda veritate*'. With Cirillo, Giannone also attended anatomical demonstrations by Porzio, where he met 'the profound Cartesian philosopher' Gregorio Caloprese.[25] As with the Investiganti, the contribution of the Medina Coeli to Neapolitan intellectual life was not limited to its own proceedings.

Another feature of late seventeenth-century Naples to which Giannone paid tribute was its libraries. Notable collections of books were held both by religious institutions and by individuals. Among those in individual hands, two collections were outstanding. One was the collection of some 20,000 volumes which Cardinal Francesco Maria Brancaccio left to the city on his death in 1675. By 1690 this had been transferred to San Angelo a Nido, where it functioned as a public library, with librarians and funds for purchases. It was here that Giannone found many of the books of Roman and ecclesiastical law and history to which Aulisio had directed his attention.[26]

Though Giannone did not use it until later, a second private collection had already assumed an even more important role in Neapolitan intellectual

[23] The membership of the academy and contents of its proceedings are analysed by Giuseppe Ricuperati, 'A proposito dell'Accademia Medina Coeli', *Rivista Storica Italiana*, 84 (1972), 57–79.

[24] As in Stone, *Vico's Cultural History*, pp. 93–109.

[25] Giannone, *Vita*, in *Opere di Giannone*, pp. 48–52.

[26] Comparato, *Valletta*, p. 97; Giannone, *Vita*, in *Opere di Giannone*, p. 32. The collection later became the core of the Biblioteca Nazionale at Naples.

life by 1690. This was the library acquired by Giuseppe Valletta himself with the wealth he had accumulated as a merchant and an advocate (just how it was accumulated remains, unfortunately, unknown). Consisting of 10–12,000 titles (many of which were in several volumes), it was a library of comparable size with that of Brancaccio, and included classical, modern, and contemporary works, as well as a number of manuscripts. The best indication of its contents appears to be the manuscript list, described as the 'Antico Catalogo', kept by the library of the Congregation of the Oratory in the convent of the Girolamini. This is believed to have been drawn up for the library in 1726, when, with the assistance of Vico, it acquired the greater part of Valletta's collection from his nephews. (The 'catalogue' itself has been ascribed to Vico, though there seems to be no positive evidence for this.)[27] The books are listed by size (folio, quarto, and duodecimo), language, and subject. By far the largest number of books were in Latin, and were divided into the categories of *Libri Ecclesiastici*; *Philosophi, Mathematici et Medici*; *Historici et Geographi*; *Lexicographi et Bibliothecarii*; *Authores Greci et Latini*; *Literatores et Antiquarii*; and *Poeti Latini recentatae*. Listed after these were all sizes of books in the category *Juridici et Politici*. Books in Italian, French, English (with a few in Dutch), and Spanish were listed separately, again by size, but with sub-headings only in the case of the Italian books.

As the classification suggests, the collection was strong in the classical authors, in theology, philosophy, history, antiquities, law, and politics. Among the Italian books poetry and politics were both prominent. By contrast the *Libri Gallici* contained a striking amount of contemporary French religious controversy and moral philosophy: besides the works of Descartes, books by the leading thinkers of Port Royal, including Pascal, Arnauld, and Nicole, and of the Oratory, including Malebranche and Simon, were present in large numbers, along with several by Huguenots such as Jurieu and Bayle. Here, clearly, was the source of Valletta's knowledge of modern French philosophy, so central to his defence of the *libertà filosofica*. In English Valletta collected histories and the libertine poetry of the Restoration, also equipping himself with dictionaries to assist in their translation; given

---

[27] The 'catalogue' which I have read has been given the title 'Antico Catalogo della Biblioteca dei Girolamini attribuito a Giambattista Vico', but originally appears to have been without a title. It was read in the library on a microfilm, in line with the current policy that manuscripts are only made available to readers on microfilm; its reference number was 27.1.10. The manuscript contained 244 folios, and was written on both recto and verso, making a total of 488 pages. It is impossible for me to be sure that this was the same manuscript as that read thirty years previously by Professor Comparato, and discussed in his study of Valletta: *Valletta*, pp. 98–105, but especially p. 99 note. But the description he gives of the 'Antico Catalogo' which was made available to him suggests that it was probably the same manuscript.

such tastes, it was perhaps fortunate that he was reputed to be the only man in the kingdom who could read English.[28] That Valletta should have been able to acquire so many foreign books, including those by notorious dissidents, heretics, and libertines, testifies to their ready availability in Naples. There was apparently little effective control over the import of books. The Index could not keep up with the flow of suspect works, hampering attempts by the ecclesiastical authorities to intervene; in any case the civil authorities resisted the church's demands for a clamp-down on the trade.[29]

Valletta's library was not just for his private use: he made his books freely available to fellow Neapolitan men of letters of all ages, from the leaders of the Investiganti, Cornelio and di Capua, to the younger generation.[30] Nor was the library simply a source of books: it was also a meeting place for the learned and curious, Neapolitans and visitors to the city. It was in his library that Valletta received Jean Mabillon and Gilbert Burnet in 1685, visitors whom he regarded as the leading lights of the Catholic and Protestant worlds of learning.[31] English visitors, another unnamed Scot and a cousin of Burnet followed in 1686, along with a Swede, a German, and a Frenchman. The pattern continued, and over twenty-five years later it is likely to have been in the library that Valletta and members of his family received the third earl of Shaftesbury, during his second visit to Naples from late 1711 until his death in 1713.[32] These visits not only enabled Valletta and his circle to make the personal acquaintance of fellow men of letters from elsewhere; they often also opened fresh channels of correspondence – Shaftesbury, for example, established contact between Valletta and Newton – and brought new books to the library as tokens of gratitude.

The most important channel of correspondence, however, was that which Valletta and others maintained with Antonio Magliabecchi, the librarian

---

[28] For Valletta's reputation as a reader of English, see the 'Elogio del Signor Giuseppe Valletta, Napoletano', published in the *Giornale de' Letterati d'Italia* in 1714 on Valletta's death, reprinted in his *Opere filosofiche*, App. v, p. 413. On the English books in the Girolamini by 1736, most of which are likely to have been Valletta's, see Mario Melchionda, 'La cultura inglese nei libri secenteschi della Biblioteca Oratoriana dei Girolamini a Napoli', *English Miscellany*, ed. Mario Praz, XXI (1970), 265–341.

[29] Maria Consiglia Napoli, 'Editoria clandestina e censura ecclesiastica a Napoli all'inizio del Settecento', in Anna Maria Rao (ed.), *Editoria e cultura a Napoli nel XVIII secolo* (Naples, 1998), pp. 333–51, esp. 339–40.

[30] 'Elogio del Valletta', *Opere filosofiche*, p. 414; Giannone used the library later, after Valletta's death, while it was still in the hands of his nephews: *Vita*, in *Opere di Giannone*, p. 54.

[31] As he wrote to Antonio Magliabecchi, in December 1685, in *Lettere dal Regno ad Antonio Magliabecchi*, ed. Amadeo Quondam and Michele Rak, 2 vols. (Naples, 1978), no. 862, p. 1070. Burnet's visit is discussed further below, pp. 139–41.

[32] Robert Voitle, *The Third Earl of Shaftesbury 1671–1713* (Baton Rouge and London, 1984), pp. 393–5.

to the grand duke of Tuscany, in Florence. Begun in 1681, when Valletta presented Magliabecchi with a copy of di Capua's *Parere*, the correspondence became the main link between Naples and the wider European, and especially the francophone, world of letters. From Magliabecchi Valletta obtained news of books and their availability, information about libraries which were coming on to the market and from which he might hope to buy, recommendations of visitors, and the sort of personal gossip which the intellectual world needs more than most to offset the isolation of scholarly work. Valletta was by no means Magliabecchi's only Neapolitan correspondent; others were Francesco d'Andrea and the publisher and bookseller Antonio Bulifon. D'Andrea also corresponded with the natural philosophers Marcello Malpighi and Francesco Redi, and maintained contact with Luc'Antonio Porzio. More than anything, it was such direct, personal correspondence, accompanied by the exchange of books, which ensured that Neapolitan men of letters were accepted and able to regard themselves as fully accredited members of the European Republic of Letters.[33]

Another less personal but increasingly important source of intellectual news was provided by the journals and reviews which sprang up in the second half of the seventeenth century, especially in northern Europe. Their value was eloquently recalled by Giannone in the *Storia civile*:

> What brought learning to the highest point of perfection among us was the commerce which, by means of *Giornali de' Letterati*, was established between us and France, Germany and Holland; for by means of the great number of journals which emanate from these countries, every one may be informed of the books which are printed in Europe, of the matters they contain, and of the news of the Republic of Letters (*Repubblica Letteraria*).[34]

All the major reviews were available in Naples in Valletta's library: the Parisian *Journal des Sçavans*, first published in 1665, the *Acta Eruditorum* published in Leipzig from 1682, and the two great rival Protestant reviews from Holland, Pierre Bayle's *Nouvelles de la République des Lettres* (1684–87), and Jean Le Clerc's *Bibliothèque universelle et historique* (1686–93) and *Bibliothèque Choisie* (1703–13). Valletta also took the Italian derivative of these, the *Giornale de' Letterati* published by Bacchini from 1686, which owed much of its material to Bayle and Le Clerc, but which also carried

---

[33] *Lettere dal Regno ad Antonio Magliabecchi*, under Valletta, Bulifon, and others; A. Borelli, 'Francesco d'Andrea. Lettere a G. Baglivi, A. Baldigiani, A. Magliabecchi, M. Malpighi, A. Marchetti, F. Redi, L. Porzio', *Archivio Storico per le Provincie Napoletane* (1997), 113–258.

[34] Pietro Giannone, *Dell' Istoria civile del Regno di Napoli Libri* XL, 4 vols. (Naples, 1723), vol. IV, lib. XL, c. v, p. 489 (my translation).

reviews of Neapolitan works; as well as being good for Neapolitan morale, this helped to make Neapolitan works better known, at least within Italy.[35] Another *Giornale de' Letterati d'Italia*, that published in Venice between 1710 and 1720 by Scipione Maffei, Antonio Vallisnieri, and Apostolo Zeno, would later perform a similar function for Neapolitan books, reviewing works by both Vico and Doria.[36]

That Neapolitan books were available for review indicated that the city was also able to support intellectual life with its own printing industry. Antonio Bulifon was one of the leading publishers from the 1680s until the end of Spanish rule in 1707: another, active from the 1670s, was the Frenchman Jacques Raillard. Raillard published the posthumous works of Cornelio in 1688 and the second and third editions of di Capua's *Parere* in 1689 and 1695; he had previously published works by the Florentine natural philosopher Francesco Redi, and later reprinted the *Saggi* of the Academy of the Cimento (1701). Other publishers active in the last quarter of the century included Ludovico Cavallo and Domenico Parrino.[37] Publishing was not unrestricted. Legitimate publication required that a book be printed with official letters of approval, and even if the crown resisted demands by the church to be given complete control, its censorship was an obstacle. While Bulifon was permitted to produce an edition of Lucretius' *De rerum natura* in 1693, the Italian translation by Marchetti, which had been completed in 1668, and was cited from manuscript by d'Andrea in his defence of the new philosophy in the 1690s, could only be published clandestinely, in 1717. Nevertheless, clandestine printing was widespread and difficult to prevent. The publisher of Marchetti's Lucretius, Lorenzo Cicarelli, successfully produced a number of works in this way, including editions of Galileo's *Dialogo intorno ai due massimi sistemi* and his *Lettera alla Granduchessa Cristina di Toscana* (1710), Jacques Rouhault's *Tractatus physicus* with notes by Samuel Clarke (1713), and the *Opere* of di Capua (1714). The most notorious Neapolitan publication of the period, Giannone's *Istoria civile del Regno di Napoli* (1723), was likewise printed unofficially, by Ottavio Vitagliano.[38]

---

[35] 'Antico Catalogo', Biblioteca dei Girolamini, Mf. 27.1.10, f. 231r; see also Comparato, *Valletta*, pp. 124–38. As with books, the dates ascribed to the holdings of the journals in the 'Antico Catalogo' do not always correspond to the actual dates of publication.

[36] Stone, *Vico's Cultural History*, pp. 156–60.

[37] Ibid., pp. 12–20; Giovanni Lombardi, 'L'attività carto-libraria tra fine '600 e primo '700', in Rao, *Editoria e cultura a Napoli*, pp. 79–96, esp. pp. 80–3.

[38] Napoli, 'Editoria clandestina e censura ecclesiastica', pp. 335–8; on the activity of Cicarelli, and the still mysterious edition of Marchetti's Lucretius, whose place of publication was given as 'London', but which other evidence suggests was produced in Naples: Vincenzo Ferrone, *Scienza natura religione. Mondo Newtoniano e cultura italiana nel primo Settecento* (Naples, 1982), pp. 466–7, and note 17. Stone, *Vico's Cultural History*, p. 56, on d'Andrea's use of the translation in the 1690s.

Well into the eighteenth century, moreover, print was supplemented by manuscript copying. It is very difficult to pin down the scale of such copying, or identify those who carried it out, but the copies were almost certainly intended for wider circulation. Among the works which survive in manuscript copies are Valletta's letters against the Inquisition and his 'Istoria filosofica', the *lezioni* of the Accademia Medina Coeli, and (as we shall see) several pamphlets concerning the future of the Spanish monarchy, some translated from printed works in French. The prevalence of copying underlines once again the extent to which Neapolitan intellectual life depended on a combination of public, semi-public, and private institutions and initiatives. Such a combination may appear to offer a precarious basis for vigorous intellectual life; in practice, it made possible the extensive circulation of ideas among the city's men of letters, and succeeded in creating space for serious intellectual debate, despite the many restrictions which the authorities had the power to impose.

STRUCTURES OF INTELLECTUAL LIFE IN SCOTLAND

The component structures of intellectual life in Scotland in this period were broadly the same: universities and voluntary institutions of learning, libraries, reviews and correspondence, and a local publishing industry. But in each case there were also differences, appreciation of which is important to the assessment of the Scots' ability to respond to new thinking. As in Naples, the oldest of these structures was the university. But where the kingdom of Naples was restricted to one university, in the capital city, Scotland had five: in order of foundation, St Andrews, Glasgow, Edinburgh, and King's and Marischal Colleges in Aberdeen. The Scottish universities were also much less beholden to the crown: in 1690 it had the power to appoint to only four out of forty-nine university posts. Instead government of the colleges was the responsibility of their respective burgh corporations. In Edinburgh, understandably, the corporation was often directed by the superior weight of the Privy Council; but it was difficult for any authority to coordinate measures in all five institutions, as the Commissioners appointed to conduct a visitation of the universities discovered in the 1690s. Another distinctive feature of the Scottish universities was the continuation into the early eighteenth century of generalist teaching in the arts: instead of there being professors for each subject, a tutor or 'regent' would take students (who were usually teenagers) through all parts of the arts course, including logic, rhetoric, and moral and natural philosophy, and would also exercise pastoral responsibilities for the boys. But individual chairs were being created in mathematics, medicine, and law before 1700; and in 1708 Edinburgh abolished regenting in favour of subject-based appointments, with Glasgow following suit in 1727. The range of subjects taught also expanded, with additional chairs in medicine, anatomy, law, and civil and ecclesiastical history.[39]

Just as in Naples, the universities of Scotland were teaching institutions, with no brief to advance the frontiers of knowledge. But the new philosophy was not thereby excluded. The first references to Descartes in teaching occur in the 1650s, and by the 1670s several regents were discussing his ideas. Newton was likewise mentioned from an early date, in the 1680s. More remarkably, the professors of mathematics included a few, notably the brothers David and James Gregory, who had immediately become committed Newtonians. It is unlikely, even so, that the majority of regents understood Descartes or Newton sufficiently to offer a systematic account of their philosophies; typically they were supplementing a syllabus whose coherence was still derived from scholasticism. The efforts of the Commissioners in the 1690s to organise common syllabi, distributing the task of designing model courses among the different universities, quickly revealed not only disagreement about what should be taught, but marked inequalities in the understanding of the sciences in particular.[40] The need for change was most apparent in moral philosophy, since the Aristotelian scholasticism prevalent before 1689 had endorsed absolute monarchy, hereditary right, and passive obedience. In its place the regents William Law and William Scott at Edinburgh, and Gershom Carmichael at Glasgow, adapted Pufendorf's theory of natural law and natural rights to the theology of reformed scholasticism to produce an acceptable – and enduring – basis for moral philosophy teaching in eighteenth-century Scottish universities.[41] On the whole the hopes of stricter presbyterians in the 1690s that the universities would become bastions of a narrow orthodoxy were disappointed; but the clergy continued to keep a watchful eye on the orthodoxy and acceptability of those teaching there.

Scottish students did enjoy an opportunity apparently not available to, or rarely taken by, their Neapolitan counterparts: they could supplement study in a Scottish university with a period of study abroad, in the Netherlands.

---

[39] Roger L. Emerson, 'Scottish universities in the eighteenth century, 1690–1800', *Studies on Voltaire and the Eighteenth Century*, 167 (1977), 453–74.

[40] Christine M. Shepherd, 'Newtonianism in Scottish universities in the seventeenth century', in R. H. Campbell and A. S. Skinner (eds.), *The Origins and Nature of the Scottish Enlightenment* (Edinburgh, 1982), pp. 65–85.

[41] James Moore, 'Natural Rights in the Scottish Enlightenment', in M. Goldie and R. Wokler (eds.), *The Cambridge History of Eighteenth-Century Political Thought* (Cambridge, forthcoming).

Both in civil law and in medicine the Dutch universities had professors among the most distinguished in the Protestant world; and Scots students went to hear them in large numbers in the last two decades of the seventeenth century and the first three of the eighteenth (after which numbers fell away sharply). By far the largest number went to Leiden, to study law under the leading professors of the 'Dutch Elegant School', or (after 1701) medicine under Hermann Boerhaave. Smaller numbers went to Utrecht, where the theology was soundly orthodox, to Franeker, and, in the 1720s, to Groningen, where they might hear modern natural law being expounded by Jean Barbeyrac.[42] Residence in the Netherlands should also have given the Scots direct access to the uniquely free intellectual worlds of Rotterdam and Amsterdam, to the publications of Bayle, Le Clerc, and their associates, and even, perhaps, to the native (and vernacular) Dutch debate over the ideas of Spinoza. Whether it in fact did so, however, is another matter: so far, little evidence has come to light to suggest that they took advantage of the opportunity.

Where Scotland was lacking by comparison with Naples was in institutions to match the academies of the Investiganti and Medina Coeli. The residence of James, duke of York and Albany, at Holyrood in the early 1680s did encourage initiatives on behalf of professional bodies, notably the Royal College of Physicians and the Faculty of Advocates. The combined efforts of Sir Robert Sibbald and Sir George Mackenzie of Rosehaugh led to the granting of a royal charter to the physicians in 1681, which enabled them to take responsibility for both a library and the town's Physic Garden. The Faculty of Advocates had recently been recognised by the Court of Session in 1672; but Mackenzie's appointment as its dean in 1682 enabled him to develop its professional character, above all through the expansion of its library.[43] As professional bodies, however, neither the college nor the faculty

---

[42] Roger L. Emerson, 'Scottish cultural change 1660–1710 and the Union of 1707', in John Robertson (ed.), *A Union for Empire: Political Thought and the British Union of 1707* (Cambridge, 1995), pp. 127–8; Robert Feenstra, 'Scottish-Dutch legal relations in the seventeenth and eighteenth centuries', in T. C. Smout (ed.), *Scotland and Europe 1200–1850* (Edinburgh, 1986), pp. 130–3. Feenstra's figures for Scottish students correct but do not entirely supersede those given by Nicholas T. Phillipson – in 'Lawyers, landowners, and civic leadership of post-Union Scotland, *Juridical Review*, new series 21 (1976), pp. 107, 120. A forthcoming study by Esther Mijers, based on her thesis 'Scotland and the United Provinces c. 1680–1730: a study in intellectual and educational relations', University of St Andrews doctoral thesis (2002), will add significantly to our knowledge of the Scottish experience of the Dutch universities. The late importance of Groningen is but one of her findings. It seems, however, that expectations of hearing Barbeyrac were often disappointed: as befits a 'star' professor, he was frequently on leave.

[43] Ouston, 'York in Edinburgh: James VII and the patronage of learning in Scotland 1679–88', in John Dwyer, Roger A. Mason, and Alexander Murdoch (eds.), *New Perspectives on the Politics and Culture of Early Modern Scotland* (Edinburgh [1982]), pp. 139–48.

was in a position to function as a general institution for the advancement of learning. Conscious of this, Sir Robert Sibbald in particular sponsored a succession of voluntary clubs of *virtuosi*, the first in 1680–1 for physicians, the second from 1700 to 1711 mainly for antiquaries. At some point between 1698 and 1701 he also attempted to persuade a group of Scottish politicians of the need to create a 'Royal Society of Scotland for Improving of Useful Arts'. Although the name recalled the Royal Society in London, Sibbald's declared models were the academies of France and Italy, and he initially hoped that such a society might encompass divinity, law, history (civil, ecclesiastical, and natural) as well as medicine, experimental philosophy, and mathematics. A second draft put more emphasis on practical improvement, and sought legal powers to require the assistance of local magistrates. Unfortunately, the politicians to whom Sibbald made the proposal (and to whom he prospectively assigned the offices of the new society) were out of royal favour, and the proposal came to nothing.[44]

If the Scots had no academies, they did pioneer another formal but voluntary institution of a distinctive kind, the masonic lodge. In the fertile mind of a William Schaw, James VI's master of works in the late sixteenth century, or of Sir Robert Moray, founder member of the Royal Society of London, freemasonry had the potential to prompt a range of exotic intellectual associations. But it seems that few members of the Scottish lodges in this period could have lived up to such expectations. The majority continued to be 'operatives', practising stone-masons, and while the numbers of non-operatives began to grow, few of the new members were from the educated classes. The lodges may have offered models of a new, ritualistic sociability; but there is no evidence that they promoted philosophical discussion.[45]

As in Naples, however, there is a good deal of evidence for the growth of Scottish libraries in the later seventeenth century. In the long term, the most significant development would be the founding of the Advocates' Library. First discussed by the faculty in 1679, the idea of the library was given practical effect through the efforts of Sir George Mackenzie in the 1680s. In an oration to inaugurate the Advocates' Library in 1689, Mackenzie set out his conviction that it should be a library of history, criticism, and rhetoric as well as of law, since these were all essential to the formation

[44] Roger L. Emerson, 'Sir Robert Sibbald Kt., the Royal Society of Scotland and the origins of the Scottish Enlightenment', *Annals of Science*, 45 (1988), 43–52.

[45] On early Scottish freemasonry, David Stevenson, *The Origins of Freemasonry: Scotland's Century 1590–1710* (Cambridge, 1988); qualified by Margaret C. Jacob, *Living the Enlightenment: Freemasonry and Politics in Eighteenth-century Europe* (Oxford, 1991), pp. 35–46.

of a good advocate. The library quickly established itself, and was used by scholars as well as the advocates themselves. Its first catalogue, in 1692, contained over 3,000 volumes; and from 1700 to 1750 it grew from 5,000 to perhaps 20,000 volumes. Initially many books were donated, but the Copyright Act of 1709 enabled the Advocates' Library to acquire a wider range of books of its own choosing. Legal works, the classics, history, and antiquities continued to predominate; philosophy and modern literature, especially from Europe, were in much shorter supply.[46]

While the Advocates' Library was in its infancy a number of individuals had already acquired sizeable private libraries. Doctors, lawyers, and clergy all collected books. Probably the most notable collection of the 1660s and 1670s was that of Archbishop Robert Leighton, who left over 1,000 volumes to the diocese of Dunblane. These included works by the Cambridge Platonists, the Port Royal philosophers, contemporary Anglicans, mystics both Protestant and Catholic, and Thomas Hobbes.[47] Still more substantial were the libraries built up in the last two decades of the century by Sir Robert Sibbald and Andrew Fletcher. Sibbald's eventual collection of over 4,000 volumes was predictably strongest in history, antiquities, and natural history, but also contained a range of modern philosophers, including Bacon, Descartes, the Port Royal thinkers, Athanasius Kircher, and the atomists Kenelm Digby and Walter Charleton.[48] Andrew Fletcher's book collecting began during his earliest travels on the continent in the 1670s, and continued unabated until his death in 1715. He bought in Amsterdam, Paris, and Leipzig, and made frequent use of the services of Alexander Cunningham of Blok, a Scot who had settled in the Netherlands, as an agent. Fletcher's manuscript catalogue lists over 5,500 titles, loosely organised under the headings *Historici, Poetae, Oratores, Theologi, Legislatores, Physici, Mathematici,* and *Juridici.*[49] Fletcher was clearly a collector, looking for good, unusual, or rare editions; the library's contents ranged well

---

[46] Ouston, 'York in Edinburgh', pp. 148–9; John W. Cairns, 'Sir George Mackenzie, the Faculty of Advocates and the Advocates' Library', in J. W. Cairns and A. M. Cain (eds.), *Oratio Inauguralis Aperienda Jurisconsultorum Bibliotheca: Sir George Mackenzie* (Edinburgh, 1989); Duncan, *Thomas Ruddiman,* pp. 24–40.

[47] Emerson, 'Scottish cultural change 1660–1710', pp. 131–2.

[48] Ibid., pp. 132–3. Other private libraries are discussed on pp. 130–1, 133–40.

[49] The catalogue is in the Saltoun Papers in the National Library of Scotland: NLS Ms. 17863, ff. 1–97. It is entitled (in the hand of Sir William Fraser) 'Catalogue of Books. Holograph of Andrew Fletcher of Saltoun'. The catalogue itself is in Fletcher's own hand: it is in fact a list, to which Fletcher made many alterations and additions. The herculean task of identifying the books and drawing up a short-title catalogue has been undertaken by Dr Peter Willems: *Bibliotheca Fletcheriana: or, the Extraordinary Library of Andrew Fletcher of Saltoun, Reconstructed and Systematically Arranged* (privately published by the author: Wassenaar, 1999). With a helpful introduction and annotation, Willems's catalogue is a major addition to the scholarship on Fletcher.

beyond the interests which he pursued in his own writings. But though he possessed works by Descartes, Gassendi, and Malebranche, the coverage of modern philosophy, and in particular of natural philosophy, was far weaker than that of European history and politics, which was very good indeed.

Both Sibbald and Fletcher lent their books, Fletcher keeping a list of such loans at the end of his catalogue. Among the most frequent borrowers of his books was Sibbald himself; others included politicians (of all parties), lawyers, landowners, and men of learning.[50] But neither Sibbald nor Fletcher appears to have played the part of Valletta, as librarian to the intellectual community as a whole. If Sibbald aspired to such a role, his tendency to quarrel, most notably with Pitcairne, undermined his capacity to fulfil it; and Fletcher always went his own way, being frequently out of Scotland.

Libraries with up-to-date holdings of the new philosophy seem to have emerged only in the second and third decades of the eighteenth century. In 1724 Robert Steuart, professor of natural philosophy at Edinburgh, created for his class the Physiological Library. It had over 400 volumes, the bulk of them in natural philosophy and mathematics. The section on natural philosophy was headed by Lucretius' *De rerum natura*, and contained works by Descartes and several other Cartesians, by Gassendi, Hobbes, Malebranche, and Locke. Barrow and Newton dominated in mathematics, while the works of Boyle were placed on their own, at the head of the catalogue. Though comparatively small, here at last was a library equipped to give its student readers, like the young David Hume, a proper grounding in the culture of modern science.[51]

How soon and how widely the Scots had access to the Huguenot literary reviews, which had quickly established themselves as the best means for learning of new books and the controversies they provoked, is still far from clear. Fletcher's library contained runs of the *Journal des Sçavans*, the *Nouvelles de la République des Lettres* and the *Bibliothèque universelle et historique*; but they do not appear in his lists of books lent.[52] As librarian at Glasgow College between 1698 and 1703, the young Robert Wodrow asked a correspondent in Utrecht and Leiden to be on the look-out for 'the Republicks', which he seems to have used as a generic term for the reviews; he specifically mentioned gaps in the library's holdings of the *Acta*

[50] NLS Ms 17863, ff. 93r–94v, 96r.
[51] Michael Barfoot, 'Hume and the culture of science in the early eighteenth century', in M. A. Stewart (ed.), *Studies in the Philosophy of the Scottish Enlightenment* (Oxford, 1990), pp. 151–60.
[52] NLS Ms 17863, f. 19r.

eruditorum.[53] From his own reading of the 'Nouvels de la republique des letters', however, he was prompted only to seek out a polyglot Bible.[54] There is no indication that he was aware of the identity of the editors of 'the Republicks', or of the implications of the arguments going on inside them. Much later, as we shall see, Hume appears to have studied the arguments of Bayle on religion in back numbers of the Dutch literary reviews; but this was probably in the late 1730s or early 1740s, and he may well have read them in London.[55] By comparison with Naples, where the journals' significance was appreciated almost as soon as they were published, it is the present paucity of evidence for Scottish interest which is striking. It may be significant that the one Scottish publication of a similar kind, John Cockburn's *Bibliotheca Universalis*, ceased after a single issue in 1688.[56]

Just as there was no Scottish counterpart to Valletta the librarian, so there was no equivalent to his correspondence with Magliabecchi in keeping the Scots in touch with the European Republic of Letters. Individual Scottish men of letters corresponded widely: David Gregory with Newton, Sibbald with both continental and English virtuosi, Fletcher with John Wallis, Christopher Wren, and John Locke, the young Wodrow with the English and Welsh scholars William Nicholson, James Sutherland, and Edward Lhuyd. No doubt much more correspondence has been lost, perhaps especially Fletcher's. But with no single figure gathering and passing on news at the centre of the Scottish intellectual community, the benefits of such correspondence were largely confined to the individuals involved. Individual intellectual horizons naturally varied. Fletcher's curiosity extended to the place of music in ancient education, and to the principles of ancient architecture; but though he mentioned to Locke his interest in the Egyptian origins of priestcraft, the substance of his correspondence with him concerned the health of members of his family, on which he sought Locke's professional advice.[57] While still in his early twenties, Wodrow pursued a correspondence with the older Nicholson and Sutherland which was traditional in both style and substance, concentrating on antiquities, and on

---

[53] L. W. Sharp (ed.), *Early Letters of Robert Wodrow 1698–1709*, Scottish History Society, 3rd series, 24 (Edinburgh, 1937), pp. 136: 'For Mr Matheu Connel at Utrecht', [19 Dec. 1700], 140: 'For Mr. M. Connell at Leyden', 24 Jan. 1701.

[54] *Early Letters of Wodrow*, p. 7: 'For Mr Matheu Simsone at Leyden', 14 Jan. 1699.

[55] See below, ch. 6, pp. 303–4.   [56] Ouston, 'York in Edinburgh', pp. 152–3.

[57] NLS Ms 16502 ff. 165–8: John Wallis to Andrew Fletcher, 18, 27 Aug. 1698 (on music in ancient education); ff. 208–9: David Gregory to Fletcher, 21 April 1707, passing on an opinion of Christopher Wren; *Correspondence of John Locke*, vol. v, no. 1851, Fletcher to Locke, 22 Feb. 1695, and Locke's reply, ibid., vol. VIII (Oxford, 1989), no. 1854A, Locke to Fletcher, 1 March 1695.

the exchange of references, coins, and specimens. Once he had qualified as a minister, he soon abandoned 'literature' (his term), and in 1706 declared himself a 'stranger' to the 'Reipublick of Letters'.[58]

The last two decades of the seventeenth century did see a marked increase in the output of Scottish printers. Aside from government publications and news-sheets, religious works were still the largest category. But contemporary Scottish writers were published alongside the classics, the most published author being Sir George Mackenzie, with twenty-one titles between 1660 and 1689. There was also a growing volume of pamphlet and polemical literature. In the 1690s much of this was focused upon the state of Scottish agriculture and on the Darien venture; in the first decade of the new century a still more vigorous debate was generated by the negotiations for union.[59] After the Union the printers Robert Freebairn and James Watson supported Thomas Ruddiman in what amounted to a considered programme of 'patriotic editing'. Together they published scholarly editions of some of the finest works of Scottish humanism, including Gavin Douglas's translation of Virgil's *Aeneid* (1710), the *Works* of William Drummond of Hawthornden (1711) and the *Opera Omnia* of George Buchanan (1715). Ruddiman's editorial labours were strongly encouraged by Pitcairne, and he also acknowledged the loan of books by Andrew Fletcher, whom he hailed as 'Cato nostri seculi'.[60] The Jacobite sympathies of Freebairn and Ruddiman underline what was evident in the Union debate: access to print for the expression of controversial political opinion was easier in Scotland than in Naples. Official controls of the press were limited, permitting genuinely public debate; there was no need for Scots to resort to the circulation of manuscript copies of their works. But it is also clear that the intellectual priorities of Scottish publishers were conservative: the commitment of Freebairn and Ruddiman was to the native humanist tradition rather than the new philosophy.

[58] *Early Letters of Wodrow*, particularly the letters to William Nicholson, archdeacon, subsequently bishop of Carlisle, to James Sutherland, and to Edward Lhuyd at the Ashmolean. Within Scotland Wodrow exchanged the news he received for information from Sir Robert Sibbald, with whom he was prepared to overlook his deep religious differences. By 1703, however, the strain was showing: pp. 251–4: Wodrow to Dr Sibbald, 18 Jan. 1703. For the letter renouncing the 'Reipublick of Letters', p. 283: Wodrow to Mr Lachland Campbell, minister at Cambeltoun in Kintyre, 4 Feb. 1706.

[59] Emerson, 'Scottish cultural change 1660–1710', pp. 140–4, incl. table 5.4 of Scottish imprints 1660–1700; for a listing of pamphlet contributions to the Union debate, W. R. McLeod and V. B. McLeod, *Anglo-Scottish Tracts 1701–1714: a Descriptive Checklist*, University of Kansas, Library Series 44 (Lawrence, Kan., 1979).

[60] Duncan, *Thomas Ruddiman*, ch. iv, 'Patriotic editing'; the tribute to Fletcher is in the 'Praefatio' to *Georgii Buchanani Opera Omnia . . . curante Thoma Ruddimano* (Edinburgh, *apud* Robert Freebairn, 1715), p. xxi.

In the relative freedom of Scottish publishing, as well as in the number and independence of its universities, Scottish intellectual life would seem to have had the advantage over that of Naples. In other respects, however, it is the Neapolitans who appear to have been better placed. Not only did the academies of the Investiganti and the Medina Coeli encourage discussion of new ideas, but the efforts of Valletta in particular ensured a far better coordination of intellectual life in the city. Through his library, his hospitality to visitors, his purchase of the literary reviews, and his correspondence, Valletta was able to connect Neapolitans with the European Republic of Letters, and more specifically to introduce them to modern French philosophy. Lacking such coordination of their activities, individual Scots had to rely on their own connections; as a result it would appear that it took significantly longer for the new philosophy to become widely available. So far, however, we have only been looking at the structures which made intellectual life possible. What we must now do is examine whether the apparent disparity between the two kingdoms at this level was reflected in the patterns and substance of Neapolitan and Scottish intellectual activity over the same period.

THE LEGACY OF HUMANISM

In both countries intellectual activity was of course shaped by the legacy of the past. Since the impact of the new philosophy needs to be assessed against the evidence for the continuity of older interests, it is important first to take the measure of these, with an outline of intellectual developments in the two kingdoms since the Renaissance. Many of the most important developments had been associated with humanism; and as even a brief survey will suggest, there had been striking similarities in the pattern of Neapolitan and Scottish humanist interests. At the outset, in the mid- and later fifteenth century, humanism had been the court culture of both kingdoms. In Naples Alfonso I (1440–58) had attracted to the city a number of humanists whose reputations rivalled those of Florence, including Panormita, Pontano, and Lorenzo Valla. The greatest of these was Valla: immensely learned and frighteningly violent, Valla had composed his most famous work, the exposure of the forgery of the Donation of Constantine, in part to strengthen his king's claim to independence from the overlordship of the pope.[61] Similarly, James IV of Scotland (1488–1513) had been the

---

[61] Jerry H. Bentley, *Politics and Culture in Renaissance Naples* (Princeton, 1987), pp. 108–22 on Valla and the Neapolitan context of his *De falso credita et ementita Constantini donatione declamatio* (1440).

patron of the great vernacular poets, William Dunbar, Robert Henrysoun, and Gavin Douglas, the translator of the *Aeneid* into Scots, while one of his councillors, Bishop Elphinstone, was the patron of Scotland's first humanist historian, Hector Boece. In neither country did humanism completely supersede scholasticism. In Naples this remained the preserve of the religious orders; but in Scotland the close connections established by the new universities with France encouraged a greater originality, manifest in the works of the logician George Lokert, the theologian John Ireland, and the great Aristotelian John Mair. While in Scotland between periods spent teaching philosophy in Paris, Mair had also written his *Historia Majoris Britanniae* (1521), a powerful challenge to Boece and to Scottish pretensions to permanent independence from England.[62]

In the sixteenth century, however, the vital connection with the court was severed, as the kings of Naples became Spanish absentees, and the Scottish crown suffered a series of minorities, whose effects were made worse by the upheavals of the Reformation. In these circumstances, humanism in both kingdoms became a culture of resistance. In Scotland this culture was embodied by George Buchanan. Reputed the finest Latin poet of his day, Buchanan was also a Stoic moralist and the author of the *De jure regni apud Scotos* (1579), a justification of resistance as radical as its celebrated contemporary, the *Vindiciae contra Tyrannos* (also 1579), if less reliant than the latter on a scholastic conceptual framework. His subsequent *Rerum Scoticarum Historia* (1582) endorsed Boece's patriotic claim that Scotland's was the oldest continuous monarchy in Europe, but ingeniously combined this with an account of repeated justified resistance to royal tyranny by the Scottish nobility.[63] A similar role was played in Naples by the historian Giovanni Antonio Summonte, the first two volumes of whose *Historia della città e Regno di Napoli* were published in 1601–2. Summonte did not explicitly argue for a right of resistance, but his comments on past episodes of disobedience implied that there were circumstances in which

---

[62] Roger A. Mason, 'Kingship, nobility and Anglo-Scottish union: John Mair's *History of Greater Britain* (1521)', and '*Regnum et imperium*: humanism and the political culture of early Renaissance Scotland', both in his *Kingship and the Commonweal: Political Thought in Renaissance and Reformation Scotland* (East Linton, 1998), pp. 36–77, 104–38; Alexander Broadie, *The Circle of John Mair: Logic and Logicians in pre-Reformation Scotland* (Oxford, 1985); J. H. Burns, *The True Law of Kingship: Concepts of Monarchy in Early Modern Scotland* (Oxford, 1996), chs. 1–2.

[63] Burns, *The True Law of Kingship*, ch. 6; Arthur H. Williamson, *Scottish National Consciousness in the Age of James VI* (Edinburgh, 1979), pp. 107–16; Roger A. Mason, '*Rex Stoicus*: George Buchanan, James VI and the Scottish polity', in Dwyer, Mason and Murdoch, *New Perspectives on the Politics and Culture of Early Modern Scotland*, pp. 9–33; for the story of Buchanan's *History*: H. R. Trevor-Roper, 'George Buchanan and the ancient Scottish constitution', *English Historical Review*, Supplement 3 (1966).

it was legitimate. Moreover his claims that twelfth-century Naples had possessed many of the features of a commune, and that the people had anciently shared its government with the aristocracy, provided a powerful justification for the aspirations of the *popolo* in city politics.[64]

Another field in which humanism was often implicated in challenges to royal authority was the law. Neither in Scotland nor in Naples, however, did legal scholarship become the battle-ground it was in France. In Sir Thomas Craig Scotland did produce one jurist of note: his *Jus Feudale* (1603) was a major contribution to a field only recently opened up by the French scholars Jacques Cujas and François Hotman.[65] Neapolitan jurists had a keen practical interest in feudal law; but despite this the importance of the work of the French school was not appreciated in the kingdom until much later in the seventeenth century.

In sharp contrast was the remarkable efflorescence of interest at the end of the sixteenth century in radical anti-Aristotelian philosophies, including full-blown neo-Platonic naturalism. Between them Bernardino Telesio, Giambattista della Porta, Giordano Bruno, and Tommaso Campanella made the kingdom of Naples the centre of late Renaissance philosophical heterodoxy. Telesio's *De rerum natura* (1565) was an explicitly un-Aristotelian account of nature, while della Porta's *Magia naturalis* (1558) went further in a neo-Platonic and hermetic direction. More radical still were Bruno and Campanella, who took full advantage of the extraordinary degree of intellectual freedom allowed to the Neapolitan Dominicans at the time, and repeatedly challenged the authorities in both church and state. Having carried his heresies and his hatred of the papacy as far afield as England, Bruno had allowed himself to be arrested in Venice in 1591, and finally died at the stake in Rome in 1600. A combative early supporter of Telesio, Campanella had thrown his rebellious energies into a messianic revolt in Calabria in 1599. But he escaped Bruno's fate by feigning madness (and defying the torture intended to prove his sanity), and had then survived twenty-six years of incarceration in all the major Neapolitan fortresses. While in prison he had passed the time by writing variously in advocacy of both Spanish universal monarchy and a utopian 'City of the Sun', and in defence of Galileo as well as of his own highly complex anti-Aristotelian philosophy.[66] A not dissimilar interest in neo-Platonism,

[64] Rosario Villari, *La rivolta antispagnola a Napoli. Le origini* (Rome and Bari, 1967), pp. 57, 106–12.

[65] John G. A. Pocock, *The Ancient Constitution and the Feudal Law: A Study of English Historical Thought in the Seventeenth Century. A reissue with a retrospect* (Cambridge, 1987), pp. 79–90.

[66] John M. Headley, *Tommaso Campanella and the Transformation of the World* (Princeton, 1997): ch. 1 discusses the intellectual universe of the kingdom in the late sixteenth century.

messianism, and astrology was shown by the contemporary Scottish mathematicians Robert Pont and John Napier. Here, as in Naples, it seemed as if the grip of scholasticism on metaphysics and natural philosophy had finally been loosened.[67]

But radical humanism had overreached itself. Even though Campanella had continued to write, imprisonment had served its purpose: when he finally emerged and went into exile in France, he found himself intellectually isolated, greeted with bafflement and mounting exasperation by his hosts.[68] Meanwhile the authorities in Naples had ruthlessly suppressed other possible sources of dissent, especially among fellow Calabrians. In Scotland it was very much a part of James VI's gradual reassertion of royal authority to repudiate the rebellious connotations of humanism. His principal target was Buchanan, his hated former tutor, whose intellectual authority James did everything in his power to undermine; but he was equally unsympathetic to the eschatological speculations of Pont and Napier.[69] By the time both kingdoms were again in revolt, in the 1640s, the contribution of humanism was less one sided. In Naples the historical defence of the role of the people in the government of the city provided by Summonte and later by Francesco de Pietri, the secretary of the Accademia degli Oziosi, still offered an intellectual reference point for the leaders of the urban revolt in 1647–8.[70] In Scotland Buchanan's works likewise continued to be regarded as the original justification of the presbyterian cause. But his account of the Scottish past was now challenged by the royalist poet and historian William Drummond of Hawthornden. Taking his cue from Mair rather than Buchanan, Drummond's *History of Scotland from 1423 until 1542* (1655) demonstrated that the same story might yield opposite political conclusions. Drummond and others also brought the Scots up to date with the thinking of Justus Lipsius and European neo-Stoicism, demonstrating

---

[67] Arthur H. Williamson, 'Number and national consciousness: the Edinburgh mathematicians and Scottish political culture at the union of the crowns', in Roger A. Mason (ed.), *Scots and Britons: Scottish Political Thought and the Union of 1603* (Cambridge, 1994), pp. 187–212.

[68] Headley, *Campanella*, pp. 117–26: though Peiresc had done his best to smooth his path, Campanella was thoroughly awkward once in Paris, and made a point of airing his differences with Gassendi in particular. Mersenne kept his distance, Descartes wanted nothing to do with him.

[69] On Buchanan and James VI: Rebecca W. Bushnell, 'George Buchanan, James VI and neo-classicism', and Roger A. Mason, 'George Buchanan, James VI and the presbyterians', both in Mason, *Scots and Britons*, pp. 91–137, the latter also in Mason, *Kingship and Commonweal*, pp. 187–214. But there is no account of James's hostility towards Buchanan to match that by Hugh Trevor-Roper, in 'Queen Elizabeth's first historian: William Camden', in his *Renaissance Essays* (London, 1985), pp. 126ff.

[70] Aurelio Musi, '*Non pigra quies*. Il linguaggio politico degli Accademici Oziosi e la rivolta napoletana del 1647–48', in Eluggero Pii (ed.), *I linguaggi politici delle rivoluzioni in Europa XVII–XIX Secolo* (Florence, 1992), pp. 87–95, on De Pietri; the last two volumes of Summonte's *Historia della città e Regno di Napoli* were published in 1640–43. See also above, ch. 2, pp. 62–3.

that Stoic ideals were just as well if not better adapted to encouraging obedience among subjects.[71] The re-emergence of a royalist humanism was met, moreover, by a significant shift in presbyterian intellectual strategy. Though still invoking Buchanan, the author of the most powerful new statement of the right to resist, Samuel Rutherford, was a scholastic theologian, whose *Lex, Rex* (1644), was framed in the terms of Calvinist jurisprudence.[72]

As we shall see, the fortunes of humanism in the two kingdoms were to have a direct bearing on intellectual developments after 1660. But it is time to examine these in more detail, looking first at Naples.

THE IMPACT OF THE NEW PHILOSOPHY: NAPLES

In a city in which law was the most lucrative profession, and the high road to ministerial office, it was to be expected that jurisprudence would have a prominent place in intellectual life. Yet it was not until the last quarter of the seventeenth century that the methods of French legal scholarship were at last introduced to Naples. For this Giannone gave the credit to Francesco d'Andrea, as the first to adopt the principles of the 'never enough celebrated' Jacques Cujas. These principles had then been applied to the teaching of the law by Giannone's beloved mentor Domenico Aulisio. Emphasising that the law must be studied in its historical context, Aulisio explained to Giannone the significance of Cujas's work on fiefs, and demonstrated the extent to which ecclesiastical law had developed from within the civil law.[73] D'Andrea also took the lead in introducing Neapolitans to the work of the Protestant Hugo Grotius on the law of nature and nations. Since in Catholic Naples the doctrine of the law of nature was still the preserve of scholastic theologians, this interest did not lead to the writing of systematic treatises of natural jurisprudence in the manner of Samuel Pufendorf or Richard Cumberland. But d'Andrea openly cited the authority of Grotius in works written to defend the territories of the Spanish monarchy against the acquisitive ambitions of Louis XIV.[74] Another to employ the arguments

[71] David Allan, *Philosophy and Politics in Later Stuart Scotland: Neo-Stoicism, Culture, and Ideology in an Age of Crisis 1540–1690* (East Linton, 2000), pp. 88–175.

[72] John D. Ford, '*Lex, rex iusto posita*: Samuel Rutherford on the origins of government', in Mason, *Scots and Britons*, 262–90.

[73] Giannone, *Storia civile*, bk XXXVIII, c. iv, app. I, and XL, c. v (vol. IV, pp. 420–1, 489–91). The reference to the 'non mai a bastanza celebrato Jacopo Cujacio' is at IV, p. 125. On Aulisio, also: *Vita*, in *Opere di Giannone*, pp. 19–32.

[74] Francesco d'Andrea, *Risposta al trattato delle ragioni della Regina Cristianissima, sopra il Ducato del Brabante, et altri stati della Fiandra. Nella quale si dimostra l'ingiustizia della guerra mossa dal Re*

of natural law was Valletta, who referred to Grotius in two manuscript tracts of the 1670s on the introduction of new money.[75]

A much stronger interest of Neapolitan humanism had been the study of history, particularly of Naples itself; but in this field too there was innovation in the later seventeenth century. The enduring importance of the history of the city and kingdom of Naples to men of letters at the end of the seventeenth century is evident in the number of works on the subject, both printed and manuscript, which Valletta collected for his library.[76] But the interest of the subject now lay less in the internal government of the city and its relation to the crown than in the status of the kingdom itself, and its relation to the papacy in particular. As the imminent failure of the Spanish Habsburg dynasty became the subject of ever more explicit discussion towards the end of the 1690s, the kingdom's history became, as we shall see in the following chapter, directly implicated in its present condition and future prospects. At the same time, the potential of historical enquiry was being given wider expression in the *lezioni* of the Accademia Medina Coeli. It may be true that there is little indication in these *lezioni* of concern with the critical use of evidence, such as was being displayed by contemporary French scholars, Mabillon in particular; in this respect his earlier visit to Naples had apparently had little effect.[77] It is probable, however, that a locally more powerful stimulus to new historical thinking was already at work, in Aulisio's championing of the need to study law in combination with history. It was Aulisio who directed Giannone's attention to the importance of the hitherto neglected *bassi tempi* of the middle ages, leading him to the scholarship of the modern 'Gallican' historians Fleury and Tillemont. When to these Giannone added the works of two Englishmen, Arthur Duck's comparative study of European civil law, and Francis Bacon's *Advancement of Learning* (1623), he found that he had formed the idea of a 'civil history', in writing which he might aspire to match the progress lately made by others in natural history.[78] The outcome, his

di Francia, per la conquista di quelle provincie; non ostante le ragioni, che si son pubblicate in suo nome, per la pretesa successione a favor della Regina Cristianissima (Naples, 1667; second edn 1676); on which Salvo Mastellone, *Francesco D'Andrea politico e giurista 1648–1698. L'ascesa del ceto civile* (Florence, 1969). Giannone underlined the significance of this work in his *Vita*, in *Opere di Giannone*, p. 44.

[75] Comparato, *Valletta*, chs. i–ii, and the appendix, which prints Valletta's 'Risposta ad amico sopra le ragioni della città di Napoli per l'assistenze domandate alla fabrica della nuova moneta', on pp. 287–337.

[76] Biblioteca Oratoriana dei Girolamini, 'Antico Catalogo', Mf. 27.1.10, ff. 161r, 165r–v (*Libri Italici*), 241v, 242v–244v (*Libri manuscripti*).

[77] Stone, *Vico's Cultural History*, p. 100.

[78] Giannone, *Vita*, in *Opere di Giannone*, pp. 25, 31, 53–4. Giannone recalled that Arthur Duck's 'golden little book', *De usu et authoritate iuris civilis Romanorum in dominiis principum christianorum* (1653),

Istoria civile del Regno di Napoli (1723), not only raised Neapolitan historical writing to a new level; it gave grievous offence to the church, and by
its consequent reputation as well as its content was an inspiration to later
Enlightenment historians.[79]

As Giannone implied, and his memoirs bore witness, these new directions in the study of law and history in late seventeenth-century Naples
were accompanied by a comparable, if not greater, interest in recent developments in philosophy. This was first apparent in natural philosophy. It
is a common misapprehension that the papal condemnation of Galileo in
1633 marked the end of the 'scientific revolution' in Italy. It was certainly
the case that discussion of the Copernican hypothesis became much more
difficult for Catholics, while ideas specifically associated with Bruno were
rigorously proscribed. But Galileo himself had continued to work after his
condemnation, and many of his specific ideas and experiments continued
to be developed by his students, notably by Torricelli and Borelli. They
were central to the activities of the Accademia del Cimento in the 1650s
and 1660s, and were likewise discussed by the Neapolitan Investiganti. In
the case of the Investiganti, however, circumstances as well as the interests
of its leaders encouraged greater attention to medical questions; and with
the academy's demise, practical, experimental science (with the exception
of anatomy) ceased to be the first interest of Neapolitan men of letters.
Instead, they were increasingly absorbed by the more general, metaphysical
issues raised by the new philosophy, whose leading exponents were now
regarded as the French.

Two strands of ancient philosophy were fundamental to this new direction in Neapolitan interests. One was scepticism, as expounded by the
second-century BC Greek philosopher Sextus Empiricus, whose works had

---

was then very rare and little known in Naples, which implies that he read it before it was published in
Naples in 1719. Sir Arthur Duck (1580–1648) had served Laud as chancellor of the diocese of London,
before writing the book in retirement during the Civil War. On Giannone and Aulisio, Giuseppe
Ricuperati, 'La prima formazione di Pietro Giannone. L'Accademia Medina Coeli e Domenico
Aulisio', in E. Sestan (ed.), *Saggi e ricerche sul Settecento* (Naples, 1968), pp. 94–171. The major study
of Giannone's formation as a historian remains Giuseppe Ricuperati, *L'esperienza civile e religiosa di
Pietro Giannone* (Milan and Naples, 1970).

[79] On the significance of Giannone's *Storia civile*, which was translated into English as early as 1729,
but was most widely read in the French translation of 1742: John G. A. Pocock, 'Giannone: jurist
and *libertin* in the central Mediterranean', *Barbarism and Religion. II: Narratives of Civil Society*
(Cambridge, 1999), pp. 29–71; H. R. Trevor-Roper, 'Pietro Giannone and Great Britain', *The Historical Journal*, 39 (1996), 657–75; for the inspiration it provided Gibbon in particular: John Robertson,
'Gibbon and Giannone', in David Womersley (ed.), with the assistance of John Burrow and John
Pocock, *Edward Gibbon: Bicentenary Essays, Studies on Voltaire and the Eighteenth Century*, 355 (1997),
3–19.

become available in Latin editions in the 1560s.[80] Of the two varieties of ancient scepticism identified by Sextus, the 'academic' and the 'Pyrrhonian' (after Pyrrho), it was the more moderate, academic version which appears to have been followed in Naples among the leaders of the Investiganti. Doubts as to the possibility of achieving 'certain' knowledge of the natural world were voiced by di Capua in his *Parere* in 1681, and by Valletta and d'Andrea in their defences of the *libertà filosofica*. But they did continue to believe in degrees of probability, maintaining that a probable understanding of nature was both achievable and worthwhile.

Closely related to scepticism, and even more important to the Neapolitans, was the ancient doctrine of atomism. The view that the world had been formed by atoms combining together in a cosmic void had been developed by the Greek philosophers Democritus and Epicurus. Though none of the latter's writings survived, many of his arguments were reported in Diogenes Laertius' *Lives of the Philosophers* and subsequently by Cicero. But by far the fullest exposition of the atomist theory of nature (and specifically of Epicurus' theory, which differed in some respects from that of Democritus) was given by the Roman poet Lucretius. In the six books of his *De rerum natura* (c.55 BC) Lucretius set out the principles of the atomic system, including atomic movement, the nature of the mind and its place within the body, the operation of the senses, the formation of the world and the development of human society, and the explanation of apparently terrifying natural phenomena such as thunder, storms, earthquakes, and volcanic eruptions. Not only the most complete, Lucretius' poem was also the most accessible account of Epicureanism, having been printed in several editions in the sixteenth and seventeenth centuries, to which were added Bulifon's Neapolitan edition of 1693, and Marchetti's Italian translation in 1717.

An interest in atomist, Democritean, and Epicurean principles of nature had been associated with Tommaso Cornelio since his return to the city in 1649, and through him extended to other members of the Investiganti. It was also clear that such principles were suspect in the eyes of the church; controversy clouded even the arrangements for Cornelio's funeral in 1684.[81] A decade later, as we have seen, the philosophy and reputation of Epicurus were vigorously defended in the aftermath of the trial of the atheists

---

[80] Richard H. Popkin, *The History of Scepticism from Erasmus to Spinoza* (Berkeley, Los Angeles, and London, 1979).

[81] Cristofolini, 'Cornelio et l'histoire du matérialisme'; Borelli, 'Franceso D'Andrea. Lettere', pp. 245–6: d'Andrea to Francesco Redi, in Florence, 25 June 1685, describing the difficulties he faced in organising Cornelio's funeral, in the face of accusations that he belonged to a sect of atomists who were secret atheists.

by Valletta and d'Andrea: atomism, they argued, not only offered a far more convincing account of nature than Aristotelianism, but was much less likely to lead its exponents into theological heterodoxy. Whatever the validity of the second of these claims, the first was supported by the interest which atomism continued to arouse in Naples. When Giannone sought to educate himself in philosophy in the later 1690s, the ancient texts which he read were those of Sextus, Diogenes, and Lucretius, exemplifying the association of scepticism with Epicureanism. Equally significant, however, was Giannone's recollection that he did so after reading the *Epitome* of the philosophy of Pierre Gassendi, the modern historian and interpreter of Epicurean doctrine.[82]

The mediation of Gassendi was crucial to the acceptance of Epicurean atomism in the later seventeenth century. For of itself the Epicurean account of the world and its formation, especially as told by Lucretius, was incompatible with the Christian. A world which had been formed only by chance, out of a universe of infinite indivisible atoms swirling in a void, and which was both eternal and one of a potentially infinite number of other worlds – this was not the world described in the biblical account of divine creation. Equally alarming was the Lucretian understanding of the mind's relation to the body, with its explicit corollary that the soul was material and therefore mortal. Gassendi, however, had dealt directly with these difficulties. A series of historical studies of Epicurus' thought culminated in the posthumously published *Syntagma Philosophicum* (1658), setting out the principles of a Christian atomism. Holding that God's will is free and absolute, Gassendi reaffirmed that God had created the world and continued to rule it through his providence; in turn the universe demonstrated God's design. It was within this framework, he argued, that atomism represented the most probable account of the natural world, especially when combined with a mechanical explanation of its workings. Gassendi also rejected Lucretius' account of the mortality of the soul: God's freedom required that man too had retained his freedom, and a capacity to make moral choices for which the soul would afterwards be held to account.[83] It was in these Gassendian terms that Valletta defended the atomist philosophy in the 1690s; Gassendi, he maintained in the 'Istoria filosofica', was the proof that an atomist could also be a good Catholic.[84]

[82] Giannone, *Vita*, in *Opere di Giannone*, pp. 33–4.
[83] Margaret J. Osler, 'Ancients, Moderns, and the history of philosophy: Gassendi's Epicurean project', in Tom Sorell (ed.), *The Rise of Modern Philosophy: the Tension between the New and Traditional Philosophies from Machiavelli to Leibniz* (Oxford, 1993), pp. 129–43; L. S. Joy, *Gassendi the Atomist: Advocate of History in an Age of Science* (Cambridge, 1987).
[84] Comparato, *Valletta*, pp. 234–5.

But Gassendi was not the only French philosopher to catch the Neapolitans' imagination. By 1700 it was clear that the impact of Descartes would be at least as great. His works, and those of his immediate followers like Rouhault, were being read in Naples even before the 1680s, when French academic culture began to present Descartes as the great modern philosopher. But the potential of Cartesian philosophic principles was perhaps most fully appreciated once Neapolitans had read the *De la Recherche de la Verité* (1674–5) by Nicolas Malebranche. To Valletta, who seems, like Giannone, to have read the work in its Latin version (*De inquirenda veritate*), this represented the most complete statement of Descartes' philosophy, and as such 'the highest expression of human genius'.[85] Strictly speaking, the Cartesian philosophy was incompatible with Gassendian atomism at several points. Descartes' dualist metaphysics, with its insistence on the separation of the mind from the body, once again made reason independent of the senses, and elevated man above the animals with whom the Epicureans had associated him. But an absolute dualism was undermined by Malebranche, who began from the premise that man's original sin, by subjecting him to his senses and passions, had strengthened the union of soul and body to the point that it seemed they were one and the same substance, and even that the body was the principal part. It was indeed the purpose of philosophy to recover the truth, by weakening the mind's union with the body and leading it back towards God; but only at death was the union of soul and body entirely broken.[86] By implication, this suggested that philosophers would find themselves placing more, not less, emphasis on the materiality of the body. In the hands of Malebranche, Cartesianism positively enhanced the credibility of Epicurean materialism as the first step in the search for truth.

Once again, Giannone's memoirs provide a revealing insight into the way in which Cartesianism was received in Naples. Impressed as he was when he read Descartes, in particular by his method, Giannone was not persuaded to repudiate his earlier enthusiasm for Gassendi. Instead he decided to adhere to no single philosophical school, but to take reason and experience alone as his guides in the investigation of nature. On Capasso's recommendation, he then read Malebranche, who showed him the manner in which he should enquire into the truth of things. But more than this, Malebranche also taught him that our enquiries into the nature of this world should always have morals as their object. If Descartes' writings on the passions had shown

---

[85] Valletta, 'Lettera in difesa della modern filosofia', *Opere filosofiche*, pp. 136–7: 'l'ultimo sforzo dell'ingegno humano'.

[86] Nicolas Malebranche, *De la Recherche de la Verité* (1674–75), preface, in the edition by G. Rodis-Lewis, in *Oeuvres Complètes de Malebranche*, 20 vols. (Paris, 1963–7), vol. I, pp. 11–12, 15.

him the baseness of human nature and the miserable figure we cut, it was from Malebranche that he learnt the need to develop a moral philosophy that would enable men nevertheless to live in this world.[87] Giannone's recollection that moral philosophy now came to matter most to him was representative of the attitude of many of the younger generation by the end of the 1690s. The shift of interest may have been a response to the church's continuing hostility towards new thinking in natural philosophy and metaphysics. But if so, it backfired: the impact of the new philosophy was even more explosive in morals than in metaphysics.

For here scepticism, Epicureanism, and Cartesianism encountered a further, enormously powerful current in late seventeenth-century francophone intellectual culture: Augustinianism. Particularly potent were the consequences of crossing Augustinianism with Epicureanism. On the face of it, the two were barely compatible. On St Augustine's account of the human condition – an account which represented orthodoxy for Catholic and Protestant alike – the Fall had condemned men and women to live in sin, driven by their passions and a self-interested desire for preservation. In such a condition it was impossible for men to attain true morality: virtue was the standard from which men and women had fallen, and to which they could return only through Christ's redemption of their immortal souls. The best fallen man could do was attempt to suppress his base passions by cultivating an ascetic disdain for their satisfaction, while seeking always to show love (charity) towards God. By contrast, Epicurus, who of course knew nothing of the Fall, held that as a creature of passions, man naturally sought pleasure in their satisfaction, and evaluated his actions by their utility, the extent to which they brought pleasure. Such a view of human motivation and moral judgement was open to caricature by critics as hedonism; but as a succession of the greatest Christian humanists, including Valla, Erasmus, and Montaigne, had sought to explain, Epicurus was better understood as teaching that pleasure lay in the moderate exercise of the passions, and was often best achieved by withdrawal from public life. Properly interpreted, the Epicurean philosophy was at least a preferable alternative to the presumptuous claim of the Stoics that virtue was to be found in displays of heroic, self-denying exertion on behalf of the public.

---

[87] Giannone, *Vita*, in *Opere di Giannone*, pp. 49–50. In the *Storia Civile*, bk xxxii, ch. v.3 (iv, pp. 113–14), Giannone had suggested that Descartes superseded Gassendi in Neapolitan philosophy as early as the 1680s; the *Vita* describes a more convincingly complex process of adaptation and differentiation between the two philosophies. On the emergence of an Epicurean, materialist Cartesianism in Naples, see the important article by Raffaele Ajello, 'Cartesianismo e cultura oltremontana al tempo dell'*Istoria Civile*', in Ajello (ed.), *Pietro Giannone e il suo tempo* (Naples, 1980), esp. pp. 96–145.

Had the moral philosophies associated with Augustine and Epicurus kept to these positions, the scope for their convergence would have remained small. Neither tradition, however, was static, and in the second half of the seventeenth century French philosophers developed both in ways which brought them into a much closer relationship. Encouraged by Gassendi's Christianisation of the Epicurean account of nature, a number of moralists, notably Saint-Evremond, argued that it was unnecessary to withdraw from society to achieve pleasure. A convincing case could be made in Epicurean terms for 'pleasing' others as well as oneself by living in society as an *honnête homme*.[88]

At the same time, far more radical developments were occurring within Augustinianism, in the thinking of Blaise Pascal and Pierre Nicole, both of whom were associated with the convent of Port Royal in Paris, the centre of the reforming movement known as Jansenism. An edition of Pascal's brilliant but notoriously elliptical *Pensées* was published by members of Port Royal in 1670; Nicole's first volume of *Essais de morale* appeared in 1671. As intensely devout Augustinians, Pascal and Nicole were fascinated by the ability of fallen, self-interested man nevertheless to live successfully in society with others. Not only did *amour propre*, the selfish pursuit of individual survival, actually seem to serve the requirements of sociability; it was arguable that a general adherence to the strictest standards of virtue would render society impossible.[89] Wrestling with this paradox, Pascal and Nicole found themselves alarmingly close to the conclusion that it was sin which sustained society. At the least it was a paradox which brought them into direct conflict with Stoicism, the dominant moral philosophy of early seventeenth-century France. By the same token, it lowered the barriers between Augustinianism and Epicureanism. Against the arrogant claims of Stoicism for the desirability of the life of virtue, a strict Augustinian was now much closer to the anti-Stoic, sceptical view of human nature associated with Epicureanism.[90]

---

[88] On Saint-Evremond, whose works were published relatively late in his life, in the 1680s, Nannerl O. Keohane, *Philosophy and the State in France: the Renaissance to the Enlightenment* (Princeton, 1980), pp. 229–35; Enrico Nuzzo, 'Antroplogia e morale in Saint-Evremond', in V. Dini and A. Taranto (eds.), *Individualismo Assolutismo Democrazia* (Salerno, 1992), 211–73.

[89] Keohane, *Philosophy and the State*, pp. 262–303; and Ben Rogers, 'In praise of vanity: the Augustinian analysis of the benefits of vice from Port-Royal to Mandeville', University of Oxford doctoral thesis (1994).

[90] Jean Lafond, 'Augustinisme et épicurisme au XVII siècle', in his *L'homme et son image. Morales et littérature de Montaigne à Mandeville* (Paris, 1996), pp. 345–68 – a particularly helpful discussion of the convergence of the two traditions, and the controversies which resulted. See also Pierre Force, *Self-Interest before Adam Smith: a Genealogy of Economic Science* (Cambridge, 2003), pp. 48–63.

The potential for a *rapprochement* between Epicurean and Augustinian moral thought was quickly perceived by those on the fringes of Port Royal, most intelligently by the duc de La Rochefoucauld, author of the *Maximes morales* (1664–80). Within Port Royal itself, however, others scented real danger. The most vigilant was the Cartesian and self-appointed champion of Jansenist orthodoxy, Antoine Arnauld, 'le grand Arnauld'. To Arnauld the point of Descartes' dualism was that it provided a firmer foundation for genuine morality: separated from the bodily passions, the mind yields moral intuitions whose truth is directly authorised by God. To his horror, however, Arnauld discovered that even a sophisticated Cartesian might find it hard to hold the line against Epicureanism. Worse still, the principal suspect was Malebranche. Though a member of the Paris Oratory rather than Port Royal, Malebranche was sympathetic to Augustinianism (like many Oratorians) as well as a convinced Cartesian. Yet as we have seen, it was precisely the Augustinian conviction of the primacy of the passions in fallen man which led him to qualify the separation of the mind from the body. Malebranche insisted that we must acknowledge the fact, the reality, of bodily pleasures, and should recognise that they bring a certain happiness to the soul. 'It is necessary to speak to men as Jesus Christ did, and not as the Stoics, who understood neither the nature nor the weakness of the human mind.'[91] Further, Malebranche not only supposed that *amour propre* was the basis of society; he accepted that since the charity (love of God) which is founded on reason is all too rare, *amour propre* must also be regarded as a source of the love of God.[92] Such errors, as Arnauld saw them, prompted him to launch a furious assault on Malebranche, carried on in a series of polemical treatises from 1683 until Arnauld's death in 1694; Malebranche's replies began almost immediately, and continued for several years after Arnauld's death. He conceded little. If he made clear his repudiation of the Epicurean denial of providence, he defended only God's 'general' providence as against Arnauld's doctrine of a divine providence prompt to intervene on 'particular' occasions. Though he insisted that he had qualified the happiness which 'sensible pleasures' brought to the soul, Malebranche did not hide his conviction that the mind 'naturally' understood pleasure in such Epicurean or *libertin* terms.[93]

---

[91] Malebranche, *Recherche de la Verité*, bk IV, ch. x, part 1, in *Oeuvres Complètes*, vol. II, pp. 76–82, with the quotation on p. 81: 'Il faut parler aux hommes comme Jesus-Christ leur a parlé, & non pas comme les Stoïciens, qui ne connoissent ni la nature ni la maladie de l'esprit humain.'

[92] Malebranche, *Recherche de la Verité*, IV.v.1, in *Oeuvres Complètes*, II, pp. 45–6.

[93] Nicolas Malebranche, *Réponse à une Dissertation de Mr Arnauld contre un Eclaircissement du Traité de la nature et de la Grace* (1685), and *Réponse du Père Malebranche à la Troisième Lettre de M. Arnauld*

Beyond Malebranche lay Pierre Bayle. A profound, if Protestant, Augustinian, Bayle was no Cartesian, but a thorough-going Pyrrhonian sceptic. In his *Pensées Diverses* (1683) – a work to which we shall need to return at greater length in ch. 5 – he had defended the possibility of a society of atheists, living in a tolerable state of sociability out of no more than self-interest, with no reference whatever to the life to come. His *Nouvelles de la République de Lettres* had immediately picked up, extracted, and commented on the exchanges between Arnauld and Malebranche: there, and again in the article on 'Epicurus' in the *Dictionnaire historique et critique* (1697), he underlined the superior honesty of the Epicurean account of human nature and its compatibility with the condition of man after the Fall. Arnauld, he pronounced, had criticised in vain the doctrine that the happiness of man consisted in pleasure.[94] It was as if Bayle would justify Arnauld's worst fears: with or without Cartesianism, Augustinianism as it was now understood (thanks not least to Arnauld's fellow Port-Royalistes) was no longer clearly distinguishable from Epicureanism.

Little of this was missed in Naples. The chief interests of the older generation may have been in natural philosophy and metaphysics; but d'Andrea and Valletta were clearly also alert to the parallel debates raging within moral philosophy. The best evidence for this lies, once again, in Valletta's library, in the lists of *Libri Gallici*. There were numerous titles by Arnauld, including several of his attacks on Malebranche, matched by the latter's replies. Alongside these were the *Essais* of Nicole and the *Oeuvres* of Saint-Evremond, Bayle's *Dictionnaire* and *Nouvelles de la République de Lettres*, and the works of several lesser French moralists.[95] Whether Valletta

Docteur de Sorbonne touchant les idées & les plaisirs (1699), both in the editions by André Robinet, in *Oeuvres Complètes de Malebranche*, vols. VI–VII, pp. 521–23, VIII–IX, pp. 976–89. The first of these passages is quoted by Lafond, 'Augustinsme et épicurisme', p. 368, also pp. 348–54, 359–60, 367. Arnauld levelled the charge of Epicureanism in his *Reflexions philosophiques et théologiques sur le nouveau système de la nature et de la Grace* (1685). Force, *Self-Interest before Adam Smith*, pp. 190–1, relates the debate to that between Fénelon and Bossuet over the possibility of a disinterested love of God.

[94] Pierre Bayle, *Dictionnaire historique et critique* (Rotterdam, 1697), article 'Epicure' in vol. I, part 2, pp. 1042–53; esp. pp. 1047–9: 'C'est en vain que Mr Arnauld a critiqué cette doctrine', with Remark G, in which Bayle rehearsed the arguments between Arnauld, Malebranche, and himself. The article was considerably extended in the second (1702) edition of the *Dictionnaire*: see *Dictionnaire historique et critique*, fourth edn (Amsterdam and Leiden, 1730), II, pp. 364–76. Once again, see Lafond, 'Augustinisme et épicurisme', pp. 353–4, 360–1.

[95] 'Antico Catalogo', Biblioteca dei Girolamini, Mf. 27.I.10, ff. 202r (Bayle, *Dictionnaire*, 1694 [?]), 207r, 211v (Arnauld), 214r (La Mothe le Vayer, *Oeuvres*), 216r (Arnauld, *Reflexions philosophiques et théologiques sur le nouveau système de la nature et de la Grace*), 216v (Malebranche, several, including the *Réponse à une Dissertation de M. Arnauld contre un eclaircissement du Traité de la nature et de la Grace*, 1688), 217r–v (controversy over Jansenism), 218v (Nicole, *Essais*), 223v (Saint-Evremond, *Oeuvres*), 224r (Arnauld, *Logique*, 1697; Montaigne, *Pensées*, 1700), 226v (Chevalier Méré, *Oeuvres*,

himself had fully taken the measure of the debate raging on his shelves is not altogether clear: his praise for Malebranche's work was matched by the encomium he bestowed upon Arnauld, whose sublime genius and excellent doctrine qualified him as 'the eagle among intellects'.[96] But if Valletta was reluctant to be drawn into that Cartesian quarrel, his own philosophic instincts inclined him to the very *rapprochement* of Augustinianism with Epicureanism which Arnauld so feared. Close to the Neapolitan Oratory, Valletta was clearly sympathetic to Augustinian moral rigorism, while his writings of the 1690s show him to have been well aware of the moral dimension of Epicurean doctrine.

It was among the next generation, however, that moral debate began in earnest in Naples. The opening round took place in the setting of the Accademia Medina Coeli, to which Gregorio Caloprese and Niccolò Capasso contributed *lezioni* in support of very different moral positions. Those of Caloprese, which appear to have inaugurated the academy, were clearly Cartesian in inspiration.[97] Their declared purpose was to recover 'la scienza del vivir civil' from those philosophers who believed that man was 'un mostro spaventoso', a terrifying monster. According to them man is absolute master of all that he does, following only his own will (his *proprio volere*); he loves only himself, coming together with others in cities out of fear; and his sole end is his own utility (*utilità*). In rejecting these assumptions Caloprese did not deny the existence of *amor proprio*, or that it frequently encourages us to neglect our duties; he conceded the Augustinian tenet that all men have an inclination to evil. But, he argued, those who have understood man solely through his *amor proprio* have looked only at the 'goods of the body' and their satisfaction, and have neglected the 'goods of the mind'. Men do also have a disposition to honesty and virtue, to love others, and to believe in divine providence. Epicurus himself acknowledged as much; indeed Epicurus' morals were so rigid that they

---

1698), 231r (Bayle, *Nouvelles*). Works not found in the list are Pascal's *Pensées* (the *Lettres Provinciales* are present, f. 213v) and Bayle's *Pensées Diverses*, though the latter was certainly known in Naples.

96 Valletta, 'Lettera in difesa della modern filosofia', *Opere filosofiche*, pp. 136–7: 'Antonio Arnaldo, uno de' maggiori Teologi della Sorbona e che per la sublimità del suo ingegno, ed eccellenza della sua dottrina, si può giustamente chiamare l'Aquila degl'ingegni, lo splendore dell'età nostra e il più gagliardo sostenitore della fede contro il Calvinismo.' The last article of the encomium suggests that Valletta may have been taking the opportunity to demonstrate at least his anti-Protestant credentials. Nevertheless, the *Libri Gallici* include many Huguenot works, from across the entire spectrum of Huguenot thinking, from Bayle to Jurieu, via Le Clerc.

97 Gregorio Caloprese, 'Dell'origine dell'imperij', in 'Delle lezione Accademiche recitate avanti l'Eccmo Sigr Duca di Medina Coeli Vice-Re', part I, lib. I, BNN Ms XIII.B.69, ff. 1–32r. The suggestion that these were the inaugural lectures derives from their being placed first in the manuscipt collection. These lectures were printed as an appendix in Silvio Suppa, *L'Accademia di Medinacoeli. Fra tradizione Investigante e nuova scienza civile* (Naples, 1971), pp. 177–212.

would have been those of a Christian had he but recognised that men do for love what he believed they do from *amor proprio*.[98]

Caloprese developed his criticism of those who would found moral-ity upon self-interest by observing that this was to treat vice as if it was praiseworthy (*lodevole*). It was to say that virtue was vice, and vice virtue, suggesting that virtue was nothing more than a name without a subject, invented by ill-designing men to deceive the simple-minded.[99] The way out of this impasse, Caloprese argued in the last lecture of his series, was to recognise that in the mind, as distinct from the body, we have inclinations to both the good and the bad, and that the key to happiness and pleasure (*godimento*) lies in possessing the good. But we need to use our free will to live according to the prompting of reason rather than appetite. The goods of the body, which we need for preservation, being few, we should seek those of the soul, and shun those of opinion, which spring from a desire to be superior to others. In this way, he concluded, we will be able to reconcile our *amor proprio* with our desire for company, and 'all will be obliged to keep within the limits of justice and honesty, which is what constitutes the nature of governments'.[100] Set in these Cartesian and Malebranchiste terms, Caloprese would argue, a recognition of the power of *amor proprio* was not incompatible with believing men also capable of the freely willed love of their neighbour and of God.[101]

Although the premises were similar, the direction of the argument in Capasso's lecture was very different. Setting himself the question 'Whether reason of state may contravene natural law?', Capasso began by denying that he was repeating the ancient error of equating the just with the useful. Nevertheless, he wanted to argue, reason of state must be allowed to over-rule the law of nature in every matter which does not relate to God. Given the ill nature of man, his subjection to laws is essential to the maintenance of society. Whether the government be by one or by many (and there were strong arguments for monarchy), subjects must give up all their rights to their prince, against whom there will be no appeal, whether under civil law, the law of nations, or the law of nature. It is for the prince to regulate the

[98] Caloprese, 'Dell'origine dell'imperij', *Lezioni prima e seconda*, in Suppa, *L'Accademia di Medinacoeli*, pp. 171–91.

[99] *Lezione terza*, ibid., p. 196: 'E nel vero, secondo l'idea di costoro niuna cosa è più vana e più ridicola e più dannosa della virtù, la quale per loro avviso non sarebbe altro che un nome senza soggetto inventato dalla malizia degli uomini per ingannare la semplicità de' sciocchi.'

[100] *Lezione quarta*, ibid., pp. 202–12: 'affine di obbligare tutti a tratenersi tra' limiti della giustizia e della onestà: che è quello che costituisce la natura degl'imperij'.

[101] Enrico Nuzzo, *Verso la Vita Civile. Antropologia e politica nelle Lezioni accademiche di Gregorio Caloprese e Paolo Mattia Doria* (Naples, 1984), esp. chs. 2–4: a subtle as well as thorough analysis of the specific Cartesianism of Caloprese, interpreted in the context of Neapolitan debate.

practice of religion, since sacraments and sacrifices are community matters. Likewise it is for the prince to determine when an act of usurpation of another's property, though certainly contrary to natural law, may nevertheless be legitimate, or when hunting, fishing, and navigation, which are naturally free to all, should be regulated. In the same way, Capasso continued, a prince may prevent the succession to a fief of a lawful heir, if the inheritance would give the subject too much power. Capasso was careful to add that this did not authorise the prince to behave out of private caprice, as Ahab did in usurping the vineyard of Naboth. But he also observed that among the Hebrews succession had been governed by divine law, implying that the example of Ahab was not applicable to a Gentile ruler. Which, as Capasso abruptly concluded, was sufficient by way of explanation of the thesis that 'the civil law is not at all subservient to natural reason'.[102]

The positions marked out by Caloprese and Capasso in their lectures were indicative of two of the main directions taken by Neapolitan moral philosophy over the next thirty years. Faced with the challenge of converging Augustinian and Epicurean accounts of human nature driven by *amor proprio*, Caloprese had responded by adapting the dualist metaphysics of Descartes and Malebranche in order to reaffirm that moral and physical pleasures were distinguishable. Like Malebranche, Caloprese was ready to accept the fact of *amor proprio*; but his insistence that the love of God and of one's fellows were goods of the mind, rationally and freely willed, suggested a determination to avoid the dangers which Arnauld had found in Malebranche's concessions to Epicureanism. As we shall see, a similarly Cartesian conviction that virtue could be distinguished from *amor proprio* would inform the much fuller account of the *Vita Civile* given ten years later by another academician, Paolo Mattia Doria, and would be reflected in his prescriptions for the renewal of the kingdom under its Austrian government, after the long years of Spanish reason of state. In Capasso's thinking, by contrast, the distinction between justice and utility was no more than a formal concession: his interest was in the world of facts. The substance of his argument that man's nature required absolute government, whose law should follow the reason of state not of nature, was almost exclusively Epicurean, even Hobbesian. It was an argument designed to equip the government of the kingdom to tackle the greatest rivals to its power, the church and the feudal baronage; and it would shortly receive

---

[102] 'Se la Ragion di Stato possa derogare alla legge Naturale del Dr Niccolò Capasso', 'Lezione Accademiche', part III, BNN Ms XIII.B.73, ff. 23–28: 'e tanto basti per interpretazion di quel testo che apertam[en]te dice, che la legge Civile non serve dell' in tutto alla Ragion Naturale'.

powerful support from Alessandro Riccardi and, above all, Giannone, who counted Capasso among his closest friends.

THE IMPACT OF THE NEW PHILOSOPHY: SCOTLAND

In Scotland as in Naples, history and the law were two fields in which one might expect to find continuities with the humanist past. These were especially marked in the study and use of history. For all that Cromwell's English army had conquered Scotland and forced its king into exile, both ends of the Scottish political spectrum continued to treat the continuity of the Scottish monarchy, and the record of the nobility as guardians of the nation's internal and external liberty, as the indispensable historical foundations of the kingdom's existence. Not surprisingly, it was the royalist version of this story which was retailed with most confidence after 1660: its leading exponent was Sir George Mackenzie, in works such as his *Brief Account of His Sacred Majestie's Descent* (1681), and in the more explicitly political *Ius Regium* (1684). Sibbald too was active in defence of Scottish history and historians, though his own work did not get beyond manuscript. In opposition to the royalists, the covenanters James Steuart and Alexander Shields maintained and even radicalised the Buchananite arguments for resistance; the *De Iure Regni* itself was republished shortly after the Revolution of 1689.[103]

The succession crisis which followed Anne's coming to the throne in 1701 required a shift of focus (just as did the Spanish succession crisis in Naples): the need now was to vindicate Scotland's historic independence from English claims to overlordship, mischievously renewed by William Atwood. At the instigation of Parliament James Anderson duly contributed *An Historical Essay shewing that the Crown and Kingdom of Scotland is imperial and independent* (1705).[104] Even after the Act of Union of 1707, the writing of history as an affirmation of the value of the national past remained a central preoccupation of many Scottish men of letters. With obvious reason Jacobite scholars took the lead, their efforts coordinated by the publishers Robert Freebairn and James Watson. It was the Jacobite sympathiser Thomas Ruddiman who at last did scholarly justice to the works

---

[103] J. C. L. Jackson, *Restoration Scotland, 1660–1690: Royalist Politics, Religion and Ideas* (Woodbridge, 2003), esp. ch. 3: 'The origins and nature of the Scottish monarchy'; Colin Kidd, *Subverting Scotland's Past: Scottish whig historians and the creation of an Anglo-British identity 1689–c.1830* (Cambridge, 1993), pp. 27–8.

[104] Kidd, *Subverting Scotland's Past*, pp. 43–50; William Ferguson, 'Imperial crowns: a neglected facet of the background to the Treaty of Union', *Scottish Historical Review*, 53 (1974), 22–44.

of Buchanan, while Patrick Abercromby contributed still another variant on the old story in the two folio volumes of his *The Martial Atchievements of the Scots Nation* (1711, 1715).[105]

If the native tradition of historical writing was thus in rude health, it was also substantially unaffected by the discussions of the nature of historical writing and of the critical treatment of evidence which were going on elsewhere. Mackenzie and Sibbald knew of the work of Mabillon and Simon; but Mackenzie's own writing showed no noticeable trace of their example, while Sibbald's projects for collecting the sources of Scottish history never came to fruition. Not until the exiled Jacobite priest Thomas Innes published his *Critical Essay on the Ancient Inhabitants of the Northern Parts of Britain, or Scotland* (1729) were the critical methods of Mabillon applied to Scottish history, removing at last the forty mythical kings which Boece and Buchanan had added to the story. Yet even then Innes had not scrupled to replace them with another, equally imaginary, Pictish genealogy for the Scottish monarchy.[106] Nor was the conservatism of Scottish historical writing evident only at the level of method. The traditional humanist ideal of history as a lesson in virtue remained pervasive, along with an apparently growing conviction that it displayed the guiding hand of divine providence in human affairs.[107] There was no thought that the nature of historical writing might need to be reconceptualised, no equivalent of Giannone's drawing from Bacon and Duck the idea for a new, 'civil' history. If anything, the tendency was in the opposite direction, towards a reaffirmation of humanist shibboleths, as in Abercromby's reduction of Scottish history to a catalogue of 'martial achievements'. Abercromby was an intelligent man: that he could think of Scottish history in no more modern terms underlines the extent to which historical writing was trapped in its humanist past.

The legacy of the past weighed less heavily on Scottish jurisprudence. Here two figures dominated the period after 1660. One was the ubiquitous Sir George Mackenzie, who combined his interests in Scots history

[105] Patrick Abercromby, *The Martial Atchievements of the Scots Nation. Being an account of the lives, characters and memorable actions, of such Scotsmen as have signalis'd themselves by the sword at home and abroad. And a survey of the military transactions wherein Scotland or Scotsmen have been remarkably concern'd, from the first establishment of the Scots monarchy to this present time*, 2 vols. (Edinburgh, printed by Mr Robert Freebairn, 1711, 1715). On this Jacobite scholarship and the Whig response, Kidd, *Subverting Scotland's Past*, pp. 80–96.

[106] Fr Thomas Innes, *A Critical Essay on the Ancient Inhabitants of the Northern Parts of Britain, or Scotland* (London, 1729); on which, and on the reception of Mabillon in Scotland: Thomas I. Rae, 'Historical scepticism in Scotland before David Hume', in R. F. Brissenden (ed.), *Studies in the Eighteenth Century*, II (Canberra, 1973), pp. 205–21; Kidd, *Subverting Scotland's Past*, pp. 101–7.

[107] David Allan, *Virtue, Learning and the Scottish Enlightenment: Ideas of Scholarship in Early Modern History* (Edinburgh, 1993), chs. 1–2.

and Stoic morals with a professional commitment to the advancement of Scottish law. To this end he contributed a number of treatises, including his short and popular manual, *Institutions of the Law of Scotland* (1684).[108] Intellectually far more ambitious, however, was James Dalrymple, Viscount Stair's *Institutions of the Law of Scotland* (1681). This was a full-scale exposition of Scots law, developed from first principles. For these principles Stair drew upon the Protestant natural lawyers, Grotius and Pufendorf, systematically presenting law as the dictate of reason. Much more than these, however, Stair was insistent that reason was subsidiary to the will of God: there was no question of repeating the Grotian formula that the law of nature would obtain even allowing the hypothesis that there was no God. Calvinist theological assumptions underpinned Stair's work throughout; his closest Scottish intellectual predecessor was the scholastic Samuel Rutherford rather than the humanist Thomas Craig.[109] As we shall see, reformed theology would also shape the thinking of the most prominent Scottish exponent of natural jurisprudence in the early years of the eighteenth century, Gershom Carmichael. But for Carmichael natural jurisprudence was a vehicle for the teaching of moral philosophy: to appreciate his broader intellectual purposes, we need first to assess the Scots' response to the new currents in natural and moral philosophy in the closing decades of the seventeenth century.

In recent years scholars have done much to dispel the notion that late seventeenth-century Scots were ignorant of the contemporary intellectual revolution in natural philosophy.[110] From 1660 the ideas of Galileo and Descartes were being mentioned by university teachers to their students, even if they were uncertain how to integrate them within a framework of scholastic metaphysics. Perhaps because of his wariness of metaphysical claims, Newton's work was to prove particularly attractive. His ideas on light and colour, gravity, matter, and astronomy began to feature regularly in regents' lectures and theses in the 1690s. More remarkably, within a few years of the publication of the *Principia Mathematica* (1687), there had

[108] On the humanist legal culture which Mackenzie's works embodied and promoted, John W. Cairns, 'The formation of the Scottish legal mind in the eighteenth century: themes of humanism and Enlightenment in the admission of advocates', in Neil MacCormick and Peter Birks (eds.), *The Legal Mind: Essays for Tony Honoré* (Oxford, 1986), pp. 258–61.

[109] On Craig: Peter Stein, 'Law and society in eighteenth-century Scottish thought', in N. T. Phillipson and Rosalind Mitchison (eds.), *Scotland in the Age of Improvement: Essays in Scottish history in the Eighteenth Century* (Edinburgh, 1970), pp. 148–51.

[110] In addition to Shepherd, 'Newtonianism in Scottish univerities', and Emerson, 'Sir Robert Sibbald', the more recent claims of Paul Wood, 'Science in the Scottish Enlightenment', in Broadie, *Cambridge Companion to the Scottish Enlightenment*, pp. 94–107.

emerged in Scotland a group of committed Newtonians, with the competence to expound and apply his ideas in a systematic fashion. Prominent among these were Sibbald's great rival, Archibald Pitcairne, and the two Gregories, David and his brother James. Professor of mathematics at Edinburgh since 1683, David Gregory transferred to the chair of astronomy at Oxford in 1691, whereupon James succeeded him in Edinburgh. Thereafter the Scottish Newtonians formed overlapping circles around Pitcairne in Edinburgh and David Gregory in Oxford; together they made substantial contributions both to the publicising of Newtonian physics and to its application to physiology. The group was Tory in politics, episcopalian or High Church in religion; nevertheless it enjoyed Newton's support and patronage.[111] Newton's approval is itself a powerful testament to the group's intellectual strength, and its existence demonstrates that there were no insuperable barriers to Scottish participation in the latest developments in natural philosophy. But whether such a specialised interest can be taken to stand for a more general Scottish engagement with the new philosophy is another matter.

In Naples, as we have seen, the crucial stimulus had come through the atomism of the natural philosophers associated with the Investiganti, which in turn had facilitated the reception of Gassendi's Christianised Epicurean ethics. By 1700 Neapolitan intellectual life had been exposed to all the main currents in contemporary French philosophy, and in particular to the confrontation between Epicurean and Augustinian views of human nature displayed in the rival philosophies of Malebranche and Arnauld, and in the writings of the Port-Royalistes, Pascal, Nicole, and their followers. Where were these in late seventeenth- and early eighteenth-century Scotland? Sir Robert Sibbald provides a clue. In the memoirs he began in 1695, he recalled that he discovered the atomist philosophy by reading books by Kenelm Digby and Thomas White at college in Edinburgh in the 1650s. But he also remembered that he was most influenced by the principal of the college at the time, Robert Leighton, afterwards archbishop of Glasgow.[112] Leighton's Augustinian piety had something in common with that of Port Royal, but he was a fierce critic of Epicurean and Lucretian atomism.[113] Since there is no sign that Sibbald maintained his interest in atomism, or ever appreciated the larger philosophical issues raised by Epicureanism, it looks as if

[111] Anita Guerrini, 'The Tory Newtonians: Gregory, Pitcairne and their circle', *Journal of British Studies*, 25 (1986), 288–311.
[112] Sir Robert Sibbald, 'Memoirs of my Lyfe' (begun in 1695), *The Memoirs of Sir Robert Sibbald (1641–1722)*, ed. Francis Paget Hett (London, 1932), pp. 54–5.
[113] Roger L. Emerson, 'Science and moral philosophy in the Scottish Enlightenment', in Stewart, *Studies in the Philosophy of the Scottish Enlightenment*, p. 15.

Leighton had successfully negated the potential of his early reading. There is evidence that a similar distrust of Epicureanism was conveyed in the earliest discussions of Descartes in Scottish universities; Cartesian mechanism was sometimes treated as a revival of Epicureanism.[114] But Leighton's hostility reflected a broader theological and philosophical commitment, one widely shared among the intellectual elite of Restoration Scotland.

In important new studies, Colin Kidd, Clare Jackson, and David Allan have brought to light two convergent currents of thought in Restoration Scotland.[115] As in Naples, one was theological, the other an ancient moral philosophy. But in Scotland the combination was different. Here the theological current was a form of latitudinarianism, the moral philosophy neo-Stoicism. Scottish latitudinarianism took shape in response to the bigotry of the more zealous covenanters and the hair-splitting of the sects. It put piety before doctrine, inclusiveness before a rigid orthodoxy; it emphasised the importance of reason in the right use of conscience, but sought to avoid a reductive Socinian reliance on reason alone to establish moral truths. Perhaps to avoid such an overreliance on reason, Scottish latitudinarianism showed a marked inclination to mysticism. The acknowledged spiritual leader of the movement was Robert Leighton; his mysticism is likely to have been shaped by the interest in neo-Platonism and in Port Royal evident in his library. Among the younger generation, the mystical tendency was strongest in Aberdeen, being strikingly expressed by Henry Scougal and George Garden.[116] Leighton also set the pattern for combining this form of latitudinarian piety with an allegiance to neo-Stoic morals. His library contained all the major ancient Stoic texts, and he was a particular admirer of Epictetus and Seneca.[117] The allegiance to neo-Stoicism was equally strong among intellectually minded laity, including Sir Robert Moray and Sir George Mackenzie. Mackenzie took up the mantle of the royalist Drummond of Hawthornden as both historian and moralist, being the author of a succession of moral writings, from *Religio Stoici* (1663) to *The Moral History of Frugality and its opposite Vices* (1691). Not surprisingly, however, the corollary of this adherence to neo-Stoicism was an implicit or – in Leighton's case – explicit hostility to Epicureanism. Leighton was

---

[114] Shepherd, 'Newtonianism in Scottish universities', pp. 66, 70.

[115] Colin Kidd, 'Religious realignment between the Restoration and Union', in Robertson, *A Union for Empire*, pp. 145–68, esp. 147–53; Jackson, *Restoration Scotland*, ch. 7, 'The defence of true religion'; Allan, *Philosophy and Politics in Later Stuart Scotland*, ch. 5, 'Reconciliation or retirement? Philosophy and political activity in Restoration Scotland'.

[116] On Scougal and his colleagues, G. D. Henderson, *Mystics of the North East* (Aberdeen, 1934).

[117] See more particularly, David Allan, 'Reconciliation and retirement in the Restoration Scottish Church: the neo-Stoicism of Robert Leighton', *Journal of Ecclesiastical History*, 50 (1999), 251–78.

adamant on the point: Epicurean materialism was the subversion of religion and an inlet for the philosophy of Hobbes.[118]

Leighton had one protégé on whom he looked with particular favour, Gilbert Burnet. Born in 1643, well connected and well educated (at Marischal College in Aberdeen, with subsequent periods of study in Cambridge, France, and the Netherlands), Burnet obtained his first charge as a minister at the parish of Saltoun, to which he was presented by Sir Robert Fletcher (Andrew's father) in 1665. Almost his first duty was to deliver a funeral address for Sir Robert. The address, which was published, portrayed him as a model of undogmatic faith and personal piety, who shunned the public eye but devoted himself to learning, particularly in mathematics and natural philosophy. Burnet made a point of evoking Sir Robert's abomination of 'that French contagion of atheism', and his rejection of those who argued that there is no certainty, and 'ranked themselves under Leviathans Banner' in mathematics.[119] In 1669 Burnet moved on to be professor of divinity at Glasgow, before withdrawing from Scottish public life and moving south in the mid-1670s. Having made friends of leading English Whigs, he felt it prudent to go abroad in 1683, and two years later took the opportunity to travel south through Switzerland to Italy. The journey took him as far as Naples, where he was received by Valletta and introduced to his circle. On his return to the Netherlands (where he joined the court of William of Orange), Burnet published a travel journal, entitled *Some Letters containing an account of what seemed most remarkable in Switzerland, Italy &c* (Amsterdam, 1686); the fourth of these letters included a lengthy account of his visit to Naples, with his impressions of Valletta and his circle. Set off against Valletta's own reports of the visit to Magliabecchi, these provide a unique opportunity to observe a direct encounter between representatives of the intellectual worlds of Scotland and Naples in the later seventeenth century.

The visit had followed the prescribed rituals of the Republic of Letters. Burnet arrived equipped with an introduction to Valletta from Magliabecchi; for his part, Valletta regarded the visit, which followed hard on one by Mabillon, as a fresh confirmation of his own status in the Republic. Burnet struck him, he reported to Magliabecchi, as 'a thunderbolt of letters'. He flattered himself (but Burnet even more) that there was no greater man of letters in the Protestant world, and made a point of showing

---

[118] As in his Theological Lectures, quoted by Jackson, *Restoration Scotland*, pp. 186–7.

[119] [Gilbert Burnet], *A Discourse on the Memory of that rare and truely Virtuous Person Sir Robert Fletcher of Saltoun: who died the 13 January last, in the thirty-ninth year of his Age. Written by a Gentleman of his Acquaintance* (Edinburgh, 1665), quoted passages from pp. 121–8.

Burnet his library.[120] The memory was still warm a year later, when Valletta received a copy of Burnet's *History of the Reformation in England* from a cousin who was visiting Naples.[121] But the book Valletta was keenest to receive was Burnet's travel *Letters*, containing his impressions of Naples. Unfortunately, by the time Valletta was able to read the book, in English, in December 1687, he already knew that it had damaged him.[122]

It was precisely the remarks about Valletta and his circle which were the problem. 'There are', Burnet had written, 'societies of men at Naples of freer thoughts than can be found in any other place of Italy. The Greek learning begins to flourish there, and the new philosophy is much studied.' In D. Joseph Valletta's library, where there was 'a vast collection of well chosen books', there was an assembly of men of true learning and good sense. But the clergy regarded them as 'a set of atheists, and as the spawn of Pomponatius his school'. Some physicians too had come under the scandal of atheism. Burnet confidently declared that he had found no such thing among them, but also observed that such disbelief was quite understandable amid so much superstition and imposture. The tactlessness of these remarks was made worse by dismissive comments on Catholic learning. Neither the Jesuits nor the Oratorians in Naples were as learned as their counterparts in France, he thought, and they were poor preachers. As for the quietist Molinos, whom Burnet believed to have had 20,000 followers in the city, he was a very ordinary divine, whose popularity was to be explained simply as a reaction against the excesses of priestly and popular (especially female) piety.[123]

Published two years before the trials of the 'atheists' began, Burnet's remarks could not fail to embarrass Valletta. Coming from a Protestant, his reassurance that the members of Valletta's circle were not atheists would count for little, and only served to publicise the charge throughout Europe. As an emissary from the Protestant to the Catholic world of letters, Burnet had behaved ungraciously and ungratefully. Yet arguably the greater loser by the episode was Burnet himself, and the culture he represented. For Burnet had spurned the opportunity he had been offered for intellectual exchange. Throughout his remarks his attitude to the inhabitants of the city

---

[120] Valletta to Magliabecchi, 21 Nov. 1685, describing Burnet as 'il fulmine delle lettere', and [Dec., 1685], in *Lettere dal Regno ad Antonio Magliabecchi*, pp. 1067, 1070.

[121] Valletta to Magliabecchi, 3 Dec. 1686, ibid., pp. 1081–2.

[122] Valletta to Magliabecchi, 1 and 16 Dec. 1687 (putting a brave face on his disappointment), in ibid., pp. 1083–4.

[123] Gilbert Burnet, *Some Letters containing an Account of what seemed most remarkable in Switzerland, Italy &c.* (Amsterdam, 1686), 'The Fourth Letter, from Rome, the 8th of December 1685', pp. 195–200.

and the kingdom was one of unmitigated condescension. Not only were they ignorant and superstitious, they were also idle and feckless, incapable of undertaking commerce.[124] Burnet was confident that he had visited an alien as well as a papist world, from which he had nothing to learn. As a result he was oblivious to the philosophical issues then exercising the Neapolitans, and completely failed to appreciate that the deficit was on his side of the intellectual balance. Loyal to a now old-fashioned Stoicism, the leading lights of Restoration Scottish intellectual life, of whom Burnet would certainly account himself one, were simply unaware of the currents of Epicurean and Augustinian thought which were already setting the agenda in Naples.

The pattern of Scottish intellectual life did change after the Revolution of 1688, but only to a limited extent did it become more receptive to the new philosophical currents emanating from France. Neo-Stoicism of the kind favoured by Leighton and Mackenzie was too closely associated with royalism to survive the regime change. It was also clear that episcopacy had no future within the Church of Scotland, and that latitudinarianism would therefore have to find a new presbyterian form, which in due course would turn out to be moderatism. (Episcopalianism became a form of dissent, within which the mystical tendency survived, under a certain amount of persecution, to bring solace to Jacobites.) In the crucial sphere of moral philosophy teaching, the initiative passed to the new generation of presbyterian regents who were redesigning the philosophy courses in the universities.

Among these the leading intellect was undoubtedly that of Gershom Carmichael. Born in 1672, Carmichael was a regent at Glasgow from 1694, and for his final two years, from 1727 to 1729, the university's first professor of moral philosophy. Unusually at the time (though the example was followed by his successors), Carmichael published the works he prepared for the instruction of his students. The first to appear were two sets of *Philosophical Theses*, in 1699 and 1707. A decade later, in 1718, he published his major work, an edition of Pufendorf's *De Officio Hominis et Civis juxta Legem Naturalem*, with an extensive commentary of his own; this was reissued in a second edition in 1724. Between the two editions Carmichael also published *A Short Introduction to Logic* (1720); he completed the series with *A Synopsis of Natural Theology* (1729). Recently translated and edited by James Moore and Michael Silverthorne, these writings indicate with striking clarity the direction in which Carmichael believed

---

[124] Ibid., pp. 191–2.

moral philosophy should now move, and the theology which should underpin it.[125]

In important respects, as Moore and Silverthorne have argued in a series of fundamental studies, the basis of Carmichael's thinking was Augustinian and Cartesian.[126] His *Logic* derived from the Port Royal logic of Arnauld and Nicole, his *Natural Theology* from earlier manuals by Gerard de Vries (a Dutch Calvinist Cartesian) and Jean Le Clerc – although the latter was treated more as a target of criticism. From an early stage, as the *Philosophical Theses* demonstrate, Carmichael was also introducing his students to Malebranche's theory of ideas, and his occasionalist account of sensation. He likewise endorsed Malebranche's enumeration of the primary passions as desire, happiness, and sadness.[127] When it came to moral philosophy, however, there was no question of Carmichael's following Malebranche on to the controversial ground of Augustinianism's affinity to Epicureanism. Instead Carmichael turned to natural jurisprudence, and in particular to Pufendorf's *Offices*, which he read with the commentaries by Leibniz and Barbeyrac. An Arminian Huguenot, follower of Jean Le Clerc, Jean Barbeyrac was a critic precisely of the tendency to scepticism and Epicureanism latent in strict Augustinianism, and explicit in the works of Bayle.[128] But Barbeyrac (like Le Clerc) was still too Pyrrhonian for Carmichael, who thought, like Leibniz, that neither Pufendorf nor Barbeyrac had attached sufficient weight to God as the object of our veneration and the source of our duties.[129] Carmichael accordingly sought to reconstruct Pufendorf's account of natural law, adapting and combining two distinct lines of

---

[125] *Natural Rights on the Threshold of the Scottish Enlightenment: the Writings of Gershom Carmichael*, ed. James Moore and Michael Silverthorne, with the texts translated from the Latin by Michael Silverthorne (Indianapolis, 2002).

[126] James Moore and Michael Silverthorne, 'Gershom Carmichael and the natural jurisprudence tradition in eighteenth-century Scotland', in Istvan Hont and Michael Ignatieff, *Wealth and Virtue: the Shaping of Political Economy in the Scottish Enlightenment* (Cambridge, 1983), pp. 73–87; 'Natural sociability and natural rights in the moral philosophy of Gershom Carmichael', in V. Hope (ed.), *Philosophers of the Scottish Enlightenment* (Edinburgh, 1984), pp. 1–12; 'Protestant theologies, limited sovereignties: natural law and the conditions of union in the German Empire, the Netherlands, and Great Britain', in Robertson, *A Union for Empire*, pp. 189–97.

[127] *Philosophical Theses* (1699), in *Natural Rights on the Threshold of the Scottish Enlightenment*, pp. 333–40; this set of *Theses* also carried an epigraph from the *Recherche de la vérité*.

[128] James Moore, 'Natural law and the Pyrrhonian controversy', in Peter Jones (ed.), *Philosophy and Science in the Scottish Enlightenment* (Edinburgh, 1988), pp. 20–38.

[129] *Supplements and Observations upon the Two Books of Samuel Pufendorf's On the Duty of Man and Citizen according to the Law of Nature, composed for the use of students in the Universities, by Gershom Carmichael* (Edinburgh, 1718, second edn 1724), in *Natural Rights on the Threshold of the Scottish Enlightenment*: on his differences with Pufendorf and Barbeyrac, see in particular the preface to the 1724 edition (printed in translation as ch. 1), and supplements I (in translation, ch. 2) and III (in translation, in ch. 7).

philosophical reasoning. On the one hand, he developed a recognisably Cartesian, or Malebranchiste, account of the human soul's longing for God, and of its happiness as lying in the love and veneration of God. On the other, he reaffirmed the scholastic propositions that the law of nature was derived from divine law, and that our obligation to it must be based on our love of God (and not on our fear of his punishment, as Pufendorf suggested). The structure of Carmichael's moral philosophy, therefore, would seem to have been a synthesis of Cartesian Augustinianism and Protestant or reformed scholasticism. It was by bringing these together that he was able to interpret the modern natural jurisprudence of Pufendorf, and also Locke, in a manner appropriate to the moral instruction of Scottish youth.

Carmichael brought a new level of sophistication and modernity to Scottish moral philosophy. When his thinking is set alongside that current in Naples at this time, however, what is striking is the effectiveness with which it shut out the challenge of an Augustinianism prepared to recognise its proximity to Epicureanism. If Leighton knew instinctively to avert his eyes from Epicureanism, lest his countrymen be contaminated by Hobbes, Carmichael, who was familiar with the work of Malebranche and Barbeyrac, must have been aware how close Epicureanism might come to the Augustinianism he professed. More particularly, it is very hard to believe that Carmichael was ignorant of the existence and the writings of Bayle. Even if he did not read Bayle for himself, he would have heard of him through Barbeyrac. Though it is no more than speculation, it does not seem unreasonable to infer that the omission was deliberate, and that Carmichael had decided not to expose his students to Bayle's array of sceptical, Augustinian, and Epicurean arguments.[130] If Carmichael had set himself to prevent the sort of debate which developed in Naples from occurring in Scotland, he could hardly have chosen his arguments better. Positing an intimate relation between Augustinian theology and the moral duty imposed by natural law, Carmichael enabled moral philosophy to be taught in terms which made it most unlikely that any student would be led to repeat the doubts which had assailed the unfortunate Aikenhead.

Carmichael did have a colleague at Glasgow, the professor of divinity, John Simson, who was intent on pursuing a less orthodox path. Attracted by the rationalism of Samuel Clarke, Simson found himself exploring the

---

[130] For example, Carmichael's arguments for the existence of God in his *Natural Theology* included universal human consensus, an argument which Bayle had singled out for criticism in the *Pensées Diverses*, criticism to which Carmichael made no reference: *A Synopsis of Natural Theology, or, the Knowledge of the existence, attributes and operations of the Supreme Deity, drawn from Nature itself* (Edinburgh 1729), in *Natural Rights on the Threshold of the Scottish Enlightenment*, p. 245.

foothills, if not the high peaks, of Socinianism. But fellow clergy were quick to invoke ecclesiastical authority to stop him. Between 1715 and 1717 Simson was investigated by the General Assembly of the Church of Scotland for teaching the Arminian doctrine that the Fall had not deprived man of his reason and free will. His own vigorous denials of unorthodoxy were sufficient to secure a qualified acquittal on the charge of unsound teaching. He was allowed to continue until 1727, when he was suspended again and subjected to further investigation, this time for Arianism. The second process against him ended, in 1729, in continued suspension from teaching. Simson was not deposed, and died in 1740 still nominally professor of divinity – a marked advance on the fate of Aikenhead. Nor was Simson without public supporters in Scotland, notably Archibald Campbell in St Andrews. Nevertheless his case was a reminder to those teaching in universities not publicly to transgress Calvinist orthodoxy, whose defenders remained loyal to the simple scriptural theology with which Halyburton had sought to exorcise the ghost of Aikenhead.[131]

But even the best efforts of Carmichael and ecclesiastical authority could not hold the line forever. In the early 1720s a group of philosophic Young Turks, including William Wishart and George Turnbull, began to chafe against philosophy teaching which seemed so lacking in 'warmth' towards virtue. Egged on from Ireland by the venerable republican Robert Molesworth, they appealed to the philosophy of the earl of Shaftesbury, and to Machiavelli and Harrington, to counter the scholastic Augustinianism they were taught at university, and Glasgow in particular. Further support came from Dublin, in the early philosophic writings of John Simson's former student, Francis Hutcheson.[132] But Hutcheson had hardly begun to praise Shaftesbury before he became aware that another contemporary, Bernard Mandeville, had let the Augustinian-Epicurean cat out of the bag in a form so provocative that no serious moral philosopher could continue to ignore it. In the *Free Thoughts on Religion, the Church and National Happiness* (1720), as, more subtly, in *The Fable of the Bees* (1714, 1723), Mandeville had effectively 'translated' Bayle for English readers. As Hutcheson quickly realised, something better than either Augustinian reformed scholasticism or even Shaftesburian benevolence would be needed to meet

---

[131] On the complex story of Simson's trials: Anne Skoczylas, *Mr Simson's Knotty Case: Divinity, Politics and Due Process in Early Eighteenth-century Scotland* (Montreal, 2001); and on the context of theological debate at the time: Stewart, 'Religion and natural theology', pp. 34–6.

[132] On the Molesworth connection, James Moore, 'The two systems of Francis Hutcheson: on the origins of the Scottish Enlightenment', in Stewart, *Studies in the Philosophy of the Scottish Enlightenment*, pp. 45–7.

this new challenge. But the challenge could not now be disarmed; indeed it may be that Carmichael's success in suppressing the potential threat of an Epicurean Augustinianism for so long only magnified the explosive force of Mandeville and Bayle when they finally struck Scottish moral philosophy – or, more specifically, when they were read by the young David Hume. In due course, it will be my contention that engagement with the Augustinian-Epicurean arguments of Mandeville and of Bayle was the key to Hume's analysis in *A Treatise of Human Nature* (1739–40) of the passions, the acquisition of morality, the historical formation of society, and the redundancy of God.

Thanks to Hume, the Scots would finally 'catch up' on their Neapolitan counterparts, and confront the challenge of modern Epicureanism. In the context of this study, however, that moment still lies in the future. There were two intermediary stages in the emergence of Enlightenment in Scotland and in Naples which require to be examined in detail before we reach Hume. The first was the debate over the predicament in which the two kingdoms found themselves at the end of the seventeenth century, when the failure of their dynasties threw open the question of their relation to the monarchies of which they had for long been part. The circumstances in which the two kingdoms found themselves, as well as their contrasting patterns of political, economic, and social development over the seventeenth century, were examined in ch. 2; as a result of the succession crises in the Spanish and British monarchies, those circumstances now became the subject of urgent, intensive discussion in both kingdoms. Keenly aware that trade was transforming traditional relations between states, both Neapolitan and Scottish commentators now revealed a common commitment to enabling their kingdoms to take advantage of the apparent opportunity to escape from the condition of provincial dependence. In each case, moreover, there was at least one contributor with the conceptual sophistication to set specific, local concerns in a larger intellectual framework: Paolo Mattia Doria in Naples, Andrew Fletcher in Scotland. There is therefore ample material for a comparative analysis of the debates, which follows in ch. 4. In turn this will provide a starting point for study (in ch. 7) of the moment, half a century later, when Antonio Genovesi in Naples and David Hume in Scotland decided to turn their attention from philosophy to political economy, making the latter the chosen intellectual instrument of the cause of Enlightenment in their respective countries.

Hume must also wait until after we have seen the *dénouement* of the Neapolitan engagement with Epicureanism. This was to come from an unexpected quarter at an unpropitious time, just when it seemed that the relative intellectual freedom which the Neapolitans had been enjoying would be brought to an abrupt end. In 1723, the new approach to legal-historical scholarship taught by Domenico Aulisio yielded its greatest fruit, Pietro Giannone's *Istoria Civile del Regno di Napoli.* Instantly the church reacted: Giannone was forced into exile, his defeat celebrated in Solimena's great fresco *Heliodorus driven from the Temple* (1725), above the doorway in the Gesù Nuovo.[133] Giannone might be driven away; but his defeat became another's opportunity. Protesting to all who would listen his desire to refute the revitalised heresies of Hobbes, Bayle, and the Epicureans, Giambattista Vico published the first version of his *Scienza Nuova* in 1725. Its author's protestations notwithstanding, the *New Science* was, I shall argue in ch. 5, the most ambitious and original of all Neapolitan engagements with Epicureanism, and a response to the challenge of Bayle in particular. It thus provides a fitting comparative foil for Hume's *Treatise of Human Nature*, which we shall reach in ch. 6.

---

[133] Romeo de Maio, *Pittura e controriforma a Napoli* (Rome and Bari, 1983), pp. 5–7, notes the coincidence between Giannone's enforced flight and the subject of Solimena's fresco.

CHAPTER 4

The predicament of 'kingdoms governed as provinces'

THE SPANISH SUCCESSION CRISIS

By 1700, it has been suggested, Neapolitan men of letters were aware that the currents of scepticism, Epicureanism, and Augustinianism flowing so strongly from France had the potential to transform the understanding of man's place in this world. Scots were slower to appreciate this potential, quite possibly because those responsible for intellectual leadership were reluctant to engage with the new thinking; nevertheless they too were to recognise it eventually. But why should Neapolitans and Scots have become particularly interested in understanding man's place in this world? What made this increasingly their chief intellectual preoccupation? An answer, I shall suggest, lies in the incentive to thought offered by the circumstances of the two kingdoms. Before Neapolitans and Scots turned to systematic reflection on human society and its history, they had already devoted their intellectual energies to discussion of the specific political and economic problems which they found in their own countries. Prompted by the onset of political, and in the Scottish case also economic, crisis in the late 1690s, both Neapolitan and Scottish observers began to consider the reasons for their countries' predicaments, and the means by which they might hope to escape them. Moreover it was not simply the subject matter of these discussions which pointed the Neapolitans and the Scots towards the more general analysis of the human condition; the debates also served as a testing ground of the existing conceptual resources for such analysis. That in the event those resources were stretched to the limits of their capacity during the debates was, it will be suggested, a further incentive to thinkers in both countries to devote their efforts to the elaboration of a new approach to the understanding of society and its improvement.

The circumstances of the two kingdoms before 1700 were outlined earlier, in ch. 2. In both kingdoms the common experience of belonging to greater, composite dynastic monarchies had been violently disrupted by revolution in the middle decades of the century. Since then the two governing elites had gradually re-established their authority and political autonomy, though where in Naples this was achieved by reinforcing the separate privileges of the feudal and the robe nobilities, in Scotland the nobility forged a new alliance with the lairds and the legal profession. A divergence was also evident in the economic outlook of the two countries. While the population of the Mezzogiorno was much larger than that of Scotland, recovering quickly from the sharp fall in the mid-century, and the city of Naples in particular was a major urban centre, the owners of wealth tended to devote it to consumption rather than investment. By contrast, the smaller Scottish economy was better integrated, and the leadership of Scottish society increasingly willing to think in terms of investment to promote agricultural reform and manufacturing and commercial enterprise. Even as the two societies were beginning to draw apart in these ways, however, events at the very end of the 1690s precipitated a fresh crisis, the common factor in which was, once again, the kingdoms' status as junior partners in larger composite monarchies.

The crisis was that of the Spanish succession. Of itself merely a matter of dynastic failure, of the imminent end of the Spanish branch of the Habsburg family, the crisis had much larger implications, which bore directly on the kingdom of Naples, and indirectly on that of Scotland. Ever since his accession to the Spanish thrones in 1665, at the age of four, it had been apparent that Charles II was likely to be the last of his dynasty. Sickly throughout his life, the prospects of his having children became increasingly remote; from the late 1660s other dynasties were calculating their own chances of the succession, and seeking to forestall those of rivals. But Charles enjoyed a long death: not until the second half of the 1690s was it clear that the end was in sight, and the jockeying for the succession became dangerously intensive. The principal claimants were the families already holding the most powerful thrones in Europe, the Bourbons of France, headed by Louis XIV, and the Austrian Habsburgs, whose head was the emperor, Leopold I. The Bourbon claim was based on Louis XIV's marriage in 1659 to Charles's older half-sister, the Infanta Maria Teresa: failing heirs of Charles himself, the succession should pass to her as the eldest daughter of Philip IV of Spain, and hence to her son. The obvious objection, that Louis had renounced any claim upon the Spanish succession for his heirs as a condition of the marriage, was circumvented (if not answered) by adopting as the Bourbon candidate one of his younger grandsons, Philip duke of Anjou, who was not in the direct line of succession to the French throne. The rival Austrian claim was that the succession should revert to the surviving (and supposedly senior) branch of the Habsburg family, whose head, Leopold, had married Charles II's older full sister, Margarita Teresa. Again, it was not expected that the emperor himself would succeed: in 1698 the Habsburg candidate was Joseph Ferdinand, prince of Bavaria, Leopold's grandson by the marriage of his daughter to the elector of Bavaria. But Joseph Ferdinand died in 1699, whereupon the claim passed to the emperor's younger son, the Arch-Duke Charles. Other, lesser, dynasties also entered claims, in case the great powers should prefer to settle for such an alternative. Among these were the Portugese house of Braganza and the house of Savoy; for various reasons the claim of the latter would be seen as the most credible.

Two other powers which were not in a position to advance dynastic claims of their own, but which had a close interest in the succession, were the Dutch republic and the British monarchy: since 1689, of course, their interests had been jointly represented by William III. The interest of the Dutch and the English was commercial: both had carved out lucrative trades with the European and overseas territories of the Spanish monarchy, which a new and more powerful ruler might well seek to terminate. From the Dutch and English viewpoints, the greatest single threat was from Louis XIV: were a member of his family to succeed to the Spanish thrones, his power in Europe would be unassailable. Following the Peace of Ryswick with Louis in 1697, William III accordingly took the lead in attempting to secure treaties which would partition the Spanish monarchy between the several claimants. Two such partition treaties were agreed, in 1698 and again, because of Joseph Ferdinand's death, in 1700. The thinking behind them was simple: an agreed division of the territories of the monarchy would be preferable to the war which all assumed would follow if the monarchy passed entire to one or other of the major claimants.

But what was intended to calm the anxieties of the great powers only intensified those of the territories which were the subject of this haggling. By the late 1690s, it was all too clear that the future of the kingdom of Naples in particular was about to be decided by others, regardless of Neapolitan interests and wishes. The likeliest alternatives had, it is true, some historical precedent. The claim of the Bourbons might be connected with that of the Angevins, rulers of the kingdom in the fourteenth and early fifteenth centuries. Perhaps more cogently, the claim of the Austrian Habsburgs recalled the monarchy of Charles V, and, distantly, of the great thirteenth-century Hohenstaufen emperor, Frederick II. The existence of minor candidates for the Spanish succession also made it just possible that a general division and exchange of territories and thrones might enable the kingdom to emerge with its own dynasty, as an independent monarchy. But even that – remote – possibility carried dangers: the claimant might be no better than an adventurer like the duke of Guise in 1647. The one certainty was that the stability so carefully restored after Masaniello's revolt was about to end, requiring the various interests within the ruling elite to adapt to new dynastic masters.

Scotland, of course, had no dynastic interest in the Spanish succession. But the implications of the crisis affected it in two vital ways, and in 1698 it even, briefly, acquired a certain territorial interest. In the first place, any increase in the power of the French monarchy, and consequent war, would lead to renewed French backing for the claims of the exiled James VII, and a reinforcement of Jacobitism. A war of the Spanish succession, in other words, could easily become a war of the Scottish (and thence British) succession. At the same time, the prospect of renewed war would put fresh strain on Scotland's relation to England. Though formally independent, with an active Parliament, Scotland since 1689 had been required to supply men for William's armies, and to contribute to their financing, while having no separate voice in the conduct of war and policy. The potential conflict of interest burst into the open in 1698, when the Scots attempted to plant a colony on Spanish territory at Darien in central America. English trading interests were alarmed, and English ministers quickly persuaded the king to take their part against his Scottish subjects: the Spanish were not discouraged from recapturing the territory, and the Scots were taught the lesson that their kingdom was the subordinate partner in the monarchy. The Scots could be in no doubt that a renewal of war over the Spanish succession would reinforce the primacy of English interests in policy-making.

In the event, Charles II settled the Spanish succession himself. Provoked by the powers' presumption in agreeing to partition his monarchy, he willed it entire to Louis XIV's grandson, Philip duke of Anjou, before dying at last in 1700. Louis promptly accepted the will and renounced the partition treaty: Anjou became Philip V of Castile and ruler by the appropriate titles of all the territories of Charles II. As soon as the news reached Naples the viceroy, the duke of Medina Coeli, proclaimed Philip as king, taking precautions to ensure that the announcement passed without protest. Despite these, a noble conspiracy on behalf of an Austrian claimant followed within a year: only after the revolt's suppression did the Bourbon monarchy seem secure in Naples. For their part, William and the emperor temporised; not until 1702 did England formally declare war on France, in the name of 'the balance of Europe'. During the interval, however, the tension within the British monarchy itself had intensified. It was now clear that the British kingdoms faced a succession problem the mirror image of the Spanish: it was extremely unlikely that Anne, who succeeded William as queen in 1702, would herself have heirs. Shortly before William's death the English Parliament passed an Act of Settlement (1701) determining that in the absence of such heirs the succession would pass to the house of Hanover. An English Act could not settle the Scottish succession; but it was plain that the Scots were expected to follow suit, and William instigated negotiations for a formal union which would ensure this. By 1702, therefore, the Scots were under mounting pressure to accept that the existing, purely dynastic, union of the two kingdoms would have to be reconstructed.

Well before then, however, intelligent observers in both Naples and Scotland had recognised that the turn of events since the late 1690s required them urgently to reconsider the future of the two countries, and to think through the options which might be available. Precedent for such a debate had been created in Naples by the manuscript tracts circulated during the atheists' affair earlier in the 1690s, while in Scotland the development of local publishing facilitated a genuinely public discussion of the issues. Since with the exception of one suggestive but fictitious connection, the debates proceeded quite separately, they will be examined accordingly. The Neapolitan debate was in two parts, the first in response to the Spanish succession crisis and its immediate outcome, the second following the capture of Naples by the Austrians on behalf of Archduke Charles in 1707. In Scotland debate began in earnest in the critical summer of 1698, and continued until the Act of Union was finalised in 1707: it is conveniently studied between the two stages of the Neapolitan debate. The separateness of the debates, however, does not undermine their comparability. As we shall see, the debates display certain striking similarities. In both cases the lead was taken by individuals who commanded the respect of contemporaries, and whose interventions shaped the course of subsequent discussion. The debates also drew on very similar conceptual resources, and shared a common analytical preoccupation, with the 'provincial' status to which the two kingdoms had been reduced. Above all, it was in the course of these debates that Neapolitans and Scots came to grips intellectually with the distinct but in vital respects similar predicaments of their kingdoms, and, in the Neapolitan case, began to draw more general conclusions for the study of *la vita civile*, or political and social life.

THE SPANISH SUCCESSION IN NAPLES: FRANCESCO D'ANDREA

The leading commentator on the predicament of Naples in the face of the Spanish succession crisis was Francesco d'Andrea. Advocate, jurist, and until recently holder of high ministerial office, d'Andrea (as we have seen) had been a leading member of the Investiganti, and was closely associated with Valletta in the defence of atomism and Epicureanism following the trial of the 'atheists'. He had also early recognised the danger which French ambitions might present to the outlying territories of the Spanish monarchy. In response to Louis XIV's very first predatory gambit, his claim to Flanders by right of 'devolution' to his wife, d'Andrea had written a *Risposta al trattato delle ragioni della Regina Cristianissima, sopra il Ducato del Brabante, et altri stati della Fiandra* (1667). Produced initially as a memorandum for Charles II, this was developed by d'Andrea into a full-length treatise rebutting the French claim. Setting aside the case against Louis as an aspiring universal monarch as 'something already too well known', he had concentrated on the juridical basis of the French claim: against it he had marshalled both historical evidence and the new jurisprudence of the Protestant Hugo Grotius. The *Risposta* was published again in 1676, with new material, in response to French intervention in Spanish territory much closer to Naples, in support of the revolt of Messina in 1672. By its success it established d'Andrea's reputation, within and beyond Naples: Giannone remembered 'the incomparable treatise on the succession of Brabant' as a model of modern jurisprudential reasoning.[1]

When d'Andrea returned to the problem of French ambition and the future of the Spanish monarchy in the 1690s, however, there was a marked change in the terms of his analysis. He now approached the problem in the language of 'interests'. A first attempt in this vein appears to have been the manuscript 'Discorso politico circa lo stato presente dell'Europa', dated March 1695, which explored the 'interests' of the various parties to the present war, including France, the emperor, Holland, England, and even Scotland, to explain why the allies did not desire a peace with the French.[2] A much fuller analysis in these terms followed in the 'Discorso politico

---

[1] Francesco d'Andrea, *Risposta al trattato delle ragioni della Regina Cristianissima, sopra il Ducato di Brabante, et altri stati della Fiandra. Nella quale si dimostra l'ingiustizia della guerra mossa dal Re di Francia, per la conquista di quelle provincie; non ostante le ragioni, che si son pubblicate in suo nome, per la pretesa successione a favor della Regina Cristianissima* (Naples, 1667; 2nd edn. 1676), 'L'informazione al lettore'. Pietro Giannone, *Vita scritta da lui medesimo*, in *Opere di Pietro Giannone*, ed. Sergio Bertelli and Giuseppe Ricuperati (Milan and Naples, 1971), p. 44: 'l'incomparabile trattato Sopra la successione del Brabante'.

[2] 'Discorso politico circa lo stato presente dell'Europa, e delle vere ragioni, per le quale i Prencipi collegati non desiderano la pace col Re di Francia, 1695, nel mese di Marzo', Biblioteca Oratoriana dei

intorno alla futura successione della monarchia di Spagna', which d'Andrea composed in 1697–8. The work survives in several manuscripts, and was presumably intended for circulation in this form.[3] In a sophisticated exposé of the issues, d'Andrea pointed to the difficulty of persuading any of the leading contenders – the prince of Bavaria, France and the emperor – to accept the success of another. Even if these were compensated by exchanges of territory, the 'interests' of the Spanish themselves had to be taken into account. Characterising the form of government in the monarchy as an *aristomanzia*, or 'aristocracy in effect', d'Andrea observed that the Castilian high nobility were accustomed to having a king who was amenable to direction by his council. He thought it likely that they would prefer a second grandson of Louis XIV to the second son of the emperor, because this would avoid war with France, while keeping the Spanish monarchy formally separate. D'Andrea was careful to state no preference of his own; but he did observe that a union of the French and Spanish monarchies was 'the road towards making one Monarchy in Europe, greater than the Roman'.[4] By contrast, an imperial succession might create a monarchy greater than that of Charlemagne, but since the French monarchy would remain separate and hostile, no single monarchy would dominate over all others. An imperial succession to the Spanish monarchy would have the further advantage of being welcomed in Italy. The emperor would be 'Imperatore Romano' in effect as well as in name, with an Italian-speaking court; and leading Italian princely and noble families could expect to become imperial princes, and even, in the cases of Savoy and Tuscany, electors.[5] D'Andrea did not explicitly mention the kingdom of Naples in this analysis; but he might well be read as implying that it would have a central place in such a reconstituted Italian Habsburg 'empire'.

Summarised thus, d'Andrea's 'Discorsi' may come across simply as acute pieces of political commentary, of no general intellectual significance. But there was more to his analysis conceptually than meets the eye. There was indeed little evidence of the Grotian jurisprudence which had distinguished the *Risposta* of 1667. But the language of the two 'Discorsi' had its own

---

Girolamini, Codice Cart. xv, op. 13, ff. 120–9, read on microfilm 28.3.28. The attribution to d'Andrea is made by Salvo Mastellone, *Francesco d'Andrea politico e giurista 1648–1698. L'acesa del ceto civile* (Florence, 1969), p. 153.

[3] It is printed as an appendix in Mastellone, *Francesco d'Andrea politico e giurista*, pp. 183–99 (and will be referred to in this version); other mss are discussed by Mastellone in ibid., p. 155, as is the version published (but attributed to another) in 1720.

[4] 'Discorso politico intorno alla futura successione', in Mastellone, *Francesco d'Andrea*, pp. 184–96, quotation on p. 196.

[5] Ibid., pp. 196–8.

intellectual pedigree, in the related analytical idioms of 'reason of state' and 'universal monarchy'. These were the idioms in which students of politics in the sixteenth and seventeenth centuries understood the actual conduct of government, and relations between the monarchies and republics of the Christian world.

The doctrine of reason of state was first effectively formulated – and named – by the Piedmontese Giovanni Botero, in his *Della Ragion di Stato* (1589); but he was only one of several Italians thinking along similar lines in the second half of the sixteenth century. Their starting point was a conviction that an understanding of politics required more than knowledge of the forms of government, and the moral qualities appropriate to them, as Aristotle had suggested; the advice given to princes could not be limited to the injunction to follow the moral virtues. Instead, Botero and others argued, rulers must add to virtue the ability to harness the resources of their peoples and territories, the better to secure and enhance their own power. They should concern themselves with their population, to ensure sufficient manpower; with the natural and material resources of their territories – minerals, but also tradeable goods; and above all with taxation and credit, since money was now the sinews of war and the prerequisite of status. In thinking in terms of resources, human, material, and financial, the reason of state theorists brought political theory closer to economics than ever before (closer, in practical terms, than Aristotle's analysis of exchange as a household activity had allowed). But they stopped short of the analysis of economic activity in its own right, and for its own sake: thus the doctrine of reason of state is not helpfully thought of as an early form of political economy. The 'reason' for maximising resources was strictly the enhancement of the 'state' of the ruler.[6]

Although Botero coined its name, there was an important sense in which the true author of this idiom of political analysis was another Italian, from the very beginning of the sixteenth century, Niccolò Machiavelli. It was Machiavelli who had made the point, with devastating clarity, that politics was not chiefly about forms of government, and certainly not about the practice of the 'virtues', Aristotelian or Ciceronian. The measure of politics, rather, was the effectiveness of those who ruled in mobilising the *virtù* – the public spirit – of subjects in order to maintain the state (*mantenere lo stato*) and to win worldly glory. Machiavelli, it is true, had been little concerned with the harnessing of resources: his *virtù* was moral not material. But his sceptical insight that politics necessarily involved a conflict of interests, and

---

[6] Richard Tuck, *Philosophy and Government 1572–1651* (Cambridge, 1993), pp. 65–9.

that the ruler must seek to identify and direct the interests which would advance his state, was the foundation on which the reason of state doctrine was constructed.

Despite this, the reason of state theorists themselves were at some pains to distance themselves from Machiavelli. There were two reasons for disguising their debt. One was Machiavelli's reputation for impiety, and in particular for hostility to the papacy. Within the Roman Catholic world, therefore, reason of state theorists presented themselves as 'anti-Machiavellians', and covered their tracks by associating their common emphasis on interest and prudence with the classical historian Tacitus rather than with Machiavelli.[7] A second reason to distinguish themselves was Machiavelli's declared preference for states which actively pursued a policy of expansion, which were 'for empire' like ancient Rome rather than 'for preservation' like Sparta or Venice. Botero explicitly reversed this order of preference, putting 'conservation' before 'aggrandisement'. But here too the difference was less than it seemed: Botero was still thinking in terms of large-scale monarchy, and he and other reason of state theorists looked to the Spanish monarchy in particular to assume responsibility for the unity and defence of Christendom.[8]

With this commitment to large-scale monarchy, it is not surprising that reason of state theory became associated with the idea of 'universal monarchy'. This term was first used systematically of Charles V's great *Monarchia*, which embraced the Holy Roman empire, the Burgundian Netherlands, the Spanish kingdoms and the New World. After Charles's division of the monarchy in 1555 the term was used less literally, to capture what was assumed (not without reason) to be the ambition of his Spanish and imperial successors to re-establish the position of dominance he had seemed to enjoy. Used to evaluate the policy of a particular monarchy, the term was almost always pejorative: few kings had the confidence openly to avow an ambition to universal monarchy, and never for long. Even Philip II did so only in the 1580s, after his annexation of Portugal.[9] But the term was never simply polemical; it was also used analytically, to characterise the tendency of monarchies to seek to enlarge their territory and power at the expense

[7] Robert Bireley, *The Counter-Reformation Prince: Anti-Machiavellianism or Catholic Statecraft in Early Modern Europe* (Chapel Hill and London, 1990).

[8] For Machiavelli's opposition of 'una republica che voglia fare uno imperio' to 'una che le basti mantenersi', his *Discorsi sopra la prima deca di Tito Livio* (c. 1517), bk I, cap. v; for Botero's between 'il conservare' and 'l'aggrandire', *Della Ragion di Stato* (1589), also bk I, cap. v.

[9] Geoffrey Parker, 'David or Goliath? Philip II and his world in the 1580s', in Richard L. Kagan and Geoffrey Parker (eds.), *Spain, Europe and the Atlantic World: Essays in Honour of J. H. Elliott* (Cambridge, 1995), pp. 245–66.

of others, and to establish what would now be called 'hegemony' in international affairs. In this sense the term, though never used by Machiavelli, was a natural extension of the Machiavellian and reason of state analysis of the competitiveness of rulers, and of the constant temptation to expand.[10]

The most explicit linking of universal monarchy with reason of state had occurred in the work of a Neapolitan, whom we have already encountered as a radical anti-Aristotelian, Tommaso Campanella.[11] Among the first works he composed during his long imprisonment had been a treatise 'Della Monarchia di Spagna', in which he had instructed the king of Spain on the steps he must take if he was to fulfil the divine promise of a universal monarchy. Even by Campanella's extraordinary standards this was a work with an almost impossibly complex history. Composed in Italian, first published in German in 1620 and 1623, it only became generally available when published in Latin as *De Monarchia Hispanica* in 1640 (English translations followed in 1654 and 1660). But at some point the manuscript had been supplemented with material taken directly from Botero's *Della Ragion di Stato*. Further enlivened by Campanella's astrological predictions and neo-Platonist metaphysics, the resulting work was an intellectual farrago on a scale rarely matched in the history of political thought.[12] But it made for a vivid statement of the potency of the ideal of universal monarchy, which was to establish a lasting association between the ideal and the city of Naples.

It was an association which Francesco d'Andrea may well have wished to avoid, even in the 1690s when he preferred the circumlocution of a monarchy 'greater than the Roman'. But the writing of his own *Risposta al trattato* in 1667 had nonetheless coincided with a fresh round of debate over the prospects for universal monarchy, provoked by the ambitions of Louis XIV. Like Philip II in the 1580s, Louis XIV in the 1660s was so confident of his strength that he had encouraged his publicists openly to advance his claim to a universal monarchy. The most brazen had been Antoine Aubery, whose *Des Justes Pretentions du Roi sur l'Empire* (1667) had maintained the claim of the Most Christian King, not only to the Spanish

---

[10] Franz Bosbach, *Monarchia Universalis. Ein politischer Leitbegriff der frühen Neuzeit* (Göttingen, 1988); with an English summary, 'The European debate on Universal Monarchy', in David Armitage (ed.), *Theories of Empire 1450–1800* (Aldershot and Brookfield, Vt., 1998), pp. 81–98. Rodolfo de Matteo, 'Il mito della monarchia universale', in his *Il pensiero politico Italiano nell'età della controriforma* (Milan and Naples, 1982), pp. 221–47.

[11] Above, p. 119.

[12] The complexity of the work's history has long baffled commentary. But see now John Headley, *Tommaso Campanella and the Transformation of the World* (Princeton, 1997), ch. VI. On the composition and publication of the work, L. Firpo, *Bibliografia degli scritti di Tommaso Campanella* (Turin, 1940), pp. 56–67.

succession, but to the empire as well, on the grounds that the king of France was the lineal heir of Charlemagne. So shameless was its reasoning that the work had promptly been reissued in a Latin abridgement by the imperial librarian, in order to alert the rest of Christendom to Louis' aims.[13] But the empire did not lack for its own publicists, and Aubery was countered in the same year by Franz von Lisola, in the *Bouclier d'Estat et de Justice. Contre le dessein manifestement decouverte de la Monarchie Universelle* (1667). In this widely cited work Lisola accused France of 'vast designs' of conquest, going far beyond the seizure of a few provinces, and including the goal of becoming 'the absolute mistress of commerce'. To this end the French would always work by the maxims of 'interest', seeking to divide their enemies in peace as well as in war. Lisola argued that the rulers of Europe must respond according to the maxims of both justice and interest. Unless the faith of treaties was upheld, nations would be reduced to the condition of lions and tigers; but it was equally necessary to maintain a 'balance' of interests in Europe between France and the house of Austria.[14]

There is good reason to suppose that the terms of this debate were familiar to later seventeenth-century Neapolitans. D'Andrea may have been keen to avoid association with Campanella, but he admired Lisola, confessing in 1676 that he might never have published the *Risposta al trattato* had he been aware of his work.[15] Three copies of the *Bouclier d'Estat* were listed in the catalogue of Valletta's library, and two of Aubery's *Justes Pretentions*. In addition the library contained several other contributions to the debate, including a manuscript translation of a work originally published in Strasbourg in 1686, 'Il vero interesse de principi cristiani opposto a'i falsi interessi, che da poco in qua' sono stati dati in luce'.[16] The manuscript itself survives in more than one copy, suggesting that it was regarded in Naples as a particularly helpful guide to the existing state of Europe. The argument of

---

[13] Antoine Aubery, *Des Justes Pretentions du Roi sur l'Empire* (Paris, 1667), and *Axiomata politica Gallicana* (1667), prepared by Peter Lambeck, the Prefect of the Imperial Library. On the relation between the two works: Franz Bosbach, 'Eine Französische Universalmonarchie? Deutsche Reaktionen auf die europäische Politik Ludwigs XIV', in Jochen Schlobach (ed.), *Vermittlungen. Aspekte der deutsch-französischen Beziehungen vom 17. Jahrhundert bis zur Gegenwart* (Berne, 1992), pp. 56–7.

[14] [Franz von Lisola], *Bouclier d'Estat et de Justice. Contre le dessein manifestement découvert de la Monarchie Universelle, sous le vain pretexte des pretentions de la Reyne de France* (1667); on which also Bosbach, 'Eine französische Universalmonarchie?', pp. 58–62.

[15] D'Andrea, *Risposta al trattato*, 'L'informazione al lettore'.

[16] Biblioteca Oratoriana dei Girolamini, 'Antico Catalogo', Segn. 27.1.10, ff. 217v, 219r, 224v (*Bouclier*); 204v, 208r (*Justes Pretentions*); other tracts on ff. 219r, 224v, 225r, 229v; and *Libri manuscripti*, f. 242r ('Il vero interesse'). The French original of the last was published as *Le vrai interêt des princes chrestiens opposé aux faux interêts qui ont été depuis mis en lumière* (Strasbourg, 1686).

the tract (which may have been of Huguenot authorship) was straightforward. Louis' ambition to 'universal monarchy', and hence his designs upon the Spanish succession, were clear from all his actions: both the papacy and the empire could expect to be reduced to a state of subordination unless they put their common 'interests' with the Dutch and English before their confessional differences, and allied to insist upon French renunciation of the Spanish crowns.[17]

It was in the same terms (albeit with a less pejorative synonym for 'universal monarchy') that d'Andrea framed his analyses of the Spanish succession issue in the 1690s. That the neo-Machiavellian idiom of 'interests' should appeal to Neapolitans is quite consistent with what we have already seen of the intellectual world of the city at the turn of the century: in d'Andrea's case it accorded with the sceptical, Epicurean views which he espoused in natural and moral philosophy. But d'Andrea's use of the idiom was only a beginning. The scope of his analysis was limited to the issue of the succession; although he had earlier written, in a juristic vein, on internal problems of the kingdom, he did not now embark on a neo-Machiavellian analysis of its condition. It was not until after Charles II's death in 1700 that others were to take up that challenge.

Before then the debate over the succession had also involved the Accademia Medina Coeli. Apparently alarmed by French pretensions, the viceroy himself commissioned members of his academy to prepare replies. Among the collected papers of the academy are two attributed to the Abate Magnati, rejecting French claims to the kingdoms of Naples and Sicily and to the papal enclave of Avignon. Another two, by Serafino Biscardi and Niccolò Capasso, were vigorous refutations of the traditional claim of the papacy to grant the kingdom by investiture.[18] Since this claim did not have

---

[17] 'Il vero interesse de principi cristiani opposto a'i falsi interessi, che da poco in qua' sono stati dati in luce. Trattato che rappresenta al vivo l'interesse, che hanno li principi cristiani d'opporsi alle pretensioni d'un re, che vorebbe rendersi soggetti tutti li stati dell'Europa', Biblioteca Nazionale di Napoli, Ms XI.c.25, ff.: 1–23; esp. ff. 6r–7v on the behaviour of the French king as a universal monarch. Another copy (probably Valletta's), in the Biblioteca Oratoriana dei Girolamini, Cod. CXXXVII, Misc. Div. no. 10 (Microfilm Segn. 28.4.3).

[18] 'Delle Lezione Accademiche', parte III, Biblioteca Nazionale di Napoli, Ms XIII.B.73, ff. 132–50: 'Risposta a un libro fatto dare in luce dal Re di Francia sopra li diritti, che pretende avere sopra molti reami, e stati, & in particolare di Napoli e Sicilia, dell'Abate Magnati'; ff. 155–66: 'Intorno alle pretensioni, che il Re di Francia pretende avere sopra la Contea d'Avignone, dell'Abate Magnati'; ff. 167–70: 'Ragioni per l'Investitura del Regno di Napoli, che si devono stendere in scrittura formata . . . Serafino Biscardi autore'; ff. 171–2: 'Circa l'Investitura sopradetta . . . D. Niccolò Capasso'. The origin and authorship of the *lezioni* attributed to the Abate Magnati are, however, unclear. The 'Risposta a un libro' carries the date 22 November 1682; and other copies of the work are to be found in Ms XI.C.25 ff. 174–97, and in the Società Napoletana per la Storia Patria, Ms XX.A.18 ff. 95–109, where it is marked as 'di Fran.co d'Andrea' and dated 22 October 1692.

a direct bearing on the outcome of the Spanish succession, it could be discussed with fewer inhibitions than the rival claims of the French and the Austrian Habsburgs. Even so, the firmness with which the academicians reasserted the historical autonomy of the kingdom was suggestive: it seems likely that d'Andrea's fears for that autonomy if the kingdom were to pass into French hands were widely shared within the Neapolitan intellectual community.

It was in this climate of opinion, which he had fostered, that Medina Coeli found himself obliged to proclaim the succession of the Bourbon Philip V in 1700. Few can have been surprised by the conspiracy on behalf of the Austrian interest a year later. Even so, it was the nobility of the *seggi*, led by the prince of Macchia, who took the initiative and framed the conspiracy's programme. The Archduke Charles was to come to Naples to rule in person; civil, military, and ecclesiastical offices were to be restricted to *regnicoli* (subjects of the kingdom); the Inquisition was to be banned and the Parliament restored; and the tariffs which restricted exports (and the profits of great landowners) were to be lifted. As a diagnosis of the needs of the kingdom this was wholly one sided, and the conspiracy attracted very little support (even from the Austrians) before its suppression. But the very attempt to identify the problems to be addressed was significant; the most valuable legacy of the Macchia conspiracy was the debate which began in its wake.[19]

From the safety of exile, several of the conspirators attempted to justify their action by reference to the plight of the kingdom under continuing Spanish rule. In a letter from Vienna dated September 1701, one of the noble conspirators, the duke of Telese, wrote that their object had been to give Naples its own king, and thus 'to liberate the kingdom from the not less ignominious than miserable condition of a province'. The long years of Spanish rule, he argued, had debilitated the kingdom, because the Spanish had divided the people from the nobility, impeded commerce, and impoverished everyone. The special pleading of a feudal noble was barely disguised; but the main line of the analysis, that the kingdom had been reduced to a province, was soon picked up and elaborated by others less identified with noble interests.[20]

---

[19] Salvo Mastellone, 'La congiura di Macchia (1701)', in F. M. de Robertis and M. Spagnoletti (eds.), *Atti del congresso internazionale di studi sull'età del viceregno* (Bari, 1977), vol. II, pp. 39–48.

[20] 'Copia di lettera scritta da D. Bartolomeo Ceva Grimaldi Duca di Telese ad un suo amico a Napoli, Vienna lo sc'mbre 1701', Società Napoletana di Storia Patria, Ms xxvii.c.10 ff. 121–31, quotation at 124r–v: 'di liberare il Regno dalla non meno ignominiosa, che miserabil condizione di Provincia'. On the author and this work, R. Colapietra, *Vita pubblica e classi politiche nel Viceregno napoletano 1656–1734* (Rome, 1961), pp. 11, 138, 152–4.

A fuller justification was forthcoming from one of the few non-noble conspirators, the *togato* Saverio Pansuti, in a 'Discorso intorno alla successione della Monarchia di Spagna dopo la morte di Carlo II', thought to have been written in Vienna in 1704. Pansuti renewed the charge that the Bourbon acquisition of the Spanish monarchy was part of Louis XIV's strategy to secure a universal monarchy in Europe. To this end, Louis had deceived the dying Charles II into accepting Philip of Anjou as his sole heir, on the specious ground that this was the only way to preserve the unity of the monarchy. But Pansuti also believed that Louis had wished to gain the kingdom of Naples in particular on account of its natural wealth – its fertile fields, its minerals, its estimable wines, its innumerable flocks, its industrious and warlike people, and above all its capital city, which had offered the Spanish 'a perpetual stage for the glorification of their power'. If the kingdom were now to fall into the hands of France, it would inevitably become an 'ignominious province'. Repeating the phrase used by the duke of Telese, Pansuti linked the condition of a province directly to the exploitation of what he believed to be the kingdom's abundant natural resources.[21]

Faced with such criticism, the Bourbon monarchy encouraged or commissioned responses on its behalf. Quickly adjusting to the new regime, Biscardi contributed an *Epistola pro Augusto Hispaniarum Monarcha Philippo Quinto*, in which he defended Philip V's right of succession under Spanish, Roman, and Neapolitan law, with supporting reference to the authority of Cujas, Hobbes, Grotius, and Pufendorf.[22] In the neo-Machiavellian idiom, the anonymous author of a set of 'Reflections' on the interests of the powers of Europe in the Spanish succession dismissed the accusation that Louis XIV sought a universal monarchy as a 'specious pretext'. There was little prospect of the monarchies of France and Spain being united, he argued, since 'reason of state' would lead the Spanish ruler to preserve the integrity of his monarchy. The king of France was best placed, however, to assist the Spanish kingdoms to counter the commercial ambitions of the English and the Dutch, whose goal was the dismemberment of the monarchy.[23]

[21] 'Discorso interno alla successione della Monarchia di Spagna dopo la morte de Carlo II, del Consiglier Conte Saverio Pansuti', Biblioteca Nazionale di Napoli, Ms x.F.72 ff. 1–44; quotations on ff. 28r–v: 'un perpetuo teatro della lor gloria della lor potenza'; 'il tutto fusse poi divenuto inevitabilmente sua ignominiosa provincia'.

[22] Serafino Biscardi, *Epistola pro Augusto Hispaniarum Monarcha Philippo Quinto qua & jus ei assertum successionis universae Monarchiae, & omnia confutantur, quae pro Investitura Regni Napoletani & pro coeteris Regnis a Germanis scripta sunt* (Naples, 1703); also Seraphini Biscardi, *Oratio . . . in Die naturali Philippi V Potentissimi, Invictissimique Hispaniarum Monarchae* (Naples, 1705).

[23] 'Riflessioni sopra li differenti interessi che la maggior parte delle potenze d'Europa hanno nel presente stato della monarchia di Spagna', Società Napoletana di Storia Patria, Ms xxvi.D.10 ff. 728–55; quotation on f. 733: 'il pretesto specioso della monarchia universale'.

The best-known defence of the Bourbon succession, however, was that commissioned from Giambattista Vico, in the form of an official history of the Macchia conspiracy. In the event, the 'Principum neapolitanorum coniurationis historia' which Vico composed in 1703 was not quite what the viceroy was looking for, and was not sanctioned for publication. This may have been because Vico was too frank about the extent of Louis XIV's ambitions: by allowing the Spanish monarchy to pass to one of his own lineage, Vico observed, Louis XIV had converted the greatest monarchy in the world into a 'colony' of the house of Bourbon. But Vico's strongest invective was reserved for the noble leaders of the conspiracy, whom he accused of seeking only to advance their own interests, at the expense of those beneath them. Vico might concede that there was, as Telese and Pansuti had contended, a real danger of the kingdom being reduced to colonial or provincial status (along with the rest of the Spanish monarchy); but it was quite mistaken to believe that restoring power to the feudal nobility would relieve the danger. On the contrary, Vico implied, the condition of the kingdom, within a Bourbon no less than a Habsburg monarchy, required magistrates and *letterati* to take the lead in reform.[24]

The suppression of Vico's history appears to have signalled the end of debate on the condition of the kingdom for the remainder of the (short) period of Bourbon monarchy. Already, however, the key terms for an analysis of its predicament had been identified. When debate began again after the Austrian takeover in 1707, the question of what it meant to have been reduced to a 'province' would be at the forefront of Neapolitan minds.

SCOTLAND BETWEEN DARIEN AND UNION: ANDREW FLETCHER

The first thing to be encountered on turning to Scotland is another 'Neapolitan' contribution to the debate over the Spanish succession: the *Discorso delle cose di Spagna scritto nel mese di Luglio 1698*, written throughout in Italian, with a title page indicating that it was published at 'Napoli' in the same year. In fact both its language and its place of publication were conceits: the pamphlet was the work of a Scotsman, Andrew Fletcher, and was almost certainly published by him in Edinburgh.[25] But why should a Scot wish to comment on the affairs of Spain as if from Naples?

---

[24] Giambattista Vico, 'Principum neapolitanorum coniurationis anni MDCCI historia', edited with a translation by Claudia Pandolfi, *La Congiura dei principi napoletani 1701* (Naples, 1992). On which, Giuseppe Giarrizzo, *Vico, la politica e la storia* (Naples, 1981), pp. 63–5.

[25] The *Discorso delle cose di Spagna* was issued separately in 1698, and reprinted in Andrew Fletcher, *The Political Works* (London, 1732; 1737), ed. John Robertson (Cambridge, 1997). On its place of publication, R. A. Scott Macfie, 'A Bibliography of Andrew Fletcher of Saltoun', *Publications of the*

The answer lies in the eccentric intelligence of Andrew Fletcher, the ablest and most learned of the contributors to the debate on the condition of Scotland between 1698 and 1704. Born in 1653, the son of Sir Robert Fletcher, Gilbert Burnet's model of undogmatic piety, Andrew Fletcher succeeded his father in 1665 as the laird of Saltoun, an estate in East Lothian, south-east of Edinburgh. Fletcher published no more than five pamphlets and a collection of speeches, all between 1697 and 1704, which when later collected formed one slim volume of *Political Works* (1732): his intelligence was economically expressed. But if his learning was lightly borne, it was nonetheless extensive, being derived from a lifetime of travel, and from the great library he acquired while travelling. Fletcher's travels had begun in his teens, when after a year at college at St Andrews he left Scotland for London and the continent in 1668, apparently not returning until 1678. He was away again in the 1680s, this time as a political exile, and was condemned for treason after participating in Monmouth's revolt in 1685. Even after the Revolution of 1689 had made it possible for him to return and live in Scotland, Fletcher was often abroad, seeking company and books in the chocolate houses and sale rooms of London, Paris, and the Netherlands. But it is likely to have been an earlier, rather different experience, of travelling incognito through Spain as a fugitive after he had abandoned Monmouth's expedition, which lay behind Fletcher's interest in that country's affairs, and inspired the *Discorso* of 1698.[26]

Even so, Fletcher's travels are not known to have taken him to Naples (unless he was the Scot who called on Valletta in 1686, in a group of three 'very literary men', one of whom was a great friend of Gilbert Burnet).[27] It was probably not personal experience, therefore, which prompted Fletcher to write about the Spanish monarchy as if he were a Neapolitan. For clues to explain this, we have to rely on the content of the *Discorso* itself. The pamphlet purported to be a dispassionate account of the present state of the Spanish monarchy, and of the prospects of the various claimants to its succession. The precipitous decline of the monarchy, it suggested, was the result of its kings' continued reliance on 'fortune', to the neglect of its real

---

Edinburgh Bibliographical Society, vol. IV (1901), pp. 117–18. The *Discorso* is translated as 'A Discourse concerning the Affairs of Spain' in Andrew Fletcher, *Political Works*; subsequent references to it, and to Fletcher's other writings, will be to this edition.

[26] Fletcher's known movements are outlined in the 'introduction' and 'Chronology of Fletcher's life', in *Political Works*, pp. xii–xv, xxxi–xxxiv. See also the entry in the new *Oxford Dictionary of National Biography*.

[27] Valletta to Magliabecchi, Naples, 20 May 1686, *Lettere dal Regno ad Antonio Magliabecchi*, no. 874, p. 1080. The 'tre litteratissimi' were 'uno scozese, uno svezese e l'altro inglese'. Fletcher knew Burnet through the latter's period as the minister of Saltoun Kirk between 1665 and 1669.

strengths. At the head of these was the incomparable advantage of its situation, between the Mediterranean and Atlantic seas; other strengths should have been its agriculture, industry, and commerce, and above all its population, which had been wasted by religious intolerance and the demands of the Indies. A change of succession, however, created an opportunity for a new prince (*un prencipe nuovo*) to reform (*riordinare*) the government by the establishment of good orders (*lo stabilire buoni ordini*). These would be headed by toleration, which by repopulating the Spanish kingdoms would in turn encourage agriculture, the mechanical arts, commerce, and navigation.

The *Discorso* also reviewed the prospects of the various pretenders to the succession. Casting the net wide, Fletcher considered not only the likely Austrian and French claimants, but lesser candidates such as the king of Portugal and the duke of Savoy; briefly he even alluded to the possibility of 'private' candidates (*privati*), offering as an example the viceroy of Naples, the duke of Medina Coeli. As he did so, Fletcher carefully considered the redistributions of territory, especially in Italy and Flanders, which would be needed to render any particular succession secure. His object, he frequently confided to his readers, was no less than to enable the new ruler of the Spanish monarchy to realise at last, without others being aware of it, the promise of a universal monarchy (*monarchia universale*) or the empire of the world (*l'imperio del mondo*).[28]

For those who could read it, the *Discorso delle cose di Spagna* offered a perceptive analysis of both the reasons for the monarchy's decline and the possible outcomes of its succession crisis. Few of these readers, moreover, are likely to have been taken in by its professed intention to facilitate the achievement of universal monarchy. (Though just in case any should still wonder, Fletcher subsequently prefixed an 'Avviso' to the pamphlet, avowing that its real purpose was to expose the danger of universal monarchy.)[29] Rather more knowledge would be required to appreciate why Fletcher adopted the esoteric devices of writing in Italian and identifying Naples as the place of publication. But here too a reader versed in the idioms of political thought outlined earlier in the chapter would have recognised the allusions. The language, at least, could hardly be mistaken. Not only

---

[28] Fletcher, 'A Discourse concerning the Affairs of Spain', *Political Works*, pp. 84–117.

[29] Fletcher, 'A Discourse', *Political Works*, p. 84, 'Advertisement'. The London Commonwealthman Walter Moyle countered irony with irony, drily asking a friend to 'tell Fletcher it was with tears in my eyes that I read the account of his apostasy; is it possible that such a surly Patriot, who all his life long had talked, writ and rebelled for Liberty, should all of a sudden turn Projector for a Universal Monarchy?', to Anthony Hammond, 26 January 1699, in Walter Moyle, *The Whole Works* (London, 1727), p. 243. (I owe this reference to Mark Goldie.)

did Fletcher twice quote Machiavelli, but his use of the terms *prencipe nuovo, riordinare* and *buoni ordini*, among many others, was transparently Machiavellian. As for the attribution of place of publication to Naples, the likely allusion was to the most notorious exponent of the ideal of universal monarchy, Campanella, whose *De Monarchia Hispanica* Fletcher possessed in his library.[30] But it is also possible that Fletcher wanted his readers to learn a more contemporary lesson: that a Neapolitan vantage point from which to discuss the affairs of Spain was comparable with a Scottish viewpoint on the monarchy of Britain.

The possibility of such an allusion is reinforced by the coincidence of the *Discorso*'s composition with the departure in July 1698 of the first Scottish expedition to Darien. As David Armitage has pointed out, at least one of the *Discorso*'s observations could well have been a direct comment on the Darien venture. When Fletcher remarked on the strategic and commercial importance of the Straits of Gibraltar to the Spanish monarchy, there was an obvious parallel with the isthmus of Darien, situated close to the narrowest stretch of land between the Atlantic and Pacific oceans (and later the site of the Panama canal).[31] The critical difference was that the Scots were not in the potentially commanding position of the Spanish monarchy; their object in the Darien venture was to break up rather than to take over the monopoly which the Spanish had asserted over trade with the Americas. In a world of would-be universal monarchs, the world which Fletcher parodied in the *Discorso di Spagna*, smaller, outlying kingdoms such as Scotland (or Naples) must find a way of developing their trade in competition with the established maritime powers. As Fletcher observed of his own country in the first of the *Two Discourses concerning the Affairs of Scotland*, written like the *Discorso* in the summer of 1698,

this nation, of all those who possess good ports, and lie conveniently for trade and fishing, has been the only part of Europe which did not apply itself to commerce.[32]

The Darien venture, to which Fletcher was giving his backing, was an attempt to remedy that neglect by a single, bold stroke; as such, as we have

---

[30] National Library of Scotland, Ms 17863 f. 59v; *Bibliotheca Fletcheriana: or the Extraordinary Library of Andrew Fletcher of Saltoun, Reconstructed and Systematically Arranged*, comp. and ed. Peter Willems (Wassenaar, 1999), p. 49.

[31] Fletcher, 'A Discourse of Spain', *Political Works*, pp. 87–8; David Armitage, 'The Scottish vision of empire: intellectual origins of the Darien venture', in John Robertson (ed.), *A Union for Empire: Political Thought and the British Union of 1707* (Cambridge, 1995), pp. 107–9.

[32] Andrew Fletcher, *Two Discourses concerning the Affairs of Scotland; written in the year 1698* (Edinburgh, 1698), in *Political Works*, p. 38.

seen, it aroused widespread enthusiasm within Scotland, Fletcher himself subscribing £1,000 at the first opportunity.[33]

By contrast, the venture was fiercely opposed by English merchants, who persuaded the king to do nothing to assist the beleaguered Scottish colony when the Spanish reclaimed their territory. Powerful vested interests were at stake, not least those of the East India Company; but their hostility to the Scottish venture also reflected an assumption of the primacy of English interests within the British monarchy. Such an assumption was elaborated by numerous English political and economic commentators at the time, with arguments which provide further reason for suggesting that Fletcher may have associated the Neapolitan and Scottish points of view.

Ever since Louis XIV's invasion of the United Provinces in 1672, English observers had denounced what they took to be his ambition of universal monarchy.[34] The accusation had been a powerful strand in the mounting criticism of James II, who was believed to be Louis' dependent ally; and it continued to be heard throughout the 1690s, gaining a fresh lease of life with the Spanish succession crisis. The two most sophisticated exponents of the danger at the turn of the century were Daniel Defoe and Charles Davenant. Both were convinced that the pursuit of universal monarchy was inherent in the rivalry of states: as Defoe put it, 'every king in the world would be the universal monarch if he might'. But what particularly exercised them about the threat of a union between the French and the Spanish monarchies was that the English, along with the Dutch, might lose 'their empire of the seas', to the grave damage of their trade. A great monarchy, Davenant explained, like a great city within a kingdom, will draw all trade to the kingdom at its centre.[35] As general propositions, these were very much in line with Fletcher's own thinking. But Davenant in particular made it quite clear that England's response to the French threat must be to assert its own commercial interest at the expense of any potential rival, including its partners within the British monarchy. By this he had in mind particularly the Irish, whose woollen industry threatened to undercut England's through cheaper labour costs. It was 'a reasonable jealousy of state'

---

[33] Above, p. 91.
[34] Steven Pincus, 'The English debate over universal monarchy', in Robertson, *A Union for Empire*, pp. 37–62.
[35] [Daniel Defoe], *The Interests of the several Princes and States of Europe consider'd, with respect to the Succession to the Crown of Spain* (London, 1698), esp. pp. 22–9; and *The two Great Questions consider'd: 1. What the French King will do, with respect to the Spanish Monarchy, 11. What measures the English ought to take* (London, 1700), quotation on p. 15; Charles Davenant, *An Essay upon Universal Monarchy* (1701), in his *The Political and Commercial Works*, coll. and rev. Sir Charles Whitworth, 5 vols. (London, 1771), IV, pp. 1–41, esp. pp. 33–4.

to bar the import of Irish woollens to England. Davenant admitted that Scotland was not in the same case as Ireland: being a 'distinct state', it was allied with, not subordinated to, the realm of England. But he foresaw ill consequences of the 'Scotch act' authorising the Darien venture, 'which ought to make us very watchful over what our neighbours do'.[36] The Scots, in other words, must expect no support from the English to develop their own trade; where their efforts to do so interfered with England's 'empire' of the sea, it would be consistent with reason of state to obstruct them.

Later, in the *Account of a Conversation* (1704), Fletcher would tackle such anglocentric reasoning head on. But his suspicions were evident in a short work which belongs to this earlier round of debate, *A Speech upon the State of the Nation, in April 1701*. There was a real danger, Fletcher argued, that William's reluctance to begin a new war against Louis XIV over the Spanish succession masked an ambition to bargain for the Spanish Netherlands, as his price for accepting a Bourbon monarch in Spain. And once William was the absolute ruler of all seventeen provinces of the Netherlands as well as the three British kingdoms, what would prevent him claiming 'the empire of the sea, with an entire monopoly of trade'?[37] The scenario might be improbable, but Fletcher's very ability to imagine it testifies to his inclination to view the problem of empire, or universal monarchy, from the vantage point of the subordinate kingdom – from Naples and from Scotland.

The failure of the Darien venture, obvious by 1700, made the Scots receptive to Fletcher's message. Angry commentators denounced the way in which English interests had prevailed on William to reverse his initial agreement, as king of Scotland, to the Act instituting the Africa Company and its project. Scotland's sovereignty had been 'trampled underfoot' declared one, probably Lord Belhaven, while George Ridpath protested that the affair had seen the greatest invasion of Scottish sovereignty and freedom since the time of Balliol.[38] Fletcher agreed, but knew that there were limits to the extent to which indignation was a prudent or sufficient

---

[36] Charles Davenant, *An Essay upon the probable methods of making a People gainers in the Balance of Trade* (1699), in *The Political and Commercial Works*, II, esp. pp. 248–54; for a thorough analysis of Davenant's thinking, see Istvan Hont, 'Free trade and the economic limits to national politics', in John Dunn (ed.), *The Economic Limits to Modern Politics* (Cambridge, 1990), pp. 57–95, reprinted in Istvan Hont, *The Jealousy of Trade: Nationalism, Global Competition, and the Wealth of Nations* (Cambridge, Mass., 2005), pp. 185–266.

[37] Andrew Fletcher, *A Speech upon the State of the Nation, in April 1701*, in *Political Works*, pp. 118–28, quotation on p. 128.

[38] [John, Lord Belhaven?], *A Defence of the Scots Settlement at Darien, with an answer to the Spanish memorial against it. And Arguments to prove, that it is the interest of England to join with the Scots, and protect it* (n.p., 1699), quoted phrase on p. 42; [George Ridpath], *Scotland's Grievances relating to Darien, humbly offered to the consideration of the Parliament* (n.p., 1700), pp. 1–27, the allusion being to Edward I of England's virtual imposition of John Balliol as king of Scotland in 1291–2.

response. Rather than give way to anglophobia, and provide the English with an excuse to break up their Parliament, the Scots should assert their interest by concentrating on issues such as the standing army which might bring them allies within the English Parliament.[39] Despite his mistrust of the English and their king, Fletcher continued to seek common ground: for example, the threat to both kingdoms represented by the growth of the standing army was open to a common solution through the institution of a militia.[40]

The implication that the remedy for a nation in the position of Scotland was not to renounce but to reform its relation with its more powerful partner was one accepted by commentators with very different views of what that relation should be. Overcoming his initial anger, the presbyterian George Ridpath envisaged a more equal and amicable alliance with England. In *The Great Reasons and Interests consider'd, anent the Spanish Monarchy* (1701), he urged the Scots not to succumb to the temptation to look to Louis XIV for help in regaining Darien. The French king's interest would only be to place the exiled Stuarts back on the thrones of Britain as his dependants, while depriving the English and the Scots of their trade. 'The ballance of power in Europe' required neighbours to ally to prevent one great power from achieving universal monarchy.[41] By contrast the young and articulate William Seton of Pitmedden, an Erastian episcopalian, thought that the best means to counter the French pursuit of 'the Empire of Europe' would be the union of Scotland and England into one monarchy. Devoting the second of three essays on *The Interest of Scotland* (1700) to the proposal, he argued that England had nothing to gain from reducing Scotland to 'a conquered province', since this would leave both vulnerable to rule by a standing army. A union of Parliaments, churches, and laws, under which both nations would enjoy the same privileges in trade, would be far more to the advantage of both kingdoms.[42]

By 1700–1, therefore, the Scots had accepted Fletcher's implied invitation to put themselves in the position of Neapolitans within the Spanish

---

[39] As in his letter to Lord Yester, 23 Sept. 1699, National Library of Scotland, Ms 7020 ff. 169–70, commenting on *A Defence of the Scots Settlement at Darien*; and in the short one-page tract, probably by Fletcher, 'A Letter from a Gentleman at London to his Friend at Edinburgh, October 13, 1700', printed and mss versions in the National Library of Scotland, the latter in Mss 17498, f. 72. Though not included in the *Political Works*, Fletcher's authorship is made likely by the presence of several copies of the tract in his library.

[40] As Fletcher had earlier argued in *A Discourse of Government with relation to Militia's* (Edinburgh, 1698), in *Political Works*, pp. 1–31.

[41] [George Ridpath], *The Great Reasons and Interests consider'd, anent the Spanish Monarchy* (n.p., 1701), esp. pp. 20–1, 36–40.

[42] [William Seton of Pitmedden], 'An Essay concerning the Union of England and Scotland into one Monarchy', *The Interest of Scotland in Three Essays* (1700; 2nd edn London, 1702), pp. 37–63, quoted phrases on pp. 56, 59.

monarchy. Commentators like Ridpath and Seton had begun to discuss their predicament in terms very similar if not identical to those being used in Naples. Like the Neapolitans, the Scots had discovered that in the modern world of would-be universal monarchies and maritime commerce, the prospect facing smaller kingdoms within greater monarchies was increasingly one of dependency – of reduction to the ignominious status of a 'province'. But the Scottish debate did not simply mirror the Neapolitan. By the early 1700s Scottish commentators were also engaged in a vigorous discussion of their country's economic condition, covering the improvement of agriculture, the promotion of trade, and the enlargement of credit; and from 1703 there was the further prospect of radical change in the kingdom's constitutional relation to England. The debates on these subjects made possible a fuller examination than any undertaken in Naples before 1707 of what it meant to be a 'province', and of how this condition might be transformed.

In the later seventeenth century, as we have seen, Scottish agriculture underwent a slow but definite process of change.[43] The two most prominent developments were the substitution of money rents for rents in kind and a reduction in multiple tenancies, the latter a trend encouraged by parliamentary legislation. Even if very few nobles and lairds yet counted themselves as 'improvers', the production of both grain and livestock was increasingly market oriented. The sudden, unexpected experience of a run of harvest failures in the mid-1690s thus came as a severe shock. The widespread hardship, and in some areas famine, with a consequent sharp increase in mortality and vagrancy, seemed to suggest that Scottish agriculture still lagged far behind that of its apparently prosperous southern neighbour. Though 1698 was in fact to be the last of these 'ill years', the coincidence of another harvest failure with the first expedition to Darien suggested an economy still acutely vulnerable to misfortune. As a result agriculture itself, and the social relations under which it was carried on, became the subject of direct public debate.

In this case too it was Andrew Fletcher who took the initiative, in the second of his *Two Discourses concerning the Affairs of Scotland* of 1698. He first addressed the most visible aspect of the crisis, the large numbers of poor and vagabonds forced onto the roads. Since the existing Poor Laws were unable to cope, Fletcher recommended that they be replaced by a regime under which the labouring poor and their families would become the property of individual masters, after the example of the domestic slaves

[43] Above, pp. 84–6.

of antiquity. Fletcher insisted that this was not slavery in the true, political sense of the term; masters would be responsible for maintaining their servants in return for owning their labour, and servants would be protected by law from physical abuse. In any case, vagabondage was a symptom, not the cause, of Scotland's 'present poverty and misery'. The 'principal and original source of our poverty', he argued, was the system of landholding, and in particular the practice of letting land at excessive rents, which discouraged investment. Fletcher's remedies for this were the general acceptance of money rents, combined with measures to limit the amount of land anyone could farm directly, and to channel investment to farmers who lacked capital of their own; a condition of these proposals, he acknowledged, would be that all tenures became 'allodial' or freehold. The proposals were complex, and it is by no means evident that their long-term outcome would be the extension of small- and medium-scale landownership, as Fletcher apparently intended. What is clear, nevertheless, is Fletcher's conviction that the root of the problem was the system of feudal tenure which enabled great landowners to manage their estates at the expense of both their tenants and, in the longer run, themselves.[44]

Not surprisingly, the severity of Fletcher's proposals won them few supporters. The dramatic proposal for a return to domestic slavery was regarded as eccentric; and the scheme for land reform was never pursued, though Fletcher apparently continued to try to refine and clarify it.[45] But his analysis of the reasons for the weakness of Scottish agriculture did command support, notably from William Seton, who likewise denounced the treatment of tenants by landowners, observing that 'we have learned that method of oppressing our peasants from the French'.[46] It is likely that Fletcher himself intended the proposals to make an analytical rather than a practical point. The terms in which he presented them suggest this. He openly avowed a classical inspiration for the proposal to institute a benevolent form of domestic servitude. It was by thus providing for their poor, and making every man useful to the commonwealth, that the ancients had been able to

---

[44] Andrew Fletcher, *Two Discourses concerning the Affairs of Scotland* (1698), 'The Second Discourse', *Political Works*, pp. 56–80. On the interpretation of his proposal for agriculture, see also Shigemi Muramatsu, 'Some types of national interest in the Anglo-Scottish Union of 1707: Scotland's responses to England's political arithmetic', *Journal of Economics of Kumamoto Gakuen University*, 3 (1996), pp. 6–7.

[45] See what are most probably his manuscript alterations to a copy of the *Two Discourses*, given in *Political Works*, pp. 76–80 and notes, 228–31.

[46] Seton, 'An Essay upon the Present State of Scotland', *The Interest of Scotland*, pp. 77–80, 88–9. Other contributions to the debate on agriculture and the responsibility of the landowners are discussed by Colin Kidd, *Subverting Scotland's Past: Scottish Whig Historians and the Creation of an Anglo-British Identity 1689–c.1830* (Cambridge, 1993), pp. 34–5.

build all those public works and monuments which had embellished their countries; wealth had been a public, not a private, good.[47] Though not made explicit, a similar inspiration can be identified for his projected reform of landownership. The elaborate proposals to ensure that the landowning class, now all freeholders, would not be divided by great inequalities of wealth amounted in effect to a form of agrarian law, of the kind which Machiavelli had regarded as the essential social foundation of the Roman republic, and which James Harrington would have instituted in the commonwealth of Oceana.[48] Unless limits were set to individual landownership, Fletcher agreed with Harrington, the emergence of inequalities would destroy the unity of the class of freeholders and subvert the clear distinction between freeholder and servant on which a stable social order depended. But by maintaining that distinction, a modern Agrarian Law would ensure the survival of the class of freeholders who made up the political community and served in the national militia.

Framed in these terms, Fletcher's analysis of the state of Scottish society, like his reflection upon the modern European political order, was recognisably neo-Machiavellian in character. It may still be thought that the impracticality of his own proposals reflects a forced, even archaic analysis of the problems. But the only other source of concepts for the analysis of a society of agrarian property-owners was the civil and feudal law; and little appears to have been done to develop their application to Scottish circumstances since the pioneering investigations of Sir Thomas Craig a century earlier. Still less analytical was the response to the crisis of the 1690s by the antiquaries and historians of the circle of Sir Robert Sibbald.[49] By his deliberate choice of the neo-Machiavellian, or in this case neo-Harringtonian, categories of freeholder and servant, Fletcher had offered a demonstration of how a critical analysis of Scottish landed society might be developed. In so doing, he opened up a major new line of enquiry within Scottish intellectual culture.[50]

---

[47] Fletcher, *Two Discourses, Political Works*, pp. 64–6.

[48] Machiavelli, *Discorsi Sopra Tito Livio*, I.xxxvii; James Harrington, *The Commonwealth of Oceana* (1656), in *The Political Works of James Harrington*, ed. J. G. A. Pocock (Cambridge, 1977), pp. 231–41.

[49] Sir Robert Sibbald's response to the harvest failures was a pamphlet, *Provision for the Poor in time of Dearth and Scarcity. Where there is an account of such food as may be easily gotten when corns are scarce, or unfit for use; and of such meats as may be used when the ordinary provisions fail, or are very dear. Written for the Relief of the Poor by R. S. Doctor of Medicine* (Edinburgh, 1699; second edn 1709): honourably practical, but quite unanalytical.

[50] Fletcher's intellectual significance was first recognised in these terms by John G. A. Pocock: see *The Machiavellian Moment: Florentine Political Thought and the Atlantic Republican Tradition* (Princeton, 1975), ch. 8: 'Neo-Machiavellian political economy'. Also, on the neo-Harringtonian analysis of

The agrarian economy was not the only focus of discussion, however. Following the failure of the Darien venture, fresh projects were advanced for the promotion of trade and the creation of credit. One proposal which attracted powerful support was that of a council of trade. Initially suggested by Seton in 1700, the proposal was given substance by William Paterson, originator of the Darien venture, in *Proposals and Reasons for constituting a Council of Trade* (1701), and was still being pursued by Seton in 1705. Both authors took it for granted that Scottish trade had declined since the Union of the Crowns a century ago: extensive dealings with northern Europe and the Mediterranean before 1603 had quickly been reduced to a 'peddling trade' thereafter. The point of a council of trade, therefore, was to restore Scottish control over the nation's commerce, and to secure a favourable balance of trade. But how the council was to work, and what policies would achieve its ends, were less easy to agree. There was a marked reluctance to promote an aggressive policy towards England, whose greater power and distinct 'interest' were readily conceded. The most such a council could be expected to do, it seemed, was to identify the commodities and manufactures in which Scotland had a competitive advantage, and encourage their development.[51] In effect Paterson and Seton were conceding that a protectionist and *dirigiste* approach to economic policy was impossible for a kingdom such as Scotland, on which its more powerful neighbour might at any time threaten to impose its interest by force.

Much more radical and clear headed in his thinking was the principal exponent of a second remedy, John Law, whose *Money and Trade Considered, with a Proposal for supplying the nation with Money* was published in 1705. To Law the root of Scotland's economic problem lay in the supply of money and credit. It was true that Scotland possessed competitive advantages in trade, particularly in low labour costs. It was perhaps 'more capable of an extended trade than any other country of Europe'. But the Scots had been unable to exploit their advantage because of a shortage of money, whereas the Dutch could still trade more cheaply, despite high labour costs,

---

property in particular: 'The mobility of property and the rise of eighteenth-century sociology', in John G. A. Pocock, *Virtue, Commerce and History: Essays on Political Thought and History, chiefly in the Eighteenth Century* (Cambridge, 1985), pp. 103–23.

[51] William Paterson, *Proposals and Reasons for constituting a Council of Trade* (Edinburgh, 1701), repr. (without 'The Introduction') in *The Writings of William Paterson*, ed. Saxe Bannister (1859; repr. New York, 1968), pp. 5–105; Seton, *The Interest of Scotland*, pp. 107–8, and *Some Thoughts on Ways and Means for making the Nation a Gainer in Foreign Commerce; and for supplying its present Scarcity of Money* (Edinburgh, 1705), esp. pp. 8–19, 51–2. On Seton's economic thinking: Muramatsu, 'Some types of national interest', pp. 8–20.

because they enjoyed easier credit.[52] Law's solution was a scheme to introduce paper money on the security of land. Unlike silver, he reasoned, land cannot easily fall in value, and cannot be exported; paper money is easier to use than silver, and its quantity can be increased and decreased in line with demand.[53] Increasing the supply of money, Law argued, was the key to quickening economic activity generally. It would increase employment (the present large number of unemployed being the consequence of the shortage of money, not a reflection of the Scots' laziness). It would thus increase output, and consequently exports, leading to a surplus in the balance of payments.[54] With considerable sophistication, Law had framed his argument to meet Scotland's situation as a small but open economy in the international market. Though short of money, the Scots did not enjoy the benefit of lower prices, because prices tended to be set on an international basis, and the oversupply of silver in Europe kept those prices high.[55] If, however, the Scots were to remedy their deficiency of silver by the introduction of land-based paper money, stimulating increased output, they would be much better able to exploit their competitive advantage.

Law's writing injected a quite new level of intellectual sophistication into Scottish economic debate. For a number of reasons, however, his immediate impact, practical and intellectual, was limited. His scheme depended on two assumptions, both of which were open to question. One was that a board of forty commissioners would have the knowledge and expertise to manage the money supply, and the land on which it was to be secured. A second was that the ensuing increase in output would go into exports, and that internal consumption would not increase.[56] Probably more serious was the confusion created by the appearance of a number of similar proposals related to money. The most widely canvassed was by Hugh Chamberlen: though Law was fiercely critical of its theoretical inadequacies, the two schemes were often discussed together.[57] In a particularly damaging episode in 1705,

[52] John Law, *Money and Trade Considered, with a Proposal for supplying the Nation with Money* (Edinburgh, 1705), pp. 15, 110–13.

[53] Law, *Money and Trade*, pp. 84–110, esp. pp. 91–3, 101–2.   [54] Ibid., pp. 102, 116–20.

[55] Ibid., pp. 73–4; on this point see Antoine E. Murphy, *John Law: Economic Theorist and Policy Maker* (Oxford, 1997), pp. 95–8.

[56] On these assumptions, Murphy, *John Law*, pp. 98–103. Aware that an increase in internal consumption was likely, Law sought to reinforce the position of exports by suggesting restrictions on internal consumption, thereby qualifying if not contradicting his insistence that remedying the shortage of money would alone be sufficient to generate a favourable balance of trade.

[57] [Hugh Chamberlen], *A Few Proposals humbly recommending the Establishment of a Land Credit* (Edinburgh, 1700); on which Law, *Money and Trade*, pp. 78–84; another proposal was that of James Hodges, *Considerations and Proposals, for supplying the present Scarcity of Money, and advancing Trade* (Edinburgh, 1705).

a debate in the Scottish Parliament on the two schemes was interrupted by Fletcher, who denounced them both as 'gibberish'. Fletcher's outburst had a political dimension, and also suggests a distaste for technical economic argument.[58] But if even he was not confident that the Scots could manage their own economy, as Law's, Paterson's, and Seton's schemes presupposed, it is not surprising that others were unconvinced. By the end of 1705 Scottish opinion was moving towards the conclusion that the country would only flourish within a political framework which allowed the Scots to trade under the same privileges as the English. A new political relation with England was increasingly seen as the prerequisite of a fresh economic start.

The opportunity to consider a new political relation between the two kingdoms had arisen two years earlier. In 1703 ministers had finally called a new Parliament, in the hope that it would agree to the same Hanoverian succession to Anne as the English Parliament had accepted in 1701. Elected to this Parliament, as he had not been to the Parliament of William, Fletcher again seized the moment. The Scots, he proposed, should agree to the same succession as England's only in return for 'Limitations' on the power of the Scottish crown and its ministers. The basis for this demand was a coruscating analysis of the condition to which Scotland and its Parliament had been reduced under the Union of the Crowns. With the court removed to London, he argued in a succession of speeches, Scottish ministers had become the servile dependants of their English counterparts, managing the Scottish Parliament in return for favours for themselves and their followers. The inevitable result was that Scotland 'from that time appeared to the rest of the world more like a conquered province, than a free independent people'.[59]

   The Limitations were designed to ensure the future independence of the Scottish Parliament by restricting the powers of any future shared sovereign. The Parliament was to choose the king's ministers, raise the national militia, and take decisions on war and peace. Limitations of this sort had earlier

---

[58] The remark was directed at Fletcher's erstwhile supporter the earl of Roxburgh, whom Fletcher challenged to a duel. The incident was variously reported by observers: by [Mungo Graham] to [the duke of Montrose], [13 July 1705], National Archives of Scotland GD 220/5/800/13; by [William Greg] to [Robert Harley], 14, 17 July 1705, *Historical Manuscripts Commission, Portland Papers*, IV (London, 1897), pp. 207–9; and by the earl of Mar to his wife, 16 July 1705, Historical Manuscripts Commission *Mar and Kellie Papers* (London, 1904), p. 234. As we shall see, however, Fletcher had already given reasons for doubting whether Scotland could have the economic independence which the various schemes presupposed: see below, p. 179.

[59] Andrew Fletcher, *Speeches by a member of the Parliament Which Began at Edinburgh the 6th of May, 1703* (Edinburgh, 1703), in *Political Works*, pp. 132–3. The speeches were actually delivered between May and September 1703, and published soon afterwards.

been imposed on Charles I by the Scottish Parliament of 1641; but although Fletcher invoked the 'antient constitution' to justify them, he was careful to dissociate himself from the religious bigotry of the covenanters.[60] A speech to a heated assembly was perhaps not the place to display the conceptual structure of his argument; but it is much more likely that here too his inspiration was Machiavellian. In effect Fletcher was seeking to renew the Scottish Constitution in the Machiavellian sense of *riordinarla* (the phrase he had used of the Spanish monarchy). By reconstituting the *ordini*, the structures, of Scottish government, he would restore freedom and independence to the Scottish political community, preventing the crown and its ministers from treating it as but a 'province'. By implication, the proposals would also change the terms of Scotland's union with England. Despite the invocation of 'a free, independent people', Fletcher did not propose to break the union entirely; but the Limitations would have turned the existing union of the crowns into a more strictly equal, 'confederal', union of the two kingdoms and their separate Parliaments.[61]

Fletcher's diagnosis of the ill consequences of the Union of the Crowns was universally accepted, even by Jacobites. 'We all own', Patrick Abercromby observed, 'that we are unhappy, and that, because our sovereigns reside in England.'[62] In Scotland (as in Naples) the conviction that the kingdom had been reduced to the status of a province was by 1703 the shared premise of all discussion of the country's predicament. Fletcher's proposed solution, measures of institutional reform which would reconstitute the union on an equal, confederal basis, also attracted support. James Hodges worked hard to provide a coherent definition of 'confederate or federal union', and discussed the merits of the available models, Poland–Lithuania, the Swiss cantons, and, probably most relevant, the United Provinces of the Netherlands.[63] But others drew the opposite conclusion from the same

---

[60] Fletcher, *Speeches, Political Works*, pp. 134–40.

[61] For earlier versions of this interpretation of Fletcher's proposals: John Robertson, 'The Scottish Enlightenment at the limits of the civic tradition', in Istvan Hont and Michael Ignatieff (eds.), *Wealth and Virtue: the Shaping of Political Economy in the Scottish Enlightenment* (Cambridge, 1983), pp. 142–51; and 'An elusive sovereignty: the course of the Union debate in Scotland 1698–1707', in Robertson, *A Union for Empire*, pp. 203–6.

[62] [Patrick Abercromby], *The Advantages of the Act of Security, compar'd with these of the intended Union: founded on the Revolution Principles publish'd by Mr Daniel Defoe* (n.p., 1706); the pamphlet was a clever but disingenuous attempt to use 'revolution principles' against incorporating union (which Defoe supported), while supporting an Act of Security which would have the effect of keeping the Scottish succession open, and hence making possible a Stuart restoration.

[63] [James Hodges], *The Rights and Interests of the Two British Monarchies, Inquir'd into, and Clear'd; with a special respect to an United or Separate State. Treatise I, shewing the different Nature of an Incorporating and Federal Union; the Reasons why all Designs of Union have hitherto prov'd unsuccessful; and the Inconsistency of an Union by Incorporation with the Rights, Liberties, National Interests, and Publick Good of Both Kingdoms* (London, 1703).

premise, arguing that the dependence of the Scottish Parliament pointed to the advantages of an 'incorporating' union of Parliaments as well as crowns. The leading proponents of this solution were Seton of Pitmedden and George Mackenzie, earl of Cromarty.

The attempt to restore the independence of the Scottish Parliament, Seton argued, was much more likely to lead to a revival of the sort of behaviour associated with the 'Gothic constitution of government', which had been so frequently attended with 'feuds, murders, depredations and rebellions'.[64] By incorporating their Parliament with the English, however, the Scots would be able to share the 'great advantages' which the English had already won for themselves: rights of liberty and property, and with them the advantages in commerce which the English enjoyed.[65] Against these gains, the loss of the kingdom's independence was strictly notional. The 'notion of a kingdom per se', as Cromarty put it, was an abstraction, when what mattered were 'the riches, honour and safety of all, and of every individual'.[66]

By 1706, when negotiations for a new union began again, it was clear that an incorporating union was politically by far the most likely outcome. Initially reluctant to concede a union of the Parliaments – they continued to refuse it to the Irish – English ministers now recognised that this was the simplest means to settle the Hanoverian (and any future) succession. They had also decided that admitting the Scots to trade on equal terms with the English was an acceptable price to pay. That they could have conquered the Scots into submission was not denied, even by Scottish opponents of closer union. But the necessary diversion of troops from the war of the Spanish succession on the continent would have been both humiliating and dangerous, since the French would gladly have transferred the theatre of war to Scotland, activating the Jacobites to rise in support of the claims of James VII's son.

The Treaty of Union which was negotiated in 1706 required the Scottish Parliament's effective dissolution, and the transfer of a limited number of its Members to the Parliament in Westminster. This was renamed the Parliament of Great Britain, but was in other respects the previous Parliament of England. Notoriously, Scottish acceptance of the Treaty was encouraged by the disbursement of money and titles to those prepared to

---

[64] Speech by William Seton of Pitmedden on the First Article of the Union, 2 November 1706, in Daniel Defoe, *The History of the Union between England and Scotland* (London, 1786), pp. 312–14.

[65] [William Seton of Pitmedden], *Scotland's Great Advantages by an Union with England; shewen in a Letter from the Country, to a Member of Parliament* (n.p., 1706).

[66] [George Mackenzie, earl of Cromarty], *Trialogus. A Conference betwixt Mr Con, Mr Pro, and Mr Indifferent, concerning the Union* (n.p., 1706), pp. 5–6.

vote in its favour.[67] But the process of negotiation, which continued as the Scottish Parliament discussed individual articles of the treaty, also resulted in significant concessions to Scottish interests. Probably most important was the Act securing the Protestant Religion and Presbyterian Church Government, which accompanied the treaty, and which was matched by a similar English Act securing the Church of England. The Act reassured presbyterians fearful of the likely actions of an Anglican-dominated British Parliament; but the Erastian implications of such legislation, which were liable to be as offensive to *jure divino* Anglicans as to presbyterians, meant that the real beneficiaries of the concession were the laity.[68] A second important set of concessions concerned trade. The opening of English markets at home and overseas gave the Scots access to the largest protected free-trade zone in the European world. At the same time, the Scots gained a series of specific concessions for individual industries, protecting them from English competition for stated periods.[69] Such concessions mattered not only in themselves. They also encouraged Scots to believe that the treaty was conditional – that were its terms subsequently broken, the Union would be dissolved. As the debate over the treaty reached its climax in 1706–7 this argument became increasingly important to its supporters, and was eloquently promoted by the English publicist Daniel Defoe.[70] In fact the treaty was deliberately ambiguous on the future alteration of its terms; but the supposition that it was conditional and therefore revocable was a fiction which the Scots were given every encouragement to believe.

Andrew Fletcher was prominent among the small but vociferous group which continued to protest and obstruct the treaty during its passage through the Scottish Parliament. But arguably he had delivered the sharpest comment on the implications of an incorporating union as early as 1704, in *An Account of a Conversation Concerning a Right Regulation of Governments for the common Good of Mankind*. Probably the last of Fletcher's published writings, it was also the most complex in form and argument. It has the form of a dialogue, whose participants, besides Fletcher himself, were the

---

[67] But see now John Stuart Shaw, *The Political History of Eighteenth-Century Scotland* (Basingstoke, 1999), pp. 1–17: 'The price of Scotland?', for a reassessment.

[68] On these acts, see Colin Kidd, 'Religious realignment between Restoration and Union', in Robertson, *A Union for Empire*, pp. 165–8.

[69] Christopher A. Whatley, 'Economic causes and consequences of the Union of 1707', *Scottish Historical Review*, 68 (1989), pp. 158–9; and *Bought and Sold for English Gold? Explaining the Union of 1707* (2nd edn East Linton, 2001), pp. 72–7.

[70] [Daniel Defoe], *An Essay at Removing National Prejudices against a Union with England. Part III* (n.p., 1706), pp. 10–33, esp. p. 26. The argument was taken up by the presbyterian lawyer Francis Grant in *The Patriot Resolved; in a letter to an Addresser, from his Friend; of the same sentiments with himself, concerning the Union* (n.p., 1707).

earl of Cromarty and two English Tory MPs, Sir Christopher Musgrave and Sir Edward Seymour. Presented as an actual encounter, the dialogue was realistic in both setting and development; but the participants were so well chosen, and the conversation so artfully conducted, as to suggest that the realism was integral to the genre. Following an introductory exchange over the pleasures and perils of London, the conversation turned to Fletcher's conduct in the 1703 session of Parliament, and the political maturity of Fletcher's young noble followers (to whom the pamphlet was formally addressed). But the greater part of the conversation looked forward, not back, as the participants discussed, with extraordinary prescience, the likely outcome of the crisis.[71]

Acknowledging that with the defeat of Limitations the case for incorporating union was likely to gain ground, Fletcher set himself to convince his listeners (and readers) that such a union was no remedy for Scotland's present ill condition, but would only increase its poverty. When the parties to such a union were as unequal as England and Scotland, and the weaker left unprotected by Limitations, the stronger would be bound, in its own interest, to take advantage. The proof of this Fletcher found in England's recent treatment of Ireland.[72] Ignoring the justified claims of the Anglo-Irish that they were not liable to be ruled as a conquered people, the English government had ruthlessly discriminated against Irish economic interests whenever these conflicted with English. There was even less reason for the English to regard the Scots as a conquered people; but the slightest disturbance following a union would be taken as the occasion to treat them as such. The Scots might seek the security of a 'guarantee' for a treaty of union; but the English would never allow a third party, such as the French or the Dutch, to assume this role, and no other guarantee could be relied on. Ultimately, any treaty of union would depend on trust; and in the face of more powerful English interests, trust was too weak a security. Effectively Fletcher had anticipated, and countered, what would become one of the key arguments of the incorporating unionists, that the treaty would entrench Scottish interests, and would be revocable if its terms were broken. If the

---

[71] Andrew Fletcher, *An Account of a Conversation Concerning the Right Regulation of Governments for the common Good of Mankind. In a Letter to the Marquiss of Montrose, the Earls of Rothes, Roxburg and Haddington, from London the first of December, 1703* (Edinburgh, 1704), in *Political Works*, pp. 175–215; see pp. 176–88 for the opening stages of the conversation. See also note 1 on p. 176 for details of the participants in and addressees of the conversation.

[72] The Irish context of Fletcher's argument has been illuminated by Hont, 'Free trade and the economic limits to national politics: neo-Machiavellian political economy reconsidered', pp. 41–120, and by David Armitage, *The Ideological Origins of the British Empire* (Cambridge, 2000), ch. 6: 'The political economy of empire'.

Scots objected once a union had been agreed, Fletcher warned, they would simply be conquered outright – a conclusion he proceeded to illustrate with a vigorous exchange of insults between himself and Sir Edward Seymour over previous battles between the two kingdoms, the most recent of which had all been won by the English.[73]

Returning to the case of Ireland, Fletcher developed a second line of argument against incorporating union. His thinking now became still more striking in its originality, to the point that it undermined not only his opponents', but even his own, previous position. Once again trade was the visible sign of the fundamental problem:

trade is now become the golden ball, for which all nations of the world are contending, and the occasion of so great partialities, that not only every nation is endeavouring to possess the trade of the whole world, but every city to draw all to itself; and the English are no less guilty of these partialities than any other trading nation.[74]

Behind the 'national' interest in trade, Fletcher had observed, lay that of the city. It was the ambitions of great cities, even more than of nations, which were fuelling the race for commercial dominance. To illustrate the point, Fletcher adapted William Petty's hypothesis of a transplantation of the population of Ireland into England. In Petty's hands the idea had been a counter-factual, intended to demonstrate the capacity of England to support a much larger population that it presently did, by employing the extra hands in manufactures.[75] As adapted by Fletcher, however, the hypothesis became a *reductio ad absurdum* of the argument that trading interests should always be put first. For there was no reason, Fletcher told his startled audience, why such a transplantation should stop at Ireland; the populations of the northern counties of England and of Wales could equally well be moved south, leaving those parts of the country to be cut off and sunk (and creating thereby a convenient 'ditch' against the Scots). The process might indeed continue until all the people of the two kingdoms had been concentrated in and around London. That city would then be as

---

[73] Fletcher, *Account of a Conversation, Political Works*, pp. 188–98, with the exchange of insults on pp. 197–8. Though Fletcher invoked Bannockburn to counter Seymour's gloating reference to his ancestor Protector Somerset's victory at Musselburgh in 1547, and argued that the later victories of Cromwell were in pursuit of a party, not a national, conflict, there was no attempt to deny recent English superiority. Fletcher's use of Seymour as an interlocutor in the conversation was exceptionally artful. Cast as the stage Little Englander, 'Seymour' more than once provides cover for arguments of Fletcher's own which were liable to give fellow-Scots particular discomfort.

[74] Ibid., p. 193.

[75] Sir William Petty, *The Political Arithmetick* (1690, but written c. 1671–6), in *The Economic Writings of Sir William Petty*, ed. C. H. Hull, 2 vols. (Cambridge, 1899), I, p. 285.

ancient Rome, with the dominion of the world in its power. But it would also become, like Rome, a centre of corruption from the very excess of its riches and power. Incapable of order and discipline, it would in due course fall to a foreign conqueror.[76]

On this analysis, the problem facing the Scots was ultimately the problem of London. Fletcher had taken Petty's point that a modern economy, in which agriculture was sufficiently developed to support a large population of manufacturers, was thereby capable of supporting much larger cities, which would in turn act as magnets drawing population and resources from the rest of the country. To Petty such cities were engines of development; to Fletcher they were a mortal threat to the economic viability of outlying territories which lacked comparable cities of their own. Within an incorporating union the Scots would be defenceless against the economic power of London. The passage of wealth southwards, begun under the Union of the Crowns, would only intensify, while the competitive advantage of cheaper labour, reiterated earlier in the conversation by Cromarty, would count for little against the pulling power of the metropolis. But the realisation that London had such power had equally devastating implications for those who still hoped that Scotland would be able to pursue an independent economic policy. A proposal such as John Law's that the Scots could manage the nation's money supply on lines quite different from those elsewhere simply flew in the face of this modern reality. To dismiss Law's scheme as 'gibberish', as Fletcher did a year later, did him no credit; but in the *Account of a Conversation* Fletcher had already given good reason to question whether any 'national' economic policy could withstand the power of a metropolitan city such as London.

This implication was dramatically confirmed by Fletcher's own solution to the problem of great cities. Called upon by Musgrave to propose his alternative, Fletcher assumed the guise of 'a second Phaleg' (after the descendant of Noah in whose days the earth was divided) and divided Europe anew into ten geographical areas, in each of which there would be ten or twelve cities with surrounding territories. These cities would be united under one prince or council for the purposes of defence, in the manner of the Achaian league in ancient Greece; but they would otherwise be the capitals of sovereign and independent countries. The cities being more or less equal, there would be a balance both within and between the leagues to which they belonged, ensuring that any war among them would be limited. Each also being of moderate size, the cities would not be

---

[76] Fletcher, *Account of a Conversation, Political Works*, pp. 198–202.

vulnerable to the corruption which now afflicted great capital cities such as London: rather the several cities would be easily governed, encouraging virtue among their citizens, improving the arts and sciences, and offering great variety of entertainment to 'all foreigners and others of a curious and inquisitive genius'.[77]

At this point Fletcher was interrupted by the irascible Sir Edward Seymour. 'What visions have we here, said Sir Edw-rd? Destroy the greatest and most glorious city of the world to prosecute a whimsical project!' Certainly, Fletcher replied, the kingdoms of Britain and Ireland should be divided between twelve cities, six in England, four in Ireland, and two in Scotland. London should be reduced to a level with Bristol, Exeter, Chester, York, and Norwich; Dublin should share Ireland with Cork, Galloway, and Londonderry; and Scotland would be divided between Stirling in the south and Inverness in the north.[78] But for all Seymour's bluster on behalf of London, the implications of the proposal for Scotland were at least as shocking. London might be demoted, but Edinburgh was to lose its capital status altogether, and the kingdom of Scotland would disappear as a political entity. It was as if Fletcher would concede that a 'free and independent' kingdom of Scotland, which he had defended so eloquently in Parliament less that a year earlier, was a chimera – that a Scotland which clung to that status was doomed to remain a province of the kingdom of England and its overmighty capital. In the modern world of commercial rivalry and great metropolitan cities, Fletcher seemed to want his readers to conclude, political objectives required radical readjustment, to the extent, if necessary, of dismantling even the most ancient of kingdoms. For only if the relation between cities and their territories was equalised, preventing any one city from gaining pre-eminence, would the destructive and corrupting potential of commerce be contained.

As remarkable as these political consequences of Fletcher's argument were its intellectual implications. Once again key concepts were identifiably Machiavellian; but now, as never before, Fletcher can be seen to have stretched the concepts to the limits of their analytical viability – and even beyond. The terms in which he analysed the relations between the three kingdoms of England, Ireland, and Scotland were those he had employed in the *Discorso delle cose di Spagna*: 'interest' was assumed to be the overriding motive of those in power. But there was a new sense of the way in which commerce had at once reinforced and complicated the pursuit of interest; it was clear that the interest of a nation, as defined by its government, was

[77] Ibid., pp. 203–11, 213–14.   [78] Ibid., pp. 212–14.

becoming an extension of the interest of those engaged in commerce. For Fletcher this realisation was exemplified in the phenomenon of the modern city. For this was not the city state of the ancient or Italian world, whose leading citizens applied their wealth to the defence and embellishment of the republic: the modern city, rather, was the creation of a novel partnership between royal courts and commercial and financial elites, whose rationale was that the revenues of the crown would increase if the profits of the merchants and financiers were maximised. The only ancient precedent for this city was Rome in its imperial corruption and decline, when it had drained the provinces of their resources; but though Fletcher invoked the parallel, Rome offered limited insight into the ambitions of the modern commercial metropolis. In recognising the challenge of this new phenomenon Fletcher, as we have seen, was following Petty, perhaps the first to take the measure of London's significance; and he was the contemporary of Boisguilbert, who likewise addressed the problem of Paris in 1705–6.[79] But none was clearer than Fletcher that this was a development which burst the bounds of Machiavellian comprehension.

The same pattern of Machiavellian concepts stretched beyond their previous usage characterises Fletcher's project for a Europe of leagues of cities. An obvious source for the scheme was Machiavelli's discussion of defensive leagues in book II of the *Discorsi sopra Tito Livio*. There Machiavelli had identified the Achaian league as the ancient model (along with the Etruscan league in pre-Roman Italy); its modern successor he had found in the league of the Swiss cantons. The characteristic feature of such leagues, he observed, was their reluctance to expand; defence was their natural priority.[80] But if this was Fletcher's inspiration, there was no denying that his scheme was also, as Seymour was allowed to point out, a 'whimsical project'. Other clues that Fletcher's argument had acquired a consciously speculative, even utopian, purpose are scattered through the work. In particular there are suggestive parallels with More's *Utopia*, not only in the form and cleverness of the dialogue, but specifically between More's description of the city of Amaurot and Fletcher's opening depiction of London.[81] Such care to advertise the utopian character of a Machiavellian project suggests that here too,

---

[79] On the genesis of this discussion, the remarkable essay by Franco Venturi, 'Napoli Capitale nel pensiero dei riformatore illuministi', in the *Storia di Napoli*, vol. VIII (Naples, 1971), pp. 3–7. Boisguilbert's manuscript writing has been entitled 'De la nécessité d'un traité de paix entre Paris et le reste du royaume' (1705–6).

[80] Machiavelli, *Discorsi sopra Tito Livio*, II.iv.

[81] Fletcher, *Account of a Conversation*, *Political Works*, pp. 177–8, also p. 186, where Cromarty remarks that Fletcher's projects 'seem rather contrived to take place in a Platonick commonwealth than in the present corruption of things'.

as in the proposals of the second of his *Two Discourses concerning Scotland* in 1698, Fletcher's purpose was chiefly analytical. Whatever he had hoped to achieve in 1703 with his Limitations, by 1704 he had virtually conceded that the reforms they embodied were unattainable.

An analytical point is especially clear in the case of the project's implications for commerce. Though the economic circumstances of the cities and their territories are not discussed, it has plausibly been suggested that Fletcher intended them to be as autarkic, or self-sufficient, as possible, minimising the need for competitive international commerce.[82] But the proposition that commercial rivalry, along with the great capital and trading cities which accompanied and fuelled that rivalry, would only be restrained by the arbitrary imposition of a new political division of Europe was tantamount to an admission that no reform of the existing political system would be enough. Governments, Fletcher was effectively admitting, were now hostage to commerce. There were, in ways Machiavelli had never imagined, economic limits to national politics.[83] Fletcher was not the only Scot to admit this; the incorporating unionists Seton and Cromarty had made the point too. But they were happy to see politics take second place. As Cromarty put it, 'the riches, honour and safety of all, and every individual' were what mattered, not the independence of a kingdom; not public virtue, but the individual's well-being and security were the modern priorities.[84] Fletcher knew as well as Cromarty that this was what the modern world had come to; but he made the point by insisting upon exemplary, impossible measures to uphold the primacy of public life and the pursuit of virtue.

Fletcher's determination to insist upon these priorities is the more remarkable given the pattern of his own life, and the pleasure he derived from the cities whose power he decried. A political activist for short periods only, Fletcher spent much of his time and most of his income in London, Paris, and the cities of Holland: he clearly relished the opportunities they offered for conversation and the consumption of coffee and chocolate, rare books, and finely cut (if austere) clothes. His project for a Europe

---

[82] Armitage, 'The Scottish vision of empire', p. 115; Muramatsu, 'Some types of national interest', pp. 7–8. See also Shigemi Muramatsu, 'Andrew Fletcher's criticism of commercial civilisation and his plan for European federal union', in T. Sakamoto and H. Tanaka (eds.), *The Rise of Political Economy in the Scottish Enlightenment* (London, 2003), pp. 8–21: I agree with his suggestion that it was only in the *Account of a Conversation* that Fletcher fully worked out the devastating implications of modern commerce for a Machiavellian politics.

[83] Hont, 'Free trade and the economic limits to national politics', pp. 114–20, for an analysis of the *Account of a Conversation* to which mine remains much indebted.

[84] See above, note 66.

of cities would have spread those pleasures more widely: so many seats of government, as he put it, would not only encourage virtue, but offer variety of entertainment to foreigners and others of 'a curious and inquisitive genius' (a nice description of himself). But Fletcher knew from personal experience that it was great cities like London, not provincial backwaters like Edinburgh, which had created that variety of entertainment in the first place. Unlike so many contemporary moralists who simply denounced the corruptions of city life, Fletcher understood, and genuinely appreciated, what he also feared.

What is most remarkable about Fletcher's thinking, however, is its intellectual single-mindedness. Along with John Law, Fletcher was probably the most intelligent Scot of his time; and he was considerably better read than the economist. Yet Fletcher showed no inclination to connect his analysis of modern politics, commerce, and rural and urban life with more general developments in moral and political philosophy. For all his awareness of the power of 'interest', national and commercial, in the modern world, there is no allusion to the problem of self-interest in human nature, then preoccupying philosophers of sceptical, Augustinian, or Epicurean inclinations. Nor, on the other hand, is there any indication that his continued insistence on the possibility of a politics of virtue derived from Stoic moral philosophical commitments. Almost certainly this single-mindedness of intellectual purpose helped to sharpen Fletcher's analyses of Europe in the age of the Spanish succession crisis, and of the predicament of Scotland as a provincial kingdom, akin to Naples within the Spanish monarchy, but under the growing shadow of the great capital city of London. But the very exclusiveness of Fletcher's focus may also be taken to reflect, and underline, the still fragmented character of Scottish intellectual life. In the absence of a core of thinkers with a common interest in the principal philosophical currents of the age – a core such as was formed by d'Andrea and Valletta, Caloprese and Capasso in contemporary Naples – individual Scots simply went their several ways. Of none was this more true than Fletcher. Though enormously respected by his contemporaries, his independent life and single-minded writings testify to the continuing absence from Scotland of the sort of collective intellectual energy already so evident among their Neapolitan counterparts.

For an indication of the rather different form which an analysis of the predicament of a provincial kingdom might take when written from within that more developed intellectual culture, we can now, however, return to Naples, and to the writings of Paolo Mattia Doria.

NAPLES AFTER 1707: PAOLO MATTIA DORIA

The year 1707 was also, unexpectedly, a decisive year for the kingdom of Naples: on 7 July, the anniversary of the outbreak of Masaniello's revolt, imperial troops entered the city, claiming it on behalf of Archduke Charles of Austria. In principle, Naples was claimed as part of the archduke's 'Spanish' monarchy, and was ruled by him from Barcelona, where he had established his court. In practice, the kingdom now formed part of the Austrian Habsburg monarchy, and received its viceroys, and their orders, from Vienna. This reality was formalised when the archduke became emperor as Charles VI in 1712, and subsequently retained the kingdom of Naples under the terms of the Treaty of Utrecht, having renounced the claim to the remaining Spanish titles. For a while after 1707 the archduke's pretension to rule Naples as if it was still part of the Spanish monarchy encouraged the Austrians to accept a large measure of continuity in its government, continuity personified in the ministerial leadership of Gennaro d'Andrea, an experienced servant of Charles II. But the change of dynasty nevertheless aroused expectations of changes in policy as well: the debate over the predicament and future of the kingdom which had begun, somewhat tentatively, before the Macchia conspiracy now received a fresh lease of life.

Not surprisingly, the barons who had led that earlier conspiracy on behalf of the Austrian claim now stepped forward to renew their demands. Their spokesman on this occasion was Tiberio Carafa. Emphasising the role of the nobility in government since the foundation of the city by the Greeks as a free republic, Carafa diagnosed the problems of the kingdom as a want of 'good order and true justice'. Several of his demands duly gave prominence to noble interests. The privileges and titles of the nobility should be respected, putting an end to the 'abomination' of granting nobility to merchants and traders (*mercadanti* and *bottegari*). More constructively, he urged that additional Neapolitan regiments be raised, to provide employment for the traditionally martial Neapolitan nobility, and to serve with Austrian forces. But other proposals presupposed the nobility's cooperation with the *togati*. Calling for the laws of the kingdom to be codified, he commented that this should be easily achieved in a city full of excellent jurists, among whom he named Argento, Biscardi, Gennaro d'Andrea, Aulisio, Giannone, Riccardi, and Pietro Contegna – a list notable for including the younger generation as well as their seniors. He also proposed the institution of a number of academies in the sciences and the arts. One of these would be a gymnasium for the nobility; but others should be in the mechanical arts and navigation, to exploit the kingdom's abundant resources of wool and silk.[85]

An altogether more radical set of demands was tabled by the lawyer Alessandro Riccardi. A keen Cartesian, who had associated with Caloprese, Riccardi was a close friend of Giannone. In place of Carafa's reference to the city's origins, Riccardi's starting point was the natural abundance of the kingdom. It was universally agreed that the kingdom was better placed to achieve the greatest happiness than any other part of Europe. Not only was it blessed with all that need and pleasure could desire; its access to the sea enabled it to carry its goods to others, while its inhabitants were capable in all the arts, manual as well as liberal. Nevertheless, this kingdom, 'which ought to exceed all others in happiness, exceeds them only in poverty'. The reasons were two. The country lived off revenue, rather than off the returns of industry; and a large part of its revenue left the kingdom, being taken by the court and, above all, by Rome. Together these two constantly drained the kingdom of its natural resources.[86] Riccardi did not use the term 'province', in its pejorative sense, to characterise this position; but his analysis pointed to that conclusion.

The remedy was equally clear: 'commerce and an abundant trade' (*la mer-catanzia, e l'abbondanza del traffico*). In particular Riccardi recommended the establishment of a free port, at either Naples or Salerno; the creation of an assembly of merchants to advise on matters of trade; and measures to encourage young lawyers and nobles to take up commerce. It was commerce alone which had made the sterile country of Holland, whose seven provinces together were barely as large as the two Calabrias, so marvellously rich: how much more, he implied, would it do for Naples. But the promotion of commerce would need to be accompanied by measures to prevent the outflow of revenue from the kingdom. Payments to Rome should be stopped by appointing Neapolitans to vacant benefices; and the court should be brought from Barcelona to Naples. If Charles was to be successful

---

[85] 'Parere di Tiberio Carafa formato d'ordine di S[ua] M[ajesta] sul sistema della Città e Regno di Napoli, l'anno 1708', in 'Raccolta di Rime, e Prose non ancora terminate di Tiberio Carafa Principe di Chiusano ec.', Biblioteca Nazionale di Napoli, Ms XIII.D.8, pp. 257–67 (but ff. 331–6); printed with an introduction by Vittorio Conti, 'Il "Parere" di Tiberio Carafa a Carlo d'Asburgo', *Il Pensiero Politico*, 6 (1973), 57–67. Conti underlines the extent to which the erstwhile conspirator now offered to compromise with the *ceto civile*.

[86] 'Memoria di Don Alessandro Riccardi', edited with an introduction by Giuseppe Ricuperati, 'Alessandro Riccardi e le richieste del "ceto civile" all'Austria nel 1707', *Rivista Storica Italiana*, 81 (1969), 745–77, with the text on pp. 770–7.

in capturing the whole Spanish monarchy, requiring the court to be moved from Naples, the interest of the kingdom should continue to be protected by the appointment of *regnicoli* to all important offices, by instituting fixed terms of office for viceroys, and by recalling the Parliament. The remedy for the reduction of the kingdom to its present position of dependence was thus the restoration of its autonomy within the Spanish monarchy, autonomy which would enable it to enjoy the fruits of its potentially lucrative commerce.[87]

In practice, one of Riccardi's demands was much easier for the Austrians to encourage than others. With the backing of the viceroy, Cardinal Grimani, the demand that all vacant benefices be filled by Neapolitans was made the subject of an aggressive campaign against the Curia in 1708 and 1709, in which Riccardi was joined by Niccolò Caravita, Gaetano Argento, and Costantino Grimaldi.[88] Riccardi's reward for such anti-curial zeal, however, was to be appointed to positions at the courts in Barcelona and Vienna – an outcome in direct contradiction of his other demand for the return of the court to Naples. An attack on the Curia might be useful, for a while, to Vienna; but the Austrian court had no similar interest in strengthening either the autonomy or the commerce of the kingdom of Naples.

Individuals within the Neapolitan government nevertheless continued to encourage discussion of the kingdom's position, and it seems to have been Gennaro d'Andrea himself who commissioned the most ambitious and interesting of all the contributions, the 'Relazione dello stato politico, economico e civile del Regno di Napoli nel tempo ch'è stato governato da i Spagnuoli prima dell'entrata dell'armi tedesche in detto Regno', more simply known as the *Massime del governo spagnolo a Napoli*, by Paolo Mattia Doria. Unfortunately, d'Andrea fell from favour in 1709, at which point Doria appears to have interrupted the work, which remained in manuscript (though in several copies). But if its practical influence was thus limited, its intellectual significance was considerable, both for its analysis of the kingdom's predicament, and for its relation to Doria's major published work of this period, the *Vita Civile* of 1710.[89]

Paolo Mattia Doria was born in Genoa in 1667; his youth and education had been those of a patrician who would be 'un perfetto cavaliere'. He

---

[87] 'Memoria di Riccardi', pp. 772–6.

[88] Harold Samuel Stone, *Vico's Cultural History: The Production and Transmission of Ideas in Naples 1685–1750* (Leiden, New York, and Cologne, 1997), pp. 144–52.

[89] On the manuscripts of the 'Relazione' or 'Massime', and the dating of the work, Vittorio Conti 'Nota al testo', in the modern edition entitled *Massime del governo spagnolo a Napoli*, ed. Giuseppe Galasso and V. Conti (Naples, 1973), pp. 5–17.

may have visited Naples in the 1680s, but settled there only in 1690, taking advantage of the existence of a Genoese community. He quickly made a double reputation as a duellist and a man of letters (a pairing of proclivities he shared with Andrew Fletcher). Through friendship with Caravita he was among the founding members of the Accademia Medina Coeli, to which he contributed *lezioni* on the art of war, fencing, and the Emperor Claudius. He also became a committed Cartesian, to the extent that he was regarded as the successor to Caloprese as the head of the school when the latter left Naples early in the 1700s. He seems likely to have begun the 'Massime degli Spagnuoli nel governo di Napoli' in 1709, returning to amend (but not to finish) the work in 1712.[90]

What makes Doria's analysis of Naples under Spanish rule so striking is its explicit conceptual premise: that Naples was 'a kingdom governed as a province', *un regno governato in provincia*. It was 'an indispensable maxim of state', Doria observed, that a newly acquired kingdom must be governed by new maxims, with new orders (*ordini*) and new customs (*costumi*). But whereas a kingdom acquired for rule in person should be governed by justice, one acquired at a distance, and ruled as a province, must be governed only by 'that reason of state, which is the opposite of a virtuous politics'.[91] In the case of Naples, the maxims of state by which the Spanish had ruled had been both general and particular. Their general maxims had been to divide and rule, and to change the 'orders' and customs of their predecessors; they had preferred these methods to the use of force. But they had also been careful to adopt maxims appropriate to the particular orders of the kingdom and the 'particular circumstances of the times' (*le particolari congiunture de' tempi*).[92] Doria's brief preliminary exposition of the terms of his analysis contained no allusion to Machiavelli; but it would have been obvious to his readers that the concept of *un regno governato in provincia* was an ingenious extension of the categories used by Machiavelli to treat the position of a 'new prince'. More explicitly even than Andrew Fletcher, Doria had set himself to apply a Machiavellian framework of analysis to the predicament of dependent, 'provincial' kingdoms within greater, composite monarchies.

There had been several stages to Spanish rule in the kingdom. Immediately following its acquisition by Charles V, the emphasis had been on

---

[90] Biographical details of Doria are derived from Salvattore Rotta, 'Nota introduttiva' to 'Paolo Mattia Doria', in R. Ajello and others (eds.), *Dal Muratori a Cesarotti*. v: *Politici ed economisti del primo settecento* (Milan and Naples, 1978), pp. 837–53.

[91] Doria, *Massime del governo spagnolo*, p. 21: 'a regni governati in provincia devono sentire un poco di quella ragione di Stato, che con la virtuosa politica in tutto non ben s'accorda'.

[92] Ibid., pp. 21–3.

changing the orders and customs of the kingdom. Noble houses associated with the previous monarchy had been reduced, and their power distributed among a more numerous lesser baronage; Spanish customs in the treatment of women had been adopted; and the authority of the viceroy strengthened. Once Spanish rule was assured, its maxims had become subtler and more divisive. Church, nobility, and jurists were treated as separate spheres of interest, while the education in virtue which should have promoted union between the orders was deliberately neglected. But by 1647 reliance on such maxims had reduced the kingdom to such a state that it took only a simple fish-seller to unite the people in revolt. Masaniello, Doria insisted, had been no more than the occasion of a revolt whose real cause was the excess of 'oppression' practised by the Spanish. After the revolt the Spanish had been obliged to alter their maxims again, lightening the burdens on the people and ensuring that the poor were provided with necessities. But justice had been sacrificed yet further to reason of state, since the barons too had been propitiated by granting them protection from their creditors, to the destruction of the 'trust' (*fede*) without which commerce could not be carried on.[93]

The final and only praiseworthy phase of Spanish rule was initiated by the viceroyalty of the marchese del Carpio in the 1680s. He had checked the licence hitherto granted the nobility, and had even begun to relax the strict Spanish customs towards women, permitting greater freedom in relations between the sexes, and removing the temptations to the sins of incest and prostitution. Doria welcomed these changes, but feared that unless they were accompanied by a fresh emphasis on virtue, young nobles would continue to be motivated by the love of pleasure, indulging or exploiting women with the arts of gallantry.[94] In a sharp criticism of the nobility's values, he went on to denounce their contempt for their inferiors, their vanity, their indifference to justice and the duties of the subject. *Amor di patria* meant nothing to them, *amor proprio* was all; their passions were their morality.[95] The consequences were visited on the rest of the population. In the country the people were kept divided and weak by the baronage. In the city of Naples itself the rivalry between the several social orders had resulted in 'a chaos of confusion, jealousy, emulation and discord'. For want of the 'civil prudence' which maintains harmony among the orders, a kingdom otherwise so favoured by nature in the amenity of its situation, and the

---

[93] Ibid., pp. 23–40.   [94] Ibid., pp. 41–3, 45–57.

[95] Ibid., pp. 57–60: 'non hanno amor di patria, ma son tutti amor proprio; e perciò formano una morale delle loro passioni'.

abundance and exquisite quality of its produce, had been reduced to a state of misery.[96]

But where was civil prudence to be sought in Naples now that the Spanish had been replaced? Perhaps because the work was interrupted when Gennaro d'Andrea fell, the *Massime* contain no positive advice for the kingdom's new rulers. An indication of where Doria expected to find the requisite prudence may nevertheless lie in his analysis of the several magistracies of the kingdom and their jurisdictions. In every case he diagnosed an alarming lack of expertise: the members of the governing and judicial councils, the *Collaterale*, the *Sommaria*, the *Vicaria*, were alike ignorant of the 'scienza dello stato' needed to understand and administer the law. But if any order was capable of restoring the government of the kingdom it was the magistrates, for whom, Doria pointed out, he had recently written just such a 'science of the state, or politics, theoretical and practical' in his *Vita Civile*.[97]

The need to rectify abuses which had developed under Spanish rule was most urgent in two areas, which were the responsibility respectively of the provincial courts, the *udienze*, and of the tribunal of the *annona* in Naples. The *udienze*, as the royal tribunals which heard appeals from the baronial courts, had failed utterly to protect the peasantry from the tyranny of their lords. Fearful of the barons, and anxious not to prejudice a future career in Naples, the provincial judges had done nothing to restrain the barons' crimes or to check their privileges. Those privileges were held in the name of liberty, but in reality they served only vice. The result was that none had suffered more in the Spanish era than 'the poor peasant': he and his kind had borne the full weight of baronial tyranny, being treated like the beasts which never taste the food they are made to carry on their backs.[98] Doria's hostility to the baronage was more openly expressed than any previous criticism; its clear implication was that more would need to be done to curb baronial privileges than the measures taken by the marchese del Carpio.[99]

---

[96] Ibid., pp. 65–70, in particular p. 69: 'si vede quanto il mal ordine sia solo bastante a rendere poco men che infelice un Regno, nel quale la natura ha versato tutti i suoi tesori in ciò che riguarda amenità di sito, abbondanza de' comestibili, ed in varie parti però ricercata esquisitezza ancora di quelli. Qual paese potrebbe reputarsi tanto da Iddio beneficato, quanto questo, se a i privileggi, che ha sortito dalla natura, quelli che dalla civile prudenza dipendono vi accoppiasse; e se le moderate, e virtuose massime seguendo, i diversi ordini tutti essendo nella diversità medesima d'animo unitissimi, in dolce e tranquilla pace vivessero?'

[97] Ibid., pp. 79ff: 'Stato presente de' magistrati di questo Regno' followed by a 'Descrizzione' of the several councils individually. The reference to the *Vita Civile* is on p. 106.

[98] Ibid., pp. 111–20.   [99] Above, ch. 2, pp. 64, 75–8.

Such abuses were not confined to the countryside. Doria was equally alarmed by the disproportionate growth of Naples and the burden which its provisioning imposed on the rest of the kingdom. This last was the responsibility of the tribunal of the *annona*, composed of the *eletti* of the city. His analysis of the defects of this tribunal was every bit as sharp as of the *udienze*. In fixing the prices at which grain was bought and bread sold, the *annona* enabled merchants to profit at the expense of both producers and the public treasury. In turn, the administration was encouraged to treat the wealth of the *piazza mercantile*, the merchant class, as a resource to be raided whenever the state required funds. The result had been to interfere with the liberty of commerce, and to undermine the trust essential to the provision of credit. It was hardly surprising that the merchant class of Naples was among the weakest in Europe, or that capital was in such short supply.[100]

But the most serious consequence of government economic policy was the shortage of money. So much was taken out of the kingdom by Rome, or by absentee feudal landlords, that the amount of money available did not match the abundance of what was produced. Attempts to remedy the deficiency of money by raising its face value had only encouraged its export, and the abuses of usury and monopolies. Invoking the remarkable early seventeenth-century Calabrian writer on money, Antonio Serra, Doria argued that unless these abuses were corrected, the trade of the kingdom would soon be reduced to barter.[101] Doria did not, in the *Massime*, take Serra's more radical point that the very fertility of the kingdom had served to discourage its inhabitants from manufactures and trade, and that the absence of these was the fundamental cause of the shortage of money. (He would later return to the problem, but in the very different circumstances of the 1730s.)[102] If Doria's interest in economic argument was still underdeveloped, however, he had clearly acknowledged its importance. Like Riccardi, he had recognised that the kingdom would never escape being governed as a province unless it developed its commerce.

Scholarly discussion of the 'Massime' has tended to concentrate upon the work's political implications. Despite the sharpness of Doria's tone, it

---

[100] Doria, *Massime del governo spagnolo*, pp. 93–4, 120–37.

[101] Ibid., pp. 137–41. Antonio Serra, author of the *Breve Trattato delle cause, che possono far abbondare li regni d'oro, & argento, dove non sono miniere. Con applicatione al Regno di Napoli* (Naples 1613), was a native of Cosenza, and among the Calabrians imprisoned on suspicion of conspiracy against the government after Campanella's revolt in 1600. He appears to have remained in prison for the best part of two decades, writing and publishing the *Breve Trattato* from there. A modern facsimile of the work was edited by Sergio Ricossa and Clemente Secondo Rije, and published by the Istituto Italiano per gli Studi Filosofici in Naples in 1986.

[102] See below, ch. 7, pp. 334–7.

is argued, the circumstances of the work's commissioning make it unlikely that he was advocating a sharp break from the policies pursued in the final years of Spanish rule.[103] But an overemphasis on the politics of the 'Massime' may have led scholars to underestimate its intellectual significance. A revealing comparison may be drawn with the writings of Andrew Fletcher on Scotland. Like Fletcher, Doria was consciously applying Machiavellian terms to the analysis of the kingdom's predicament. Sharing the conviction that a formally independent kingdom had effectively been reduced to the condition of a 'province', Doria had explicitly added the concept of a *regno governato in provincia* to the Machiavellian lexicon. Characteristic of that condition, Doria had found (again like Fletcher), was not only the loss of political independence, but the corruption of the ruling orders of society, the outflow of revenue, and the virtual exclusion of the kingdom from international commerce. Where Doria differed from his Scottish contemporary was in the assessment of the prospects for the reordering of the kingdom of Naples. In Scotland Fletcher had thought in terms of a radical reconstruction of rural society, in which great feudal landowners ceded their power to the freeholders, while there emerged a substantial class of middle-rank tenants; these would then secure the existence of an independent Parliament and a national militia. Faced with the entrenched privileges of the feudal nobility of the kingdom of Naples, and the bestial poverty of the peasantry, Doria (like Vico in his history of the Macchia conspiracy) had to look elsewhere for leadership, to the magistracy of the city, the *ceto civile*. Even these required a re-education in virtue; but a virtuous magisterial ruling order was at least conceivable, where a rural nobility remained (as for Machiavelli himself) incompatible with any politics of virtue.[104]

What Doria understood by a politics of virtue was much more fully discussed, however, in the work he completed just as he drafted the 'Massime', the *Vita Civile*. In this work, as we shall now see, Doria moved on to ground before which Fletcher stopped short, with a philosophically informed investigation of the limits of a Machiavellian analysis of modern society.

---

[103] See especially the judgements of Giuseppe Galasso, 'Introduzione' to the *Massime del governo spagnolo*, esp. pp. xxx–xxxv, reprinted in his *La filosofia in soccorso de' governi*, pp. 216–21; Raffaele Ajello, 'Diritto ed economia in Paolo Mattia Doria', in Aa. Vv., *Paolo Mattia Doria fra rinnovamento e tradizione* (Galatina, 1985), pp. 111–12; and Giuseppe Giarrizzo, 'Un "Regno governato in provincia": Napoli tra Austria e Spagna (1690–1740)', in *Paolo Mattia Doria*, pp. 316–17.

[104] Cf. Galasso, 'Introduzione' to the *Massime del governo spagnolo*, pp. xxxvi–xlvii, or in *La filosofia in soccorso de' governi*, pp. 221–32. Machiavelli's dismissal of rural nobilities, that of the kingdom of Naples in particular, is in the *Discorsi Sopra Tito Livio*, I. lv.

La Vita Civile, e L'Educazione del Principe was published in two editions in 1710, the first in duodecimo in three volumes, the second in one quarto volume; both editions bore German imprints, but were almost certainly published in Naples. Doria himself much preferred the larger format, fearing that the duodecimo would encourage readers to regard the work as 'a romance for passing the time during hours of leisure'.[105] As it was, his 'introduction' should have removed all doubts as to his seriousness of purpose. There was a clear distinction, he began, between the 'vulgar' and those who profess 'true philosophy'; and in any state it is the latter who should be at the head. In recent times, however, politics had been treated as the sphere of the man of practice, who ruled on the assumption that men were evil, driven by *amor proprio*. This had been the error of Tacitus, and then of Machiavelli; and it had led to the reduction of politics to the false and malicious doctrine of 'reason of state'. Doria did not believe that Machiavelli had actually counselled this doctrine, but his work was like a 'farmacopeia', open to interpretation, and his advice had been taken to reinforce evil rather than virtue. Doria's purpose, accordingly, was to present a politics which would once again make possible 'la buona vita civile'. Founded on an understanding of human nature, the various forms of government and the several orders of civil life, his work would offer 'a perfect idea of politics, justice and economy', thereby retrieving the damage done by those whose excessive regard for Tacitus and Machiavelli had led them to reduce all politics to reason of state.[106]

Beginning with what he called the 'natural light' (*il lume naturale*) in men, Doria observed that the first object of our desires was human happiness (*umana felicità*): 'we all aspire to this most useful end' (*questo utilissimo fine*). This in turn gave us our natural inclination to union with each other, and to the *vita civile*. But our natural inclination for civil life was not to be attributed solely to the prompting of the senses. Humans sought their happiness through their own and their children's preservation, but also through understanding the truth of things, by imagination and reasoning, and through seeking remedies for life's ills. Even if the vulgar will not recognise it, reason is a part of man's *lume naturale*. Nevertheless Doria was equally insistent that reason does not often conquer the passions. Sensible

---

[105] Paolo Mattia Doria, *La Vita Civile, distinta in tre parti aggiuntovi un trattato della Educazione del Principe, seconda edizione, dall'autore ricorretta, ed accresciuta* (second edn Augusta [probably Naples], 1710), 'L'Autore a chi legge': the phrase was 'a guisa di romanzo per passatempo nell'ore oziose'. Subsequent references to the *Vita Civile* will be to this edition. The first edition was entitled *La Vita Civile, e L'Educazione del Principe*, 3 vols. ('Frankfurt' [probably Naples], n. d. [1710]).

[106] Doria, *Vita Civile*, 'Introduzione', pp. 1–20.

things are men's first preoccupation, and even the wise may be deceived in their reasoning by the pleasures of the senses. More than once Doria distinguished his argument from that of the Stoics: no man could abstract himself entirely from the senses, as the Stoics supposed (unless by God's grace, which was extremely rare). Happiness, therefore, lay in the good use of the passions, regulating them by reason, and choosing the virtuous passions over the vicious.[107] In effect what Doria sought to supply in these early chapters of the *Vita Civile* was what Descartes had failed to provide: a Cartesian ethics, sceptical without being Epicurean in its recognition of the strength of sense impressions and the force of the passions, rational but not Stoic in the conviction that virtue could be identified and pursued.

Having given this account of human nature, Doria proceeded to outline the course of human social development. Despite their natural inclination to union, men were only at peace before the Fall; thereafter increasing numbers and the shortage of necessities generated conflict, and obliged men to seek protection from the strongest. As under the 'shepherd kings' of Egypt, they gave obedience in return for defence. But since evil did not cease under the strong, men looked instead for rulers with prudence, and in due course for those who would rule according to law. They thus began to receive their forms of government from law-givers wise in philosophy. Initially the government was still likely to be a monarchy; but as monarchs allowed their absolute power to degenerate into tyranny, new forms of government would be introduced, including oligarchy and democracy. As these in turn were corrupted, monarchy might be restored – as it had been in Naples following the extreme democracy of the time of Masaniello. Alternatively, a mixed form of government might be adopted, after the example of ancient Sparta, which had from the first put preservation before conquest (unlike Rome, whose popular form of government was framed for conquest).[108]

The development of the *vita civile*, however, was not simply a history of forms of government. Equally essential had been the emergence of *ordini* or distinctions of rank. These had their origin, Doria believed, in man's need for *ordine*, order, amid the sea of infinite passions, if he was to achieve happiness. The first *ordini* to emerge were likely to be those associated with government – commanders, law-givers, and magistrates. But these had been followed by distinctions among the governed, between masters, or *padroni*, who owned the land, and servants, the *servi* or 'rustic plebeians' who worked

---

[107] Ibid., part I, chs. i–ii, pp. 21–89; the comments on the Stoics occur on pp. 39, 74–5.
[108] Ibid., part I, ch. iii, pp. 90–104.

on it. The landowners formed the order which became identified as 'noble', and whose support was regarded as most important by their rulers, whether in monarchies or in republics. Later these had been joined by further *ordini*, the merchants and the men of letters. It was by this division into *ordini*, Doria observed, that the tasks necessary to the life of a state were justly distributed, according to the abilities of its members; their harmonious combination was the basis of civil life.[109]

Together with the forms of government, it was the *ordini* which gave a state what Doria termed its *forma di vivere*. Where there was no government and no law, there could only be the *forma di vivere barbara*, a barbarous mode of living, a condition well illustrated by Italy during the barbarian invasions. The *vita civile*, by contrast, might take one of two forms, the *civile economica*, and the *civile pomposa*. The first was characterised by frugality and by moderate wealth and poverty. If commerce was pursued it would be for the benefit of the public rather than for private gain, as in the case of the Dutch; but there were others in this condition, for example the Swiss or the Japanese, who had rejected commerce as a source of corruption. In this *forma di vivere* men will defend the state with their own arms, religion will serve the *patria*, and the magistrates can be expected to be learned and uncorrupt. In the condition Doria termed *civile pomposa*, by contrast, men's objects were pomp and ornament, arts and letters, private as well as public wealth and pleasure. There was no necessary progression from one *forma di vivere* to another: movement might be forwards or backwards. But the danger of corruption was particularly great for those whose condition was *civile pomposa*, especially if its government engaged in conquest.[110]

The second and much the longest part of the *Vita Civile* was devoted entirely to magistrates, to the maxims by which they should rule and the objects which they should pursue in government. Fundamental to Doria's conception of magistracy was the understanding of human nature set out in the opening chapters of the work: it was the magistrate's task to direct the passions of the vulgar, to subordinate *amor proprio* to prudence and duty. For this purpose magistrates needed to be 'men of the utmost virtue' (*virtuosissimi uomini*), with the prudence to recognise and take the opportunities which fortune offers. The greatest number of responsibilities attached to those Doria classed as *magistrati di politica*. They were charged with inculcating respect for religion (whose civil purpose Doria underlined), love of the *patria* and, as its indispensable basis, love of the family. They should also supervise the people's diversions, encouraging public games and

---

[109] Ibid., part I, ch. iv, pp. 105–16.   [110] Ibid., part I, ch. v, pp. 117–29.

theatre. To these ends Doria would have magistrates pay particular attention to the formation of good habits, since habit is so much more powerful than reason among the generality of men; these habits should be appropriate to the form of government and the variety of men's circumstances.[111]

More specific responsibilities were attributed to the magistrates responsible for justice and the economy. In the case of justice, Doria argued that magistrates should regard themselves as 'legislators' and not simply as 'legists'. They should take as their model the mandarins of China, and set themselves to combine prudence with learning in the philosophy of the law. Rather than compilations of laws, magistrates should study Plato and Aristotle, and even the discourses of Machiavelli, where general maxims were drawn from particular examples. For in administering justice the magistrate must always proceed from the universal to the particular, conceding nothing to 'reason of state'.[112]

To administer economic life, by contrast, required a mind both orderly and specific. It was a sphere which tended to be despised by politicians, but, Doria pointed out, it was taken much more seriously by the people. The object of the economy (*l'economia*) Doria defined as *la conservazione del proprio avere*, by which he meant the harvest, increase, and just distribution of one's natural resources. An *economia naturale* was one in which the fruits of the land were improved by industry, and taxed moderately and equitably by the prince. But this conception of economic activity was increasingly under threat from another, which Doria termed *economia astratta*, whose object was the accumulation of wealth in the imaginary form of money. Those who pursued wealth in this form were *cabalisti* (a term difficult to translate, but which seems intended to carry connotations of intrigue, monopoly, and deception): typically such wealth was sought by trade rather than agriculture. Doria was clearly alarmed at the pressure which these *cabalisti* now exerted on magistrates; in the third edition of the *Vita Civile*, which he brought out in 1729, he added a section to this chapter in which he traced the rise of their influence to the discovery of the Indies, and the resulting influx of gold and silver into Europe. To avert the danger which they represented Doria urged magistrates to ensure that trades and wealth were distributed among the people rather than concentrated in the hands of a few; likewise there should be a good distribution of inhabitants in all the parts of a kingdom, to prevent their gathering in great cities.

---

[111] Ibid., part II, ch. i, pp. 137–304. On Doria's conception of the proper relation between politics and religion: Vincenzo Ferrone, 'Seneca e Cristo: la "Respublica Christiana" di Paolo Mattia Doria', in *Paolo Mattia Doria fra rinnovamento e tradizione*, esp. pp. 239–51.

[112] Doria, *Vita Civile*, part II, ch. ii, pp. 305–18.

For such cities all too easily became dependent on being supplied from a distance, rendering them vulnerable to famine and siege. But above all the magistrates responsible for the economy should maintain trust (*fede*), as the indispensable condition of the agreements on which all commerce is founded. The greatest of the dangers represented by the *cabalisti* was that they undermined such trust, ruining the 'natural' no less than the 'abstract' economy.[113]

The third and shortest part of the work opened with a strong argument against conquest as an object of state. Though regarded by princes as a mark of their state's greatness, the pursuit of conquest was directly contrary to the purposes for which men entered civil life, in other words, to human happiness. The conquering nation itself all too often suffered a loss of population and resources, while the conquered had to be held in continuing subjection. When the conquered state was large, and not only distant from the state of the conqueror, but quite distinct in language and customs, the conqueror would be obliged to rule it as *un regno governato in provincia*, following maxims calculated to promote weakness and vice. Without elaborating further on the problems of governing *in provincia*, Doria indicated his preference for leagues and unions between states, both principalities and republics. Leagues were better adapted to defence than conquest, and depended on the maintenance of trust among their members.[114]

In the end, Doria concluded, all states were liable to decline from the imprudence or inconstancy of their rulers. Being a compound of human passions, a state could not always avoid disorder. But with good maxims, the continuous correction of errors and good direction of the passions, order could frequently be restored. It had been Doria's purpose to delineate the qualities of 'the true statesman' who could remedy the ills of a state: in the *Vita Civile*, he believed, he had achieved this by taking the best principles and maxims of Machiavelli, and with the help of good philosophy putting them in their true place in *la scienza politica*.[115]

When a copy of the *Vita Civile* finally reached that indefatigable reviewer Jean Le Clerc in Amsterdam in 1716, he would hail it as the first work

---

[113] Ibid., part II, ch. iii, pp. 319–37; with the additional particella x, in the third edition of the work: *La Vita Civile, con un Trattato della Educazione del Principe*, third impression, corrected by the author, and adorned with many additions (Naples 1729), pp. 334–50. On the concept of *fede*, trust, in Doria, see Anthony Pagden, '*Fede pubblica* and *fede privata*: trust and honour in Spanish Naples', in his *Spanish Imperialism and the Political Imagination: Studies in European and Spanish-American Social and Political Theory 1513–1830* (New Haven and London, 1990), pp. 65–89.

[114] Doria, *Vita Civile*, part III, chs. i, iii, pp. 359–84 (esp. p. 383 for the *regno governato in provincia*), 400–9.

[115] Ibid., part III, chs. iv, v, pp. 410–34, with the final reference to Machiavelli on p. 434.

by an Italian to follow the example of Grotius, Hobbes, and Pufendorf in examining the fundamental principles of civil society (*la société civile*), in war and in peace. The Italians, Le Clerc acknowledged, had shown a natural talent for politics; but hitherto they had derived their conception of it from Machiavelli, taking its object to be the satisfaction of the passions rather than the inculcation of virtue. Those who read this work, however, would find in it a much nobler and juster understanding of the subject: it deserved to take its place in libraries among the best books of politics.[116] Not surprisingly, the review gave Doria considerable pleasure; but it was also not inaccurate as an assessment of his book's intellectual significance.

For the *Vita Civile* was a work of genuine intellectual ambition. In its characterisation of the principles of human nature, and of the development of what Doria called *la vita civile*, and Le Clerc translated as *la société civile*, it did indeed reveal interests very similar to those of the Protestant natural jurists. In the absence of explicit reference to them, it is impossible to gauge the extent of Doria's acquaintance with their work, but given the availability and reputation of the writings of Grotius, Hobbes, and Pufendorf in contemporary Naples, it is not unlikely that Doria modelled his enterprise on theirs. Le Clerc was equally justified, however, in observing that the *Vita Civile* was written in a recognisably Italian idiom. The conviction that Machiavelli's principles still provided the starting point for 'political science' was reaffirmed in Doria's closing words: in criticising the reductionist use made of Machiavelli's concepts by later exponents of reason of state (such as Francesco d'Andrea), Doria evidently believed that he could adapt and develop them in ways which would continue to be appropriate to the circumstances of the eighteenth century.

Above all, Le Clerc was right to identify an ambition to reinstate virtue in political life at the heart of Doria's work. The foundations of this were laid in the early chapters of the *Vita Civile*, and informed the argument throughout. In his Cartesian conviction that reason could act independently of the passions, directing them to virtuous ends, but equally in his respect for the power of the passions, and careful dissociation of his idea of virtue from the artificial virtue of Stoicism, Doria offered an individual synthesis of themes central to the moral-philosophical culture of late seventeenth- and early eighteenth-century Naples. But he also saw the need to take the discussion of virtue in new directions, beyond the generalities of his Cartesian

---

[116] Reprinted from the *Bibliothèque ancienne et moderne pour servir de suite aux Bibliothèques universelle et choisie* (Amsterdam, 1716), vol. V, pp. 54–125, by Enrico Vidal, in *Il pensiero civile di Paolo Mattia Doria negli scritti inediti* (Milan, 1953), pp. 19–20.

master, Caloprese. Above all, he responded to the challenge of commerce. The distinction between 'natural' and 'abstract' commerce, and his hostility to the latter, suggest that Doria had absorbed the critique of the corrupting power of luxury recently developed in Archbishop Fénelon's *Télémaque* (1699).[117] A restoration of virtue was now as urgent in the economic as in the political sphere, for on it depended the trust which was essential to the continued existence of society.

Confident that he had secured the philosophical basis of virtue, Doria was also able to identify the *ordine* best equipped to govern according to its principles. This was certainly not the nobility, for whose petty rural tyranny Doria shared, and amplified, the contempt once shown by Machiavelli. Rather, it was the magistracy, an *ordine* not singled out by Machiavelli, who instead attributed the potential for *virtù* to an undifferentiated 'people'. Only an educated magistracy, Doria believed, could be expected to possess the philosophic understanding of human nature which virtuous government required. The similarity of Doria's conception of magistracy to the ministerial governing class of Naples, the *togati*, would have been apparent to most of his readers. But the difference between Doria and Machiavelli was not simply that one was thinking of *settecento* Naples, the other of *cinquecento* Florence. When Machiavelli identified the *popolo* as the bearers of *virtù*, the quality he had in mind was that of political and martial energy rather than moral wisdom as such. Doria, by contrast, respected and feared the political energy of a provoked populace: the memory of Masaniello was still vivid. But the conditions in which the mass of the people lived, whether in town or countryside, gave no ground to suppose that they were capable of what Doria understood by true virtue. As Le Clerc rightly observed, it was Doria's confidence that such virtue was not only conceivable, but should be expected of the magistracy, that distinguished him most clearly from Machiavelli as well as from the Florentine's reason of state successors.

In its intellectual ambition, and in particular in its exposition of the philosophic foundations of virtue, Doria's *Vita Civile* also adds a dimension to the comparison with Andrew Fletcher. Between Fletcher's writings on Scotland in the age of the Spanish succession crisis and Doria's 'Massime del governo spagnolo a Napoli', it was suggested earlier, there was significant

---

[117] On Fénelon, Lionel Rothkrug, *Opposition to Louis XIV: the Political and Social Origins of the French Enlightenment* (Princeton, 1965), pp. 249–86; Istvan Hont, 'Commerce and Luxury', in Mark Goldie and Robert Wokler (eds.), *The Cambridge History of Eighteenth-Century Political Thought* (Cambridge, forthcoming).

conceptual common ground. Both exhibited a commitment to understanding the predicament of kingdoms governed as provinces in recognisably neo-Machiavellian terms. But not only had the *Vita Civile* no equivalent in Fletcher's writing, there is not the slightest indication that Fletcher ever contemplated such a work. When set alongside Doria's achievement, what stands out is Fletcher's intellectual reticence: his reluctance to extend himself beyond political and economic analysis, and his unwillingness to give the idea of virtue a philosophical content. The contrast may be one between individuals only; but (especially in the absence of any contemporary Scottish work to compare with the *Vita Civile*), it is at the least symbolic of the gulf in philosophical sophistication between Neapolitan and Scottish intellectual cultures at the outset of the eighteenth century.

Even so, the two contemporaries had something of the utmost importance in common, which the *Vita Civile* only serves to underline. This was the conviction that the pre-eminence of politics, and the practice of virtue in political life, axioms at the heart of Machiavellian thinking, now faced a challenge of which Machiavelli had remained quite unaware. The challenge was that of commerce. Not only did those engaged in commerce naturally think in terms of self-interest; as long as the trust which sustained their agreements was upheld, they had no reason to consider either the political or the moral consequences of their actions. The efforts of governments to control commerce to their individual advantage, moreover, had only added to the damage, inciting wars of conquest on an unprecedented scale, and encouraging the growth of great capital cities at the expense of the rest of the state, and in particular the rural economy. Against this threat, both Doria and Fletcher would attempt to renew and reinforce political limitations upon economic activity for its own sake. Fletcher would do so by a reordering of Scottish society, prescribing what was virtually an agrarian law to secure the basis for a free and independent Scottish political community, and also by redrawing the political map of Europe, and in the process dividing almost all existing political communities (including the Scottish) into smaller parts. Doria, by contrast, put his faith in the rule of a magistracy educated in jurisprudence and philosophy. In both cases, a strain of conscious idealism is not far from the surface. Fletcher openly acknowledged that his proposals were liable to be viewed as utopian; Doria cast his philosopher magistrates as Chinese mandarins. In different ways, it would seem, both were suggesting that only a deliberate decision to put virtue and politics first, and to check the acquisitive passions and selfish interests which drove economic activity, could reverse the damage which commerce was doing to civil life. To what extent either Fletcher or Doria expected their pleas to be heeded in practice may be impossible to determine; but the admission that commerce now set the terms of political discourse could not have been clearer.

In Fletcher's case, the admission may be regarded as confirmed by his reluctance to commit himself to print after publishing the *Account of a Conversation* in 1704, even though the Scottish crisis was not resolved until 1707. Living longer, Doria was to pursue the opposite course, protesting ever more noisily against what he saw as his age's acceptance of a false morality. Over the two decades between the publication of the first two and the third editions of the *Vita Civile* in 1710 and 1729, he not only turned against Descartes, but engaged in a vehement polemic against the new philosophy of Locke, openly avowing his allegiance to Plato. Later still, at the end of the 1730s, Doria would return to the economic issues first touched on in the 'Massime', but his commitment to the ideal of a virtuous magistracy remained, as we shall see in the final chapter, firm to the very end.

But by then another, much greater, Neapolitan mind had taken up the challenge represented by the new philosophy, and sought to counter it with a radically different, genuinely 'new science' of human affairs: Giambattista Vico. With Vico, as with the young David Hume after him, the attention shifts from politics and the economy to philosophy, from commerce to human nature, to the conditions, including the religious conditions, of sociability, and to the historical development of societies. But the questions raised by the debate over the predicament of kingdoms governed as provinces did not disappear from the Neapolitan and Scottish agendas. They would return to the forefront of intellectual interest in both countries in the 1750s, in the political economy of Antonio Genovesi and David Hume. By then, however, political economy had been put on a new intellectual basis. Where Fletcher and Doria strained against the conceptual limitations of neo-Machiavellianism, Genovesi and Hume were able to build upon fresh conceptual foundations, adapted from modern Epicureanism. In this guise, political economy would become, for Genovesi and Hume alike, the chosen vehicle of Enlightenment in their respective countries. It is to understand how this became possible that we turn next to Vico, and after him to Hume, and to an examination of the extraordinarily fertile engagement with modern sceptical Epicureanism which is to be found in both the *Scienza Nuova* and the *Treatise of Human Nature*.

CHAPTER 5

Vico, after Bayle

THE QUESTION OF VICO'S 'CONTEMPORARIES'

Over October and November 1725 Giambattista Vico dispatched presentation copies of his newly published *Princìpi di una Scienza Nuova* (the *New Science*) to a number of friends, fellow men of letters, and potential patrons. In the letters which accompanied the book he expressed his hopes for its success, and took the opportunity to point out the targets against whom it was directed. Writing to one of his closest friends among the Neapolitan clergy, the Capuchin Father Giacco (then out of the city for health reasons), Vico contrasted the *New Science* with his previous works. Those had been written to demonstrate his suitability for the university chairs for which he had been a candidate; now that he had been judged unworthy of such positions, he had been free to write the new book as he chose, for the benefit of the few who were truly wise. With this work, he told Giacco, he felt as if he had dressed himself as 'a new man'.[1]

Another, much more distant recipient of a presentation copy of the *New Science* was Jean Le Clerc. In his accompanying letter Vico fulsomely thanked Le Clerc for his review of Vico's previous publications in his *Bibliothèque Ancienne et Moderne* in 1722; it was Le Clerc's favourable judgement which had encouraged Vico to continue with the new work. In particular, Le Clerc's review had drawn favourable attention to Vico in Rome, where Cardinal Fabroni had publicly declared Vico's work to be a necessary defence of the Christian religion against the maxims of Thomas Hobbes and the advice to rulers of Bayle, 'who would have it that nations could be governed without religion'.[2] Vico made the same point more directly to a recipient of the book in Rome itself. To Cardinal Lorenzo Corsini (who

---

[1] Vico to Padre Giacco, 25 Oct. 1725, in *Giambattista Vico: Opere*, ed. Andrea Battistini, 2 vols. (Milan, 1990), pp. 308–10 (hereafter referred to simply as *Opere*).

[2] Vico to Jean le Clerc, 5 Nov. 1725, in *Opere*, pp. 311–12. The works reviewed by Le Clerc were the *De uno universi iuris principio et fine* and the *De constantia iurisprudentis* (1720–1), the first two of three volumes known together as the *Diritto Universale*.

201

would become Pope Clement XII in 1730) Vico wrote that he intended the *Scienza Nuova* to refute both the 'Hobbesian philosophers' and the 'Baylean philologists', by demonstrating that 'the world of nations could not be ruled for an instant without the religion of a provident divinity'. At the same time, he added, the work destroys 'the three systems of the natural law of the gentes' of Grotius, Pufendorf, and Selden, none of which had been founded on divine providence.[3] Further letters to correspondents in Rome in 1726 reinforced and elaborated the message Vico wanted to convey. To one he portrayed his work as an antidote to the corruption of the times, upholding the idea of providence in a world fluctuating between the 'chance' of Epicurus and the 'necessity' of Descartes. Among modern philosophers who had adopted the philosophy of Epicurus he singled out Gassendi and Locke for particular criticism.[4] To another Vico lamented the predominance of Cartesian philosophy in Naples, along with the taste for secondhand knowledge, exemplified in dictionaries and journals such as those of Moréri and Bayle.[5]

In part Vico's letters and presentation copies reflected the time-honoured strategy of an author seeking recognition from his peers in the Republic of Letters. He clearly hoped that his efforts would gain reviews for the book and fresh patronage for himself. But Vico's insistence on identifying the targets of his work suggests that he may also have wished to make an intellectual point. Le Clerc illustrates the scope for both motives. In writing to him, Vico was requesting a notice from the leading reviewer in the Republic of Letters. Le Clerc was, it is true, a Protestant whose liberal, Arminian, and perhaps Socinian leanings in theology certainly did not make him sympathetic towards Roman Catholicism. But his broad, catholic interests in the world of learning ensured that his reviews in the *Bibliothèque ancienne et moderne* carried weight among Protestants and Roman Catholics alike. At the same time, Le Clerc was particularly interested in the debate over the nature and antiquity of the early pagan religions, and their relation to the religion of the Old Testament Hebrews, a subject directly relevant to the argument of the *New Science*. Perhaps most important to Vico,

---

[3] Vico to Cardinal Lorenzo Corsini in Rome, 20 Nov. 1722, in *Opere*, pp. 313–14: 'Nella quale . . . si truovano tali princìpi convincere di falso e i filosofi obbesiani e i filologi baileani, con dimonstrar loro che'l mondo delle nazioni non abbia retto pur un momento senza la religione d'una divinità provedente . . .'

[4] Vico to the Abbate Esperti in Rome [Naples, early 1726], in *Opere*, pp. 322–5.

[5] Vico to Padre de Vitry, Naples, 20 Jan. 1726, in *Opere*, pp. 326–29. On the references to Bayle in these letters: Lorenzo Bianchi, '"E contro la practica de' governi di Baile, che vorrebbe senza religioni poter reggere le nazioni". Note su Bayle nella corrispondenza di Vico', *Bollettino del Centro di Studi Vichiani*, 30 (2000), 17–30. The four references to Bayle in Vico's correspondence were all made in the period 1724–6.

Le Clerc had been a public antagonist of Bayle, whom he had attacked as a sceptic, perhaps even an atheist. The presentation to him of a copy of the *New Science* was thus both a statement of Vico's desire to be recognised in the Republic of Letters, and a taking of intellectual sides.

In the case of Corsini, the hope of patronage was almost certainly a motive. Vico had already sought a subvention from the cardinal for an earlier version of the book, the so-called 'Scienza Nuova in forma negativa'; despite a rebuff, he clearly hoped that Corsini might think better of the new work. Vico's need was the greater since he lacked effective patrons in Naples itself.[6] For all his claim to Giacco that the rejection for his candidacy for a professorship of law had been a liberation, Vico had been hurt in reputation and income. In these circumstances his emphasising that the new book refuted an array of heretical philosophers and jurists might well have been calculated to win favour in the Vatican – especially at a time when Neapolitan men of letters were under suspicion in Rome following Giannone's publication of his *Civil History* two years earlier.[7] Yet there is reason to think that Vico was not simply being opportunist in announcing the targets of his book: there was in Rome at the time an intellectual context in which the *New Science* could be expected to have an impact.

In particular, there was a group of theologians keenly interested in issues which were relevant to the subject matter of Vico's book. Among these were Celestino Galiani, Domenico Bencini, Francesco Bianchini, and Biagio Garofalo. Bencini appears to have been the group's coordinator, being secretary of the Accademia dei Concili, which had been revived by Pope Clement XI specifically to combat heresy in modern philosophy, and which met at the *De Propaganda Fide* where Bencini taught theology. Central preoccupations of these theologians were the relation of sacred to profane history, the status of the Bible as history, and the nature of pagan or Gentile religions.[8] The challenges they now faced in this area were several. They were headed by Isaac de La Peyrère's *Praeadamitae* (1655), which argued that there must have been men in the world before Adam, thus casting doubt on the historical credibility of the creation story in Genesis. Reinforcing La Peyrère was the new critical biblical scholarship of Benedict Spinoza and Richard Simon, who questioned Moses' authorship of the Pentateuch (the first

---

[6] Vico continued to seek patronage from Corsini in later years, requesting it for his sons Gennaro and Filippo in 1726 and 1737: Fabio Tarzia, 'Una supplica inedita di Giambattista Vico al papa Clemente XII del 20 novembre 1737', *Bollettino del Centro di Studi Vichiani*, 30 (2000), 303–8.

[7] See above, pp. 123–3, 146.

[8] The group is identified and its interests surveyed by Ferrone, *Scienza natura religione. Mondo Newtoniano e cultura italiana nel primo Settecento* (Naples, 1982), pp. 366–94.

five books of the Old Testament). Further complicating the picture were the comparative studies of the religion of the ancient Egyptians, Chaldeans, and Hebrews by John Spencer, John Marsham, and more recently Jean Le Clerc, which suggested that the Hebrew religion was not necessarily the oldest of the three. All of this heterodox scholarship was known and studied in Rome in the first three decades of the century.

One of this group was of particular importance to Vico: his fellow Neapolitan, Celestino Galiani, to whom he also sent a presentation copy of the *New Science*. Galiani was born in 1681 near Foggia, in the Capitanata; orphaned at seven, he entered the order of the Celestini (whence his adopted name) at sixteen, and was sent to Rome to continue his studies in 1701. He quickly established himself as one of the ablest of the Vatican's theological scholars, and though he visited Naples in 1708 and was well connected with its intellectual life, he himself remained in Rome until 1731, when he was appointed bishop of Taranto and *Cappellano Maggiore* in Naples, with responsibility for the direction of the university. Galiani's one published work was a strictly orthodox treatise on biblical chronology, refuting La Peyrère. But his many writings in manuscript tell a different story, whose significance has been elucidated by Vincenzo Ferrone. In these he is seen to have accepted Spinoza's and Simon's rejection of Mosaic authorship of the Pentateuch, to have engaged with the works of the heterodox Protestants Grotius, Toland, and Locke, and to have taken a particular interest in English experimental and mathematical philosophy, that of Newton above all.[9] Galiani also had a keen interest in modern Epicureanism. He played a leading role in the project to publish the *Opera Omnia* of Gassendi, which came out in Florence in 1727, canvassing support for it in Rome and in Naples (there with the assistance of Bartolomeo Intieri, of whom we shall hear more in ch. 7). The edition was prefaced by a statement from the printer (but more probably a collective manifesto) in which Gassendi's atomism was harnessed to the cause of Galilean experimentalism, and the advantages of Epicurean morals were set against the dangers of Stoicism.[10]

Ferrone has drawn attention to the intellectual interest of one in particular of Galiani's manuscript writings, the 'Ricerche intorno alle primi origini della scienza morale' ['Enquiries into the first origins of moral science'].[11] The manuscript survives in two versions, one evidently a fair copy of the

---

[9] Ferrone, *Scienza natura religione*, pp. 382–420.

[10] Ibid., pp. 155–66.

[11] Ibid., pp. 420–42. For a first interpretation of this work, see Koen Stapelbroek, 'Moral philosophy in Ferdinando Galiani's early political economy', University of Cambridge doctoral thesis (2004), ch. 1. 'Celestino Galiani: the moral power of commerce'.

other, among Galiani's papers in Naples. Internal evidence suggests that it was written in Rome, probably in the early 1720s.[12] The 'Scienza morale' reveals Galiani's wide acquaintance with modern philosophy: Descartes, Malebranche, Locke, and Bayle are all cited by name. Galiani's purpose in writing the treatise appears to have been to steer a path between Cartesian dualism, with its strict separation of mind from body, and the Spinozist or Stratonist view of thought as being embedded within matter (a view then being applied to the Newtonian concept of attraction by the Venetian Antonio Conti).[13] Rejecting Descartes' concept of innate ideas, and in particular the suggestion that we have an innate idea of God, Galiani offered instead an account of ideas and their foundation in the senses which seems closely based on that of Locke. So doing, he was careful to reject the Epicurean idea of eternal matter, deploying several arguments to show that the world was yet young, the result of a recent act of creation. But the proof of God's creating mind was derived from nature itself: Galiani's was an explicitly natural theology.[14] This in turn provided the basis for a theory of morals which likewise denied that they were innate: a man falling from the clouds would acquire his ideas of virtue and vice only through his senses. What he would learn, moreover, is the pleasure and convenience (*comodo*) to be derived from the company of others: if man is 'by nature a sociable animal' (*per natura un animale sociabile*), making it possible to say that God created man with 'sociability' (*la sociabilità*), it is because he finds pleasure in the society of others. Likewise the laws of nature are God's commands, but they are adapted to man as he is, and to his need to live in society.[15] In the course of this account of sociability, Galiani also touched on several issues which had been the subject of extended discussion by Bayle: the

---

[12] The manuscripts are among the papers of Celestino Galiani in the Società Napoletana per la Storia Patria, Mss xxx.C.16, ff. 1r–68r (fair copy), and xxxi. B.1, ff. 197r–249r (draft). References are to the fair copy, Ms xxx.C.16. Evidence suggesting that the work was written in Rome is in the reference to waterfalls and cataracts 'come quelle da noi poco discoste di Tivoli nel Teverone' (ff. 51r–v), i.e. the falls of Tivoli; that it dates from the early 1720s is suggested by the author's remark that he cannot remember his thinking 'prima di trentacinque in quarant'anni' (f. 45r), that is (as I understand the passage), it is only for thirty-five of his forty years that he can remember thinking – he cannot remember his thinking in his first five years. (The philosophic point being that he is unable to claim that he has always existed as a thinking being.) Since Galiani was born in 1681, this would place the date of composition around 1721. See also Ferrone, *Scienza natura religione*, pp. 354–5 n. 25.

[13] On Conti, see ibid., pp. 338–54.

[14] 'Della scienza morale', SNSP Ms xxx.C.16, ff. 23v–43v, and 34r–58r (the foliation of the manuscript goes back to 34 after 43, and thus repeats 34–43 before carrying on). The chapter headings in this part of the work are: 'Della religione naturale', 'Dell'idea di Dio', 'Dell'esistenza di Dio', and 'Alcune difficoltà intorno alle riferite ragioni sopra l'esistenza di una mente eterna'.

[15] 'Della scienza morale', SNSP Ms xxx.C.16, ff. 1r–23r; the discussion of 'sociability' is on ff. 17v–18v. The chapter headings here are: 'Come han potuto acquistare le idee della virtù o de vizio', 'Delle Legge di Natura', and 'De' doveri, che prescrive la Legge di Natura in ordine a noi stessi'.

question of whether animals have souls, and thus whether they are radically different from humans; the authority to be attached to common opinion; and the observation (explicitly attributed to Bayle) that it is common to find orthodox Christians living immorally and the unorthodox living virtuously.[16] Although the 'Scienza morale' remained unfinished, petering out in fragmentary remarks, there is more than enough to suggest that its author was committed to a moderate, Christian Epicureanism, in which morality and natural law were in accordance with men's natural desire for the pleasures and conveniences of society.

It is not known whether the manuscript circulated in Naples in the 1720s; there appears to be no evidence that Vico himself was acquainted with it. Nor is it clear whether Vico regarded Galiani as friend or foe when he sent him a copy of the *New Science* in 1725. (Later, after Galiani's return to Naples in 1731, they would be ranged on opposite sides of Neapolitan intellectual culture, but apparently without personal rancour.) What the manuscript 'Scienza morale' does confirm, however, is that Vico was justified in supposing that there were in Rome at the time thinkers interested in modern philosophy and natural law, more particularly in Epicureanism and in Bayle, and who might therefore be expected to respond to the terms in which he announced the *New Science*.

But perhaps Vico was so keen to attract potentially sympathetic readers in Rome because he knew that he would not find them in Naples. Many scholars have been inclined to think so, and to suppose that Vico was a prophet without honour in his own city. This view has been particularly favoured by English-speaking Vico scholars, led by Isaiah Berlin and Giorgio Tagliacozzo. Pointing to the frequent complaints of isolation to be found in Vico's *Autobiography*, these have been happy to use his supposed neglect by his contemporaries to set off their own claims for his universal significance. Vico, it is suggested, was the classic case of a thinker 'born before his time'.[17] Among Italian scholars Benedetto Croce had his own

---

[16] 'Della scienza morale', SNSP Ms xxx.C.16, ff. 40v–44r (ff 40–43 in the second, repeated foliation) (on animal souls), 46r (on 'il comun consenso delle gente'), 63v (Bayle on the morals of orthodox Christians). See Ferrone, *Scienza natura religione*, pp. 427–9, for a not quite identical list of references.

[17] Isaiah Berlin, 'The philosophical ideas of Giambattista Vico', in *Vico and Herder: two Studies in the History of Ideas* (London, 1976), pp. 1–142, with the observation that he was 'born before his time' in the opening sentence, p. 3. For Giorgio Tagliacozzo, leader of Vico studies in the United States, Vico's significance would only be realised in our times, when his philosophy was recognised as providing the unifying framework for all the advances in the humanities and social sciences since 1875: 'Introductory remarks' to Giorgio Tagliacozzo, Michael Mooney, and Donald Phillip Verene (eds.), *Vico and Contemporary Thought* (Atlantic Highlands, N.J., 1976), pp. 1–8. By the 1990s Tagliacozzo was sufficiently confident of the state of Vico studies to believe in Vico's 'resurrection': *The 'Arbor Scientiae' Reconceived and the History of Vico's Resurrection* (Atlantic Highlands, N.J., 1993).

reasons for thinking along the same lines; but from the mid-twentieth century a more historical approach prevailed, and scholars increasingly ran in the opposite direction, identifying 'contemporaries' for Vico all across late seventeenth- and early eighteenth-century Europe. For this, however, they were sharply called to order in 1981, when Paolo Rossi put the simple question: 'who are the contemporaries of Vico?' In a direct challenge to his fellow scholars, Rossi questioned their inclination to connect Vico with any and every 'contemporary' thinker who might serve to magnify his originality, irrespective of whether Vico could be shown to have read and responded to that 'contemporary's' work. In principle, Rossi conceded, Vico's contemporaries might be taken to include all who published between the late 1680s and the early 1740s. But in the *New Science* Vico cites no more than fourteen works published in the 1680s and 1690s, and a further seven published after 1700. Arguably, Rossi observed, the writers of most interest to the author of the *New Science* were those whose works appeared earlier in the seventeenth century, between 1600 and 1680. The evidence of Vico's *Autobiography*, Rossi added, must reinforce the need for caution in connecting Vico with his immediate context. The modern authors whom Vico singled out as important for his philosophical development – Descartes, Bacon, and Grotius – were all from the earlier part of the century. Even more telling was Vico's apparent admission that he could not read French, which must have ruled out direct engagement with many of the philosophers and scholars of his time. The burden of the evidence, Rossi concluded, was clear. Vico was not up to date in his reading; his learning, as Momigliano had previously suggested, was in important respects archaic.[18]

Vico's letters to Le Clerc and to Corsini and others in Rome have already suggested that such scepticism may be exaggerated. Vico himself clearly felt that he had something important to say to his contemporaries at the centre of the Catholic intellectual world. Is there reason to believe that Naples was different? A closer look at the *Autobiography* suggests that his self-depicted isolation may have been misinterpreted. Commissioned in 1721 by a Venetian publisher to be one of a series of lives of contemporary writers, the *Vita di Giambattista Vico scritta da se medesimo* (hereafter the

[18] Paolo Rossi, 'Chi sono i contemporanei di Vico?', *Rivista di Filosofia*, 62 (1981), 51–82; the use of the present tense underlined the challenge to Rossi's contemporaries. The paper is reprinted in Paolo Rossi, *Le sterminate antichità e nuovi saggi vichiani* (Florence, 1999), pp. 275–303. The same volume contains a sequel 'Ancora sui contemporanei di Vico', ibid., pp. 387–96 (a response to Eugenio Garin's claim that Vico had an understanding of advances in the physical sciences, from Galileo to Newton), along with several other instances of Vico's 'archaisms', pp. 305–86, 399–405, 473–9. Anticipating Rossi was Arnaldo Momigliano, 'Vico's *Scienza Nuova*: Roman "Bestioni" and Roman "Eroi"', in Momigliano's collected *Essays in Ancient and Modern Historiography* (Oxford, 1973), pp. 253–76.

Autobiography) was probably composed in 1723 and supplemented in 1728, with a further 'Addition' in 1731. It was consciously written 'da filosofo'; and though Vico denied the resemblance, it followed the model established by Descartes in his *Discours de la Méthode*.[19] Like Descartes, Vico devoted most of the work to an account of how he had reached his philosophical position at the time of writing. As intellectual history, therefore, the *Autobiography* is liable to be foreshortened, narrowing the focus on to what Vico thought was necessary to explain his existing preoccupations. But since its writing coincided closely with Vico's decision to devote himself to the *New Science*, the *Autobiography* may nevertheless tell us much about Vico's thinking just as he launched himself on that project. Specifically, I suggest, it reveals Vico's familiarity with the dominant current in late seventeenth- and early eighteenth-century Neapolitan intellectual culture: Epicureanism.

This is evident, first of all, in the negative: in Vico's repeated efforts to distance and dissociate himself from that dangerous philosophy. The distancing was literal: it was, he reminded his readers, while he was staying at Vatolla in the Cilento, and therefore out of Naples, that the 'vogue' for studying Epicurus 'sopra (through) Pier Gassendi' was at its height.[20] Though he did not say so, the years of his absence, between 1686 and 1695, also coincided with the 'trial of the Atheists', several of whom had been Vico's acquaintances; by implication, his absence from the city conveniently absolved him of any association with that affair. When he studied Epicurus' philosophy for himself (which he did by reading its most comprehensive ancient exponent, Lucretius), Vico discovered that it was, as he puts it, fit only for the weak and limited intellects of women and children. He particularly objected to its reduction of mind to body, and body to indivisible particles. On the basis of a mechanical physics, Epicurus had constructed a metaphysics from the senses alone (one exemplified by the metaphysics of John Locke), and an ethics of pleasure, good only for men who live in solitude. Whatever satisfaction Vico remembered deriving from Epicurean explanations of the forms of corporeal nature, their accounts of the workings of the human mind seemed to Vico quite ridiculous. In his view it was vital to recognise those 'eternal truths' which are in our mind and not at all dependent on our body, having been placed there by an 'eternal idea' itself quite separate from body. Such were the truths of physics in Plato's *Timaeus*. These must be distinguished from what we understand

---

[19] *Vita di Giambattista Vico scritta da se medesimo*, in *Opere*, pp. 3–85; English translation as *The Autobiography of Giambattista Vico*, transl. M. H. Fisch and T. G. Bergin (Ithaca, 1944). Henceforth cited in these editions as *Vita* and *Autobiography*: thus, *Vita*, pp. 7, 69; *Autobiography*, pp. 113, 182.
[20] *Vita*, p. 18; *Autobiography*, p. 126.

through the body alone, when we use our imagination, memory, passions, and senses. The knowledge we acquire in this way we do so by 'making' it ourselves.[21]

Given the importance Vico attached to distinguishing truths of the mind from purely corporeal knowledge, it may come as a surprise that he proceeds immediately to attack the philosophy of Descartes, since the French philosopher had proposed just such a mind–body dualism. But Vico turned to Descartes after reading Lucretius, having become aware of Descartes' fame in Naples. He read, he tells us, the exposition of Cartesian natural philosophy by Regius, assuming it to be the work of Descartes himself. What he discovered was that the physics of Descartes was all too similar to that of Epicurus. Both believed that matter was already formed in the beginning. Their disagreements were over lesser, specific issues, culminating in the difference that where Epicurus proposed a world at the mercy of chance, Descartes would subject it to fate. Descartes' claim to have established two types of substance, one of (material) extension, the other of intelligence, had simply been a device to win him approval 'tra i chiostri', among the theologians. An Epicurean physics led to a purely corporeal, Epicurean metaphysics, from which, not surprisingly, Descartes had been unable to derive a morals compatible with Christianity. Not even Malebranche, Vico added, had been able to erect a system of Christian morals on a Cartesian foundation. Reading Regius, therefore, only reinforced the lesson Vico had drawn from reading Lucretius, pointing him back once more to Plato. As a result, Vico recalled, he had returned to Naples to find himself a stranger in his own country, left to languish in obscurity.[22]

On this account, there is no need to doubt Vico's disaffection with Neapolitan intellectual life – or, perhaps, his capacity for self-pity. But disaffection does not entail that Vico was cut off from or indifferent to the main currents of thought in his city; on the contrary, it would seem that Vico was all too well aware of the intellectual trends prevailing among his contemporaries. When he complained to one of his Roman correspondents about the prevalence of Cartesianism in Naples, what he had in mind was the prevalence of Epicureanism.

A further reason to suppose that Vico was familiar with the dominant trends in Neapolitan intellectual culture, one not mentioned in the *Autobiography*, is the commission he received in 1722 to value the library of Giuseppe Valletta, which was subsequently sold by Valletta's heirs to the

[21] *Vita*, pp. 19–20; *Autobiography*, pp. 126–7.
[22] *Vita*, pp. 20–23, 26; *Autobiography*, pp. 128–30, 132, 134.

Oratorians. The range and depth of Valletta's holdings in seventeenth-century French metaphysical and moral philosophy were highlighted earlier.[23] They were particularly rich in works of an Augustinian or Epicurean tendency. To what extent Vico was able – or permitted himself – to read the books listed as *Libri Gallici* is impossible to know. But he is unlikely to have been left ignorant of their existence and general character. For all his complaints of neglect and isolation, there is no good reason to continue to believe that Vico was cut off from the intellectual culture of late seventeenth- and early eighteenth-century Naples, a culture which on his own account was particularly fascinated by the Epicurean philosophy.[24]

Vico, then, had a very good idea who his contemporaries were, and where he stood in relation to them. It is true that most of those singled out in his letters of 1725–6 as the targets of his book – Hobbes, Descartes, Gassendi, Grotius, Selden, and Pufendorf – belonged to an earlier period, and were not strictly his contemporaries. But this was not the case with all those he named: the lifespans of Locke and Bayle both overlapped with that of Vico. Moreover all those earlier thinkers continued to be read in a 'contemporary' perspective: Vico's Descartes, as we have seen, was an Epicurean, and therefore a contemporary, even if the original Descartes was not. A reading of the *New Science* in Vico's Neapolitan historical context has, accordingly, all that we should expect to commend it, and we may reasonably approach that work with its designated targets in mind. This is not to assume that Vico's hostility to Epicurean philosophy, and to Hobbes and Bayle in particular, was simple and obvious in its effects. The extent to which the *New Science*, in its successive versions, drew on the resources of Epicurean philosophy at the same time as it sought to repudiate their damaging implications will be a question central to the investigation which follows. But we may begin by supposing that arguments which Vico associated with Hobbes and Bayle, and with Epicureanism more generally, were among those most at issue in his new work.

---

[23] On the library of Giuseppe Valletta, see above, ch. 3, pp. 105–6; on Vico's role in its sale: Antonio Bellucci, 'Giambattista Vico e la Biblioteca dei Girolamini', *Quaderni della Biblioteca dei Girolamini di Napoli*, First Series 2 (1955).

[24] A recent study of Vico in English which does assert the importance of his Neapolitan context is Harold Samuel Stone, *Vico's Cultural History: the Production and Transmission of Ideas in Naples 1685–1750* (Leiden, New York, and Cologne, 1997). Stone, however, overlooked the contemporary interest in Epicurean philosophy, and thereby omitted what it is being argued here was the most important single aspect of that context. Fundamental studies of Vico in Neapolitan context in Italian include Eugenio Garin, 'Da Campanella a Vico', in Garin, *Dal Rinascimento all'Illuminismo. Studi e ricerche* (Pisa, 1970), pp. 79–117 (first published in 1968–9), and Enrico Nuzzo, 'Il congedo della "sagezza moderna" nella cultura napoletana tra '600 e '700. Vico e la tradizione dei "moralisti"', *Bolletino del Centro di Studi Vichiani*, 17–18 (1987–8), 25–114.

VICO'S TARGETS: HOBBES AND SPINOZA

In pursuing Vico's reasons for singling out Hobbes, Bayle, and Epicure-anism as his targets, it remains important to bear Rossi's warnings in mind. It is one thing to show, as I have sought to do, that Vico had an acute sense of contemporary philosophical trends; it is another to suggest that he possessed a detailed knowledge of the works of individual contemporaries. Not only references, even identifiable allusions to contemporary authors are rare. At no point in the *New Science*, in any of its surviving versions, is there sustained engagement with the arguments of another philosopher. Nevertheless, it may be helpful to amplify the context established so far, by providing outlines of the philosophy of Hobbes and (more fully) of Bayle, and indicating their relation to Epicureanism. Between the two will be inserted a – brief – account of Spinoza's philosophy of nature, because Bayle's account of Epicureanism was inseparable from his response to Spinoza, and because Vico would subsequently oppose Hobbes and Spinoza as representatives of the Epicurean and Stoic philosophies. The purpose of amplifying Vico's context in this way is not to revive the sugges-tion that he 'must have read' the works of these philosophers in detail, or to claim that his counter-arguments apply exclusively to them. It is, rather, to help to clarify the nature and direction of Vico's own arguments, when we get to them, and thus to achieve a fuller historical understanding of the *New Science*.

According to Thomas Hobbes (1588–1679), the world we know, both natural and human, is constituted by matter in motion. What we know and how we behave can only be understood by building on that foun-dation. It is through motion that our senses are aroused, and our sense impressions are then taken up by the imagination, retained in the memory, and developed in the understanding. Understanding also requires speech, by which things are named, and reason, which is the reckoning of the con-sequences of our definitions: the outcome of understanding is knowledge of those consequences, which is 'science'. In so far as such knowledge depends upon our (arbitrary) use of language, therefore, it is an artificial, human creation; but what we know, the content of our science, can only ever be a representation of matter in motion.[25]

---

[25] Thomas Hobbes, *Leviathan* (1651), in the edition by Richard Tuck (Cambridge, 1991), chs. 1–5, in Latin (1668), in the edition by Sir William Molesworth, *Thomae Hobbes Opera philosophica omnia*, vol. III (London, 1841); *De Corpore* (1655), English version *Elements of Philosophy. The First Section, concerning Body* (1656) respectively in Molesworth (ed.), *Opera philosophica*, vol. I (London, 1839), and *The English Works of Thomas Hobbes*, vol. I (London, 1839).

It is likewise through our senses that we are moved by our passions to act. In response to the senses and the imagination, our passions express appetite (for pleasure) or aversion (to pain), and determine or 'will' that we act accordingly. The process of deciding to act is therefore a physical one throughout: the passions, like the imagination, are corporeal, belonging to the body. As is well known, this account of how we act left no room for free will, a concept which Hobbes derided as a verbal confusion. What we call the 'will' is simply the last appetite (or aversion) in deliberating; freedom is a purely physical condition, the absence of obstacles to moving in the way that we wish to do. Less well known, but equally important to Hobbes's thinking about the passions, was his explanation of motion within the mind – the process of willing. Descartes, who sought to separate mind from body, had suggested that there might be a motion which was purely mental, and not corporeal. Hobbes, by contrast, insisted that motion within the mind was corporeal. The term he used to denote such motion was 'endeavour', in Latin *conatus*. It is by endeavour or *conatus* that our passions move us to avoid pain or achieve pleasure.[26] In Hobbes's terms, therefore, human actions have a consistently corporeal, material explanation.

Hobbes's philosophy had dramatic implications for the explanation of how men came to live together in society. Appetite for pleasure and aversion to pain did not make men naturally sociable. On the contrary, man's natural state was one of war, of every man against every man. For the overriding fear of death and desire for self-preservation, coupled with radical uncertainty about the lengths to which everyone else would go to ensure their own preservation, encouraged the individual to take pre-emptive action against his fellow men. The only escape from such a mutually destructive condition was for each individual to recognise, by reasoning from consequences, that his preservation would be better secured by an agreement to transfer all his powers (except that of immediate self-defence) to a civil sovereign. Such an agreement would take the form of a contract, or covenant, between the participating individuals; alternatively, the contract might be imposed on each individual by a conqueror. Subsequently the interpretation of the contract (up to the point of the individual's self-preservation) would be entirely in the hands of the sovereign. By Hobbes's account, therefore,

---

[26] Hobbes, *Leviathan*, chs. 6, 21; *De Corpore*, ch. xxv, sects. 12–13. I am indebted to the lucid discussion by Susan James, *Passion and Action: the Emotions in Seventeenth-century Philosophy* (Oxford, 1997), pp. 126–36. For a critical analysis of the physics of *conatus*, on which Hobbes was interrogated by Leibniz: J. W. N. Watkins, *Hobbes's System of Ideas* (London, 1973), pp. 85–96. See too Mario Papini, 'Vicenda seicentesca di minimi e conati', *Bollettino del Centro di Studi Vichiani*, 22–23 (1992–93), pp. 146–55.

human society was anything but natural: it was an artificial creation, and to keep it in being required an authority possessed of arbitrary, discretionary powers.[27]

Equally dramatic were the implications of Hobbes's philosophy for the understanding of religion. An account of the mind in purely corporeal terms made it very difficult to conceive of an incorporeal, immortal soul. Hobbes may have avoided explicit affirmation of the mortality of the soul; but he regarded the term to which the theologians had resorted, 'incorporeal substance', as another instance of verbal confusion, and he saw no basis for supposing that humans have an innate longing for immortality. Rather, the natural cause of religion was anxiety for the future, which made men fear the power of invisible things. The poets were therefore right to depict the gods (that is, the gods of the Gentiles) as created by human fear. Once men began to think rationally, and desired to know causes, they would then acknowledge 'one God Eternall, Infinite, and Omnipotent'. For they would recognise that there must be one 'First Mover', and identify God as the first and eternal cause of all things.[28] There was no suggestion, however, that the First Mover was a mind which continued to direct the world and the affairs of men: Hobbes made no mention of a divine providence. Nor was there any question of God taking responsibility for the naturally hostile behaviour of men towards each other. Since 'the Desires, and other Passions of man, are in themselves no Sin',[29] there was no need to invoke the Fall or to construct a theodicy to explain why God permitted evil in the world. Hobbes did not directly question the status of Scripture as the revealed Word of God. He did, however, set strict limits to the significance of Scripture by insisting that its interpretation was rightly a matter for the civil sovereign alone, and should not involve the churches. He also reduced the articles of Christian belief to the proposition that 'Jesus is the Christ' – although even this did not need to be publicly affirmed.[30]

Hobbes did not present his philosophy under an Epicurean banner. In the first half of the seventeenth century, when Hobbes's thinking took shape, it was Stoicism, not Epicureanism, which was intellectually reputable. The case for Epicureanism, in a form in which it could be discussed openly within a Christian culture, had still to be made. But Hobbes was personally close and intellectually sympathetic to the philosopher who would do more

---

[27] Brusquely summarised, this was the argument of Hobbes's *De Cive* (1647), modern critical edition by Howard Warrender (Oxford, 1983), English translation as *On the Citizen*, by Richard Tuck and Michael Silverthorne (Cambridge, 1998), chs. 1–14, and subsequently also of *Leviathan*, chs. 13–30.

[28] Hobbes, *Leviathan*, ch. 12 'Of Religion'.   [29] Hobbes, *Leviathan*, p. 89.

[30] Hobbes, *De Cive*, chs. XV–XVIII; sharpened in *Leviathan*, part III, 'Of a Christian Commonwealth'.

than anyone to make that case, Pierre Gassendi; and followers of Gassendi, such as Samuel Sorbière, were among Hobbes's greatest admirers. It was not difficult, subsequently, to understand major features of Hobbes's philosophy in Epicurean terms.[31] His doctrine that men seek pleasure through the passions, and thus understand pleasure in corporeal terms, was readily characterised as Epicurean, as was the proposition that men's natural condition was solitary, brutish, and violent. Hobbes did maintain that everything had a cause: he did not portray a world created and governed by chance, as Epicurus had done. But Hobbes's causes were arbitrary in their operation: necessity was not purpose, still less evidence of continuing divine oversight. It did not require a great leap to equate so radical a denial of divine providence with the Epicurean doctrine of chance.

Hobbes is often linked in histories of philosophy and of political thought with his Jewish and Dutch contemporary, Baruch or Benedict Spinoza (1632–1677). Vico did not identify Spinoza as an antagonist in the *Autobiography*, or in the letters which accompanied the first presentation copies of the *New Science*, but he did attack him, and still more his doctrine, on several occasions in the *New Science* itself. This has encouraged scholars – and particularly English-speaking scholars – to see the relation between Vico and Spinoza as important, and to suggest varying degrees of indebtedness on the part of Vico.[32] Drawing on their arguments, Jonathan Israel has recently drafted Vico into his great panorama of 'Radical Enlightenment', as further proof that Spinoza was the seminal intellect of this pre- or early Enlightenment period.[33] Even if there is little to support such claims, Spinoza, and arguments which were regarded as Spinozist, do feature at important points in the *New Science*, not least in contradistinction to Epicurean arguments. A short sketch of Spinoza's philosophy will make it easier to appreciate these when they are encountered.

[31] On Hobbes's links with Gassendi and his circle in Paris, Noel Malcolm, 'Hobbes and the European Republic of Letters', *Aspects of Hobbes* (Oxford, 2002), pp. 497–8. Epicurean philosophy may have played a larger part in keeping Hobbes within the mainstream of European thought in the later seventeenth century than Malcolm allows.

[32] Frederick Vaughan, '*La Scienza Nuova*: orthodoxy and the art of writing', *Forum Italicum*, 2 (1968), 332–58, has been surprisingly influential in suggesting that Vico was a covert Spinozist; among those to follow Vaughan's lead have been James C. Morrison, 'Vico and Spinoza', *Journal of the History of Ideas*, 41 (1980), 49–68; J. S. Preus, 'Spinoza, Vico and the imagination of religion', *Journal of the History of Ideas*, 50 (1989), 71–93; and Gino Bedani, *Vico Revisited: Orthodoxy, Naturalism and Science in the Scienza Nuova* (Oxford, 1989), pp. 86–90. Bedani cast the net wider, and also drew attention to Vico's interest in Lucretius (pp. 90–3); but his search for 'covert levels of meaning' in Vico's writing was an emphatic renewal of Vaughan's approach, accompanied by repeated references to Vico's 'indebtedness' to Spinoza (pp. 267–74).

[33] Israel, *Radical Enlightenment*, pp. 664–70.

It was in the first of his two major works, the *Tractatus Theologico-Politicus* (1670), that Spinoza challenged the assumption of Moses' authorship of the Pentateuch. Setting aside the assumption of divine inspiration which Moses personified, Spinoza subjected the Bible to historical criticism. He argued that the Mosaic books must have been compiled much later, and that they, and indeed the whole of the Old Testament, were no different in kind from the early historical records of any other literate nation.[34] Even more controversial, however, was the *Ethics* (published in the *Opera Posthuma* in 1677–8), in which Spinoza set out his radically monist philosophy. According to Spinoza, nature, man, and God can be explained in terms of the one concept of substance. Since both God and nature are contained within substance, they can be treated as identical, while thought and extension can be understood as different modes of the one substance. From this it follows that mind, as a mode of the substance which contains God, is both divine and human: all human knowledge, therefore, ultimately corresponds with the divine intellect. Further, the order and connection of ideas being the same as the order and connection of things, the powers of mind and body are one. *Conatus*, as Spinoza used the term, characterised the striving of both mind and body to preserve and increase their power, and thus to enhance the individual's joy or diminish his sadness.[35]

It is certainly possible to read Spinoza, like Hobbes, as a philosopher of materialism. But Spinoza's monist concept of substance, which incorporated the divine intellect, went far beyond Hobbes's straightforward insistence on the corporeality of the passions and of *conatus*, and his identification of God as (simply) the first cause. These differences were significant: not the least of their consequences was that it would be difficult subsequently to represent Spinoza as an Epicurean. Rather, his philosophy was commonly associated with Stoicism.[36] As we shall see, this was how Vico understood him. In opposition to Hobbes the Epicurean, Vico placed Spinoza with the Stoics, as an adherent of the doctrine that fate (rather than chance) ruled the world. But we shall be better placed to appreciate why Vico should have understood the arguments of Spinoza and the Epicureans as he did once we have reviewed the discussion of them in the work of Bayle.

[34] Spinoza, Baruch or Benedict, *Tractatus Theologico-Politicus* (1670), English transl. R. H. M. Elwes as *A Theologico-Political Treatise* (New York, 1951).

[35] Spinoza, *Ethics* (1667–68), transl. R. H. M. Elwes (New York, 1955). I am again indebted to James, *Passion and Action*, pp. 136–56.

[36] Spinoza's philosophy had identifiable Stoic sources: see Susan James, 'Spinoza the Stoic', in Tom Sorell (ed.), *The Rise of Modern Philosophy: the Tension between the New and Traditional Philosophies from Machiavelli to Leibniz* (Oxford, 1993), pp. 289–316.

VICO'S TARGETS: BAYLE

Vico's relation to Pierre Bayle (1647–1706) is the most debated of all. It has become, in effect, a test case of whether Vico had any close 'contemporaries'. In modern Vico scholarship, the first observation of Bayle's apparent importance for Vico was made by Eugenio Garin. Detailing the successive allusions and references to Bayle in Vico's writings from the 1720s onwards, Garin suggested that Bayle was one of Vico's deepest preoccupations; specifically, the *New Science* should be seen as the most important Italian response to Bayle's hypothesis of a society of atheists.[37] The suggestion was pursued by Gianfranco Cantelli, in a study which set off Vico's treatment of pagan religion in the *New Science* against the contrasting discussions of the same subject by Bayle and by Le Clerc. Vico's engagement with the arguments of Bayle's works on the comet, the *Continuation* as well as the original *Pensées Diverses*, Cantelli believed, was such as to leave no doubt that Vico had read both with attention.[38] To this Rossi objected in his strongest terms. There was nothing to indicate exactly which works by Bayle Vico had read (and one of which Cantelli had made much, the *Continuation des Pensées Diverses*, was not available in any Neapolitan library). Moreover Vico's statement in the *Autobiography* that he never cared to learn French made it most unlikely that he could have given sustained attention to any work only available in that language.[39] Rossi's was not, however, the last word.

In a lengthy and notably balanced review of the issues, Enrico Nuzzo has pointed out that historical assessment of the relation between Bayle and Vico is not reducible to evidence of Vico's reading. (Even in that connection, Nuzzo suggests, the extent to which Vico was able to read French remains an open question, the declaration in the *Autobiography* notwithstanding.) In a broader historical perspective, the overlap between several of Bayle's and Vico's interests and arguments is sufficient to warrant further investigation. Whether Vico can be shown to have read Bayle closely is less important than the light which the comparison may shed on the modernity of Vico's arguments: his contribution to contemporary debates about the origin and nature of religion, the sociability of man, and the historical process of society's development, Nuzzo suggests, could not have been what it was

---

[37] Eugenio Garin, 'Per una storia dei rapporti fra Bayle e l'Italia', in Garin, *Dal Rinascimento all'Illuminismo*, pp. 178–82 (the article first appeared in 1958–9).

[38] Gianfranco Cantelli, *Vico e Bayle. Premesse per un confronto*, Studi Vichiani 4 (Naples, 1971). The conviction that 'there is therefore no doubt that Vico had read the *Pensées Diverses* and the *Continuation* with a certain attention' is expressed on p. 71.

[39] Rossi, 'Chi sono i contemporanei di Vico?', 72–6, *Le sterminate antichità*, pp. 295–8; for Vico's declaration that he never learned French, *Vita, Opere*, p. 25, *Autobiography*, p. 134.

unless he was up to date in his awareness of the issues under discussion.[40] Nuzzo's observations provide the starting point and justification for what will be attempted here. My object in what follows is not to revisit the question of Bayle's 'influence' upon Vico; it is simply to reconstruct a context in which the text of the *New Science* may be read and, perhaps, better understood.

Vico associated Bayle with one supremely dangerous idea: that it is possible to conceive of a society without religion. Bayle advanced this hypothesis in the context of a discussion of the relative merits of a society of idolaters and a society of atheists, in the *Pensées Diverses*, first published in 1682, and in a second, enlarged edition in 1684. After an interval a third edition appeared in 1699, with an *Addition* appended to it; and when it a fourth edition was published in 1704 it was accompanied by the separate *Continuation des Pensées Diverses*, which was longer than the original. Since the *Continuation* was apparently not available in Naples, the following exposition concentrates on the *Pensées Diverses*.[41]

Bayle's *Pensées Diverses* was exactly what it purported to be: a collection of diverse thoughts on the implications of the comet of 1680. Bayle published the work anonymously, and wrote in the guise of a Roman Catholic, not as the Huguenot exile living in the United Provinces which he had become in 1681. The unsystematic character of the work may have served a number of purposes; but it did not mean that its arguments were selected at random. Bayle's objective was clear: he would refute and disabuse those who believed, or feared, that the comet was a portent of disaster to come. To this end he began by refuting any suggestion that there was either a natural or a historical connection between the appearance of comets and the incidence of disasters on earth. A connection of physical causation was impossible to demonstrate, in corpuscular or qualitative terms (ix–xv). The claims of the astrologists that their science could demonstrate such a connection Bayle dismissed as ridiculous: that many professed to believe them only discredited the doctrine that weight of opinion was a criterion of truth (xvii–xxii). But historians had been equally at fault in recording and giving credence to supposed disasters following the appearance of comets (v–vi).

---

[40] Enrico Nuzzo, 'Attorno a Vico e Bayle', in Nuzzo, *Tra ordine della storia e storicità. Saggi sui saperi della storia in Vico* (Rome, 2001), pp. 165–239; an earlier version was published in 1996. For the response to Rossi in particular, see pp. 174 ff., and n. 43 on pp. 220–2. Rossi has acknowledged Nuzzo's balance: *Le sterminate antichità*, p. 475n.

[41] The full title is *Pensées Diverses. Ecrites à un Docteur de Sorbonne, A l'Occasion de la Comète qui parut au mois de Decembre 1680*. I have used the 'nouvelle édition corrigé' published by the heirs of Reinhard Leers (Rotterdam, 1721), vols. I–II. References will be to section numbers (not pages), and these will be given in brackets in the text (in lower case Roman numerals).

In fact, Bayle pointed out, examination of events before and after the comets which had appeared earlier in the century would show that what occurred after them was no worse than what went before (xxiv–xliv).[42] Bayle brought this first part of his discussion to a close by reiterating and generalising his objections to claims for the efficacy of comets based on popular opinion: 'la persuasion générale des peuples' should carry no weight at all as a proof (xlv–xlix).

But the arguments to which Bayle devoted most attention were those drawn from 'theology'. Although any attempt to order them runs counter to Bayle's preference for apparently haphazard presentation, the arguments may be arranged in three stages. First, since comets are not the natural cause of events on earth which follow their appearance, they must, if they are to be understood as portents, be evident miracles. God's laws, Bayle maintains, citing 'un des plus grands philosophes de ce siècle' (identified in a note as Malebranche), are simple, general, and uniform. His providence is general, and is not disrupted by the exercise of 'volontés particulières' – except when he performs miracles. But there has been nothing to indicate that he has designated comets, for which there are several plausible natural explanations, as miracles (lvii–lx; cciv–ccxxxiv).

Second, Bayle argued that even if we allow comets to be miraculous portents, their greatest effect will be to encourage idolatry, which is surely offensive to God. There was no reason to suppose that the original belief that comets were portents was restricted to a small corner of Judaea. On the contrary, pagans had everywhere shown themselves susceptible to portents. Comets had always encouraged superstition and multiplied deities. The ancients, Bayle pointed out, had been liable to make gods out of anything, even, in the case of Marcus Aurelius, out of an unfaithful wife – a curious instance, Bayle remarked, of 'debonnairêtê philosophique' (cv). Characteristically, the pagans had assumed that their gods must be as keen on sensual pleasure as they were themselves, and had then pretended to punish them for it, with a presumption which amounted to 'leze-majesté divine' (cxxiii, cxxxii).

A Protestant might well read Bayle's criticism of pagan idolatry as an attack on Roman Catholic superstition. But the argument could equally have derived from a Roman Catholic standpoint, as a rigorist critique of moral and theological laxity, pagan or Christian. Although a Protestant himself, there is some reason to think that Bayle was sympathetic to this attitude, which was associated with the Augustinian, Jansenist wing of

---

[42] Bayle returned to this point at the end of the work: ccxxxv ff.

French Catholicism.[43] Nevertheless, it is clear that a critique of idolatry is not, in itself, Bayle's priority in the *Pensées Diverses*; at least as important is the argument which it is used to offset, the argument which forms the third stage of Bayle's 'theological' case against treating comets as portents.

This was the proposition that the idolatry which was encouraged by the fear of comets is not obviously preferable to atheism. In the course of the *Pensées Diverses* (and again in the *Continuation*), Bayle came at this proposition from constantly shifting angles. But certain points are recurrent. One was *ad hominem*. Bayle identified several idolaters (Nero and Alexander were two prominent examples) whose behaviour had been far worse than that of any known atheists. To these he counterposed examples of virtuous atheists, including the philosopher Epicurus, whose manner of living had been exemplary, the Sadducees, a Jewish sect who denied the immortality of the soul, yet lived more 'honestly' than the Pharisees, and 'the detestable Vanini', the young man burnt for atheism at Toulouse in 1619, despite his strict morals (clxxiv). These cases demonstrated that it was perfectly possible to have an idea of *honnêteté* (a translation of Cicero's *honestum*, signifying morality in general), without believing that there was a God (clxxviii).

An alternative, more general point of departure was supplied by observation of human nature. Bayle believed that all men are driven by their passions rather than governed by their opinions and beliefs:

> The true principle of man's actions (I except those in whom the grace of the Holy Spirit is deployed with all its efficacy) is no other than the temperament, the natural inclination towards pleasure, the taste which he acquires for certain objects, [and] the desire to please someone else, a habit he gains through the commerce of his friends.[44]

Certain passions – ambition, avarice, envy, revenge, lust – are found to rule men in every country and every century; they are the same in the Jew and the Muslim, the Turk and the Moor, the Christian and the infidel, the Indian and the Tartar (cxxxvi). There is nothing in our experience to suggest that a knowledge of God can check these vicious inclinations (cxxxiv, cf. cxliii). What does do so, however, is the force of human

---

[43] The identification of Bayle as a 'rigorist' is made by Cantelli, *Vico e Bayle*, pp. 15–17; it is endorsed by Nuzzo, 'Attorno a Vico e Bayle', pp. 205, 216.

[44] 'Le veritable principe des actions de l'homme, (j'excepte ceux en qui la grace du Saint Esprit se deploye avec toute son efficace) n'est autre chose que le temperament, l'inclination naturelle pour le plaisir, le goût que l'on contracte pour certains objets, le désir de plaire à quelqu'un, une habitude gagnée dans le commerce de ses amis', *Pensées Diverses*, cxxxvi (vol. 1, p. 372 of the 1721 edition): my translation.

law – a proposition which Bayle proceeded to demonstrate by reference
to the laws against indecency, so much more effective with both men and
women than religious prohibitions (clxii–clxx). From this it follows that
so long as crimes are severely punished, and moral and infamous actions
are clearly distinguished from each other, a society of atheists will be as
civil and as moral as any other (clxxii). Bayle was careful to emphasise that
there was no record in history of a society entirely atheist: it was, therefore,
impossible for him to disprove the conjecture that such a society would lack
all moral virtue. But given that the inclination to ill-doing is rooted deep
in human nature, and is no greater among atheists than among those who
believe in a heaven and a hell, the conjecture is, at the least, very uncertain
(cxlv). There is no good reason to suppose atheists any less capable of living
sociably than those who profess a religion.

The more Bayle developed this argument, the clearer became its foundation in a certain view of human nature. Man is a creature of his passions, driven by 'amour propre, that passion inseparable from our nature',
devoted to the pursuit of riches and to obtaining the praise of others. It is
this 'accursed passion' which makes us take pleasure in everything which
flatters our vanity (clxxi).[45] Given such a nature, man's moral standard is
naturally that of 'l'utile et l'agréable' – what is useful, advantageous, and
agreeable. Against these inclinations, Bayle would argue, religion – or any
set of principles – is of no avail. It will only reinforce them. This was as
true of atheism as of Christianity. Individual atheists might have displayed
notable 'honnêteté', but they were not exempt from vanity. Spinoza's care
to protect his reputation when he was close to death was one example;
Vanini's decision to accept execution rather than dissemble was another.
Even if Vanini had acted contrary to his own 'particular utility' in putting
the reputation for honesty before his own life, he would have had the pleasure of believing that his conduct brought glory to himself while being
useful to others (clxxxi–ii).

Bayle's arguments in the *Pensées Diverses* combined elements of Augustinian rigorism with a recognisably Epicurean understanding of human
nature and moral practice. The rigorism was apparent in his contempt for
idolatry; the Epicureanism in his portrayal of human nature as dominated
by the passions, and naturally inclined to a morality of 'l'utile et l'agréable',
a recognisable echo of the Epicurean poet Horace's *utile* and *dulce*.[46] Bayle's

---

[45] 'Il faut donc dire, que c'est l'amour propre, cette passion inséparable de notre nature, qui nous rend
avares. Car cette maudite passion nous faisant trouver du plaisir à tout ce qui flatte notre vanité . . .',
Pensées Diverses, clxxi (vol. II, p. 46).
[46] Horace, *Ars Poetica*, 343.

engagement with Epicureanism, however, was to go rather further than this. His great *Dictionnaire historique et critique*, published first in 1697, then in a second, considerably expanded edition in 1702, contained extended discussions of the philosophical and theological issues raised by Epicurean materialism, and of its relation to the philosophy of Spinoza. Although it was the hypothesis of a society of atheists to which Vico would specifically respond, an examination of Bayle's broader treatment of Epicurean ideas in the *Dictionnaire* will help to clarify the underlying philosophical foundations of the *New Science*.

In its original form, the article on 'Epicurus' in the *Dictionnaire* concentrated on his morals.[47] His teaching on the gods might be impious, Bayle conceded, but his doctrine of happiness, though open to misrepresentation, was 'au fond... tres raisonnable'. It should not be denied that the happiness of man consists in pleasure. A lengthy 'remark' elaborated this proposition (remark G in the first edition, H in the second).[48] It depended on the recognition that pleasure is a mental state, secured by physical health and ease – not, as Epicurus' enemies charged, by sensual indulgence. In his support Bayle summarised the arguments of his debate with Arnauld in his journal the *Nouvelles de la République des Lettres* in 1685, when he had defended Malebranche on just this point. Later in the article he observed that Epicurus' position had been traduced by the Stoics, whom he labelled the 'Pharisees' of paganism, and likened to the modern *dévots*. By contrast, Epicurus' morals had been ably defended by Gassendi, La Mothe le Vayer, Sorbière, and St-Evremond.[49] In the second edition Bayle added a new remark D on the school of Epicurus, commenting on his followers' capacity for friendship, honesty, and mutual support, without practising community of goods.

---

[47] There is a valuable analysis of the importance of this article in the context of French philosophical debate by Jean Lafond, 'Augustinisme et épicurisme au XVII siècle', in his *L'homme et son image. Morales et littérature de Montaigne à Mandeville* (Paris, 1996), pp. 345–68.

[48] The articles in the *Dictionnaire* contained three elements: (1) the main body of the article; (2) 'remarks', which were often lengthy, printed in columns beneath the main article; and (3) references, printed in the margins of the text and remarks. As is well known, Bayle took full advantage of the flexibility which this format created, using the 'remarks' in particular to engage in substantial discussions of issues which interested him, but which might take him well beyond the matter in the main article. There is an excellent discussion of Bayle's strategies as an author by David Wootton, 'Pierre Bayle, Libertine?', in M. A. Stewart (ed.), *Studies in Eighteenth-Century European Philosophy* (Oxford, 1997), pp. 197–226.

I have used the first edition, *Dictionnaire Historique et Critique*, 4 vols. (Rotterdam, chez Reinier Leers, 1697), and the fourth, also 4 vols. (Amsterdam and Leiden, 1730). Unless otherwise stated, references are to the latter. The article 'Epicure' is in vol. II of this edition, pp. 364–76; remark H is at pp. 368–9.

[49] *Dictionnaire*, 'Epicure', remarks M, N (in the first edition: L, M), II, pp. 368–71.

It was a clear proof of the ability of those who deny providence to live in society.[50]

Other additions to the article in the second edition of the *Dictionnaire* broke new ground. The most substantial were a series of remarks on the consequences of Epicurus' doctrine of the eternity of matter. Although the doctrine was common to all the pagan philosophers, Bayle was surprised that he could find no book which discussed it. The problem, he explained in remark S, was that the doctrine of eternal matter precluded the idea of divine providence. It did so because it was incompatible with God's creation of the world. No pagan physicist, Bayle pointed out, had disputed the eternity of matter (even if they did not all accept Epicurus' atomism), for they were all agreed that it was impossible to make something out of nothing. It was true that some pagan philosophers had attempted to combine the doctrine of the eternity of matter with the idea of a God who formed and preserved the world. But they were arguing the impossible: that pre-existent, self-sufficient matter should have been remade by an external agent. Bayle tried to imagine the best arguments which a Platonist might come up with to support such a position, but concluded that Epicurus would have found difficulties in them all. Given the eternity of matter, the roles of creator and of director of the course of nature were equally redundant. Epicurus had been quite consistent to deny the existence of divine providence.[51]

What this demonstrated, Bayle hastened to point out in his next remark, was that 'the System of Scripture' could alone provide solid foundations for the doctrine of providence and the perfections of God. The objections of Epicurus vanish like smoke before the revelation of Scripture that God did create matter – that he did create something out of nothing. This truth is of unequalled importance, Bayle went on: it is the source of the most sublime and fundamental dogmas. Above all, it vindicates divine providence. As the creator of matter, God acquires the highest possible authority to dispose of the universe as he sees fit. By a simple act of will he may do all that pleases him; nothing occurs which is not part of his plan. There are those – the Socinians – who attempt to dispense with the creation as an incomprehensible mystery (like the doctrine of the Trinity); but they are in the same position as the Platonists who argued against Epicurus. They cannot consistently maintain both the idea of eternal, uncreated matter and the doctrine of divine providence. (It is not surprising, Bayle observed in a marginal note, that there have been reports of Socinians turning Spinozist

---

[50] *Dictionnaire*, 'Epicure', remark D, II, pp. 365–6.   [51] Ibid., remark S, II, pp. 372–4.

because of the difficulty they have had in maintaining the idea of a material principle distinct from God.) Against them Bayle invoked the authority of Malebranche, again described as 'one of the greatest philosophers of the century': he too had defended the consistency of Epicurus. In passing, Bayle conceded that if everything which occurred did so by God's providence, it must also be responsible for the evil in the world. But this was not what was at issue. The point here was the necessary connection between the doctrines of the creation and of divine providence, and the dependence of both on the truth of Scripture.[52]

Bayle's readiness to vindicate Epicurus' consistency in the matter of providence did not extend to every feature of his philosophy. In the last of this series of remarks, Bayle turned to Epicurus' belief that the world was formed and developed by chance. This was absurd. Epicurus appeared to have adopted it out of a misapprehension that he would otherwise have to deny all liberty to men. As Democritus had realised, however, an atomist theory of matter entailed the operation of eternal and necessary laws of motion. In order to deny this, Epicurus had had to invent the supposition that atoms moved with an arbitrary, downwards 'swerve' (as if infinite space contained an 'above' and a 'below', or its swerve somehow made an unthinking atom 'free'). Various proposed solutions to Epicurus' dilemma were reported by Cicero, the best being that offered by the sceptic Carneades; but none undid the determinist implications of atomism. It was these which were fatal to divine providence.[53]

Bayle, then, did not leave his defence of Epicurus' consistency unqualified. When he examined Spinoza's philosophy, however, the emphasis on inconsistency was far more prominent. Concentrating on the *Opera Posthuma* of 1677, which contained the *Ethics*, Bayle opened by observing that Spinoza's doctrine of a single substance, within which God and the world are one being, was by no means as original as his followers (called 'sectateurs' by Bayle) would suppose. It shared common ground with the philosophy of Strato and with the Stoic idea of the Soul of the World; versions of it were also to be found in Indian and Chinese philosophy. But these parallels did not prevent it from being 'the most monstrous hypothesis imaginable'.[54] For one thing, it was contrary to the clearest notions of human understanding, according to which matter or extension was

---

[52] Ibid., remark T, II, pp. 374–5.   [53] Ibid., remark U, II, pp. 375–6.

[54] *Dictionnaire*, 'Spinoza', vol. IV, pp. 253–71; the quoted remark is in the main article, at pp. 258–9: 'la plus monstrueuse hypothèse qui se puisse imaginer'. There is an English translation of most of this article in Pierre Bayle, *Historical and Critical Dictionary: Selections*, transl. and ed. Richard H. Popkin (Indianapolis, New York, and Kansas City, 1965), pp. 288–338.

composed of particles. Bayle noted that the greatest mathematicians of the time – he named Huygens, Leibniz, Newton, Bernouli, and Fatio – all subscribed to the multiplicity of substances.[55] It also led to manifest inconsistency. If God and matter were contained within one substance then God would be both perfect and corruptible. If the human mind partook of the divine intellect the latter must be the subject of all the inconsistencies in men's thoughts. Most bafflingly of all, God would be both the agent and the subject of all men's crimes.[56] Bayle concluded by remarking that while Spinoza agreed with Epicurus in rejecting providence, their systems were otherwise as different as fire and water.[57] The Epicurean system merely made providence redundant; the Spinozan involved the idea of God itself in egregious absurdity and contradiction.

The format of the *Dictionnaire* exempted Bayle from the need to bring any of his arguments to a definite conclusion; unless he had previously committed himself, he did not have to appear to take sides on an issue. But of course Bayle had previously committed himself, both by his intervention in the controversy between Malebranche and Arnauld, and in the *Pensées Diverses* (whose authorship he now acknowledged); and he indicated in the 'clarifications' which he added to the second edition of the *Dictionnaire* that he stood by the argument concerning atheists in the *Pensées Diverses*.[58] There is no reason to suppose, therefore, that he did not wish readers of the *Dictionnaire* to draw certain conclusions. Two conclusions concerning divine providence could be derived from his discussions of the philosophies of Epicurus and Spinoza. First, the doctrine of providence depended on the truth of God's creation of nature, and therefore on repudiating the ancient consensus in favour of the eternity of matter. The one source for this truth was Scripture: if this were compromised, as it was by the Socinian attempt to rationalise its mysteries, the doctrine of divine providence would have no foundation. Second, the operation of divine providence could only be general, never particular. Miracles apart, it must accord with the observably law-bound behaviour of nature (an argument already encountered in the *Pensées Diverses*). As Bayle casually admitted in remark T in the article on Epicurus, this means that providence is as responsible for evil as for good in the world, and does nothing particular to promote morals over depravity. So indiscriminate a providence would hardly provide the basis for a credible

---

[55] *Dictionnaire*, 'Spinoza', remark N, in vol. IV, at pp. 259–60, and main article at pp. 270–1.
[56] Ibid., pp. 259–62.   [57] Ibid., main article, IV, p. 271.
[58] *Dictionnaire*, 'Eclaircissemens', 'I: Sur les Athées', nos. xii, xv, in vol. IV, p. 618; English translation in *Bayle: Political Writings*, ed. Sally L. Jenkinson (Cambridge, 2000), pp. 315–16, 320.

theodicy, or justification for the prevalence of evil in the world.[59] Secure as the truth of providence might be, therefore, its effective contribution, whether to the course of nature or to the direction of human affairs, was so general as to be insignificant.

The beauty of Bayle's method, leaving it to readers to draw the author's conclusions, was that he did not have to decide for them how far they should go. Another step, and the reader might infer that Bayle's account of Epicureanism left the philosophical and moral defences of Christianity dangerously exposed. All that stood in its way was the status of Scripture as revealed truth. If that truth were undermined, Epicurean principles would provide a sufficiently persuasive account of the world and human behaviour. Epicurus' philosophy was not free from difficulties: the supposition that the world was governed by chance was incoherent. In principle, however, an atomist theory of matter provided a secure foundation for the new mathematical and mechanical explanations of nature as subject to certain laws. It was the doctrine of the creation which was an arbitrary addition to an otherwise plausible natural philosophy. Likewise, the Epicurean account of human nature, according to which individuals are driven by their passions to seek their own preservation and advantage, could explain why men naturally behave badly towards each other. At the same time, it also showed how men might make the best of their situation, by living peaceably under the restraint of the law, and contenting themselves with what was useful and agreeable. There was no need, therefore, to invoke the Fall or await Christ's act of redemption to explain and justify man's predicament. Finally, the Epicurean philosophy negated what was left of the doctrine of divine providence. Since its operation must correspond to the general laws of nature and of human behaviour, it was superfluous to invoke divine providence at all.

THE FIRST *NEW SCIENCE* (1725)

In his letters of 1725–6, Vico characterised Bayle as a philologist and, more dismissively, as a purveyor of secondhand knowledge. Analysis of Bayle's discussions of Epicurus and Spinoza, however, has revealed that he was also very much a philosopher. Vico too was both: a philologist – a humanist legal scholar – who would be a philosopher. As we shall now see, Vico wrote

---

[59] At this point a theologian might suggest that it was the role of Christ to redeem sin. But this too faced difficulties. As Bayle pointed out elsewhere, the amount of evil in the world did not seem to have diminished following Christ's initial appearance. See the article 'Xenophanes', remark E, *Dictionnaire*, vol. IV, p. 518; and in *Bayle: Political Writings*, p. 291.

philosophy using the same terms and addressing many of the same issues as Bayle. He probably had not read any of Bayle's works carefully (though I do not think the evidence allows us to be sure of this); but for our purposes what will matter is evidence in the *New Science* of Vico responding to issues associated with Bayle. What is to be investigated is the extent to which Vico was able to take up arguments which Bayle had explored, to engage with the implications of modern Epicureanism, and to take the debate forward on to new ground of his choosing. For Vico was right to think that his own ambition was greater, or at least more systematic, than Bayle's. Where Bayle had compiled a dictionary, Vico set himself to construct a complete new science. In that new science, moreover, the idea of divine providence was to have pride of place.

Published in 1725, the first version of the *New Science* (hereafter the first *New Science*) opened unequivocally:

The natural law of nations was certainly born with the common customs of nations; nor was there ever a nation of atheists in the world, because all nations began with some one religion (8).[60]

These religions, Vico continued, all had their roots in the natural desire of men to live eternally, a desire which derives from a 'common sense', hidden in the depths of the human mind, that human souls are immortal. Faced with the pains of death, we desire a force superior to nature to overcome them and offer us that prospect of immortality – which force 'can only be

---

[60] For both the 1725 and the 1744 versions of the *Scienza Nuova* I have used the edition by Andrea Battistini in *Giambattista Vico: Opere*, which also includes the *Vita* and the letters cited previously. Equipped with excellent notes, this is widely recognised as the best available edition. References to both versions of the *Scienza Nuova* will be given in brackets in the main body of my text above (as were references to Bayle's *Pensées Diverses*), and will be to paragraph numbers, not pages. The paragraph numbering is not Vico's own, and was introduced by the great Vico editor Fausto Nicolini; but it is conventionally used by Vico scholars, and makes it easy to identify a reference in different editions, and in translations.

There are now English translations of both the first and the third *New Science*: Vico, *The First New Science*, edited and translated by Leon Pompa (Cambridge, 2002); and *The New Science of Giambattista Vico*, transl. T. G. Bergin and M. H. Fisch, revised, unabridged edition, including the 'Practic of the New Science' (Ithaca and London, 1984). There is another translation of the (third) *New Science* by David Marsh, with an introduction by Anthony Grafton (Harmondsworth, 1999). Where I provide translations from the Italian, I have been guided by those of Pompa and Bergin and Fisch, but have taken my own decisions.

The full title of the first *New Science*, known as the *Scienza Nuova Prima*, was *Princìpi di una Scienza Nuova intorno alla natura delle nazioni per lo quale si ritruovano i princìpi di altro sistema del diritto naturale delle genti*, in Pompa's translation: *The Principles of a New Science of the Nature of Nations through which the principles of a new system of the natural law of the gentes are discovered*. The passage quoted above, which opens [chapter] i of book i, reads in the original: 'Il diritto naturale delle nazioni egli è certamente nato coi comuni costumi delle medesime; né alcuna giammai al mondo fu nazion d'atei, perché tutte incomminciarono da una qualche religione.'

found in a God who is not nature itself, but superior to nature, that is, an infinite and eternal mind' (8).[61] Vico does not refer to Bayle in this opening paragraph – he will in the very last paragraph of the work – but the allusion is indisputable. The *New Science* began from a rejection of the hypothesis of a society of atheists, as something not only unknown but impossible. It was impossible because there was a consensus among men on the need for a religion, to satisfy their conviction that their souls may be immortal. That aspiration for immortality, in turn, can only be fulfilled by a mind distinct from and superior to nature; evidently, Vico would not be taken for a Spinozist.

Men not only desire immortality, however; they wish to know what only God who is infinite and eternal mind can know: the future. This curiosity, forbidden by nature, precipitated the fall of the first two members of the human race, and God's consequent decision to found the religion of the Hebrews on the cult of his 'infinite and eternal providence'. By the same providence, he condemned the whole human race to labour, pain, and death. Curiosity to know the future likewise explained how all the other, false religions arose through 'idolatry', that is the cult of imaginary deities which are falsely believed to possess strengths superior to nature, and thus to be able to assist men in their afflictions. With idolatry was born divination, a vain science of the future through the interpretation of signs supposedly sent by the gods. Vain as it was, however, this science hid 'two great principles of truth'. First, that there is a divine providence which governs human affairs; second, that men possess free will, by which they may, if they choose, avoid what would otherwise befall them. This second truth explains why men have chosen to live in accordance with justice – a 'common sense' that is corroborated by the common desire of men to have laws, where these do not conflict with their self-interest (9).

It is not only the dense, jerky style of these two opening paragraphs (8–9) which is liable to bewilder the reader. In the course of them, Vico also abruptly alters the subjects of his enquiry. Initially it is men's common need for religion which precludes the possibility of a society of atheists. Then it is God who is responsible for both the Fall and the founding of the Hebrews' religion on the cult of his providence. Thereafter, however, the focus moves back to those who do not have the benefit of revelation, and who are left to the devices of 'idolatry'. Blurred by the rapidity of these shifts of focus, two points are being made. One is that the primacy of

---

[61] '. . . negli estremi malori di morte, desideriamo esservi una forza superiore alla natura per superargli, la quale unicamente è da ritruovarsi in un Dio che non si essa natura ma ad essa natura superiore, cioè una mente infinita ed eterna; . .', *Scienza Nuova* (1725), 8.

sacred history is acknowledged: the Fall defined man's condition on earth, and only to the Hebrews did God vouchsafe true religion. But the second is that Vico's repudiation of the Baylean hypothesis will rest equally on accepting that idolatry is also religion, and that idolaters too seek 'divine' providence.

Vico proceeds by observing that the 'humanity' manifest in the willingness to live according to an idea of justice derives from three 'common senses' of mankind. The first of these is the existence of providence. The second is that men father 'certain' children by 'certain' women (that is, should take wives in order to be sure of the identity of their children); this practice will also be the foundation of a common civil religion, since children will be brought up in conformity with the laws and religion under which they are born. The third 'common sense' is that the dead be buried, and not left to lie on the earth. Together these demonstrate that there was never a nation of atheists, and that all nations have treated matrimony and burial as religious ceremonies. This is the 'vulgar wisdom' (*sapienza volgare*) of mankind, which begins with religion and laws, and perfects and completes itself in the sciences and the arts (10).

The proper relation between this 'vulgar wisdom' of nations and the 'esoteric wisdom' (*sapienza riposta*) of philosophers, however, had yet to be established. No one had yet fixed the αχμη, or state of perfection, which would make it possible to measure the stages through which humanity must make its course; nor had anyone identified the 'practices' (*pratiche*) by which it might achieve that state of perfection. To do this would require the philosophers to work with those who upheld the vulgar wisdom of their nations, supporting the latter's science of civil affairs, both divine and human, with a science of the same things according to nature and reason (11). Yet this was precisely what certain philosophers had not done, instead abandoning vulgar wisdom. The Epicureans were the first to do so, by their teaching that human affairs are ruled by chance, that human souls die with the body, that the passions are driven by the senses to seek pleasure, and that utility (which constantly changes) is the rule of justice. The Stoics, by contrast, had done so by teaching that a fatal necessity determines everything, including the will, that souls enjoy a temporal life after death, and by setting men a standard of 'honesty' (*l'onestà*) too burdensome for the passions, leaving men to despair of virtue (12). Plato alone had the wisdom to accept the doctrine of divine providence and the immortality of the soul, and to place virtue in the moderation of the passions. But even he lost sight of providence when he measured natures which he scarcely knew against his own idea of the perfect state. For his was an ideal of the just beyond the common sense of men, exemplified in his proposal for community of women (13).

Initially the jurists had done better than the philosophers. Recognising that vulgar wisdom was the basis for a system of justice, the ancient Roman jurists had exactly defined the natural law of the gentes as 'the law ordained by divine providence through the dictates of human necessities or utilities, as observed equally among all nations' (14).[62] But this truth had subsequently been forgotten by modern jurists, and in particular by the three founders of the natural law of nations, Hugo Grotius, John Selden, and Samuel Pufendorf. They had failed to found their systems on divine providence (15). Grotius, indeed, had committed the unpardonable error of stating that his system might stand even without a knowledge of God; as a Socinian, he had also proposed that man was not originally evil, but simply weak and needy. On his account men entered society only from a sense of its utility, 'which is, in fact, the hypothesis of Epicurus' (16). Selden, meanwhile, had committed the different error of treating God's commands to Noah as the basis for a law for all peoples. He had forgotten that the Hebrews, descendants of Shem, had ever since kept their own law distinct from that of the Gentile descendants of Ham and Japhet (17). Finally Pufendorf, for all his intention to respect providence, had still adopted 'an Epicurean or rather Hobbesian hypothesis (which is the same thing)' of man cast into the world without divine assistance, and left to follow utility alone (18). All three, therefore, had failed to appreciate how the natural law of the gentes had originated from the customs of nations, in particular their religious customs, and how it had developed through certain 'sects of times' (*certe 'sètte di tempi'*), a Vichian phrase for epochs or historical stages. The jurists also had a misplaced confidence in their authorities, failing to realise how unreliable these were as guides to the most obscure and fabulous periods of nations' histories. They had thus been unable to recognise the 'occasions' by which human necessities or utilities had brought the nations of men to accept the same natural law, or the various modes and times in which this had occurred (19–22). In short, the modern jurists had failed to understand the providential, customary, historical character of the law they professed.

---

[62] Vico adopts the formula 'natural law of the gentes' (*il diritto natural delle genti*) to refer to the natural law of the ancient nations; the 'natural law of the nations' (*il diritto natural delle nazioni*) refers to the natural law of the modern jurists. He keeps the two distinct because he does not believe that the modern jurists have an adequate understanding of the earlier form of natural law. 'Genti' might be translated 'peoples', but I adhere to the standard translation 'gentes' because Vico uses the formula as a term of art. The quoted definition is '"Diritto ordinato dalla provvedenza divina coi dettami di esse umane necessità o utilità, osservato egualmente appo tutte le nazioni"', *Scienza Nuova* (1725), 14.

The unfortunate reason for this, Vico told his readers, was the absence until now of a science which was both a history and a philosophy of humanity. The philosophers had not thought to provide one, because they assumed that human nature had always been at the level it only attained once it had been civilised by religion and law. Accordingly they supposed that the Gentile nations must have been founded by individual wise men, the Assyrians by Zoroaster, the Egyptians by Hermes, the Greeks by Orpheus, who ensured that their nations had been civilised from the beginning (23, 27–31). By contrast the philologists (poets, historians, orators, and grammarians) believed that the histories of the Gentile nations were the work of individual 'theological poets'. Failing to recognise that the 'vulgar theology' (*teologia volgare*) of the poets should be understood as the beliefs of the 'vulgar' concerning divinity, they accepted the poets' most fantastic accounts of the Gods and their scandalous misdeeds, and endowed the ancient nations with a common antiquity of which they themselves had no knowledge (23–4, 32–9).

A different starting point was needed, one provided by sacred history. Vico identified it, not in the Fall, but in the aftermath of the great Flood. After the Flood the posterity of Noah had been reduced to the level of beasts, wandering over the waterlogged, forest-covered earth. In that savage state men abandoned their women and mothers their children; the language of Adam was forgotten; the need to satisfy hunger, thirst, and lust suppressed any sense of humanity. Yet just then, 'in that long, dense night of darkness', a single light shone out, which provided the first truth of Vico's science: that the world of the Gentile nations was certainly made by men. The principles of his science were to be found, therefore, in the nature of the human mind itself. What was needed was a metaphysics which would study that mind, not in the individual, to lead him back to God (the province of divine philosophy), but in that common sense which is the mind of nations, in order to connect it with God as eternal providence (40). Likewise needed was a jurisprudence which would study the mind of man as he emerged from the state of solitude, in which he had thought only of his preservation, and entered into marriage and thus into the state of families and cities. In this way study of the natural law of nations would also follow 'the natural order of ideas' (41).

How this new science should be developed Vico proceeded to discuss more fully in book II, 'The Principles of this Science concerning ideas'. Vico began by explaining why human society could not have begun, as John Locke and others maintained, with a promise. For men will only regard a promise as binding if they already possess an idea of truth – and this can only be the idea of God through the attribute of providence: that is, 'an eternal and infinite Mind' (*una mente eterna ed infinita*) which foresees everything. Divine providence, Vico reiterated, was the architect of this world of nations: it directs the particular ends of men and peoples to a universal end, an end beyond and often contrary to their own intentions (45). It was providence which had founded the world of nations on the vulgar wisdom which is the common sense of every nation, and it was this common sense which directed men to live sociably (46).

Under the divine architect, however, it is human will (*l'umano arbitrio*) which is the maker or artificer (*il fabbro*) of the world of nations. By its nature highly uncertain in individuals, in mankind as a whole the will is determined by the 'utilities or necessities' which are common to all men's natures. It was to identify those utilities and necessities that Vico directed attention to the state into which Cain and Seth had fallen before the Flood, Ham, Japhet, and a little later Shem, after it. For in turning their backs on the God of their fathers Adam and Noah, who had alone kept them in society, they had been reduced to a condition of bestial liberty, without language or any other sociable custom, condemned to wander over the face of the earth. Such was indeed the state of solitude which Grotius had imagined, the predicament of man abandoned by God as Pufendorf described it. But the jurists had erred by misunderstanding the significance of this moment in sacred history. Selden had confused Hebrew and Gentile history; Pufendorf had ignored sacred history altogether; Grotius, worst of all, had adopted the Socinian hypothesis of man as originally a simpleton, thereby failing to recognise the depths to which human nature had fallen (47).[63]

As a result, the modern jurists were unable to recognise what was immutable and universal in the natural law of the gentes. They had forgotten that the seeds of justice are buried in sin: there is a necessary correlation between the doctrine of original sin and the idea of an eternal justice. This is what makes the natural law of the gentes immutable, 'an eternal law which runs through time' (*un diritto eterno che corre in tempo*) (49). They had also taken too literally the idea of a state of solitude, forgetting the universal need for men to join themselves with women for assistance and

---

[63] What Vico says is that 'Grozio vi peccò più di tutti, perché dà un'ipotesi sociniana del suo uomo semplicione, e poi si dimenticò affatto di ragionarla'. Pompa translates the last part of the sentence as 'and then utterly failed to work out its consequences', which is as far as Vico's words can be taken. The point, however, seems to be that suggested in paragraph 16, that as a Socinian, Grotius failed to comprehend the original depravity of man. On Vico's characterisation of Grotius as a 'Socinian', Francesco Piro, 'I presupposti teologici del giusnaturalismo moderno nella percezione di Vico', *Bollettino del Centro di Studi Vichiani*, 30 (2000), 125–49.

the reproduction of children. For this, Vico argued, was the critical step in leading men out of their post-diluvian depravity and towards a state in which the universality of the natural law was acknowledged (55).

Sketched in the remainder of book II, Vico's account of how this occurred was a *tour de force* of historical imagination. His masterstroke was the portrayal of post-diluvian men as giants. This was an old story, which Vico put to dramatic new use. Genesis relates that there had been giants among the people of God before the Flood (Genesis, 6.4; cited by Vico at 95); that they also existed after the Flood is suggested by the characterisation of Nimrod, a grandson of Ham, as 'a mighty one' (Genesis, 10.8–10). The significance of these giants had been authoritatively discussed by Augustine; after him, medieval and Renaissance commentators had developed a virtual science of 'gigantology'.[64] Vico's twist to the story was to identify the giants with all the Gentile descendants of Noah's children. For a time these Gentile giants had wandered the still-sodden earth in isolation from one another, living at no better than the level of animal necessity, acknowledging no gods, taking no wives, and recognising no children. (The Hebrews, meanwhile, lived cleanly and reverted to normal stature (101–2).) Gradually, however, the earth began to dry out, and as it did so, the exhalations generated thunder and lightning in the skies. Fearful of what they did not understand, the giants imagined the thunderbolts to be the weapons of a deity, whom they characteristically named Jove, and they hid themselves away from him in caves.[65] So universal was this experience, Vico observed, that Joves proliferated among the ancient nations: the Egyptians, the Greeks, and the Romans all had their Joves (104–5).

Jove induced more than fear: the giants also felt an acute sense of shame when they coupled with women in the open, under the skies from which Jove looked down. So they dragged the women too back to their caves, married them, and began to found definite families (55–6). Reverting back for a moment to the Fall, Vico pointed out that shame was also at the heart of the story of Adam and Eve. From the beginning, shame had been the instrument chosen by divine providence to bring men to acknowledge God and adopt the institution of matrimony (58).[66] The Joves of the Gentiles were only reproducing the punishment which the true divine providence

---

[64] Augustine, *City of God* (426), XV.23, XVI.3–4; Walter Stephens, *Giants in those Days. Folklore, Ancient History, and Nationalism* (Lincoln, Nebr., 1989).

[65] The wonderfully evocative term used by Vico for 'cave' or 'den' was 'spelonca', in the plural 'spelonche': *Scienza Nuova* (1725), 55 ff.

[66] Vico went on in para. 58 to remark that the story of Adam and Eve was one of those origins beyond which it is foolish to seek others before them, which is the most important mark of the truth of origins. For even if we did not stop with Adam and his Creator, the question would still arise of

had inflicted on the first man and woman. Without the renewal of that sense of shame which Jove induced, however, humanity would never have emerged from the state of feral depravity which followed the Flood.

As they settled with their families in their caves, the giants passed on their ideas of Jove, and required their children to worship him. Their worship reflected their anxiety to know the future: by the use of auspices they sought to 'divine' what providence had in store for them. Particularly important were the auspices taken at the time of marriage, the key institution in maintaining the certainty – the identity – of families (59, 61–6, 107). Vico did not attempt to deny that the worship of divine providence in this form was idolatry (109–11). But he suggested that it was a form of idolatry which tended to a belief in one god: that each nation originally had its own Jove encouraged them to acknowledge that they shared the same Jove. Humanity is thus contained within the unity of God, while the truth and antiquity of the Christian religion, which had always had one God, continues to be affirmed separately (60, 105).

Vico pursued his history of the ancient nations by describing the giants' emergence from their caves, and their descent, along with their families, to the coasts and plains. There they diminished in stature and settled as the heads of clans. The clans were still fiercely exclusive: although they attracted to their settlements those who had yet to form families, the heads of the clans were vigilant in refusing strangers the right to marry into them. The clans further reinforced their position by burial of their dead, and by the division of the land into fields whose cultivation was for the maintenance of their members alone. All this they did under the aegis of their religion (113–16).

As specific evidence of how a nation formed itself out of a group of clans, Vico drew on the ancient Roman law of the Twelve Tables, to which he had already devoted an extended analysis in his previous work, the *Diritto Universale*. In a lengthy 'corollary', Vico repeated his view that the Twelve Tables were the original law of Rome. They had not been brought from Athens: rather, they exemplified the way in which every nation must be presumed to have generated its own code of laws, each embodying similar general principles (79–89). Change had continued to take place after the introduction of the Twelve Tables: the heads of the ruling families had acquired the names and status of nobles, and had introduced new forms of property by which to keep the plebs in dependence on them as their 'clients'

when men began to feel shame. The point seems to be that those who would argue for the existence of men before Adam, as in the *Praeadamitae* of La Peyrère, would be unable to explain the course of human sexual relations without a version of the Fall.

(73–4, 117–23, 145–50). In return, however, the plebs had at last gained the right of marriage, and thus of citizenship; increasingly they were able to ensure that they were governed according to the rules of justice (76–7, 151).

The point of telling this story was its demonstration of the unity of human history. Out of the separate histories of the many Gentile nations (and the one chosen people of God) had emerged one 'humanity'. Vico underlined his opposition to the philosophers who would deny this. Pyrrhonism destroyed humanity, because it denied the principle of unity evident in the existence of common human utilities or necessities. Epicureanism dissipated unity by leaving the judgement of utility to each individual. Stoicism annihilated it, by refusing to recognise any common needs or utilities of a corporeal nature, but only those of the soul. Only Plato had upheld the idea of one justice, 'il giusto uno', which is the principle of natural law (71).

In defiance of the sceptics, Epicureans, and Stoics, Vico was confident that he had vindicated the eternity and universality of the natural law of the gentes. He had done so by constructing a science which combined philosophy and history to establish both 'an ideal eternal history' (*una storia ideale eterna*) and a new 'ars critica'. As an 'ideal eternal history' the new science uncovered the origins and 'progresses' (Vico used the plural *progressi*) of all nations, and made possible the writing of a 'universal history with certain origins and certain continuity' (*la storia universale con certe origini e certa perpetuità*) – these being the two things which universal history has hitherto lacked (90). Such a history, he added in the disappointingly short book IV, would identify the successive stages of necessity or utility through which humanity must pass (391, 397). As a new 'ars critica', the new science also provided a method with which to discern the truth within the histories which the Gentile nations told of themselves (91–3). In book III Vico would enlarge upon this method by applying it to specifically linguistic evidence – to hieroglyphs, coats of arms, and the various kinds of language. He proposed the composition of various etymologicons to trace the history of the terms through which nations express their common ideas, and a dictionary of mental words common to all nations. Methodically interpreted, Vico believed, all such evidence could be used to establish the common elements in the histories of the Gentile nations.

Vico had less to say about the projected outcome of the ideal eternal history. He had suggested in book I that his science would establish an αχμη or state of perfection at which religion and law would be fully supported by theology and morals, and from which the levels of humanity achieved by nations could be measured. This in turn would yield a set of 'practices' by which a nation might be brought up to that state of perfection (11). But when the perfect state is mentioned again, at the very end of book II, it is clear that if it were ever achieved, it would be unlikely to endure. The philosophies of the Epicureans and Stoics, the sceptics and the atheists present a constant challenge to religion and order. Nations which succumb to these will become incapable of governing themselves, and will return to an earlier stage of development (247). The implication that the ideal eternal history will follow a cyclical course is reinforced by an earlier set of aphorisms describing the limits within which the customs of nations will be contained. At first seeking only to satisfy necessity, men's wants will gradually extend through what is convenient to the pleasurable and the luxurious, before they lay waste their substance by extravagance (125). Initially barbarous, men are by turns severe, humane, noble and delicate, and finally dissolute and corrupt (129). The new science may posit the idea of a state of perfection, but it does not suggest that the history of nations will be a history of progress.

In a brief 'conclusion' Vico took the opportunity to fire parting shots at his chosen antagonists. By uncovering the uniform origins of all the ancient nations, he had exposed the failings of the modern jurists, who constructed their systems in ignorance of those origins, and had given the lie to both the Epicureans, who attributed them to chance, and the Stoics, who ascribed them to fate (474). By demonstrating the importance of auspices in establishing the natural law of the gentes, he had refuted the claims of Polybius and Bayle that nations might be governed without religion. Without a providential God, there would only ever have been the state of bestial, brutish wandering, of violence, depravity, and blood; possibly, even certainly, mankind would not now exist (475–6).

Such, then, is the content of Vico's first *New Science*. In what ways does it relate to the context suggested by Vico's *Autobiography* and correspondence at the time of its publication? Specifically, does the content of the *New Science* explain why Vico singled out Hobbes and Bayle as its principal targets? At one level the answer is clear. The first *New Science* is framed as a rejection of Bayle's hypothesis of a society of atheists. Specifically, Vico contradicted two of the arguments on which Bayle had placed particular emphasis in the *Pensées Diverses*. Bayle had represented idolaters as no more sociable than atheists. Vico retold the history of the Gentiles to show that it was precisely idolatry which had made them sociable. Solitary and bestial in their post-diluvian state, the Gentile giants had only become sociable because they personified thunder as the god Jove, and felt shame at fulfilling their sexual desires in his presence, instead taking their women off into the darkness of caves. Denied the revelation granted to the Hebrews, the Gentiles in their idolatry had nonetheless recognised and worshipped divine providence. Another of Bayle's key arguments was the rejection of proofs based on a consensus of opinion. Yet Vico maintained that the evidence that every nation had its Jove was a proof of the universal acceptance of providence. There was a 'common sense' of a need for religion, as for matrimony and burial: the presence of this common sense in every ancient nation, Gentile as well as Hebrew, made it possible to think of this as the common sense of all mankind.[67]

At a deeper philosophical level, however, it is less immediately obvious why Vico should have made so much of his opposition to Hobbes and Bayle. A hostility to Epicureanism is expressed throughout the first *New Science*. But in most cases it is superficial, concentrating on the Epicurean doctrine of chance. There is no indication that Vico had taken the point, discussed at length by Bayle in the final remark of his article on Epicurus, that the doctrine was inconsistent with the materialist premises of Epicurean philosophy, and therefore marginal in its significance. More acute were Vico's comments on the Epicurean elements in the thought of Grotius and especially Pufendorf, whose view of man in the state of nature he equated with that of Hobbes. But if this were all, we would have to conclude that the part played by Epicureanism in Vico's thinking was slight and inconsequential, and that he remained unaware of, or unconcerned by, the profounder challenge which Hobbes and Bayle had shown it to present to Christian philosophy in general and the idea of divine providence in particular.

In fact, there have been indications that Vico's engagement with Epicureanism went further. Alongside his explicit criticisms, certain identifiably Epicurean themes continue to be evident in Vico's own arguments. In drawing attention to these, I do not wish to suggest that Vico's criticism was diversionary, that he was 'really' an Epicurean, and was trying to disguise this from his readers. (This is the sort of interpretation which has repeatedly been placed upon his relation to Spinoza.) Much more likely is that he recognised the force, the explanatory power, of certain characteristically Epicurean arguments, and sought to accommodate or even to harness them to his own purposes, the better to defend what he thought was really important. It is here that comparison with Bayle, and to a lesser

---

[67] For the identification of Vico's concept of 'common sense' as a rejection of Bayle's critique of 'consensus', see particularly Cantelli, *Vico e Bayle*, pp. 79–83. A possible difficulty with Cantelli's interpretation is that Bayle's reasons against proof by consensus, while outlined in the *Pensées Diverses*, are much more fully elaborated in the *Continuation*, which may not have been available in Naples.

extent Hobbes, becomes important in helping to establish the depth of
Vico's engagement with contemporary Epicurean thinking.

One area in which Epicurean themes are prominent is the account of the
earliest human nature. Vico's Gentile giants have the attributes of Hobbesian man in the state of nature: their condition was one of bestial isolation
and mutual hostility. But their passionate, needs-driven nature also enabled
them to escape this condition, as both Hobbes and Bayle suggested it would.
Fear and shame drove men to acknowledge and worship God, while the
search for the utilities or necessities of life drew them into society and taught
them the importance of justice. Vico's treatment of these issues suggests
that he knew how close he was to Epicurean thinking, for he took some
trouble to emphasise his differences from it. Thus he distinguished his
account of human nature from that of Hobbes or Pufendorf by pointing
out that he thought in terms of the common needs and utilities of nations,
where those Epicurean philosophers reduced everything to the level of the
individual. (Celestino Galiani had done exactly as the Epicureans in his
'Scienza morale', when he began his account of sociability with a solitary
individual.) Vico also denied the efficacy of a contract unsupported by
the idea of God, although he (mistakenly) identified the idea with Locke
rather than Hobbes.[68] Finally, Vico insisted on the indispensability of the
Fall, which Hobbes had effectively denied. But the compatibility of the Fall
with an Epicurean account of human nature (and its incompatibility with
Stoicism) was almost a commonplace of late seventeenth-century philosophy, and was amply demonstrated in the work of Bayle. Vico's account of
early human nature, and of the formation of morals and justice, it may be
suggested, was a not dissimilar blend of Augustinianism with Epicureanism,
cast in an anti-Stoic mould.

The challenge represented by modern Epicureanism is perhaps still more
important in understanding Vico's treatment of divine providence. It seems
that Vico was aware of the issues which had exercised Bayle in the *Dictionnaire* article on Epicurus. When in the very first paragraph of his work he
upheld the existence of a God who is an infinite and eternal mind, separate from and superior to nature, he not only pre-empted any suspicion of
Spinozism, he met what Bayle had identified as the first, essential condition of the idea of divine providence, the complete separation of God from
matter. Bayle had also pointed out that our knowledge of this God, of the
creation and hence of his providence depends upon the truth of Scripture.

---

[68] Contrary to Vico's supposition, the efficacy of Locke's concept of contract depended precisely upon
a prior acknowledgement of obligation to God under natural law. Locke too denied the possibility
of a society of atheists.

Vico accepted this too when he insisted on the primacy of sacred history, as revealed in Scripture. The Fall must be the starting point of human history, as the occasion of man's sin and shame; and the aftermath of the Flood marks the beginning of Gentile history, separate from that of the Hebrews. But a difference is also apparent. When Bayle insisted that the credibility of the idea of providence depended on assumptions about the nature of God and the status of Scripture, subversive implications were not far from the surface. If those assumptions were compromised, he might be read as suggesting, the credibility of providence would be undermined. There is little to indicate, however, that Vico was concerned by this prospect (and still less to indicate that it might have appealed to him). Apart from underlining the significance of the Fall as the origin of the sense of shame, he devotes little space to reinforcing the truth of Scripture. What he does, rather, is shift the focus of the enquiry away from sacred history, and on to that of the Gentiles.

Vico treats divine providence among the Gentiles as a human belief, and contrasts it with the revelation accorded to the Hebrews. Although the point is not developed, the evidence for the universal belief in divine providence among the Gentiles is natural, not transcendental: it lies in a common 'sense' found in the early history of all nations. That this common belief is characteristically monotheist, which reduces its distance from the truth of the Christian God, does not affect the difference between them. The foundation of the Gentiles' belief in divine providence is in the senses, that is in human nature, and the belief itself is a form of idolatry. But by writing a history of religion on the basis of human nature, Vico is able to vindicate idolatry as a manifestation of a common belief in divine providence. Further, he is able to show that this 'common sense' is not simply a 'consensus' of opinion – the form of evidence Bayle had derided – but a historically observable characteristic of nations in the earliest stages of their development. Such a history of early Gentile religion might do nothing for the truth of Christianity, beyond confirming that it depended on the truth of sacred history, as that was revealed in Scripture. But it was enough to challenge Bayle's supposition that the idea of divine providence had no foundation independent of the 'system of Scripture'.

THE THIRD *NEW SCIENCE* (1744)

Between 1725 and 1730 the *New Science* underwent a major recasting, and the second version, published in 1730, had a new structure. Still Vico was unhappy, and he continued to make revisions, most of which were incorporated into the final version, published posthumously in 1744, the

Scienza Nuova Terza, or third *New Science*. In structure, however, the third version remained close to the second. An immediately obvious consequence of the revision was that Bayle no longer provided Vico with his starting point. As we shall see, he continued to argue that the universality of the idea of divine providence refuted Bayle's hypothesis of a society of atheists. But the negative, polemical orientation of the first *New Science* disappeared. In this Vico was continuing a process which had begun when he discarded the first draft of the work, the so-called 'Scienza Nuova in forma negativa', whose publication Cardinal Corsini had refused to subsidise, and which was subsequently lost. Evidently Vico had occasional second thoughts about diminishing the negative emphasis of his work: after the second version had appeared he drafted a short section which spelt out anew his opposition to leading modern philosophers, Descartes, Spinoza, and Locke in particular.[69] But this was not included in the eventual third edition of 1744, when the decision to adopt a more 'positive' form of presentation was maintained.

In moving on to the third *New Science*, the focus of the exposition will be on what was new and additional to the argument by comparison with the first *New Science*. More particularly, I shall be alert to evidence bearing on Vico's engagement with the issues which have been identified as associated with Epicureanism: the nature of man and his motives for entering society; and the grounds of the universal belief in divine providence.[70]

The third *New Science* begins with an introduction in the form of an 'Explanation of the Picture placed as a Frontispiece' to the work. The first feature of the picture to be explained is a seeing eye within a triangle, which

---

[69] Entitled 'Riprensione delle metafisiche di Renato delle Carte, di Benedetto Spinosa e di Giovanni Locke', the manuscript was given the paragraph numbers 1212–17 by Niccolini. There is an English version by Donald Phillip Verene, 'Giambattista Vico's "Reprehension of the Metaphysics of René Descartes, Benedict Spinoza, and John Locke": an addition to the *New Science* (translation and Commentary)', in *New Vico Studies*, 8 (1990), 2–18. The paragraphs were intended to form a short chapter added to the section on 'Poetic Metaphysics' in book II of the third *New Science*.

The criticisms are trenchant and precise. Descartes is charged with failing to recognise that the idea of God as 'true Being' is eternal, infinite and free, and must therefore be quite distinct from body. Descartes' confusion brought about that of Spinoza, who made substance both mind and body, establishing a God of infinite mind in infinite body, therefore operating by necessity. Finally Locke embellished the metaphysics of Epicurus, holding that all ideas are projections of body, and thus offering a God all body and operating by chance. This explicit identification of Locke with Epicureanism also appears in another draft revision from the same period (para. 1122), and was prominent in the *Autobiography*; but is not present in either the first or the third *New Science*, where Hobbes continues to do duty as an Epicurean philosopher. Locke's philosophy was a focus of controversy in Naples in the early 1730s (Ferrone, *Scienza natura religione*, pp. 429–38, 442–50, 503–10), which may explain Vico's comment; but over the three editions of the *New Science* it is Hobbes and Bayle who provide the explicit reference points for his engagement with Epicureanism.

[70] As with the first, references to the third *New Science* will be by paragraph number (not page), and will be given in the body of the text. I have again used the Italian edition by Battistini. Translations will be indebted to, but not always identical with, those of Bergin and Fisch. See above, n. 60, for details of these editions.

represented God in his aspect of providence. This leads Vico straight to a definition of his science as 'una teologia civile ragionata della provvedenza divina' – a rational (or reasoned) civil theology of divine providence, a formula he had not used in 1725. It was a 'civil' theology, Vico explained, as distinct from a natural one. Hitherto philosophers had concentrated on the order of nature at the expense of that part of God's providence most proper to men, their human nature as 'sociable' beings. By contrast Vico would seek to establish how providence has ordered matters so that men, having fallen from justice by original sin, should yet have emerged from the state of bestial solitude to live in justice and society (2). At the same time, Vico's was a 'reasoned' rather than a revealed theology of divine providence. It was a theology valid for the Gentiles as well as the Hebrews, which took as its starting point their common belief in a God able to tell the future, and whose providence might therefore be 'divined' by the use of auspices (9).

Vico's confidence that he was now able to begin with a formal definition of his 'new science' was backed up by other novel features of the third *New Science*. The first of these was a chronological table, placed at the beginning of book I, followed by a series of 'annotations' (43–118). The table set the histories of seven ancient nations – the Hebrews, Chaldeans, Scythians, Phoenicians, Egyptians, Greeks, and Romans – alongside each other in columns, with two further columns giving the years of the world and of Rome. The first recorded event, the Flood, was placed in Hebrew history, and dated to the 1656th year of the world. Only a hundred years after that did the first event in another nation's history occur, with Zoroaster and the kingdom of the Chaldeans. Scholars such as Marsham or Spencer, who had suggested that the Egyptians or the Chaldeans might have been older than the Hebrews, were quite mistaken: there was no possibility that these nations, or any other (such as the Chinese), were of greater antiquity than the people of God (44, 54). As Paolo Rossi has underlined, Vico's position in the great seventeenth- and early eighteenth-century debate over the antiquity of the world and its peoples was absolutely clear. Sacred history had priority: the time-scale for all history remained that laid down in the Bible.[71]

A second new feature since 1725 was the deliberate use of 'degnità' or axioms to set out what Vico called the 'elements' of the new science

---

[71] Paolo Rossi, *The Dark Abyss of Time: the History of the Earth and the History of Nations from Hooke to Vico*, transl. L. G. Cochrane (Chicago and London, 1984), pp. 168–90. Originally published as *I segni del tempo. Storia della terra e storia delle nazioni da Hooke a Vico* (Milan, 1979). Also Rossi, *Le sterminate antichità*, pp. 227–53.

(119–329, forming the second section of book I). These axioms were accompanied where appropriate by 'corollaries', explaining and elaborating their point. Vico drew a distinction between those axioms which were 'philosophical' and those which were 'philological', basing this in turn on the distinction between 'the true' (*il vero*) and 'the certain' (*il certo*). This last was a distinction implicit in the first *New Science*, and discussed in works before that; but Vico now spelt out its significance for the understanding of his work as a 'science'. According to axiom x, philosophy contemplates reason, whence comes knowledge (*scienza*) of the true; philology observes the authority of the human will (*umano arbitrio*), whence comes consciousness (*coscienza*) of the certain (138). Vico added two corollaries, in one of which he indicated that the subjects of philology were the languages and deeds (*fatti*) of peoples, their customs and laws, wars, alliances, voyages, and commerce. (The subject matter of philosophy was not further defined.) He also commented that the philosophers and the philologists were equally at fault for working in isolation from each other: had they combined reason and authority, they would have anticipated Vico's new science (139–40). The recourse to axioms, and the distinction between the true and the certain, were clearly intended to fix and formalise the propositions of this science. But complete clarity was still elusive: an exposition of the content of the science continues to require the reader to reconstruct and reorder Vico's arguments.

Vico had stated at the outset, in the introduction, that the subject of this new science would be man's social nature, or natural sociability, and the conduct of divine providence in its realisation (2). Axiom VII takes up the argument. Legislation considers man as he is in order to make good use of him in society. Thus out of ferocity, avarice and ambition, the three great vices found across the human race, it creates the military, merchant and governing classes which provide the strength, wealth and wisdom of states; out of vices which could destroy mankind, in other words, it makes civil happiness (132). This axiom, Vico immediately explains,

> proves that there is divine providence and that it is a divine legislative mind, which out of the passions of men, all devoted to their private utility, for the sake of which they would live as wild beasts in a state of solitude, has made civil institutions by which they may live in human society (133).[72]

---

[72] 'Questa degnità pruova esservi provvedenza divina e che ella sia una divina mente legislatrice, la quale delle passioni degli uomini, tutti attenuti alle loro private utilità, per le quali viverebbono da fiere bestie dentro le solitudini, ne ha fatto gli ordini civili per gli quali vivano in umana società': *Scienza Nuova* (1744), 133. The translation adapts that of Bergin and Fisch in the direction of more awkward literalness.

Axiom VIII continues: 'things out of their natural state neither settle nor endure' (134).[73] In the first of two corollaries, Vico observes that this axiom alone settles the great dispute, still being waged by the best philosophers and moral theologians against Carneades the Sceptic and Epicurus (and which not even Grotius could settle), whether there is law in nature, or – which is the same thing – whether human nature is sociable. It does so because the human race, for as long as there has been memory of the world, has lived and continues to live 'comportevolmente' in society; it has accepted the requirements of social life (135). In other words, sociability is natural because it has lasted over time: it is a natural-historical fact. A further corollary adds that this and the previous axiom prove that man has free will, however weak, to make virtues of his passions; but that he is aided naturally by God with divine providence, and supernaturally with divine grace (136). Man may choose to make himself sociable over time; but he does so with the assistance of divine providence. Both are natural processes.

After the axioms devoted to definition of the true and the certain (IX–X), the thread is picked up again in axioms XI–XIII. Axiom XI states that human will, by its nature most uncertain, is made certain and determined by the 'common sense' of men concerning human necessities or utilities, which are the sources of the natural law of the gentes (141). In axiom XII common sense is defined as 'a judgement without reflection' (*un giudizio senz'alcuna riflessione*), commonly felt (*communemente sentito*) by an entire order, people, nation or the entire human race (142).[74] Axiom XIII adds that uniform ideas born among entire peoples not known to each other must have a common ground of truth (144). A corollary then explains that this axiom establishes the common sense of mankind as the criterion taught to nations by divine providence to define what is certain in the natural law of the gentes, and thereby to ascertain its substantial unity (145). Thus understood, Vico continues, the concept of a common sense of nations destroys the traditional idea that the natural law of the gentes derived from a single source, as the Twelve Tables were supposed to have been brought from Greece to Rome. On the contrary, natural law had separate origins among peoples who knew nothing of each other; its common nature was established only as they came into contact through wars, embassies, alliances, and trade. For the natural law of the gentes was a law instituted naturally by divine providence along

---

[73] 'Le cose fuori del loro stato naturale né vi si adagiano né vi durano': *Scienza Nuova* (1744), 134.

[74] It is important to note that common sense, as an unreflective judgement, is 'commonly felt' – 'communemente sentito': the translation of this as 'shared' (Bergin and Fisch) misses the point that common sense is a (bodily) feeling.

with human customs, not a civil law communicated to other peoples by human initiative (146).

Taken together, axioms VII–VIII and XI–XIII seem to contain a clear account of how divine providence works with human nature to establish society and law. The human passions, by themselves anti-social, are naturally assisted by divine providence to form a common sense of human needs and utilities, on which basis men will accept the need for law, and accustom themselves to living in society. But what does it mean to say that the passions are naturally assisted by divine providence? How does this occur?

Vico's immediate answer is historical. Axiom XIV puts this in the most general terms: 'the nature of institutions is nothing but their coming into being at certain times and in certain guises' (147).[75] In the subsequent axioms XV–XXI (individually almost equally gnomic), Vico indicates that the key to understanding this 'coming into being' of human civil institutions is to be found in the vulgar traditions, laws, languages, and poetry of ancient nations (148–60). Finally, in axioms XXIII–XXXI, he descends to particulars, and identifies the essential moments of the story. Everywhere the world of peoples began with religion. In the case of the Hebrews, of course, it was a religion founded by the true God, who prohibited the divination on which the Gentile nations arose. Among the Gentiles, by contrast, it was the terror of an imagined divinity which prompted the earliest wild and violent men to begin to put themselves into some order, and institute the first nations. These were the giants who occupied the world after the Flood (and whom he now likened to the wild creatures reported by travellers in the country of *los patacones* at the foot of America); before they had gods to fear they had lived a bestial, lawless existence (165–78). In a revealing comment, Vico adds that it was Hobbes's failure to recognise that his own 'fierce and violent men' were made sociable by religion which made him fall into error with the 'chance' of his Epicurus. The implication is that Hobbes's characterisation of the original condition of men was valid: he had rightly sought to go further than Greek philosophy by studying man 'in the whole society of the human race'. What he had overlooked was that without religions, no commonwealths could be born (179).[76]

---

[75] 'Natura di cose altro non è che nascimento di esse in certi tempi e con certe guise': *Scienza Nuova* (1744), 147. Here I follow Bergin and Fisch in translating 'cose' as institutions and 'nascimento' as coming into being.

[76] At this point (179) Vico referred to the discussion of Hobbes by the Lutheran Georg Pasch, *De eruditis huius saeculi inventis*, i.e. *Schediasma de curiosis huius saeculi inventis* (Kiel, 1695; 2nd edn 1700). On Pasch, Malcolm, 'Hobbes and the European Republic of Letters', pp. 480, 511–12 and note 202: Pasch stopped short of accusing Hobbes of atheism, but linked him to Epicurus.

Summarily stated here in book I, and elaborated later in book II, this was a fresh version of the argument Vico had offered in the first *New Science*. Bayle was not now singled out as its target (though his hypothesis was criticised a little later, at 334); alongside Hobbes, it was Polybius who was arraigned for suggesting that had there been philosophers at the beginning of the world there would have been no need of religions (179). But the argument was close to that with which Vico had earlier refuted Bayle. The working of divine providence was evident in the course of human history: society had 'come into being' because, in their fear of the gods and desire for the necessities and utilities of life, men had submitted to providence and accepted the need for law in their relations with each other. The existence of providence was not itself described as a 'common sense', as it had been in the first *New Science*; instead it is providence which worked over time to assist the passions to form men's common sense of their needs and utilities. Being formed over time, and grounded in men's needs and utilities, this 'common sense' could not be equated with the kind of arbitrary 'consensus' so criticised by Bayle; on the contrary, it was integral to the historical process by which divine providence had ensured man's natural sociability. Such a historical account of the working of divine providence was not, however, the only explanation which Vico offered in the *Third New Science* of the way in which our passions combine with divine providence to form a 'common sense' of our humanity. Another, rather different explanation is also identified.

The new explanation referred to a specific feature of human nature, the 'conato', in Latin *conatus*, in English 'endeavour'. The concept is first mentioned in the final section of book I, entitled 'Of method'. Vico asks how the terrifying thought of a divinity was able to impose 'form and measure' (*modo e misura*) on the bestial passions of the first wild men, and transform them into human passions. It did so, he suggests, by arousing the *conato* proper to the human will, which holds in check the motions impressed on the mind by the body. This act of restraining the motions of the body is certainly, Vico continues, an effect of the liberty of the human will (*la libertà dell'umano arbitrio*), and hence of free will (*la libera volontà*), which is the seat of all the virtues, including justice. To attach *conato* instead to bodies would be to imply that bodies have the freedom to regulate their own motions, when all bodies are by nature necessary agents. What 'the mechanical philosophers' (*i meccanici*) call 'powers', 'forces', 'endeavours', are insensible motions of bodies, not the *conato* as Vico understands it, which is proper to the will (340).

The *conato* activated by the frightful thought of a divinity cannot, however, be effective without assistance. Corrupt as men's nature is, tyrannised by *amor proprio*, men follow principally their own utility (*la propria utilità*), and are unable by themselves to impose *conato* on the passions. Therefore it must be by divine providence that men are checked sufficiently to accept the institutions of family, civil society, and finally human society as a whole. Which shows that what regulates all justice among men is divine justice, which is administered by divine providence to preserve human society (341). In suppressing and transforming the bestial passions into human ones, in other words, the *conato* of human free will must be assisted by divine providence. The point is reinforced by Vico's subsequent observation that divine providence acts without any human involvement or counsel, and often against the designs of men (342). Divine providence is neither Epicurean accident nor Stoic fate: it is above and beyond the reach of human intention, but acts with the *conato* of the will to check men's selfish passions, and direct them to sociable ends.

As his allusion to 'the mechanical philosophers' indicated, Vico was well aware that he was exploiting a concept previously used by his antagonists. Hobbes's definition of *conatus* or 'endeavour' as a function of body in particular matched the one which Vico attributed to the mechanical philosophers.[77] Vico had previously discussed the concept in *On the most ancient wisdom of the Italians* (1710), where he had reclaimed it for metaphysics, insisting that *conatus* derived from God; but it did not feature at all in the first *New Science*.[78] Having reintroduced it into the third *New Science*, he underlines its importance by referring to it on several further occasions. On two of these it is to emphasise that *conato* is not in the body, but part of the liberty of the mind. It is quite distinct from the motion of bodies as necessary agents (388, 689). Its principle and agent is the 'spirit' (*l'animo*), which acts 'in the soul' (*nell'anima*) (696).[79] Elsewhere he explains that it was by *conato* that the giants learned to check their bestial lust, and to

---

[77] See above, pp. 212; cf. p. 215 for Spinoza's usage of *conatus* as a power of mind and body as one substance – a definition no less incompatible with Vico's.

[78] *De antiquissima italorum sapientia ex linguae Latinae originibus eruenda. Liber primus: metaphysicus* (1710), cap. IV, sections ii–iii; in the edition of Vico's *Opere filosofiche* by Nicola Badaloni and Paolo Cristofaro (Florence 1971), pp. 84–97; translated by L. M. Palmer, *On the most ancient wisdom of the Italians* (Ithaca and London, 1988), pp. 68–79. Vico's earlier use of *conatus* is discussed by Mark Lilla, *G. B. Vico: the Making of an Anti-modern* (Cambridge, Mass. and London, 1993), pp. 37–45, and by Rossi, *Le sterminate antichità*, pp. 155–9, who emphasises the difference of his usage in the third *New Science*.

[79] At 696 Vico distinguishes 'l'animo' from 'l'anima': Bergin and Fisch translate these respectively as 'spirit' and 'soul'. But the divorce between the 'spirit' and the body is not absolute, for 'spirit is the vehicle of sensation' ('l'animo 'l veicolo sia del senso'), and is identified with the animal spirits present in the nerves. The passage is discussed by Bedani, *Vico Revisited*, pp. 269–70, who draws attention to parallels with Hobbes's earlier discussion of 'conatus'. My interpretation, however, gives more weight to Vico's evident determination to distinguish his use of the concept from that of the 'mechanical philosophers'.

take one woman with them into their caves, which was the beginning of moral virtue (504, 1098). Reinforcing the initial definition of the term, these uses of *conato* make it clear that Vico would have it understood to be an aspect of free will. *Conato* is a capacity of the mind, not the body, and as such is free of the necessity inherent in body. Because of this, it is inferred, the *conato* is the chosen medium by which the divine mind itself provides providential guidance to men. It thus provides Vico with a new and coherent explanation for the operation of divine providence upon the human passions.

It is not possible, however, to leave the matter here. For Vico also introduces into the third *New Science* a discussion of the sources of human knowledge. Here too he develops ideas which received little or no attention in the first *New Science*. In the course of this discussion, it is strongly suggested that the human mind is corporeal, and that it is moved by the senses alone. It is not clear where this leaves the idea of *conato*.

It is one of Vico's axioms (LXIII) that the human mind is naturally inclined by the senses to see itself externally in the body, and is only with difficulty able to understand itself by reflection (236). Referring back to this axiom later in book I, he remarks that it is this weakness (*miseria*) of the mind, buried in the body, which explains why philosophers have hitherto studied the world of nature, and have neglected that made by themselves (331). At the outset of book II, 'Of Poetic Wisdom', Vico introduces a different distinction, between the first vulgar wisdom of the poets, and the later esoteric wisdom of the philosophers. The former may be said to be the sense and the latter the intellect of mankind. He explains the distinction by observing that the human mind does not understand anything for which it has not had a prior impression (*motivo*) from the senses – what the metaphysicians of today would call an 'occasion'.[80] The mind uses the intellect, by contrast, when, from something it senses, it proceeds to apprehend something which does not fall under the senses (363).

What Vico understands by poetic or vulgar wisdom is further elaborated in the discussion later in book II of 'poetic metaphysics'. To the extent that human nature is like that of animals, the senses are its only way of knowing things. But the first men were also able to create things, as children do, in their minds. They did not create as God creates, by knowing things out of his pure understanding, and, by knowing them, creating them. In their ignorance, the first men created by virtue of a wholly corporeal imagination

---

[80] An allusion, almost certainly, to Malebranche's doctrine that sense impressions are the 'occasions' for God's causal agency. Although the doctrine preserved God's general causal agency or providence, it also underlined the immediate corporeality of knowledge.

(*una corpolentissima fantasia*). Out of fear and astonishment they began to exercise the natural curiosity which gives rise to wonder (*maraviglia*). In the skies above them they imagined a God, Jove, whom they pictured in the only terms their senses understood, as a great, enormously strong body. In this way Jove was born in poetry as a 'naturally divine character' or 'imaginative universal' (*un universale fantastico*). It was the beginning of the poetic wisdom of the ancient gentile nations, a wisdom entirely grounded in the senses, or body (374–84).

For Vico, this wisdom was exemplified in the poetry of Homer, barely mentioned in the first *New Science*, but the subject of a separate book (III) in the third *New Science*. Famously Vico argued that 'the true Homer' was the Greek peoples themselves, and that his two poems were to be regarded as 'two great treasure stores of the customs of early ancient Greece' ('due grandi tesori de' costumi dell'antichissima Grecia') (875, 904). But what was exemplified in Homer's poetry was also demonstrated by the history of philosophy. The evidence of the senses was the basis of men's earliest, crude philosophising, after which it was used by Epicurus, for whom the mere exhibition of things to the evidence of the senses was sufficient. The same evidence was used by Aesop and the so-called 'vulgar' moral philosophers. Later the medical philosophers, Socrates, and Plato had all contributed to enhancing the evidence of the senses by the use of induction. The teachings of Aristotle and of Zeno, by contrast, had added nothing of value, though the latter's resembled the method of many modern philosophers. Against them the great philosopher and statesman Verulamius (Bacon) was to be commended for once again advancing the method of induction in his *Organum* – a method, Vico added, which was still being followed by the English with great profit in experimental philosophy (499). Vico followed this account of the development of philosophy as reflection on the evidence of the senses with a brief discussion of what he called 'intelligible universals' (*universali intelligibili*). These constituted the higher form of philosophical wisdom which he had distinguished from poetic wisdom at the outset of book II: an example of an intelligible universal was the recognition that it was the essential property of law to be universal (501, cf. 363). But he remained sceptical of philosophers' access to a higher knowledge in the mind separately from the body. They were all too likely to confuse themselves in abstractions, thereby disabling themselves from entering the vast imagination of the first men, while gaining no more philosophical wisdom for themselves (378).

Vico returned to the problem of the relation between divine providence and the senses for the last time in the 'Conclusion' to the third *New Science*

as a whole. He restated his conception of divine providence. While it
is true that men have themselves made this world of nations (the first
incontestable principle of this science), it is also beyond doubt that this
world has issued 'from a mind often diverse, at times quite contrary, and
always superior to the particular ends that men had proposed to themselves'
(1108).[81] At the same time (and with a final reference to Bayle), he reaffirmed
his fundamental proposition that society is impossible without religion,
by emphasising that religions alone bring peoples to virtue by an appeal
to their 'senses' (*sensi*). Specifically, providence makes itself felt in three
senses, wonder, veneration and curiosity (1110–11). This was accompanied,
however, by a distinction. In the Christian religion, which is true, divine
grace causes virtuous action for the sake of an infinite and eternal good.
Such a good cannot fall under the senses, Vico says, and in consequence it
is the mind of itself which moves the senses to virtuous actions. In all other
religions, which are false, the goods sought are finite and fleeting, whether
in this life or in the other (where they anticipate a beatitude of corporeal
pleasures). In these, accordingly, the senses must draw the mind into doing
virtuous works (1110). In the end, therefore, Vico leaves the reader with a
clear affirmation that divine providence issues from a mind distinct and
always superior to the minds of men, but also with the admission that only
the divine grace accorded to Christians can reach the minds of men directly.
In all other cases divine providence must work through the senses.

How then are we to understand the proposition that divine providence
assists the passions to enable men to form a common sense of their needs
and utilities, which is the foundation of sociability? In particular, what are
we to make of the apparently separate propositions that providence operates
upon the passions through the *conato*, and that providence draws men to
virtue through the senses? On the face of it, the two propositions are not
readily complementary. In defining the *conato*, Vico was insistent that as
an aspect of free will it is a mental, not a bodily power; but he is equally
insistent on the corporeality of the senses, and hence of the knowledge
and motivation derived from them. Such knowledge includes the common
'sense' of human utilities and necessities, while it is the motive of utility, of
self-advantage, which leads us to recognise the virtue of justice and hence
to live with others in society. Despite Vico's best efforts with *conato*, the
opportunity for the exercise of free will by a mind so beholden to the senses
seems limited.

---

[81] '. . . è questo mondo, senza dubbio, uscito da una mente spesso diversa ed alle volte tutta contraria
e sempre superiore ad essi fini particolari ch'essi uomini sì avevan proposti;' *Scienza Nuova* (1744),
1108.

The problem is compounded by Vico's late admission that it is divine grace alone which enables the mind to move the senses. For much earlier, in book I, he had drawn a clear distinction between divine grace and divine providence. Divine grace, he had indicated, acts on the will supernaturally, where divine providence assists it naturally (136). Further on in book I Vico referred back to this passage, as explaining why his account of divine providence is compatible with the Catholic doctrine of grace. The paragraph (310) is particularly obscure, but Vico's point seems to be that divine grace can release men's potential for good works, and hence make possible their (supernatural) salvation; in doing so it does not detract from the natural operation of divine providence.[82] Divine grace and divine providence, it is suggested, are quite different manifestations of the divine intellect, acting separately upon the human will. Divine grace acts directly, through the mind; divine providence, however, must go through the senses, with or without the assistance of *conato*.

VICO'S EPICUREANISM

As Vico himself observed, the third version of the *New Science* was set out following a different method from the first (873). He was now more explicit in the formal presentation of his ideas as a 'science'. He had also altered the definition of its primary subject matter. In the first version, historical argument took precedence, as he sought to demonstrate that it was impossible to conceive of societies without religion. The worship of a provident divinity, by whose auspices men might seek to know their future, was one of the three common senses observable in the history of mankind, along with marriage and burial of the dead. By contrast, in the third version Vico was sufficiently confident to take as his subject matter the civil theology of divine providence itself. It remained essential to his exposition of this theology that societies were founded on religion; but the third *New Science* turns on the claim that divine providence works with the passions of men to form the 'common sense' of the needs and utilities which constitute their 'humanity', and which make them naturally sociable. To secure this claim, however, Vico also had to make explicit certain assumptions which had been latent or under-developed in the first *New Science*, and to extend his discussion much further into the workings of the human mind. In doing

[82] By distinguishing the operation of divine grace from that of divine providence in this way, Vico could circumvent the objection raised by Arnauld against Malebranche, that his doctrine of a divine providence which was general ('une volonté générale') rather than particular ('une volonté particulière') was unable to explain why God saved some but not all men.

so, he may be seen to have confronted the challenge of Epicureanism more directly than before, the better to accommodate its account of human nature within his 'reasoned civil theology' of the operation of divine providence in human affairs. He may also be seen to have taken his difference from Bayle to a still deeper level.

As Bayle had pointed out, the idea of divine providence presupposes a certain conception of God as a divine mind, capable of creating and directing the material world. Acknowledged at the outset of the first *New Science* (8), the point was reiterated and amplified by Vico in the third version of the work. Divine providence is an aspect of an eternal and infinite mind, distinct from and superior to the corporeal world of nature and of men (third *New Science*, 2, 342–45, 1108). There was no room for confusion between the two: a God not completely independent of matter could not exercise his providence over nature or men. In Vico's opinion this was Descartes' error: he had failed in his attempt to separate mind from matter, and thus had lapsed into Epicureanism. Spinoza had gone still further. In combining the divine and human minds with nature in one substance, he had perpetrated a confusion worse than that of Descartes, and aligned himself with the Stoics (335). (In other words, Vico could not have been in more fundamental disagreement with Spinoza: why so many scholars have persuaded themselves otherwise becomes ever harder to explain.) If the divine were inseparable from matter, the operation of providence would be impossible, and the world would be ruled by fate.

Vico also, of course, rejected Epicurean materialism, identifying its doctrine that the world was formed and developed by chance as the antithesis of a theology of divine providence. But at least the Epicureans had not confused the divine mind with matter, as Spinoza and Descartes had done. The problem – but also the fascination – of Epicureanism, as Bayle had pointed out, was that its principles of nature and human nature had a cogency independent of the working of divine providence. Vico too felt that fascination, and acknowledged that cogency. Again and again he can be seen to explain human behaviour in terms close to, if not identical with, those of Epicureanism. The Epicurean account of human nature was consistent, as Vico acknowledged Hobbes to have demonstrated, with the originally violent and bestial nature of men. But it also explained why men driven by self-interested passions should be capable of forming societies, by recognising that they possessed a common sense of their needs and utilities. It further explained why men were so dependent on their senses for knowledge: as the passions were activated by corporeal, material needs, so the imagination and the memory were stimulated by sense impressions.

There was no better instance of this process than the need men felt for religion itself. Out of fear men imagined the existence of a deity with the power to foretell and determine the future; and they naturally imagined that deity as possessing an exaggerated version of the corporeal qualities they recognised in themselves. The same Epicurean philosophy which purported to make the operation of providence redundant thus also suggested a coherent explanation of why men nevertheless imagined it to exist. Hobbes had previously indicated how such an explanation might be developed; and Vico had devoted much of the first *New Science* to what was effectively a natural history of Gentile religion as the cult of divine providence. In the third *New Science* he renewed and reinforced that account, by treating the Joves of the Gentile nations as the imaginative universals of poetic wisdom, and explaining that wisdom in Epicurean terms, as rooted in the senses.

Bayle had suggested that the only plausible response to Epicureanism's denial of divine providence was the truth of Scripture. Vico continued to concede nothing on this vital point, defending the priority of sacred history in the third *New Science* as he had in the first. The chronological table fixed the priority of the Flood, making it clear that the history of all Gentile nations began after that of the Hebrews. Less may have been made of the Fall in the third *New Science*; but there was no suggestion of dispensing with it as the explanation for man's earliest, depraved, and violent nature. Nevertheless, Vico could not be content with Bayle's suggested reliance on Scripture alone. For Vico's was a reasoned, not a revealed theology of providence: it was specifically concerned with the operation of providence among those who had not had the benefit of revelation, and who did not have access to the truths of Scripture. Vico underlined the difference when he insisted that the operation of divine providence be distinguished from that of divine grace. Christians (at least Roman Catholics) believed that salvation was the province of divine grace, which acted supernaturally, while divine providence concerned itself with the natural affairs of men in this world. Divine providence therefore carried no responsibility for the incidence of sin among men, as Bayle had thought it should; a 'reasoned civil theology of divine providence', as Vico defined his new science, was under no obligation to provide a theodicy.

Vico's concept of divine providence was like that of Bayle (and of Malebranche and Gassendi before him) in being uniformly general in its operation.[83] As the aspect of an infinite, eternal mind, quite distinct from the

---

[83] See above ch. 3, p. 129; and Gianni Paganini, 'Vico et Gassendi. De la prudence à la politique', in Sylvia Murr (ed.), *Gassendi et l'Europe 1592–1792* (Paris, 1997), pp. 347–67.

mind of man, divine providence will often contradict men's designs; but there is not the slightest suggestion that this will extend to miraculous dispensations from the normal course of natural and human affairs. Again, however, Vico contrasts with Bayle in seeking to turn this feature of providence to its advantage. Bayle had left it open to the reader to infer that the generality of providence was also its limitation: in its operation it must accord with the otherwise observable laws of nature and human behaviour. Vico, by contrast, would have it understood that providence actively allies itself with the passions of men, and reinforces their exercise of free will. Even where it might seem that men's behaviour could be sufficiently explained in natural, Epicurean terms, providence too will be at work. As we have seen, Vico offered more than one account of the way in which providence acts upon men, whether through the *conato* or by means of the senses, without clearly establishing their compatibility. What is clear, nevertheless, is Vico's determination that explanations which might seem to be sufficient in material, Epicurean terms, should not exclude the operation of divine providence. He might acknowledge that Epicurean principles provided the best available explanations for human behaviour; but he was confident that such principles could be accommodated within his reasoned civil theology of divine providence.

Neither in his accommodation of Epicurean principles nor in his defence of the idea of divine providence was Vico in any sense 'backward looking'. On the contrary, it was precisely his willingness to recognise the force of Epicurean explanations of human nature, sociability, and men's need for religion, and to combine them with a renewed case for the operation of divine providence, which made his thinking contemporary. The *New Science* may not have attracted the attention for which its author had hoped in 1725, but this did not mean that it was written in intellectual isolation, or that its concepts must have been incomprehensible to more than a handful of sympathetic contemporaries. On the contrary, the *New Science* was a work conceived and written at the leading edge of intellectual debate in early eighteenth-century Europe, and in Vico's Naples in particular. In using Epicurean principles to defend the agency of divine providence in human affairs, Vico was not only defying Bayle; he was also thinking, in Nuzzo's unequivocal phrase, 'modernamente'.[84]

But if this was Vico's achievement, a puzzle remains: why was it so difficult for contemporaries (let alone later scholars) to recognise Vico as a

---

[84] Nuzzo, 'Attorno a Vico e Bayle', *Tra ordine della storia e storicità*, p. 220. 'Modernamente' might be translated 'modernly', or 'in a modern manner'; neither quite captures the positivity of the Italian.

'modern'? Vico certainly did not make it easy for his readers. The *New Science* itself, in any of its three versions, was a difficult, perhaps wilfully esoteric work, which covered its tracks by refusing to engage directly or at any length with the arguments of those with whom Vico disagreed, yet required its readers to recognise the wider debates to which it was a contribution. Within contemporary Naples, moreover, Vico positioned himself among the 'ancients', the *veteres*, opposed to the cultural and intellectual initiatives of the 'moderns', the *novatores*. The *Autobiography* avowed his friendship with Paolo Mattia Doria, who by the 1720s had become a bitter critic of every 'modern' philosopher from Descartes to Locke and Newton. Devoting himself to the *New Science* and its revision, Vico never became an activist in the anti-modern cause in the manner of Doria; but he did become a member of the Accademia degli Oziosi, founded in 1733 in response to the modernising Accademia delle Scienze. The latter was the initiative of Celestino Galiani, who had returned to Naples two years earlier as Cappellano Maggiore, and who had quickly made common intellectual cause with local *novatores*, including Bartolomeo Intieri. Inspired by the Académie Royale des Sciences in Paris, Galiani's academy was devoted to natural philosophy rather than metaphysics, and open to discussion of Locke and Newton in that context. It is not surprising that Vico found neither the subject matter nor the philosophy to his taste.[85]

Vico's isolation within Naples in the 1730s and early 1740s should not be exaggerated. In 1732 Galiani himself intervened on Vico's behalf with cardinal Neri Corsini, nephew of Pope Clement XII (to whom Vico had presented a copy of the second *New Science* to follow his gift of the first in 1725), in a further effort to secure financial subvention.[86] Public recognition followed in 1735, when Vico was appointed Historiographer Royal by the new king of the Sicilies, Carlo Borbone, for whom he composed laudatory sonnets. The *New Science* was read – and read seriously – by the next generation of Neapolitan men of letters, notably by the thinker who would emerge as the leading voice of Enlightenment in the kingdom, Antonio Genovesi. In turn Genovesi passed on a sense of the interest and significance of the *New Science* to his pupils: one of them, Francesco Mario Pagano, would produce in his *Saggi politici* (1783–5) the most sustained engagement with Vico's historical ideas undertaken in the eighteenth century. That the significance of Vico's work was not appreciated further afield may be put down to the absence of a French translation. (There was none until 1827,

---

[85] Ferrone, *Scienza natura religione*, pp. 486–545; Ferrone emphasises that Vico was never a 'militant' for the *veteres* in the manner of Doria.
[86] Ferrone, *Scienza natura religione*, p. 529.

when Michelet published an abridged translation.) Vico's book was held out to visiting foreign men of letters, from Montesquieu to Goethe, for their admiration; unable to read it, however, they tended to reinforce the misleading impression of its author as a misunderstood, esoteric sage.

If Vico's isolation in his last years can be exaggerated, it is none the less true that he showed no interest in the topic which became the dominant preoccupation of the modernisers, Galiani and especially Intieri, in the 1730s: the economic condition of the kingdom. As we shall see in ch. 7, Doria, for all his hostility to modern philosophy, did engage with this issue, taking up where he had left off in the *Massime del governo Spagnolo*. But the initiative in introducing political economy to Naples would lie with Galiani and Intieri, and with their young protégés Ferdinando Galiani (Celestino's nephew) and Antonio Genovesi. Their initiative, moreover, had a markedly Epicurean inspiration: the text which Intieri used to propagate political economy in Naples was the *Essai politique sur le commerce* by Jean-François Melon, a student of Bayle and Mandeville.[87] It was not an application of Epicureanism which Vico was minded to endorse.

A final glance at the *New Science* will make this easier to understand. Vico, it has been argued, sought to defend the idea that divine providence directed the world of men on grounds which acknowledged the force of the Epicurean explanation of human behaviour. In his account divine providence operated by naturally assisting the passions: it was through, not against, men's needs and utilities that divine providence could be shown to have made men naturally sociable. But while Vico thought of sociability as something which developed naturally over time, with the assistance of divine providence, he stopped short of regarding its development as progress. In the first *New Science*, it is true, he spoke of the 'progresses' of nations within an 'ideal eternal history', and he projected the possibility of an αχμη or state of perfection, towards which nations might be thought to ascend. But he also made it clear that a nation will usually follow a course of development running from an initial condition of necessity to one of corruption, and culminating in a return to an early stage of barbarism.[88] This idea of a 'return' became much more explicit in the second and third editions of the *New Science*, to which Vico added a book (v) explicitly devoted to a theory of the 'course' (*corso*) and 're-course' (*ricorso*) of nations.[89] A modified version of Machiavelli's cyclical theory of history,

---

[87] Below, ch. 7, pp. 340–7.   [88] Above, pp. 228, 234–5.

[89] *Scienza Nuova* (1744), Libro Quinto, 'Del ricorso delle cose umane nel risurgere che fanno le nazioni' (translated by Bergin and Fisch as 'The recourse of human institutions which nations take when they rise again'), paragraphs 1046–96.

Vico's theory has been characterised as an arbitrary addition to his historical philosophy, belatedly introduced into the *New Science* to give point to his warnings about the corruption present in modern nations.[90] But it is more plausible to read it as a logical consequence of Vico's sceptical, Epicurean account of human nature, reinforced by the doctrine of the Fall. Mankind was too vulnerable to its corporeal desires, too prone to sin, to be capable of permanent improvement. Modern as he was in his appreciation of the process by which men's utilities provided the basis for their sociability, Vico could not accept that this process would lead to human betterment. Presiding over the *corso* and *ricorso* of nations, the divine providence of the *New Science* left no scope for the 'progress of society'.

By contrast, it was to be a crucial distinguishing feature of the Scottish road to Enlightenment that the philosopher who took the lead in engaging with the inheritance of modern Epicureanism, and with Bayle in particular, did not shy away from the prospect of progress. This philosopher was David Hume, to whom we turn next.

[90] This is the argument of Mark Lilla, in *Vico: the Making of an Anti-modern*, pp. 217–31.

CHAPTER 6

Hume, after Bayle and Mandeville

FINDING 'DIVERSION AND IMPROVEMENT' IN BAYLE

At some point in the spring or early summer of 1729, the eighteen-year-old David Hume experienced 'a new Scene of Thought', which inspired him 'to throw up every other Pleasure or Business' to devote himself entirely to it. The 'new Scene of Thought' was almost certainly the germ of the *Treatise of Human Nature*. But for reasons he would explain at length in the 'Letter to a Physician' of March 1734, Hume was unable to realise the promise of that revelatory moment for over five years. A succession of physical complaints prevented him devoting himself to sustained work; but Hume also observed that his attempts to console himself with 'peevish Reflections on the vanity of the World & of all humane Glory' – the shibboleths of Stoic philosophy – had been to no avail.[1] If he found any relief during this period, it was apparently in a work by Bayle, which he recommended to his friend Michael Ramsay in 1732 as 'a Book you will yourself find Diversion & Improvement in'.[2] What this book was is not known. It may have been the *Dictionnaire historique et critique*, but it may also have been the collected *Oeuvres Diverses*, recently published at The Hague in four volumes between 1727 and 1731.[3] It may not be coincidental that during this period Hume also filled what he later described as a 'Manuscript Book',

---

[1] Hume to ? [March or April 1734], in *The Letters of David Hume*, ed. J. Y. T. Greig, 2 vols. (Oxford, 1969), I, pp. 12–18. Now known as the 'Letter to a Physician', its addressee was thought by Greig to be George Cheyne and by E. C. Mossner, *The Life of David Hume* (second edn Oxford, 1980), pp. 83–8, to be John Arbuthnot. Neither attribution can be confirmed, and it is not known whether Hume ever sent the letter.

[2] Hume to Michael Ramsay, March 1732, *Letters of Hume*, I, p. 12.

[3] The *Oeuvres Diverses* was available in Scotland through Thomas Johnson, a bookseller in The Hague with strong Scottish connections. But as M. A. Stewart observes, neither it nor the *Dictionnaire* is exactly described as 'a book', so it is also possible that Hume was referring to one of Bayle's earlier works: M. A. Stewart, 'Hume's intellectual development 1711–1752', in M. Frasca-Spada and P. J. E. Kail (eds.) *Impressions of Hume* (Oxford, 2005), p. 35. Stewart also canvasses the possibility that Michael Ramsay, who was nine years older, had been Hume's tutor before he went up to College.

in which he recorded the gradual progress of his thoughts (or doubts) on religion.[4]

The reference to Bayle as a source of 'Diversion and Improvement' in a moment of physical and intellectual crisis is one of the few surviving clues to Hume's formation as a philosopher. Shortly before his death in 1776 Hume did write an autobiographical essay, 'My own Life'; but this had no pretension to be more than 'the History of my Writings', from the early failure of the *Treatise* to the eventual success of the *History of England*. It offered none of the clues to its author's intellectual development which can be found in Vico's *Autobiography*.[5] We know that Hume would have studied philosophy while at the university in Edinburgh between 1721 and 1725; thanks to M. A. Stewart and Michael Barfoot, we now also have some idea what he may have been taught. In the third year he would have followed the classes of Colin Drummond, professor of logic and metaphysics. But Drummond taught the scholastic philosophy favoured by orthodox Calvinists, and there is no sign that it left any but a negative trace in Hume's thinking.[6] More promising was the fourth-year natural philosophy class of Robert Steuart, who taught Newtonian optics, mechanics, and astronomy, and reproduced Boyle's experiments. Steuart also created for his students a Physiological Library, of which David Hume was a member. Headed by multiple works by Boyle, the library's catalogue also listed Lucretius, *De rerum natura*, and the modern interpreters of Epicureanism, notably Gassendi, along with the *Recherche de la Verité* of Malebranche and Locke's *Essay concerning Human Understanding*.[7] Yet whether even Hume was able to take full advantage of this opportunity must be doubted: he was still only fourteen when he completed the class, and later remembered his college education as extending little further than the languages.[8]

Still less is known about the four years between Hume's leaving college and experiencing the 'new Scene of Thought'. By 1727 he was avowing a conscious inclination towards philosophy and letters (rather than the law, his family's preference), and it is known that in 1726 he had purchased a

---

[4] Hume to Gilbert Elliot of Minto, 10 March 1751, *Letters of Hume*, I, p. 154. Hume told Elliot that he burned the book 'not long ago'.

[5] David Hume, 'My own Life', written in April 1776 and first published in 1777; reprinted in many places. I have used the annotated edition by Eugene F. Miller, included in his edition of the *Essays, Moral, Political, and Literary* (1741–1777) (Indianapolis, 1985), pp. xxxi–xli.

[6] Stewart, 'Hume's intellectual development', pp. 11–16.

[7] Michael Barfoot, 'Hume and the culture of science in the early eighteenth century', in M. A. Stewart (ed.), *Studies in the Philosophy of the Scottish Enlightenment* (Oxford, 1990), pp. 151–90.

[8] Hume to ['a physician'?], [March or April, 1734], *Letters of Hume*, I, p. 13.

copy of the 1723 edition of Shaftesbury's *Characteristicks.*[9] But if Shaftesbury was an early inspiration, the appeal of his philosophy was evidently tested during the years of crisis after 1729: the contrast between the 'Diversion and Improvement' to be found in Bayle and the uselessness of 'peevish Reflections' on the vanity of the world suggests that Hume's thinking may already have begun to turn away from Stoicism.

Towards the end of his crisis Hume resolved to take a break from study, to leave Scotland and move to Bristol to work in the office of a merchant. That expedient was soon abandoned – Hume's efforts to improve the grammar and spelling of his employer's letters were not appreciated – and in the summer of 1734 Hume went on to France. In Paris he was received and advised by the Chevalier Ramsay, fellow Scot, Catholic convert, freemason, Jacobite, and metaphysician. Though Hume thought Ramsay too whimsical to be a philosopher, he would later take ironic advantage of the Chevalier's ingenuousness in matters of religion. After a few weeks in Paris Hume moved out into the provinces, to Rheims and later to La Flèche, in order to live more cheaply and to concentrate on his studies. There he was at last able to compose the *Treatise of Human Nature*. At La Flèche he had access to the library of the Jesuit College, and could familiarise himself with French philosophy; while in France he may also have had the opportunity to read works in the clandestine irreligious tradition. But the only contemporary indication of the philosophers who mattered most to him while he was composing the *Treatise* was another letter to the friend of his youth, Michael Ramsay, in August 1737. Hume advised Ramsay that he might prepare for the metaphysical parts of the work by reading the *Recherche de la Verité* of Malebranche, Berkeley on human knowledge, some of the more metaphysical articles in Bayle's *Dictionary*, such as those of Zeno and Spinoza, and the *Meditations* of Descartes; but the remaining parts of the work were so little dependent on 'all former systems of Philosophy', that Ramsay would have to rely on his own sense to understand them.[10]

When he published the *Treatise*, Hume acknowledged a few more precursors. In the introduction to the work he identified five philosophers in England, 'who have begun to put the science of man on a new footing': Locke, Shaftesbury, Mandeville, Hutcheson, and Butler.[11] Otherwise Hume

---

[9] Hume to Michael Ramsay, 4 July 1727, *Letters of Hume*, i, pp. 9–11; for comment on the Stoic character of the philosophy in the letter, and on Hume's dated copy of the *Characteristicks*, Stewart, 'Hume's intellectual development', pp. 28–32, 37–8.

[10] Hume to Michael Ramsay, 26–31 August 1737, printed in Mossner, *Life of Hume*, 626–7.

[11] David Hume, *A Treatise of Human Nature* (1739–40), ed. David Fate Norton and Mary J. Norton (Oxford, 2000), p. 5 ('Introduction'). Hume repeated these names in the 'Abstract' which he published in 1740 in an attempt to draw attention to the *Treatise*; on this occasion he also mentioned Malebranche, Leibniz and the *Art de Penser* of Arnauld: ibid. pp. 407–8 ('Abstract').

was sparing in expressions of debt to fellow philosophers. The reticence was almost certainly deliberate: in his first published work, Hume would allow as little as possible to detract from the novelty of his own arguments. But this does not mean that Hume avoided engagement with the arguments of his contemporaries. On the contrary, as historians of philosophy have increasingly recognised, the *Treatise of Human Nature* had a rich intellectual context: the detailed argument of the work reveals that Hume had educated himself thoroughly in both British and French philosophy of the previous hundred years.

The chapter which follows will explore Hume's engagement with two in particular of those whom he identified as sources or predecessors, Pierre Bayle and Bernard Mandeville. Having alerted Michael Ramsay to the interest of Bayle in the letters of 1732 and 1737, Hume would cite him on several occasions in the *Treatise* and subsequent philosophical works, and would make use of a number of recognisably Baylean devices in the presentation of his arguments. Although there is no evidence which would make it possible to date when Hume read Mandeville, he evidently did so while preparing the *Treatise*, where Mandeville is included among Hume's precursors in the study of a science of man. If thereafter in the *Treatise* Hume tended to allude to Mandeville rather than cite him by name, the accuracy with which Mandeville's arguments are rehearsed is testimony that Hume had studied them carefully. In both cases, Hume was engaging with exponents of a sceptical, Epicurean approach to morals and sociability. Bayle has already been encountered in this guise; Mandeville, as we shall see, explicitly presented himself as Bayle's expositor to an English readership, rehearsing his arguments and restating his conclusions (often rather more emphatically than Bayle himself). Study of Hume's engagement with Bayle and Mandeville thus offers an opportunity to test the extent to which his account of human nature and morals was also built upon sceptical Epicurean foundations. Potentially still more revealing is the scope for comparison of Hume's response to Bayle and Mandeville with Vico's response to Bayle. If Hume is seen to have been responding to questions similar to those which Vico confronted in the *New Science*, we may find ourselves in the unexpected position of finding that even David Hume was one of Vico's contemporaries.

The relationship of Hume to Mandeville, as to Bayle, has already been investigated by a number of scholars, and the interpretation to be developed here will build upon their findings.[12] More generally, the interpretation of

---

[12] Richard H. Popkin, 'Bayle and Hume', in R. A. Watson and J. E. Force (eds.), *The High Road to Pyrrhonism* (1980, repr. Indianapolis, 1993) 149–59; James Moore, 'Natural Law and the Pyrrhonian

Hume offered here is indebted to that outlined in recent years by James Moore and M. A. Stewart, both of whom have emphasised the presence of sceptical and Epicurean themes in Hume's philosophy.[13] As in the previous chapter's analysis of Vico's response to Bayle, the object of the enquiry is not to trace influence as such; rather, it is to construct a context for the interpretation of a number of Hume's works, in particular the *Treatise of Human Nature*, the *Enquiry concerning Human Understanding*, and the *Natural History of Religion*. To make this possible, the chapter will have a similar structure to its immediate predecessor, in which exposition and interpretation of Vico's *New Science* were preceded by an account of relevant passages in the philosophical writing of Bayle. In this chapter, I shall begin with a similar account of Mandeville's thought, paying particular attention to his elaboration of Baylean themes. Appended to this discussion of Mandeville will be a shorter account of William Warburton's *Divine Legation of Moses*. Warburton's attack on Bayle and Mandeville in this work, it will be suggested, highlights the connection between the two; further, it offers an instructive comparison with Vico's response to Bayle.

We have seen, however, there was an important difference between Vico's intellectual context and Hume's. The intellectual culture of late seventeenth- and early eighteenth-century Naples was rich in modern French philosophy and Epicureanism, making it unsurprising that Bayle should have had such an impact on Vico. In Scotland, by contrast, knowledge of French and Epicurean philosophy was much weaker; and there are even indications that those responsible for teaching moral philosophy and natural theology kept their students away from Bayle. Hume's discovery of Bayle, first documented in 1732, seems to have been his own initiative. But if Bayle could be ignored, Mandeville could not. The furore surrounding the publication of the second edition of the *Fable of the Bees* in 1723 soon extended to Scotland. In particular it drew in Francis Hutcheson; and while Hutcheson's first attacks on the *Fable of the Bees* were written in Dublin, he kept up the assault after transferring to the chair of moral philosophy

controversy', in Peter Jones (ed.), *Philosophy and Science in the Scottish Enlightenment* (Edinburgh, 1988), 20–38; Dario Castiglione, 'Considering things minutely: reflections on Mandeville and the eighteenth-century science of man', *History of Political Thought*, 7 (1986), 463–88; M. M. Goldsmith, 'Regulating anew the moral and political sentiments of mankind: Bernard Mandeville and the Scottish Enlightenment', *Journal of the History of Ideas*, 49 (1988), 587–606; E. J. Hundert, *The Enlightenment's Fable: Bernard Mandeville and the Discovery of Society* (Cambridge, 1994), esp. pp. 59–60, 75–96.

[13] James Moore, 'Hume and Hutcheson', in M. A. Stewart and J. P. Wright (eds.), *Hume and Hume's Connexions* (Edinburgh, 1994), pp. 23–57; and M. A. Stewart, 'Two species of philosophy: the historical significance of the First *Enquiry*', in Peter Millican (ed.), *Reading Hume on Human Understanding* (Oxford, 2002), pp. 67–95.

at Glasgow in 1730, in a debate which also involved Archibald Campbell, a professor at St Andrews. Hutcheson's response to Mandeville will accordingly be the subject of another section of this chapter, adding a Scottish dimension to the development of a Mandevillian context for Hume.

In the end, however, the test of Hume's relation to Mandeville and Bayle, and the basis for any comparison with Vico, will lie in his arguments themselves. These will be examined over the remainder of the chapter. It will be seen that while Hume was critical of specific arguments associated with Mandeville, his response to Mandeville, and still more to Bayle, was far more positive than Vico's. Many of Hume's most radical arguments on morals and religion will be found to take up those of Bayle and Mandeville, the better to clarify their implications and sharpen their conclusions. Under their impetus, Hume would go on to conceive of human society, its moral values, and even its religious beliefs, as something for which humanity alone was responsible. As he did so, it will be suggested in the chapter's conclusion, Hume, unlike Vico, reached the threshold of Enlightenment.

BERNARD MANDEVILLE

Free Thoughts on Religion

Born in Rotterdam in 1670 to a family of doctors, Bernard Mandeville attended the Erasmian or Illustrious School in the city, and was thus in all probability a pupil of Pierre Bayle, who taught there alongside his orthodox Calvinist rival Pierre Jurieu.[14] At the age of fifteen Mandeville went on to the university of Leiden to study philosophy and medicine, eventually presenting theses in both subjects, and gaining his doctorate. Early in the 1690s he moved to London and began practising as a doctor, his profession until his death in 1733. But he was clearly more interested in securing recognition as a writer. His earliest publications were in verse, and included a translation of La Fontaine's fables and his own *The Grumbling Hive* (1705). Making little impact, Mandeville switched to prose, writing in the name of the female authors of *The Female Tatler* (1709–10). None of these early writings was marked by an obvious allegiance to Bayle. This changed when *The Grumbling Hive* was reissued in *The Fable of the Bees: or, Private Vices, Publick Benefits* (1714), accompanied by an 'Enquiry into the Origin of Moral Virtue' and twenty 'Remarks' or notes on the poem. As we shall

---

[14] The most up-to-date biography is that by Maurice Goldsmith, in the *Oxford Dictionary of National Biography*. The name notwithstanding, the Mandevilles were a native Dutch and not a Huguenot family.

see, the premise of the 'Enquiry' was radically Baylean. But the *Fable* did not make a major impact until 1723, when it was published in a second edition, further enlarged by the inclusion of an 'Essay on Charity and Charity Schools' and 'A Search into the Nature of Society'. Three years before that Mandeville had published another work which was, explicitly, an attempt to apply the arguments of Bayle to English affairs: *Free Thoughts on Religion, the Church and National Happiness* (1720). Given that the *Fable* at first passed relatively unnoticed, it makes sense to begin the exposition of Mandeville's arguments with the *Free Thoughts*.

The immediate context of the *Free Thoughts* was the financial crisis known as the South Sea Bubble of the same year, when the collapse of the South Sea Company's stock after a speculative mania threatened to ruin hundreds of investors, as well as the government's credit. As in the original *Grumbling Hive*, Mandeville wrote to rebut those who lamented the unhappy state of the country, and specifically those who sought to blame it on others' religious failings. He recorded his debt to Bayle at the outset, writing in the preface that he had made 'great use of Monsieur Baile'. He had borrowed many of his citations from Bayle's *Dictionary*, and in places had translated and incorporated passages from it without acknowledgement. In a passage added to the second edition in 1729 he explained that he had done so because of Bayle's skill 'in shewing what might plausibly be said for many heterodox opinions'. Since there was no indication which those passages were, however, only a reader with a thorough knowledge of Bayle's *Dictionary* could distinguish when Mandeville spoke for himself, and when he merely reported Bayle.[15]

Adapting a strategy employed by Bayle in the *Pensées Diverses sur la Comète*, the author of the *Free Thoughts* presented himself as a broad-minded Anglican, addressing all Christians. His first task was to explain what religion is, and why it is practised by outward signs of devotion. In

---

[15] B[ernard] M[andeville], *Free Thoughts on Religion, the Church and National Happiness* (London, 1720; second edn London, 1729). I have used the modern edition by Irwin Primer (New Brunswick and London, 2001), which reprints the first edition, giving the original pagination in the text. I will use this original pagination, and hereafter will give the page references in brackets in the main text. The page references for the passages quoted above from the preface are i, xv–xvi; the passage added to the preface in the second edition is given by Primer in his introduction, p. xxvii.

Primer did not attempt a variant edition, but he observes that the changes to the second edition were far fewer than might be expected from the advertisement that it was 'revised, corrected, and enlarged, with many Additions by the Author'. Primer's edition has the value of identifying the articles in the *Dictionary* where Bayle had provided the references to the classical authors whom Mandeville appears to cite directly in his footnotes; Primer does not, however, identify the passages which Mandeville simply copied out of Bayle. Mandeville indicated that these occurred particularly in ch. V, but was not more specific.

general, he began, religion consists in 'an acknowledgement of an immortal power, that, superior to all earthly dominion, invisibly governs the world', and in a 'respectful endeavour' to discharge the duties required by that power. This definition, he added, is good for Mahometans and pagans as well as for Jews and Christians (1). In addition to a belief in providence and obedience to its commands, Christians are more particularly required to believe in the mysterious as well as the historical truths of the Gospel, and to live up to its rules, the chief of which is self-denial. The problem facing Christians, however, is that it is easy for them to believe what their religion requires, and at the same time to lead wicked lives. Self-denial is almost impossible when men and women everywhere are driven by their passions, and when it is to their own and society's worldly advantage that they act accordingly. Even when they do restrain themselves, it is because one passion prevails over another: when women resist seduction and single men abstain from fornication, they do so, Mandeville observed, out of pride and prudence, not to avoid sin (2, 6–15). Nor do individuals worry unduly at the sacrifice of their eternal welfare to worldly advantage. They may fear the prospect of future punishment; but if they are in health, a future state seems a long way off. Instead, they seek an immediate means to allay their fears, and find it in going to church. The reputation of being a strict church-goer is enough to cover even the most notorious sins (17–36). Recognising this, the clergy have exploited and encouraged the laity's need, by multiplying the signs and ceremonies of outward devotion (38–41). Even after the Reformation, the several Protestant churches had each continued to insist on certain ceremonies, damning those who differed from them. But to Mandeville, the clergy's insistence on their own ceremonies was simply an encouragement to superstition, hypocrisy, and intolerance. If Christians would only recognise that their outward devotion was a cover for their failure to live by self-denial, they would cease to take their differences seriously (42–61).

Consideration of the 'mysteries' to which Christians were expected to subscribe reinforced the point. It was in the successive chapters on the doctrine of the Trinity and on free will and predestination that Mandeville made most extensive use of Bayle, and he did not hesitate to state conclusions which Bayle himself had been happy to leave his readers to draw if they chose. At issue in both doctrines was the proper relation between philosophy and theology. Philosophy is concerned with knowledge, which derives from the senses, the understanding, and reason. From these we may be assured that there is a first cause, and consequently that there is a God (63). But we have no such knowledge of the divinity of Christ and of the

Holy Ghost, as revealed in the New Testament. Contradicting the necessary unity of God, this is something which 'shocks our understanding' (65–6). Instead of leaving it to revelation, however, the clergy have attempted to explain the mystery of the Trinity by insinuating philosophy into theology. In so doing, they have not only made the contradiction clearer; they have made the Trinity a cause of contention ever since the quarrel of Arius and Athanasius, to the ruin of millions of laymen (66–76). The public peace required that the two should be kept separate: 'how useful soever philosophy may be to the society, and the affairs of human life; it is the worst guide to eternity, and ought never to be mix'd with theology' (84–5).

The same argument underlay the discussion of God's will. According to human reason or philosophy, 'what we call the will is properly the last result of deliberation'. As such the will can never be free, 'for as soon as the will is made, the thing will'd is determined'. Moreover though we may wish as we please, the will is influenced and seduced by our appetites and inclinations; it is subject to the passions (88–91).[16] But the Gospel states in no uncertain terms that man's eternal fate is predestined, already willed, by God. Men and women are punished for sins which God knows and has decreed they will commit. In other words, the Gospel makes God the author of evil (92–3). In an attempt to save God from this absurdity, the theologians have again had recourse to philosophy, in the form of 'the system of free will'. They have suggested that men still had to choose to sin. But as 'a celebrated author' (already identified in the preface as Bayle) has pointed out, this does not remove the difficulty. Only the Epicurean hypothesis of eternal, uncreated matter could absolve God of his responsibility for evil in the world, since it was incompatible with the existence of a divine providence. Otherwise the one hypothesis capable of explaining the presence of evil was the Manichean doctrine of the two eternal principles of good and evil. The Fathers may have crushed the uneducated Manicheans; but they had never found a better answer to the argument of Epicurus (93–105). Still less had the Socinians, with their implausible claim that unforeseen contingencies had prevented God from using his grace to rescue Adam and Eve. In a passage which Mandeville transcribed directly from Bayle's article on the Paulicians, the Socininians are represented as taking God for an irresponsible mother, who leaves her daughters at a ball though she knows that they are liable to be seduced in the course of it (106–10).[17]

---

[16] The definition is strikingly close to Hobbes's in *Leviathan*, ch. 6.
[17] The debt to Bayle's article on the Paulicians (remark F) is noted by Primer; but he does not alert the reader to the full extent of Mandeville's direct translation and copying of Bayle's words.

Mandeville's immediate conclusion was Bayle's: the word of God alone, the Old and the New Testaments, could cut this Gordian knot (105). Faced with the impossibility of reconciling either the system of predestination or that of free will with the necessary attributes of God, men should desist from quarrelling, and accept the mysteries of revelation (114). But Mandeville did not confine himself to this conclusion: in the setting of the *Free Thoughts* as a whole, his argument had a larger purpose. On Mandeville's analysis, it was the clergy who had taken the mysteries of the Gospel to the point of absurdity, by mixing philosophy with theology. In subsequent chapters, he proceeded to explain how the clergy had made the church the instrument of their authority over the laity. At every stage, he drew on Bayle's *Dictionary* for telling examples of the inconsistency between the clergy's conduct and Christian principles of self-denial.

The great trick had been to exploit the vast disproportion between the momentary duration of this life and the eternity of the pains or pleasures which were supposed to await men in the next. This the clergy had done by making themselves the sole interpreters of the sacred oracles, and masters of the church (146–8). Properly the church signified all believers in Christ; moreover, since actual churches are built at public expense, churches are national institutions (117–21). But the clergy had spared no effort to make the church their own, and the secular power their servant. Above all, they had used the charge of heresy to legitimate persecution of their enemies. However manifest the absurdity of most heresies – a point illustrated by a host of examples from Bayle – absurdity was no obstacle to persecution (180–6). The success of the Protestant schism had only multiplied the occasions for persecution, Lutherans attacking Calvinists, and Calvinists everyone who crossed their path (199–213). On the evidence of the policy of Calvin and Béza at Geneva, Mandeville remarked, 'persecution seems to be a manifest tenet of Calvinism'; again Bayle furnished the examples (219–22). But all national clergy were persecutors, even in England; none could admit the sincerity of dissenters or schismatics (223–35).

Mandeville did not think that the laity need despair. The clergy were not invincible. To turn the tables, the laity need only recognise that the clergy were really motivated by self-interest. Clergymen were like any other profession: to advance their interests they formed themselves into societies, and adopted titles which linked them to their ancestors (albeit in their case their ancestors were the apostles) (252–67). Above all, the laity should not make the mistake of overrating the personal worth of the clergy. For this only encouraged them to pursue their own ends with greater licentiousness (272). 'The reason why we ought to apprehend the encroachments of the clergy more than any other profession is, because they have greater opportunities, and are less mistrusted' (274). The remedy was to adopt the policy of the city of Amsterdam: to grant the clergy the comforts of life, but to deny them any jurisdiction over the laity, and strictly to prevent all seditious preaching (275–94).

To reinforce the point, Mandeville ended the *Free Thoughts* by pointing out that exactly the same assumptions should apply to those who govern us. The best constitution is the one which 'preserves itself firm and remains unshaken, though most men should prove knaves' (297). Fortunately, Mandeville judged, the present constitution of Britain met this condition. Yet the English still expected more of courtiers and ministers than human nature and the situation they were in would permit. 'To expect ministries without faults, and courts without vices is greatly betraying our ignorance of human affairs' (355). If only we would acknowledge this – and keep the clergy of all communions in check, prohibiting all religious disputes – we would then appreciate our real blessings: a happy climate, the skill and productivity of our labouring people, especially in London, and, the greatest happiness of all, our liberty under the law (356–7, 330–4).[18]

The Fable of the Bees

In its attempt to persuade the English that they were in a much better condition than they feared, the *Free Thoughts* represented a reworking of the original message of *The Grumbling Hive*. But Mandeville had of course not abandoned that early work; instead, he had reissued it in 1714 with additional material under the new title *The Fable of the Bees*. The new material was to make all the difference. Even if the public did not at first recognise it, the *Fable* was the most provocative work of moral theorising since Hobbes's *Leviathan*. This was due in no small part to its unacknowledged adoption of a notorious argument of Bayle.

The first new element in the *Fable* (apart from the preface) was a short essay, 'An Enquiry into the Origin of Moral Virtue'.[19] It seemed clear to Mandeville that men, as creatures of their appetites, had no natural sense of virtue. Of all species of animal, he observed, men were the least capable

---

[18] Mandeville's commendation of the 'slaving people' of London explicitly included the productivity of their labour: 'there is more bodily strength exerted to the best advantage, and more work done in London, than by the same number of hands you shall find perform'd anywhere else . . .' (332).

[19] I have used the standard edition of *The Fable of the Bees, or Private Vices, Publick Benefits. By Bernard Mandeville*, ed. with a commentary by F. B. Kaye, 2 vols. (Oxford, 1924; reprinted by the Liberty Fund, Indianapolis, 1988). Page references will be to the volume and pages of Kaye's edition, and will be given in the main text, in the form: I, 41–51.

of living together in large numbers, and they could not be made tractable by force. They therefore had to be persuaded by law-givers and moralists to distinguish between virtue and vice, as the basis on which they might live sociably with each other. This had come about when it was realised than men could be flattered by notions of honour and shame. 'Skilful politicians' had identified honour with restraint of the appetites and shame with their indulgence, and had called such restraint 'virtue' and indulgence 'vice'. The distinction corresponded to a division within the human species, between the class of 'heroes' in whom pride was strong enough to have made them master their appetites, and the remainder who were always hunting after immediate enjoyment, but who could be rendered sufficiently ashamed of their weakness to proclaim their allegiance to the same definition of virtue and vice. This, Mandeville argued, 'was (or at least might have been) the manner after which savage man was broke': morality, government, society itself were all artifices, imposed by a few upon the many. 'Moral virtues are the political offspring which flattery begot upon pride' (I, 41–51).

Alongside this argument was another, which Mandeville stated with only a little less bravado. In defining virtue as self-denial, he was identifying it with what in the *Free Thoughts* he would represent as the duty of a Christian. But in the *Fable* he explicitly rejects the proposition that the distinction between virtue and vice is owing to religion. He spoke, he insisted,

neither of Jews or Christians, but man in his state of nature and ignorance of the true deity; and then I affirm – he continued – that the idolatrous superstitions of all other nations, and the pitiful notions they had of the Supreme Being, were incapable of exciting man to virtue, and good for nothing but to aw and amuse a rude and unthinking multitude. (I, 50)

Morality was not discovered in the New and the Old Testaments; and no heathen idolatry, be it Egyptian, Greek, or Roman, was capable of teaching it. Six years before he acknowledged his debt to Bayle in the preface to the *Free Thoughts*, Mandeville had relaunched the most disquieting of all Bayle's theses: that a society of atheists was not only possible, but preferable to one of idolaters. It was not from their religious beliefs, but by the skilful management of their natural appetites that savage men were persuaded to adopt rules of morality.

In the 'remarks' with which Mandeville proceeded to annotate the original *Grumbling Hive*, the focus switched to modern society. The definition of virtue as self-denial was now applied to expose the hypocrisy at the heart of the way men and women lived in a great city such as London. A prominent case was that of luxury. Luxury was the antithesis of self-denial, and hence by definition a vice (remark L: 1, 107–8). But its benefits were enjoyed by almost every inhabitant of the city. The desire for luxuries was the engine of industry and commerce, encouraging the nation's manufactures, and enabling it to trade them for goods from abroad (remark L: 1, 108–15). The constant changing of fashions set the poor to work, and encouraged the artificer to yet further improvements (remark M: 1, 130). Luxury particularly appealed to women; and their desire for trinkets drove demand to the extent that a considerable portion of the prosperity of London 'depends entirely on the deceit and vile stratagems of women' (remark T: 1, 227–8). What intrigued Mandeville most of all, however, was the pleasure which luxury gave. In a great city, where a man may hourly meet with fifty strangers to one acquaintance, men and women could fashion themselves by their clothing, and be esteemed, 'not as what they are, but as what they appear to be: which is a greater temptation than most people want to be vain' (remark M: 1, 128). When the benefits of luxury were enjoyed by so many, the hypocrisy of those who still affected to denounce it as immoral was all the more ridiculous, as Mandeville took every opportunity to point out. But if the author of the *Fable* delighted in satire, he also wanted to explain why hypocrisy was unavoidable, especially in modern society. We must accept, Mandeville argued, 'what Mr Bayle has endeavour'd to prove at large in his Reflexions on Comets: that man is so unaccountable a creature as to act most commonly against his principle' (remark O: 1, 167). As Epicurus had recognised, men's delight is in their pleasure, even if this is not what they have been persuaded to regard as virtue (remark O: 1, 147–8).[20]

The various threads of the *Fable*'s argument were gathered up in the essay which Mandeville added as a conclusion in 1723, 'A Search into the Nature of Society'. He now made it explicit that he had written to counter the philosophy of Lord Shaftesbury, who had believed that man is made for society, and that he is born with an affection of benevolence towards the whole. To Mandeville virtue and vice were not 'permanent realties', any more than beauty (1, 323–4). Even the most apparently natural social relations might be warped by custom: polygamy was not shocking to a Mahometan, while in the east sisters once married brothers, and men their mothers. Hunting after 'the *Pulchrum & Honestum*' with Shaftesbury was therefore not much better than 'a wild-goose-chace' (1, 330–1). Moreover Shaftesbury's notion that one may be virtuous without self-denial vastly increased the scope for hypocrisy, by underestimating the power of the

---

[20] Edward Hundert, 'Mandeville, Rousseau and the political economy of fantasy', in Maxine Berg and Elizabeth Eger (eds.), *Luxury in the Eighteenth Century: Debates, Desires and Delectable Goods* (Basingstoke and New York, 2003), esp. pp. 28–33, an interpretation which gets beyond the obvious.

passions. The calm virtues are no match for strong inclinations, which can only be subdued by passions of greater violence (1, 331–4). We also need to recognise that sociability requires a measure of dissimulation, for we cannot say openly what we think and desire without giving offence. It is by flattery and persuasion that men and women seek to gain from one another: the imagined 'conversation between a spruce mercer and a young lady his customer', Mandeville's wonderful portrayal of the rules of shopping, is an epitome of civilised sociability (1, 349–53). Mandeville did not discount the role of the 'skilful politician' in a commercial society: 'dextrous management' of the balance of trade and the supply of cheap labour was necessary to ensure a thriving economy. But it was our unabated pursuit of pleasure through the satisfaction of our appetites which he emphasised most of all:

. . . what we call evil in this world, moral as well as natural, is the grand principle that makes us sociable creatures, the solid basis, the life and support of all trades and employments without exception. (1, 369)

Though the most radical features of Mandeville's argument in the *Fable* had been present in 1714, it was the second edition of 1723 which provoked a clamour of indignation. As well as the wrath of a host of pamphleteers, the *Fable* brought on its publisher a formal presentment by the grand jury of Middlesex. The charge associated the book with those who denied the Trinity and providence, and, more generally, with the propagation of libertinism and the running down of virtue at the expense of the church, universities, and social order. In the 'Vindication' which he issued in the same year, Mandeville strongly denied that he had denigrated virtue. But what most disturbed him was the failure to recognise the seriousness of the *Fable* as a work of philosophy. The prose – 'hardly intelligible to any that have not been used to matters of speculation' – even the price of 5 shillings, should have made it plain that he was not attempting to scatter dangerous tenets among the people (1, 404–6).

Infuriated contemporaries may have focused on the libertine satire of the *Fable*; but historians have less excuse for overlooking its deeper philosophical commitments.[21] These may be identified as a renewed and reinvigorated combination of the Epicurean and Augustinian accounts of man developed by French moral philosophers at the turn of the century, above all by Bayle. Mandeville's thinking was Epicurean in its assumption that men are driven by their appetites to pursue pleasure and advantage, and also in the assumption that law-givers had been required to reduce them

---

[21] Especially in the light of Hundert's study, *The Enlightenment's Fable*.

to order. Like Hobbes, Mandeville did not believe that sociability came naturally to man.[22] A debt to the French Augustinians was likewise evident in Mandeville's keen sense of man's capacity for hypocrisy in pursuit of the satisfaction of the ends of self-love, and of the manifold, unintended ways in which hypocrisy nonetheless enables men to live together in society.[23] As Bayle had observed, men characteristically live their lives in defiance of their moral principles. But Mandeville departed radically from the Augustinians in refusing to equate vices with sins. The sociability which interested him in the *Fable* (at least up to this point) was unrelated to religion, whether Judaeo-Christian monotheism or pagan idolatry; he wrote for a society of atheists. More than this, Mandeville rejected the preoccupation with evil which so marked the thinking of Bayle himself.[24] 'What we call evil in this world', he dismissively observed, is precisely what makes us sociable. In effect, Mandeville offered his readers a secularised theodicy: an explanation of why what we call 'evil' – our wants – makes society happy and flourishing in this world. (No wonder he provoked clergymen in particular.) The explanation of this worldly flourishing lay in his dynamic account of human social interaction, as driven by our limitless appetites. But it was not, at this stage, a complete account: there were still gaps and weaknesses in the argument, notably the simple equation of virtue with self-denial, and the absence of any historical explanation for the passage from savage to civilised man. Evidently aware of this, Mandeville set himself to develop his argument in these and other respects in a further series of works, published in the last years of his life: part II of the *Fable of the Bees* (1729), *An Enquiry into the Origin of Honour* (1732), and finally *A Letter to Dion* (1732).

The Fable part II

What Mandeville called *The Fable of the Bees part II* was in fact a new work, in a new form. It consisted of six dialogues, all except the opening pages of the first between two characters, Cleomenes and Horatio. Cleomenes is identified as speaking for Mandeville, while Horatio is a representative of the *beau monde*, and an admirer of Lord Shaftesbury. The 'manner

---

[22] Mandeville's debt to Epicureanism is explored by Hundert, *The Enlightenment's Fable*, pp. 45–9; see also the same author's 'Bernard Mandeville and the Enlightenment's maxims of modernity', *Journal of the History of Ideas*, 56 (1995), 587–91.

[23] On Mandeville's Augustinianism: Ben Rogers, 'In Praise of Vanity: the Augustinian analysis of the benefits of vice from Port Royal to Mandeville', University of Oxford doctoral thesis (1994), ch. 7: 'Bayle and Mandeville', pp. 207–25.

[24] Mandeville's abandonment of Augustinian premises at this point is emphasised by Hundert, *The Enlightenment's Fable*, 36–8.

of writing' is attributed to the example of Gassendi ('The preface', II, 3–28).[25] The rhetorical strategy of the dialogues is straightforward enough: Cleomenes is seeking to persuade Horatio that the arguments of the *Fable* make better sense of our behaviour in society than those of Shaftesbury. The outcome is a sophisticated reworking of points made in the first part of the *Fable*, with many freshly imagined examples. But Mandeville also took the opportunity to move his arguments on, and it is to the new features of the *Fable part II* that I wish to draw attention.

One of these was a greater analytical interest in the nature of the passions. (There is, correspondingly, much less emphasis on satirical exposure of their prevalence over virtue.) In the third dialogue, Mandeville focused on 'the self', convinced that 'in our own species every individual person likes himself better than he does any other . . . it is that *self* we wish well to' (II, 137). Within the self he distinguished two passions, self-love and self-liking. Self-love is a passion common to all animals: it is the drive to acquire what we need for our subsistence, and to make our young secure. Self-liking is what gives us 'that relish we have for life': it is the instinct which man has to a greater degree than any animal for valuing himself above his real worth. It is the same as, or at least the cause of pride, and generates rivalry between men (II, 129–37).[26] It is also what prompts us to cultivate politeness, the avoidance of giving offence (II, 138). The art of good manners, Cleomenes assures Horatio, has nothing to do with virtue and religion, and seldom clashes with either; it requires no more than the outward appearance of virtue, and a seeming conformity in outward worship. It is not surprising, he adds, if those who 'to outward appearance' have devoted themselves to obtaining happiness in this world, should regard what may become of them in the next as the least of their concerns (II, 146–7).

Mandeville's confidence that he could now explain how the passions are responsible for our conduct in society may in turn explain his offering a remarkably blunt test of the desirability of anything which brings happiness: 'the question is not, whether it is true, but whether this happiness is worth having at the rate it is only to be had at' (II, 106). If our

---

[25] References to part II are in the same format as to the original *Fable*, and indicate the volume and page number of Kaye's edition. Kaye observes (II, 21 n. 1) that Gassendi is not known to have written dialogues. Mandeville may have been thinking of the *Disquisitio metaphysica seu dubitationes et instantiae adversus Renati Cartesii Metaphysicam et responsa* (1644), in which Gassendi set Descartes' answers to one of his previous works off against further, longer responses by himself.

[26] Strictly speaking, self-love is not to be equated with self-preservation, for Mandeville insists that it is self-liking which gives us that 'relish we have for life' even when it is not worth living, and self-love might prompt us to end it (II, 135–6). Mandeville thus avoided Hobbes's difficulty in being obliged to deny that man might ever regard suicide as preferable to life.

passions lead us desire something, we must simply weigh the pleasure of having it against the price to be paid in flouting our moral conventions.[27] Well might Horatio immediately ask how it appears that the author of the *Fable* was addressing Christians, as Cleomenes claims. To which the latter replies simply, 'from his writing it in English, and publishing it in London' (II, 107). The circumstances of its publication mean that the book's readers will be those who regard themselves as Christians; but its argument does not suppose that they really are.

Mandeville returned to the analysis of the self in the fourth dialogue, where Cleomenes and Horatio discuss the relation of the mind to the body. Though persuaded that the thoughts and affections of the mind have a more certain, mechanical influence on several parts of the body than had hitherto been discovered, Mandeville admitted that this influence was unlikely ever to be known. Faced with the mysterious structure of the brain, the skills of the anatomist were inadequate (II, 161–6). Mandeville knew too much medicine to have recourse to the metaphysical notion of the *conatus*, with which Hobbes, Spinoza, and Vico had attempted to explain the mind's influence upon the body.[28] Instead, he concluded that useful knowledge about man is only to be had *a posteriori*, by arguing from experience. It was this method which had laid open the nature and usefulness of self-liking, and it would easily account for all the rest of the passions (II, 175–7).

On this foundation, Mandeville proceeded in the latter part of the fourth dialogue to re-examine the cause of man's sociableness. Man has neither a natural affection nor a natural aversion towards others: he simply seeks his own happiness, and stumbles by chance on useful discoveries (II, 177–9):

The love man has for his ease and security, and his perpetual desire of meliorating his condition, must be sufficient motives to make him fond of society; considering the necessitous and helpless condition of his nature.[29] (II, 180)

In other words, men become sociable through their desire of improving their condition, and as they learn that this is best achieved by association with others. Mandeville still presupposes that society needs government; but this requires that men be governable – that they have learnt to recognise being ruled as to their advantage (II, 183–4). Sociableness, therefore, is a process of learning over time, in which man reasons by experience, *a posteriori*

---

[27] The question thus posed in general terms derived from a specific, graphic example: whether the preserving and strengthening the voices of youths merited their castration (II, 105–6).

[28] On their use of *conatus*, see above, ch. 5, pp. 212, 215, 244–6.

[29] The phrase 'meliorating our condition' is then repeated by Horatio (II, 181).

(knowing *a priori* belongs to God only) (II, 186). Such learning advances by slow degrees, and is slowest among those who live in remote parts, nearer the state of nature; it is most extensive among those who live in or near 'great cities or considerable towns' (II, 189–90). London, it may be inferred, is the acme of sociability.

By this stage, Mandeville had come a long way from the account in 'The Origin of Moral Virtue' of the 'breaking' of savage man by a few 'skilful politicians'. Far from abandoning the savage to the obscurity of the state of nature, however, Mandeville devoted the final two dialogues of the *Fable part II* to an extended discussion of his 'steps to society'. These fifth and sixth dialogues are not only the longest in the work; they are also the least studied and understood. It is not difficult to see why. For alongside a naturalistic account of how the earliest men formed societies out of the need to defend themselves from wild beasts and from each other, Mandeville's two protagonists repeatedly return to the question of the compatibility of such an account with the Bible story of the creation, the Fall, and the Flood. Moreover the roles of Cleomenes and Horatio appear to be, if not reversed, then realigned: Horatio has become a sceptical *provocateur*, while Cleomenes shifts, apparently awkwardly, between affirmations of the Bible's literal truth, arguments from probability, and protests that there are mysteries which should not be meddled with.[30]

The savages depicted at the outset of the fifth dialogue were quite unsociable. They had no idea of justice, and the only authority among them was that claimed by a father over his children and grandchildren. But since the savage propagated by instinct, with no regard for consanguinity, children owed their parents no reciprocal obligation (II, 199–205, 224–9). Nor would religion have served to strengthen family ties to the point that they became social ones. Among savages religion could be no more than a fear-induced notion of an invisible power, responsible for the evils which afflicted them (II, 207–12). Though Cleomenes initially rejects Epicurus' maxim that 'Fear makes Gods', he soon acknowledges that religion and the fear of God were synonymous; it is certainly not gratitude for what (little) they do enjoy which makes men religious (II, 207, 214–18). The first step to society occurred only when savages began to cooperate to defend themselves against wild beasts. The importance of the danger was attested by the many accounts of conflicts with beasts in profane history. But while

---

[30] Kaye believed that the roles of Cleomenes and Horatio were reversed, and that in these dialogues Horatio was Mandeville's 'real mouthpiece' (II, 21–2, n. 2). I shall suggest that the matter may have been more complicated.

in those myths it was heroic individuals who slew monsters and dragons, in real life men had found that they could best overcome the danger from other animals by combining their strength and skills. In this way savage men had gradually established their dominance over the temperate regions of the earth (II, 230–61).

Accompanying this naturalistic sketch of the pre-social life of savages, however, was a running commentary on its implications for the authority of the Bible. Repeatedly Horatio directed Cleomenes' attention to the issues. How could the numbers of savages known to exist in the world all be the descendants of Adam, Noah, and his posterity (II, 196–9)? How had the lion, whom Milton described in Paradise, dandling the kid in his paw, become man's ferocious enemy (II, 233–4)? Having ducked the first question, Cleomenes answered the second by appeal to the literal truth of the Mosaic account of Paradise: Milton had been imagining things, because there simply had not been enough time for the goat to produce kids. Horatio pounced: in that case, the lion, endowed with all its strength and weaponry, must have been created for purposes out of Paradise, indicating that 'the Fall of Man was determin'd and predestinated' (II, 235–6). Cleomenes had to admit God's foreknowledge, but maintained that the questions of predestination and the origin of evil were inexplicable mysteries, into which he would not be drawn. It was enough to affirm that the danger from beasts, and savage man's ability to overcome it by combining with others, were the work of providence, and a sign of 'the unalterable wisdom of the Supreme Being . . . the fountain of that incomprehensible chain of causes, on which all events have their undoubted dependance' (II, 236–9, 251–2; quoted passage at 239). Eventually Horatio declared himself persuaded – at which point Cleomenes took the opportunity to answer Horatio's first question, declaring that he was also fully satisfied that all the nations in the world, and every individual, were derived from the sons of Noah (II, 263–4).

In the sixth and final dialogue Mandeville proceeded to discuss the second and third steps to society, respectively the danger men found themselves in from one another, and the invention of letters. The former divided men into bands and companies, each under different leaders, and the latter had made possible written law (II, 266–70). Once men were governed by written law, the rest came on apace. Property could be secured, labour divided and subdivided (II, 283–4). As important, speech itself would be improved, and with it men's ability to persuade others to do as they wished. For the origin of language, Mandeville believed, lay not in the communication of knowledge for others' benefit, but in the desire to subordinate others without having to fight them (II, 285–96).[31] Following the invention of letters, the superiority of man's understanding over that of animals was so evident, there was no temptation to return to the savage state; self-love now reasons us into content with society (II, 299–300).

Just as he appeared to complete the task of explaining historically how savage man had become sociable, however, Mandeville reopened the question of his story's compatibility with the Bible. If we are to dismiss the idea of an early Golden Age as unhistorical, enquires Horatio, why should we still accept the story of Adam and Eve, when the latter must be as much a miracle as the former (II, 309)? Again Cleomenes is given the case for the defence. Of all the accounts of creation, that in the Bible is the least improbable. The alternative explanations of the Epicureans and Spinozists, that the world derived from a fortuitous concourse of atoms, or has existed from eternity, are alike absurd (II, 309–12). Moses' account has the merit of showing an extraordinary knowledge of both nature and human nature. As the universe betrays the unity and greatness of its creator, so the Ten Commandments reveal their author's deep insight into human nature (II, 315–16, recapitulating 272–83 on the decalogue). Nobody, Cleomenes concludes, 'can disprove any thing that is said in the *Pentateuch* in the most literal sense' (II, 317).

The constant juxtaposition of naturalistic and biblical arguments in these dialogues defies straightforward explanation.[32] This may well have been as Mandeville intended. The dialogues could serve more than one possible purpose. Through Horatio, Mandeville could air the manifold objections to the plausibility of the Bible story, demonstrating his thorough acquaintance with an accumulating sceptical literature. At the same time, Cleomenes' credit as Mandeville's spokesman had been sufficiently established in the first four dialogues for the author to claim that he himself upheld the orthodox line, and that another prosecution of his work would be unjustified. Under this cover, Mandeville could then exploit the ironic potential of Cleomenes' defences of the Bible. There is reason to suggest, however, that Cleomenes' awkwardness may have been genuine. The positions which Cleomenes defends were close to those which Bayle had suggested were essential to the defence of revelation itself. The critical doctrines of revelation, divine providence, and the perfections of God, Bayle had seemed to

---

[31] On Mandeville's account of the origin of language, and its Epicurean foundation: Hundert, *The Enlightenment's Fable*, 86–96.

[32] Aside from the commentary in Kaye's notes, there have been remarkably few attempts at interpretation of these dialogues. The interesting pages devoted to them by Rossi, *The Dark Abyss of Time*, 227–36, do not engage with the discussion of the Bible.

say, were all dependent on acceptance of the literal truth of Scripture, and on rejection of the Socinians' attempts to reason away its difficulties.[33] As we have seen, most notably when examining the *Free Thoughts on Religion*, Mandeville was a close student of Bayle – but also one inclined to present as definite conclusions what in Bayle's work were no more than implications or possibilities. Mandeville's problem was that in the context of his discussion of man's passage from savagery to sociability, such conclusions threatened to leave him with very little room for manoeuvre in relation to the Bible. Mandeville could use the dialogue form, and the figure of Horatio in particular, to give himself the freedom to raise the questions; but his loyalty to Bayle would seem to have left him little scope but to give Cleomenes' answers.

Mandeville's difficulties with the Bible may be illuminated by a comparison with the way in which Vico constructed his very different response to Bayle. On Paolo Rossi's strict criteria, Mandeville may not count as one of Vico's contemporaries: neither was aware of the other's work.[34] Nevertheless, they had something vital in common: they had recognised the challenge which Bayle had thrown down to anyone interested in explaining how men became social. With Bayle, both accepted that man is driven by his passions. In consequence, both presupposed that man is not naturally sociable, and set out to explain how he becomes sociable over time, by learning that his selfish passions are most fully satisfied in society. Separately, but almost simultaneously, Vico and Mandeville forged these insights into strikingly original historical accounts of man's passage from a condition of savagery to that of sociability. As they did so, however, they had parted ways. Vico developed his account of the history of nations explicitly to refute Bayle's thesis that a society might exist without religion. Religion, which among the Gentiles had indeed taken the form of idolatry, had been essential from the first to the formation and preservation of society, and divine providence had determined the course of nations at every stage. Mandeville, by contrast, had marginalised the contribution of religion. Idolatry, he agreed with Bayle, was the expression of fear, and did nothing to make men moral. Nor did the development of sociable out of savage man owe anything to either Jewish or Christian moral precepts; instead it was quite compatible with the hypothesis of a society of atheists, which Mandeville had endorsed in the account of the origin of virtue in the first edition of the *Fable*. Yet Mandeville had then found it impossible to avoid the question of the truth of the biblical account of the creation and Fall. Cleomenes' defence of that

---

[33] See above, ch. 5, pp. 222–5.   [34] For Rossi's criteria, see above, ch. 5, p. 207.

truth, and of the action of God's providence, plainly lacked the conviction, let alone the ingenuity, of Vico's rational civil theology of divine providence. Mandeville had found, it seems, that his adherence to Bayle had locked him into a defence of revelation which Vico, as Bayle's antagonist, had been able to sidestep. Vico was free not only to choose the ground on which he answered Bayle – man's capacity to divine providence rather than Revelation itself – but also to choose when he began his account of human history. If nothing else, Mandeville's difficulties over the Fall allow us to appreciate Vico's wisdom in starting the history of humanity after the Flood, with the Gentile descendants of Noah's sons, whose doings were not in the Bible.

Honour and *Dion*

Though it had a new title, *An Enquiry into the Origin of Honour and the Usefulness of Christianity in War* (1732) was in form a continuation of *The Fable part II*, being a further series of dialogues between Horatio and Cleomenes. In the opening dialogue (the only one to be examined here), Mandeville consolidated and reformulated his idea of honour. Previously Mandeville had characterised honour as a passion induced by the opinion of others, and thus distinct both from pride, a passion we are born with, and from virtue, an artificial convention.[35] Returning to the subject, he now made it clear that the origin of honour lay in self-liking, 'that great value which all individuals set upon their own persons' (1–3).[36] When the passion of self-liking is excessive, it gives offence and is called pride; but when it is moderate it excites us to actions which earn praise. Honour is the 'term of art' which we have learned to use to express our agreement with the self-estimation of others; shame is the corresponding term for their ignominy (6–12). Honour and shame are sentiments which depend on the judgement of others, and are therefore social sentiments; but they depend on self-liking for their effectiveness. (Public disgrace has no effect on the shameless) (41–2). Mandeville also emphasised that while honour and shame, like virtue and vice, were the invention of moralists and politicians, the invention had been the joint labour of many, over a long period of time (29, 39–41). Once appreciated, moreover, honour was far more beneficial to

---

[35] *Fable*, remark C: I, 63–80; *part II*: second dialogue: II, 91–4.
[36] I have used the first edition, *An Enquiry into the Origin of Honour and the Usefulness of Christianity in War. By the Author of the Fable of the Bees* (London, 1732); page references in brackets within the text above. A photographic reprint of this edition, misleadingly called the second edition, with an introduction by M. M. Goldsmith, was published in London in 1971.

civil society than virtue. Men might still indulge their appetites without transgressing the principle of honour, whereas virtue required strict self-denial (42–4). Honour, therefore, was a principle far better adapted to the prevalence of the passions in human nature, regulating and directing rather than seeking to suppress them, as virtue would.

Honour was also a more effective principle than religion for keeping men in awe. The better to explain this, Mandeville set Horatio and Cleomenes to review men's need for religion. The fear of an intelligent, invisible cause, they agreed, extended to men in every society, civil as well as savage. It was not an invention of rulers, like morality, but it could be managed by them to strengthen their subjects' allegiance. For this purpose the deity might be of any form or number. It might be identified with animals, with the two principles of good and evil, with three persons, or with 50,000 (17–25). For most men, indeed, idolatry and a belief in a mischievous God are easier than a belief in one all-wise and perfectly good being, even if the latter is more rational (26). Against idolatry, Cleomenes points out, Christianity insists on one God; it also has the advantage of revelation, while its mysteries gain credit from the strictness of its morality (30). But these merits are precisely what undermine its political utility. Christians have proved that the profession of religion and the practice of wickedness are perfectly compatible. Christian self-denial flies in the face of the fact that men are constantly seeking to improve their condition in this world. It is here and now that men seek security and reputation, for reputation cannot be enjoyed after death (36–8). This is why moralists and politicians do better to cultivate the principle of honour rather than religion. By making man an object of reverence to himself, they can hope to make him tractable in a way that a belief in God and a future state never could (39–40).

Mandeville's last work, *A Letter to Dion, occasion'd by his Book call'd Alciphron* (1732), was also a continuation of an earlier one, in this case the 'Vindication' of the first *Fable*. Its target was George Berkeley, who had ridiculed the argument of the *Fable* in the second dialogue of *Alciphron*, published earlier in the same year. Clearly incensed at being traduced by a fellow philosopher, Mandeville accused Dion of failing to read the book he purported to criticise. Both the prose and the price of the *Fable*, he repeated, should have shown that it was a work of philosophy (1–15).[37] Two points in particular he insisted on. First, nowhere had he contradicted Bayle's observation that the utilities of vice do not prevent it being bad. In

---

[37] *A Letter to Dion, occasion'd by his Book call'd Alciphron, or the Minute Philosopher. By the author of the Fable of the Bees* (London, 1732); page references in brackets.

maintaining that luxury had become necessary to the greatness of a nation, he had simply observed that poverty and self-denial held very little attraction for most people (15–34). Second, Mandeville insisted that religion had very little effect on men's behaviour. 'In many actions, and even the most important affairs, they are not more influenced by what they believe of a future state, than they are by the name of the street they live in' (56). Men brought up as Christians will not disown the name, but very few show any enthusiasm for the severe manners which Christianity requires. Modern Christians, he added, in a final, splendid insult, are just like Freemasons, who attend their lodges, and pretend to mysteries, but who, as far as Mandeville could learn, had nothing more to do there than to be Freemasons (62–4).

If the final dialogues of *The Fable part* II draw our attention to the common ground between Mandeville and Vico, these last works underline the gulf which eventually separated them. Notwithstanding his difficulties over the truth of the Bible, Mandeville's loyalty to Bayle had carried him on to ground which Vico never wished to reach. The power of the passions was too strong to be checked by our conventional notion of virtue as self-denial. Only the derivative but still self-regarding sentiments of honour and shame were effective in regulating (not suppressing) our appetites. Equally, the passions were too strong for any religion. Idolatry, itself a product of the passion of fear, could do little to contain them. Christianity, with its ascetic virtues, simply encouraged hypocrisy and put a misguided trust and authority in the hands of the clergy. Men's desire to meliorate their condition in this world, along with their desire for reputation, meant that they discounted the prospect of a future state of reward or punishment. They were heedless of the retribution which Christianity tried to teach them would follow their devotion to worldly pleasure. In any discussion of society, Mandeville was arguing, it was not only plausible, it was essential to accept Bayle's shocking hypothesis, and to begin by supposing that its members would be atheists.

Nowhere were these findings better displayed, Mandeville believed, than in his adopted city of London. It was in that teeming, stinking, prosperous city that the advantages of sociability were most visibly enjoyed.[38] Had Vico, living in the equally teeming, stinking, but significantly less prosperous, city of Naples, been able to read the *Fable*, we may suppose that he would have understood Mandeville's reasoning, since he shared the same

---

[38] Mandeville had commented on the filthy, stinking streets of London at the very outset of the *Fable*: 'Preface', I, 10–12.

Epicurean conviction of the power of the passions. But he would certainly have recoiled from Mandeville's conclusions. If anything could have illustrated the danger which the *New Science* was designed to counter better than Bayle's hypothetical society of atheists, it was the London which Mandeville celebrated. Alas, however, Vico could not read *The Fable of the Bees*.

William Warburton, *The Divine Legation of Moses*

However suggestive, these comparisons between Mandeville and Vico will seem arbitrary, even unhistorical, if it is thought that they belonged to completely different intellectual worlds. It is very much the argument of this study that they did not. Corroboration of this claim is provided by what may seem an unlikely source, William Warburton's *The Divine Legation of Moses Demonstrated* (1738, 1741). William Warburton (1698–1779) was an Anglican clergyman, who had already written *The Alliance between Church and State* (1736), a vigorous statement of Erastianism. The subject of the *Divine Legation of Moses* was rather different.[39]

Warburton had a singular thesis to advance: that the absence of the doctrine of the immortal soul, and of a future state of rewards and punishments, from the Jewish religion adumbrated by Moses, was a proof of that religion's divine inspiration.[40] It was a response to the argument of deists like John Toland, who in turn was inspired by Spinoza, that there was no trace of the doctrine of the immortality of the soul in the Old Testament, though it was to be found in ancient Egypt. With their hieroglyphs and fables, Toland had maintained, the Egyptians were the real source of all the wisdom and religion in the ancient pagan world. As his subtitle indicated, Warburton's strategy was to turn the deists' arguments against themselves. Not only was the absence of the doctrine of the immortality of the soul and a future state from the Old Testament a proof of that work's divine inspiration (and, in the by-going, disproof of the Socinian thesis that the truth of Christianity was independent of the Old Testament). But the doctrine's earlier presence in Egypt represented no danger to the truth of Christianity. There was no

---

[39] On Warburton's life, see the memoir by B. W. Young in the *Oxford DNB*. Mark Pattison, 'Life of Bishop Warburton', in *Essays by the late Mark Pattison*, ed. Henry Nettleship, 2 vols. (Oxford, 1889), II, 119–76, is evocative; Brian W. Young, *Religion and Enlightenment in Eighteenth-century England: Theological Debate from Locke to Burke* (Oxford, 1998), ch. 5, 'William Warburton, a polemic divine', makes a case for the defence.

[40] William Warburton, *The Divine Legation of Moses Demonstrated, on the principles of a religious Deist, from the omission of the doctrine of a future state of reward and punishment in the Jewish dispensation, in six books*, 2 vols. (London, 1738, 1741).

hidden wisdom in the Egyptian hieroglyphs, a case Warburton supported with his own account of the origin of writing in images, linked to the origin of language in sounds and gestures.[41]

In the context being reconstructed here, however, another of Warburton's targets is of most interest. Having outlined his intended argument, 'the necessity of religion in general, and the doctrine of a future state in particular, to civil society', Warburton devoted the remainder of book 1 to identifying a succession of thinkers who had denied that necessity, and who had, in effect, defended atheism. The latest of these was Mandeville. Like so many others, Warburton became splenetic at the prospect of discussing the *Fable*. Its argument was 'a monstrous paradox', 'an unheard-of impiety'; its author 'a wordy declaimer' of 'low impure buffoonery and childish rhetoric'. In daring to maintain that private vices were public benefits Mandeville had broken the essential connection between virtue and religion, and specifically between virtue and the doctrine of reward and punishment in a future life. Further, he had misrepresented virtue itself by equating it with the misanthropic values of monks and ascetics. He had thus confused true Christianity with the beliefs of bigots and fanatics. No wonder he had then denied that consumption could be advantageous without becoming luxury, and refused to recognise that luxury still represented a danger.[42]

Immediately behind Mandeville, Warburton knew, stood Bayle. The analysis of Bayle's errors occupied Warburton rather longer. He concentrated on the central question of the *Pensées Diverses* and the *Continuation*, which of atheism and ancient idolatry or polytheism was the least hurtful to mankind. Acknowledging that Bayle's arguments were 'occasionally and confusedly dispersed throughout that large work', he identified and attacked the four he considered most damaging. The first was that an atheist might understand the moral difference between good and ill – an argument all the more dangerous, Warburton pointed out, because none of the existing schools of moral philosophy had an adequate answer. A second was that an atheist might have as strong an appetite for glory, praise, and reputation as other men, the danger here being that these could be gained merely by counterfeiting the real virtues. The third dangerous argument was that men do not act according to their principles, while the fourth was

---

[41] Warburton, *Divine Legation*, I, pp. 1–8, summarising the argument to come. Rossi, *The Dark Abyss of Time*, pp. 236–45, is a lucid guide.
[42] Warburton, *Divine Legation*, I, pp. 78–86.

Bayle's claim that examples of virtuous atheists ranged from philosophers to savages.[43]

Consistent with his general strategy, Warburton built his case for the necessity of the doctrine of future rewards and punishments on selected presuppositions of his opponents. The state of nature, he accepted, was just as the Hobbists represented it, a condition in which men's appetite for self-preservation led to mutual violence. Against this religion alone was an insufficient check, and the magistrate was required to establish civil society. But the magistrate's authority too was insufficient, because one sided. He could punish, but he could not reward. (Only in the utopia of Lilliput did the government reward as well as punish.) Without the prospect of rewards, the incentive for subjects to fulfil their 'imperfect' obligations of gratitude, hospitality, and charity was diminished. But the necessary sanction was provided by religion, which teaches that there is an overriding providence, which rewards the good and punishes the ill. A religion which included this doctrine, therefore, was essential to the maintenance of civil society.[44]

The remaining books of volume I were given over to a demonstration that the necessity of the doctrine had been well understood by the legislators and philosophers of antiquity. Evidence from Egypt, Greece, and Rome all pointed in that direction, but the best evidence, Warburton believed, was the account of the mysteries given by Virgil in the sixth book of the *Aeneid*. It was true, of course, that mysteries were a common feature of the ancient pagan religions, and hence the product of idolatry. But they were not characteristically polytheist, since they had insisted on the unity of the godhead. Bayle had been wrong to equate all pagan religion with polytheism, and to maintain that idolatry was of no benefit to morals. The idolatry of the ancients had been conducive to civil society, as atheism could never be.[45] If the Jews did not possess the doctrine of a future state with rewards and punishments, it was because God had given them a special dispensation. Christ, for his part, had simply enabled his followers to rejoin the rest of humanity in upholding the doctrine.

In the course of this argument, and especially in the second volume of the *Divine Legation*, Warburton would cover ground which was also familiar to Vico, notably when discussing ancient language, hieroglyphs and emblems. Observing this, some Vico scholars have added Warburton's name to the list of 'Vico's contemporaries'. In this case too, Rossi enters reservations: not only were Vico and Warburton unacquainted with each other's work, there were marked differences between them, not least in

[43] Ibid., pp. 33–78.   [44] Ibid., pp. 9–24.   [45] Ibid., pp. 111–231.

the evaluation of Egyptian superstitions. Nevertheless, there was also a remarkable congruence of purpose: both Warburton and Vico were seeking to refute Bayle through a reinterpretation of the history of ancient nations, using the Old Testament as their starting point.[46] There is a striking – if double-edged – sense in which Warburton was the closest eighteenth-century English intellectual culture came to producing a Vico.[47]

If Warburton's *Divine Legation of Moses* demonstrates that the threat from Bayle could be understood and answered in not dissimilar ways in England and in Naples, it nevertheless also registers that the debate had now moved on, beyond Bayle, and into the pages of the *Fable of the Bees* and its sequels. Where Bayle had been subversive by implication, 'the indulgent foster-father of infidelity',[48] Mandeville was unequivocal: his work embodied an open challenge to the relevance and credibility of the doctrine of a future state. Nor was Warburton the only writer to recognise the threat in Mandeville's radicalisation of Bayle. Among the many who had seen the danger, there was one in particular whose connections with Scottish intellectual life were rather closer than Warburton's.

FRANCIS HUTCHESON

There was no immediate response to the *Fable of the Bees* from Scotland. But there was from a Scottish-educated Irish presbyterian philosopher, Francis Hutcheson (1694–1746). The son of a presbyterian minister in Ulster, Hutcheson had attended a dissenting academy in County Down before proceeding to Glasgow in 1710 to complete the basic university curriculum. He stayed on in order to train to be a minister, studying under the controversial Arminian and perhaps also Arian professor, John Simson. Returning to Ireland in 1718, Hutcheson moved south to Dublin to take charge of an academy. There he forged several close personal and intellectual connections, with Church of Ireland as well as presbyterian clergy, with the Old Whig politician Robert Molesworth, and with the journalist James Arbuckle and the publishers of the *Dublin Weekly Journal*.[49] By this time, if

---

[46] Rossi, *The Dark Abyss of Time*, pp. 243–6, 252–3, 269.

[47] An observation which John Pocock might, or might not, regard as support for his proposition that the *Divine Legation of Moses* was one of the two major works of England's Enlightenment, the other being the *Decline and Fall*: 'Clergy and commerce: the conservative Enlightenment in England', in Rafaelle Ajello and others (eds.), *L'età dei lumi. Studi storici sul settecento europeo in onore di Franco Venturi* (Naples, 1985), vol. I, p. 554.

[48] Warburton, *Divine Legation*, I, p. 88.

[49] The most accurate biography of Hutcheson is that by James Moore, in the *Oxford DNB*. See also Michael Brown, *Francis Hutcheson in Dublin 1719–1730: the Crucible of his Thought* (Dublin, 2002), which is organised, a little awkwardly, around his friendships.

not earlier, Hutcheson had become thoroughly disillusioned with the moral philosophy of the schoolmen, of which Gershom Carmichael had been the leading exponent in Scotland, and was keen to promote the philosophy of Shaftesbury in its stead. In 1725 he published *An Inquiry into the Original of our Ideas of Beauty and Virtue; in Two Treatises. In which the principles of the late Earl of Shaftesbury are explain'd and defended, against the author of the Fable of the Bees: and the ideas of moral good and evil are establish'd, according to the sentiments of the antient moralists* (1725). Notwithstanding the subtitle, Hutcheson did not explicitly engage with Mandeville in this work. But the assault was only delayed: in 1726 Arbuckle's *Dublin Weekly Journal* published three letters 'to Hibernicus', in which Hutcheson set about exposing the weaknesses of the *Fable*.

Hutcheson's attitude to the book was clear from his opening declaration that it was 'unanswerable', by which he meant that its arguments were too absurd for coherent response. Nevertheless he managed to restrain himself sufficiently in the first two letters to engage in philosophical criticism. The root of the problem, Hutcheson suggested, lay in the definition of pleasure. All men of reflection, from the age of Socrates to that of Addison, had agreed that the truest pleasure 'consists in kind affections to our fellow creatures, gratitude and love to the deity, submission to his will, and trust in his providence, with a course of suitable actions'.[50] If we cannot be sure of the continuation of such pleasure, and suffer any 'present seeming disorders and calamities', he added, we have the hope of a future state as compensation.[51] Only the Epicureans had defied the consensus of heathen moralists that kind affections were natural to man, and that consulting the public good was the way to individual happiness.[52] The second letter extended the argument to luxury. Mandeville's treatment of luxury as a vice had plainly relied on too severe a notion of virtue. All ancient and modern moralists, including the Stoics, allowed the use of pleasures above what was strictly necessary, and Christian law did not contradict them.[53] Luxury, therefore, was properly only expenditure on dress, table, and equipage beyond what a person's wealth would bear, if he was also to fulfil his responsibilities to his family, friends, country, and the poor. From his observation of Dublin society, Hutcheson was confident that on this definition only a small part of our consumption would be found owing to our vices.[54] By the third letter,

---

[50] I have used the later, separately published edition of the letters: Francis Hutcheson, *Reflections upon Laughter and Remarks upon the Fable of the Bees* (Glasgow, 1756), p. 45. Hereafter, *Remarks upon the Fable*.

[51] Hutcheson, *Remarks upon the Fable*, pp. 47–8.   [52] Ibid., p. 53.

[53] Ibid., pp. 58–9.   [54] Ibid., pp. 66–7.

Hutcheson's patience had given out, and he resorted to *ad hominem* abuse. The author of the *Fable* was a 'penetrating swaggerer', who had probably been struck by a fanatic sermon on self-denial in his youth, and had never got it out of his head. His contempt for pedantry and the clergy was that of a writer keen to give himself free-thinking airs. His pretension was apparent in his easy talk of 'meliorating our condition', while his inconsistencies, most glaring in his treatment of pride, undermined his argument at every turn.[55]

Hutcheson's other major engagement with Mandeville's legacy occurred following his translation back to Glasgow in 1730, to succeed Gershom Carmichael in the recently established chair of moral philosophy. Departing slightly from custom, Hutcheson chose to devote his inaugural lecture to a substantive problem: the natural sociability of mankind.[56] From the content of the lecture it seems reasonable to suppose that Hutcheson now had part II of the *Fable* in his sights as well. Another fresh element in the context was a work by the professor of ecclesiastical history at St Andrews, Archibald Campbell's *An Enquiry into the Original of Moral Virtue*.[57] Campbell wanted to defend the view that self-love causes all our actions from the misuse made of it by Hobbes, Spinoza, and Mandeville. According to Campbell self-love exerts itself in a desire for esteem, and thus leads us to pursue moral virtue.[58] Human nature was misrepresented by those, such as Hobbes, who drew their observations from courts and cities, where the natural balance of our nature is disturbed; Mandeville had also mistaken virtue for austerity.[59] As his book's subtitle implied, however, Campbell was equally critical of

---

[55] Ibid., pp. 68–82.

[56] Francis Hutcheson, *De naturali hominum socialitate oratio inauguralis* (1730), translated as 'Inaugural lecture on the social nature of man', in *Francis Hutcheson: Two Texts on Human Nature*, ed. Thomas Mautner (Cambridge, 1993), pp. 124–47, and as 'On the natural sociability of mankind' in James Moore and Michael Silverthorne (eds.), *Francis Hutcheson: Logic, Metaphysics and Natural Sociability* (Indianapolis, 2005).

[57] Archibald Campbell, *An Enquiry into the Original of Moral Virtue. Wherein it is shewn (against the author of the Fable of the Bees & co.) that virtue is founded in the nature of things, is unalterable, and eternal, and the great means of private and publick happiness; with some reflections on a late book, intitled, An Enquiry into the Original of our Ideas of Beauty and Virtue* (Edinburgh, 1733). This was first published in curious circumstances in 1728, in the name of one Alexander Innes, who had claimed it as his own. Campbell exposed the deceit in 1730, and issued the work again, under his own name and with a new preface, in 1733. (To complicate matters, Innes had also impersonated Mandeville, staging a public renunciation of the *Fable* by throwing it into a bonfire; Mandeville had been obliged to clear up this confusion in the preface to the *Fable part II*, pp. 23–8.)

[58] Campbell, *Enquiry into the Original of Moral Virtue*, pp. 12–48; in his support (p. 30), Campbell quoted Spinoza on the bias of our nature to do all we can to relieve our fellow men from misery.

[59] Campbell, *Enquiry into the Original of Moral Virtue*, pp. 234–7, 528–34.

Hutcheson, accusing him of denying that benevolence is prompted by the prospect of divine reward.[60]

Hutcheson told his Glasgow audience that he had chosen the topic of his lecture because recent writers had not sufficiently explained which aspects of the human mind make us sociable. He began by defining 'nature' in teleological terms: the nature of a thing is given by its end, the completed structure. It may be evident, however, even in an impaired form, as a house which has fallen into disrepair.[61] This conception of nature as purposive was one Hutcheson had outlined in the second of his philosophical works published in Dublin, *An Essay on the Passions* (1728), where he associated it with God's providential design.[62] Applied to society, it entailed that the term 'state of nature' ought to denote either the ordinary condition of man, or the most perfect state he could attain; its use by Hobbes and Pufendorf to describe a state of solitary wretchedness was an abuse of words which slandered human nature. Hutcheson himself would avoid the problem by counterposing the civil state and the state of freedom, in which there is no authority. He then devoted the remainder of the lecture to discussing whether sociability was natural to man in the state of freedom.[63]

Hutcheson took the point, made by Mandeville and others, that there was more to human sociability than the herd instinct of animals. What he wanted to refute, however, was the Epicurean thesis that men were brought together out of weakness. This had been the belief of Pufendorf, who supposed that men had discovered that they needed the help of others to realise the ends they sought out of self-love. Against this, Hutcheson argued that men are also driven into society for higher ends, for the pleasures of praise and honour, and for the exercise of the many benevolent affections and passions which are also implanted in our nature.[64] Hutcheson acknowledged the existence of desires which led men to compete against one another for wealth and reputation, and he admitted that these desires were natural and found in the state of liberty. The desire for private advantage had been implanted by God himself: human nature is in many respects fallen, weak, and corrupted. But God's providence was not thereby inconsistent, for it had endowed men with reason, enabling them to recognise that their

---

[60] Ibid., pp. 404–34. On Campbell, see M. A. Stewart, 'The Scottish Enlightenment', in Stuart Brown (ed.), *British Philosophy in the Age of Enlightenment* (London and New York, 1995), pp. 280–1.

[61] Hutcheson, 'Inaugural Lecture', *Two Texts on Human Nature*, pp. 127–30.

[62] Francis Hutcheson, *An Essay on the Nature and Conduct of the Passions and Affections, with Illustrations on the Moral Sense* (London, 1728), ed. Aaron Garrett (Indianapolis, 2002), treatise I, sect. VI, part vii. On Hutcheson's conception of nature and God's providential design: David F. Norton, *David Hume: Common Sense Moralist, Sceptical Metaphysician* (Princeton, 1982), pp. 87–92.

[63] Hutcheson, 'Inaugural Lecture', *Two Texts on Human Nature*, pp. 130–3.   [64] Ibid., pp. 133–7.

advantage lay in the modest pleasures of society and friendship. Sociability, therefore, was not the creation of education and statecraft: it was not an artifice. The existence of benevolent, social affections in human nature was the precondition of men's coming together in society: without them politicians would not have found people so tractable and willing to be governed.[65]

Hutcheson made it clear that the targets of his lecture were the advocates of the Epicurean doctrine that self-love is the spring of all our actions. He did not identify Mandeville as one of these, naming only Hobbes and Pufendorf; but he did cite in his own support Mandeville's *bête noire*, 'the elegant Lord Shaftesbury'.[66] The importance of natural jurisprudence as the didactic basis of the moral philosophy Hutcheson was appointed to teach may explain why Pufendorf rather than Mandeville was now his principal target. Nevertheless the lecture laid the foundations of an explicitly anti-Epicurean account of sociability, and man's passage from the state of freedom to civil society. Had Hutcheson been able to complete the project with an account of sociability in civil society, as he intended, he would have been in a position to match Mandeville head on.

Unfortunately, he was unable to do so. It seems that once Hutcheson was settled in Glasgow the familiar burdens of teaching and administration sapped his energies; and he may have been wary of exposing himself to accusations of heresy in a university still much exercised by the lapses of Professor Simson. Two of his student manuals, in Latin, on morals and metaphysics, were published in 1742 by the Glasgow firm of Robert Foulis; but they may well have been written in Dublin in the 1720s. A more original venture was a collaboration with his Glasgow colleague James Moore and with Foulis to publish translations of ancient Stoic texts, beginning in 1742 with the *The Meditations of the Emperor Marcus Aurelius*. The introduction to the translation spoke of the work as uplifting the hearts of those with any sense of goodness, and warming them with the emotions of piety, gratitude, and resignation to God. The paganism of the emperor was qualified by the observation that, like all Stoics, he had been a monotheist, while his persecutions of Christians had been less zealous than those Christians had perpetrated on each other. The compatibility of Stoic morals with biblical precepts was further underlined in the notes.[67]

[65] Ibid., pp. 140–7.   [66] Ibid., pp. 131, 134–5.

[67] *The Meditations of the Emperor Marcus Aurelius*, newly translated from the Greek: with Notes, and an Account of his Life [by Francis Hutcheson and James Moore] (Glasgow: printed by Robert Foulis, 1742), 'Introduction', pp. 2, 35–45; examples of notes on pp. 207, 238. On the Stoic and Shaftesburian publishing of the Foulis Press, Isabel Rivers, *Reason, Grace, and Sentiment: a Study of the Language of Religion and Ethics in England, 1660–1780*. vol. II: *Shaftesbury to Hume* (Cambridge, 2000), pp. 185–7.

The other new undertaking of Hutcheson's Glasgow years was a work which would only be published after his death, *A System of Moral Philosophy, in Three Books* (1755). Recently re-examined by James Moore, this work shows Hutcheson engaging with the problem of which Bayle had made so much: God's responsibility for the existence of evil as well as good in the world. Even in this case, however, it seems that Hutcheson was writing primarily for his Irish friends, prompted by the translation of Bishop William King's *Of the Origin of Evil* (1731), the 1702 Latin original of which had been a reference point for Bayle. In the *System of Moral Philosophy* Hutcheson attempted to argue at length what he had previously suggested only in passing: that divine providence would order our passions and desires to ensure the ultimate prevalence of good over evil, and that the prospect of a future state offering everlasting happiness was our consolation for present ills. Given this, he concluded, it was needless to enquire whether a society of atheists could exist, or would be better or worse than one devoted to superstition.[68] As a response to Bayle, however, such a defence of divine providence was quite different from that offered by Vico, by Warburton, or even (however half-heartedly) by Mandeville. Hutcheson was uninterested in exploring the history of religion, or in discussing the role of idolatry in fostering sociability. Where Vico, and even Warburton, had accepted that early man was driven by self-love, Hutcheson avoided lines of enquiry in which it was difficult to deny the plausibility of Epicurean moral assumptions. Hutcheson could not escape the questions which Bayle and Mandeville had raised, and clearly recognised the threat presented by the *Fable of the Bees* in particular. But he would not engage with the questions on the ground chosen by those two predecessors.

There are signs that Hutcheson was uncomfortably aware that the genie was out of the bottle. His uneasiness may be seen in his relations with colleagues who discussed the controverted issues. Archibald Campbell complained in the preface to the 1733 reissue of his *Enquiry into the Original of Moral Virtue* of the way in which Hutcheson insisted on branding him an Epicurean. Hutcheson may not have been reassured by Campbell's

---

[68] Francis Hutcheson, *A System of Moral Philosophy, in Three Books*, 2 vols. (Glasgow and London, 1755), book I, part II, chs. ix–xi, in vol. I, pp. 168–226; earlier in the first 'Hibernicus Letter', *Remarks upon the Fable*, pp. 47–8, and in *Essay on the Passions*, sect. VI, parts iii–iv. See James Moore, 'Hutcheson's theodicy: the argument and the contexts of *A System of Moral Philosophy*', in Paul Wood (ed.), *The Scottish Enlightenment: Essays in Reinterpretation* (Rochester, N.Y., and Woodbridge, Suffolk, 2000), pp. 239–66; and James A. Harris, 'Answering Bayle's question: religious belief in the moral philosophy of the Scottish Enlightenment', in D. Garber and S. Nadler (eds.), *Oxford Studies in Early Modern Philosophy*, vol. I (Oxford 2004), pp. 242–3.

declaration of loyalty and indebtedness to Professor Simson.[69] Then there was David Hume. At some point in 1739 Hume sent Hutcheson a draft of book III of the *Treatise of Human Nature* for his comments. Although Hutcheson's own contributions to the ensuing correspondence are missing, he plainly told Hume that he found the work lacking 'a certain warmth in the cause of virtue'. It has also been suggested that Hutcheson may have helped to write the review of book III of the *Treatise* which appeared in the *Bibliothèque Raisonnée* published by William Smith in Amsterdam in 1741: the review highlighted differences between Hume's and Hutcheson's treatments of morals.[70] Hume himself made no effort to persuade Hutcheson to the contrary, pointedly telling him in response that his founding his definition of 'natural' on final causes was to rely on a consideration 'pretty uncertain & unphilosophical'.[71] For these and other reasons Hutcheson had decided by 1744 that Hume was unfit to teach moral philosophy in a Scottish university, and actively opposed his candidacy for the vacant chair of moral philosophy at Edinburgh.[72] Turning now to examine Hume's *Treatise*, we shall see how justified Hutcheson was in his diffidence.

DAVID HUME

A Treatise of Human Nature: the passions and the natural virtues

Two famous phrases characterise Hume's project in *A Treatise of Human Nature* (1739–40). His subject, he explained in the introduction, was no less than 'the science of man' (Introduction.4).[73] And in studying this subject, Hume likened his procedure to 'the accurate anatomy of human nature', or 'the anatomy of the mind' (1.4.6.23; II.1.12.2). He returned to this image in the very last paragraph of the work, when he drew a distinction between the anatomist and the painter, and insisted that his own ambition was only

---

[69] Campbell, *Enquiry into the Original of Moral Virtue*, 'Preface', pp. x–xiv: 'Is a thing false, because Epicurus maintained it? Or is a thing true, because the late Earl of Shaftesbury (whose principles Mr Hutcheson professes to explain and defend) was pleased to declare for it[?] I should think that truth and falsehood, or the agreement and disagreement of things, have no dependence on the opinions of men' (pp. xiii–xiv).

[70] M. A. Stewart and James Moore, 'William Smith (1698–1741) and the Dissenters' book trade', *Bulletin of the Presbyterian Historical Society of Ireland*, 22 (1993), 20–7. The attribution is contested.

[71] Hume to Francis Hutcheson, 17 Sept. 1739, *Letters of Hume*, I, pp. 32–5.

[72] M. A. Stewart, *The Kirk and the Infidel* (Lancaster: inaugural lecture at the University of Lancaster, 1995).

[73] I have used the new Oxford Philosophical Texts edition of *A Treatise of Human Nature*, ed. David Fate Norton and Mary J. Norton (Oxford, 2000). References, in brackets in the main text, will be to book.part.section.paragraph.

to be the former. Were an anatomist to emulate a painter, he would risk sacrificing the accuracy of his dissections to the need to give his figures a graceful and engaging expression (III.3.6.6).[74] But the self-image of the anatomist was also potentially misleading, since in other passages Hume had disclaimed it. When at the beginning of book I he resolved the perceptions of the human mind into 'ideas' and 'impressions', and presented these as the building blocks of the whole *Treatise*, he made it clear that he would not be examining the sensations which first give rise to impressions, since this 'belongs more to anatomists and natural philosophers than to moral' (I.1.2.1). The disclaimer was repeated at the outset of book II (II.1.1.2).

In the science of man, or moral philosophy, investigation of natural and physical causes was set aside in favour of reasoning based on observation and experience. More specifically, Hume proposed to base his science on experiments derived from 'a cautious observation of human life', as it appears in men's behaviour in company, in affairs, and in their pleasures. 'Where experiments of this kind are judiciously collected and compar'd, we may hope to establish on them a science, which will not be inferior in certainty, and will be much superior in utility to any other of human comprehension' (Introduction.6). In book I, 'Of the Understanding', Hume analysed the rules of causal necessity according to which human behaviour must be understood; and he repeated them, in summary form, at the beginning of part 3 of book II. The observation of a constant conjunction between causes and effects, motives and actions in human behaviour gives us confidence that there is a general course of nature in human actions, as there is in the operations of the sun and the climate. Even where a constant conjunction is not observable, there are many inferior degrees of evidence and probability. We thus acknowledge the force of 'moral evidence', and draw conclusions about the actions of men from consideration of their motives, temper, and situation (II.3.1.1–18).

Given causal necessity, Hume continues, we must acknowledge an important conclusion: that the will is no exception to its rules – in other words, that there is no 'free' will. All human behaviour must be understood as determined, or caused; were it not, an individual's actions

---

[74] Hume had drawn the same distinction for Hutcheson's benefit, when defending himself from Hutcheson's charge that the draft of book III lacked 'warmth in the cause of virtue': *Letters of Hume*, I, pp. 32–3. Hume could have added the remark about the anatomist and the painter to the final paragraph of the *Treatise* after the exchange with Hutcheson. But since he had used the term 'anatomy' in books I and II, which were already in print, it did not originate in the exchange. Hume elaborated the contrast in the opening section of *An Enquiry concerning Human Understanding* (1748): 'Of the different Species of Philosophy'. On Hume's use of the contrast, Stewart, 'Two species of philosophy', pp. 70–4.

would be arbitrary, and he could not be held responsible for them. The persistent supposition that moral responsibility depends upon the possession of free will is a mistake. It is a mistake explicable from our reluctance, after we have performed an action, to admit that we were governed by necessity in doing it. But the mistake has also been encouraged by those who believe that the doctrine of necessity has dangerous consequences for religion and morality. Religion, Hume thought, 'has been very unnecessarily interested in this question' (II.3.1.18, II.3.2.1–8).

Although the doctrine of causality as the observation of a constant conjunction of like causes with like effects was of course Hume's own, the general principles of his approach to the study of man were congruent with Mandeville's. Like Mandeville, Hume believed that we must reason *a posteriori* concerning human behaviour, on the basis of experience and observation. Hume also agreed with Mandeville that our knowledge of the physical operation of the mind and the passions is insufficient to offer the moral philosopher any reliable knowledge concerning the actions of men. (There is in Hume, as in Mandeville, no trace of the idea of *conatus*, or endeavour, to explain the working of the passions.) A moral philosopher might style himself an anatomist of human nature, but his sphere of enquiry was separate from that of the medical anatomist. Like Mandeville too Hume insisted on causal necessity and, as its consequence, on denying the freedom of the will. The determination of so many philosophers to uphold free will, Hume and Mandeville agreed, was a clear example of the confusion which arose when religious considerations were brought into philosophical argument.

Before this suggestion of congruence between the moral philosophies of Hume and Mandeville can be taken any further, however, it faces an obvious difficulty. For when Hume came to consider 'the origin of the natural virtues and vices' in part 3 of book III, he explicitly differentiated himself from 'some philosophers', who

have represented all moral distinctions as the effect of artifice and education, when skilful politicians endeavour'd to restrain the turbulent passions of men, and make them operate to the public good, by the notions of honour and shame.

This system, Hume judged, 'is not consistent with experience' (III.3.1.11). The allusion is much too specific for there to be any doubt that he had Mandeville in mind, and is indeed only a repetition of a previous criticism of 'certain writers on morals', who have made the artifice of politicians the sole cause of the distinction we make between vice and virtue (III.2.2.25). Hume gave two reasons for his judgement. First, there are virtues and vices besides those with a tendency to the public advantage and loss; and second, if men had not had a natural sentiment of approbation and blame, the sense of virtue and vice could never have been excited in them by politicians. Then Hume added a rider:

But tho' this system be erroneous, it may teach us, that moral distinctions arise, in a great measure, from the tendency of qualities and characters to the interest of society, and that 'tis our concern for that interest, which makes us approve or disapprove of them. Now we have no such extensive concern for society but from sympathy; and consequently 'tis that principle, which takes us so far out of ourselves, as to give us the same pleasure or uneasiness in characters which are useful or pernicious to society, as if they had a tendency to our own advantage or loss. (III.3.1.11)

The interest of society, or utility, was indeed one of the most important sources of moral distinctions; but it was established by the capacity of members of society for sympathetic appreciation of each other's characters, not by the arbitrary decree of manipulative politicians.

In these terms, Hume's rejection of Mandeville's account of the origin of moral distinctions was emphatic but not unqualified. It was mistaken to suppose that definitions of virtue and vice were simply imposed by a few upon the many, because the latter could not have understood them unless they already had an inclination towards approval or blame; nevertheless, Mandeville had recognised the importance men attach to utility in their judgements. We have seen, however, that Mandeville had formulated the principle of utility in a certain way, as 'whether this happiness is worth having at the rate it is only to be had at'. In other words, utility was to be traded off against virtue. Mandeville put it this way because he identified virtue with the suppression of the passions, happiness with their indulgence. Hume, by contrast, wished to argue that utility makes a direct contribution to the way we draw moral distinctions, which cannot simply be opposed to the passions. As E. J. Hundert has observed, his fundamental criticism of Mandeville, in the passages quoted above, was that Mandeville had been insufficiently naturalistic in his account of human behaviour. In insisting that moral distinctions were imposed on men, Mandeville had missed the extent to which men had (and must have) developed moral sentiments compatible with human nature, and hence with the passions.[75] In what follows, I shall confirm, but also modify, this interpretation. It has already been suggested that in his later writings Mandeville showed a greater awareness of the way in which the sentiments of honour and shame

[75] Hundert, *The Enlightenment's Fable*, pp. 84–5.

develop from rather than against the passions. Hume, it will be argued, was to advance much further in that direction.

Hume's analysis of the passions in book II of the *Treatise* is more technically philosophical than Mandeville's. In Hume's terms the passions are impressions rather than ideas, and he distinguishes between direct and indirect passions. The direct passions are those which arise immediately from good or evil, pleasure or pain, such as desire and aversion, hope and fear (II.1.1.1–4). Hume reserves these to the end of book II, and finds relatively little to say about them (II.3.sect. 9). It is the indirect passions which are of primary interest, beginning with that of pride.

Hume defines pride, and its contrary, humility, in relation to the objects and their causes. The object and the causes of pride are distinct. The object of pride is always 'self, or that succession of related ideas and impressions, of which we have an intimate memory and consciousness' (II.1.2.2). Self is the 'natural' object of pride (II.1.3.2). But it is not the cause of pride. The causes of pride are the ideas which produce it. These ideas may refer to qualities of mind or body, or to objects (such as property), or to attributes (of virtue, beauty, or wealth). The liveliness of these ideas in turn stimulates impressions or feelings which arouse the passion of pride (II.1.sects. 2–6). In this way it can be seen that the self experiences pride because of its relation to such advantages as moral virtue, physical beauty and health, family, nationality, the possession of property and wealth (II.1.sects. 7–10). An example (one appropriate to this author if not to Hume) might be a father's pride in his beautiful daughters: they are its cause, his self its object. By contrast, Hume was suggesting, an account of pride such as Mandeville's, which treated it as an immediate expression of 'self-liking', could not explain why pride is aroused by certain qualities or attributes.

In any case, Hume continued, there was a further, secondary cause of pride and humility, in the opinions of others:

> Our reputation, our character, our name are considerations of vast weight and importance; and even the other causes of pride; virtue, beauty and riches; have little influence, when not seconded by the opinions and sentiments of others.

This 'seconding' of pride by the opinion of others occurred by means of 'sympathy' (II.1.11.1). Sympathy too was an impression, created by the lively idea of another person's sentiments: we sympathise with others when we receive their inclinations and sentiments, and render them 'intimately present' to ourselves. Hume added that we are liable to reinforce this impression by reasoning, persuading ourselves that the sentiments of others amount to a judgement, and thus possess authority. But it is the principle of sympathy which most intrigued Hume. No quality of human nature, he thought, is more remarkable than this propensity. It explains the great uniformity we observe in the humours and turn of thinking of a whole nation. More immediately, it explains why the passion of pride is strengthened most of all by 'fame' – by the praise of others: 'the pleasure, which we receive from praise, arises from a communication of sentiments' (II.1.11.2–19). Mandeville had tried to capture the process whereby the opinion of others reinforces our self-liking by the term 'honour'; by introducing a principle which had no direct association with pride, Hume further distanced pride from a single, original selfish passion.

The operation of sympathy was similarly crucial to Hume's explanation of the other indirect passions of love, hatred, and their derivatives. In all cases it is sympathy which explains that 'ardent desire for society', which is so conspicuous in man, even more than in other creatures. 'Whatever other passions we may be actuated by; pride, ambition, avarice, curiosity, revenge or lust; the soul or animating principle of them all is sympathy; nor wou'd they have any force, were we to abstract entirely from the thoughts and sentiments of others' (II.2.5.15). This was to take the analysis of the passions well beyond the level attained by Mandeville. Where Mandeville had recognised the importance of the opinion of others in turning self-liking into pride, Hume was giving the principle of sympathy a much more general application, making it equally the key to the cluster of passions denominated love, benevolence, and esteem, and hence to our very desire for society.

Hume's account of the passions not only made Mandeville's assumption that all human behaviour could be reduced to self-love and self-liking look facile; it also undermined Mandeville's treatment of virtue and vice. On Hume's analysis of the passions, it made little sense to think of virtue simply as self-denial, and vice as the indulgence of the passions. Hume's immediate concern when he opened his account of morals in book III of the *Treatise* was not, however, with Mandeville. Instead, he was at pains to distinguish his approach from those who thought that moral distinctions were discerned by reason. Hume objected that it was impossible for reason to distinguish virtue and vice from matters of fact, and hence to distinguish what we ought to perform from what is; in any case, as he had already shown in book II, reason itself was unable to produce or prevent our actions, being the slave not the master of the passions (III.1.1.2–27; II.3.3.4). Moral distinctions, therefore, must be derived from 'a moral sense'. That is, they must be felt, and take the form of 'moral sentiments'. Unless it is understood that such sentiments arise within us, exciting either pleasure or uneasiness, we will be unable to explain why men are moved to act in accordance with moral principles (III.1.2.1–5). Hume was of course using the same term, 'moral sense', as Hutcheson had done, but evidently not to the same purpose. Hume was not suggesting that we have a distinct 'moral sense' which naturally inclines us to be benevolent towards others. Rather, Hume would show how the moral sentiments (in the plural) are aligned with the passions.[76]

This is clearest in the case of the 'natural' virtues and vices. Hume explains that we identify natural virtues by their usefulness and agreeableness, either to the person who displays them or to others; and that we do this by the operation of sympathy. More exactly, we judge moral character by observing a person's qualities, and sympathising with the pleasure or pain they give. Pleasure or pain may arise from qualities fitted to be useful or agreeable either to ourselves or to others (III.3.1.1–30). In other words, Hume argues that we take men's passions as they are, and by sympathy with the pleasure or pain they produce, denominate them virtuous or vicious by the criteria of usefulness and agreeableness.

Thus pride, where a person really has the qualities that are valuable, is agreeable both to the person himself and to others; it is also useful to us in life. The rules of good breeding may require modesty in the expression of pride; but humility need not go beyond the outside. A 'genuine and hearty pride', if both well concealed and well founded, is essential to the character of a man of honour (III.3.2.1–11). Similarly, we naturally approve of goodness and benevolence in all their manifestations: 'generosity, humanity, compassion, gratitude, friendship, fidelity, zeal, disinterestedness, liberality'. Indeed we praise all the passions which are immediately agreeable to the person actuated by them (III.3.3.3–4). We even esteem men's natural abilities, where these are useful to the person or to others, or simply agreeable (III.3.4.1–14). A teasing example was the case of what Hume called 'women's men', whose physical advantages are esteemed even by women whose virtue prevents any design of ever giving employment to the men's abilities (III.3.5.1–4).

In many cases, therefore, the passions and other qualities of men are naturally counted virtuous, because they are useful and agreeable to the person who exhibits them or to those affected by them. There was no

---

[76] There is an excellent, lucid account of Hume's moral theory in Rivers, *Reason, Grace, and Sentiment*. Vol. II. *Shaftesbury to Hume*, pp. 288–308; the exposition covers the *Enquiry concerning Morals* as well as the *Treatise*, but scrupulously notes the differences between them. Also the concise but lucid account by Luigi Turco, 'Moral sense and the foundations of morals', in Alexander Broadie (ed.), *The Cambridge Companion to the Scottish Enlightenment* (Cambridge, 2003), pp. 141–6.

ground for Mandeville's supposition that virtue required the suppression of the passions, and derived from the artifice of politicians and moralists. Mandeville had qualified this view in his later writings, in recognising that men had learned to honour qualities originating in the passions. But Hume could go much further – and thus reach simpler, consistently naturalistic conclusions. The key to men's ability to derive moral sentiments from their passions lay in the operation of sympathy, through which they could make the pleasure or pain of others their own, and judge the merit of the behaviour which had produced that pleasure or pain. Our natural capacity for sympathy, in short, rendered the artifice of politicians secondary if not redundant in the formation of moral sentiments; men recognised what was virtuous for themselves, simply by assessing the passions according to the criteria of usefulness and agreeableness. Hume had cut through the difficulties which Mandeville brought upon himself by opposing virtue to the passions – and had returned to the subtler moral Epicureanism of Bayle. For Bayle, it will be recalled, the passions were moral to the extent that they were 'utile et agréable'; Hume used the self-same formula, having added his explanation of the process whereby the passions naturally become moral sentiments.[77]

Hume did not, however, believe that all moral sentiments are natural in this straightforward sense. Some are, by comparison, artificial.

A Treatise of Human Nature: justice

The virtue which Hume believed is artificial, not natural, was of course justice. His discussion of justice, along with property, promises, and government, occupied part 2 of book III of the *Treatise*. Immediately beforehand, Hume had discussed the several possible definitions of the 'ambiguous and equivocal' term 'nature'. If by natural we mean anything not miraculous, he observed, then not only moral distinctions, but every event in the world, 'excepting the miracles on which our religion is founded', is natural. Even if we mean only the opposite of rare and unusual, our moral sentiments must surely be natural, since there was never a person utterly devoid of them. The only distinction a philosopher might draw, accordingly, is that between nature and artifice: it was possible that our sense of some virtues is artificial, of others natural (III.1.2.6–9).[78] Justice must be such an artificial

---

[77] On Bayle, see above, ch. 5, pp. 220–1. For a comparable Epicurean reading of Hume's argument: Moore, 'Hume and Hutcheson', esp. pp. 29–33, 39–47.

[78] Hume added that nothing could be more unphilosophical than those systems which asserted virtue to be natural and vice unnatural (III.1.2.10): a thrust, the Nortons suggest, at Seneca and Shaftesbury, *Treatise*, Annotations, p. 539.

virtue, Hume proceeded to argue, because man has no natural motive to act honestly and therefore justly. Neither the public interest nor private benevolence provides such a motive. The sentiment of justice, therefore, does not arise in the natural course of our passions. Hume was quick to add that to call the rules of justice artificial is not to make them arbitrary; they were an obvious and necessary invention (III.2.1.7–19).

Before he explained the artifice of justice, however, Hume carried the analysis of the problem a stage further. Not only have men no natural sense of justice; they are not naturally sociable. In general, 'there is no such passion in human minds, as the love of mankind, merely as such' (III.2.1.12). The condition of man, Hume explained, is characterised by a discrepancy between his 'numberless wants and necessities', and 'the slender means' which nature affords of relieving them. Society alone allows him to bridge this gap, in three ways. It enables men to combine their forces, to divide their labour, and to assist each other in the face of fortune and accidents. Behind these advantages lies a more basic necessity, which supplies the original principle of human society: the natural appetite of the sexes, and their concern for their common offspring. Yet despite the necessity and the advantages of society, selfishness still keeps men apart. Even if men's selfishness has been wildly exaggerated by 'certain philosophers' (among them, almost certainly, Hobbes and Mandeville), it produces 'an opposition of passions' which endangers the union of society; and the effects of this are exacerbated by the scarcity of goods and the instability of their possession (III.2.2.2–7). The resulting competition for goods makes men positively unsociable:

this avidity alone, of acquiring goods and possessions for ourselves and our near-est friends, is insatiable, perpetual, universal, and directly destructive of society. (III.2.2.12)

So partial are our affections in favour of ourselves and our nearest relations, our morals can only follow suit, making it impossible for justice to be taken for a natural principle, capable of inspiring men to treat each other equitably (III.2.2.8):

The remedy, therefore, must be found in an artifice.

This can be done after no other manner, than by a convention enter'd into by all the members of the society to bestow stability on the possession of those external goods, and leave every one in the peaceable enjoyment of what he may acquire by his fortune and industry. (III.2.2.9)

Both the nature and the purpose of such a convention are carefully clar-ified. A convention is not a promise, for promises themselves arise from conventions (as Hume will shortly explain). It is rather 'a general sense of the common interest', or, as he puts it a little later, 'a sense of interest, suppos'd to be common to all' (III.2.2.10, 22). This 'general sense' of interest in maintaining the rule concerning stability of possession arises gradually, and acquires force by a slow progression, and by repeated experience of the inconveniencies of transgressing it. It may be compared with the conventions which establish languages or money, neither of which can be supposed to derive from an original promise (III.2.2.10). The purpose of the convention is to check the heedless and impetuous movement of men's passions, making it possible for them to live in society and obtain the advantages of doing so. Hume emphasised that such restraint of the passions is perfectly compatible with the individual's self-interest. Indeed it is only from 'the selfishness and confin'd generosity of man' in conditions of scarcity that justice does derive. It may not always be in an individual's immediate or direct interest to behave justly towards his fellows; but this does not alter the fact that justice, and hence society, are in every individual's interest (III.2.2.9–22).

If interest forms a 'natural' obligation to justice, it cannot, however, create a moral obligation, and render justice into a moral sentiment. As justice requires the artifice of a convention to be established, so the moral obligation must also arise indirectly. To explain it, Hume anticipated the fuller analysis of the operation of sympathy in part 3. Even though acts of injustice may be committed at a distance from us, we share the uneasiness they cause by sympathy, and join in condemning them as vices. This sympathy with the public interest is the source of the moral approbation which attends justice (III.2.2.23–4). At this stage – and not before – sentiments of justice may also be encouraged by 'the artifice of politicians' and by education. Here too Hume made clear his opposition to 'certain writers' (who must include Mandeville) who would make the artifice of politicians the sole source of our moral distinctions: the most politicians can perform, he insisted, is to extend our natural sentiments beyond their original bounds (III.2.2.25).

The treatment of justice as an artificial virtue is reinforced by the subsequent account of promises. Promises, Hume pointed out, cannot be the expression of a natural moral obligation. Of itself a promise is unintelligible unless there already exists a convention establishing what it is. Deriving from a convention, moreover, promises must be founded on 'the necessities and interests of society'. Since men are naturally selfish, they are not easily induced to perform any action for the interest of strangers, unless with a view to reciprocal advantage. Promises, therefore, develop as 'the sanction of the interested commerce of mankind'; once again politicians and moralists can only reinforce, never themselves create the obligation which attaches to them (III.2.5.1–12).

Hume argued, then, that society is held together by the purely human and artificial conventions of justice and promising, which are able to defeat the destructive tendency of our avidity for goods and possessions. Justice and promising have done this, he went on to explain, by providing the artificial moral basis for the institutions of property and government. In both cases, Hume sought to trace the general rules on which the obligations to respect property and obey government were founded. Taking property to have preceded government, he suggested that present possession is likely to have provided the initial grounds for a claim of ownership; but this would later have been superseded by prescription or long possession, and by rules governing accession, succession, and the transfer of property by consent (III.3.3.1–11; 4.1–2). By contrast, government may be supposed to have been established at first by a promise; but as soon as the advantages of government became known, the grounds of allegiance would shift, and would derive from those advantages (III.2.8.3; 10.2–3). The 'objects of allegiance', as Hume called them, would become long possession, or, failing that, present possession. With government as with property, long possession gives the strongest claim, but in this case it is also right to submit quietly to the power established in the country where we happen to live, in the interest of the preservation of peace (III.2.10.4–7).

In emphasising long possession, Hume made a point of explaining why it exerted such an influence on men's sentiments:

Possession during a long tract of time conveys a title to any object. But as 'tis certain, that, however every thing be produc'd in time, there is nothing real, that is produc'd by time; it follows, that property being produc'd by time, is not any thing real in the objects, but is the offspring of the sentiments, on which alone time is found to have any influence. (III.2.3.9)

The term which Hume used to characterise time's influence on the sentiments was custom. The force of custom, he argued, was felt particularly in the case of allegiance owed to government by long possession. Even though there was hardly a dynasty or commonwealth which was not founded on usurpation or rebellion, time nevertheless

gives solidity to their right; and operating gradually on the minds of men, reconciles them to any authority, and makes it seem just and reasonable. Nothing causes any sentiment to have a greater influence upon us than custom, or turns our imagination more strongly to any object . . . (III.2.10.4)

It is custom, experience accumulated to the point that it becomes habitual, which exerts the strongest influence on men to support the institutions of property and government on which society depends for its continuing existence.

In reading the *Treatise*, there is always the danger that the meticulous care with which Hume clarified the details of his argument may detract from appreciation of its larger point. The matter of justice, however, went to the heart of the problem of human sociability. On Hume's account, the intractability of the problem facing men was matched only by the ingeniousness of their solution. He reminded readers of this in section 6, midway through the discussion of justice. Even though society was 'absolutely necessary for the well-being of men', their passions constantly led them to put the interests of themselves and those close to them before those of others, in ways which made the maintenance of society impossible. Yet the solution to the problem derived from the self-same passions. For the rules of justice 'are only a more artful and refin'd way' of satisfying the passions. Unless they restrained their passions by certain rules, men observed, they would be unable to live in society and enjoy its advantages. At the same time, the operation of sympathy, by enabling men to take pleasure in actions which tend to the peace of society, led them to regard these rules of justice as moral duties (III.2.6.1, 11).

The whole process was seemingly paradoxical. Justice was a necessary invention, for without it there could be no society, yet it was 'entirely artificial' (III.2.6.1). It was advantageous to the public, since it comprehended the interest of every individual, yet it was not intended for that purpose by its inventors (III.2.6.6). The beauty of Hume's explanation of justice was that it dissolved those paradoxes. At the heart of this explanation was the insight that sociability was a historical development. Though Hume allowed that the idea of a *state of nature* had its uses as a 'philosophical fiction', it was based on the error of supposing men capable of forming all at once reflections 'which in fact arise insensibly and by degrees' (III.2.2.14–15; 3.3). Men learned from experience, and incorporated what they learned into conventions, which in due course acquired the force of custom. The key to the development of justice, therefore, was the influence of time on the sentiments. Justice was not a natural virtue, in the sense of being an original principle of the mind, or one whose utility and agreeableness were immediately apparent. It owed its origin to the artifice of self-interested men, recognising, over time, that they shared a common interest, and that the rules of justice were, after all, useful and even, by the operation of sympathy, agreeable to everyone. Moreover once it was appreciated that human nature, if at first unsociable, became sociable over time, it could be seen that those artificial rules of justice were also, in another sense of the term, 'natural'. The rules of justice were not only useful; they were also '*laws of nature*' (III.2.1.19, 6.1).

In treating justice as an artificial virtue, Hume put himself clearly on the side of Mandeville, and before him, of Hobbes, against those who held that men were naturally sociable. But his explanation for the artificiality of justice was far removed from the naive propositions of Mandeville. Hume allowed that sentiments of justice might helpfully be fostered by the artifices of moralists and politicians; and government was certainly required to enforce its rules. But it was absurd of Mandeville to have suggested that men could have had those rules imposed upon them, in the absence of prior conventions establishing their purpose. There was the same degree of difference in Hume's understanding of the utility of justice. Mandeville had been right to emphasise the importance of the principle of public utility, but wrong to trade utility against moral standards. Hume, by contrast, could show that the usefulness of justice was intimately related to the pleasure it gave to observers. Justice might be an artificial invention, but it too was found to be useful and agreeable, and hence became a moral sentiment. In Hume's terms, Mandeville's defect was to have been incompletely naturalistic and insufficiently historical in his understanding of human behaviour. Although he had taken over the Epicurean account of human nature as driven by the passions, in constant pursuit of self-interest, Mandeville had failed to appreciate the varied ways in which self-interest led men, unintentionally, to become sociable. For all his satirical alertness to the unintended consequences of self-interest, Mandeville had remained wedded to the simple Lucretian view that legislators had been necessary to make men sociable. Instead, Hume argued, the artifice of justice was of general human invention, over time.

In one important respect, however, Hume may appear to have been less completely naturalistic than Mandeville. From the *Free Thoughts on Religion* to the *Letter to Dion*, a constant feature of Mandeville's writing on morals was his open scorn for the sanctions of a future state. By contrast, in the *Treatise*, Hume all but avoided the topic. Two passing references, however, suggest where his sympathies lay. In one of these he commented on 'the universal carelessness and stupidity of men with regard to a future state', which he explained by its lack of resemblance to our present life. It is true that in matters of religion men take a pleasure in being terrified, flocking to preachers who excite the gloomy passions. But the pleasure is the same as we experience from a dramatic performance arousing fear and terror:

in both cases the pleasure reflects the sense of their unreality (1.3.9.13–15). The second reference to a future state lies in a mischievous addendum to the discussion of promises. The operation of promising, Hume observed, was even more 'mysterious and incomprehensible' than the sacraments of *transubstantiation*, or *holy orders*. In the case of the sacraments, intention is required to make the form of words effective. But in the case of a promise, intention to perform is not essential to its being regarded as obligatory. As mere priestly inventions, of no use to society, the sacraments have been given an appearance of rationality by the theologians' insistence on intention. By contrast a promise, as an invention for the interest of society, has been warped into as many different forms as that interest requires. The contrast was explained by the difference in men's attitudes to the present and future life. 'Men are always more concern'd about the present life than the future; and are apt to think the smallest evil, which regards the former, more important than the greatest, which regards the latter' (III.2.5.14). Like the other, it was no more than a throw-away remark, but it strongly implied Hume's agreement with Mandeville. A future state, where there would be rewards and punishments for behaviour while on earth, was irrelevant to moral obligation, because men do not in fact pay any serious attention to it.

There is good evidence, moreover, that Hume had not always intended to be so reticent on this and related topics in the *Treatise*, and in later writings he would make his position much clearer. To see what this position was – and thus to take further the analysis of Hume in relation to Mandeville and Bayle – we need now to move on, beyond the *Treatise*. As we do so, the full scope of the potential for a comparison between Hume and Vico should become apparent.

The omitted 'nobler parts' of the *Treatise:* miracles and divine providence

In a letter written in December 1737, shortly after he had returned from France to London with the draft of the *Treatise*, Hume informed Henry Home that he was engaged in 'castrating' the work, 'cutting off its nobler parts'. He was doing so in the hope of limiting the offence the book might cause, and, in particular, because he wanted to present a copy of it to the philosopher-bishop, Joseph Butler. Hume gave one clue as to the content of these 'nobler parts', mentioning some 'Reasonings concerning Miracles', on which he sought Henry Home's judgement.[79] These were almost certainly

---

[79] Hume to Henry Home, 2 Dec. 1737, *Letters of Hume*, I, pp. 24–5.

the basis for an essay he published eleven years later. Before turning to this, however, there are two other relevant pieces of unpublished evidence, which have been dated to the period in which Hume was finalising the *Treatise*, or to its immediate aftermath.

One, which has only recently come to light, is a manuscript fragment on evil. It was edited for publication by M. A. Stewart, who drew attention to indications that it may have been part of a draft of the *Treatise*; if it was not, it was most probably written soon afterwards.[80] In the fragment Hume considered the arguments against endowing the deity with moral attributes. Even allowing that the intelligence of the deity is proved by phenomena, this permits no inference concerning his benevolence. The benevolence of the author of nature can only be proved by evidence that good predominates over evil in the universe. But it is very difficult, if not impossible, to determine the facts, and compute the happiness and misery that is in the world. The most we can say is that pains outweigh pleasures in the degree to which they are felt, though pleasures tend to be felt more frequently than pains. On balance, Hume was inclined to think that 'Evil predominates in the world'; but even if pleasure predominated in a small degree, this would still be no proof of the deity's benevolence. The manuscript ends at this point; but however keenly we might wish for more, the evidence that Hume was engaging with these issues as or shortly after he completed the *Treatise* is of some significance. For the fragment clearly shows Hume confronting the Baylean conundrum of evil in the world, and accepting that it casts doubt on God's good intentions.

The likelihood that Hume was actively reflecting on Bayle's arguments at this time is enhanced by the evidence of his manuscript notebook, known as the 'Early Memoranda'. Mossner, who edited, reordered, dated and entitled the 'Early Memoranda' for publication, was confident that they were begun as early as 1729, and that those which he categorised as 'philosophy' belonged to the period 1730–4, before Hume went to France. They were therefore preparatory to the drafting of the *Treatise*.[81] On examination of the paper, the hand, and the content of the notebook, Stewart has dismissed this dating (and much else in Mossner's editing), and points instead to the period immediately after the *Treatise*, in the early 1740s.[82] Of particular interest

[80] M. A. Stewart, 'An early fragment on evil', in Stewart and Wright, *Hume and Hume's Connexions*, pp. 160–70; the text of the fragment is both printed and photographically reproduced on pp. 165–8. For a further comment, Stewart, 'Hume's intellectual development', pp. 46–7.

[81] Ernest Campbell Mossner (ed.), 'Hume's Early Memoranda, 1729–1740: the complete text', *Journal of the History of Ideas*, 9 (1948), 492–518.

[82] M. A. Stewart, 'The dating of Hume's manuscripts', in Wood, *The Scottish Enlightenment*, pp. 267–314, esp. pp. 276–88 and note 5 on p. 309.

here are the several notes deriving from 'Baile'. These need not have been taken from Bayle's individual works; instead it has been suggested by J. P. Pittion that Hume is likely to have been working from periodicals of the first decade of the century, which printed articles by Bayle and his critics.[83] Whatever his exact sources, Hume may well have been encouraged and guided in his reading by Pierre Desmaizeaux, Bayle's editor and biographer, with whom Hume had struck up an acquaintance while he was living in London and preparing the *Treatise* for its publication.[84]

Of the notes which specifically refer to Bayle, the following are, for the purposes of this analysis, particularly striking. They are quoted in the order they appear in the notebook (Mossner's enumeration is given solely for purposes of reference):

Tho the Antients speak often of God in the singular Number, that proves not they believed in his Unity, since Christians speak in the same manner of the Devil. Baile (11.4)

The Testimony of Idolaters cannot be united to that of Christians against the Atheists; since they never form'd one Proposition that there is a God & afterwards that there is more than one. These two Propositions were always the same. Id. (11.5)

The Center of Unity of all Men with Relation to Religion is, That there is a first Cause. As you augment the Propositions you find Non-conformists, Atheists, Epicureans, Idolaters, those who maintain the Extension, Composition, Necessity of the first Cause &c. Id. (11.8)

Atheists plainly make a Distinction betwixt good Reasoning & bad. Why not betwixt Vice & Virtue? Baile[85] (11.10)

Other notes derived from Bayle discuss the dangers of Strato's atheism in particular (11.14, 15), the origin of ill in the world (11.18–20), the inconsistencies of arguments concerning God's liberty (11.22–5, 30–4), and the fact that the first supreme deity of the Romans was not Jupiter but Summanus, to whom they attributed thunder by night (11.29). What these notes demonstrate is that by the early 1740s Hume was acquainted not merely with the general argument on behalf of a society of atheists, but with Bayle's detailed analysis of the weaknesses of idolatry and of arguments for God's benevolent providence.

[83] J. P. Pittion, 'Hume's reading of Bayle: an enquiry into the source and role of the Memoranda', *Journal of the History of Philosophy*, 15 (1977), 373–86.
[84] The connection is attested by Hume's letter to Desmaizeaux of 6 April 1739, asking his opinion of the newly published *Treatise*; *Letters of Hume*, 1, pp. 29–30.
[85] Mossner, 'Hume's early memoranda', p. 500; the entries are among those reprinted and sourced by Pittion, 'Hume's reading of Bayle', p. 385; the first three of the four quoted above are reproduced photographically as fig. 8 in Stewart, 'The dating of Hume's manuscripts', p. 283.

Not until later in the decade, however, did Hume actually publish anything which may have derived from the excised 'nobler parts' of the *Treatise*. The *Philosophical Essays concerning Human Understanding* (1748), later retitled as *An Enquiry concerning Human Understanding* (1756), contained two essays or sections directly concerned with religion. The first, 'Of Miracles' (section 10), very probably derived from the earlier 'Reasonings concerning miracles' which he had sent to Henry Home in 1737. As David Wootton has pointed out, issues of probability, which underpinned the arguments of 'Of Miracles', had been much more prominent in the *Treatise* than they were in the *Philosophical Essays* as a whole; along with other evidence, this suggests that the essay as it was published in 1748 had been conceived in a French context, while Hume was drafting the *Treatise*. It was only in the second, 1750 edition of the *Philosophical Essays* that Hume added references to the English debate over miracles.[86] The focus of Hume's analysis was the reliability of testimony on behalf of miracles. He did not argue that miracles are a natural – physical – impossibility. On his own principles causes do not inhere in the nature of objects; rather our knowledge of causes and effects, and hence of nature, is itself based on a species of testimony, the recorded evidence of observation and experience. The argument, therefore, was one of the balance of probability. The evidence in favour of miracles is outweighed by the evidence for nature pursuing a regular course. This argument from probability was reinforced by a second, to the effect that the testimony in favour of miracles was itself characteristically unreliable, since it came from those with an interest in their occurrence.[87]

The strengths and weaknesses of Hume's arguments against miracles have provoked sharp debate among philosophical commentators, and continue to do so. For our purposes, however, the viability of the arguments is much less important than their implication. For Hume, unlike Conyers Middleton, whose *Free Inquiry into the Miraculous Powers* (1748) caused a much more immediate stir, did not except from his analysis the miracles performed by Christ himself. All testimony on behalf of miracles, including that of the Old and New Testaments, was suspect in Hume's terms, and fell far short of the probability in favour of nature pursuing its regular course. Hume made the point explicit at the very end of the essay, when he ridiculed the 'prodigies and miracles' recounted in the Pentateuch, and

---

[86] David Wootton, 'Hume's "Of Miracles": probability and irreligion', in Stewart, *Studies in the Philosophy of the Scottish Enlightenment*, pp. 191–229.

[87] David Hume, *An Enquiry concerning Human Understanding*, ed. Tom L. Beauchamp (Oxford, 1999), sect. 10, 'Of Miracles', pp. 169–86; and the exposition by Wootton, 'Hume's "Of Miracles"', pp. 203–6.

proceeded to declare that 'upon the whole, we may conclude, that the Christian religion not only was at first attended with miracles, but even at this day cannot be believed by any reasonable person without one'.[88] What Hume had done was critically weaken what Bayle always treated as the one secure bulwark against the Epicurean, atheist account of nature and man: the truth of Scripture as God's revelation to man. Bayle was well aware of the accumulating threats to the credibility of the Bible's truth status, not least those arising from disputed authorship of the Pentateuch. In the face of these he had insisted that Christianity depended on acceptance of the truth of the Bible as it stood. Hume's argument on miracles amounted to saying that whatever their authorship, the Scriptures could never be accounted reliable testimony.

Bayle had upheld the truth of Scripture as necessary to the existence of a divine providence. Hume turned to the matter of providence in the essay immediately following that on miracles in the *Philosophical Essays*. It is not known whether this essay, originally titled 'Of the Practical Consequences of Natural Religion', and in 1750 renamed 'Of a Particular Providence and of a Future State', also originated in the 'nobler parts' of the *Treatise*. But it dealt directly with what Hume called 'the religious hypothesis' – the claim that the order and beauty of the universe demonstrated the existence of a divine intelligence, whose providence continued to rule over it, and offered men the prospect of a future life. The essay thus took up the proposition which Hume had noted in his memoranda and attributed to Bayle, that 'the Center of Unity of all Men with Relation to Religion is, That there is a first Cause'. In form too the essay had a Baylean character. It was framed as a discussion between the author and 'a friend who loves sceptical paradoxes' (1).[89] The two begin by reflecting on the contrast between the freedom enjoyed by philosophers in the ancient world, and the 'bigotted jealousy' to which they are subject in the present age. The friend observes that this bigotry is the offspring of philosophy herself, by her alliance with superstition. To prove that there is nothing in speculative philosophy which should make a magistrate jealous, he offers to demonstrate that even Epicurus could easily have defended himself before the Athenians against the charge of subverting morality (2–5). At this point Hume took the opportunity to rename the friend 'Epicurus', and to put the ensuing argument into his mouth (6–23). Philosophical ventriloquism of this sort

---

[88] 'Of Miracles', *Enquiry concerning Human Understanding*, paragraphs 40–1, p. 186.
[89] 'Of a Particular Providence and of a Future State', *Enquiry concerning Human Understanding*, pp. 187–98. References in brackets in the text are to paragraph numbers.

was a technique which Bayle used repeatedly in the 'remarks' to the text of the *Dictionary*; he often followed it by reverting to the authorial voice to deliver the final, clinching argument. As we shall see, Hume does exactly the same at the end of his essay.[90]

'Epicurus' begins by allowing the argument of those who ask whether the order, beauty, and wise arrangement of the universe, which form such a glorious display of intelligence, could possibly proceed from the fortuitous concourse of atoms. Their argument, 'Epicurus' points out, is one from effect to cause, whereby they infer from the order of nature that there must have been 'project and forethought in the workman' (10–11). 'Epicurus' reminds them, however, that even if such a cause can be inferred from the effect, no additional quality can be attributed to the cause as a result. There is no reason to assign to the deity any greater perfection than is to be found in the world. Rather, 'we must acknowledge the reality of that evil and disorder, with which the world so much abounds', even if it limits the perfection of God (12–17). Nor does the religious hypothesis give us any reason to associate the deity with a system of distributive justice, by which providence has undertaken to reward the good. The idea that this life is merely 'a porch, which leads to a greater, and vastly different building', is derived only from the conceit and imagination of those who maintain it; it has no basis in observed phenomena (20–2). In consequence, 'Epicurus' concludes, the religious hypothesis has no practical, and certainly no moral consequences (23). To question that hypothesis, therefore, can do no harm to human society.

So far, 'Epicurus' has carefully limited the application of the hypothesis, but he has not yet questioned it outright. At this point, however, Hume interrupted the essay and reinstated the authorial voice. He did so to raise a seeming objection to the argument of 'Epicurus'. The objection is the argument from a half-finished building: when we see such a building, we infer that it is the work of design, and that the designer has the finished house in mind. By analogy, therefore, we may regard the world and the present life as an imperfect building, which the superior intelligence of providence will render perfect in some distant point of space or time (24).[91] The objection is no sooner stated, however, than 'Epicurus' and the author together proceed to demolish it. The analogy between human and divine design is invalid.

---

[90] Stewart, 'Two species of philosophy', p. 93 note 43, suggests another Baylean model for the speech of 'Epicurus' in the *Continuation des Pensées Diverses*.

[91] Hutcheson had used a variant of this argument to support the proposition that nature is purposeful: above, p. 286.

In the case of men, we know by repeated experience how they build: they and their productions form two 'species' of objects constantly conjoined. But the deity is known only by his unique productions: since neither can be replicated, the requirement on which the principle of constant conjunction depends, that effect and cause bear a similarity to other effects and causes, cannot be met. It appears, therefore, that the argument which 'Epicurus' was at first willing to allow is, after all, open to doubt: the proposition 'That there is a first Cause' cannot be demonstrated by reasoning from observation and experience. The hypothesis of a divine providence and a future state, Hume closed by suggesting, is *both* undemonstrable and of no practical consequence (25–7, 30).

In the terms of the discussion with which Hume had opened the essay, the religious hypothesis has been shown to be one of those 'speculative dogmas' which arose from the misalliance of philosophy and superstition, and which have encouraged bigotry at the expense of freedom and toleration. Like Mandeville in the *Free Thoughts*, Hume would underline the danger of mixing philosophy with theology (although Mandeville had accepted the idea of a first cause itself on philosophical grounds). In the manner of Bayle, however, it was left to the reader to decide whether such speculative dogmas of religion were not more dangerous than atheism.[92]

The Natural History of Religion

There are some signs that the *Philosophical essays concerning Human Understanding* were intended to be Hume's answer to, if not revenge upon, those, led by Hutcheson, who had denied him the chair of moral philosophy in Edinburgh in 1745. Hume's willingness to include the two essays on miracles and providence, and thus to publish at least some of the omitted 'nobler parts' of the *Treatise*, indicates a determination not to be deterred from applying his philosophy to religion. Nor was he satisfied with the publication of those two essays. In the years immediately after the appearance of the *Philosophical Essays*, he was at work on one and perhaps both of two further works devoted to religion. He is known to have written a draft of

---

[92] One other topic may have been among the 'nobler parts' omitted from the *Treatise*: the doctrine of the immortality of the soul. James Moore has pointed out to me that Hume's discussion of 'the immateriality of the soul' in the *Treatise* (1.4.5.1–35) reaches a curiously ambivalent conclusion, whereas the argument of the posthumously-published 'Of the Immortality of the Soul' was much more decisive (*Essays, Moral, Political, and Literary*, pp. 590–8). Along with 'Of Suicide', the essay was set up in print in 1755, for inclusion in the projected *Five Dissertations*, but was then suppressed by Hume. They were eventually published anonymously as *Two Essays* in 1777.

the *Dialogues concerning Natural Religion* by 1751, when he sent a 'sample' to Gilbert Elliot; he probably began *The Natural History of Religion* soon afterwards.[93]

Of the two, the *Dialogues* were the more direct in their challenge to contemporary Christian doctrine. They contained a fully developed discussion of the argument from design, and of the attributes of the deity, in which the sceptical participant, Philo, probed ceaselessly at the weaknesses in the reasoning of his theist opponents, Cleanthes and Demea. To his chagrin, however, Hume was unable to overcome his friends' reluctance to allow the *Dialogues* to be published. Having tweaked the noses of the academics and divines who had denied him the chair, Hume could not afford to lose the support of the laity and the younger, 'moderate' clergy on whom his position in Edinburgh society now depended. The *Dialogues*, therefore, were not published in his lifetime. He had to content himself with taking them out of the drawer every so often to sharpen and polish his arguments, and with leaving clear instructions for their publication after his death. (They finally appeared in 1779.) By contrast, he could and did publish *The Natural History of Religion*, as one of *Four Discourses* in 1757. Relatively neglected by scholars, perhaps because it is less obviously of philosophical interest, the *Natural History of Religion* is arguably of more interest in the present context.[94] For it shows Hume taking up several more issues derived from Bayle (and the notes Hume had taken from him) and from Mandeville. Specifically, it shows Hume addressing the issues of the nature of idolatry, its relation to monotheism, and thence the fundamental question of the

---

[93] On the *Dialogues*: Hume to Gilbert Elliot, 10 March 1751, *Letters of Hume*, I, pp. 153–7; the story of their composition is re-assessed by Stewart, 'The dating of Hume's manuscripts', pp. 288–304. On the *Natural History*: Hume to Andrew Millar, 12 June 1755, *Letters of Hume*, I, p. 223, offering Millar 'four short Dissertations, which I have kept some Years by me, in order to polish them as much as possible'. This suggests that he had begun them at the beginning of the 1750s, if not earlier. After some vicissitudes, including the printing and suppression of the alternative of *Five Dissertations*, and an attempt by Warburton to stop their publication, the *Four Dissertations* were eventually published in 1757.

[94] Among recent studies: Michel Malherbe, 'Hume's *Natural History of Religion*', *Hume Studies*, 21 (1995), 255–74, who observes that 'if we try to understand the text more systematically and attempt to rationalize its composition or its argumentation, we cannot help feeling at a loss to determine Hume's real intentions and to precisely evaluate the *Natural History*'s general import' (p. 255). Also Christopher Barnard, 'Hume and the madness of religion', in Stewart and Wright, *Hume and Hume's Connexions*, pp. 201–23, which examines the *Natural History* in relation to Hume's account in the *Treatise* of 'imagination' and 'belief'; and Christopher J. Berry, 'Rude religion: the psychology of polytheism in the Scottish Enlightenment', in Wood, *The Scottish Enlightenment*. pp. 315–34, which compares Hume's account of polytheism with others by his Scottish contemporaries. None of these is concerned, except incidentally, with historical explanation of Hume's purposes. By contrast James Harris, 'Answering Bayle's question', pp. 247–53, is closer to this concern; but although he discusses several relevant aspects of Hume's philosophy, he discusses the *Natural History* only briefly.

relation between religion and morals. It is in the *Natural History*, in other words, that Hume engages with the key elements of Bayle's hypothesis of a society of atheists. In so doing, *The Natural History of Religion* supplies a final, vital dimension of Hume's account of sociability.

Hume introduced the *Natural History* by accepting the foundation of religion in reason. 'The whole frame of nature bespeaks an intelligent author; and no rational enquirer can, after serious reflection, suspend his belief with regard to the primary principles of genuine Theism and Religion' (Introduction, 309).[95] There is little reason to doubt that Hume made this concession for the sake of argument. In the essay on providence, after all, 'Epicurus' and the author had undermined the validity of reasoning from a single effect to a unique cause. Nevertheless, the purposes of argument for which Hume admitted the rationality of theism were important: the admission freed him to concentrate on the question of the origin of religion in human nature – the better, gradually, to show the irrelevance of its supposed foundation in reason. Turning therefore to the origin of religion in human nature, Hume immediately observed that there was insufficient evidence to assume that a belief in invisible, intelligent power was universal in the human race. Sentiments of religion could not be regarded as 'an original instinct or primary impression of nature'; they were secondary principles, whose operation may easily be perverted by accidents or causes, or even be prevented altogether (Introduction, 309–10).

In these terms, Hume suggested, 'the first and most ancient religion of mankind' must necessarily have been 'polytheism or idolatry'.[96] About 1700 years ago, 'all mankind were idolaters'. That there had been a few sceptical philosophers, and one or two nations who subscribed to – a 'not entirely pure' – theism, formed 'no objection worth regarding'. (In other words, the Jews of the Old Testament could be discounted.) The further we went back into antiquity, the more we would find mankind plunged into idolatry (1, 310). Hume dismissed the suggestion that men might have fallen into polytheism having originally been theists. The ignorant multitude

---

[95] I have used the version in *Essays Moral, Political, and Literary, by David Hume*, ed. T. H. Green and T. H. Grose, 2 vols. (London, 1898), vol. II, pp. 307–63. This edition was based in the 1777 edition of the *Essays and Treatises on Several Subjects*, the last which Hume had corrected; editorial footnotes indicate changes which Hume had made to the text. References are given in brackets in the text, by section number (roman) and page number (arabic).

[96] The pairing 'polytheism or idolatry' occurs throughout the text. In later editions Hume sometimes dropped 'idolatry' and 'idolaters', or substituted 'polytheism' and 'polytheists'; such occasions are noted by Green and Grose. But this was not a systematic policy on Hume's part: elsewhere he continued to use the terms, sometimes on their own, sometimes paired with 'polytheism'. It is clear that he regarded (and expected readers to understand) polytheism as idolatry. In my quotations I have reinstated idolaters and idolatry, in line with the original 1757 version of the work.

would never have stretched to conceive of one perfect being before they had thought of beings who bore some similarity to themselves. Rather than viewing the design of nature as a whole, uninstructed mankind were preoccupied with the events of daily life, and transferred their hopes and fears to the agents they believed were directly responsible for these events. These agents men naturally conceived of as like themselves, and thus they ascribed human powers and even human features to natural forces. Having identified these 'secret intelligent powers', men supposed that their fortunes depended entirely on them, and sought every method of appeasing them (I–III, 311–19).

Hume next emphasised the distance between such idolatry and genuine theism. The gods of polytheists were no different from the elves and fairies, goblins and sprites in which so many of our ancestors in Europe had believed before the revival of letters. Our ancestors might have professed to believe in one supreme God, but by admitting the interposition of angels and other subordinate ministers, and believing in elves and fairies, they had brought themselves down to the level of polytheism. At that level, Hume suggested, men were really 'a kind of superstitious atheists', and acknowledged no being that corresponds to our idea of a deity (IV, 320). By way of illustration, he cited examples of polytheists attempting to coerce or even 'punish' their deities for their failures. At greater length, he showed that no polytheist or idolater had entertained the idea of 'divine contrivance or intention in the fabric of the world'. The ancient mythologists, he observed, seem to have favoured the idea of generation to account for the origin of the universe, and to have discounted the idea of creation. It had been philosophers who had first asked the question of the origin of the world, and it was long before they thought of a mind of supreme intelligence. Even then few of the ancient philosophers had been genuine theists, least of all, Hume remarked, Marcus Aurelius and his fellow Stoics, whose creed 'may justly be said to exclude a deity, and to leave only angels and fairies' (IV, 320–5). (So much for Hutcheson's efforts to claim Marcus Aurelius for monotheism.) The difference between idolatry and theism was further underlined by the characteristic tendency of polytheists to allegory and hero worship. Gods were given genealogies, attributes, and adventures, while the vulgar deified those they regarded as heroes. Painters and sculptors profited by supplying sensible representations of these deities in human form, giving the vulgar something more tangible to worship than an invisible spiritual intelligence (V, 325–8).

Many of Hume's observations on the nature and practices of polytheism echoed Bayle's account of idolatry. Several may be correlated with the notes which Hume had taken from Bayle and jotted in his 'Memoranda'. Above all, Hume may be seen to have endorsed Bayle's point that 'the Testimony of Idolaters cannot be united to that of Christians against the Atheists' (note 11.5, quoted above). A subtle shift in his argument underlay this conclusion. At the outset, as we saw, he had denied that sentiments of religion were a primary impression of nature; they were secondary principles, easily perverted by accidents. But by the end of his account of polytheism Hume was apparently prepared to concede that its general principles were 'founded in human nature, and little or nothing dependent on caprice and accident' (v, 327). The implication was that polytheism or idolatry was at least more natural than theism; and if, as Hume also argued, such idolatry was really a kind of superstitious atheism, then atheism, too, must be regarded as more characteristic of human nature than theism. It was the testimony of idolaters and atheists which was naturally united.

Having examined polytheism, Hume turned to the rise of theism. When the doctrine of one supreme deity did begin to take hold among great and populous nations, he reiterated, it was not because the vulgar had been persuaded by 'those invincible reasons, on which it is undoubtedly founded', that is, by the beauty of final causes (vi, 328). It was because a particular deity had gradually become the favoured object of worship by a particular nation. As it did so, the deity's votaries would cry up its attributes, seeking to outdo each other in its praise, until in the end, by chance, they arrived at the notion of a perfect being, the creator of the world (vi, 330). (Hume's insistence that it was 'by chance' that men arrived at an idea of God which coincided with the principles of reason and true philosophy underlined the point that theism was not a primary impression of nature.) He then offered an example of the process. 'Thus, notwithstanding the sublime idea suggested by Moses and the inspired writers, many vulgar Jews seem still to have conceived the supreme being as a mere topical deity or national protector' (vi, 331 n.1).[97] In other words, the acres of print devoted by Warburton and his many predecessors to the special dispensation of the Jews were beside the point; they were just one example of a common historical phenomenon. Another was provided by Mahometanism, although here the process had varied in that the depiction of the deity in the most sublime colours, as

---

[97] It was a sentence, however, which Hume rewrote at least twice: from 1764 it read even more simply 'Thus, the God of Abraham, Isaac, and Jacob, became the supreme deity or Jehovah of the Jews'. See Green and Grose, *Essays Moral, Political, and Literary*, p. 331: the sentence as it read in 1757 (and which is quoted in my text above) is given in note 1, which also gives a proof variant; the sentence as it read from 1764 onwards (quoted in this note) is the one printed in the main text by Green and Grose and subsequent editors.

creator of heaven and earth, had been combined with his degradation to an almost human level, at which he was supposed liable to 'infirmities, passions, and partialities, of the moral kind'. Nothing would prove more strongly the divine origin of a religion, Hume added, than to find it free of such contradiction, so characteristic of human nature (and happily, a parenthesis suggested, this was the case with Christianity) (vi, 332). In fact, as Hume went on immediately to demonstrate, no monotheism, and least of all Christianity, had been able to resist for long the countervailing temptations of idolatry, or what he called 'the flux and reflux of polytheism and theism' (viii, 334–6). Though he did not say so directly, a judicious choice of examples in these chapters indicated that he had Roman Catholic Christianity particularly in mind.[98]

Despite this tendency for even the best of monotheisms to lapse back into polytheism, Hume argued, the two species of religion encouraged very different behaviour among their followers. By elevating the deity above men, monotheisms tended to sink the human mind, encouraging 'the monkish virtues of mortification, penance, humility, and passive suffering'. One need only contrast the abject submission and slavish obedience displayed by the Christian saints with the monster-slaying deeds of the heroes of paganism (x, 339–40). Worse, monotheisms were characteristically intolerant, condemning the worship of other deities as impious, and thus unleashing on each other 'that sacred zeal and rancour, the most furious and implacable of all human passions' (ix, 337). Jews, Mahometans, and Christians all displayed such intolerance; if, among Christians, the Dutch and the English had adopted the principles of toleration, this was only because the civil magistrate had enforced it over the continued efforts of 'priests and bigots' (ix, 338). The authority of the magistrate, Hume would agree with Mandeville, was the sole effective check on the inclination of all Christian clergy to persecute those who disagreed with them.

Perhaps the danger to which Hume was most sensitive, however, was the tendency of monotheism to suborn and corrupt philosophy. Pagan divinity had been founded on traditional stories, which could fill only a few volumes, and gave little scope for philosophical controversy. Theism, by contrast, attracts philosophy by its seeming reasonableness, only to pervert it into serving the purposes of superstition. Its 'popular theology', Hume remarked, has 'a kind of appetite for absurdity and contradiction'. It was as if its doctrines would appear too easy, if they did not go beyond reason

---

[98] As, for example, in the remark that it was not long before the Virgin Mary began to usurp many attributes of the Almighty (vi, 331). By contrast, the Jews and Mahometans had at least attempted to banish the arts of statuary and painting (viii, 335).

and common sense. In proof of this tendency, Hume observed that in any theological controversy it was always those who inclined more to the side of reason who were branded with heresy. Arian, Pelagian, Erastian, Socinian – all stood condemned before the sophisms of scholastic theology. To oppose the torrent of scholastic philosophy was like pretending to stop the ocean with a bullrush; and the same fires which were kindled for heretics, Hume warned, will serve also for the destruction of philosophers (XI, 340–2). But it was not only heretics and philosophers who were in danger from monotheist theology.

The real threat from the theist alliance of philosophy and superstition lay in its ambition to impress itself upon the affections and understanding of all men. Like Bayle and Mandeville, Hume was keenly aware of the discrepancy between belief and behaviour. In most men religious conviction is more affected than real, and scarcely ever approaches 'that solid belief and persuasion, which governs us in the common affairs of life'. For this reason, those who would employ the chisel to engrave theological tenets on the mind of man rarely leave a lasting impression. Nevertheless, a 'systematical, scholastic' religion was much more likely to succeed than a 'traditional, mythological' one (XII, 347–52). This was above all because the former exploited men's fear of the future by insisting on the idea of a vengeful God. Naturally, Hume thought, men represent the deity as both dreadful and excellent. Idolaters tend to emphasise wicked and detestable qualities, theists the more elevated ones. But as the latter exalt their idea of the divinity, they enhance his power and knowledge at the expense of his goodness, and attribute to him an implacable vengeance. The lengths to which Christianity in particular had gone in representing the divinity in an 'immoral and unamiable light' were illustrated in a footnote, in which Hume quoted a long passage from the Chevalier Ramsay. By the doctrine of predestination, Ramsay had observed, the Christian philosophers had divinised cruelty, vengeance, and all the blackest vices; the pagans had merely divinised lust, incest, and adultery. As Ramsay had added, moreover, neither the Arminian nor the Molinist schemes could mend the matter (XIII, 352–7, and n. 2 on 355–6). The note, which took the words of one who, Hume acknowledged, had a laudable inclination to be orthodox, and turned them against Christianity, was a curious way of repaying Ramsay for his hospitality when Hume first arrived in Paris in 1734. But it was also a classically Baylean device, using another's voice to serve the author's subversive purpose.

Even then, Hume's purpose went further than exposing the vengefulness of the theists' God. The more serious issue was the contradiction between this representation of God and our natural ideas of generosity and justice. 'The genuine principles of morals', Hume reminded his readers, derive from their 'absolute necessity . . . to the existence of society' (XIII, 355–6). Moreover, all virtue, once men are reconciled to it by a little practice, is agreeable, whereas all superstition is odious and burdensome (XIV, 358). Moral sentiments, in other words, correspond to what is useful and agreeable to us in this world. To a theist, however, acts of virtue are no substitute for devotion. Theism therefore increases its demands upon men for devotion, at the expense of morals. In this it has a willing ally in popular prejudice, whose preference for superstitious devotion is such that even were an order of priests to inculcate that nothing but morality could win divine favour, the people would make attendance at their sermons the essential of their religion, rather than virtue and good morals. The inevitable outcome of this emphasis on devotion is hypocrisy. Thus 'it is justly regarded as unsafe to draw any certain inference in favour of a man's morals, from the fervour or strictness of his religious exercises, even though he himself believe them sincere'. The most criminal, indeed, are commonly the most superstitious (XIV, 359–60). Mandeville had made a similar point about devotion, and the opportunities which this afforded the clergy, at the beginning of the *Free Thoughts on Religion*; but he had explained devotion as a cover for men's failure to live up to an austere standard of morality. Hume's point was that theism was responsible for both: it attached an exaggerated importance to devotion, at the same time as it fostered the austere, 'monkish' virtues. In *both* respects, theism was at odds with our natural moral sentiments, as we recognise – or develop – them through the experience of living in society. Theism encouraged men to allay their fears by submissiveness and superstition; Hume thought men would do far better to rely on 'a manly, steady virtue', which either preserves us from accidents, or teaches us to bear them. As long as we enjoy what he called, in a wonderful phrase, the 'calm sunshine of the mind', the spectres of false divinity need never make their appearance (XIV, 360).

One of the notes which Hume had taken from Bayle stated simply 'Atheists plainly make a Distinction betwixt good Reasoning & bad. Why not betwixt Vice & Virtue?' In the *Natural History of Religion*, Hume had not merely answered the question; he had turned it round, suggesting that it is theists who cannot be relied upon to recognise the distinction between vice and virtue. It was not those who lived in fear of punishment in a future state, and therefore devoted this life to assuaging the deity by their devotions, who were moral and sociable; it was those who followed their natural moral inclinations, and who judged their own and others' behaviour by

its usefulness and agreeableness in the present. Hume had already demonstrated, in the first part of the work, that idolatry or polytheism could not
be regarded as the ally of Christianity in demonstrating the universal necessity of religion to society: in many respects, idolatry was closer to unbelief
than to strict theism. To this Hume had now added, in the second half
of the book, a positive proposition: that it was atheists, not monotheists,
who were most naturally sociable. It was a proposition which Mandeville
had asserted before him, repeatedly and memorably, in all his works from
the *Fable of the Bees* to the *Letter to Dion*. But while Mandeville might
recognise that in most of their affairs men pay no more attention to the
idea of a future state than to the name of their street, he was less certain
of the explanation, pointing either to men's capacity for hypocrisy or to
a concern for worldly honour. Hume's argument, by contrast, was clear
and straightforward. He had masked it in the *Treatise of Human Nature*, by
excluding all but the most passing of references to the idea of a future state
from his account of morals. By the end of the *Natural History of Religion*,
however, the point was much clearer. The theists' doctrine of a future state
was not simply superfluous, it was contrary to morality, because our moral
sentiments, natural and artificial, really accord with what we find useful
and agreeable in this world. In our morals, we are – and we are the better
for being – sociable atheists.

HUME, VICO, AND THE EPICUREAN FOUNDATIONS OF ENLIGHTENMENT

So far as I am aware, no one has seriously argued that Hume was Vico's
contemporary in more than the obvious chronological sense.[99] Against
Paolo Rossi's strict criteria of contemporaneity, the suggestion is likely to
seem a *reductio ad absurdum*. None the less, it is what is being argued
here. Hume was Vico's contemporary, despite all the obvious differences
between their philosophies, in that he was responding to the same set of
issues as Vico. These issues derived from the work of Pierre Bayle, and,
in particular, from his question whether idolaters were morally in a better
position to form a society than atheists. In Vico's case, we cannot count
on his having had a detailed knowledge of Bayle's arguments; yet it has
been seen that he framed the *New Science*, and most explicitly the first
New Science, to demonstrate the historical and moral impossibility of a

---

[99] Leon Pompa, *Human Nature and Historical Knowledge: Hume, Hegel and Vico* (Cambridge, 1990),
discusses the two within the covers of the same book, but for the purposes of analytical contrast, not
historical comparison.

society of atheists. In Hume's case, by contrast, we have evidence that he read and reflected on Bayle's arguments from an early stage, and that he also engaged closely with the writings of Bayle's most original disciple in England, Bernard Mandeville. My purpose in this long chapter has been to show the extent to which these encounters shaped Hume's 'science of man', and in particular his analysis of the contributions of morals and religion to human sociability. What has emerged, I suggest, is a striking degree of comparability between the enterprises of Hume and Vico.

Hume's response to Bayle and to Mandeville, it has been argued, had three aspects. The first was his extended account of the passions, and of the relation between them and the moral sentiments. Although this offers the least scope for direct comparison with Vico, the contrasting accounts which Vico and Hume gave of the passions had substantial implications for the direction each would take towards the understanding of human society. Vico possessed a keen sense of the power of the passions, and of their origin in the physical senses; he acknowledged the force of the Epicurean account of human nature. But he sought to offset this by an Augustinian morality by which, as a result of the Fall, sin was equated with indulgence of the passions, and virtue with their restraint. This was combined with a determination to retain the concept of free will. With the aid of his interpretation of the concept of *conatus*, or endeavour, Vico would demonstrate that the influence of the passions was compatible with the exercise of free will, and that this in turn was quite consistent with the operation of divine providence in human affairs.

By contrast Hume, like Mandeville, insisted that even on a sceptical account of causality, the will must be regarded as determined; if it were not – if the will were arbitrary – there would be no basis on which to hold men morally responsible. Hume's purpose in book ii of the *Treatise of Human Nature* was thus to explain how the passions (including the will) were determined. His account gave pride of place to those passions (technically the indirect passions) which express our self-esteem in relation to others, and which depend, in part, on the opinion of others, as we become aware of that opinion through the operation of sympathy. This analysis of the passions was in turn closely related to the discussion of the natural virtues in the final part of book iii of the *Treatise*, where Hume maintained that many of our moral sentiments derive naturally from our passions, as we find them to be 'useful and agreeable'. In adopting the useful and agreeable as the standard of morality, Hume was endorsing and elaborating the Epicurean theory of Bayle, but repudiating the Augustinian residue still present in Mandeville, who (like Vico in this respect) had persisted in identifying virtue with a strict idea of self-denial. To accept an Epicurean account of the passions, Hume sought to show, did not entail setting morals to tame the passions: a coherent account of morals must itself be based in human nature, rather than treating them as an arbitrary invention to be imposed upon men. As it was, the distance between Hume and Mandeville was diminished by the latter's increasing readiness to recognise that the sense of honour was more important to men's relations with each other than virtue itself; in particular, men's care for their honour helped to explain why they gave so little thought to their prospects in a future state. Despite Hume's irritation at Mandeville's adherence to an unnatural concept of virtue, therefore, what they had in common was more important than what separated them. In their characteristically Epicurean appreciation of the pleasure and utility to be derived from the self-regarding passions, Hume and Mandeville stood together against the neo-Stoic moral philosophy championed by Shaftesbury and Hutcheson. By the same token, Hume's understanding of the moral possibilities of an Epicurean account of human nature would in due course (though not in the *Treatise*) lead him in directions which Vico was determined to reject.

Before their paths diverged decisively, however, the second aspect of Hume's response to Bayle and Mandeville, his explanation of justice and sociability, reveals a striking parallel with Vico. An Epicurean awareness of the power of the passions meant that neither Vico nor Hume could take sociability for granted. Vico painted a dramatic picture of the earliest Gentiles as giants whose lives were solitary and brutish, without gods or families, or any of the benefits of society. Only after a long period of wandering in isolation had the giants established families, and the families gathered into nations. As they did so, Vico suggested, there emerged in each nation a 'common sense' concerning human needs and utilities, which was the source of the natural law of the gentes, and thus of the idea of justice. Only after the idea of justice had taken root in each nation would men become aware of their common humanity, and nations be able to 'settle and endure'; and only then would men be naturally sociable, recognising the law of the gentes as a 'natural' law.

Hume made no attempt in the *Treatise* to sketch the condition of the earliest men (he had none of Vico's or Mandeville's interest in their attributes, thoughts, language, or behaviour). He simply observed that however naturally men value what is useful and agreeable, they do not naturally form and maintain societies. For society requires justice, and men's natural avidity for goods and possessions for themselves, their families, and friends is inconsistent with a constant respect for the possessions of others, and with the fulfilment of promises. Hume's response to this problem, in the second part of book III of the *Treatise*, was to accept, with Hobbes and Mandeville, that justice was an artificial, not an immediately natural virtue; its rules were the product of human artifice. But Hume could not accept the further supposition, derived from Lucretius and endorsed by Mandeville, that justice must therefore have been imposed upon mankind by far-sighted legislators, for this did not explain how men came to be in a position to understand and accept its rules. Instead, Hume argued that justice must have derived from a convention, 'a general sense of the common interest' in preserving society in order to secure its benefits. This 'general sense of the common interest', it may be suggested, bears a more than verbal resemblance to Vico's 'common sense' concerning human needs and utilities. Like Vico's 'common sense', Hume's 'general sense of the common interest' developed over time: as a convention it was not an arbitrary creation, like a contract, but an understanding or agreement which has been acquired by experience. Men became sociable, Hume thought, as they accustomed themselves to live according to rules of justice, respecting property, keeping promises, and owing allegiance to government. In due course such sociability would come to seem natural, and its rules would be regarded as 'Laws of Nature'. But this was because the rules of justice endured and were universally accepted, not because men were originally sociable. Separately but contemporaneously, Vico and Hume had put the problem of sociability (and with it the concept of natural law) on a new foundation, by setting the Epicurean understanding of human nature in a properly historical framework.[100]

The third aspect of Hume's response to Bayle and Mandeville focused upon what he and Vico regarded as the most important question of all: whether society, and the morality required to sustain it, was possible without religion and the direction of divine providence. For whatever reason, Hume decided to omit all but the most fleeting indications of his answer from the *Treatise*, leaving it to his readers to infer what it was likely to be. But he soon thought better of such reticence (which had not deceived the clergy), and in two works published in the 1740s and 1750s, the *Philosophical Essays*

---

[100] The extent to which Hume should be regarded as an exponent of natural jurisprudence has been the subject of considerable discussion. Among those who have emphasised Hume's differences with the natural law tradition are James Moore, 'Hume's theory of justice and property', *Political Studies*, 24 (1976), 103–19, and 'Natural law and the Pyrrhonian controversy'; and Pauline C. Westerman, 'Hume and the natural lawyers: a change of landscape', in Stewart and Wright, *Hume and Hume's Connexions*, pp. 83–104. By contrast, the connections between Hume, Pufendorf, and other exponents of the tradition have been emphasised by Duncan Forbes, *Hume's Philosophical Politics* (Cambridge, 1975), chs. 1–2; and by Knud Haakonssen, *Natural Law and Moral Philosophy: from Grotius to the Scottish Enlightenment* (Cambridge, 1996). The comparison with Vico seems to me to lend weight to those who emphasise Hume's differences from the tradition.

concerning the Human Understanding and *The Natural History of Religion*, he laid out his answer. On each of three critical issues, the status of Scripture, the role of providence, and the morals of idolatry and atheism, that answer, we can now see, was diametrically opposed to Vico's.

Vico had trodden a careful path over Scripture. He affirmed its truth, as history and divinity. He accepted the Fall and adopted the chronology laid down in the Bible as the framework of his own history. But he did so the better to exploit the opportunity within that chronology (and particularly in the length of time occupied by the aftermath of the Flood) for a conjectural history of the earliest Gentiles. On this ground he could answer Bayle without invoking the rest of the Old Testament history of the Hebrews, and having to meet the objections which were being raised to the authorship and reliability of the Old Testament, and the Pentateuch in particular. The wisdom of this strategy is thrown into relief by the difficulties which faced Mandeville's Cleomenes in attempting to defend a literal interpretation of Paradise, or, on a much greater scale, Warburton in the *Divine Legation*. Warburton's ambition was indeed no less than Vico's – the refutation of Bayle by means of a study of ancient religion; but a focus upon the religion of the Hebrews and the Egyptians created hostages to fortune which Vico was careful to avoid. Hume, by contrast, had no interest in following either Vico or Warburton into the thickets of Old Testament scholarship. His attack in 'Of Miracles' on the credibility of the testimony of the Scriptures was direct and comprehensive. All testimony on behalf of divine, miraculous intervention contrary to the ordinary course of nature and human affairs was implausible. If the Bible had any value as testimony, it was as the record of the history of the various peoples it concerned, shorn of all claims for their special status by divine revelation or providence. This is why Hume was so dismissive of the Jews in the *Natural History*: far from being a special case, they were simply one example among several of the tendency for particular nations to pretend that their local deity was the supreme god. A people to whose divine dispensation Warburton had devoted volumes merited from Hume a single sentence.

A defence of divine providence and its role in human affairs was of course at the heart of Vico's *New Science*. It was clearly designed to refute the alternative Epicurean and Spinozist accounts of the world, whose merits and defects had been discussed by Bayle. Vico's providence was an aspect of an eternal and infinite mind, quite separate from the material world; only thus could providence be responsible for the creation and direction of that world. Providence was general in its operation, working through the normal course of nature and human affairs: miracles (subsequent to those recorded in the Bible) were no part of its brief. It was not to be confused with divine grace: providence was not responsible for salvation – or for the sin from which men needed to be saved. Providence, in short, is strictly concerned with what happens in this world: it is what gives human affairs the degree of order they possess. Without recognising its existence there can be no coherent understanding of the history of men and nations – no 'New Science' as Vico envisaged it.

Hume's conception of providence likewise presupposed a higher intelligence, separate from the universe it had created. But Hume broke away from Bayle's formulation of the question as an alternative between a divine creator-providence and a purely materialist explanation of the world.[101] Instead Hume concentrated on the proposition that there is a first cause, and questioned both its validity and its implications. As a causal proposition, the inference from the universe to its creator was concerned with unique entities, and therefore could not meet the usual requirements of causal reasoning based on constant conjunction. (We are not in a position to observe a relation between other creators and other universes, as would be required by the rules of constant conjunction.) Even if the inference were allowed, Hume continued, it authorised no further inferences concerning the attributes of God. We cannot ascribe to the deity a perfection greater than that of the world itself; and we certainly cannot ascribe to divine providence the capacity to reward and punish us in a future state. The 'religious hypothesis' of a divine providence and a future state is neither demonstrable nor of any practical, moral relevance to human life. It therefore has no place in the 'science of man'.

For both Vico and Hume, however, the most provocative, the most stimulating of all Bayle's questions concerned the possibility of a society of virtuous atheists. The formulation of the question was critical. What Bayle had asked was whether religious idolaters could satisfy the moral requirements of living in society any better than atheists. On the face of it, the question was innocuous in its implications for Christianity: if the choice was between idolatry and atheism, the answer, even one unfavourable to idolatry, would leave true (Christian) religion unaffected. As Vico, Hume, and many others were all too well aware, however, the implications of such

---

[101] In Hume's terms it made absolutely no sense to think of a causal power within nature, since causes can only be ascribed on the basis of human observation of a constant conjunction between events. A Spinozist materialism, according to which divine agency operates in nature itself, is therefore inconceivable. (It may be worth recalling that Hume recommended his friend Michael Ramsay to read Bayle's critical discussion of Spinoza as preparation for reading the metaphysical part of the *Treatise*.) Epicurean materialism is not open to the same objection, but offers no account of causality at all.

an answer would be almost as damaging to Christianity as to idolatry. Not only were some Christians (most obviously Roman Catholics) regularly accused of idolatry; but if idolatry were no better than atheism, all the religions of the ancient world (except the Jewish) and most of those in the modern would stand condemned, and it would have to be assumed that the one true God was content to leave the great majority of mankind in a state of religious error and moral degradation.

In successive versions of the *New Science*, Vico set himself to demonstrate that there had never been a society of atheists. To this end he focused on the Gentile, not the Hebrew, descendants of Noah, showing, first, that their abandonment of the true God was followed by their dispersal to wander isolated across the post-diluvian wasteland, and second, that they only came together again when their frightened imaginations led them to acknowledge Jove as the divinity of thunder and lightning. In turn, the fear of Jove had driven the giants to carry women off to their caves, to marry them, and to bring up their offspring to acknowledge the power of divine providence. It was idolatry, therefore, which was directly responsible for the socialisation of the Gentiles, by encouraging the primitive rudiments of morality. Like Warburton, Vico was keen to strengthen his argument still further by emphasising the tendency of even the simplest idolatry to monotheism. But the crucial point in both men's answer to Bayle was the capacity of idolatry to satisfy the moral requirements of society.

Though unaware of Vico, Hume had studied Bayle's argument closely, and he was very probably also familiar with the claims of Warburton. His answer to Bayle's question in the *Natural History of Religion* was two pronged. On the one hand, he would demonstrate that idolatry offered no support to theist religions against atheism. For idolatry was polytheism, and polytheism was little better than a kind of 'superstitious atheism'. Polytheism, moreover, was more natural than theism; the latter owed far more to the artifices of priests and theologians. On the other hand, Hume was confident of the possibility of a society of virtuous atheists. Audaciously, he turned the argument against the theists, accusing them of undermining the values by which men do actually live in society. By their preference for the monkish virtues, and the importance they attached to devotion under the direction of priests, the theists sought to undermine the useful and agreeable values which men would otherwise recognise and create for themselves. Like Mandeville, Hume was confident that men's conduct was normally unaffected by whatever they might imagine awaited them in a future state (however much they might relish a good preacher's account of its horrors). But Hume was still bolder than Mandeville in answering Bayle's question in the affirmative: a society of atheists was morally preferable not only to one of idolaters, but also, even more so, to one of Christian theists.

Comparison with Vico draws attention to one further aspect of Hume's thought in the works under consideration here. The preceding chapter on Vico ended with the observation that his understanding of history precluded a concept of historical progress. By contrast, it might be expected that such a concept would be present, even prominent, in Hume's 'science of man'. Mandeville, after all, had attributed to man a 'perpetual desire of meliorating his condition'. A similar thought would seem to be present in the *Treatise*, when Hume refers to men's 'avidity . . . of acquiring goods and possessions'. Yet the thought, if it is such, is surprisingly muted. The historical account of the formation of justice and hence of society is not otherwise framed in terms of a desire among men to improve their condition; and neither in the *Treatise* nor in the *Natural History of Religion* is there a concept of the progress of society, against which to measure the moral or religious condition of men.[102] If a concept of 'the progress of society' is held to be a feature of Enlightenment thinking, then Hume too, it seems, was not of the Enlightenment.

Nevertheless Hume, not Vico, had reached the threshold of Enlightenment, and stood ready to open the door. This chapter's analysis of the *Treatise of Human Nature* and its subsequently published 'nobler parts' has revealed the extent to which Hume belonged in the world of Bayle, of Mandeville, of Warburton, and even of Vico – the world, in short, of the immediate pre-Enlightenment. But it has also shown that Hume, building on Epicurean foundations which he shared with Vico, had constructed a quite different account of human sociability, according to which men alone were responsible for the world in which they lived. With this as his new starting point, Hume (who, it is easy to forget, was not yet thirty when he published the *Treatise*) would quickly move on to open up two fresh lines of enquiry. One, to which he turned immediately after completing the *Treatise*, was politics, the principal subject of the first two volumes of *Essays, Moral and Political*, published in 1741–4. The other, about which Hume began to think hard later in the 1740s, was political economy, the subject of the *Political Discourses* of 1752. It was in this second line of enquiry that Hume may be seen to have adopted the principle of melioration: political economy was the means to achieve the betterment of human life on this earth.

---

[102] The absence of a progressive principle from the *Natural History of Religion* is noted by Berry, 'Rude religion', in Wood, *The Scottish Enlightenment*, p. 325.

When Hume took up political economy, and encouraged his contemporaries to engage in its discussion, he brought Enlightenment fully to Scotland. At almost exactly the same time, Antonio Genovesi was to do the same in Naples. How they introduced political economy into Scotland and Naples, what they argued and how they presented the new discipline form the subject of the next chapter of this book.

CHAPTER 7

The advent of Enlightenment: political economy in Naples and Scotland 1730–1760

CONTEXTS AND EXPECTATIONS

The preceding, extended comparison of the philosophies of Vico and Hume ended by emphasising difference. Vico had developed in successive versions of his *New Science* an account of human sociability in which men's actions manifested the guiding hand of divine providence, and from which it was impossible to infer a principle of progress. What Hume elaborated in the *Treatise of Human Nature*, by contrast, was an account of morality and society as purely human creations, the outcome of a remarkable combination of human nature and artifice. But no less important to the comparison was the identification of common ground between the two philosophers; without this, indeed, the comparison would have had little historical point. Vico and Hume, it was argued, shared a common preoccupation with the Augustinian-Epicurean account of the human condition, according to which men were weak and driven by their passions, to the extent that their pursuit of their own utility was barely compatible with the maintenance of society. Likewise common to Vico and to Hume was the conviction that the problem of unsociability could only be resolved in the course of history, in a process of socialisation. It was on these common foundations – in an important sense Epicurean foundations – that Vico and Hume built their different philosophies; and the same foundations, I now want to argue, provided the platform from which the Enlightenment was brought to Naples and Scotland in the middle of the eighteenth century. To see how this happened, we need now to turn to another field of intellectual activity, which came to the fore in both countries in the crucial early years of the Enlightenment, between 1730 and 1760. The new field was political economy. What marked the advent of Enlightenment in Naples and in Scotland was the emergence of political economy as a systematic explanation of economic behaviour and guide to policy, on the basis of more or less explicitly Epicurean assumptions about human nature.

It was in these terms that the case for Enlightenment was made in the two countries.

To grasp the contexts in which political economy developed in Naples and Scotland, however, it is necessary first to pick up the threads of the earlier chapters devoted to the economic and social condition of the two countries, and to the discussions of their predicament as 'kingdoms governed as provinces'. By the late seventeenth century, it was seen, both Naples and Scotland were on the economic periphery of Europe. Agriculture just about sustained population, which in the Neapolitan case was once again rising, to make up for the terrible losses of 1656. But there was no margin of error: in the 1690s a series of harvest failures in Scotland had resulted in famine and, in the worst-affected parts, a loss of population of 10–15 per cent. Manufacturing capacity was small, limited both by low domestic demand and by the absence of opportunities for large-scale exports. The latter weakness was in turn related to a lack of native shipping, and to the vulnerability of both countries' coasts to privateers and corsairs. If the two kingdoms were alike in economic weakness, however, there was a marked contrast in the outlooks of their ruling elites. The structure of Neapolitan society, with its rigid status divisions between the feudal, landowning nobility and the city-based lawyers and magistrates, militated against the taking of economic initiative: this was an elite with a propensity to consume, not to invest. By comparison the Scottish elite was marked by a much closer association between landowners and lawyers, who together were increasingly explicit in their commitment to the economic welfare of the kingdom. The Scottish elite, moreover, was willing to put its money behind its words, demonstrating its willingness to invest in a succession of speculative ventures, culminating in the Darien scheme.

In both countries, a recognition of the importance of the economy to the health of the nation was precipitated by political crisis. Not surprisingly, given the outlook of the elite, the response was greatest in Scotland. The kingdom's economic prospects were a major theme in the debate over its constitutional relationship to England in the years between the Darien venture and the Union of 1707. Whether the Scots should accept incorporating union was inseparable from negotiation over the extent of (and exceptions to) the free trade which was to accompany it. What divided participants in the Scottish debate, moreover, was perhaps less important than what united them. There was almost universal agreement that the future health of Scottish society depended on ending the power of the feudal baronage, and on promoting agricultural improvement and commercial activity. Such a broad-based consensus was absent from the Neapolitan debate, which was on a much smaller scale, being conducted by the circulation of manuscript memoranda, and dependent on the intellectual initiative of a few jurists and men of letters. Despite these limitations, participants in the Neapolitan debate were able to take advantage of the political uncertainty caused by the Spanish succession crisis to focus on the subordinate, provincial status of the kingdom within the greater Spanish monarchy; in particular, they drew attention to the kingdom's exclusion from the commerce over which the European powers now competed. From this discussion two convictions had formed: that the kingdom possessed the natural advantages of fertility and access to the sea; and that it was unable to benefit from them because its provincial status had deprived it of the ability to participate in maritime commerce. Even if the outcome of the crisis was simply a change of dynastic masters, the kingdom falling under Austrian Habsburg rule in 1707, these convictions indicated what an independent kingdom should seek to do in the economic sphere, and fuelled expectations that the Austrian viceregal regime would be more aware of Naples' economic interest than its Spanish predecessor had ever thought to be.

Of the two, Scotland appeared to be much better placed than Naples in the immediate aftermath of the events of 1707. The financial consequences of the Union with England were favourable, the Scots being compensated with the 'Equivalent' for assuming a share of the English national debt. In practice, the funds made available through the Equivalent were used to compensate Darien stockholders, restoring liquid funds to the Scottish economy.[1] Yet there were several grounds for uncertainty about the future. The unanticipated abolition of the Scottish Privy Council shortly after the Union deprived government in Scotland of its traditional head, and left a confusing vacuum above the level of local shire and burgh administration. More provocative, the Toleration and Patronage Acts of 1712, passed by English Tory majorities in Westminster, were held by many Scots to be in direct breach of the Treaty of Union, as undermining the authority and altering the government of the presbyterian Church of Scotland. Directly opposed to the Union and the Hanoverian succession, moreover, were the Jacobites, who continued to plot on behalf of the exiled pretender. These were behind a motion in the House of Lords to dissolve the Union in 1713; and two years later they succeeded in instigating a full-scale rising in Scotland in the name of James VIII and III. The rebellion, as historians have pointed out, was far from being the desperate throw of a backward Highland

---

[1] On the uses to which the Equivalent was put: John Stuart Shaw, *The Political History of Eighteenth-Century Scotland* (Basingstoke, 1999) ch. 1 'The price of Scotland?'

society.[2] It drew support from many parts of Scotland, and particularly from the north-east, where episcopalianism was strong; it was led by a nobleman, the earl of Mar, who had supported the Act of Union; and it reflected the integration of the Highland economy into the lowland rather than their separation. Once defeated, however, the rebellion did concentrate minds. The loyal Protestant elite learnt that the Union would not of itself resolve the nation's problems: improvement and social transformation still had to be worked for. As a variety of interests had reason to reflect, the economic consequences of the Union had been mixed, and by no means all disappointing.

Historians used to believe that the short-term consequences were limited, and that any benefits were slow to materialise. As a more detailed picture comes into focus, however, it is clear that there were both gainers and losers.[3] Among the latter were the linen industry and coastal fishing, though fishing suffered more from the sudden and uncontrollable movement of herring. But hard negotiation over several clauses in the Union treaty had resulted in effective protection for some Scottish industries, including coal and salt, while freer access to markets in the south encouraged others. Grain exports in particular appear to have doubled in the second decade of the century; and cattle exports from the south-west probably also rose. Assisted by the provision of convoys, coastal trade benefited from grain exports, as well as from the re-export of tobacco southwards from Glasgow. By 1720 grain exports from Fife had sparked a wave of riots in the coastal villages of east Fife, as unemployed linen-workers protested against higher prices.[4] More important in the longer term, structural change in relations between landowners and tenants was now continuous. Rents were increasingly paid in cash rather than kind; multiple tenancies were replaced by single ones; and longer, nineteen-year leases became common. There was no immediate transformation in agricultural productivity; but the foundations of radical change later in the century were being laid.[5]

The existence of a process of change in agriculture, alongside shorter-term opportunities, was accompanied by a renewed commitment on the part of the elite to the cause of 'improvement'. Landowners founded The Honourable the Improvers in the Knowledge of Agriculture in Scotland in 1723, and 300 members joined the society. The burghs followed not far

---

[2] Bruce Lenman, *The Jacobite Risings in Britain 1689–1746* (London, 1980).

[3] Christopher A. Whatley, *Scottish Society 1707–1830: beyond Jacobitism, towards industrialisation* (Manchester, 2000), pp. 51–61.

[4] Christopher A. Whatley, 'The Union of 1707, integration and the Scottish burghs: the case of the 1720 food riots', *Scottish Historical Review*, 78 (1999), 192–218.

[5] T. M. Devine, *The Transformation of Rural Scotland: Social Change and the Agrarian Economy 1660–1815* (Edinburgh, 1994), ch. 2 'Before improvement: rural society and economy c. 1700–1750'.

behind: after several years of pressure on behalf of the linen manufacture, the Annual Convention of the Royal Burghs secured legislation in favour of the industry in 1727, and the establishment of the Board of Trustees for Fisheries and Manufactures. The willingness of the government in London to respond to such solicitation reflected continued concerns over political and social instability in Scotland: the prime minister, Sir Robert Walpole, was ever alert to the Jacobite threat, and ready to make concessions. It was in response to the malt tax riots in 1725 that he agreed to channel revenue from the tax to the Board of Trustees.[6] But the way to both government and Parliament was smoothed by the efforts of Scots in London, and above all by the earl of Ilay, brother of the second duke of Argyll (and eventually himself third duke). Ilay's commitment to improvement went deeper than that of a politician responsive to the expectations of his native power base; with his large library and interests in natural history Ilay was a patron of cultural as well as economic development, and in due course of Enlightenment itself.[7]

These initiatives naturally intensified expectations, and their immediate fruit was meagre. There was no marked expansion in either linen manufacture or the tobacco trade until the 1740s. Agricultural change continued, but there was still an embarrassing shortage after the harvest of 1740, albeit one whose effects were far less harmful than those of the 1690s. (A better internal market as well as orderly poor relief averted disaster, and ensured that the failure was without longer-term consequences.)[8] The uncertainty of this period was reflected in the writings of a number of commentators. Consciously picking up the threads of the union debate in which he had himself been a participant, Sir John Clerk of Penicuik drew up a manuscript of 'Observations on the present circumstances of Scotland' in 1730. Clerk expressed no regret for the loss of Scotland's Parliament, but he did lament a decline in patriotism and virtue – qualities he illustrated by quotations from Andrew Fletcher's speeches. Clerk was particularly exercised by the volume of luxury imports, most perniciously of French wine and brandy, but also of cloths, laces, silks, soap, and paper. Since Scottish manufactures for export were not sufficient to compensate, the balance of trade was in deficit, resulting in a shortage of specie. Clerk divided the blame for this

---

[6] Whatley, *Scottish Society 1707–1830*, pp. 60–1.

[7] R. L. Emerson, 'Catalogus Librorum A.C.D.A., or, the library of Archibald Campbell, third duke of Argyll', in R. L. Emerson and others, *The Culture of the Book in the Scottish Enlightenment* (Toronto, 2000), pp. 13–39; and 'The scientific interests of Archibald Campbell, 1st Earl of Ilay and 3rd Duke of Argyll 1682–1761', *Annals of Science*, 59 (2002), 21–56.

[8] T. C. Smout, 'Where had the Scottish economy got to by the third quarter of the eighteenth century?', in Istvan Hont and Michael Ignatieff (eds.), *Wealth and Virtue: The Shaping of Political Economy in the Scottish Enlightenment* (Cambridge, 1983) p. 49.

sorry situation between merchants and manufacturers. The former dishonestly evaded duties designed to deter luxury imports; the latter did nothing to encourage a spirit of industry among the people.[9]

A more colourful, if deeply eccentric commentator was Sir Alexander Murray of Stanhope. Murray was convinced that the people of Scotland were being kept in ignorance of their true misery 'by the great powers, and various Machiavellian, Gabriel Naudlean, and Padre Paolo's oligarchick maxims and artifices of the leaders of our factions in Scotland'.[10] His particular *bête noire* was the heritable jurisdictions still maintained by the aristocracy, which he denounced in extravagant, interminable sentences. It is unlikely that Murray's tirades held the attention of many readers for long, or lent plausibility to his principal contention, that Scotland's mineral resources were the key to its future.[11] But his critique of the aristocracy was by no means exceptional; the point, which can be traced back to Fletcher and Seton, was also made by the far soberer Patrick Lindsay, an Edinburgh merchant. Lindsay's *The Interest of Scotland Considered* (1733) was chiefly a plea for the development of the linen industry as Scotland's staple manufacture. By concentrating on this one manufacture, and realising its export potential, Scotland would earn the means to pay for its imports. Lindsay recognised the stimulating effects of luxury imports on retail as well as wholesale trade:

are not the purcelain of China and Japan, and the curious workmanship brought from thence, the coffee of Turkey, spices of Arabia, the luscious sugar of the American islands, high-pric'd wines, and even the insipid tea of China, now universally used? All so many subjects of commerce that serve to support numbers of merchants, and greater numbers of retailing shop-keepers, who deal in these commodities.[12]

But luxury was damaging when it spread too far down the social scale. It was essential to keep the lower classes to labour, encouraging their industry, and

---

[9] Sir John Clerk of Penicuik, 'Observations on the present circumstances of Scotland, 1730', ed. T. C. Smout, *Scottish History Society*, Fourth Series 2, *Miscellany X* (1965), pp. 175–212, esp. pp. 188–9, 198–200, 206–8. For comment, Gentaro Seki, 'Policy debate on economic development in Scotland: the 1720s to the 1730s', in T. Sakamoto and H. Tanaka (eds.), *The Rise of Political Economy in the Scottish Enlightenment* (London, 2003), pp. 23–6.

[10] Sir Alexander Murray of Stanhope, Bart., *The True Interest of Great Britain, Ireland and our Plantations* (London, printed for the author, 1740), 'An Apology to the Reader, Jan. 1ˢᵗ 1740/41', p. 7.

[11] On the aristocracy, ibid., p. vi: 'those bastard lions, leopards, wolves in sheep's clothing, bellers of the cat, dragons of Wantley, destroyers of whole provinces, and eaters-up of the people;' – the semicolon a mere drawing of breath before he continued his denunciation (and the sentence) for many more lines. On minerals, paper vi; and *An Abstract of an Essay on the Improvement of Husbandry and Working of Mines, in a Letter to the Right Honourable Sir Robert Walpole* (London [1733]).

[12] [Patrick Lindsay], *The Interest of Scotland Considered, with regard to its Police in imploying the Poor, its Agriculture, its Trade, its Manufactures, and Fisheries* (Edinburgh, 1733), p. 64. The work was dedicated to the earl of Ilay. See also Seki, 'Policy debate', pp. 30–3.

forcibly retraining beggars and thieves to become good weavers.[13] Unlike Clerk, who kept his grumbles to himself, Lindsay deliberately published his work, appealing to his readers to take up the discussion.[14] His refusal simply to condemn luxury on moral grounds brought a degree of sophistication to Scottish economic debate, but his argument was still dependent on the suppositions of a clear separation of ranks, and the long-run necessity of a favourable balance of trade.

In Naples, meanwhile, the Austrian viceroyalty did respond to the arguments of the economic reformers with at least two institutional initiatives. In 1710 the viceroy Grimani established a *Giunta di Commercio*, whose purpose was subsequently defined in revealing terms in a memorandum of 1714:

> to promote the trade of this kingdom, which is the best adapted to trade of all the provinces of Italy, being itself so fertile a province that over and above what it needs for its own purposes, it abounds in many commodities needed by the other nations of Europe, and is inhabited by the most industrious of peoples, qualified in every profession.[15]

The memorandum acknowledged, however, that the fruits of so fertile a territory and industrious a people would not be enjoyed until the contempt in which commerce was held by the nobility had been overcome. Another initiative was taken under the viceroyalty of Cardinal Althann, with the establishment of the Banco di San Carlo in 1725. The bank was intended to provide the crown with an instrument to buy back alienated fiscal rights, and to provide capital for promising enterprises. But it quickly ran into fierce opposition from the church and the nobility, who now held the fiscal rights; and despite the support of senior *togati*, lawyers were reluctant to work for the bank for fear of losing their noble clients. Althann himself was distracted by the continuing furore over the publication of Giannone's *Storia Civile* in 1723, and sided with the church (although ironically Giannone himself was against the scheme). His successor as viceroy, Harrach, eventually conceded defeat in 1732, and the bank closed.[16]

Two years later, the Austrians were expelled. Taking advantage of the Polish succession crisis, Carlo Borbone, son of Philip V of Spain by his second wife, Elizabeth Farnese, marched from Tuscany to Naples and claimed the kingdom, along with the kingdom of Sicily. Quite unexpectedly, the kingdom of Naples had regained its independence. Carlo Borbone, who

---

[13] Ibid., pp. 1–31.   [14] Ibid., 'The preface', pp. xxxiv–xxxv.

[15] Quoted by Giuseppe Ricuperati, 'Napoli e i Vicerè austriaci 1707–1734', in Aa. Vv., *Storia di Napoli*, Vol. vii (Cava dei Tirreni, 1972), pp. 392–4 (my translation of the quoted passage).

[16] Ricuperati, 'Napoli e i Vicerè austriaci', pp. 405–12, 428–9.

became Carlo VII of the Sicilies, brought with him a coterie of ministers assembled by Elizabeth Farnese. The three most important were the duke of Santesteban, the king's tutor and maggiordomo of the court, Joachim de Montealegre, marquis of Salas, the principal secretary of state, and Bernardo Tanucci, an able Tuscan administrator of rigorist inclinations, who became second secretary of state, and served the monarchy until 1776. As the leader of a group of francophile Spanish administrators committed to fiscal and economic reform, Montealegre allied himself with leading reformers among the *togati*, including Francesco Ventura and Pietro Contegna, thereby establishing continuity with the policies which had produced the Banco di San Carlo. Brushing aside an effort by the feudal nobility to recover political power, the new administration initiated a range of reforming measures in the second half of the 1730s. These included centralisation of the tax administration and the proposal of a fiscal census; reform of the law courts, and the appointment of a commission to codify the laws of the kingdom (projects particularly associated with Tanucci); and restrictions on clerical immunity, fiscal and legal. At least as important, however, was the replacement of the viceregal *Giunta di Commercio* with a new *Supremo Magistrato di Commercio*.[17]

The foundations of this new magistracy were laid and its purpose set forth in two conferences held by the secretary of state, Montealegre, in June and July 1739. The previous neglect of the commerce of the two kingdoms was unsurprising, Montealegre explained, given that for two centuries they had been ruled in the absence of their kings, by viceroys. But now that their sovereign resided in the kingdoms, there was every reason to believe that their advantageous situation and natural fertility would enable them to prosper. Specifically, the Supreme Magistracy would be expected to encourage silk manufacture, to reform the customs, and to provide justice for merchants by establishing and supervising maritime consuls in the main ports.[18] Developing themes incipient in the memorandum on the purpose of the previous *Giunta di Commercio*, Montealegre's discourse on the new Supreme Magistracy enshrined the two principles which would thereafter

[17] Elvira Chiosi, 'Il regno dal 1734 al 1799', in G. Galasso and R. Romeo (eds.), *Storia del Mezzogiorno*. Vol. VI, tomo ii: *Il Regno dagli Angioini ai Borboni* (Naples, 1986), pp. 373–96. But in their very different ways, the most evocative accounts are those of Harold Acton, *The Bourbons of Naples 1734–1825* (London 1956, repr. 1974), pp. 11–47 (on the new court and its tastes); and Franco Venturi, *Settecento riformatore*. Vol. I, *Da Muratori a Beccaria 1730–1764* (Turin, 1969), 1. 'Gli anni trenta del settecento' (on the great expectations of reform).

[18] Archivio di Stato di Napoli (hereafter ASN), Tribunali Antichi, fasc. 1728: *Supremo Magistrato del Commercio*, 'Registro delle deliberazioni prese nelle conferenze, ordinate da S[ua] M[ajesta] tenersi nella Secreteria di Stato, Guerra e Marina, circa il commercio, a Di 10 Giugno 1739', ff. 3–12; 'A Di 8 Luglio 1739', ff. 43–7. See also Chiosi, 'Il regno dal 1734 al 1799', pp. 386, 390–3.

be accepted as the axiomatic premises of the political economy of Naples. First, that this was a land whose natural fertility was such that it ought to be able to meet the food needs of all its inhabitants, as well as providing materials for manufactures and, once manufactured, products for export. Second, that independence, by ending the kingdom's former 'provincial' dependence, had established the necessary conditions for taking advantage of these natural resources, to the benefit of both the inhabitants and the crown. Not before the last quarter of the century did these propositions begin to wear thin, although they were still to be heard even then. But throughout the 1740s and 1750s they were everywhere repeated, with no trace of scepticism, let alone irony.

One of the first to articulate a programme of reform inspired by these premises was a young lawyer, Giovanni Pallante, in a manuscript 'Memoria per la riforma del Regno' (1735–7). Hailing 'the passage from province to independent realm', Pallante compared it to the end of Spanish rule in Holland: the difference was that the kingdom of Naples was worth fifty Hollands in terms of its situation, resources, and people. He surveyed the damage which the Spanish viceroyalty had done to Naples. The military strength of the kingdom had been run down; the crown had lost control of taxation; the barons had been left free to oppress the rural communities, despite the proliferation of laws and lawyers; the city of Naples had been privileged at the expense of the provinces, which became ever more subservient to it. But now that there was an independent monarchy, its subjects could expect 'increase, abundance and commerce'. Pallante's remedial programme was fourfold, covering the administration of justice, the creation of a national army with compulsory military service, and a thorough reform of the fiscal system, as well as measures to ensure 'security and protection' for commerce. Shipping should be provided with ports and refuges; inland transport with roads and bridges, while baronial monopolies which disrupted the passage of goods should be abolished. The production of grain should be encouraged by permitting its export; and domestic manufactures should be promoted at the expense of imports by royal example and by the instituting of trading companies. The proposals offered a timely conspectus of the practical needs of the kingdom, without aspiring to connected economic analysis. The premise of natural fertility was taken to imply that increase and abundance would follow directly from better and safer transport and the removal of baronial obstructions to commerce, and this was combined with the common assumption that it was better to export manufactured goods than raw materials. Nevertheless, Pallante's memorial was indicative of the relative importance which a new generation attached to economic reform, alongside the jurists' more traditional concerns with the immunities of the church and the feudal prerogatives of the nobility.[19]

A few years later a more experienced and sophisticated commentator entered the debate. Paolo Mattia Doria's manuscript 'Del commercio del regno di Napoli', dated April 1740, was specifically addressed to Francesco Ventura, as president of the *Magistrato di Commercio*, although it almost certainly had a wider circulation in the course of time. Referring back on several occasions to both the *Vita Civile* and the *Massime del governo spagnolo*, Doria made it clear that his approach to commerce was based on his earlier work. He began with a definition of commerce as 'mutuo soccorso', mutual assistance: the exchange of goods between those who possess and those who want them is what sustains civil society. As such commerce requires both liberty and security of contracts, which in turn depend on trust (*fede*) and justice. To ensure that trust exists, there must be a magistracy responsible for education, discipline, and customs as well as for justice, along the lines he had discussed in the *Vita Civile*.[20]

Doria unhesitatingly endorsed the assumption of the kingdom's natural fertility. It was like 'a shop full of all the goods necessary for life', to whose ports all the nations of the world might be drawn to purchase its produce.[21] Its objectives in commerce, he thought, should be three. First, agriculture should encouraged to produce in abundance. Second, good arts and man-ufactures should be introduced in order not only to free the inhabitants from dependence on foreign goods, but to supply the foreigners themselves. Finally the sale of the kingdom's produce should be promoted, internally and externally. Given these objectives, Doria believed it clear that for the kingdom of Naples internal commerce should take preference over exter-nal.[22] For reasons he would elaborate in other writings of this time, Doria was strongly opposed to the sort of commerce practised by those he called *cabalisti*, whose priority was the acquisition of specie. Naples had no need

---

[19] Giovanni Pallante, *Memoria per la riforma del regno* (1735–7), ed. Imma Ascione (Naples, 1996). An earlier edition was published in 1885, using Pallante's private, disillusioned title 'Lo Stanfone'. The introduction by Ascione examines Pallante's motives in writing the memorial, which was apparently intended for the attention of Tanucci. By the time it was finished, however, Montealegre was in charge of economic policy, and the memorial was never circulated. See pp. 103–9 for the remarks about the passage from provincial status and the comparison with Holland; p. 129 for the expectation of 'l'accrescrimento, l'abbondanza e' l commercio'; and part ii, 'Della sicurezza e protezione', pp. 171–95, for the discussion of commerce and manufactures.

[20] Paolo Mattia Doria, 'Del commercio del regno di Napoli . . . Lettera del Signor D. Paolo Mattia Doria diretta al Signor D. Francesco Ventura, degnissimo Presidente del Magistrato di Commercio. Napoli. 2 Aprile dell' anno 1740', in Enrico Vidal (ed.), *Il pensiero civile di Paolo Mattia Doria negli scritti inediti. Con il testo del manoscritto 'Del commercio del regno di Napoli'* (Milan, 1953), pp. 161–206; introductory remarks, pp. 161–4.

[21] Doria, 'Del commercio del regno', p. 165.   [22] Ibid., pp. 165–6.

of such an 'ideal' commerce, since it could always acquire money by the export of its produce. Even were the kingdom to lose all its money, and be reduced to barter, it would soon return as foreigners exchanged money for goods.[23] Standing in the way of these objectives, however, were a multitude of obstacles. One was the power of the barons, and the oppression of the 'popolo minuto' who had the misfortune to be their vassals. The scale of the barons' abuses and the violence with which they enforced them Doria blamed on the concessions which the Spaniards had made to the nobility when they ruled the kingdom as a province.[24] A second obstacle was the excessive population of the city of Naples. It was the most important cause of the disorders to which the kingdom was prone, while the monopolies granted to ensure its provisioning resulted in severe distortion of the grain trade. There were too many tradesmen, medical practitioners, and 'dottori' (jurists) in Naples. The city's population should be reduced by encouraging the relocation of manufactures in the provinces, raising the status of the provincial law courts, creating new educational institutions in the other cities of the kingdom, and raising the standard of the doctorate.[25] Finally Doria recommended breaking the stranglehold of Neapolitan merchants on foreign trade by designating three ports in which it could be carried on (Brindisi, Taranto, and Naples), and by creating a new company to conduct it, organised along the 'republican' lines of the Casa di San Giorgio in Doria's native Genoa.[26]

The reasons for Doria's hostility to extensive Neapolitan participation in foreign trade emerge much more clearly from two other manuscript tracts of this period, 'Il politico all moda' ('The fashionable politician'), and 'Il commercio mercantile', both dated 1739–40.[27] The tone of these two works is noticeably more aggressive than in the tract on the commerce of the kingdom; they are not known to have been addressed to anyone in particular. Doria was convinced that there was now an alliance between the *cabalisti* who pursued an 'ideal' commerce devoted to the acquisition of specie, and princes who were bent on achieving domination in Europe without having to go to war. The distinction between real and ideal

---

[23] Ibid., pp. 166–8.   [24] Ibid., pp. 173–5.   [25] Ibid., pp. 168–71, 186–90.

[26] Ibid., pp. 190–205. The force of Doria's analysis of the ills of the kingdom is best conveyed by Venturi, *Settecento riformatore. Da Muratori a Beccaria*, pp. 42–5.

[27] Paolo Mattia Doria, 'Il politico alla moda di mente adeguata e prattica' (1739–40), edited by Vittorio Conti, and printed as an appendix to *Paolo Mattia Doria. Dalla repubblica dei togati alla repubblica dei notabili* (Florence, 1978), pp. 130–259; and 'Il commercio mercantile. Ragionamento nel quale si dá l'idea dell'origine e dell'essenza del commercio e si dimostrano gli utili e li danni che quello ha cagionato nel mondo', printed in *Manoscritti Napoletani di Paolo Mattia Doria*, vol. IV, ed. Pasquale di Fabrizio (Galatina, 1981), pp. 277–410.

commerce was one which Doria had drawn in the third edition of the *Vita Civile*, published in 1729, where he traced the rise of ideal commerce to the discovery of the Indies.[28] What was new was the 'furioso amor di commercio' now being displayed by the leading powers of Europe. Doria was particularly alarmed by the policy of Cardinal Fleury, the first minister of Louis XV, accusing him of renewing Louis XIV's ambition to make France a universal monarchy by commerce alone.[29]

Examination of the present state and prospects of other European powers did not allay his fears. The English enjoyed a liberty which frequently degenerated into licence, and did not possess the virtue required to counter France.[30] Italy, meanwhile, was especially vulnerable to such aggression. The Austrians had already plundered it for themselves. Doria did observe that the king of Sardinia (the duke of Savoy) might aspire to make the whole of Italy his kingdom, but he clearly did not expect it to happen.[31] Nowhere could he identify a secure bulwark against the predatory ambitions of princes and their merchant allies. The jurists Grotius, Pufendorf, and Doria himself (in the *Vita Civile*) might have agreed that all peoples were free under the laws of nature; but to the rulers and 'mercadanti' of Europe they were just sheep to be traded.[32] The one empire which had showed itself superior to such ambition was that of China, where the mandarins ensured that the emperor ruled wisely, without seeking to dominate his neighbours. But the distortions of the Jesuits in their reports from China had prevented this model from being properly understood, and there was no counterpart to China in Europe.[33]

It is not easy to categorise Doria's economic thinking. He had a clear view of the importance of economic activity to the future of the kingdom. Its abundant resources for both agriculture and manufactures would require encouragement and security if the kingdom was to flourish and sustain its new-found independence; otherwise it would be at the mercy of predatory commercial powers, France above all. Doria also had a clear order of priorities: agriculture came first, followed by manufactures which used the raw materials of the kingdom; the exchange of agricultural and manufactured products then needed to be encouraged by provision of a secure, unobstructed internal market. The kingdom might also export both produce and manufactures, and receive in return the money it needed for

---

[28] Paolo Mattia Doria, *La Vita Civile*, third impression (Naples, 1729), parte II, Cap. III, part. x 'Nella quale si ragiona del commercio in genere, e poi del presente usato in Europa', pp. 334–50.

[29] Doria, 'Il politico alla moda', pp. 148–70; 'Il commercio mercantile', p. 304.

[30] Doria, 'Il politico alla moda', pp. 179–82.

[31] Ibid., pp. 171–8, 187–99.   [32] Ibid., pp. 247, 254.   [33] Ibid., pp. 231–40.

its internal commerce; but it should deter expensive imports. Since Doria referred to no earlier writers on the subject besides himself, identification of the sources of his thinking is difficult. It was suggested earlier that his preference for self-sufficiency echoed the position of Fénelon and his circle of critics of the French monarchy's aggrandising ambitions at the very beginning of the century. As we shall see, Doria was not mistaken in his belief that French economic thinking under Fleury had become more aggressive: he was evidently more aware of contemporary developments in economic thought than he admitted. Nevertheless, he clearly preferred to treat the kingdom of Naples as a case apart.[34]

If Doria attached no names to the economic doctrines he discussed, he left no doubt about the identity of the underlying philosophy of the *cabalisti* to whom he was so opposed. Repeatedly in 'Il politico alla moda' and 'Il commercio mercantile' he associated these with the Epicureans and sceptics who discounted any idea of virtue in favour of 'the poisonous seed of *amor proprio*'.[35] Epicureanism and scepticism had been the source of the politics of Machiavelli, Hobbes, and the Jesuits, who in turn were the inspiration of Richelieu, Louis XIV, and Fleury. The rise of commerce, these statesmen had realised, had made luxury and effeminacy better instruments with which to undermine the morals of peoples than armies themselves.[36] In Doria's mind, ideal commerce and Epicureanism were in turn closely linked to the philosophy of Locke and the natural philosophy of Newton, and thence to deism and even to Spinozism. Against all such 'pernicious philosophy of the senses' Doria appealed to the authority of Plato. Only in his philosophy were to be found the true metaphysical foundations of virtue, religion, and magistracy.[37]

---

[34] The existing literature on Doria's economic writing has little to say on the subject of his sources. Studies which have given particular attention to his economic thought are those by Salvatore Rotta, 'Paolo Mattia Doria. Nota Introduttiva', in *Dal Muratori al Cesarotti*. v: *Politici ed economisti del primo Settecento*, in R. Ajello and others (Milan and Naples, 1978), pp. 837–72; and 'Paolo Mattia Doria rivisitato', in Giovanni Papuli and others, *Paolo Mattia Doria fra rinnovamento e tradizione* (Galatina, 1985), pp. 389–431; and by Raffaele Ajello, 'La critica del regime in Doria, Intieri e Broggia', in his, *Arcana Juris* (Naples, 1976), pp. 389–427, and 'Diritto ed economia in Paolo Mattia Doria', in *Doria fra rinnovamento e tradizione*, pp. 93–126. Most recently Maria Luisa Pesante has discussed Doria against the background of an analysis of Renaissance republican thinking on economic issues, without explaining how the 200-year interval between them may have been bridged: 'Il commercio nella repubblica', *Quaderni storici*, 105 (2000), 655–95. Vincenzo Ferrone is (as far as I can see) the one scholar to have mentioned (even if only in passing) Doria's affinity with Fénelon's 'Christian agrarianism': Ferrone, *Scienza natura religione. Mondo Newtoniano e cultura italiana nel primo Settecento* (Naples, 1982), p. 599. Cf. ch. 4 above, pp. 195–8.
[35] Doria, 'Il politico alla moda', pp. 134–8; 'Il commercio mercantile', p. 314.
[36] Doria, 'Il politico alla moda', pp. 140–6.
[37] Doria, 'Il commercio mercantile', pp. 299–302, 407–10.

In the *Vita Civile*, it was argued,[38] Doria had sought to steer a path between Epicureanism and Stoicism, adapting rather than wholly repudiating the Machiavellian tradition of political analysis. In 1724 and 1732–3, however, he had published explicit attacks on the philosophies of Descartes and Locke, in which he had vehemently denounced Epicureanism.[39] It was at the same time that Vico had focused on the threat posed by Epicureanism, and set himself to counter it in the *New Science*. Vico also acknowledged Doria in his *Autobiography* as one of the few contemporaries with whom he felt an intellectual affinity.[40] Later, in the 1730s, the two were members of the Accademia degli Oziosi, founded in 1733 as a response to the modernising Accademia delle Scienze.[41] But it is an exaggeration to portray Vico and Doria as forming a common ideological front against the Epicurean menace. As we have seen, Vico's philosophy was far from a complete rejection of Epicureanism: he acknowledged and built on the power of the Epicurean account of human nature as grounded in utility even as he sought to render it compatible with the operation of divine providence. Vico, moreover, was never an active member of the Accademia degli Oziosi. By contrast, the stridency of Doria's late works was a telling reflection of his philosophical isolation. By the time of his death in 1746, at the age of seventy-nine, he had experienced the double disappointment of seeing his best hopes dashed, and his worst fears vindicated.

Doria's hope that Ventura would be able to make the *Supremo Magistrato di Commercio* a model of virtuous magistracy had been disappointed even before the ink was dry on his memorandum on the commerce of the kingdom. The detailed minutes of its early proceedings tell a tale of almost immediate frustration. Instituted in the summer of 1739, its first meeting was convened by Ventura as its president on 5 November. Provision had been made for a membership consisting of nobles (though their regular attendance was not counted on), five *togati* (including Pietro Contegna as well as Ventura) and three merchants, who were not to vote on matters of law.[42] It was to meet twice a week, in the early evening. Two items were discussed at the first meeting: the establishment of *consolati di mare* in the principal cities of the kingdom, and the black dye used in silk manufacture,

---

[38] See ch. 4 above pp. 197–8.

[39] Paolo Mattia Doria, *Discorsi critici filosofi intorno alla filosofia degli antichi e dei moderni, ed in particolare alla filosofia di Renato Des Cartes con un progetto di metafisica* (1724); *Difesa della metafisica degli antichi contro il Signor Giovanni Locke ed alcuni altri moderni filosofi* (1732–33).

[40] Vico, *Vita*, in *Opere*, I, p. 29; *The Autobiography of Giambattista Vico*, transl. M. H. Fisch and T. G. Bergin (Ithaca, 1944), p. 138.

[41] Ferrone, *Scienza natura religione*, pp. 525–45: 'La controrivoluzione scientifica di Paolo Mattia Doria'.

[42] ASN, Tribunali antichi 1728 f. 45v, on its composition.

a problem apparently inherited from the *Giunta di Commercio*. The meeting also considered a memorial on the commerce of the kingdom which had been deposited in the archives of the city.[43] Thereafter the Magistracy met regularly throughout November and into December. The question of the consulates was its major preoccupation, and it quickly became clear that their establishment would not be straightforward, since they would interfere with existing baronial jurisdictions.[44] It was decided to make a start in Naples itself – only for a new difficulty to be raised: merchant consuls, it was argued, would not have a proper knowledge of the law they were to administer.[45] By the end of November the consulate in Naples had been approved, but the Magistracy was no nearer to a resolution of the obstacles to its institution elsewhere. Now yet another dispute halted proceedings altogether: two noble members, the dukes of Corigliano and Fragnito, quarrelled over precedence, and the three *togati* present (including Contegna) insisted that since precedence was a matter of law, they alone could resolve the issue. When this was denied by the president, they threatened to resign.[46] The fractious magistrates were summoned to a conference by Montealegre two days later, rebuked in the name of the king, and urged to concentrate on the business of commerce.[47] Returning to work, they showed a little more urgency over the establishment of the consulates, and considered a miscellany of other items and requests.[48] But by the middle of December it was clear that the problems of competing jurisdictions and legal competence would not be resolved quickly; as for formulating a more general economic policy, especially in relation to silk manufacture, there was nothing to show at all.[49] Far from being the virtuous mandarinate of Doria's ideal, the *Supremo Magistrato do Commercio* had conducted itself no differently from similar magistracies since the sixteenth century, unable to rise above questions of jurisdiction and precedence. Its difficulties were not unique. The commission set up at the same time to codify the laws

---

[43] ASN, Tribunali antichi 1728 (new foliation) ff. 1–2: 'Relazione succinta di quanto e stato agitato, deliberato, ed oprato nella prima sessione del supremo magistrato del commercio tenuta il Di 5 Novembre 1739'. The meetings, on Mondays and Thursdays, were to begin at 23 hours and last until 2 at night in winter; provision was made to begin earlier in summer if convenient. These were 'Italian hours', according to which the hours of the day were calculated to begin at or just before sunset. See Roberto Colzi, 'Che ora era? Raffronto tra le ore all'italiana e alla francese a Roma', *Studi Romani*, 43 (1995), 93–102. The memorial on the commerce at the kingdom discussed at this first meeting has not been identified.

[44] ASN, Tribunali antichi 1728, ff. 41–2: 9 Nov. 1739. (Hereafter the foliation becomes regressive.)

[45] Ibid., ff. 39–40, 37–8: 13, 16 Nov. 1739.   [46] Ibid., ff. 31–2: 23 Nov. 1739.

[47] Ibid., ff. 25–30: 'Conferenza coll'intervento del Magistrato supremo di commercio, a Di 25 9bre 1739'.

[48] Ibid., ff. 23, 21–2, 17–18, 19–20: 26 Nov., 1, 3, 7 Dec. 1739.

[49] Ibid., ff. 15–16, 13–14: 10, 14 Dec. 1739.

of the kingdom was also racked by disputes over precedence.[50] But the emasculation of such a key instrument of reform was a clear indication that independence alone would solve little.

Nor did the frustration of Montealegre and the economic reformers in the administration end there. The weakness of the Neapolitan position in relation to the maritime powers was brutally exposed by the appearance of a British fleet in the Bay of Naples in 1742, forcing the kingdom to remain neutral in the war between Britain and Spain. By 1744 Montealegre had been obliged to withdraw key initiatives, including the readmission of the Jews and the attempt to limit feudal jurisdictions. Others which survived, like the Magistracy for Commerce and the Codification Commission, had lost their impetus. The king's personal position had been strengthened by victory over the Austrians at Velletri in the same year, and in 1746 he dispensed with Montealegre, to rely instead on Tanucci, whose priorities were anti-curial rather than economic.[51]

But by then the failure of the *Supremo Magistrato di Commercio* was not the worst news which Paolo Mattia Doria could have received.

THE IMPORTANCE OF JEAN-FRANÇOIS MELON

Over the autumn and winter of 1738 to 1739, the correspondence of two leading figures in Neapolitan intellectual life, both of them identified with the reformers, had returned repeatedly to a recent book by a French author on the subject of commerce. The correspondents were Bartolomeo Intieri and Celestino Galiani. A Tuscan by origin, Intieri had settled in Naples as a young man, prospering as an administrator of the estates of several of the largest landowning families. Galiani had returned to Naples in 1731 after thirty years in Rome in order to take up appointments as bishop of Taranto and, more important, Cappellano Maggiore. As Cappellano Maggiore, Galiani had responsibility for the direction of the university of Naples. The friendship between Intieri and Galiani was an old one, and in the intervals when Galiani had to return to Rome on diplomatic missions, Intieri wrote to keep him informed of developments in the kingdom. The book about which Intieri now wrote so enthusiastically – he called it a 'golden book', which could never be sufficiently praised – was the *Essai politique sur le commerce* by Jean-François Melon, first published

---

[50] Raffaele Ajello, 'Legislazione e crisi del diritto commune nel Regno di Napoli. Il tentativo di codificazione Carlino', in E. Sestan (ed.), *Studi e ricerche sul Settecento* (Naples, 1968), pp. 220–1.

[51] See Chiosi, 'Il regno dal 1734 al 1799', pp. 397–404 for details.

in 1734, and reissued in a second edition with several additional chapters in 1736.[52]

Two features of this book particularly excited Intieri. The first was its frank recognition that in a naturally fertile, agricultural territory (such as Intieri believed the kingdom to be), abundance was an even greater danger than famine. For abundance depressed prices and reduced the incentive to the agricultural producer. Melon, Intieri noted, had identified the obvious remedy: the removal of obstacles to the export of grain.[53] The second cause for excitement was the simple fact that this was a published book on the subject of commerce. Intieri's point was that such a thing was unknown in Naples. With the exception of Doria's *Vita Civile*, which included a brief general discussion of commerce, no work devoted to the subject had been published in Naples. The increasing number of memoranda devoted to the economic prospects of the kingdom were all written for circulation in manuscript, for the eyes of ministers and a few others directly interested in the topic. The economy was simply not regarded as a legitimate subject for public discussion. It was precisely this lack of publicity, Intieri believed, which made it so easy for ministers to discount the subject's importance. Only by the printing and reprinting of 'treatises, dissertations, reflections, essays, considerations and similar titles on the elements of commerce', he told Galiani, would it be made impossible to ignore economic affairs any longer. The publicity surrounding Melon's book, which had prompted replies from Voltaire, Dutot, and others, was just what they needed to generate in Naples itself.[54]

As we have seen, Galiani and Intieri were already associated with an intellectual standpoint on the side of the *novatores*, the 'moderns'.[55] Shortly after returning to Naples, Celestino Galiani had taken the initiative in founding the Accademia delle Scienze in 1732; and Intieri was from the first one of its most committed members.[56] But their collaboration went back further than that: in the 1720s they had joined others in Florence and Rome in promoting the new six-volume Florentine edition of Gassendi's *Opera Omnia* (1727). The edition had carried an introduction which set out

[52] The letters of Intieri to Galiani are in the collections of the Società Napoletana per la Storia Patria (hereafter SNSP): collocazione XXXI.A.7: 'Galiani, Celestino: Corrispondenza Vol. 7'. For Intieri's praise of Melon's book: ff. 19 (letter of 29 Nov. 1738), 40 (letter of 14 April 1739).

[53] SNSP XXXI.A.7, ff. 27–8, 29–30, 31–4: letters of 13, 25, 31 Jan. 1739.

[54] SNSP XXXI.A.7, ff. 13–15, 36–7: letters of 11 Nov. 1738, 7 Feb. 1739.

[55] Above, chapter 5, pp. 204, 206; and Ferrone, *Scienza natura religione*, pp. 486–525 (on the Accademia delle Scienze), 546–83 (on their interest in economic reform, esp. 556–60 on their enthusiasm for Melon).

[56] His letter to Galiani of 11 Nov. 1738 mentions several instruments acquired for the academy: SNSP XXXI.A.7 ff. 14–15.

the case for a new experimental eclecticism in method, and for re-evaluating Epicurean morals at the expense of Stoicism.[57] There is no suggestion that this interest in Epicureanism extended to religious heterodoxy. Galiani had read Bayle, as he had read all the major philosophers of his day, but his manuscript treatise 'Della scienza morale' was an attempt to blend Epicurean ideas of man with a natural theology. He clearly cast himself as a modernising Catholic.[58] Intieri was a layman, and after his death was accused of free thinking, but there is no suggestion that an attack on the faith was high among his priorities.[59] Nevertheless, the association of the two men with the Epicurean philosophy was calculated to put them at odds with Vico, and even more so with Doria. If Doria knew of Intieri's enthusiastic discovery of Melon's book on commerce in 1738–9, he would have had good reason to be alarmed.

Jean-François Melon has been underestimated by historians.[60] A native of Bordeaux and a member of its academy, Melon moved in the same intellectual circles as Montesquieu; his first work, *Mahmoud le Gasnévide* (1729) was an imitation of the *Persian Letters*. He had been secretary to the *Compagnie des Indes*, the principal vehicle of John Law's ambitious but disastrous financial speculations on behalf of the Regency. The *Essai politique sur le commerce* was a defence of Law's financial strategy, and in particular of the policy of devaluation. But Melon did not confine the book to these issues, and presented the *Essai politique* as a general account of a commercial economy, and of the prospects for national economic competition. The analytical ambition of the work was evident in its opening with a model of four distinct islands, each specialising in one commodity; and it was reinforced in the second edition with extra chapters on political arithmetic and political 'systems'. By no means simply another piece of economic writing devoted to a specific issue, the *Essai politique sur le commerce* was, in ambition and in effect, a treatise of political economy.

---

[57] Ferrone, *Scienza natura religione*, pp. 155–64.
[58] See above, chapter 5, pp. 204–6; also Ferrone, *Scienza natura religione*, pp. 420–42.
[59] The charge of free-thinking on religion was levelled by his former protégé Carl-Antonio Broggia in a letter of 1765: see below, p. 360.
[60] His neglect might be explained by his falling midway between the agrarian critics of Louis XIV, studied by Rothkrug, *Opposition to Louis XIV*, and the physiocrats, the only French exponents of political economy in the period to have received extensive attention from scholars. Melon is discussed by Catherine Larrère, *L'invention de l'économie au XVIIIe siècle. Du droit naturel à la physiocratie* (Paris, 1992), pp. 95–134, but as an exemplar of a mercantilism whose principal exponent is taken to be Forbonnois. However, see now Istvan Hont, *Jealousy of Trade: International Competition and the Nation State in Historical Perspective* (Cambridge, Mass., 2005), whose introduction makes a powerful case for the importance of Melon's text.

In setting out his model of four islands, the first two of which were identified respectively with the production of grain and of wool, Melon's first concern was to explore their capacity for growth at the others' expense. The issue was national competitiveness, with the island of grain implicitly representing France and that of wool England.[61] Melon argued that since grain was a product needed by all, the island specialising in its production had a crucial advantage. The other islands would be dependent on it for their subsistence, while it had the possibility of using any surplus production to develop its own manufactures. This advantage would translate into a higher population (the second objective of the legislator, after the production of grain), and would also enable it to acquire a larger proportion of the money available to facilitate commerce (the third objective of the legislator).[62] Melon's point was that commerce was a better instrument of national aggrandisement than war and conquest. In subsequent chapters he reassessed policies traditionally associated with commercial rivalry, including colonies, slavery, and exclusive companies such as the East India Companies. In each case his criterion was strictly that of utility: the question (even in the case of slavery) was whether, and in what forms, such policies assisted the commercial ambitions of the nations which pursued them.[63] His conclusion was set out in a chapter on 'military government'. The spirit of conquest and the spirit of commerce, he argued, were mutually exclusive; furthermore, it was clear that a commercial nation was much better placed to preserve its position than a military one. The conquests of Rome, like those of the Arabs, Ghengis Kahn, and Tamurlaine, had always been precarious, because its citizens had never applied themselves to commerce.[64] But a modern nation which did might reduce its neighbours to dependence without ever having to cross their frontiers. In these terms the *Essai politique* was virtually a manifesto for the reassertion of French power at the expense of English by means of commerce; as such, it might seem of limited relevance to the case of Naples.

Derived from the model, however, was a secondary strand of argument which was of direct interest to his Neapolitan readers. For all its advantage over its rivals, the island of grain had a paradoxical weakness: the very abundance of its product would reduce its price, depriving farmers of the

[61] Hont, *Jealousy of Trade*, pp. 31–2.
[62] Jean-François Melon, *Essai politique sur le commerce* (1734); I have used the edition, described as a 'Nouvelle Édition, revue et corrigée', published in Amsterdam, 1754. This is equivalent to the second edition of 1736. In this edition, pp. 1–12: ch. 1: 'Principes'.
[63] Melon, *Essai politique*, ch. 4: 'Des colonies', 5: 'De l'esclavage', 6: 'Des compagnies exclusives'.
[64] Ibid., ch. 7: 'Du gouvernement militaire'.

incentive to produce, and making the island vulnerable to shortages. The solution, Melon argued, was to ensure that grain was traded freely within a nation, since it was unlikely that all of its provinces would be equally abundant, and to permit its export unless the price rose above a certain level.[65] Simultaneously the nation should encourage manufactures, to offer farmers the incentive of a market for their produce, and goods to purchase for themselves. Melon pointed to the way in which mechanisation and specialisation could increase the number of manufactures by reducing the amount of labour required in each, and emphasised the flexibility of female labour in particular. Whether it relied on physical strength or on the skill of its fingers, labour could always be redeployed; and the pace with which fashion now changed required that it should be.[66] Melon was also sanguine about luxury, 'that object of so many vague declamations'. After all, he observed, in a Baylean phrase, it is the passions which govern men's behaviour in society, not the maxims of religion. Luxury provided men of every rank with the incentive to better themselves, and was the best possible preventative of idleness. He dismissed the objection that luxury reduced military effectiveness, and ridiculed the idea that sumptuary laws might still be effective. But since the term continued to be abused by those who condemned it, Melon concluded that it would be better to do without it, and to banish 'luxury' from all discussions of 'police and commerce'.[67] Such enthusiasm for the manufactures of fashion and luxury notwithstanding, a comment added to the second edition of the work indicated that Melon still thought of the manufacturing sector of an agricultural economy as limited in size. In France, he calculated, as many as sixteen in twenty inhabitants were employed in agriculture, while only two were artisans (the remaining two were in the church, the courts, the army, trade and finance).[68]

Above any but the most basic level of existence, the exchange of agricultural for manufactured goods required money. Accepting that the growth of commerce was closely linked to the increase of a nation's stock of money, Melon was none the less keen to dispel mistaken notions of what this entailed. It was not simply a matter of ensuring a favourable balance of trade. Not only was the balance extremely difficult to calculate with any accuracy, a favourable balance was of little value if the volume of

---

[65] Ibid., ch. 2: 'Du Bled'.   [66] Ibid., ch. 8: 'De l'industrie', esp. pp. 83–7.

[67] Ibid., ch. 9: 'Du luxe'; and see Istvan Hont, 'Commerce and luxury', in Mark Goldie and Robert Wokler (eds.), *The Cambridge History of Eighteenth-Century Political Thought* (Cambridge, forthcoming).

[68] Melon, *Essai politique*, ch. 22: 'De la balance du commerce' (added in 1736), pp. 267–8.

commerce was kept low in order to secure it.[69] He corrected other articles of conventional wisdom as well. It might be a general rule that the export of primary goods should be discouraged when these were capable of being manufactured and subsequently exported at greater profit. But it was a rule with many exceptions: it would not disadvantage France if the English were allowed to export their manufactured cloth to France in return for importing French wines.[70] It was likewise a general rule that exclusive companies could help to protect infant industries. But this should not lead to merchants being granted monopolies on request, since their effect was to maintain the merchants' profits at the expense of the nation.[71] Commerce, Melon thought, required a balance of liberty and protection; but of the two, liberty should have the preference.[72] Nevertheless, he commended the protection given to national shipping by the English Navigation Acts. Although it might be cheaper to use Dutch shipping, a nation which would vindicate its independence must support its own marine – and might resort to pressing to obtain the seamen it required.[73]

Other means of increasing the supply of money which Melon considered included devaluation of the currency, managing the exchange rate, and the raising of public credit.[74] The last, Melon argued, was by no means disadvantageous to commerce; it was simply a passing of funds from the right hand to the left. It was republics, he pointed out, which had first set up public banks, and to them they owed their wealth and power. 'Compare them' – he went on – 'with Naples and Sicily, fertile countries where the want of circulation condemns their inhabitants to permanent poverty.'[75] It was money's circulation, not its absolute quantity, which was vital for commerce; but there were means of adding to the amount in circulation, and by these means the volume of commerce could be increased.

As Intieri's letters indicate, the impact of Melon's work was enhanced by awareness of the debate it provoked in France. Apart from Voltaire's reflections on luxury, concerned with its implications for arts and manners rather than commerce, the most direct response was that of Charles de Ferrare Dutot, in *Réflexions politiques sur les finances et le commerce* (1738). Much of the work was given over to an extended critique of Law's currency manipulation, which Melon had attempted to defend; Dutot supported his criticism with invaluable information on the working of Law's scheme.

[69] Ibid., ch. 22, pp. 246–50.
[70] Ibid., ch. 10: 'De l'exportation et de l'importation' (added in 1736), pp. 121–3.
[71] Ibid., ch. 6, p. 55; ch. 10, pp. 136–7.   [72] Ibid., ch. 2, pp. 25–6.
[73] Ibid., ch. 11: 'De la liberté de commerce', pp. 141–5; ch. 10, pp. 130–1.
[74] Ibid., chs. 12–16, 18–20, 23.   [75] Ibid., ch. 23: 'Du crédit public', pp. 274, 281.

But Dutot also made it clear that he was at one with Melon in his general understanding of the French economy and its priorities. Endowed with fertile land and an industrious people, France had the potential to be a great commercial power: the key to achieving it was the maximum 'circulation' of its products, internally and internationally.[76] Less focused but more widely known were the economic observations of Montesquieu. There is some reason to believe that Melon and Montesquieu were close students of each other's work. Melon's remarks on the economic weakness of ancient Rome echo those of Montesquieu in his *Considérations sur la grandeur des Romains et de leur décadence* (1734), while in the *Esprit des Lois* (1748) Montesquieu reiterated Melon's concern that liberty in commerce should not be equated with a licence for merchants to do as they wished.[77] But Montesquieu differed from Melon in his scepticism of French ambitions to overtake England. A monarchy such as that of France, in which the nobility offset the power of the crown, should not open itself to commerce to the same extent as a republic without fertile territory of its own. The nobility in particular should continue to be discouraged from engaging in commerce, lest luxury should undermine respect for rank.[78] Still deeply suspicious of any attempt to renew Louis XIV's ambition to universal monarchy, Montesquieu preferred to leave England as the arbiter of European peace, confident that the English pursuit of 'empire of the sea' implied no territorial ambition.[79]

The *Esprit des Lois* was published in Naples in an Italian translation as early as 1751. Its questioning whether commerce should be the priority of a territorial monarchy and its nobility, however, was not what Neapolitan reformers wanted to hear; and it did not diminish the appeal of the *Essai politique sur le commerce*. At the same time, Melon's book was also attracting interest in northern Europe. Evidence of its appeal was its early translation into English, by the Irish economic writer David Bindon. The *Political Essay upon Commerce* was published in Dublin in 1738 with the support of 535 subscribers, including the bishops of the Church of Ireland, peers, members of the Irish administration, landowners, and leading figures from the Dublin literary world. In his preface, Bindon explained the work's significance. It contained, he wrote 'a general plan of commerce', whose principles 'will hold universally true in all countries'. Bindon was not blind

---

[76] Charles de Ferrare Dutot, *Réflexions politiques sur les finances et le commerce* (1738), ed. Paul Harsin, 2 vols. (Liège, 1935), pp. 1–2 ('Avertissement de l'auteur'), 238–76 (ch III, article vii).

[77] Charles Secondat, Baron de Montesquieu, *De l'esprit des lois* (1748), book XX, ch. 12, in *Oeuvres Complètes*, ed. Roger Caillois, Bibliothèque de la Pléiade (2 vols. Paris, 1951), II, p. 593.

[78] Ibid., book XX, chs. 4, 21–2: II, pp. 587–8, 598–9.   [79] Iibid., book XIX, ch. 27: II, p. 579.

to the work's context in French aspirations to find a new, economic basis on which to re-establish their power in Europe following the failure of Louis XIV's bid for universal monarchy. But he believed that Melon's emphasis on the priority of agriculture made the work relevant to the circumstances of Ireland, where there was a pressing need to find employment for the poor, both on the land, through the creation of smaller farms, and in industry.[80] There was no suggestion that Melon's arguments might similarly apply in Scotland, where the preoccupations of economic commentators were, as we have seen, rather different. Nevertheless, it will be argued that in Scotland as well as Naples, the terms in which political economy, and with it Enlightenment, were introduced to the public owed much to Melon's 'golden book'.

POLITICAL ECONOMY IN NAPLES: FERDINANDO GALIANI AND ANTONIO GENOVESI

Neither Bartolomeo Intieri nor Celestino Galiani would seek to write on commerce themselves (the closest either came to the subject was a short tract by Intieri on the conservation of grain).[81] Their crucial role was to pass on their conviction of the importance of the subject, and their enthusiasm for Melon in particular, to two younger protégés, Celestino Galiani's nephew Ferdinando Galiani (1728–87) and Antonio Genovesi (1713–69). Of the two, it was the younger Ferdinando Galiani who was the first to publish on the subject. His *Della moneta* appeared anonymously in 1751, when he was only twenty-three. How Galiani came to write the work is only beginning to be studied. Early writings in manuscript indicate an interest in moral philosophy which is likely to have been shaped by his uncle; they suggest still another attempt to rework the Epicurean account of sociability on Christian terms.[82] He himself covered his tracks in the preface to *Della moneta*, mentioning only a handful of previous writers on the subject, and declaring his intention neither to rely on authorities nor to engage in debate

---

[80] [J.-F. Melon], *Political Essay upon Commerce*, written in French by Monsieur M***, translated, with some annotations, and Remarks, by David Bindon Esq. (Dublin, 1738). 'The Preface' occupies pp. i–xxxiv, and is preceded by the list of subscribers. The translation was made from the first edition of the *Essai politique*, and does not contain the supplementary chapters added in 1736. The translation was reprinted in 1739. Bindon's notes to Melon's text were chiefly explanatory, adding information on a number of topics.

[81] *Della perfetta conservazione del grano. Discorso di Bartolomeo Intieri* (Naples, 1754).

[82] Koen Stapelbroek, 'Moral philosophy in Galiani's early political economy' (University of Cambridge doctoral thesis, 2004), is a pioneering analysis. See especially ch. 3: 'Galiani's moral philosophy: self-deceptive love as the principle of society'.

with opponents.[83] He was only a little more forthcoming in the introduction to the second edition in 1780. He had published anonymously, he explained, in order to keep the secret of the book's authorship from his uncle; and for the same reason he had not acknowledged his debt to the conversation of Bartolomeo Intieri.[84] Among the few predecessors mentioned in the first preface, however, was Melon, of whom Galiani remarked that his ideas on money were accepted by fewer than anyone's. Galiani evidently did not share this assessment: the *Della moneta* was in important respects a development of Melon's arguments.

Although Galiani's own route to *Della moneta* remains unclear, a broader context for the work is identifiable. Throughout Italy the 1740s had seen a vigorous debate on money and public finance, a debate vividly reconstructed by Franco Venturi. One of the most important contributions to this debate was that of the Neapolitan Carlantonio Broggia. Broggia had attacked the widespread resort to devaluation to reduce debt payments, and had already identified Melon as one of the most dangerous proponents of this remedy. In the specifically Neapolitan context – which Galiani accentuated when he dedicated his work to the king – *Della moneta* was a refutation of Broggia, and a vindication of Melon. A policy of devaluation, and hence of inflation, Galiani argued, was the best means of dealing with an accumulation of wartime debt, doing the least damage both to the state and to the wider economy.[85]

The focus on money in relation to the state's finances did not prevent Galiani from commenting on its place in the wider economy, and on the economy of the kingdom of Naples in particular. He turned to this in book IV. As a general principle, the 'conservation' of society depended on the acquisition of a sufficient quantity of money.[86] But this did not mean, Galiani agreed with Melon, that quantity alone was important. What mattered was its circulation (*corso*), its speedy, regular, and well-distributed movement through the economy in commercial transactions. Naples, he believed, was a case in point: the quantity of money in the kingdom was sufficient, but it ought to be better distributed, and circulate more quickly. It was because of poor circulation that too much money was retained in the hands of merchants, 'the tyrants of commerce', resulting in the oppression of the poor peasants and farm labourers, forced to take payment in kind,

[83] Ferdinando Galiani, *Della moneta libri v* (1751), in *Opere di Ferdinando Galiani*, ed. Furio Diaz and Luciano Guerci, *Illuministi Italiani*, vol. VI (Milan and Naples, 1975), pp. 21–4: 'Proemio'.

[84] Galiani, *Della moneta*, pp. 269–75: 'Avviso dell'editore'.

[85] Venturi, *Settecento riformatore*. I: *Da Muratori a Beccaria*, ch. 7 'Il dibattito sulle monete', esp. pp. 483–8 (on Broggia), 490–504 (on Galiani).

[86] Galiani, *Della moneta*, book IV 'Of the circulation of money', introduction, pp. 200–1.

and in the ruin of farmers, who received only low prices for their produce. Galiani identified two major obstacles to the flow of money which were peculiar to the kingdom: the disproportionate size of the capital, and the disproportionate number of its courts and magistracies. There were several possible remedies, including the encouragement of fairs and markets, and properly regulated use of contracts *alla voce* (a form of credit by payment of producers in advance) – though Galiani acknowledged that these were open to abuse. But he was confident that the obstacles to improved circulation were already diminishing, simply as a result of the return of 'a prince of our own' (*un principe proprio*). In perhaps the frankest of all the many Neapolitan professions of faith in the powers of an independent monarchy, Galiani declared that 'the mere presence of the prince is sufficient to cure a state of every infirmity'.[87]

A resident prince, he continued, would stimulate trades of all sorts, and hence give rise to luxury. This was not necessarily something to be condemned, as it had been by historians, orators, and poets for so long. Though Galiani would not endorse the view he attributed to Melon that luxury was the origin of every good, he regarded it as an attribute of all societies which were no longer barbarous. Luxury was the offspring of peace, good government, and the useful arts, and could only grow when improvement in the arts made possible greater specialisation and efficiency in manufactures. As least as long as luxury was the product of domestic manufactures, its consumption would be far less harmful than its critics supposed.[88]

Large, fertile countries such as France, Spain, and much of Italy, Galiani argued, had less need for money, and therefore for foreign commerce and the trading companies which were regarded as essential to its pursuit. The nations which needed to trade were those with only restricted or mountainous territory, such Genoa, Venice, Holland, or Switzerland. But it was important to recognise that what these countries were doing by means of commerce was taking control over territory, or tracts of sea, in order to acquire the products and the subject (often enslaved) populations which their own lands could not provide. It was conquest in the guise of commerce:

Great conquests made, great territories, great fruits, and a great number of slaves. But because they are far-off, we cry commerce, commerce, instead of saying arms and military virtue. On maps we would be able to measure the least of their colonies, and find it almost greater than the whole of the kingdom of Naples.[89]

[87] Ibid., pp. 201–11.   [88] Ibid., pp. 211–13: 'Digressione intorno al lusso considerato generalmente'.
[89] Ibid., p. 246; also pp. 221–2.

Galiani illustrated the point with a remarkable counterfactual hypothesis. To increase their commerce in this way, the Neapolitans would have to discover a stretch of the Mediterranean rich in whales, herring, and cod, or cut through the straits of Suez to make themselves masters of the Moluccas, Ceylon, Batavia, and the Cape. In reality, however, the basis of commerce was a flourishing agriculture; without this, to pursue commerce was to hunt after a shadow. If Neapolitan agriculture was still languishing, despite the existence of just government and an ample population, effort should be concentrated on its improvement, not on the creation of trading companies.[90]

There was one respect, Galiani thought, in which Naples had an advantage over France: its private banks. These were quite differently organised from the banks associated with the schemes of John Law (correctly identified as 'Scozzese'), which Galiani judged 'one of the strangest productions of the human intellect'. They also contradicted Montesquieu's opinion that such banks were inappropriate to monarchies. Montesquieu was mistaken in generalising from the experience of a monarchy subject to the seditious remonstrances of parlements and clergy, disorders unknown in the absolute monarchy of Naples, where the sovereign's decrees were promptly obeyed.[91] In Galiani's eyes, the economy of the kingdom of Naples not only exemplified the case of a fertile agricultural country, which should follow the path of development previously recommended by Melon; under its own king it was in a far better position to do so than France itself.

Galiani's anonymity as author of *Della moneta* was not maintained for long. As soon as the brilliance of the work's arguments was recognised, he acknowledged authorship and set off on a tour of Italy to meet the other leading participants in the money debate. But his initial reserve, and reluctance to present the work as an exemplar of the importance of political economy for Naples, meant that it had a limited public impact. In Intieri's terms, one published treatise on the subject of commerce was unlikely to be sufficient to persuade ministers that this was the most important question of the age. Later, when in Paris as a diplomat in the 1760s, Galiani would find himself at the centre of the Enlightenment, enjoying the company of the *philosophes* (and of the *salonnières* who were their patrons). But neither in 1751 nor later did he seek to use political economy to make the case for Enlightenment in his own country.

That was the appointed task of Antonio Genovesi, who became the favoured protégé of Intieri in the early 1750s. Born in 1713 near Salerno, Genovesi early showed an interest in theology, and was ordained a priest.

---

[90] Ibid., pp. 247–8.   [91] Ibid., pp. 234–46.

When a legacy enabled him to move to Naples in 1737, he quickly developed his interests in philosophy, and by 1741 he had been appointed a professor of metaphysics at the university by Celestino Galiani. Four years later he moved to the chair of ethics. He published on metaphysics in 1743, and on the arts of logic and criticism in 1745; in the latter year he also published a discourse on the history of the physical sciences from the ancients to Newton, to accompany a Neapolitan edition of Musschenbroek's elements of physics.[92] By the end of the 1740s, it seems that Genovesi fully expected to crown his academic career by promotion to a chair of theology. But he faced insurmountable opposition from within the church. Questions had been asked of his orthodoxy as early as 1741, when he was accused of deism, and of being a follower of Bayle or of the Socinians. They were asked again in the light of a work he had written (in manuscript) in 1745 reviewing the various trends in modern theology, and defending the freedom to discuss them.[93] There is no evidence that the suspicions were well founded. Genovesi was an anti-dogmatic, modernising Catholic in the mould of Celestino Galiani, though without the depth of the latter's scholarly interests. It was almost certainly ecclesiastical politics, and the desire of Cardinal Spinelli, the archbishop of Naples, to assert his authority, which prevented Genovesi from getting the chair in theology.[94]

The rebuff was none the less decisive. It was now that Genovesi, with Intieri's encouragement, developed his enthusiasm for political economy. Scholars have divided over whether this 'turn' was a development of lines of thought already present in his philosophy, or marked a radical new departure.[95] There is no sign that Genovesi regarded his new interest as

---

[92] Antonio Genovesi, *Elementa Metaphisicae* (Naples, 1743); *Elementorum artis logico-criticae* (Naples, 1745); *Disputatio physico-historica de rerum corporearum origine et constitutione*, published with Pieter Van Musschenbroek, *Elementa physicae conscripta in usus academicos* (Naples, 1745).

[93] The work was published posthumously, as *Universae christianae theologiae elementa dogmatica, historica, critica* (Venice, 1771).

[94] Characteristically evocative outlines of Genovesi's life are provided by Franco Venturi, 'Antonio Genovesi. Nota introduttiva', *Illuministi italiani* v: *Riformatori napoletani* (Milan and Naples, 1962), pp. 3–15; *Settecento riformatore*. 1: *Da Muratori a Beccaria*, pp. 523–33. A balanced assessment of his religious thinking is that of Giuseppe Galasso, 'Il pensiero religioso di Antonio Genovesi', *Rivista Storica Italiana*, 82 (1970), 800–23.

[95] The original protagonists in the debate were Franco Venturi, the rhetoric of whose *Settecento riformatore*. 1: *Da Muratori a Beccaria*, pp. 523–644: 'La Napoli di Antonio Genovesi', suggested a radical break, and Paola Zambelli, *La formazione filosofica di Antonio Genovesi* (Naples, 1972), esp. pp. 707–94: part III, '"Da metafisico a mercatante"? Le variazioni di un piano di studi', who made the case for continuity. Further comment was offered by Eluggero Pii, *Antonio Genovesi. Dalla politica economia alla 'politica civile'* (Florence, 1984); and Richard Bellamy, '"Da metafisico a mercatante": Antonio Genovesi and the development of a new language of commerce in eighteenth-century Naples', in Anthony Pagden (ed.), *The Languages of Political Theory in Early Modern Europe* (Cambridge, 1987), pp. 277–99.

incompatible with his earlier philosophy, and he continued to add to his work on metaphysics. His philosophical thinking was in any case eclectic, being broadly based in both the ancients and the moderns, the latter including Descartes, Gassendi, and Bayle, but with an inclination towards the empirical, sense-based philosophy associated with Locke and the Newtonians. What Genovesi found congenial in Intieri's outlook was his dislike of useless abstraction, and preference for subjects which would bear real fruit. Over dinner or out walking at Intieri's rural retreat at Massa Equana, on the steep slopes above Vico Equense on the Sorrento peninsula, what they had talked about, Genovesi recalled, was the progress of human reason, of the arts, commerce, and the economy of the state, and of physics and mechanics.[96] Evidently Genovesi was untroubled by Intieri's association with Epicureanism, and welcomed the opportunity to set aside theology in favour of the new subjects of commerce and the economy. At the same time, as Venturi pointed out, Genovesi's decision was taken in the context of a series of attempts by the church to reassert its authority over Neapolitan intellectual life in the years immediately before and after 1750. A demand by the archbishop for the reintroduction of the Inquisition had been beaten off; but he had successfully obtained the suppression of the masonic lodge founded in the city in 1750 by the colourful, intellectually inquisitive Raimondo di Sangro, prince of Sansevero.[97] By the early 1750s Genovesi had every incentive to turn away, if not from philosophy, then certainly from religious controversy, and to look for a fresh outlet for his intellectual energies.

The first fruit of Genovesi's new interests was his edition in 1753 of a work by the Florentine agronomist and founder of the Accademia dei Georgofili, Ubaldo Montelatici, to which he attached a *Discorso* of his own.[98] In the following year he fulfilled Intieri's last wish, by becoming the first holder of the chair which Intieri endowed at the university, for the teaching of 'meccanica e gli elementi di commercio' (mechanics and the elements of commerce). It was effectively the first chair of political economy at any university in Europe. The choice of Genovesi to fill it reflected Intieri's high opinion of his character and teaching ability.[99] Genovesi gave the first

---

[96] 'Vita di Antonio Genovesi', composed by Genovesi between 1757 and 1760; printed in Venturi, *Illuministi Italiani*. v: *Riformatori napoletani*, pp. 47–83. See esp. pp. 72–5.

[97] Venturi, *Settecento riformatore*. I: *Da Muratori a Beccaria*, pp. 537–44.

[98] *Ragionamento sopra i mezzi più necessarii per far rifiorire l'agricoltura. Del P. Abate D. Ubaldo Montelatici . . . con un Discorso di Antonio Genovesi Regio Professore d'Etica sopra il vero fine delle lettere e delle scienze. Il tutto dedicato al Signor D. Bartolomeo Intieri* (Naples, 1753).

[99] An opinion expressed in a series of letters to his friend Antonio Cocchi, of 12 Dec. 1752, 16 Jan., 20 Feb 1753, 18 June 1754: ed. Franco Venturi, and printed in 'Alle origini dell'illuminismo napoletano. Dal carteggio di Bartolomeo Intieri', *Rivista Storica Italiana*, 71 (1959), pp. 441, 443, 444, 449–50.

lecture of his course, entitled 'Elementi di commercio' (the words Intieri had first used in 1738, writing to Celestino Galiani) in November 1754, in Italian, as Intieri had instructed.

The *Discorso sopra il vero fine delle lettere e delle scienze* (*Discourse on the true end of letters and sciences*), which Genovesi published along with Montelatici's *Ragionamento* in 1753, was described by Franco Venturi as 'a true manifesto of the new school' in Naples.[100] It was not itself a work of political economy; instead it set the need to understand the subjects of agriculture and commerce in the perspective of a revolution of philosophy. The earliest philosophers, who were legislators, teachers, and priests, had understood that true philosophy consisted in ethics, economics, and politics. But their successors, Genovesi believed, had enlarged their ambitions and complicated their thinking, forming schools of philosophy and filling their heads with useless abstractions like knight-errant Don Quixotes. Only after seven or more centuries had Francis Bacon restored philosophy to its original concerns; at the same time the Italian Galileo had applied geometry to mechanics, rescuing astronomy from astrology, and physics from magic. Genovesi emphasised the way in which Bacon's arguments had been reinforced by the opportune discovery of the printing press, whose effect on the human mind he likened, in a Vichian image, to the shield of Achilles, embarrassing it with the reflection of its past errors and delusions.[101] With the advent of the new king, the effects of this revolution should at last have been felt in Naples, as they had been in Louis XIV's France and in Peter the Great's Russia. Yet here, Genovesi found, the useful sciences were still being neglected in favour of speculation and litigation.[102]

There was every reason to think that the kingdom could do better: 'we are in the finest part of Europe', Genovesi declared. It was in a position to meet all five of Xenophon's conditions for a nation to acquire wealth and greatness. First, its government was in the hands of its own prince; 'the sad days of being a province' were over. Second, its soil and climate made the kingdom fertile, rich not only in the necessaries and conveniences of life, but in many of the materials of luxury, like silk, wines, fruits, and fine foods. Third, the situation of the kingdom was ideal for commerce: surrounded by the sea, possessed of excellent sites for ports, it had neighbours anxious to obtain the goods in which it abounded. Neapolitans needed simply to recognise that commerce is an art, with 'ends, rules, and

---

[100] Venturi, *Settecento riformatore*. I: *Da Muratori a Beccaria*, p. 560.

[101] Antonio Genovesi, *Discorso sopra il vero fine delle lettere e delle scienze* (1753), included in the excellent edition by Maria Luisa Perna of *Antonio Genovesi. Scritti economici* (Naples, Istituto Italiano per gli Studi Filosofici, 1984), 2 vols. (but with continuous pagination), pp. 11–21.

[102] Ibid., pp. 21–5.

principles', which must be learnt and practised; those who still imagined otherwise, Genovesi observed, should be sent to 'the great Melon' to be disabused. The fourth condition too was readily met. The number of the kingdom's inhabitants was more than sufficient to exploit its advantages; again he invoked 'the wise Melon' on the importance of population. Only in the fifth condition, the industry of its inhabitants, was the kingdom still deficient. It was imperative to revive this, and there was no better way to do so than to follow the inspiration and example of 'don Bartolomeo' Intieri.[103]

In the hope of arousing such a spirit of industry, Genovesi addressed the final part of the *Discorso* to three classes in particular. The first was 'our great ones', the nobility. These he urged to renew their ties with the people below them, and to set an example of justice, trust, honesty, and useful knowledge. The second was the clergy, which of all the learned professions had the most time to devote to the study of agriculture and commerce, and the opportunity to pass on their knowledge to the people. The third, in which Genovesi placed his greatest hopes, was that of 'studious youth'; these were to be the *terzo mezzo* – third force – of reform in the kingdom. Genovesi called particularly for the institution of an academy of the learned in Naples, to which 'the enlightened youth' of the provinces could contribute their knowledge and observations. In conclusion, Genovesi added a sixth condition of success to the five originally set down by Xenophon: good morals. Challenging Montesquieu's opinion that virtue was useless in monarchies, Genovesi argued that it was this above all which men of letters should seek to instil, for the greater glory and utility of the *patria*. Education, conducted in good Italian, was the key to the kingdom's prospects of happiness; it was the true agriculture of men.[104]

Genovesi quickly set an example of such teaching from his chair, and attracted growing audiences. But his approach to educating the Neapolitan public was not confined to lecturing. He added to this an ambitious programme of translation and publication, specifically of writings on economics. Here Genovesi showed himself alert to developments in French political economy more recent than the works of Melon, Dutot, and Montesquieu. For in the years around 1750, a group of administrators and economic writers had taken what in the French context was a radical and original initiative, designed to transform political economy into a subject of open, public discussion. The group was led by Vincent de Gournay, and included Georges-Marie Butel-Dumont, François Véron de Forbonnois,

[103] Ibid., pp. 25–44.   [104] Ibid., pp. 44–57.

Plumard de Dangeul, Claude-Jacques Herbert, and the young Turgot.[105] Gournay's object was to gain publicity for political economy by the simple and obvious (but not necessarily easy) means of publishing books on the subject. Some of these had previously only circulated in manuscript, like Cantillon's work. Others were works which had been published abroad, like those by the Spanish economic writers Uztáriz and Ulloa, and by the English Joshua Gee and John Cary. It was the translation of John Cary's 1695 *Essay on the State of England* by Gournay and Butel-Dumont, with additional chapters as well as notes of their own, which was of particular interest to Genovesi. The French translation appeared in 1755, and Genovesi promptly decided on its translation into Italian. The translation was published in Naples in three volumes in 1757–8 as the *Storia del commercio della Gran Bretagna, scritta da John Cary, mercatante di Bristol*. The translation itself was the work of Genovesi's brother, Pietro; but Antonio added extensive new notes, in which he brought to bear his own wide knowledge of earlier and contemporary economic literature, French, English, and Spanish. He also took the opportunity to print a version of his inaugural lecture as professor as an introduction to the translation.

The *Ragionamento sul commercio in universale* (*Reasoning on commerce in general*) outlined Genovesi's conception of political economy. He began by drawing a clear distinction between 'the science of commerce' (*la scienza del commercio*) and 'the practice of business' (*la pratica della mercatura*). The former was his subject; the latter was not. He would not be teaching merchants the arts of marketing, accounting, and the exchange. His object was to demonstrate that there was a 'science of commerce and the economy', for which he himself used the term 'political economy' (*economia politica*). It was a science with its own principles, from which derived certain, specific practical consequences.[106] In the *Ragionamento* as in his later writings on the subject, however, Genovesi preferred a discursive to a systematic mode of presentation: what followed was a series of propositions, whose analytical connection was not always made clear. He defined the 'ends' (*fini*) of political economy as two: to increase the population, and to procure the subsistence, wealth, and power of the nation. (Within a nation the wealth of the people was the source of that of the sovereign.) The means of increasing population were both physical and moral; where the physical conditions were favourable, as in a fertile country, it was important not to neglect the

[105] On this group and the significance of their initiative: Robin Ives, 'Political economy and political publicity in eighteenth-century France', *French History*, 17 (2003), 1–18.
[106] Antonio Genovesi, *Ragionamento sul commercio in universale* (1757), also in Perna, *Scritti economici*, pp. 119–63; for the initial definitions, pp. 124–7.

moral incentives which were also required if numbers were to rise to the level the land would support.[107]

The sources of the wealth of a nation were its agriculture, manufactures, and commerce, internal and external. In the case of agriculture, two factors were crucial if its product was to be maximised. One was the extent and fertility of the land under cultivation, and the scope for adding to and improving it. The second was the distribution of land among its cultivators. A grossly unequal distribution would be a disincentive to both great and small landholders. The ancients had prevented this by agrarian laws; but Genovesi did not say whether the moderns should do the same. Other obstacles to improving cultivation included unequal tax and other burdens, excessive luxury, a shortage of money in circulation, and high rates of interest.[108] In discussing manufactures, Genovesi emphasised the extent to which they must be supported by an agricultural surplus: even 'necessary manufactures', he estimated, would occupy a sixth of the population.[109] But manufactures benefited agriculture in return. Machinery improved cultivation, a point illustrated by English examples; and in a lengthy note appended to the text of the translation Genovesi spelt out the vital importance of manufactures in increasing demand for agricultural produce.[110] A subsequent note discussed luxury, which he defined as the desire of men to distinguish themselves and emulate the ranks above them, and defended against Montesquieu as appropriate both in republics and in monarchies. Citing Melon and Hume, among others, Genovesi argued that 'moderate' luxury increased consumption, to the benefit of both agriculture and manufactures. Even the consumption of foreign luxuries might be useful, if it served to increase the export of domestic produce and manufactures.[111] But before discussing foreign trade Genovesi emphasised the fundamental importance of internal commerce, especially to a kingdom such as Naples. Good roads and security from robbers were essential; but the key to internal commerce was the ready circulation of money and its proportionate distribution.[112]

Like Doria and Galiani, Genovesi clearly believed that, for the time being, the kingdom's internal commerce should take priority over foreign trade, the better to encourage both agriculture and manufactures. But he

[107] *Ragionamento*, in ibid., pp. 127–32.   [108] Ibid., pp. 133–40.   [109] Ibid., pp. 140–2.

[110] Ibid., pp. 143–5; and Annotazione n. 32 to vol. 1 of the *Storia del commercio*, ibid., p. 349.

[111] Annotazione n. 26 to vol. 1 of the *Storia del commercio*, in ibid., pp. 372–80. Till Wahnbaeck, *Luxury and Public Happiness: Political Economy in the Italian Enlightenment* (Oxford, 2004), pp. 59–66, discusses Genovesi's understanding of luxury.

[112] *Ragionamento*, in Perna, *Scritti economici*, pp. 149–52.

did not discount the potential of foreign trade, suggesting that the English provided the best example of its conduct. He praised the way in which since the revolution of 1689 they had deliberately sought to produce a surplus for export, treating agriculture as a form of merchandise, rather than simply as the means of subsistence. The English had also recognised that it was preferable to export finished goods and import primary materials; a nation which relied for its luxuries on foreign goods alone would soon be reduced to dependence on its neighbours.[113] Admiration for English commercial practices was implicit in the choice of Cary's book for translation; but Genovesi was not naive in his judgement. Several of the notes to the translation reveal an acute awareness of the extent to which English maritime commerce depended on the exercise of naval power – and of the inability of the disunited states of Italy to defend themselves against it.[114] In these notes he also frequently cited French authors, Melon prominent among them, to qualify the lessons of English experience. It is clear that Genovesi continued to follow Melon in thinking in terms of an agricultural economy, whose potential should be maximised by removing the obstacles to the sale of its produce, in the internal market and by export, without allowing merchants to treat liberty of commerce as a licence to do as they wished.[115]

Genovesi concluded the *Ragionamento* by posing two questions: first, whether the current proliferation of economic writings throughout Europe would contribute to the rejuvenation of its nations; second, whether in a world in which commerce had become the preserve of a few nations, others could still distinguish themselves in it, or must 'go backwards' (*andar dietro*) and remain in a subordinate condition. He was confident that he could answer both questions in the affirmative. To the first, he responded that the writings on the subject were the reason why almost all the nations of Europe had turned to the promotion of commerce. As to the second, it was no longer possible for one nation to acquire 'the empire of commerce' (*l'imperio del commercio*) at the expense the rest, precisely because agriculture, manufactures, and navigation were no longer regarded as mysteries, but were arts understood by all the peoples of Europe. There was therefore still time for a nation in a condition of mediocrity to distinguish itself among the others, if to the possession of natural, internal strengths it added

---

[113] Ibid., pp. 153–60.

[114] Annotazioni n. 4 to vol. II, n. 2 and n. 7 to vol. III of the *Storia del commercio*, ibid., pp. 476–80, 826–7, 830.

[115] Annotazioni n. 8 and n. 25 to vol. I, n. 4 to vol. II of the *Storia del commercio*, ibid., pp. 297–305, 367–72, 476–80, all of which quote or cite Melon, among others.

study and application. The kingdom of Naples might be 'confined in an angle of the world', but Genovesi did not doubt that it had the resources necessary to follow this path. If he never went quite as far as Galiani in suggesting that the kingdom was even better placed than France to take advantage of its natural, agricultural potential, he had a still more urgent sense that now was the moment to do so.[116]

But it is perhaps the first of Genovesi's questions which is most revealing of his purposes – and his achievement. The spread of economic writing was important for two reasons. On the one hand, it added to the resources available for understanding political economy. By learning and passing on the knowledge to be found in French, British, and Spanish economic writers, Genovesi demonstrated the need to treat the subject from a cosmopolitan standpoint. As a science with its own 'ends, rules, and principles', political economy was universal in its scope: if each nation presented specific problems, it was vital to approach these comparatively. Much more explicitly than Galiani, Genovesi recognised the need to dispel the prejudice that the situation of the kingdom on Naples was unique, and appreciated the value of political economy in teaching this lesson. Such intellectual cosmopolitanism was characteristic of the Enlightenment as a European intellectual movement: in urging his fellow countrymen to study political economy, Genovesi was making the case for Enlightenment in Naples.

The availability of economic writings served a second purpose, likewise consciously pursued by Genovesi. In a small, *ancien régime* society such as Naples, publication itself had potentially far-reaching implications. Hitherto, in Naples even more than in France, the economy had been treated along with the monarchy's finances as an affair of state – a 'reason of state' – on which interested men of letters might be more or less welcome to offer advice to government ministers in private, in manuscript memoranda; it had not been regarded as a suitable subject for public discussion. Following the wish of Intieri and the example of Gournay in France, Genovesi set out to subvert that assumption. He would not plead his case within the secretive 'private' sphere of the Neapolitan court, whose new lease of life under an independent king meant that it was, if anything, seeking to extend its control over other forms of social association in the city.[117] (The contrast with Galiani, who was always attracted by the ways of the court, is here particularly sharp.) Instead Genovesi addressed, and in

---

[116] *Ragionamento*, in Perna, *Scritti economici*, pp. 161–3.

[117] Giovanni Montroni, 'The court: power relations and forms of social life', in Girolamo Imbruglia (ed.), *Naples in the Eighteenth Century: the Birth and Death of a Nation State* (Cambridge, 2000), pp. 22–43.

so doing began to create, a 'public' sphere in educated Neapolitan society at large. This was the public for whom Genovesi wrote the *Discorso sopra il vero fine delle lettere e delle scienze* in 1753, and it was the public he intended to reach by his lectures and publications thereafter.

When Genovesi began, early in the 1750s, such a public barely existed even in the city of Naples. Between them the court, the church, and the law policed the sites and mechanisms of intellectual exchange – and, by licences and exclusive rights, the printers and publishers of books.[118] Beyond Naples, in the remote provinces of the kingdom, the opportunities for discussion were even more curtailed. Voluntary societies, even for agricultural improvement, were unknown; any independent, lay initiative was regarded with deep suspicion by the authorities. (Tanucci was as hostile to Freemasonry as Cardinal Spinelli.) This was the context in which – and the reason why – Genovesi appealed particularly to the youth of the kingdom, and attached such importance to education and to the creation of institutions of learning and the arts. His objective was to gain the attention of those who came from all over the kingdom to the city for their education, before they acquired the prejudices of a profession, or returned to the barren wildernesses of the provinces. If he could persuade the young of the importance of political economy, of the need for application to understand it and commitment to put it into practice, he might indeed create a *terzo mezzo*, a 'third force', in the kingdom, independent of, but ultimately more influential than the traditional royal and ecclesiastical authorities. The appeal to the clergy to associate themselves with the cause of economic renewal was similarly calculated. Bypassing the traditional antagonism of the jurists and civil authorities towards the church, Genovesi would turn the ordinary clergy into the footsoldiers of improvement. In the Neapolitan context these were a unprecedented ambitions, and the publication and teaching of political economy was their chosen vehicle. Combined with its inherently cosmopolitan perspective, the public orientation of political economy was fundamental to Genovesi's case for Enlightenment in Naples. This is why political economy signalled the advent of Enlightenment in Naples, and why the Neapolitan Enlightenment was Genovesi's, not Galiani's achievement.

The measure of Genovesi's achievement was perhaps most revealingly taken by the one Neapolitan thinker besides Galiani who might have challenged Genovesi, Carlantonio Broggia (1698–1767). As a young man with

---

[118] On the confused, multiply regulated but never altogether controlled world of Neapolitan publishing and bookselling in the eighteenth century: Anna Maria Rao (ed.), *Editoria e cultura a Napoli nel XVIII secolo* (Naples, 1998), especially the editor's 'Introduzione', pp. 3–55.

an intellectual interest in commerce, Broggia too had been befriended and assisted by Intieri; but in the 1730s he had followed Doria in becoming increasingly alarmed by the Epicurean associations of the new political economy.[119] His first publication, the *Trattato de' tributi* (1743), had been an attack on Melon's defence of devaluation, and made him an important (if largely unacknowledged) target of Galiani's *Della moneta* (Broggia subsequently repaid the slight by treating Intieri, not Galiani, as its author). His second publication in 1754 also contained an attack on Melon, as one of the 'sophistical sceptical Epicureans' who had attempted to provide an apologia for luxury. In Broggia's view luxury had none of the economic benefits claimed for it, and epitomised the moral threat inherent in Epicurean economics.[120] In a later correspondence, in the 1760s, Broggia would denounce both Intieri and Genovesi. His former mentor was a libertine who had promoted Epicureanism, materialism, and the career of Antonio Genovesi. As for the latter's achievement, to Broggia it amounted to no more than stealing ideas from ultramontane writers, and spreading them indiscriminately from his chair. Those who wish for the public good, Broggia thought, should address only princes, and those of their ministers whose intentions they knew to be good.[121] Genovesi stood condemned, in short, for association with Epicureanism, for cosmopolitanism, and for daring to address a public beyond the prince and his ministers: the very features of political economy which made it, in Genovesi's hands, the ideal vehicle of Enlightenment.

POLITICAL ECONOMY IN SCOTLAND: DAVID HUME

If the impact of Melon on the Neapolitan political economists is well attested, the same cannot be said for their Scottish counterparts. Nevertheless, Melon's intellectual presence was felt there too. In a moment I shall suggest that arguments from the *Essai politique sur le commerce* provided David Hume with a vital critical foil as he wrote the economic essays

[119] On Broggia's life and thought: Raffaele Ajello, 'Carl Antonio Broggia. Nota introduttiva', in R. Ajello and others (eds.), *Dal Muratori al Cesarotti* v: *Politici ed economisti del primo settecento* (Milan and Naples, 1978), pp. 971–1034; also the same author's 'La critica del regime in Doria, Intieri e Broggia', in his *Arcana Juris*, pp. 389–472. The 'Nota introduttiva' contains a particularly acute discussion of Melon's significance for Broggia: pp. 1012–15.

[120] Carlantonio Broggia, *Memoria ad ogetto di varie politiche ed economiche ragioni* (1754), 'Trattato primo intitolato: Del lusso, o sia abuso delle richezze', printed in *Dal Muratori al Cesarotti*, pp. 1041–59.

[121] Carlantonio Broggia to Giovan Giuseppe Fontanesi, 26 March 1765, in *Dal Muratori al Cesarotti*, pp. 1125–51. Fontanesi was Secretary of State to the elector palatine in Mannheim, a reasonably safe distance from which to listen to Broggia's resentments.

published in the *Political Discourses* in 1752. Before we explore the essays' content, however, Hume's venture into political economy needs to be set in biographical context, and specifically in the context of his move to Edinburgh in 1751.

As long as he was active as a philosopher, the guise in which we have met him hitherto, Hume could never feel entirely comfortable in Scotland. It was only after leaving the country and going abroad in 1734, following five years of intellectual solitude and frustration, that he was able to write the *Treatise of Human Nature*; and on returning from France with the manuscript in September 1737, he stayed on in London until February 1739 while the first two volumes were published. He was away again for most of the four years between 1745 and 1749, during which he wrote and published the *Philosophical Essays concerning Human Understanding*. Just before this period of absence, in the spring of 1745, he had been rejected for the professorship of moral philosophy at Edinburgh. Although his expectations of the post had always been misplaced, he seems to have felt the disappointment keenly, and was happy to get out of Scotland. Shortly after he had completed the *Enquiry concerning the Principles of Morals*, in 1751, he was rejected a second time for a chair of moral philosophy, at Glasgow, although in this case the disappointment probably came as less of a surprise. Even while in Scotland, he had lived in relative seclusion at the family home at Ninewells, near Berwick, reading and writing by himself, with occasional forays to visit friends. But 1751 brought a decisive change in his circumstances. His older brother married, and Hume (and his sister) could no longer stay at Ninewells. He therefore took a house in Edinburgh, removing, as he put it in 'My Own Life', 'from the country to the city, the true scene for a man of letters'.[122] In fact he had by now acquired sufficient means to live as an independent man of letters; and on arrival in Edinburgh he immediately set himself to take a central role in the intellectual and literary life of the Scottish capital.

He arrived at an opportune moment, as the pace of intellectual life began to quicken. In 1748 his older kinsman and correspondent Henry Home (elevated to the bench of the Court of Session in 1752 as Lord Kames) had taken the initiative of organising a series of extra-mural lectures on rhetoric, which were given by the young Adam Smith.[123] The Philosophical Society of Edinburgh was also active, and before the end of 1751 Hume had become its

---

[122] David Hume, 'My Own Life', written in 1776, and first published in 1777, reprinted in David Hume, *Essays Moral, Political, and Literary* (1741–1777), ed. Eugene F. Miller, rev. edn. (Indianapolis, 1985), p. xxxvi.

[123] Ian Simpson Ross, *The Life of Adam Smith* (Oxford, 1995), pp. 84–7.

joint secretary, with responsibility for its publications. Early the following year he was elected Keeper of the Advocates' Library, and in 1754 he was one of the founders (and first treasurer) of the Select Society, which immediately established itself as the leading forum for serious discussion in the city. Hume undertook these commitments on his own terms. He was determined to maintain his independence, and was quite prepared to make mischief to get his way (as when he threatened to resign from the library over an attempt by the curators to block his purchases of modern French literature). But he also recognised that he must accept certain limits. Although amused by an attempt by hostile clergy to have him excommunicated in 1756–7, he knew that he was not actually living in a society of atheists, and avoided embarrassing his friends among the Moderate clergy by public expression of his unbelief. It mattered to him that men of letters upheld appropriate standards of civility when they engaged in public debate among themselves. Given that there were no official restrictions on publication and intellectual debate such as existed in France or in Naples, Hume was anxious that men of letters should not abuse their freedom and undermine their intellectual authority in the eyes of the wider public by allowing personal antagonism to distort their exchanges.[124] It was in this context, and in this spirit, that he published the *Political Discourses* in Edinburgh in 1752.

Hume had of course published two volumes of essays on moral and political topics at the beginning of the previous decade, to which he added a further three essays (and from which he removed others) for a 'third edition' in 1748.[125] What distinguished the *Political Discourses* from the earlier essays was their concentration on economic topics: eight out of the original twelve essays in the volume were in this vein. Hume introduced the new collection with a warning to his readers that reasonings on such subjects were necessarily general rather than particular: he was concerned with 'universal propositions, which comprehend under them an infinite number of individuals, and include a whole science in a single theorem'. Subtlety and refinement were therefore to be expected: these essays were not for the lazy reader.[126] How Hume came to write on economic topics is,

[124] For further discussion of this, see my entry for Hume in the new *Oxford Dictionary of National Biography*. A good example is his rebuke to [John Stewart], [February 1754], in Hume, *Letters*, I, pp. 185–6, over a contribution which Stewart had submitted anonymously for a volume of essays Hume was editing for the Philosophical Society.

[125] *Essays, Moral and Political*, in 2 vols. (Edinburgh, 1741, 1742); and in a 'third edition' (Edinburgh and London, 1748).

[126] 'Of Commerce', first published in the *Political Discourses* (Edinburgh, 1752), here in the modern edition of the *Essays Moral, Political, and Literary*, ed. Eugene F. Miller, pp. 254–56 (hereafter cited as *Essays*).

if anything, even less clearly signposted than his route into philosophy. A section of the so-called 'Early Memoranda' contains notes from a number of economic writings, French and British; the most authoritative dating of these, by M. A. Stewart, attributes them to the years 1740–5. Stewart observes that these entries do look forward to the *Political Discourses*, but cautions that they by no means contain all the reading Hume had to do for the 1752 essays.[127] In the notes to the essays themselves, references to classical authors far outnumber any others; but there are a few indications of disagreement with French economic writers in particular, those named including Melon, Dutot, Paris-Duverney and (in a French context) John Law. The clearest answer to the question of Hume's sources, however, may be found in the arguments of the essays themselves: on closer examination, I shall now suggest, they reveal a frequent if not continuous engagement with the arguments of Melon's *Essai politique sur le commerce*.

'The bulk of every state', Hume stated early in 'Of Commerce', 'may be divided into *husbandmen* and *manufacturers*.' '*At first*', he conceded, the arts of agriculture will employ the majority. Over time, however, the land will easily maintain a much greater number of men than are required for its cultivation, or for supplying the manufactures needed for cultivation. To this Hume added a footnote:

Mons. MELON, in his political essay on commerce, asserts, that even at present, if you divide FRANCE into 20 parts, 16 are labourers or peasants; two only artizans, one belonging to the law, church, and military; and one merchants, financiers, and bourgeois. This calculation is certainly very erroneous. In FRANCE, ENGLAND, and indeed most parts of EUROPE, half of the inhabitants live in cities; and even of those who live in the country, a great number are artizans, perhaps above a third.[128]

If those surplus to the requirements of agriculture applied themselves to those arts which are commonly denominated the arts of luxury, Hume continued, they would add to the happiness of the state by giving many more people access to enjoyments which they would otherwise never have experienced. What Hume feared was that the state would instead claim the surplus population for its fleets and armies, following the example of

---

[127] M. A. Stewart, 'The dating of Hume's manuscripts', in Wood (ed.), *The Scottish Enlightenment: Essays in Reinterpretation*, pp. 276–88; Mossner decided that this section of the memoranda should be titled 'Section III General', and printed it accordingly in 'Hume's early memoranda, 1729–40', pp. 503–18.

[128] 'Of Commerce', *Essays*, p. 256 and note. The passage quoted was from ch. 22 of the *Essai politique*, which was added in the second edition. Hume must therefore have read a French edition, since Bindon's English translation was made from the first edition.

the ancient republics. His point was that the ancient policy was unnatural, being based on a complete misunderstanding of the logic and benefits of commerce. Fortunately, what had actually happened was that foreign trade had introduced the nations of the modern world to 'the *pleasures* of luxury and the *profits* of commerce'. Foreign luxuries had proved so attractive that they had stimulated the manufacture of domestic counterparts by a process of 'imitation'. Thus 'domestic manufactures emulate the foreign in their improvements, and work up every home commodity to the utmost perfection of which it is susceptible'.[129] The threat of a return to ancient virtue, still held up as the standard by so many modern moralists, had been averted by the knock-on effects of the trade in foreign luxuries.

The significance of Hume's casual – and itself 'certainly very erroneous' – recalculation of Melon's estimate of the proportions employed in agriculture and manufactures can now be seen.[130] What the note signalled was a rejection of the main argument of the *Essai politique*. It was not the economy of the island of grain which had the best prospects of development (and hence of power), but that which was most open to foreign trade. Contrary to Melon's agriculture-based model of development, Hume set out a trade-led model:

Foreign trade, by its imports, furnishes materials for new manufactures; and by its exports, it produces labour in particular commodities, which could not be consumed at home. In short, a kingdom that has a large import and export, must abound more with industry, and that employed upon delicacies and luxuries, than a kingdom which rests contented with its native commodities. It is, therefore, more powerful, as well as richer and happier. The individuals reap the benefit of these commodities, so far as they gratify the senses and appetites. And the public is also a gainer, while a greater stock of labour is, by this means, stored up against any public exigency; that is, a greater number of laborious men are maintained, who may be diverted to the public service, without robbing anyone of the necessaries, or even the chief conveniencies of life.[131]

Not only the process, but the outcome, of development are made plain in this passage. The riches and happiness of a nation consist, first, in individual benefit, defined, in Epicurean terms, as gratification of the senses and

---

[129] 'Commerce', *Essays*, p. 264.

[130] If Melon erred, Hume was even more mistaken: modern estimates suggest that in the mid-eighteenth century perhaps 10 per cent of the population of France lived in towns, 21 per cent of the population of England and 35 per cent of the population of Holland. See E. A. Wrigley, *People, Cities and Wealth: the Transformation of Traditional Society* (Oxford, 1987), pp. 170, 182, 184.

[131] 'Commerce', *Essays*, p. 263.

appetites, and, second, in the accumulation of resources which the state may draw on in emergency.

Nevertheless, before Hume had finished the essay, he appeared to make a significant concession. He admitted that the poverty of the common people in France, Italy, and Spain was in some measure due to the superior fertility of the soil and happiness of the climate in those southern regions of Europe. Since agriculture there was easy, and required no stock or art, the peasants had no incentive to produce more than was needed for their subsistence.[132] Though Hume gave no indication of a source for this observation, the point is suspiciously close to Melon's observation that fertile, agricultural countries are at risk of shortages. Was Hume admitting the existence of a distinct category of agricultural economies, as Melon and his Neapolitan followers had proposed? Hume's answer, which was negative, emerges from his subsequent essays.

The next essay was 'Of Luxury' (from 1760 re-titled 'Of Refinement in the Arts'). Having just demonstrated the economic benefits of luxury in 'Of Commerce', Hume did no more than summarise them here. The increase and consumption of all commodities which serve to give ornament and pleasure to life are beneficial to society, he reiterated, because they both multiply the 'innocent gratifications' of individuals, and constitute 'a kind of storehouse of labour' which is available in 'exigencies of state'.[133] Most of the essay was devoted instead to turning the standard moral objections to luxury on their head. Luxury did not undermine, it refined manners, improved knowledge, and increased sociability. 'Thus *industry, knowledge,* and *humanity,* are linked together by an indissoluble chain.'[134] Luxury was also favourable to liberty, because it undermined the sharp division between landed proprietors and their vassals, freeing the latter from dependence.[135] Hume allowed that it was possible for luxury to be 'vicious'. But only in a specific sense, consistent with his own principles of morals: 'no gratification, however sensual, can of itself be esteemed vicious'. Gratification was only vicious when a man deprived himself of the ability to perform such acts of duty and generosity as his situation and fortune required – that is, when his actions no longer merited sympathetic approval. Even so, to try to eliminate vicious luxury without also eradicating the contrary vice of sloth would only diminish industry.[136] In these terms, Hume's defence of luxury was even more unequivocal than Melon's, since Hume saw no need to drop the

---

[132] Ibid., pp. 266–7.   [133] 'Of Luxury', from 1760 'Of Refinement in the Arts', *Essays*, p. 272.
[134] 'Refinement', *Essays*, p. 271.   [135] Ibid., p. 277.   [136] Ibid., pp. 279–80.

term, as Melon suggested. It was also more consistent than Mandeville's, Hume sharply rebuking the author of the *Fable of the Bees* for claiming that vice might be advantageous.[137] Luxury was not only a beneficial feature of a commercial economy, Hume was arguing: it was also morally defensible.

Having digressed to settle the disputed question of luxury, Hume returned to more specifically economic issues. The third of the *Political Discourses* was 'Of Money'. Money, in Hume's definition, was not one of the subjects of commerce; nor was it the wheels of trade. 'It is the oil which renders the motion of the wheels more smooth and easy.' In any one state, he continued, the greater or lesser plenty of money is of no consequence, since the prices of commodities are always proportioned to the amount of money available.[138] The question which interested Hume, however, was the position of one country relative to another: specifically, the prospects of a poor country in competition with a rich one. A country without an extensive commerce or much gold and silver has the advantage of the low price of its labour, which will enable it gradually to attract manufactures from richer countries. With this advantage, Hume argued, the poor country would be ill advised to increase its supply of money by the artificial means of banks and paper credit.[139] But Hume then qualified this conclusion with two observations. One was that a gradual increase in the supply of money could have the effect of stimulating economic activity in the short term, before prices caught up. This was an argument, he noted with satisfaction, that the French writers – he named Melon, Dutot, and Duverney – had overlooked.[140] His second observation, by contrast, referred to the long term. Once a nation had become fully commercial, and required money for all its transactions, it was imperative to ensure the 'thorough concoction and circulation' of money through the state. As long as money circulated, the volume of economic activity could continue to increase, even without an increase in the supply of money; indeed, the resulting lower prices would help maintain the nation's competitiveness. But if money did not circulate extensively, there was a danger that parts of the economy would revert to the lower levels of economic activity associated with barter.[141] The point was elaborated in the following essay 'Of Interest', when Hume discussed the role of merchants, 'one of the most useful races of men'. They facilitate industry, he observed, both by conveying a product from one part of a state to another, and by accumulating the funds to carry it on. As commerce

---

[137] Ibid., p. 280.   [138] 'Of Money', *Essays*, p. 281.   [139] Ibid., pp. 283–5.
[140] Ibid., pp. 255–8, with n. 7.   [141] Ibid., pp. 289–94.

increases and their profits fall, so their frugality increases, permitting the lowering of interest rates.[142]

In these and later essays, Hume's arguments on money exemplified his conviction that economic subjects required subtlety and refinement. But despite the jibe at French expense, on this subject he and Melon were not so far apart. Both were agreed that nations should not seek quantity of money for its own sake, and further agreed on the importance of the circulation of money throughout an economy, to ensure its greatest possible commercialisation. They also agreed, though Hume refined the argument into a short-term framework, that an increase in money supply could be beneficial. What was distinctive about Hume's position was his concern to emphasise the advantages of a poor nation in competition with a richer one. Istvan Hont has emphasised the centrality of this argument to Hume's economic thinking, and its implicit reference (noticed by contemporaries) to Scotland's prospects in relation to England.[143] But the argument may also be seen as Hume's answer to the suggestion that there was a distinct agricultural form of economy, requiring a different model of development. The fertile but poor agricultural nations of southern Europe were not excluded from Hume's model of a commercial economy, for they were subject to the same general rules governing the operation of money. There was no reason why they too should not take advantage of lower labour costs, and attract manufactures from countries whose costs had become much higher. If circumstances were favourable, they might benefit from a controlled, short-term increase in money supply. They should certainly do everything possible to improve the circulation of money through their economies, to maximise their commercialisation. In these respects, the position of agricultural economies was no different from others in less fertile territories. Fully to refute the suggestion that agricultural economies were different, however, Hume also needed to elaborate his argument for the benefits of foreign trade.

He did so across a further series of essays, in which he attacked the phenomenon of 'jealousy of trade'. He first tackled the doctrine of 'the balance of trade', according to which a nation must prevent its imports exceeding its exports, in order to preserve and augment its quantity of money. He underlined the difficulty of accurately calculating the balance: calculations which had seemed to show a grave imbalance of trade, such as

---

[142] 'Of Interest', *Essays*, pp. 300–7.

[143] Istvan Hont, 'The "rich country–poor country" debate in Scottish classical political economy', in Hont and Ignatieff, *Wealth and Virtue*, pp. 271–315; see also Hont's 'Introduction' to *Jealousy of Trade*, pp. 63–77. The original essay is also reprinted in this volume.

those by Gee and Swift, had proved to be wildly mistaken.[144] Dispensing with calculation, Hume chose instead to demonstrate the fallacy of the doctrine with a general, hypothetical argument. The level of money in a kingdom is taken to be in proportion to the labour and commodities within it. Were the level suddenly to fall, prices would fall with it, the nation would then be able to sell its products abroad more cheaply, and the money would return. It is therefore unnecessary, and may be damaging, to seek to prevent an adverse balance of trade when trade itself provides an automatic correcting mechanism. It is not even in a nation's interest to retaliate when another bans its exports. The French excluded English woollens, and in response the English had deprived themselves of French wines. Melon had noticed that the damage was mutual, and should have been avoided; but Hume went further, pointing out that the English could still circumvent it. By continuing to purchase French wine, and even increasing their demand for it, they would require more land to be taken under cultivation for vines, obliging the French to import English grain for their subsistence.[145]

Although the balance of trade doctrine was a major cause of jealousy of trade, it was still primarily concerned with money. Hume needed to explain why free trade would benefit all nations, and not simply strengthen those already more advanced. This he sought to do in the essay specifically entitled 'Of the Jealousy of Trade', which he added to the collection in 1758, inserting it between the original essays on the balance of trade and the balance of power. No nation, Hume contended, ought to fear the increasing wealth and trade of another, for the richer nation cannot continue to prosper without promoting the riches and commerce of its neighbours. He reiterated his conviction that the domestic industry of a nation would be improved by emulation and imitation of foreign manufactures. But he now also argued that a nation was most unlikely to find its neighbours so improved that they had no demand for its products. This was not simply because of the diversity of natural endowments. A nation whose inhabitants become opulent and skilful will desire a higher standard of quality, and as they have plenty of commodities of their own to exchange, will be happy to import others which are better manufactured elsewhere. Trade between nations, in other words, creates opportunities for specialisation in quality production, which need not be confined to richer countries.[146] Hume was careful to distinguish this argument for specialisation from the traditional preference for a 'staple' product, such as England's woollen manufacture. If other

---

[144] 'Of the Balance of Trade', *Essays*, pp. 310–11.   [145] Ibid., pp. 311–16.
[146] 'Of the Jealousy of Trade' (1758), *Essays*, pp. 327–9.

nations entered the industry, there was no point in attempting to preserve the staple; better to transfer those employed in it to other manufactures, such as linen, silk, or iron, for which there was demand. Labour flexibility and product diversity were to be desired, not feared:

The emulation among rival nations serves rather to keep industry alive in all of them: And any people is happier who possess a variety of manufactures, than if they enjoyed one single great manufacture, in which they are all employed. Their situation is less precarious; and they will feel less sensibly those revolutions and uncertainties, to which every particular branch of commerce will always be exposed.[147]

The only nation which had reason to fear the improvement of its neighbours, Hume added, was one such as that of the Dutch, who had no extent of territory or number of native commodities. Even then the capital and commercial expertise of such a nation should enable it to profit from the flourishing of its neighbours for quite some time, as indeed the Dutch had demonstrated.[148]

Istvan Hont has pointed out that Hume was effectively articulating the principle of comparative advantage.[149] It is in the interest of even the most advanced nation to specialise, and to exchange what it produces best – most efficiently and profitably – for what it does less well. It was a principle from which not only Scotland, but also the agricultural regions of southern Europe, ought to have been able to benefit. To his fellow Scots, such as Patrick Lindsay, Hume was saying that it was a mistake to believe they must develop a staple product in which to concentrate their exports, or should continue to worry about the balance of trade. Rather they should exploit their price advantage as long as it lasted, take the opportunity to improve their manufactures by imitation of those they now imported, and learn to specialise in products for which there was an international demand. But Hume was also in a position to disabuse Melon and those who followed him of their belief that fertile agricultural economies should adopt a separate path of development. To their argument that such economies must first build up the internal market for their agriculture and manufactures, while protecting them from imports, Hume would respond that without 'the pleasures of luxury and the profits of commerce' which only foreign trade could bring, the incentives to invest in agriculture and to develop manufactures would be felt much more slowly. Were the agricultural countries to open their trade, however, they could expect (like the Scots) to take

---

[147] Ibid., pp. 329–30. [148] Ibid., pp. 330–31.
[149] Hont, *Jealousy of Trade*, introduction, pp. 68–70.

advantage of their lower prices, and find markets for the products with which nature had endowed them so abundantly.

Hume's case against jealousy of trade was admittedly contingent. It pre-supposed that no one nation would acquire the political and military power forcibly to distort the pattern of trade over a long period. The essay 'Of the Balance of Power' gave his reasons for thinking that such a threat no longer existed. Not only did the moderns explicitly acknowledge the concept of a balance of power; there was no longer a state in Europe which seriously aspired to its antithesis, the goal of universal monarchy. If France had ever entertained such an ambition, Hume agreed with Montesquieu, it was incapable of it now.[150] But while the threat of universal monarchy could be discounted, Hume would become increasingly aware of danger from another, perhaps unexpected, quarter: Great Britain itself. Having stood foremost against France in a succession of wars, the British people were now over-eager to counter imagined French aspirations, and were diverting excessive resources into the struggle.[151] The most obvious and dangerous manifestation of this was the growth of the public debt. In a separate, extended (and several times revised) essay, 'Of Public Credit', Hume sub-jected the arguments used to defend such schemes to sustained criticism. Several of these arguments were Melon's. To say that public debts amounted to transferring money from the right hand to the left, Hume remarked, was but one of numerous 'loose reasonings and specious comparisons' which bedevilled the subject.[152] Another was the supposed benefit of public credit to 'circulation': Hume claimed that he had never been able to discover the meaning of the term as it was used in the present subject.[153] But these were asides. Hume's real targets in the essay on public credit were the English statesmen whose hostility towards France was in danger of becoming an ambition to acquire a commercial empire by force, and their uncritical foreign admirers, like the excessively anglophile Montesquieu.[154]

---

[150] 'Of the Balance of Power', *Essays*, pp. 337–8.

[151] Ibid., pp. 338–40. The point was sharpened in a revision to the 1770 edition of the *Essays*, when Hume dropped a passage which seemed to take French power and ambition seriously; but the comments on the excessive response by the British people were there from the first edition. The deleted passage is printed on pp. 634–5 of the edition of the *Essays* used here.

[152] 'Of Public Credit', *Essays*, p. 356.

[153] Ibid., pp. 636–7, for the passage as originally published; it was removed (from p. 353 in the edition of the *Essays* used here) in 1770. A footnote to the original passage ascribed this use of 'circulation' to 'MELON, DU TOT, LAW, in the pamphlets published in FRANCE'.

[154] On Hume's critique of the debt: Istvan Hont, 'The rhapsody of public debt: David Hume and voluntary state bankruptcy', in Nicholas Phillipson and Quentin Skinner (eds.), *Political Discourse in Early Modern Britain* (Cambridge, 1993), pp. 321–48; and on his scepticism over universal monarchy: John Robertson, 'Universal monarchy and the liberties of Europe; David Hume's critique of an English Whig doctrine', in ibid., pp. 349–73.

The essay 'Of the Jealousy of Trade' should therefore be read in the context of Hume's mounting anxiety over the direction of British policy. This anxiety provided an immediate, urgent reason to include the essay in 1758. It was because he realised that the case for free trade was about to be submerged under an aggressive British (not French) military and naval imperialism that Hume set down, as plainly and succinctly as possible, the benefits of such trade for all nations. 'Not only as a man', he concluded,

> but as a BRITISH subject, I pray for the flourishing commerce of GERMANY, SPAIN, ITALY, and even FRANCE itself. I am at least certain, that GREAT BRITAIN, and all those nations, would flourish more, did their sovereigns and ministers adopt such enlarged and benevolent sentiments towards each other.[155]

Jealousy of trade would be damaging to Britain itself; to Scotland, as part of Britain; and to the southern regions of Europe, not least the small, agricultural states of Italy. As presented in the *Political Discourses*, Hume's model of trade-led development may have been contingent upon the political context of a balance of power, which he knew to be fragile. But this did not alter the *general* validity of the model, or the desirability of adopting it rather than pursuing commercial aggrandisement by military means. Commerce was not an alternative means to achieve empire, as Melon had suggested; it was an alternative to empire *tout court*. This was why, ultimately, it was the best hope of a Scotland, or a Naples.[156]

POLITICAL ECONOMY AS THE CASE FOR THE ENLIGHTENMENT

When Hume published the *Political Discourses*, I wish to argue, he was making the case for Enlightenment in Scotland just as Genovesi was in Naples. In making his case, Genovesi deployed political economy to serve two larger purposes. With the aid of the best available writing on the subject from the advanced nations of Europe, he would bring a cosmopolitan, comparative perspective to bear on the economic prospects of the kingdom. At the same time, he sought to create a 'public sphere' in Naples, by presenting political economy as a subject urgently in need of the widest possible public discussion, where before it had been treated as a secret of state, to be confined to the 'private' sphere of ministerial memoranda. In a

---

[155] 'Jealousy of Trade', *Essays*, p. 331.
[156] John Robertson, 'The Enlightenment above national context: political economy in eighteenth-century Scotland and Naples', *The Historical Journal*, 40 (1997) esp. pp. 676–82, represents an earlier version of this interpretation of Hume in relation to Melon.

rather different context, Hume may be seen to have pursued not dissimilar ends.

Matching Genovesi's commitment to a cosmopolitan perspective, Hume wrote his economic essays on the basis of a range of reference far wider than that hitherto used in Scottish economic debate, whether at the time of the Union or more recently, in the 1730s. More systematically than Genovesi, he made the arguments of Melon's *Essai politique* a foil for his own; and he engaged with a variety of other English, Irish, and French writers. Towards the French, it is true, Hume was noticeably less generous than Genovesi. His dismissals of several of Melon's weaker arguments belied the seriousness with which he responded to the French writer's central propositions; and he was always unwilling to engage directly with Montesquieu, whether he agreed with him or not. But the cosmopolitan implication of Hume's essays was clear: no nation should expect to rely on its own intellectual resources when discussing the economy. Hume may have been merely mischievous when he decided that Edinburgh advocates ought to be offered modern French novels as diversionary reading in their library. But in political economy a willingness to look to France and beyond for inspiration, comparison, and constructive disagreement was essential.

In making the case for Enlightenment, Hume did not have to create a public sphere in Scotland, as Genovesi did in Naples. Political and economic issues had been more or less freely debated in print in Scotland as in England since the 1690s, and those who wished to influence government policy had learnt they might do so by appealing to public opinion as well as, or better than, by writing privately for ministers. Hume himself published the *Political Discourses* through the booksellers Kincaid and Donaldson in Edinburgh, and he later recalled with satisfaction that 'it was the only work of mine that was successful on the first publication. It was as well received abroad and at home.'[157] The recollection may not have been strictly accurate. The comment on its reception abroad was fully justified, following the appearance of two translations of the *Discours politiques* in Amsterdam in 1754.[158] But success 'at home' is more likely to have come the following year, when the essays were included in the first cheap, multi-volume edition of Hume's *Essays and Treatises on Several Subjects*, whose principal publisher was Andrew Millar, in London, although Kincaid and Donaldson retained

---

[157] 'My Own Life', *Essays*, p. xxxvi.

[158] The translations were the work of J.-B. Le Blanc and Eléazar Mauvillon. They naturally did not include 'Of the Jealousy of Trade'. An Italian translation, the work of the Venetian Matteo Dandolo, appeared as *Discorsi politici* in 1767: on which, Maria Luisa Baldi, *David Hume nel Settecento italiano. Filosofia ed economia* (Florence, 1983), pp. 9, 174–8.

an interest.[159] As he was to learn, definitively, from the débacle of the Edinburgh publication of the first volume of his *History of Great Britain* in 1754, Hume needed direct access to the London market to achieve good sales (and the financial rewards he felt were his due). But the limitations on the market for books published in Edinburgh do not mean that Scotland had failed to develop a 'public sphere' of its own.

Since the Union, when the Scots lost their Parliament, a variety of voluntary societies had sprung up to provide opportunities for discussion, and, in some cases, for practical improving initiatives. Some, such as The Honourable the Improvers in the Knowledge of Agriculture (1723–46), were dominated by landowners; others, such as The Philosophical Society of Edinburgh (founded in 1737), were chiefly for academics and laity with an active interest in letters and sciences. But by far the most important voluntary institution in Edinburgh in the 1750s, the Select Society, drew its members from both the literary and the landed elites. Belying its name, the society grew from an original 15 members in 1754 to 135 by 1759. The great majority of landed members were heirs-apparent, indicating that the society contained those who expected soon to become the leaders of Scottish society. Its constitution barred discussion of revealed religion and any question which might offer an opportunity to express Jacobite principles; but otherwise the topics proposed for debate ranged across politics, morals, economics, and the arts. Within a year of its foundation, the practical, improving inclinations of the society's members also resulted in the formation of a subsidiary, the Society for the Encouragement of Arts, Sciences, and Manufactures.[160] Nor were such initiatives confined to Edinburgh. The Glasgow Literary Society was founded in 1752, and the Wise Club or Philosophical Society in Aberdeen in 1758, alongside the Gordon's Mill Farming Club. Across Scotland, therefore, the 1750s saw a multiplying of opportunities for the discussion of issues of public concern, unfettered by the state. The *Political Discourses* were almost guaranteed an active readership.

If Hume did not need to create a public for the discussion of political economy in Scotland, his writing implied a definite conception of the level

[159] Richard Sher, 'The book in the Scottish Enlightenment', in Emerson and others, *The Culture of the Book in the Scottish Enlightenment*, pp. 43–7: a foretaste of important work to come from Sher.
[160] R. L. Emerson, 'The social composition of Enlightened Scotland: the Select Society of Edinburgh 1754–64', *Studies on Voltaire and the Eighteenth Century*, 114 (1973), 291–329; Nicholas T. Phillipson, 'Culture and society in the eighteenth-century province: the case of Edinburgh and the Scottish Enlightenment', in Lawrence Stone (ed.), *The University in Society*, 2 vols. (Princeton, 1874) II, pp. 444–5; John Robertson, *The Scottish Enlightenment and the Militia Issue* (Edinburgh, 1985), pp. 85–6.

at which discussion should take place. It was observed that immediately on his move to Edinburgh in 1751 Hume had placed himself at the centre of its intellectual life, and had sought to impose certain standards of behaviour on his fellow men of letters. It is also noticeable, however, that he was wary of involvement in activities which went beyond his strictly intellectual expertise, and even, perhaps, his ability to control: despite his role in founding the Select Society, he kept his distance from its offshoot, the Society for the Encouragement of Arts, Sciences, and Manufactures. His priority, it seems, was to set a standard of intellectual discussion, and then to try to ensure that this was not compromised by men of letters themselves. When his favourable view of the prospects of poor countries was challenged later in the 1750s by Josiah Tucker, who used Lord Kames as an intermediary, Hume went to some lengths in correspondence to ensure that his arguments had been properly understood before Tucker expressed his criticisms in print.[161] Given his insistence on the necessarily 'refined and subtle' character of economic principles, Hume was certainly expecting a good deal of the readers of the *Political Discourses*. But this was the point: for Hume, Enlightenment was a serious intellectual exercise.

Hume's seriousness of purpose in writing on political economy marked, and perhaps also masked, a major change of intellectual direction. By the 1750s he had recognised that he could not expect to make the case for Enlightenment as if he were addressing a society of atheists; but he could make it to a society of improvers. Hume never quite gave up hope of the former, publishing the *Natural History of Religion* as one of the *Four Dissertations* in 1757, and making careful testamentary provision (more than once revised) to ensure that the *Dialogues of Natural Religion* were published after his death.[162] But he now recognised that a direct, public assault on the assumption that religious faith was the necessary basis of morality would be counterproductive, isolating himself and fatally prejudicing the case for Enlightenment. The promotion of political economy, as the means to achieve human betterment in *this* world, was far more likely to command the attention of the Scottish public.

---

[161] On this exchange, Hont, 'The "rich country–poor country" debate', *Wealth and Virtue*, pp. 275–6, 284–9.

[162] The persistence of hope over probability on this score was nicely acknowledged by Hume himself, in his imaginary conversation with Charon, when he begged for a little more time in this world, that he might have 'the satisfaction of seeing the downfal of some of the prevailing systems of superstition', only for Charon to reply, 'that will not happen these many hundred years', and order Hume forthwith into his boat. Adam Smith reported this whimsy of the dying Hume in his 'Letter from Adam Smith, LL. D. to William Strahan, Esq., Kirkaldy, Fifeshire, Nov. 9, 1776', printed in *Essays*, pp. xlv–xlvi.

It would nevertheless be a mistake to conclude that political economy was chosen to make the case for Enlightenment solely because it illustrated the desirability of a cosmopolitan perspective, and facilitated the creation and intellectual leadership of a sphere of public discussion independent of the state. For the case for Enlightenment was not simply about a willingness to learn from others; it was not simply about the creation and enlargement of opportunities for public discussion beyond the privileged sphere of government. It was about ideas, and the importance of good argument for understanding and, in time, changing the societies of Europe. As a system of ideas, political economy was not merely a means to an end, arbitrarily chosen from a range of possible intellectual disciplines. There were more fundamental, intellectual reasons for its emergence as the agent of Enlightenment in Naples and in Scotland. Political economy was chosen because it addressed what since the beginning of the century had been recognised as the most pressing problem to face the two countries: their backwardness relative to the richer and more powerful nations of Europe, and their urgent need for economic and social transformation. And it addressed this problem in terms – in concepts and arguments – which carried methodological and philosophical conviction.

In the first place, political economy provided concepts with which to address the specific circumstances of the two countries, whether understood (as by Genovesi and Galiani, after Melon) as those of a fertile, agricultural economy, or (as by Hume, against Melon) as those of poor countries in general. At the same time, it could be presented as a coherent, general, science. In Genovesi's formulation, it was a science with its own 'ends, rules, and principles', in Hume's, a science composed of 'universal propositions' which were capable of being set out in a single theorem. Even more important than its methodological coherence, however, were the foundations of both Neapolitan and Scottish political economy in a broad current in philosophy which seemed, in the first half of the eighteenth century, to offer the most compelling approach to thinking about human nature and sociability. From Celestino Galiani and Intieri, via Melon, both Ferdinando Galiani and Genovesi inherited assumptions about human nature characteristic of the Augustinian and more especially Epicurean strands of philosophy prevalent in Neapolitan intellectual culture since the early eighteenth century. These were the same assumptions whose power Vico had recognised and sought to transcend, and which Doria and Broggia still sought to repudiate. For his part, Hume founded his political economy on his own radical reworking of Epicurean moral philosophy, shaped as that was by close engagement with Bayle and Mandeville; and when he turned to political economy in the *Political Discourses*, it was to engage with the arguments of another student of Bayle and Mandeville, Melon. Ultimately, the case for Enlightenment in Naples and Scotland rested on the strength of these foundations, and on the coherence and relevance of the political economy which Genovesi, Galiani and Hume constructed upon them. In both countries, the Enlightenment stood or fell on its intellectual merits.

Conclusion: the Enlightenment vindicated?

TWO CONTEXTS, ONE ENLIGHTENMENT

In the two very different 'national' contexts of Scotland and Naples, it has been argued, there emerged one Enlightenment. More precisely, there emerged in the two countries in the middle decades of the eighteenth century thinkers who saw themselves as members of a wider, European intellectual movement, dedicated to understanding and publicising the cause of human betterment on this earth. In both cases, the terms in which this objective was articulated were those of political economy. To Antonio Genovesi and Ferdinando Galiani in Naples, as to David Hume in Scotland, political economy furnished the concepts required to understand the economic and social predicament of their respective countries. At the same time, the arguments of political economy could be more or less freely aired in print, and thus set before a 'public' much wider than the narrow circles of rulers and their ministerial advisers who had hitherto monopolised the discussion of such matters, reserving them to 'reason of state'. As a coherent intellectual discourse, even discipline (in the sense that it bound its exponents to certain forms of argument), which could also be addressed to the public at large, political economy supplied the terms in which the case for Enlightenment could be made both in Naples and in Scotland. In these two cases, it would seem, we do not need to follow John Pocock in supposing that different contexts fashioned plural Enlightenments. Instead we may do better to think, with Franco Venturi, of one Enlightenment in which patriotic and cosmopolitan impulses were combined: the patriotic inspiring the exponents of political economy to identify and publicise solutions adapted to the particular circumstances of their countries, the cosmopolitan encouraging them to think comparatively, and to frame their arguments for the general benefit of humanity.

With the argument that political economy was the vehicle of a single Enlightenment has been associated a second: that Enlightenment was not

377

successfully articulated by radical irreligion. The clearest proof of this lies in the fate of one who has featured only marginally in this book: the Neapolitan historian Pietro Giannone. His exile from Naples after the publication of the *Storia Civile*, and his later capture and imprisonment by the duke of Savoy, amounted to an unambiguous statement that in the Catholic world open irreligion, whether of a Spinozist or other variety, would not be tolerated, and would certainly not be permitted public expression. But there is an important sense in which the work, and perhaps also the frustrated career, of Giannone's Neapolitan contemporary, Giambattista Vico, has told the same tale. For all Vico's professions of orthodox intent, for all his – it has been argued here – genuine determination to reinstate and vindicate the historical reality of divine providence, Vico had explored subjects and adapted arguments whose further public discussion would very probably have created difficulties. The history of the early peoples of the Bible, the proposition that men were not naturally sociable, the need to defend the superiority of idolatry over atheism, these combined with his recognition of the explanatory power of Epicurean concepts of human nature took Vico down an intellectual path which no one in the next generation was able to follow. As the leader of that generation, Genovesi admired Vico and Giannone; but he knew that their intellectual choices could not be those of Enlightenment. In Naples, at least, it was simply not true that – in Jonathan Israel's phrase – 'the real business was over' by the 1740s. For all the extraordinary achievements of Giannone and Vico, the case for Enlightenment, as Genovesi realised, had yet to be made.

It might be thought that the writing and career of David Hume prove that the same was not true in the Protestant world. Like Mandeville, Hume was free to write about morals as if divine providence and the afterlife had no bearing on our conduct in this world: he could publish the *Treatise of Human Nature* and even the *Natural History of Religion* without fear of official censure. (Even the *Dialogues of Natural Religion*, it seems, were withheld from publication in his own lifetime more out of a reluctance to embarrass his friends.) Yet Hume's case was not completely different. He himself thought it wise to cut off the 'nobler parts' of the *Treatise* before publication, in an attempt to enhance its philosophical acceptability in the eyes of Joseph Butler and, perhaps, Francis Hutcheson. Even then, his prudence was in vain; Hutcheson in particular was not deceived. When Hume applied for a chair in moral philosophy at Edinburgh a few years later, Hutcheson moved swiftly to stop him, well aware that the rank-and-file clergy of the Scottish church would be roused against him. Hume might argue that atheists made better, more moral members of society than believers, but when he finally settled among his fellow countrymen in Edinburgh, he knew that he could not address them as if they were or could be expected to become atheists. Far better, he recognised, to address them in the terms of political economy (demanding as he emphasised these were), as members of a nation of improvers.

The adoption of political economy as the discourse of Enlightenment in the two countries cannot, however, be attributed simply to the coincidental intuition of a few thinkers. Comparative study of Naples and Scotland has done more than identify political economy, rather than radical irreligion, as the vehicle for Enlightenment; it has also suggested reasons why this should have been so. Two explanations have emerged. One derives from the specific political and economic circumstances of the two kingdoms, and the repeated attempts by observers within them to understand their predicament, and identify ways by which they might escape it. Preceding the engagement of Galiani, Genovesi, and Hume with political economy in the 1740s and 1750s, it has been shown, were the efforts of Francesco d'Andrea, Paolo Mattia Doria, and others in Naples, Andrew Fletcher, John Law, and William Seton in Scotland, as they strove to comprehend the crises facing their respective societies in the 1690s and 1700s. In both cases, there was a preoccupation with the dependent status of 'kingdoms governed as provinces', and a determination to discover how they might catch up with the more advanced nations of Europe, whose commerce was recognised to be the key to their prosperity and power. As an examination of the economic and social condition of the two kingdoms had revealed, the extent to which this preoccupation was shared across the two societies was not equal: the leaders of Scottish society, landowners and lawyers, were much more unified in their commitment to economic development than their Neapolitan counterparts. This did not deter Doria and others from stating their case; but before the 1750s they had to do so in manuscript, for the eyes of sympathetic ministers only. When Genovesi turned from philosophy to political economy in the 1750s, he had consciously to create a 'public' for the subject, by a programme of publication and lecturing. By contrast, Hume was able to devote more energy to refining and enhancing the understanding of economic principles among a public which in Scotland already existed. In addition, it was seen that the particular circumstances of the Neapolitan economy led its observers from the first to emphasise the potential of the kingdom's natural resources, and to put the encouragement of agriculture before commerce itself. It is not surprising that the priorities of Galiani and Genovesi should have differed markedly from those of Hume when they constructed their models of economic development.

The second, no less important explanation for the appeal of political economy to Neapolitan and Scottish thinkers was intellectual rather than circumstantial. It is to be found in the extent to which the political economy of Galiani, Genovesi, and Hume derived intellectual credibility from a specific conjunction of ideas: the encounter of rigorist Augustinianism with the modern Epicurean philosophy of morals. The encounter made it possible to construct an account of human sociability on the basis of the earthly utility and pleasure which men and women derived from commerce (as well as sexual relations) with each other. As Vico's case demonstrates, this by no means led necessarily or directly to political economy. Even though it was a recurrent interest of his friend Doria, the new discipline was ignored by Vico, who instead devoted every ounce of his extraordinary intellect to demonstrating that an Epicurean account of human sociability did not exclude the role of divine providence. In his fear of corruption and interest in the possibility of a relapse into 'barbarism', Vico also denied the possibility of progress, and hence of lasting human betterment. Yet even as he did so, Vico made no attempt to disguise the this-worldliness of the Epicurean account of sociability: indeed his distinction of the operation of divine providence from the action of divine grace clearly separated the question of how humans come to live in society, and why they persist in doing so, from that of individuals' fates in the world to come. It is perhaps not surprising, therefore, that Vico failed to deter those among his Neapolitan contemporaries whose enthusiasm for Epicurean principles was less qualified by theological ambivalence. Foremost among these were Celestino Galiani and Bartolomeo Intieri, the first of whom had found no obstacle to combining an Epicurean account of sociability with a natural theology and a God-given natural law. It was their enthusiasm for the economic writing of Jean-François Melon, whose Epicurean inspiration was evident in his debt to Bayle and Mandeville, which inspired the younger Galiani and Genovesi to take up political economy for themselves, and apply it to the Neapolitan case.

By contrast, Hume, who thought the idea of divine providence of no value in explaining men's behaviour in this world (and in any case undemonstrable as a causal proposition), could be much more direct. Our sociability was indeed explicable on the Epicurean grounds of usefulness and agreeableness, he argued, once the paradoxes of Mandeville were superseded by the explanation of moral judgement based on sympathy and convention which he offered in the *Treatise of Human Nature*. In Hume's hands, scepticism and modern Epicurean moral philosophy thus provided the ideal intellectual foundations for political economy, as the discourse *par excellence* of human betterment on this earth.

Enlightenment in Scotland as in Naples, therefore, may be seen to have built on Epicurean intellectual foundations. But we have also seen that those foundations were of much longer and securer standing in Naples than they were in Scotland. Vico, still thought of by some as an isolated genius, 'born before his time', was in fact the product of a rich and up-to-date intellectual culture, in which Epicureanism had been a predominant current since the late seventeenth century. By contrast, Epicureanism came late to Scotland, and Hume seems to have picked it up on his own initiative, first by reading Bayle for 'diversion and improvement', then by moving to France to find the confidence and the freedom to write the *Treatise of Human Nature*. But the delay in the reception of Epicureanism only enhanced and focused its eventual impact. Contrary to much recent wishful thinking by students of Scottish intellectual culture in the late seventeenth and early eighteenth centuries, there was precious little basis for Enlightenment in Scotland before Hume discovered the intellectual pleasures of Epicureanism. Here, even more than in Naples, it makes no sense at all to suppose that 'the real business was over' by 1740. It had only begun a year earlier, with the publication of books I and II of the *Treatise*, and it was not formulated in terms widely acceptable to the Scottish 'public' until the 1750s, when Hume published the *Political Discourses*, followed by his *History*. Comparative study of the intellectual history of Scotland and Naples between 1680 and 1760 thus points to one more conclusion. It was David Hume who initiated Enlightenment in Scotland; without him, Scottish participation in the European intellectual movement dedicated to human betterment would have been much weaker, and might never have occurred.

ENLIGHTENMENT AFTER 1760

If the political economy of Genovesi and Hume marked the advent of Enlightenment in Naples and Scotland, what followed? More to the point, does the course of intellectual development in the two countries after 1760 continue to support the thesis that there was one Enlightenment in both? It would require another volume to answer the question at convincing length; here it is possible only to outline some of the main avenues of intellectual enquiry in the two countries in the last four decades of the eighteenth century, as an indication of the evidence on which a future judgement may be based.[1]

[1] In what follows I shall give details of editions of the primary sources cited in the text, but will refer only selectively to relevant secondary scholarship, which in many areas is already considerable. What is offered here is no more than a sketch of the later Enlightenment in the two countries, and it would be misleading if detailed references were to give the impression of a comprehensive engagement with the subject.

One element of continuity, at least, seems clear: the importance attached to political economy. In the independent kingdom of Naples the vital importance of economic prosperity, and the costs of failing to secure it, were dramatically brought home by the terrible famine of 1764. Genovesi responded immediately, publishing another work by a member of the Gournay circle, Claude Herbert, on the subject of the grain trade, and following it with two editions in quick succession of his own *Lezioni di commercio, o sia d'economia civile* (1765–67; 2nd edn. 1768–70), a collected and developed version of the lectures he had been giving as professor of commerce and mechanics.[2] After his death in 1769, several of his pupils took up the baton: political economy was a central interest of Francesco Longano (who succeeded to Genovesi's chair), Giuseppe Maria Galanti (Genovesi's biographer, and a publisher as well as a writer), Domenico Grimaldi, and Giuseppe Palmieri.[3] Two preoccupations marked their writings.

The first was publicity: Genovesi's efforts to create a 'third force' among the younger generation in favour of economic reform were redoubled by Giuseppe Galanti and Domenico Grimaldi in particular. Their chosen instrument was the survey, urged by Grimaldi in his *Piano di riforma per la pubblica economia delle provincie del Regno di Napoli* (1780), but pioneered in practice by Galanti in his *Descrizione dello stato antico ed attuale del contado di Molise* (1781), later extended to the whole of both Sicilies in his *Nuova descrizione storica e geografica delle Sicilie* (1786–94). The object of these extraordinary efforts was to determine the resources available for economic development, and the persisting obstacles to their fruitful realisation.[4] At the same time, both Galanti and Grimaldi urged the establishment of agricultural societies and academies in the provinces, to disseminate knowledge of good practice: as early as 1772, Galanti cited as examples to be followed the societies which had been established in Dublin and in Edinburgh to

---

[2] *Riflessioni sull'economia generale dei grani, tradotte dal Francese, con un discorso preliminare del Signor Abbate Genovesi* (Naples, 1765), a translation of Claude Herbert, *Essai sur la police générale des grains* (1754), reprinted in *Antonio Genovesi. Scritti economici*, ed. Maria Luisa Perna (Naples, 1984), II, pp. 1131–235. Antonio Genovesi, *Lezioni de commercio, o sia d'economia civile* (Naples, 1765–7; 2nd edn. Naples, 1768–70); a critical edition is in preparation by Maria Luisa Perna.

[3] Biographical information on all of these, and on Francescantonio Grimaldi, Gaetano Filangieri, and Francesco Mario Pagano (to be discussed shortly), may be found in Franco Venturi (ed.), *Illuministi italiani*. Vol. V: *Riformatori Napoletani* (Milan and Naples, 1962).

[4] Domenico Grimaldi, *Piano di riforma per la pubblica economia delle provincie del Regno di Napoli, e per l'agricoltura delle due Sicilie* (Naples, 1780). Giuseppe Maria Galanti, *Descrizione dello stato antico ed attuale del contado di Molise*, 2 vols. (Naples, 1781); and *Nuova descrizione storica e geografica delle Sicilie*, 5 vols. (Naples, 1786–94), subsequent references being to this edition. There is a modern edition by F. Assante and D. Demarco, *Della descrizione geografica e politica delle Sicilie*, 2 vols. (Naples, 1969).

promote manufactures.[5] The call was widely repeated, and if independent provincial initiatives were few, the monarchy itself was persuaded to take the initiative in founding patriotic societies in three northern centres by 1790.[6]

The second preoccupation of these Neapolitan economists was a continued effort to harness the conceptual resources of contemporary French political economy to identify the path of development appropriate to an agricultural economy. Melon's *Essai politique sur le commerce* long remained a primary point of reference: an Italian translation was published in Naples in 1778 with a lengthy introduction and notes by Francesco Longano, and a fresh translation was published in Naples as late as 1795.[7] Writers associated with the outlook of the Gournay group likewise continued to be read, while a new contribution was made by the Physiocrats, whose writings came too late for Genovesi to consider, but whose prescriptions for agriculture were explicitly discussed by Galanti and by Giuseppe Palmieri in his *Riflessioni sulla pubblica felicità relativamente al Regno di Napoli* (1787). A favoured intermediary between the French economists and the Neapolitans was the Swiss legislative theorist, Schmidt d'Avenstein, whose *Principii della Legislazione Universale* was published in an Italian translation (from the French edition of 1776) in Naples in 1791, having been commended by both Galanti and Palmieri.[8]

Galanti was the most consistently radical of the new generation of economists. Repeatedly in his surveys he drew attention to the oppression of the peasantry, and the shamefully debased, illiterate condition to which they were condemned by government and their social superiors. His principal remedies were three. The first was to extend the right of private property to all agricultural land, breaking up communal holdings and enabling the peasantry to follow the example of English farmers. Second, and again following the English example, he would free the grain trade,

---

[5] Giuseppe Maria Galanti, *Elogio storico del Signor Abate Antonio Genovesi, pubblico professore del civil economia nella Università di Napoli* (Naples, 1772), p. 154; also his *Descrizione del contado di Molise*, II, pp. 92–5, and *Nuova descrizione delle Sicilie*, III, pp. 286–90. Grimaldi, *Piano di riforma*, pp. lvi–xci.

[6] Marta Petrusewicz, *Come il Meridione divenne una Questione. Rappresentazioni del Sud prima e dopo il Quarantotto* (Soveria Mannelli, Catanzaro, 1998), p. 42. The monarchy resumed the initiative, with added energy, after the restoration of 1815.

[7] [Jean-François Melon], *Saggio politico sul commercio, tradotto dal francese colle annotazioni dell' Ab. Longano*, 2 vols. (Naples, 1778); *Saggio politico sul commercio del Signor Melon. Tradotto dal francese. Nuova edizione con note* (Naples, 1795).

[8] Galanti, *Descrizione del contado di Molise*, II, pp. 83–4; Giuseppe Palmieri, *Riflessioni sulla pubblica felicità relativamente al Regno di Napoli* (Naples, 1787) 2nd edn. 'dall autore accresciuta' (Naples, 1788), pp. 223–31. Georg Ludwig Schmidt d'Avenstein, *Principii della legislazione universale del Sign. Schmidt. Traduzione dal francese*, 4 vols. (Naples, 1791), with a dedication to D. Giuseppe Palmieri. Italian translations had previously been published in Siena in 1777 and at Massa in 1787.

allowing free export and removing all internal tolls and price controls; to this end the system of contracts *alla voce* (payment to producers in advance, at a heavy discount) should be replaced by more reasonable forms of credit. Third, he would radically reform taxation, so that it fell directly on the land. Galanti was confident that this physiocratic principle could be applied to the kingdom of Naples, because the fertility of the land was such as to enable it to support the entire weight of public taxes, as long as arts and industry were free. Citing the work of Schmidt d'Avenstein, he argued that the antique preference for indirect taxes had been a mark of weak government. These measures were to be supported by a cultural transformation, by which the nobility would be persuaded to identify their status with the practice of agriculture, and the church would renew the bond which once existed between religion and agriculture. Finally, the uncertainty which surrounded title to property and the security of commercial transactions would be removed by a codification of the law and comprehensive reform of the kingdom's tribunals.[9]

By contrast, Palmieri's instincts were more conservative. Several chapters of his *Riflessioni sulla pubblica felicità* made clear his hostility to the radical tendencies of the early Enlightenment. Religion, and Christianity in particular, was fundamental to human happiness; a republic of atheists was a practical impossibility, and Bayle must have been aware of the weakness of his arguments. The 'useful' of the Epicureans was no substitute for virtue, and luxury was the enemy of happiness, substituting the pleasures of opinion for those of nature, and multiplying needs which could not be satisfied.[10] But if his philosophical instincts were conservative, Palmieri's engagement with political economy was serious and up to date. There were two clear points of difference from Galanti. First, Palmieri was less hostile to great proprietors. It was not inequality of property-holding which mattered, he thought, but the incentives offered to the peasantry to overcome their tendency to idleness. What was crucial to them was the availability of credit; the contract *alla voce* required reform, not abolition. Second, Palmieri was hostile to the idea of a single direct tax on land, and contradicted the arguments of both the Physiocrats and Schmidt d'Avenstein in its favour. The local circumstances of the kingdom made it almost impossible to achieve the exact census of landownership on which it must be based; more important, such a tax would obstruct the accumulation of

---

[9] Galanti, *Descrizione del contado di Molise*, II, pp. 59–124; the argument for direct taxation of the land is on pp. 76–86.
[10] Palmieri, *Riflessioni sulla pubblica felicità*, pp. 29–37, 165–79.

stock by landowners. It was stock, 'spese d'anticipazione', which was the key to improving agriculture.[11]

Increasingly, however, the research conducted by Neapolitan economists made them aware that a critical presupposition of the new political economy might not actually exist in the kingdom of Naples: private property. Between the communal property of the *università*, the rural communities, and the multiple feudal rights of the baronage, private property in the strict sense was almost impossible to discern, and was clearly going to be difficult to create. As a result, Neapolitan political economy became ever more preoccupied with the problem of feudalism.[12] The damage done to the kingdom by the introduction of the 'governo feudale' after the fall of the Roman empire was a persistent theme of Galanti's study of the Molise, and of his subsequent large-scale survey of the Sicilies. Anxious to secure the support of the nobility, Galanti observed, successive foreign dynasties had purchased it by reinforcing feudal jurisdictions, compromising their own authority and ruining the nation's agriculture.[13] But the crucial contribution to the Neapolitan debate was made by a younger man, Gaetano Filangieri, in his *Scienza della legislazione* (1780–5). With a flair that was inspirational, Filangieri resumed and radicalised the two dimensions of Genovesi's case for Enlightenment in Naples, his appeal to public opinion, and his deployment of the arguments of political economy.

As his title indicated, Filangieri's commitment was to reform through legislation. Explicitly presenting himself as Montesquieu's heir, but radicalising the emphasis on legal change which had rendered Montesquieu palatable to Europe's absolute monarchs, Filangieri advocated legislation which would alter the social structure and engineer economic development. For legislation to have the desired effect, however, it was not enough simply for the ruler to enact it. It was not even enough to do so under the guidance of philosophers. It was essential that legislation be supported by public opinion: the arguments for change, Filangieri, insisted, must be seen to arise

---

[11] Ibid., pp. 98–104, 213–47, 275–82; also Giuseppe Palmieri, *Della ricchezza nazionale* (Naples, 1792), pp. 12–66, 84–100.
[12] For an excellent introduction to the problem of feudalism, in theory and in politics, in the later eighteenth century: Anna Maria Rao, 'The feudal question, judicial systems and the Enlightenment', in Girolamo Imbruglia (ed.), *Naples in the Eighteenth Century: the Birth and Death of a Nation State* (Cambridge, 2000), pp. 95–117; this also serves as an introduction to her own published work on the subject. For an earlier survey of the debate, Pasquale Villani, 'Il dibattito sulla feudalità nel Regno di Napoli dal Genovesi al Canosa', in Sestan, *Saggi e ricerche sul Settecento*, pp. 252–331.
[13] Galanti, *Descrizione del contado di Molise*, I, pp. 142–3, 177–85, 215–16; II, pp. 19–32, 59–63, 120–1. Likewise in his *Nuova descrizione delle Sicilie*, III, pp. 263–70. Palmieri, by contrast, resisted the temptation to blame the baronage: *Riflessioni sulla pubblica felicità*, pp. 98–100, 342 and note.

from 'opinion itself'.[14] Following Genovesi and Galanti, Filangieri believed that such a public opinion would only emerge through an extended programme of education. But to this condition Filangieri added another, a free press: this was the 'court' before which the 'tribunal' of public opinion must be able to plead its case. Only a free press would ensure that sovereignty lay 'constantly and really in the people'. The role of philosophers, accordingly, had become that of guiding public opinion, while rulers ought to govern only by its suffrage.[15] It was perhaps the clearest statement in the eighteenth century of the principle that public opinion should determine the actions of governments.[16]

Having set out his general principles, the first set of laws to which Filangieri turned his attention were those relating to political economy. At the heart of his analysis, as the historian Giuseppe Galasso has observed, was the problem of property, and in particular feudal property, 'la gran macchina de' feudi' – the great machinery of fiefs. To this Filangieri traced the greatest obstacles to both population growth and the increase of wealth. Every agricultural nation in Europe, he believed, displayed the same symptoms: a gross disproportion between those who owned land and those who were propertyless, and among those with land, an equally damaging inequity between great and small proprietors. On top of which (in Catholic kingdoms) the church possessed as much of two-thirds of available property in perpetuity. Filangieri envisaged a programme of legislation to eliminate these evils. Primogeniture, entails, and the array of other devices which kept land in the hands of few families would be abolished. Feudal jurisdictions too would be abolished, the baronage being compensated with private property in land; at the same time the communal *demani* would be divided between small proprietors. Finally all rights to exact tolls on internal trade would be removed, as would the privileges and protection which capital cities claimed at the expense of the countryside. The outcome, Filangieri expected, would be the securing of private property, its possession by many more members of society, and in consequence a much more equitable distribution of wealth. Absolute equality was not to be expected, but 'when every

---

[14] Gaetano Filangieri, *Scienza della legislazione*, 6 vols. (Naples, 1780–1785), with a seventh volume published posthumously in Naples in 1791. I have used the edition in six volumes, published in Milan in 1822: in this edition, book I, 'Delle regole generali della scienza legislativa', ch. vii, vol. I, pp. 88–90. A new critical edition of *Scienza della legislazione*, dir. Vincenzo Ferrone, edit. Antonio Trampus, Maria Teresa Silvestrini and others, has been published by the Centro di Studi sull'Illuminismo europeo 'Giovanni Stiffoni', in 7 vols. (Venice, 2003–4).

[15] Filangieri, *Scienza della legislazione*, book IV, ch. xliii, vol. VI, pp. 30–9.

[16] A recent, important study of Filangieri which presents his conception of public opinion in a more radically political, constitutionalist framework than I do here is Vincenzo Ferrone, *La società giusta ed equa. Repubblicanesimo e diritti dell'uomo in Gaetano Filangieri* (Rome and Bari, 2003).

citizen can by the reasonable labour of seven or eight hours a day comfortably supply the needs of himself and his family, this will be the condition the happiest on earth, and the model of a well-ordered society'.[17] Quite why the institution of private property should lead to this outcome Filangieri did not have the economics to explain; but the fierceness of his hostility to feudalism impressed itself on the entire later Neapolitan Enlightenment.

Alongside Genovesi, the name of Ferdinando Galiani also continued to command respect among the second generation of economists.[18] Following the publication of *Della moneta*, however, Galiani's career had followed a very different course to Genovesi's. Always ambitious for a larger stage than that offered by the kingdom of Naples, Galiani had seized the opportunity offered by a diplomatic posting to Paris in 1759. For nearly ten years he enjoyed the life of the salons, talking much and writing little. Shortly before he was recalled to Naples, in 1769, he was provoked into writing the *Dialogues sur le commerce des bleds*, which his friends published in his absence in 1770. A witty assault on the physiocratic dogma of free trade in grain, the work sent shock waves through the Parisian community of *philosophes*. But though the *Dialogues* were composed in France, the strength of feeling which gave them their edge owed at least as much to Italian circumstances, specifically to the Tuscan and Neapolitan famines of 1764, whose effects Galiani had witnessed on a visit to the kingdom.

The principal argument of the *Dialogues* was that when it came to grain, a country's individual circumstances were all important. France should not model its policies on those of England, or even on those of the states of Italy. It should also be recognised that in time of want people would go where bread was to be had, flocking to the cities in expectation. A government's response must therefore be guided by reason of state, taking whatever steps were necessary to ensure a supply in the particular case, rather than by universal principles.[19] As the dialogues proceeded, however, Galiani introduced a further argument, which looked beyond immediate contingencies. He drew a distinction between industrious countries with sterile land, and 'pays agricoles et fertiles'. An agricultural people he likened to 'a nation of gamblers', whose faith in the land was not matched by energy

[17] Filangieri, *Scienza della Legislazione*, 'Introduzione', vol. I, p. 5; book II 'Delle leggi politiche ed economiche', vol. II, pp. 21–52, 87–127, 262–9, translated quotation on p. 266; book III, 'Delle leggi criminale', chs. xvii–xviii, in vol. III, pp. 204–41.

[18] In a lengthy footnote Filangieri declared his admiration for Galiani's *Dialogues sur le commerce des grains*, contrasting it with the incoherence of Melon: *Scienza della Legislazione*, vol. II, pp. 98–9n.

[19] Ferdinando Galiani, *Dialogues sur le commerce des bleds* (Paris, 1770), in the edition by Furio Diaz and Luciano Guerci, *Opere di Ferdinando Galiani*, *Illuministi Italiani*, vol. VI (Milan and Naples, 1975), dialogues 1–3.

in cultivation. Over time a small number of seigneurs would take control of the land, dividing it into a system of fiefs. Thus a purely agricultural people became the unhappiest of all, locked into servitude, superstition, and indigence. Such was now the condition of Turkey, Poland, and 'several other countries of Europe which it is not necessary to name'. It had also been the condition of France, until it was rescued by the genius of Colbert, who had recognised that the best means to encourage agriculture was to develop manufactures and internal trade, and to check the import of foreign luxuries.[20] Though Naples and Sicily were not mentioned in this context, it would be reasonable to infer that they too were 'pays agricoles et fertiles'.

Even so, Galiani did not apply the argument directly to the kingdom after his recall thither in 1769. Instead he courted ministers and the royal family rather than public opinion, and obtained a series of administrative posts, culminating in his appointment as assessor to the new *Supremo Consiglio delle Finanze* in 1784. In these capacities he turned his attention to commerce, writing a series of memoranda on the diplomatic and trading prospects of the kingdom. Hostile towards the demands of France and to a lesser extent England for commercial treaties, he saw more hope in Russia, whose entry into the Mediterranean in the 1780s offered a counterweight to the north-western maritime powers.[21] Although the focus was on commerce, however, the policy recommendations were consistent with the Colbertiste prescriptions of the *Dialogues*. A fertile, agricultural nation like Naples could ill afford the luxury of foreign commerce: a secure supply of grain depended on encouraging and protecting its domestic manufactures. Galiani's preoccupation with trade contrasted with Filangieri and Galanti's insistence on the overriding importance of feudalism; but as the respect accorded Galiani indicated, there was substantial common ground too. No Neapolitan economist could be unaware of the weakness of the kingdom in the competitive world of modern international commerce, and none was an advocate of complete free trade.

At first glance, the situation of political economy in later eighteenth century Scotland would seem to have been very different. In the 1760s and 1770s the Scottish agricultural economy 'took off', with prices and rents rising

[20] Galiani, *Dialogues*, nos. 4–5, quotation on pp. 455–6. On the significance of the fifth dialogue, Franco Venturi, 'Galiani tra Enciclopedisti e fisiocratici', *Rivista Storica Italiana*, 72 (1960), 45–64.

[21] Ferdinando Galiani, 'Considerazioni sul Trattato di Commercio tra il Re e il Re Cristianissimo' (c. 1777), in *Opere di Galiani*, pp. 717–34; 'Relazione di Galiani circa un progetto di trattato fra la Russia e il Regno di Sardegna e le prospettive di un trattato fra Russia e Regno di Napoli' (1783), printed as an appendix to F. Diaz, 'L'Abate Galiani consigliere di commercio estero', *Rivista Storica Italiana*, 80 (1968), 887–92.

sharply.[22] Scottish political economists therefore had increasing reason to believe that the cause of improvement was won, and that their country was no longer a special case, requiring the close examination and specific remedies to which their Neapolitan counterparts were obliged to devote so much of their energy. Neither of the major works of political economy published by Scots in these decades gave much space to Scottish problems. In his *Principles of Political Oeconomy* (1767), Sir James Steuart repeatedly engaged with Hume's economic essays, but his evidence was drawn from across Europe, where he had spent more than fifteen years as a Jacobite exile.[23] Even less was heard of Scotland in Adam Smith's *Wealth of Nations* (1776). This was explicitly a work universal in scope, an account of the operation of the commercial economy, and a theory of economic growth, or 'the natural progress of opulence'.

In the *Wealth of Nations* Smith moved beyond the arguments of Hume and the French economists alike. Although he credited Hume with understanding the connection between commerce and the securing of individual liberty,[24] Smith rejected Hume's model of trade-led development. It was historically true that overseas trade in luxury goods had undermined the power of the landowners, making possible the development of a properly commercial agriculture in much of Europe. But what had happened in Europe was a reversal of the natural progress of opulence, according to which agriculture will be developed first, because it offers the highest returns on capital invested, while external commerce should be developed last, since it offers the lowest.[25] At the same time, Smith believed that the Physiocrats had been mistaken in supposing that the land was the sole source of revenue and wealth in a nation.[26] Manufactures and trade also added to the wealth of nations, and their development in turn offered a constant stimulus to agricultural productivity. A further necessary condition of realising a nation's economic potential was of course free trade, which would permit the maximum division of labour and the optimum allocation of capital between the sectors. Given free trade, there was no reason why all nations, and all a nation's inhabitants, should not benefit from increasing wealth.

[22] T. M. Devine, *The Transformation of Rural Scotland: Social Change and the Agrarian Economy 1660–1815* (Edinburgh, 1994), ch. 3: 'The transformation of the rural economy'.

[23] Sir James Steuart, *Principles of Political Oeconomy*, 2 vols. (London, 1767), with a modern edition by A. S. Skinner, with N. Kobayashi and H. Mizuta, 2 vols. (London, 1998).

[24] Adam Smith, *An Inquiry into the Nature and Causes of the Wealth of Nations*, 2 vols. (London, 1776); modern critical edition by R. H. Campbell, A. S. Skinner, and W. B. Todd, 2 vols. (Oxford, 1976), book III, ch. iv, para. 4 (hereafter in the form, III.iv.4).

[25] Smith, *Wealth of Nations*, II.v; III.i–iv.   [26] Ibid., IV.ix.

The universal scope of Smith's argument was tempered by his own interest in specific, empirical problems, several of which he discussed at length
in order to exemplify his general arguments. These have offered historians contexts in which to place his contribution. One contemporary issue
addressed by Smith was the status of Britain's North American colonies,
and the value of the commercial regulations applied to them. Another was
the grain trade. In the latter case, Smith can be seen to have responded
to the French debate which had been sparked by Galiani's *Dialogues sur le
commerce des bleds*.[27] As an answer to Galiani, the *Wealth of Nations* was
crushing. Smith was prepared to concede that the argument for complete
free trade in grain might not apply in some cases of 'the most urgent necessity'. In great states, he continued to maintain, the freedom to export grain
was unlikely to be dangerous even in such circumstances. But in a Swiss
canton, or in 'some of the little states of Italy', restraint 'may, perhaps, sometimes be necessary'. In those cases only should the ordinary laws of justice
be sacrificed 'to an idea of publick utility, to a sort of reasons of state'.[28] On
Smith's horizon, the little states of Italy featured as no more than a tiny,
inconsequential exception to the general rule. Like Hume, Smith repudiated any suggestion that an 'agricultural and fertile country' was somehow
subject to different economic rules from a commercial society. In Scottish
political economy, it would appear, cosmopolitanism now needed to make
only the minimum of concessions to patriotism.

Nevertheless, it would be wrong to infer that the relevance of political
economy to Scotland no longer needed demonstration. However flourishing the lowland economy, the problem of the Highlands remained: in
searching for the key to their development, commentators such as James
Anderson had to adapt and modify the arguments of Hume, Steuart, and
Smith in specific ways.[29] More generally, the problem of the economic,
social, and political power of great landowners – of feudal property –
continued to preoccupy a range of Scottish thinkers. Here the lead had
been taken by the jurists and legal historians Lord Kames and Sir John
Dalrymple, whose *Essay towards a general history of Feudal Property in Great*

[27] Istvan Hont and Michael Ignatieff, 'Needs and justice in the *Wealth of Nations*: an introductory
essay', in Hont and Ignatieff (eds.), *Wealth and Virtue: The Shaping of Political Economy in the
Scottish Enlightenment* (Cambridge, 1983), pp. 1–44; Emma Rothschild, *Economic Sentiments: Adam
Smith, Condorcet, and the Enlightenment* (Cambridge, Mass., 2001), pp. 72–86 – valuable in noting
the limits to Smith's contribution to the debate, by comparison with those of Turgot and Condorcet.
[28] Smith, *Wealth of Nations*, IV.v.b.39.
[29] James Anderson, *Observations on the means of exciting a spirit of national industry; chiefly intended to
promote the agriculture, commerce, manufactures, and fisheries of Scotland* (Edinburgh, 1777); on which
see A. J. Youngson, *After the 'Forty-Five: the Economic Impact on the Scottish Highlands* (Edinburgh,
1973), ch. 3: 'Aims and principles of economic policy'.

Britain (1757) was the pioneering contribution to debate. That the Scots too should have been interested in the question of feudal property should be no surprise: as Arnaldo Momigliano once remarked, Edinburgh, like Naples, was a very good place from which to observe the legacy of feudalism.[30] Yet despite the efforts of Colin Kidd to draw attention to the importance of this theme, the centrality of feudalism to the economic, political, and historical thinking of the Scots in the mid and later eighteenth century remains under-explored.[31]

The neglect is the more remarkable, because the economic power of great proprietors was a central preoccupation of Adam Smith. Like Galanti and Filangieri, Smith explained that power historically, tracing it back to the conquest of the Roman empire by the barbarians, and the engrossing of uncultivated lands by a few great proprietors. These had then secured their possession by the devices of primogeniture and entails, while reducing the cultivators of the land to a condition of virtual slavery. Strictly speaking, Smith thought, the feudal law had been introduced to moderate the authority of the great lords, but in the event it had only strengthened their hold on the land and its cultivators.[32] Even when the system had been ended by the lords' need for increased income to pay for the 'trinkets and baubles' offered by the merchants, the great proprietors had continued to obstruct the full commercial development of agriculture. In principle, Smith argued, the real wealth of the landlord must increase with every improvement in the circumstances of society, since this will tend directly or indirectly to raise the real rent of land.[33] In practice, however, 'it seldom happens . . . that a great proprietor is a great improver'.[34] The problem as Smith understood it was not exactly analogous to that facing the Neapolitans. Whatever the position under feudal law, Smith assumed that the great proprietors did now own their land as private property. The problem therefore was not the absence of private property as such, but the way in which the great proprietors still sought to shield their property, by the devices of primogeniture and entails, from full exposure to the free market. They were not alone: merchants, manufacturers, and labourers all sought to do the same, by monopolies, restrictive practices, and combinations. But Smith seems to have regarded great proprietors almost as severely as he did merchants.

[30] Arnaldo Momigliano, 'Gibbon from an Italian point of view', *Daedalus*, 105 (1976), p. 127, listing Edinburgh alongside Geneva and Lausanne as vantage-points from which to appreciate the anti-feudal message of Giannone's *Storia Civile*.

[31] Colin Kidd, *Subverting Scotland's Past: Scottish Whig Historians and the Creation of an Anglo-British identity 1689–c.1830* (Cambridge, 1993), esp. pp. 150–62, 165–84.

[32] Smith, *Wealth of Nations*, III.ii, iv.8–9.   [33] Ibid., I.xi.p. 1–8.   [34] Ibid., III.ii.7.

His ideal improver was the small farmer, and he was consequently far more confident of rapid economic growth in North America, where there were no great proprietors, than in Great Britain.[35] Moreover even if Smith supposed property to be better established in Britain than the Neapolitans found it to be in their kingdom, he was not confident that it could easily be rid of its remaining encumbrances. At best, legislative initiative on the part of governments should be gradual and piecemeal.[36] Smith never believed that the problem of property, especially on the land, could be resolved as quickly or as completely as Filangieri appeared to hope.

Neither in Scotland nor in Naples did political economy and the critique of feudalism exhaust the energies of the leading Enlightenment thinkers. To the contrary, the interest in human nature, sociability, and the historical development of society which had been central to the thinking of Vico and the young (and indeed the older) Hume was maintained by their successors. In both countries, moreover, a fresh intellectual challenge served to concentrate minds on the issues once again. That challenge was a single, short book – Jean-Jacques Rousseau's *Discours sur l'origine et fondemens de l'inégalité parmi les hommes* (1755). As Adam Smith immediately recognised, the challenge of the book derived from its author's reading of Mandeville.[37]

Rousseau's response to Mandeville was both an appropriation and a critique. He agreed with Mandeville that man was not naturally sociable. The earliest men and women were solitary beings, their only passions being *amour de soi*, a desire for preservation, and pity, a sympathy for the suffering of other creatures which fell far short of sociability. As population grew, however, men and women were forced into more frequent contact. Gradually they formed families, then small societies, developing language to persuade each other to meet their needs. As they communicated, they began to identify with each other, estimating themselves in the eyes of others. To *amour de soi* they added the passion of *amour propre*. Resembling Mandeville's 'self-liking', Rousseau's *amour propre* was a reflexive passion, based on the judgement of others. But Rousseau also attributed to man a

[35] Ibid., III.iv.19.

[36] For a nuanced analysis of Smith's approach to legislative intervention in the economy, see Donald Winch, *Riches and Poverty: An Intellectual History of Political Economy in Britain, 1750–1834* (Cambridge, 1996), pp. 90–123: 'The wisdom of Solon'.

[37] In the letter to the first *Edinburgh Review* in 1756 in which he summarised Rousseau's new work, Smith remarked that an attentive reader would recognise its debt to the second volume of the *Fable of the Bees*: 'A letter to the Authors of the *Edinburgh Review*' (March, 1756), *Adam Smith: Essays on Philosophical Subjects*, ed. W. P. D. Wightman, J. C. Bryce, and I. S. Ross (Oxford, 1980), para. 11, p. 250. Smith presumably took it for granted that Rousseau had done much more reading than he acknowledged.

quality completely absent from Mandeville's account, a capacity to choose, or will, his values, a capacity which Rousseau called man's 'perfectibility'.[38] By equipping natural man with this capacity, Rousseau reopened a question which Mandeville had treated far less seriously, the question of men's capacity for hypocrisy.

For Mandeville, hypocrisy arose from the discrepancy between the arbitrary definitions of virtue and vice established by the first legislators and the actual passions governing men's behaviour. It was harmful, he suggested, only when those definitions were taken at face value by overzealous moral reformers, or when clergymen were given free rein to impose their ascetic values on the laity. Hume had countered that even this was to exaggerate the problem. The clergy, to be sure, were hypocritical preachers of self-denial. But ordinary men derived their values from their passions, not against them, judging moral worth by what was 'useful and agreeable'. Rousseau did not engage with Hume, but his response to Mandeville demonstrated his hostility to such straightforward Epicureanism. His objection was that it ignored the force of the Augustinian insight into man's capacity for moral deception. The multifarious ways in which men deceive their fellows, professing certain values while pursuing the gratification of their passions, had been explored at length by the late seventeenth-century moralist La Rochefoucauld, and were the subject of renewed attention by French dramatists in the 1730s and 1740s. What Rousseau now added was an interest in language as the instrument of such deception. It was an interest Mandeville had anticipated, but Hume had ignored. The crucial case of linguistic deception, Rousseau argued in the *Discours sur l'inégalité*, was that which produced the institution of property, when one man not only appropriated a piece of land to his own use, but persuaded others to accept his claim. It was property which entrenched inequality at the heart of modern society, and thereby enlarged almost infinitely the scope for hypocrisy, as men competed to pretend to be what they were not. From that moment, Rousseau argued, moral corruption was unavoidable, and was destined steadily to advance until men fell under the yoke of despotism. Only by a wholly new act of will, he subsequently argued in *Du Contrat Social* (1762), could they

---

[38] Jean-Jacques Rousseau, *Discours sur l'origine et fondemens de l'inégalité parmi les hommes* (1755), part I, in the *Oeuvres complètes* III: *Du Contrat Social. Écrits politiques*, ed. B. Gagnebin and M. Raymond (Bibliothèque de la Pléiade, Paris, 1964), pp. 134–63. The parallel between Mandeville's concepts of self-love and self-liking, and Rousseau's of *amour de soi* and *amour propre* is questioned by Pierre Force, *Self-Interest before Adam Smith: A Genealogy of Economic Science* (Cambridge, 2003), p. 65. Force observes that Mandeville's self-liking is a first principle of human nature, where *amour propre* is not. The important point, however, is that both required the judgement of others, and took man in society to be other-regarding.

hope to rediscover the possibility of virtue, and realise the promise of their original perfectibility.[39]

Smith first responded to the challenge of Rousseau in *The Theory of Moral Sentiments* in 1759; he continued the argument in the *Wealth of Nations*. Even then, however, Smith was not satisfied. Returning to the *Theory of Moral Sentiments* at the very end of his life, his final revisions show him still wrestling over his answer. How this response to Rousseau should be understood is now central to Smith scholarship.[40] At the heart of the problem, Smith agreed with Rousseau, was inequality. Smith had no illusions about the scale of inequality in modern societies, and no society, he recognised, was more unequal than a fully commercial society. But such inequality was not incompatible with a distribution of wealth which enabled the poorest classes to live better than ever before. Smith first made this point in the *Theory of Moral Sentiments*, observing, with the aid of the metaphor of the 'invisible hand', that the surplus wealth of the rich was redistributed to the poor through the purchase of their labour.[41] A much fuller economic explanation was subsequently offered in the *Wealth of Nations*.[42] Inequality was justified, Smith seemed to be arguing, by the very real improvement in the condition of the labourer which commercial society made possible. For all the material force of this argument, however, Smith never quite shrugged off Rousseau's criticism that such inequality must be morally corrupting. He finally conceded the point in the last edition of the *Theory of Moral Sentiments* he prepared himself, adding a chapter on 'the corruption of our moral sentiments, which is occasioned by this disposition to admire the rich and the great, and to despise or neglect persons of poor or mean condition'.[43] Smith's sensitivity to Rousseau's challenge is not surprising. He had long been an admirer of La Rochefoucauld. He also took a close interest in the debate on the origins of language initiated by Condillac, adding an essay of his own on the subject to the third edition of the *Theory of Moral Sentiments* in 1767.[44] However strong his commitment to the

---

[39] Rousseau, *Discours sur l'inégalité*, part II; *Du Contrat Social* (1762): both in *Oeuvres Complètes*, vol. III, pp. 164–94; 347–470.

[40] As in Force, *Self-Interest before Adam Smith*, passim.

[41] Adam Smith, *The Theory of Moral Sentiments* (1759), ed. D. D. Raphael and A. L. Macfie (Oxford, 1976), part IV, ch. i, para. 10 (hereafter IV.i.10).

[42] Smith, *Wealth of Nations*, 'Introduction and Plan of the Work', and I.i.

[43] Smith, *Theory of Moral Sentiments*, I.iii.3, a chapter added to the sixth edition in 1790.

[44] Nicholas Phillipson, 'Language, sociability, and history: some reflections on the foundations of Adam Smith's science of man', in S. Collini, R. Whatmore, and Brian Young (eds.), *Economy, Polity and Society: British Intellectual History 1750–1950* (Cambridge, 2000), pp. 70–84. The 'Dissertation on the Origin of Languages' was first published in the *Philological Miscellany* in 1761. Smith added it to the third edition of the *Theory of Moral Sentiments*, and it remained in the subsequent editions for which he was responsible. In the modern Glasgow edition of Smith's works it is printed with the *Lectures on Rhetoric and Belles Lettres*, edit. J. C. Bryce and A. S. Skinner (Oxford, 1983).

economic benefits of commercial society, he could not ignore the problems of inequality and hypocrisy which they threw up.

Smith did not follow Rousseau in attributing to man a capacity for voluntary moral choice, as a means of escape from corruption. But he did suggest that men might rise above the ordinary moral conventions of their society, by cultivating the idea of an 'impartial spectator'. Where the ordinary spectator represents what we take to be the opinions of our fellows, the impartial spectator is quite literally a figment of the imagination; nevertheless, Smith suggested, it is by adopting its point of view that we may learn to distinguish being praiseworthy from being merely praised. One who understood that distinction would be much better placed to judge the moral value of his actions than one who judged himself simply by the approval of others. Smith never disguised the difficulty of attaining the viewpoint of the impartial spectator, and wrote in elevated tones of the few who achieved it. They combined 'the study of wisdom and the practice of virtue'; above all, they possessed the great virtue of 'self-command'.[45] The Stoic associations of this virtue, together with the explicit invocations of the ancient Stoics in the *Theory of Moral Sentiments*, have led several scholars to interpret Smith as a neo-Stoic in moral philosophy. The suggestion that he was following Rousseau in attempting to reassert the possibility of living virtuously in the face of the corruption prevalent in modern society reinforces this reading. So too does Smith's repeated invocation of the idea of a natural moral order, presided over by a provident deity, whose interventions are like an 'invisible hand'.[46]

Yet there is reason to doubt whether Smith was so persuaded by Rousseau's critique that he abandoned completely the Epicurean analysis of commercial society developed by Mandeville and Hume.[47] His was, after all, a theory of moral sentiments. If his explanation of how we evaluate our passions is more complex than Hume's, it shares the same starting point. The virtues which we acknowledge in ourselves and others arise from the passions, and it is by imagining spectators of our behaviour, whether ordinary or impartial, that we learn to moderate those passions and assign to them moral value. Virtues are not separately conceived as the product of

---

[45] Smith, *Theory of Moral Sentiments*, I.iii.3.2, VI.iii. The concept of the impartial spectator itself cost Smith a good many pains to work out, as he modified it in every edition of the work: D. D. Raphael, 'The impartial spectator', in A. S. Skinner and T. Wilson (eds.), *Essays on Adam Smith* (Oxford, 1975), pp. 83–99.

[46] Thus Raphael and Macfie, in their introduction to the Glasgow edition of the *Theory of Moral Sentiments*, pp. 5–10; Force, *Self-Interest Before Adam Smith*, pp. 63–75, 89, 225–41; Phillipson, 'Language, sociability, and history', pp. 80–4.

[47] On Smith's relation to Mandeville, contrast the nuanced interpretation offered by Hundert, *The Enlightenment's Fable*, pp. 219–36, with that of Force, *Self-Interest before Adam Smith*, where the differences are repeatedly emphasised.

a distinct moral will. It is true that Smith distinguished the natural from the historical, where Hume treated the historical as the natural. The historical development of commerce in Europe had been almost the reverse of the 'natural progress of opulence'. But it is by no means clear that Smith gave effective priority to that natural order. As Emma Rothschild has pointed out, Smith never suggested that an understanding of the natural order, or of the natural progress of opulence, would entitle a ruler – or a philosopher – to impose it on society.[48] To do so would be to act as 'a man of system, . . . wise in his own conceit', who forgets that 'in the great chessboard of human society, every single piece has a principle of motion of its own',[49] in other words, that every individual acts upon his own interest. Moreover Smith's invocations of a benevolent, provident deity are almost always of an 'idea', a figment of the imagination like the impartial spectator itself.[50] Both might be ideas of which humans made good use, but this is not the same as saying that benevolent outcomes were the work of an actual deity, or an independent natural design.[51] When Smith invoked the 'invisible hand' to underline the capacity of human self-interest unintentionally to achieve an economically beneficial outcome, it was indeed self-interest which he was celebrating; it is not necessary to suppose that he was also worshipping Stoic nature, still less propounding a theodicy.

There is no doubt that Smith recognised in Rousseau's *Discours sur l'inégalité* a challenge which Hume's Epicureanism had blithely set aside. Modern commercial society had enormously increased the scale of inequality, with moral consequences which it was difficult not to characterise as corrupting. In the speed and thoroughness with which he responded to this challenge, Smith may be seen to have launched the second phase of Enlightenment in Scotland. He shaped the terms in which Ferguson, Millar, Dunbar, and others would conduct their enquiries from the 1760s to the 1780s. But the claim that he had done so by joining Rousseau in advancing a 'neo-Stoic critique' of the Epicurean-Augustinian understanding of human nature and moral virtue seems, to this writer, unconvincing.[52] Smith admired aspects of Stoic morals, but his analysis of commercial society, of the human passions which sustained it, and the values which it engendered, also displays important continuities with the Epicurean philosophy of David Hume.

No Neapolitan was as prompt in responding to Rousseau's challenge, or did so in terms which joined moral philosophy and political economy

---

[48] Rothschild, *Economic Sentiments*, pp. 124–5, and, more generally, 116–56.
[49] Smith, *Theory of Moral Sentiments*, VI.ii.2.17.   [50] As at ibid., III.5.7, 11; VI.ii.3.5–6.
[51] Harris, 'Answering Bayle's question', pp. 240–1, takes Smith's 'providential naturalism' more seriously.
[52] The claim advanced by Force, *Self-Interest before Adam Smith*, p. 63.

as closely as Smith was able to do. Genovesi himself was apparently more provoked by Rousseau's first discourse, the *Discours sur les sciences et les arts* of 1750, to which he replied in his *Lettere accademiche* of 1764.[53] But for his pupils, it was the question of inequality which was paramount. The question was tackled most directly and fully by Francescantonio Grimaldi (the younger brother of Domenico), in his three-volume *Riflessioni sopra l'ineguaglianza tra gli uomini* (1779–80). Rousseau might have treated the subject with 'supreme eloquence'; Grimaldi's approach was to be different. His subject was 'man as he is', his field 'the science of man'. Grimaldi disavowed any intention to project remedies for what he regarded as part of the divinely ordained 'immutable order of things'. He wished simply to explain inequality, devoting a volume apiece to its physical, moral, and political aspects.[54]

Grimaldi believed that the critical error of Rousseau and those who thought like him had been to start from a certain idea of 'nature', and then to argue that the problem of inequality would be corrected by a return to the 'state of nature'.[55] For as he explained at the start of Volume II, 'Of moral inequality', a state of nature distinct from society has never existed. Society is man's natural condition. Grimaldi emphasised that he was not the first to make this point. Voltaire and Adam Ferguson, in his 'lauded work on the origins of society', had already shown the idea of the state of nature to be 'chimerical, useless, and harmful'.[56] So well had Ferguson put it, indeed, that the remainder of Grimaldi's chapter was little more than a paraphrase of the opening chapter of Ferguson's *Essay on the History of Civil Society* of 1767, devoted to 'the question relating to the state of nature'. Grimaldi ended with a direct translation of Ferguson's words: 'If we are asked therefore, Where the state of nature is to be found? We may answer, It is here; and it matters not whether we are understood to speak in the island of Great Britain, at the Cape of Good Hope, or the Straits of Magellan.'[57] Thereafter Ferguson's work was a frequent point of reference throughout volumes II and III of the *Riflessioni sopra l'ineguaglianza*; alongside it, moreover,

[53] Antonio Genovesi, *Lettere accademiche su la questione se sieno più felici gl'ignoranti che gli scienziati* (Naples, 1764; 2nd rev. edn 1769).
[54] Francescantonio Grimaldi, *Riflessioni sopra l'ineguaglianza tra gli uomini*, 3 vols. (Naples 1779–80), vol. I, 'Introduzione', pp. xi–xix.
[55] Grimaldi, *Riflessioni*, I, pp. vii–viii, xviii.
[56] Ibid., II, pp. 21–45, with the reference to Voltaire and Ferguson in a note on p. 27.
[57] Ibid., pp. 44–5, translating from Adam Ferguson, *An Essay on the History of Civil Society* (1767), in the edition by Fania Oz-Salzberger (Cambridge, 1995), p. 14: 'Se ci vien domandato, dove lo stato della natura si può trovare, noi possiam rispondere: egli è qui; nè la natura si briga in qual parte l'uomo abbia appresa di parlare, o nelle Isole della gran Brettagna, o al Capo di Bonosperanza, o allo stretto Magellanico . . .' The passage is preceded by a reference to Ferguson, but is not within quotation marks.

Grimaldi also often referred to the histories of David Hume and William Robertson.

Francescantonio Grimaldi's interest in these Scottish writers was neither unique nor accidental in the Naples of the late 1770s and 1780s. For it was now that knowledge of the Scots' works became widespread among the Neapolitans, thanks above all to the publishing initiatives of Giuseppe Galanti. Over and above his tireless efforts to report on the economic condition of the kingdom, Galanti was also a determined intellectual entrepreneur. His first initiative was the Società letteraria di Napoli, founded in 1777. A year later it was re-formed as the Società letteraria e tipografica, with Francescantonio Grimaldi as an associate. At first Galanti attempted to be both a bookseller and a publisher, importing books from the Société Typographique de Neuchâtel, publishers of the *Encyclopédie*. But from 1780 financial difficulties forced him to concentrate on publishing, and in the same year he launched his *Collezione di storia filosofica e politica delle nazioni antiche e moderne*. The first volumes were a translation Millot's *Elements d'histoire générale*, which Galanti supplemented with notes and translated extracts from a range of other histories, including Ferguson's *Essay* and Robertson's *Charles V*. Later in the series he published a translation of Robertson's *View of the Progress of Society in Europe* (in 1781), and the *Dissertazione sopra il governo feudale del Signor David Hume* (1782), a translation of the appendix on 'the feudal and Anglo-Norman government' in volume 1 of Hume's *History of England*. Subsequently other Neapolitan publishers produced complete translations of Robertson's Histories of *Charles V* (in 1787–9) and of *America* (in 1789).[58] Over the 1780s, therefore, major works of the Scottish Enlightenment became directly available in Naples.

The interest which Galanti and Grimaldi took in the Scots serves to highlight one final area of common interest between the two branches of the Enlightenment: the historical study of society. Among the Scots Hume had turned to the writing of a major narrative history in the 1750s; in both narrative and conjectural forms history was subsequently to be the dominant interest of William Robertson, Adam Ferguson, John Millar, and James Dunbar. In Naples history was a major interest of Galanti, Grimaldi, and Filangieri; it was also the subject of Francesco Mario Pagano's *Saggi politici. De' principii, progressi e decadenza delle società*. First published in 1783–5, with a second, corrected and enlarged edition in 1791–2, the

---

[58] Maria Luisa Perna, 'Giuseppe Galanti editore', in Aa. Vv., *Miscellanea Walter Maturi* (Turin, 1966), pp. 221–58; Franco Venturi, 'Scottish echoes in eighteenth-century Italy', in Hont and Ignatieff *Wealth and Virtue*, pp. 360–2.

Saggi Politici may be regarded as the *capolavoro* or masterwork of the late Neapolitan Enlightenment. The potential for a comparative analysis of these works is only enhanced by the circumstance that the Neapolitans had read their Scottish counterparts. Even more than in the case of political economy, there is the opportunity for a direct confrontation between their historical thought. At a generation's remove, the Neapolitans may even make it possible to study the Scottish historians in the company of Vico. For in the works of Grimaldi and Pagano in particular, the insights of the Scots are frequently combined with those of 'il nostro Vico', 'our Vico'. The Vico of Grimaldi and Pagano was of course not the original Vico: they were interested in his insights into the earliest states of society, and into the history of feudal law, not in his attempt to vindicate the historical role of divine providence. Nevertheless, the coincidence of Scottish and Vichian insights in their work offers perhaps the best opportunity to answer a question which has always tantalised scholars of the Scottish Enlightenment: what if the Scots had read Vico?

To exemplify the scope for comparison, three areas of common interest may be identified in the historical writings of the Scots and Neapolitans. One is the interest in the earliest history of the family and of sexual relations. It is clear that neither the Scots nor the Neapolitans accepted Rousseau's benign view of the first couplings between men and women. Among the former, John Millar and William Robertson agreed that the condition of women in the earliest stages of society was one of servile dependence. And when a savage possesses such unlimited power, 'it cannot fail, upon many occasions, to be grossly abused'. Neither Scot explicitly discussed sexual violence (and comments by Millar appeared to discount its likelihood); but in all other respects they depicted the earliest form of family as a cruel and brutal institution.[59] If anything, Pagano was even sharper. The first encounters between men and women were rapes, and the first families were created by abduction. As he pointed out, the heroic histories of every nation were full of these, the gods committing far more rapes than miracles. On this matter, he added, even Vico had shown excessive reserve.[60]

---

[59] John Millar, *Observations Concerning the Distinction of Ranks in Society* (1771); here in the third edition, entitled *The Origin of the Distinction of Ranks* (1779), ed. W. C. Lehmann, in his *John Millar of Glasgow* (Cambridge, 1960), pp. 183–98: ch. 1 'Of the rank and condition of women in different ages', section i 'The effects of poverty and barbarism, with respect to the condition of women'. William Robertson, *The History of America*, 2 vols. (London, 1777), 1, pp. 318–19, on 'the domestic state' of the native Americans.

[60] Francesco Mario Pagano, *Saggi politici. De' principii, progressi e decadenza delle società. Edizione seconda, corretta ed accresciuta*, 2 vols. (Naples 1791–2), in the modern edition by Luigi Firpo and Laura Salvetti Firpo (Naples, 1993), 11, pp. 147–51: Saggio 11, cap. iv.

Equally intriguing to both the Scots and the Neapolitans was the apparent transformation of sexual relations achieved by the cult of chivalry. The Scottish historians had no doubt that this was 'a valuable improvement', as Millar put it, even if it was the product of Gothic institutions and manners.[61] As modern scholars have observed, the implications of this enthusiasm for chivalric sexual mores were decidedly ambiguous for the status of women: translated into the eighteenth-century ideal of 'gallantry', it rested on a view of women's nature as unchanging, and limited in its moral and political capacity.[62] By contrast, Pagano was once again more open, articulating his ambivalence. Under the influence of gallantry, he believed, modern society had recovered its 'lost half' by honouring and educating women. But chivalric gallantry none the less bore the marks of its origins in 'that absurd and monstrous body of contradictory usages, laws and customs of the middle age'. Moreover there was a very real danger that the present respect for women would degenerate into effeminacy and servility.[63]

A second common strand in Scottish and Neapolitan historical writing was the preoccupation with feudalism. In Scotland William Robertson devoted part of the introductory book of his *History of Scotland* to explaining 'the feudal system of laws and policy, that stupendous and singular fabric', as the key to understanding the weakness of the Scottish monarchy.[64] Two years later Hume published his appendix on 'The Feudal and Anglo-Norman Government and Manners' in which he characterised the feudal law in similar terms as a 'prodigious fabric', but argued that its effect on English government had been more equivocal. There it had 'for several centuries, preserved such a mixture of liberty and oppression, order and anarchy, stability and revolution, as was never experienced in any other age or any other part of the world'.[65] Robertson returned to the subject in

---

[61] Millar, *Origin of Ranks*, p. 218.

[62] Mary Catherine Moran, '"The commerce of the sexes": gender and social sphere in Scottish Enlightenment accounts of civil society', in Frank Trentman (ed.), *Paradoxes of Civil Society: New Perspectives on Modern German and British history* (2nd rev. edn New York and Oxford, 2003), pp. 61–84; Silvia Sebastiani, 'Race, women, and progress in the Scottish Enlightenment', and Barbara Taylor, 'Feminists versus Gallants: manners and morals in Enlightenment Britain', both in Barbara Taylor and Sarah Knott (eds.), *Women, Gender, and Enlightenment* (London, 2005), pp. 75–96, 30–52.

[63] Pagano, *Saggi politici*, pp. 369–72: Saggio v, cap. xxx–xxxi.

[64] William Robertson, *The History of Scotland during the Reigns of Queen Mary and King James VI*, 2 vols. (London, 1759), pp. 12–32.

[65] David Hume, *The History of England from the Invasion of Julius Caesar to the Revolution in 1688*, vol. 1 (1761), appendix 11, 'The Feudal and Anglo-Norman Government and Manners' in the six-volume edition by W. B. Todd, based on the edition of 1778, (Indianapolis, 1983), pp. 455–88, quotation on pp. 455–6. See John G. A. Pocock, *Barbarism and Religion* 11: *Narratives of Civil Government* (Cambridge, 1999), pp. 241–57 for discussion of Hume's ambivalence towards the mediaeval English constitution.

the 'View of the Progress of Society in Europe, from the subversion of the Roman Empire, to the beginning of the Sixteenth Century', which occupied the first volume of his *History of the Reign of the Emperor Charles V* (1769). If anything, his tone was even sharper, and his critique of 'this pernicious institution' now extended from government to civilisation, as he attributed to the effects of feudal anarchy the profound depression into which the human mind had fallen in Europe by the eleventh century.[66]

In Naples the pioneer historian of feudalism was Galanti. Endorsing Genovesi's view that Giannone's *Storia civile* had been too indulgent towards the baronage, Galanti put the history of feudal law at the centre of his historical introduction to the *Descrizione del contado di Molise* (1781).[67] A similar desire to clarify the historical roots of feudal law marked the work of both Grimaldi and Filangieri.[68] By contrast, Pagano's treatment of feudalism owed more to Vico, whom he followed in tracing the origin of feudal government to the noble–client relationship established in the ancient Greek and Roman republics. Given such evidence of its antiquity, Pagano suggested that 'aristocratic feudal government' should be regarded as characteristic of all the barbarian nations, and was not confined to the middle ages. The feudal government, he believed, would have been established among us even without the invasion of the northern barbarians.[69]

For all his insistence on the universality of feudalism, however, Pagano also believed that the Neapolitan experience of feudalism had been exceptionally severe. The 'spirit of feudalism', he observed in the 'General view of the history of the kingdom' with which he concluded the first edition of the *Saggi politici*, formed a major part of the 'national spirit' of the kingdom.[70] The fierce rhetoric which Filangieri directed against what he called the 'squalid spectre' of feudalism, or 'the night of feudal anarchy' reflected a similar conviction of its uniquely damaging consequences for his own country.[71] Yet the Scots thought exactly the same about their experience.

---

[66] William Robertson, *The History of the Reign of the Emperor Charles V*, 3 vols. (London, 1769), vol. I, 'A View of the Progress of Society in Europe, from the Subversion of the Roman Empire, to the beginning of the Sixteenth Century', pp. 14–20.

[67] Galanti, *Descrizione del contado di Molise*, I, chs. v–ix. See Galasso, *La filosofia in soccorso de' governi*, pp. 485–506: 'Galanti: storiografia e riformismo nell'analisi dell'ultimo feudalesimo'.

[68] Grimaldi, *Riflessioni*, vol. III: 'Dell'ineguaglianza politica', *passim*, citing Robertson, Hume, and Vico on the subject; Filangieri, *Scienze della Legislazione*, III, pp. 204–41: book III, part i, chs. xvii–xviii.

[69] Pagano, *Saggi politici*, pp. 224–9, 239–41: Saggio III, cap. x, xiv; p. 397: Saggio VI, cap. vii.

[70] Francesco Mario Pagano, *Saggi politici* vol. II: *Del civile corso delle nazioni* (1st edn Naples, 1785), p. 262.

[71] Filangieri, *Scienza della Legislazione*, I, pp. 45, 88.

The Scottish nobility, Robertson observed, had enjoyed an 'exorbitant and uncommon power', and moreover had kept it for long after the feudal system had been undermined elsewhere.[72] The coincidence of this conviction that their experience had been exceptional further underlines the comparability of Neapolitan and Scottish historical thinking.

A third theme of interest to Scottish and Neapolitan historians was that of corruption. Here the challenge of Rousseau was most persistent; as we have seen, even Adam Smith eventually found himself conceding Rousseau's point. The first Scot to treat the problem historically, however, was Adam Ferguson, whose *Essay on the History of Civil Society* ended with sections devoted to 'the decline of nations' and 'corruption and political slavery'. The force of Ferguson's language, his frequently avowed liking for the martial virtues, and his evident hostility to Epicureanism in morals immediately marked out the *Essay* as a new and distinctive contribution to the Scottish debate. Yet the *Essay* was by no means a simple jeremiad: it did not, for example, equate luxury directly with corruption. Ferguson endorsed the study of political economy, though he cautioned that commerce and wealth should not be considered as making 'the sum of national felicity'. What exercised Ferguson was the prospect of political corruption, the loss of willingness to participate in public affairs, and in particular to undertake military service, on the part of those marked out for such responsibilities by their fortune and rank in society. Once the active, independent spirit was lost, he argued, political slavery – 'despotism' – would soon follow.[73]

In Naples it was, once again, Pagano who had the most interesting things to say on this subject. In what may have been an echo of Ferguson, he gave the title 'Della decadenza delle nazioni' to the last of the *Saggi*, and began it with a chapter on the corruption of society. Pagano was certainly no enemy of political economy.[74] Yet he saw a very real danger that ignorance and a lack of education would allow a healthy *amor proprio* to be corrupted into egoism, personal interest, and insensibility toward others, leading men towards 'the abyss of despotism'. Pagano's sense of the danger was heightened by the Vichian idea that nations followed a 'corso' through history, exemplified by the collapse of Rome into a second barbarism. If it was some reassurance that Europe had not reverted to a state of complete

---

[72] Robertson, *History of Scotland*, pp. 21–32.

[73] Ferguson, *Essay on Civil Society*, pp. 140, 194–264.

[74] Pagano was also the author of a *Ragionamento sulla libertà del commercio del pesce in Napoli* (Naples, 1789), reprinted in Venturi, *Illuministi Italiani* v: *Riformatori Napoletani*, pp. 842–53, in which he argued for the abolition of all exclusive privileges in the marketing of fish, and further, for the abolition of the 'iniquitous contracts' by which the fishermen were bound in advance to sell at a price which was unrelated to the quantity of fish for sale.

savagery – a fate which would require a natural catastrophe – the example of Rome remained salutary.[75] In Pagano as in Ferguson, as indeed in Smith, this refusal to discount the threat of corruption was an acknowledgement that Rousseau's challenge was unavoidable. Both Ferguson and Pagano had endorsed the idea of man's perfectibility, Ferguson referring to 'a principle of progression, and a desire of perfection', Pagano to *perfettibilità*, 'that is, the wish to improve oneself', as the single quality which makes men sociable.[76] Though neither attributed to this quality the utopian potential glimpsed by Rousseau in the *Social Contract*, it was an idea which could only intensify a sensibility to corruption. For all their commitment to political economy, Rousseau ensured that neither the Scots nor the Neapolitans could take the progress of society for granted.

Even from a brief overview, therefore, we can find evidence of a continuing identity of interests among the Scottish and Neapolitan thinkers of the later Enlightenment. On the face of it, the existence of one Enlightenment in two national contexts remains at least a plausible hypothesis for the period 1760–90, open to further exploration and testing. What cannot be denied, however, is that the outcomes of the Enlightenment were very different in the two places. By 1800 Scotland had been more or less comfortably integrated into the political system of the United Kingdom, and was making an increasingly important contribution to the economic transformation now known as the industrial revolution; Scotsmen, moreover, were disproportionately represented in the administration, military service, and commercial activities of the British empire overseas.

By contrast, the formally independent kingdom of Naples ended the century locked into what seemed an inescapable cycle of reform and reaction, revolution and renewed reaction. A monarchy which by 1790 seemed increasingly set on reform, determined at last to assert itself at the expense of the church and the feudal nobility, was transformed by the events of 1792–3 in France into a simple force of reaction, as the king and queen sought to ensure that they themselves did not suffer the fate of their French counterparts (and relatives). In the event, however, their efforts were in vain. A combination of the French advance into Italy from 1796 and their own arrogance (abetted by the British ambassador, Sir William Hamilton, and his friend, Horatio Nelson) ensured that revolution extended even to Naples, where it broke out in January 1799.

---

[75] Pagano, *Saggi politici*, pp. 379–400. The reference to the 'baratro del dispotismo' is on p. 386.
[76] Ferguson, *Essay on Civil Society*, p. 14; Pagano, *Saggi politici*, p. 156: 'La sola qualità di *perfettibilità*, cioè l'attitudine a divenir meglio, socievoli rende gli uomini.'

The Neapolitan revolutionaries, who included Pagano as well as a younger generation of Italian 'Jacobins', worked fast to institute a new, republican form of government in the city and the provinces, to abolish entails and primogeniture, to reform the judicial system, and to announce a radical reform of the entire feudal system. Hard as they tried to consolidate the new regime, however, they remained dependent on French military support, and the withdrawal of French troops at the end of April was quickly followed by surrender and royal (and British) retribution. A fresh round of reaction followed, until the French returned in 1806, this time to remain for almost ten years, long enough to undertake and, to an extent, to carry through a number of the reforms projected in 1799. With Napoleon's defeat and surrender, however, this regime too collapsed, and the Bourbons were restored again in 1815. The cycle of reform, revolution, and reaction was by no means as negative as its repetitiveness might suggest: during the *Decennio* of French rule between 1806 and 1815 several reforms were achieved, notably in the consolidation of private landownership, which would not afterwards be reversed. But there is also no denying the disruption caused by regime change and military occupation, above all in the bandit-infested provinces.[77] The gap between the economy and society of the kingdom of Naples and that of an industrialising society such as Scotland was widening all the time.

Despite this marked discrepancy in outcomes, to think in terms of an Enlightenment successful in Scotland, and defeated or failed in Naples, is unlikely to be helpful. Causal links between intellectual movements and economic and political developments are notoriously difficult to pin down: if it is an oversimplification to give the Scottish Enlightenment the credit for the subsequent Scottish contribution to industrialisation and overseas empire, it is no more plausible to blame the Neapolitan revolution of 1799, or its failure, on the Enlightenment which preceded it. Individual Enlightenment thinkers, most notably Pagano, may have taken a leading role in the revolution, and paid for it with their lives. But it is not at all obvious that the arguments of the *Saggi politici* pointed to revolutionary conclusions; Pagano is much more likely to have been led to these under the pressure of the events of the 1790s, which in his case included imprisonment for

---

[77] For an authoritative account of the period of the revolution and French rule: Anna Maria Rao and Pasquale Villani, *Napoli 1799–1815. Dalla repubblica alla monarchia amministrativa* (Naples 1995). An up-to-date conspectus of scholarly opinion is provided by the collection of papers deriving from the principal conference held in 1999 to mark the bicentenary of the revolution: Anna Maria Rao (ed.), *Napoli 1799. Fra storia e storiografia* (Naples, 2002). In English, see the major new work by John Davis, *Naples and its Kingdom before the Making of Italy* (Oxford, forthcoming).

defending accused Neapolitan Jacobins and freemasons in 1796, followed in 1798 by exile to Rome, then under its own revolutionary republic.[78] Meanwhile others equally active in the earlier Enlightenment, such as Giuseppe Galanti, positively declined to participate in the revolution. There was no high road from Enlightenment to revolution in Naples, any more than from Enlightenment to industrial revolution and empire in Scotland.

It has frequently been emphasised here that Enlightenment philosophers, whether in Scotland or in Naples, thought about the progress – and possible decline – of society in the long not the short term. They advanced good reasons to believe that individuals, even governments, had limited power to affect the course of such development, which worked best when it was the outcome of multiple individual decisions, taken in the self-interested expectation of bettering one's condition on earth. There were indeed many obstacles to development, the most entrenched in both countries being the privileges linked to feudal landownership, and the philosophers agreed that legislative action would be required to remove them. But if the remedies were not to be worse than the existing obstacles, governments would have to learn to act in line with public opinion, which itself should be informed by sound principles of political economy. It was an additional fear of many Scots and Neapolitans that self-interested decision-making might have adverse moral consequences; but this did not mean that there should be a simple reassertion of virtue at the expense of economic betterment, such as the Jacobins proclaimed. In their confidence that they understood the requisites of progress, the Enlightenment philosophers certainly underestimated the power of politics, and especially of French revolutionary politics, to change not only regimes but whole societies in a very short space of time. But this does not make them mistaken in their conviction that political economy and the progress of society represented, in the longer term, the best available prospect for their countries, the kingdom of Naples just as much as Scotland. That was their case for the Enlightenment; it is also mine.

[78] See my 'Enlightenment and Revolution: Naples 1799', *Transactions of the Royal Historical Society*, sixth series 10 (2000), 17–44, esp. pp. 40–44, for cautionary remarks on this head.

Bibliography

MANUSCRIPTS

EDINBURGH

National Archives of Scotland

GD 220/5/800/13 (Montrose correspondence): letter relating to Andrew Fletcher.

National Library of Scotland (NLS)

Ms 7020 (Yester papers), ff. 169–70: letter of Andrew Fletcher to Lord Yester, 1699.
Ms 16502 (Saltoun papers): correspondence of Andrew Fletcher.
Ms 17498 (Saltoun papers), f. 72: 'A Letter from a Gentleman at London to his Friend at Edinburgh, October 13, 1700'.
Ms 17863 (Saltoun papers): 'Catalogue of Books. Holograph of Andrew Fletcher of Saltoun'.

NAPLES

Archivio di Stato di Napoli (ASN)

Tribunali Antichi, fasc. 1728: Supremo Magistrato del Commercio.

Biblioteca Nazionale di Napoli (BNN)

Ms x.F.72, ff. 1–44: 'Discorso interno alla successione della Monarchia di Spagna dopo la morte di Carlo II, del Consiglier Conte Saverio Pansuti'.
Ms xi.C.25: ff. 1–23: 'Il vero interesse de principi cristiani opposto a'i falsi interessi, che da poco in qua' sono stati dati in luce. Trattato che rappresenta al vivo l'interesse, che hanno li principi cristiani d'opporsi alle pretensioni d'un re, che vorebbe rendersi soggetti tutti li stati dell'Europa'.
Mss xiii.B.69–73: 'Delle Lezioni Accademiche de' diversi valentuomini de' nostri tempi recitate avanti l'Eccmo. Sig. Duca di Medina Coeli'.
Ms xiii.D.8: 'Raccolta di Rime, e Prose non ancora terminate di Tiberio Carafa Principe di Chiusano'.

Biblioteca Oratoriana dei Girolamini

Microfilm 27.1.10: 'Antico Catalogo della Biblioteca dei Girolamini attribuito a Giambattista Vico'.

Microfilm 28.3.28 (of Codice Cart. xv, op. 13, ff. 120–9): 'Discorso politico circa lo stato presente dell'Europa, e delle vere ragioni, per le quale i Prencipi collegati non desiderano la pace col Re di Francia, 1695, nel mese di Marzo', attributed to Francesco D'Andrea.

Microfilm 28.4.3 (of Cod. cxxxvii, Misc. Div. no. 10): 'Il vero interesse de principi cristiani' (another copy of the work in BNN Ms xi.c.25).

Società Napoletana per la Storia Patria (SNSP)

Ms xx.A.18, ff. 95–109: 'Risposta a un libro . . . dell'Abate Magnati' (another copy of a work in BNN Ms xiii. B. 73, ff. 132–50).

Ms xxvi.D.10, ff. 728–55: 'Riflessioni sopra li differenti interessi che la maggior parte delle potenze d'Europa hanno nel presente stato della monarchia di Spagna'.

Ms xxvii.c.10, ff. 121–31: 'Copia di lettera scritta da D. Bartolomeo Ceva Grimaldi Duca di Telese ad un suo amico a Napoli, Vienna lo sc'mbre 1701'.

Mss xxx.C.16, ff. 1–68, xxxi. B.1, ff. 197–249: copies of Celestino Galiani, 'Ricerche intorno alle prime origini della scienza morale'.

Ms xxxi.A.7: 'Galiani, Celestino: Corrispondenza Vol. 7': letters of Bartolomeo Intieri to Celestino Galiani.

PUBLISHED PRIMARY WORKS

Abercromby, Patrick, *The Martial Atchievements of the Scots Nation. Being an account of the lives, characters and memorable actions, of such Scotsmen as have signalis'd themselves by the sword at home and abroad. And a survey of the military transactions wherein Scotland or Scotsmen have been remarkably concern'd, from the first establishment of the Scots monarchy to this present time*, 2 vols. (Edinburgh, 1711; 1715).

[Abercromby, Patrick], *The Advantages of the Act of Security, compar'd with these of the intended Union: founded on the Revolution Principles publish'd by Mr Daniel Defoe* (n.p., 1706).

Anderson, James, *Observations on the means of exciting a spirit of national industry; chiefly intended to promote the agriculture, commerce, manufactures, and fisheries of Scotland* (Edinburgh, 1777).

Arnauld, Antoine, *Reflexions philosophiques et théologiques sur le nouveau système de la nature et de la Grace* (1685).

Aubery, Antoine, *Des Justes Pretentions du Roi sur l'Empire* (Paris, 1667).

Axiomata politica Gallicana (1667).

Augustine, *The City of God against the Pagans* (426), ed. R. W. Dyson (Cambridge, 1998).

Bayle, Pierre, *Pensées Diverses. Ecrites à un Docteur de Sorbonne, A l'Occasion de la Comète qui parut au mois de Decembre 1680* (1682), nouvelle édition corrigé (Rotterdam, 1721).

Dictionnaire historique et critique (Rotterdam, 1697; second edn Rotterdam, 1702; fourth edn Amsterdam and Leiden, 1730).

Historical and Critical Dictionary: Selections, ed. and transl. Richard H. Popkin, (Indianapolis, New York, and Kansas City, 1965).

Bayle: Political Writings, ed. Sally L. Jenkinson (Cambridge, 2000).

[Belhaven, John, Lord (?)], *A Defence of the Scots Settlement at Darien, with an answer to the Spanish memorial against it. And Arguments to prove, that it is the interest of England to join with the Scots, and protect it* (n.p., 1699).

Biscardi, Serafino, *Epistola pro Augusto Hispaniarum Monarcha Philippo Quinto qua & jus ei assertum successionis universae Monarchiae, & omnia confutantur, quae pro Investitura Regni Napoletani & pro coeteris Regnis a Germanis scripta sunt* (Naples, 1703).

Oratio . . . in Die naturali Philippi V Potentissimi, Invictissimique Hispaniarum Monarchae (Naples, 1705).

Broggia, Carlantonio, *Memoria ad ogetto di varie politiche ed economiche ragioni* (1754): 'Trattato primo intitolato: Del lusso, o sia abuso delle richezze', in R. Ajello and others (eds.), *Dal Muratori al Cesarotti.* V: *Politici ed economisti del primo settecento* (Milan and Naples, 1978), pp. 1041–59.

Buchanan, George, *Georgii Buchanani Opera Omnia . . . curante Thoma Ruddimano* (Edinburgh, 1715).

Burnet, Gilbert, *A Discourse on the Memory of that rare and truely Virtuous Person Sir Robert Fletcher of Saltoun: who died the 13 January last, in the thirty-ninth year of his Age. Written by a Gentleman of his Acquaintance* (Edinburgh, 1665).

Some Letters containing an Account of what seemed most remarkable in Switzerland, Italy & c. (Amsterdam, 1686).

Campbell, Archibald, *An Enquiry into the Original of Moral Virtue. Wherein it is shewn (against the author of the Fable of the Bees & co.) that virtue is founded in the nature of things, is unalterable, and eternal, and the great means of private and publick happiness; with some reflections on a late book, intitled, An Enquiry into the Original of our Ideas of Beauty and Virtue* (Edinburgh, 1733).

Carmichael, Gershom, *Natural Rights on the Threshold of the Scottish Enlightenment: the Writings of Gershom Carmichael*, ed. James Moore and Michael Silverthorne (Indianapolis, 2002).

[Chamberlen, Hugh], *A Few Proposals humbly recommending the Establishment of a Land Credit* (Edinburgh, 1700).

Clerk, Sir John, of Penicuik, 'Observations on the present circumstances of Scotland, 1730', ed. T. C. Smout, *Scottish History Society*, Fourth Series 2, *Miscellany* X (1965), pp. 175–212.

d'Andrea, Francesco, *Risposta al trattato delle ragioni della Regina Cristianissima, sopra il Ducato del Brabante, et altri stati della Fiandra. Nella quale si dimostra l'ingiustizia della guerra mossa dal Re di Francia, per la conquista di quelle provincie; non ostante le ragioni, che si son pubblicate in suo nome, per la pretesa successione a favor della Regina Cristianissima* (Naples, 1667, 1676).

The Darien Papers, ed. J. H. Burton, for the Bannatyne Club (Edinburgh, 1849).

Davenant, Charles, *The Political and Commercial Works*, ed. and rev. Sir Charles Whitworth, 5 vols. (London, 1771).

Defoe, Daniel, *The Interests of the several Princes and States of Europe consider'd, with respect to the Succession to the Crown of Spain* (London, 1698).

The two Great Questions consider'd: I. What the French King will do, with respect to the Spanish Monarchy, II. What measures the English ought to take (London, 1700).

An Essay at Removing National Prejudices against a Union with England. Part III (n.p., 1706).

The History of the Union between England and Scotland (London, 1786).

Doria, Paolo Mattia, *La Vita Civile, distinta in tre parti aggiuntovi un trattato della Educazione del Principe, seconda edizione, dall'autore ricoretta, ed accresciuta* (second edn Augusta [Naples?], 1710; third edn Naples, 1729).

Massime del governo spagnolo a Napoli, ed. Giuseppe Galasso and Vittorio Conti (Naples, 1973).

'Del commercio del regno di Napoli, 1740', in *Il pensiero civile di Paolo Mattia Doria negli scritti inediti. Con il testo del manoscritto 'Del commercio del regno di Napoli'*, ed. Enrico Vidal (Milan, 1953), pp. 161–206.

'Il politico alla moda di mente adeguata e prattica' (1739–40), ed. Vittorio Conti, printed as appendix to *Paolo Mattia Doria. Dalla repubblica dei togati alla repubblica dei notabili* (Florence, 1978), pp. 130–259.

Manoscritti Napoletani di Paolo Mattia Doria, vol. IV, ed. Pasquale di Fabrizio (Galatina, 1981).

Dutot, Charles de Ferrare, *Réflexions politiques sur les finances et le commerce* (1738), ed. Paul Harsin, 2 vols. (Liège, 1935).

Ferguson, Adam, *An Essay on the History of Civil Society 1767*, ed. Fania Oz-Salzberger (Cambridge, 1995).

Filangieri, Gaetano, *Scienza della legislazione*, 7 vols. (Naples, 1780–85, 1791), in the edition in 6 vols. (Milan, 1822); modern critical edition by Vincenzo Ferrone, Antonio Trampus, Maria Teresa Silvestrini and others, 7 vols. (Venice, 2003–4).

Fletcher, Andrew, *The Political Works* (London, 1732, 1737), ed. John Robertson (Cambridge, 1997).

Bibliotheca Fletcheriana: or, the Extraordinary Library of Andrew Fletcher of Saltoun, Reconstructed and Systematically Arranged, comp. and ed. Peter Willems (Wassenaar, 1999).

Galanti, Giuseppe Maria, *Elogio storico del Signor Abate Antonio Genovesi, pubblico professore del civil economia nella Università di Napoli* (Naples, 1772).

Descrizione dello stato antico ed attuale del contado di Molise, 2 vols. (Naples, 1781).

Nuova descrizione storica e geografica delle Sicilie, 5 vols. (Naples, 1786–94); *Della descrizione geografica e politica delle Sicilie*, 2 vols., ed. F. Assante and D. Demarco (Naples, 1969).

Galiani, Ferdinando, *Opere di Ferdinando Galiani*, ed. Furio Diaz and Luciano Guerci, *Illuministi italiani*, vol. VI (Milan and Naples, 1975).

'Relazione di Galiani circa un progetto di trattato fra la Russia e il Regno di Sardegna e le prospettive di un trattato fra Russia e Regno di Napoli' (1783), in F. Diaz, 'L'Abate Galiani consigliere di commercio estero', *Rivista Storica Italiana*, 80 (1968), pp. 887–92.

Genovesi, Antonio, *Lezioni di commercio, o sia d'economia civile* (Naples, 1765–67; second edn 1768–70).

Lettere accademiche su la questione se sieno più felici gl'ignoranti che gli scienziati (Naples, 1764; second rev. edn 1769).

'Vita di Antonio Genovesi', in F. Venturi (ed.), *Illuministi Italiani* V: *Riformatori napoletani* (Milan and Naples, 1962), pp. 47–83.

Antonio Genovesi. Scritti economici, ed. Maria Luisa Perna, 2 vols. (Naples, 1984).

Giannone, Pietro, *Dell'Istoria civile del Regno di Napoli Libri* XL, 4 vols. (Naples, 1723).

Vita scritta da lui medesimo (composed 1736–7), in *Opere di Pietro Giannone*, ed. Sergio Bertelli and Giuseppe Ricuperati (Milan and Naples, 1971).

Gibbon, Edward, *The Autobiographies of Edward Gibbon*, ed. John Murray (London, 1896).

[Grant, Francis,] *The Patriot Resolved; in a letter to an Addresser, from his Friend; of the same sentiments with himself, concerning the Union* (n.p., 1707).

Grimaldi, Domenico, *Piano di riforma per la pubblica economia delle provincie del Regno di Napoli, e per l'agricoltura delle due Sicilie* (Naples, 1780).

Grimaldi, Francescantonio, *Riflessioni sopra l'ineguaglianza tra gli uomini*, 3 vols. (Naples, 1779–80).

Harrington, James, *The Commonwealth of Oceana* (1656), in *The Political Works of James Harrington*, ed. J. G. A. Pocock (Cambridge, 1977).

Historical Manuscripts Commission: Portland Papers, vol. IV (London, 1897).

Historical Manuscripts Commission: Mar and Kellie Papers (London, 1904).

Hobbes, Thomas, *De Cive* (1647), ed. Howard Warrender (Oxford 1983); English translation *On the Citizen*, by Michael Silverthorne, ed. Richard Tuck (Cambridge, 1998).

Leviathan (1651), ed. Richard Tuck (Cambridge, 1991); Latin version (1668), in *Thomae Hobbes Opera philosophica omnia*, ed. Sir William Molesworth, vol. III (London, 1841).

De Corpore (1655), *Opera philosophica*, vol. I (1839); translation: *Elements of Philosophy. The First Section, concerning Body* (1656), in *The English Works of Thomas Hobbes*, vol. I (London, 1839).

[Hodges, James], *The Rights and Interests of the Two British Monarchies, Inquir'd into, and Clear'd; with a special respect to an United or Separate State. Treatise I, shewing the different Nature of an Incorporating and Federal Union; and the Reasons why all Designs of Union have hitherto prov'd unsuccessful; and the Inconsistency of an Union by Incorporation with the Rights, Liberties, National Interests, and Publick Good of Both Kingdoms* (London, 1703).

Considerations and Proposals, for supplying the present Scarcity of Money, and advancing Trade (Edinburgh, 1705).

Horace, *Ars Poetica* (Loeb Classical Library: Cambridge, Mass., 1926; repr. 1999).

Hume, David, *A Treatise of Human Nature* (1739–40), ed. David Fate Norton and Mary J. Norton (Oxford, 2000).

Essays, Moral, Political, and Literary (1741–1777), ed. Eugene F. Miller (rev. edn Indianapolis, 1985).

Philosophical Essays concerning Human Understanding (1748), subsequently *An Enquiry concerning Human Understanding*, ed. T. L. Beauchamp (Oxford, 1999).

'The Natural History of Religion' (1757), in *Essays Moral, Political, and Literary, by David Hume*, ed. T. H. Green and T. H. Grose, 2 vols. (London, 1898), vol. II, pp. 307–63.

The History of England from the Invasion of Julius Caesar to the Revolution of 1688 (1778), ed. W. B. Todd, 6 vols. (Indianapolis, 1983).

The Letters of David Hume, ed. J. Y. T. Greig, 2 vols. (Oxford, 1969).

New Letters of David Hume, ed. R. Klibansky and E. C. Mossner (Oxford, 1969).

'Hume's Early Memoranda, 1729–1740: the complete text', ed. E. C. Mossner, *Journal of the History of Ideas*, 9 (1948), pp. 492–518.

'An early fragment on evil', ed. M. A. Stewart, in M. A. Stewart and J. P. Wright (eds.), *Hume and Hume's Connexions* (Edinburgh, 1994), pp. 160–70.

Hutcheson, Francis, *An Essay on the Nature and Conduct of the Passions and Affections, with Illustrations of the Moral Sense* (London, 1728), ed. Aaron Garrett (Indianapolis, 2002).

A System of Moral Philosophy, in Three Books, 2 vols. (Glasgow and London, 1755).

Reflections upon Laughter and Remarks upon the Fable of the Bees (Glasgow, 1756).

Francis Hutcheson: Two Texts on Human Nature, ed. Thomas Mautner (Cambridge, 1993).

Francis Hutcheson: Logic, Metaphysics and Natural Sociability, ed. James Moore and Michael Silverthorne (Indianapolis, 2005).

[Hutcheson, Francis and Moore, James], *The Meditations of the Emperor Marcus Aurelius*, newly translated from the Greek: with Notes and an Account of his Life (Glasgow: printed by Robert Foulis 1742).

Innes, Fr Thomas, *A Critical essay on the Ancient Inhabitants of the Northern Parts of Britain, or Scotland* (London, 1729).

Intieri, Bartolomeo, *Della perfetta conservazione del grano. Discorso di Bartolomeo Intieri* (Naples, 1754).

James VI and I, *The Political Works of James I*, ed. C. H. McIlwain (Cambridge, Mass., 1918; repr. New York, 1965).

Kant, Immanuel, 'An answer to the question: What is Enlightenment?' (1784), in James Schmidt (ed.), *What is Enlightenment? Eighteenth-Century Answers and Twentieth-Century Questions* (Berkeley, Los Angeles, and London, 1996), pp. 58–64.

Law, John, *Money and Trade Considered, with a Proposal for supplying the Nation with Money* (Edinburgh, 1705).

[Lindsay, Patrick], *The Interest of Scotland Considered, with regard to its Police in imploying the Poor, its Agriculture, its Trade, its Manufactures, and Fisheries* (Edinburgh, 1733).

Lisola, Franz von, *Bouclier d'Estat et de Justice. Contre le dessein manifestement découvert de la Monarchie Universelle, sous le vain pretexte des pretentions de la Reyne de France* (1667).

Locke, John, *The Correspondence of John Locke*, ed. E. S. De Beer, vol. v (Oxford, 1979).

John Locke: Selected Correspondence, ed. Mark Goldie (Oxford 2002).

Lucretius, *De rerum natura* (Loeb Classical Library: Cambridge, Mass., 1975; repr. 1997).

Machiavelli, Niccoló, *Discorsi sopra la prima deca di Tito Livio* (c. 1517), ed. Sergio Bertelli (Milan, 1960; fourth edn 1973).

[Mackenzie, George, earl of Cromarty], *Trialogus. A Conference betwixt Mr Con, Mr Pro, and Mr Indifferent, concerning the Union* (n.p., 1706).

Magliabecchi, Antonio, *Lettere dal Regno ad Antonio Magliabecchi*, ed. Amadeo Quondam and Michele Rak, 2 vols. (Naples, 1978).

Malebranche, Nicolas, *De la Recherche de la Verité* (1674–5), in *Oeuvres Complètes de Malebranche*, ed. G. Rodis-Lewis, vol. I (Paris, 1963).

Réponse à une Dissertation de Mr Arnauld contre un Eclaircissement du Traité de la nature et de la Grace (1685); *Réponse du Père Malebranche à la Troisième Lettre de M. Arnauld Docteur de Sorbonne touchant les idées & les plaisirs* (1699), both in *Oeuvres Complètes de Malebranche*, vi–vii, viii–ix, ed. A. Robinet (Paris, 1966).

Mandeville, Bernard, *Free Thoughts on Religion, the Church and National Happiness* (London, 1720; second edn London, 1729), modern edn Irwin Primer (New Brunswick and London, 2001).

The Fable of the Bees, or Private Vices, Publick Benefits (1723, 1728), ed. F. B. Kaye, 2 vols. (Oxford, 1924; repr. Indianapolis, 1988).

An Enquiry into the Origin of Honour and the Usefulness of Christianity in War (London, 1732), ed. M. M. Goldsmith (London, 1971).

A Letter to Dion, occasion'd by his Book call'd Alciphron, or the Minute Philosopher (London, 1732).

Melon, Jean-François, *Essai politique sur le commerce* (1734; second edn. 1736, in the 'Nouvelle Edition, revue et corrigée' published in Amsterdam, 1754).

Political Essays upon Commerce, translation (of the first edition) by David Bindon (Dublin, 1738).

Saggio politico sul commercio, tradotto dal francese colle annotazioni dell' Ab. Longano, 2 vols. (Naples, 1778).

Saggio politico sul commercio del Signor Melon. Tradotto dal francese. Nuova edizione con note (Naples, 1795).

Millar, John, *The Origin of the Distinction of Ranks* (1771, third edn. 1779), ed. W. C. Lehman, in *John Millar of Glasgow* (Cambridge, 1960).

Montesquieu, Charles Secondat, Baron de, *De l'esprit des lois* (1748), in *Montesquieu: Oeuvres Complètes*, vol. II, ed. Roger Caillois (Bibliothèque de la Pléiade, Paris, 1951).

Moyle, Walter, *The Whole Works* (London, 1727).

Murray, Alexander, of Stanhope, *An Abstract of an Essay on the Improvement of Husbandry and Working of Mines, in a Letter to the Right Honourable Sir Robert Walpole* (London [1733]).

The True Interest of Great Britain, Ireland and our Plantations (London, 1740).

Pagano, Francesco Mario, *Saggi politici*, 2 vols. (Naples, 1783–5).

Saggi politici. De' principii, progressi e decadenza delle società. Edizione seconda, corretta ed accresciuta, 2 vols. (Naples, 1791–2), ed. Luigi and Laura Salvetti Firpo (Naples, 1993).

Pallante, Giovanni, *Memoria per la riforma del regno* (1735–37), ed. Imma Ascione (Naples, 1996).

Palmieri, Giuseppe, *Riflessioni sulla pubblica felicità relativamente al Regno di Napoli* (Naples, 1787).

Della ricchezza nazionale (Naples, 1792).

Paterson, William, *Proposals and Reasons for constituting a Council of Trade* (1701), in *The Writings of William Paterson*, ed. Saxe Bannister (1859; repr. New York, 1968).

Pereira, Juan de Solórzano, *De Indiarum Iure* (Madrid, 1629).

Política Indiana (1647; repr. Madrid, 1972).

Petty, William, *The Economic Writings of Sir William Petty*, ed. C. H. Hull, 2 vols. (Cambridge, 1899).

Register of the Privy Council of Scotland: Vol. VII, 1604–1607 (Edinburgh, 1885).

[Ridpath, George], *Scotland's Grievances relating to Darien, humbly offered to the consideration of the Parliament* (n.p., 1700).

The Great Reasons and Interests consider'd, anent the Spanish Monarchy (n.p., 1701).

Robertson, William, *The History of Scotland during the Reigns of Queen Mary and King James VI*, 2 vols. (London, 1759).

The History of the Reign of the Emperor Charles V, 3 vols. (London, 1769).

The History of America, 2 vols. (London, 1777).

Rousseau, Jean-Jacques, *Oeuvres complètes*. III: *Du Contrat Social. Écrits politiques*, ed. B. Gagnebin and M. Raymond (Bibliothèque de la Pléiade, Paris, 1964).

Schmidt d'Avenstein, Georg Ludwig, *Principii della legislazione universale del Sign. Schmidt. Traduzione dal francese*, 4 vols. (Naples, 1791).

Serra, Antonio, *Breve Trattato delle cause, che possono far abbondare li regni d'oro, & argento, dove non sono miniere. Con applicatione al Regno di Napoli* (Naples, 1613), ed. S. Ricossa and C. S. Rije (Istituto Italiano per gli Studi Filosofici: Naples, 1986).

Seton, William, *The Interest of Scotland in Three Essays* (1700; second edn London, 1702).

[Seton, William], *Some Thoughts on Ways and Means for making the Nation a Gainer in Foreign Commerce; and for supplying its present Scarcity of Money* (Edinburgh, 1705).

Scotland's Great Advantages by an Union with England; showen in a Letter from the Country, to a Member of Parliament (n.p., 1706).

Sibbald, Sir Robert, *Provision for the Poor in time of Dearth and Scarcity. Where there is an account of such food as may easily be gotten when corns are scarce, or unfit for use; and of such meats as may be used when the ordinary provisions fail, or are very dear. Written for the Relief of the Poor by R.S. Doctor of Medicine* (Edinburgh, 1699; second edn, 1709).

'Memoirs of my Lyfe', ed. Francis Paget Hett, *The Memoirs of Robert Sibbald (1641–1722)* (London, 1932).

Smith, Adam, *The Theory of Moral Sentiments* (1759; sixth edn 1790), ed. D. D. Raphael and A. L. Macfie (Oxford, 1976).

An Inquiry into the Nature and Causes of the Wealth of Nations (1776), ed. R. H. Campbell, A. S. Skinner, and W. B. Todd, 2 vols. (Oxford, 1976).

Essays on Philosophical Subjects, ed. W. P. D. Wightman, J. C. Bryce, and I. S. Ross (Oxford, 1980).

Lectures on Rhetoric and Belles Lettres, ed. J. C. Bryce and A. S. Skinner (Oxford, 1983).

Spinoza, Baruch or Benedict, *Tractatus Theologico-Politicus* (1670), transl. R. H. M. Elwes, *A Theologico-Politico Treatise* (New York, 1951).

Ethics (1667–8), transl. R. H. M. Elwes (New York, 1955).

Steuart, James, *Principles of Political Oeconomy*, 2 vols. (London, 1767), ed. A. S. Skinner, with N. Kobayashi and H. Mizuta, 2 vols. (London, 1998).

Valletta, Giuseppe, *Opere filosofiche*, ed. Michele Rak (Florence, 1975).

Vico, Giambattista, *The Autobiography of Giambattista Vico*, transl. M. H. Fisch and T. G. Bergin (Ithaca, 1944).

Opere filosofiche, ed. Nicola Badaloni and Paolo Cristofaro (Florence, 1971).

The New Science of Giambattista Vico, transl. T. G. Bergin and M. H. Fisch, rev. unabridged edn (of the third *New Science*), (Ithaca and London, 1984).

On the most ancient wisdom of the Italians, transl. L. M. Palmer (Ithaca and London, 1988).

Giambattista Vico: Opere, ed. Andrea Battistini, 2 vols. (Milan, 1990).

'Giambattista Vico's "Reprehension of the Metaphysics of René Descartes, Benedict Spinoza, and John Locke": an addition to the *New Science* (translation and commentary)', by Donald Phillip Verene, *New Vico Studies*, 8 (1990), pp. 2–18.

'Principum neapolitanorum coniurationis anni MDCCI historia', ed. and transl. Claudia Pandolfi, *La Congiura dei principi napoletani 1701* (Naples, 1992).

New Science, translation of the third edition by David Marsh, with an introduction by Anthony Grafton (Harmondsworth, 1999).

The First New Science, ed. and transl. Leon Pompa (Cambridge, 2002).

Warburton, William, *The Divine Legation of Moses Demonstrated, on the principles of a religious Deist, from the omission of the doctrine of a future state of reward and punishment in the Jewish Dispensation*, 2 vols. (London, 1738, 1741).

Wodrow, Robert, *Early Letters of Robert Wodrow 1698–1709*, ed. L. W. Sharp, Scottish History Society, Third Series xxiv (Edinburgh, 1937).

PUBLISHED SECONDARY WORKS

Aa. Vv., *Storia della Università di Napoli* (Naples, 1924).

Acton, Harold, *The Bourbons of Naples 1734–1825* (London, 1956; repr. 1974).

Ajello, Raffaele, 'Legislazione e crisi del diritto commune nel Regno di Napoli. Il tentativo di codificazione Carlino', in E. Sestan (ed.), *Studi e ricerche sul Settecento* (Naples, 1968), pp. 172–223.

Arcana Juris (Naples, 1976).

'Cartesianismo e cultura oltremontana al tempo dell'*Istoria Civile*', in R. Ajello (ed.), *Pietro Giannone e il suo tempo* (Naples 1980), pp. 1–181.

'Diritto ed economia in Paolo Mattia Doria', in Aa. Vv., *Paolo Mattia Doria fra rinnovamento e tradizione* (Galatina, 1985), pp. 93–126.

Una società anomala. Il programma e la sconfitta della nobiltà napoletana in due memoriali cinquecenteschi (Naples, 1996).

Ajello, Raffaele and others (eds.), *Dal Muratori al Cesarotti*. V: *Politici ed economisti del primo settecento* (Milan and Naples, 1978).

Allan, David, *Virtue, Learning and the Scottish Enlightenment: Ideas of scholarship in early modern history* (Edinburgh, 1993).

'Reconciliation and retirement in the Restoration Scottish Church: the neo-Stoicism of Robert Leighton', *Journal of Ecclesiastical History*, 50 (1999), pp. 251–78.

Philosophy and Politics in Later Stuart Scotland: Neo-Stoicism, Culture, and Ideology in an Age of Crisis 1540–1690 (East Linton, 2000).

Armitage, David, 'The Scottish vision of empire: intellectual origins of the Darien venture', in John Robertson (ed.), *A Union for Empire: Political Thought and the British Union of 1707* (Cambridge, 1995), pp. 97–118.

'Making the Empire British: Scotland in the Atlantic World 1542–1707', *Past and Present*, 155 (1997), pp. 34–63.

The Ideological Origins of the British Empire (Cambridge, 2000).

Astarita, Tommaso, *The Continuity of Feudal Power: the Caracciolo of Brienza in Spanish Naples* (Cambridge, 1992).

Baker, Keith M., *Condorcet: from Natural Philosophy to Social Mathematics* (Chicago and London, 1975).

Inventing the French Revolution: Essays on French Political Culture in the Eighteenth Century (Cambridge, 1990).

Baker, K. M., and Reill, P. H. (eds.), *What's Left of Enlightenment? A Postmodern Question* (Stanford, 2001).

Baldi, Maria Luisa, *David Hume nel Settecento italiano. Filosofia ed economia* (Florence, 1983).

Barfoot, Michael, 'Hume and the culture of science in the early eighteenth century', in M. A. Stewart (ed.), *Studies in the Philosophy of the Scottish Enlightenment* (Oxford, 1990), pp. 151–90.

Barnard, Christopher, 'Hume and the madness of religion', in M. A. Stewart and J. P. Wright (eds.), *Hume and Hume's Connexions* (Edinburgh, 1994), pp. 201–23.

Bedani, Gino, *Vico Revisited: Orthodoxy, Naturalism and Science in the Scienza Nuova* (Oxford, 1989).

Bellamy, Richard, '"Da metafisico a mercatante": Antonio Genovesi and the development of a new language of commerce in eighteenth-century Naples', in Anthony Pagden (ed.), *The Languages of Political Theory in Early Modern Europe* (Cambridge, 1987), pp. 277–99.

Bellucci, Antonio, 'Giambattista Vico e la Biblioteca dei Girolamini', *Quaderni della Biblioteca dei Girolamini di Napoli*, First Series 2 (1955).

Bentley, Jerry H., *Politics and Culture in Renaissance Naples* (Princeton, 1987).

Berlin, Isaiah, *Vico and Herder: two Studies in the History of Ideas* (London, 1976).

The Crooked Timber of Humanity: Chapters in the History of Ideas (London, 1991).

Berry, Christopher J., 'Rude religion: the psychology of polytheism in the Scottish Enlightenment', in Paul Wood (ed.), *The Scottish Enlightenment: Essays in Reinterpretation* (Rochester, N.Y., and Woodbridge, Suffolk, 2000), pp. 315–34.

Berti, Silvia (ed.), *Trattato de tre impostori. La vita e lo spirito del signor Benedetto Spinoza* (Turin, 1994).

Bianchi, Lorenzo, '"E contro la pratica de' governi di Baile, che vorrebbe senza religioni poter reggere le nazioni". Note su Bayle nella corrispondenza di Vico', *Bollettino del Centro di Studi Vichiani*, 30 (2000), pp. 17–30.

Bireley, Robert, *The Counter-Reformation Prince: Anti-Machiavellianism or Catholic Statecraft in Early Modern Europe* (Chapel Hill, N.C., and London, 1990).

Bloch, Marc, 'Pour une histoire comparée des sociétés européennes', in his *Mélanges Historiques*, 2 vols. (Paris, 1963), I, pp. 16–40.

Borelli, A., 'Francesco d'Andrea. Lettere a G. Baglivi, A. Baldigiani, A. Magliabecchi, M. Malpighi, A. Marchetti, F. Redi, L. Porzio', *Archivio Storico per le Provincie Napoletane* (1997), pp. 113–258.

Bosbach, Franz, *Monarchia Universalis. Ein politischer Leitbegriff der frühen Neuzeit* (Göttingen, 1988), Ital. transl. *Monarchia Universalis. Storia di un concetto cardine della politica europea (secoli xvi–xviii)* (Milan 1998).

'Eine Französische Universalmonarchie? Deutsche Reaktionen auf die europäische Politik Ludwigs XIV', in Jochen Schlobach (ed.), *Vermittlungen. Aspekte der deutsch-französische Beziehungen vom 17. Jahrhundert bis zur Gegenwart* (Berne, 1992), pp. 53–68.

'The European debate on Universal Monarchy', in David Armitage (ed.), *Theories of Empire 1450–1800* (Aldershot and Brookfield, Vt., 1998), pp. 81–98.

Brancaccio, G., 'La geografia ecclesiastica', in G. Galasso and R. Romeo (eds.), *Storia del Mezzogiorno*. IX: *Aspetti e problemi del medioevo e dell'età moderna* (Naples, 1991), pp. 233–76.

Broadie, Alexander, *The Circle of John Mair: Logic and Logicians in Pre-Reformation Scotland* (Oxford, 1985).

The Tradition of Scottish Philosophy (Edinburgh, 1990).

Broadie, Alexander (ed.), *The Cambridge Companion to the Scottish Enlightenment* (Cambridge, 2003).

Brockliss, Laurence, *Calvet's Web: Enlightenment and the Republic of Letters in Eighteenth-century France* (Oxford, 2002).

Brown, Keith M., 'From Scottish lords to British officers: state building, elite integration and the army in the seventeenth century', in N. Macdougall (ed.), *Scotland and War AD 79–1918* (Edinburgh, 1991), pp. 133–48.

Kingdom or Province? Scotland and the Regal Union 1603–1715 (Basingstoke and London, 1992).

Brown, Michael, *Francis Hutcheson in Dublin 1719–1730: the Crucible of his Thought* (Dublin, 2002).

Buckroyd, Julia, *Church and State in Scotland 1660–1681* (Edinburgh, 1980).

'Anticlericalism in Scotland during the Restoration', in Norman Macdougall (ed.), *Church, Politics, and Society: Scotland 1408–1929* (Edinburgh, 1983), pp. 167–85.

Burke, Peter, 'The Virgin of the Carmine and the revolt of Masaniello', *Past and Present*, 99 (1983), pp. 3–21.

Burns, J. H., *The True Law of Kingship: Concepts of Monarchy in Early Modern Scotland* (Oxford, 1996).

Bushnell, Rebecca W., 'George Buchanan, James VI and neo-classicism', in Roger A. Mason (ed.), *Scots and Britons: Scottish Political Thought and the Union of 1603* (Cambridge, 1994), pp. 91–111.

Cairns, John W., 'The formation of the Scottish legal mind in the eighteenth century: themes of humanism and Enlightenment in the admission of advocates', in Neil MacCormick and Peter Birks (eds.), *The Legal Mind: Essays for Tony Honoré* (Oxford, 1986), pp. 253–77.

'Sir George Mackenzie, the Faculty of Advocates and the Advocates' Library', in J. W. Cairns and A. M. Cain (eds.), *Oratio Inauguralis in Aperienda Jurisconsultorum Bibliotheca: Sir George Mackenzie* (Edinburgh, 1989), pp. 18–35.

Calabria, Antonio, *The Cost of Empire: the Finances of the Kingdom of Naples in the Time of Spanish Rule* (Cambridge, 1991).

Calaresu, Melissa, 'Images of ancient Rome in late eighteenth-century Neapolitan historiography', *Journal of the History of Ideas*, 58 (1997), pp. 641–61.

Cañal, Vicente Lleó, 'The art collection of the ninth Duke of Medinaceli', *The Burlington Magazine*, 131 (1989), pp. 108–16.

Cantelli, Gianfranco, *Vico e Bayle. Premesse per un confronto*, Studi Vichiani 4 (Naples, 1971).

Carpanetto, D., and Ricuperati, G., *Italy in the Age of Reason 1685–1789* (London, 1987).

Carter, J. J., and Pittock, J. H. (eds.), *Aberdeen and the Enlightenment* (Aberdeen, 1987).

Cassirer, Ernst, *Die Philosophie der Aufklärung* (Tübingen, 1932); English transl. *The Philosophy of the Enlightenment* (Princeton, 1951).

Castiglione, Dario, 'Considering things minutely: reflections on Mandeville and the eighteenth-century science of man', *History of Political Thought*, 7 (1986), pp. 463–88.

Champion, Justin, *The Pillars of Priestcraft Shaken: the Church of England and its enemies 1660–1730* (Cambridge, 1992).

Chartier, Roger, *The Cultural Origins of the French Revolution* (Durham, N.C., and London, 1991).

   'The man of letters', in M. Vovelle (ed.), *Enlightenment Portraits* (Chicago and London, 1997), pp. 142–89.

Chiosi, Elvira, 'Il regno dal 1734 al 1799', in G. Galasso and R. Romeo (eds.), *Storia del Mezzogiorno*. Vol. IV, tomo ii: *Il Regno dagli Angioini ai Borboni* (Naples, 1986), pp. 373–467.

Chorley, Patrick, *Oil, Silk, and Enlightenment: Economic Problems in XVIIIth-century Naples* (Naples, 1965).

Clark, J. C. D., *English Society 1688–1832: Ideology, Social Structure and Political Practice during the Ancien Régime* (Cambridge, 1985).

Cobban, Alfred, *Aspects of the French Revolution* (London, 1968).

Colapietra, R., *Vita pubblica e classi politiche nel Viceregno napoletano 1656–1734* (Rome, 1961).

Colzi, Roberto, 'Che ore era? Raffronto tra le ore all'italiana e alla francese a Roma', *Studi Romani*, 43 (1995), pp. 93–102.

Comparato, Vittor Ivo, *Giuseppe Valletta. Un intellettuale napoletano della fine del Seicento* (Naples, 1970).

Conti, Vittorio, 'Il "Parere" di Tiberio Carafa a Carlo d'Asburgo', *Il Pensiero Politico*, 6 (1973), pp. 57–67.

   Paolo Mattia Doria. Dalla repubblica dei togati all repubblica dei notabili (Florence, 1978).

   Le leggi di una rivoluzione. I bandi della repubblica napoletana dall'ottobre 1647 all'aprile 1648 (Naples, 1983).

Cooper, J. P. (ed.), *The New Cambridge Modern History*. IV: *The Decline of Spain and the Thirty Years' War 1609–1648/59* (Cambridge, 1970), 'General Introduction'.

Cowan, Ian B., *The Scottish Covenanters 1660–1688* (London, 1976).

Cristofolini, Paolo, 'Tommaso Cornelio et l'histoire du matérialisme', in Sylvia Murr (ed.), *Gassendi et l'Europe (1592–1792)* (Paris, 1997), pp. 335–46.

Darnton, Robert, 'In search of the Enlightenment: recent attempts to create a social history of ideas', *Journal of Modern History*, 43 (1971), pp. 113–32.

   'The high Enlightenment and the low-life of literature in pre-Revolutionary France', *Past and Present*, 51 (1971), pp. 81–115.

   The Business of the Enlightenment: a Publishing History of the Encyclopédie (Cambridge, Mass., 1979).

   The Forbidden Best-Sellers of Pre-Revolutionary France (London, 1996).

'George Washington's false teeth', *New York Review of Books* (27 March, 1997), pp. 34–8.

'Two paths through the social history of ideas', in H. T. Mason (ed.), *The Darnton Debate: Books and Revolution in the Eighteenth Century* (Voltaire Foundation, Oxford, 1999), pp. 251–94.

George Washington's False Teeth: an Unconventional Guide to the Eighteenth Century (New York and London, 2003).

Daston, Lorraine, 'The ideal and reality of the Republic of Letters in the Enlightenment', *Science in Context*, 4 (1991), pp. 367–86.

Davidson, Neil, *Discovering the Scottish Revolution 1692–1746* (London, 2003).

Davie, George Elder, *The Scottish Enlightenment* (Edinburgh 1991).

Delille, Gérard, 'Agricultural systems and demographic structures in the kingdom of Naples', in A. Calabria and J. A. Marino (eds.), *Good Government in Spanish Naples* (New York, 1990).

'Demografia', in G. Galasso and R. Romeo (eds.), *Storia del Mezzogiorno*. VIII: *Aspetti e problemi del medioevo e dell'età moderna* (Rome, 1991), pp. 17–49.

Delon, M. (ed.), *Dictionnaire européen des lumières* (Paris, 1997).

Delpiano, Patrizia, *Il trono e la cattedra. Istruzione e formazione dell'élite nel Piemonte del Settecento* (Turin, 1997).

Devine, T. M., 'The Scottish merchant community 1680–1740', in R. H. Campbell and A. S. Skinner (eds.), *The Origins and Nature of the Scottish Enlightenment* (Edinburgh, 1982), pp. 26–41.

'The social composition of the business class in the larger Scottish towns 1680–1740', in T. M. Devine and David Dickson (eds.), *Ireland and Scotland 1600–1850: Parallels and Contrasts in Economic and Social Development* (Edinburgh, 1983), pp. 163–76.

The Transformation of Rural Scotland: Social Change and the Agrarian Economy 1660–1815 (Edinburgh, 1994).

Dodghson, Robert A., *Land and Society in Early Scotland* (Oxford, 1981).

'"Pretense of blude" and "place of thair duelling": the nature of highland clans 1500–1745', in R. A. Houston and I. D. Whyte (eds.), *Scottish Society 1500–1800* (Cambridge, 1989), pp. 169–98.

Donati, Claudio, 'The Italian nobilities in the seventeenth and eighteenth centuries', in H. M. Scott (ed.), *The European Nobilities in the Seventeenth and Eighteenth Centuries*. I: *Western Europe* (London and New York, 1995), pp. 237–68.

Douglas, Norman, *Old Calabria* (1915; Harmondsworth, 1962).

Dülmen, Richard van, *The Society of Enlightenment: The Rise of the Middle Class and Enlightenment Culture in Germany* (1986, English transl. Cambridge and Oxford, 1992).

Duncan, Douglas, *Thomas Ruddiman: a Study in Scottish Scholarship of the Early Eighteenth Century* (Edinburgh, 1965).

Dupront, Alphonse, *Qu'est-ce-que les lumières?* (Paris, 1996).

Dwyer, Philip G. (ed.), *The Rise of Prussia 1700–1830* (Harlow and London, 2000).

Elliott, J. H., *Imperial Spain 1469–1716* (Harmondsworth, 1970).

'A Europe of composite monarchies', *Past and Present*, 137 (1992), pp. 48–71.

Emerson, Roger, 'The social composition of Enlightened Scotland: the Select Society of Edinburgh 1754–64', *Studies on Voltaire and the Eighteenth Century*, 114 (1973), pp. 291–329.

'Scottish universities in the eighteenth century, 1690–1800', *Studies on Voltaire and the Eighteenth Century*, 167 (1977), pp. 453–74.

'Sir Robert Sibbald Kt., the Royal Society of Scotland and the origins of the Scottish Enlightenment', *Annals of Science*, 45 (1988), pp. 41–72.

'Science and moral philosophy in the Scottish Enlightenment', in M. A. Stewart (ed.), *Studies in the Philosophy of the Scottish Enlightenment* (Oxford, 1990), pp. 11–36.

'Scottish cultural change 1660–1710 and the Union of 1707', in John Robertson (ed.), *A Union for Empire: Political Thought and the British Union of 1707* (Cambridge, 1995), pp. 121–44.

'Catalogus Librorum A.C.D.A, or, the library of Archibald Campbell, third Duke of Argyll (1682–1761)', in Roger Emerson and others, *The Culture of the Book in the Scottish Enlightenment* (Toronto: Thomas Fisher Rare Book Library Exhibition Catalogue, 2000), pp. 13–39.

'The scientific interests of Archibald Cambpell, 1st Earl of Ilay and 3rd Duke of Argyll 1682–1761', *Annals of Science*, 59 (2002), pp. 21–56.

Epstein, S. R., *An Island for Itself: Economic Development and Social Change in Late Medieval Sicily* (Cambridge, 1992).

'The peasantries of Italy 1350–1750', in Tom Scott (ed.), *The Peasantries of Europe from the Fourteenth to the Eighteenth Centuries* (Harlow, 1998), pp. 74–108.

Feenstra, Robert, 'Scottish-Dutch legal relations in the seventeenth and eighteenth centuries', in T. C. Smout (ed.), *Scotland and Europe 1200–1850* (Edinburgh, 1986), pp. 128–42.

Ferguson, William, 'Imperial crowns: a neglected facet of the background to the Treaty of Union', *Scottish Historical Review*, 53 (1974), pp. 22–44.

Scotland's Relations with England: a Survey to 1707 (Edinburgh, 1977).

Ferrone, Vincenzo, *Scienza natura religione. Mondo Newtoniano e cultura italiana nel primo Settecento* (Naples, 1982); English translation: *The Intellectual Roots of the Italian Enlightenment: Natural Science, Religion, and Politics in the Early Eighteenth Century* (Atlantic Highlands, N.J., 1995).

'Seneca e Cristo: La "Respublica Christiana" di Paolo Mattia Doria', in Aa. Vv., *Paolo Mattia Doria fra rinnovamento e tradizione* (Galatina, 1985), pp. 227–88.

La società giusta ed equa. Repubblicanesimo e diritti dell'uomo in Gaetano Filangieri (Rome and Bari, 2003).

Ferrone, Vincenzo, and Roche, Daniel (eds.), *L'Illuminismo. Dizionario storico* (Rome and Bari, 1997); French translation: *Le Monde des Lumières* (Paris, 1999).

L'Illuminismo nella cultura contemporanea. Storie e storiografie (Rome and Bari, 2002).

Firpo, Luigi, *Bibliografia degli scritti di Tommaso Campanella* (Turin, 1940).

Fisch, M. H., 'The Academy of the Investigators', in E. A. Underwood (ed.), *Science, Medicine and History: Essays in Honour of Charles Singer*, 2 vols. (London, 1953), I, pp. 521–46.

Flinn, Michael, and others, *Scottish Population History from the 17th Century to the 1930s* (Cambridge, 1977).

Forbes, Duncan, *Hume's Philosophical Politics* (Cambridge, 1975).

Force, Pierre, *Self-Interest before Adam Smith: a Genealogy of Economic Science* (Cambridge, 2003).

Ford, John D., '*Lex, rex iusto posita*: Samuel Rutherford on the origins of government', in Roger A. Mason (ed.), *Scots and Britons: Scottish Political Thought and the Union of 1603* (Cambridge, 1994), pp. 262–90.

Furbank, P. N., *Diderot: a Critical Biography* (London, 1992).

Galasso, Giuseppe, 'Il pensiero religioso di Antonio Genovesi', *Rivista Storica Italiana*, 82 (1970), pp. 800–23.

Napoli Spagnola dopo Masaniello, 2 vols. (Florence, 1982).

La filosofia in soccorso de' governi. La cultura napoletana del Settecento (Naples, 1989).

Gardiner, S. R. (ed.), *The Constitutional Documents of the Puritan Revolution 1625–1660* (Oxford, 1936).

Gardner, Ginny, *The Scottish Exile Community in the Netherlands 1660–1690* (East Linton, 2004).

Garin, Eugenio, *Dal Rinascimento all'Illuminismo. Studi e ricerche* (1968–9; second edn. Pisa, 1970).

Gay, Peter, *The Enlightenment: an Interpretation*. I: *The Rise of Modern Paganism*; II: *The Science of Freedom* (New York, 1966–9).

Giarrizzo, Giuseppe, *Vico, la politica e la storia* (Naples, 1981).

'Un "Regno governato in provincia": Napoli tra Austria e Spagna (1690–1740)', in Aa. Vv., *Paolo Mattia Doria fra rinnovamento e tradizione* (Galatina, 1985), pp. 311–25.

Massoneria e illuminismo nell'Europa del Settecento (Venice, 1994).

Gibson, A. J. S. and Smout, T. C., *Prices, Food and Wages in Scotland 1550–1780* (Cambridge, 1990).

Goldgar, Anne, *Impolite Learning: Conduct and Community in the Republic of Letters, 1680–1750* (New Haven and London, 1995).

Goldsmith, M. M., 'Faction detected: ideological consequences of Robert Walpole's decline and fall', *History*, 64 (1979), pp. 1–19.

'Regulating anew the moral and political sentiments of mankind: Bernard Mandeville and the Scottish Enlightenment', *Journal of the History of Ideas*, 49 (1988), pp. 587–606.

Goodman, Dena, *Criticism in Action: Enlightened Experiments in Political Writing* (Ithaca and London, 1989).

'The Hume–Rousseau affair: from private *Querelle* to public *Procès*', *Eighteenth-Century Studies*, 25 (1991–92), pp. 171–201.

'Public sphere and private life: towards a synthesis of current historiographical approaches to the Old Regime', *History and Theory*, 31 (1992), 1–20.

The Republic of Letters: a Cultural History of the French Enlightenment (Ithaca and London, 1994).

Gordon, Daniel, *Citizens without Sovereignty: Equality and Sociability in French thought 1670–1789* (Princeton, 1994).

'The great Enlightenment massacre', in H. T. Mason (ed.), *The Darnton Debate: Books and Revolution in the Eighteenth Century* (Voltaire Foundation, Oxford, 1999), pp. 129–56.

Graham, Eric J., 'In defence of the Scottish maritime interest, 1681–1713', *Scottish Historical Review*, 71 (1992), pp. 88–109.

Guerrini, Anita, 'The Tory Newtonians: Gregory, Pitcairne and their circle', *Journal of British Studies*, 25 (1986), pp. 288–311.

Haakonssen, Knud, *Natural Law and Moral Philosophy: from Grotius to the Scottish Enlightenment* (Cambridge, 1996).

Haakonssen, Knud (ed.), *Enlightenment and Religion: Rational Dissent in Eighteenth-century Britain* (Cambridge, 1996).

Habermas, Jürgen, *The Structural Transformation of the Public Sphere: an Inquiry into a Category of Bourgeois Society* (1962; English transl. Cambridge, Mass., 1989).

Hampson, Norman, *The Enlightenment* (Harmondsworth, 1968).

Will and Circumstance: Montesquieu, Rousseau, and the French Revolution (London, 1983).

Harris, James A., 'Answering Bayle's question: religious belief in the moral philosophy of the Scottish Enlightenment', in D. Garber and S. Nadler (eds.), *Oxford Studies in Early Modern Philosophy*. 1 (Oxford, 2003), pp. 229–53.

Haskell, Francis, *Patrons and Painters: a Study in the Relations between Italian Art and Society in the Age of the Baroque* (London, 1963).

'The patronage of painting in seicento Naples', in C. Whitfield and J. Martineau (eds.), *Painting in Naples from Caravaggio to Giordano* (London, 1982).

Hazard, Paul, *La crise de la conscience européenne* (Paris, 1935); English trans. *The European Mind 1680–1715* (1953; Harmondsworth, 1964).

Headley, John M., *Tommaso Campanella and the Transformation of the World* (Princeton, 1997).

Henderson, G. D., *Mystics of the North East* (Aberdeen, 1934).

Hirschman, Albert O., *The Passions and the Interests: Political Arguments for Capitalism before its Triumph* (Princeton, N.J., 1977).

Hollinger, David A., 'The Enlightenment and the genealogy of cultural conflict in the United States', in K. M. Baker and P. H. Reill (eds.), *What's Left of Enlightenment? A Postmodern Question* (Stanford, 2001), pp. 7–18.

Hont, Istvan, 'Free trade and the economic limits to national politics: neo-Machiavellian political economy reconsidered', in John Dunn (ed.), *The Economic Limits to Modern Politics* (Cambridge, 1990), pp. 41–120, and in Hont, *The Jealousy of Trade*.

'The rhapsody of public debt: David Hume and voluntary state bankruptcy', in Nicholas Phillipson and Quentin Skinner (eds.), *Political Discourse in Early Modern Britain* (Cambridge, 1993), pp. 321–48, and in Hont, *The Jealousy of Trade*.

Jealousy of Trade: International Competition and the Nation State in Historical Perspective (Cambridge, Mass., 2005).

'Commerce and luxury', in Mark Goldie and Robert Wokler (eds.), *The Cambridge History of Eighteenth-Century Political Thought* (Cambridge, forthcoming).

Hont, Istvan, and Ignatieff, Michael (eds.), *Wealth and Virtue: the Shaping of Political Economy in the Scottish Enlightenment* (Cambridge, 1983).

Hook, Andrew, and Sher, Richard B. (eds.), *The Glasgow Enlightenment* (East Linton, 1995).

Horkheimer, Max, and Adorno, Theodor, *Dialektik der Aufklärung. Philosophische Fragmente* (Amsterdam, 1947); English transl. E. Jephcott, ed. G. Schmid Noerr, *Dialectic of Enlightenment: Philosophical Fragments* (Stanford, 2002).

Houston, R. A., *Social Change in the Age of the Enlightenment: Edinburgh 1660–1760* (Oxford, 1994).

Hundert, E. J., *The Enlightenment's Fable: Bernard Mandeville and the Discovery of Society* (Cambridge, 1994).

'Bernard Mandeville and the Enlightenment's maxims of modernity', *Journal of the History of Ideas*, 56 (1995), pp. 577–93.

'Mandeville, Rousseau and the political economy of fantasy', in Maxine Berg and Elizabeth Eger (eds.), *Luxury in the Eighteenth Century: Debates, Desires and Delectable goods* (Basingstoke and New York, 2003), pp. 28–40.

Hunter, Michael, '"Aikenhead the atheist": the context and consequences of articulate irreligion in the late seventeenth century', in Michael Hunter and David Wootton (eds.), *Atheism from the Reformation to the Enlightenment* (Oxford, 1992), pp. 221–54.

Imbruglia, Girolamo (ed.), *Naples in the Eighteenth Century: the Birth and Death of a Nation State* (Cambridge, 2000).

Im Hof, Ulrich, *Das gesellige Jahrhundert. Gesellschaft und Gesellschaften im Zeitalter der Aufklärung* (Munich, 1982).

The Enlightenment (Oxford, 1994).

Ingrao, Charles, 'The smaller German states', in Hamish Scott (ed.), *Enlightened Absolutism: Reform and Reformers in Later Eighteenth-century Europe* (Basingstoke and London, 1990), pp. 221–43.

Insh, George Pratt, *The Company of Scotland Trading to Africa and the Indies* (London and New York, 1932).

Israel, Jonathan I., *Radical Enlightenment: Philosophy and the Making of Modernity 1650–1750* (Oxford, 2001).

Ives, Robin, 'Political economy and political publicity in eighteenth-century France', *French History*, 17 (2003), pp. 1–18.

Jackson, J. C. L., *Restoration Scotland, 1660–1690: Royalist Politics, Religion and Ideas* (Woodbridge, Suffolk, 2003).

Jacob, Margaret C., *The Newtonians and the English Revolution 1689–1720* (Hassocks, 1976).

The Radical Enlightenment: Pantheists, Freemasons, and Republicans (London, 1981).

Living the Enlightenment: Freemasonry and Politics in Eighteenth-century Europe (Oxford, 1991).

'The mental landscape of the public sphere: a European perspective', *Eighteenth-Century Studies*, 28 (1994), pp. 95–113.

The Enlightenment: a Brief History with Documents (Boston and New York, 2001).

James, Susan, 'Spinoza the Stoic', in Tom Sorrell (ed.), *The Rise of Modern Philosophy: the Tension between the New and Traditional Philosophies from Machiavelli to Leibniz* (Oxford, 1993), pp. 289–316.

Passion and Action: the Emotions in Seventeenth-century Philosophy (Oxford, 1997).

Jones, W. Douglas, '"The Bold Adventurers": a quantitative analysis of the Darien subscription list (1696)', *Scottish Economic and Social History*, 21 (2001), pp. 22–42.

Joy, L. S., *Gassendi the Atomist: Advocate of History in an Age of Science* (Cambridge, 1987).

Kaiser, Thomas E., 'Enlightenment, public opinion and politics in the work of Robert Darnton', in H. T. Mason (ed.), *The Darnton Debate: Books and Revolution in the Eighteenth Century* (Voltaire Foundation, Oxford, 1999), pp. 189–206.

Keohane, Nannerl O., *Philosophy and the State in France: the Renaissance to the Enlightenment* (Princeton, N.J., 1980).

Kidd, Colin, *Subverting Scotland's Past: Scottish Whig Historians and the Creation of an Anglo-British Identity 1689-c.1830* (Cambridge, 1993).

'Religious realignment between the Restoration and the Union', in John Robertson (ed.), *A Union for Empire: Political Thought and the British Union of 1707* (Cambridge, 1995), pp. 145–68.

Kitromilides, Paschalis M., *The Enlightenment as Social Criticism: Iosipos Moisiodax and Greek Culture in the Eighteenth Century* (Princeton, 1992).

Koenigsberger, H. G., *The Government of Sicily under Philip II of Spain: a Study in the Practice of Empire* (London and New York, 1951).

Kontler, László, 'William Robertson and his German audience on European and pan-European civilisations', *Scottish Historical Review*, 80 (2001), pp. 63–89.

Kors, A. C., 'The atheism of D'Holbach and Naigeon', in Michael Hunter and David Wootton (eds.), *Atheism from the Reformation to the Enlightenment* (Oxford, 1992), pp. 273–300.

Kors, A. C. (ed.), *Encyclopedia of the Enlightenment*, 4 vols. (New York and Oxford, 2003).

Koselleck, Reinhart, *Critique and Crisis: Enlightenment and the Pathogenesis of Modern Society* (1959; English transl. Oxford, New York and Hamburg, 1988).

Labrot, Gérard, 'Le comportement collectif de l'aristocratie napolitaine du seizième au dix-huitième siècle', *Revue Historique*, 258 (1977), pp. 45–71.

Labrot, Gérard, and Ruotolo, Renato, 'Pour une étude historique de la commande aristocratique dans le royaume de Naples espagnol', *Revue Historique*, 264 (1980), pp. 25–48.

Labrousse, Elisabeth, *Pierre Bayle*, 2 vols. (The Hague, 1963–4).

Lafond, Jean, 'Augustinisme et épicurisme au XVII siècle', in J. Lafond, *L'homme et son image. Morales et littérature de Montaigne à Mandeville* (Paris, 1996), pp. 345–68.

Larrère, Catherine, *L'invention de l'économie au XVIIIe siècle. Du droit naturel à la physiocratie* (Paris, 1992).

Laursen, John Christian, 'The subversive Kant: the vocabulary of "public" and "publicity"', in James Schmidt (ed.), *What is Enlightenment? Eighteenth-Century Answers and Twentieth-Century Questions* (Berkeley, Los Angeles and London, 1996), pp. 253–69.

Lee, Maurice, Jr., *The Road to Revolution: Scotland under Charles I 1625–1637* (Urbana and Chicago, 1985).

Lenman, Bruce, *The Jacobite Risings in Britain 1689–1746* (London, 1980).

'Militia, Fencible men and home defence, 1660–1797', in Norman Macdougall (ed.), *Scotland and War AD79–1918* (Edinburgh, 1991), pp. 170–92.

'The Scottish nobility and the Revolution of 1688–1690', in Robert Beddard (ed.), *The Revolutions of 1688* (Oxford, 1991), pp. 137–62.

Lepre, Aurelio, *Feudi e masserie. Problemi della società meridionale nel '600 e nel '700* (Naples, 1973).

Lilla, Mark, *G. B. Vico: the Making of an Anti-modern* (Cambridge, Mass., and London, 1993).

Lombardi, Giovanni, 'L'attività carto-libraria tra fine '600 e primo '700', in Anna Maria Rao (ed.), *Editoria e cultura a Napoli nel XVIII secolo* (Naples, 1998), pp. 79–96.

Lough, John, 'Reflections on "Enlightenment" and "Lumières"', in Raffaele Ajello and others (eds.), *L'età dei lumi. Studi storici sul Settecento europeo in onore di Franco Venturi*, 2 vols. (Naples, 1985), pp. 35–56; also in *British Journal for Eighteenth-Century Studies*, 8 (1985), pp. 1–15.

Lynch, Michael, 'Continuity and change in urban society, 1500–1700', in R. A. Houston and I. D. Whyte (eds.), *Scottish Society 1500–1800* (Cambridge, 1989), pp. 85–114.

Macaulay, T. B., *History of England* (Albany edn, London, 1897).

Macfie, R. A. Scott, 'A Bibliography of Andrew Fletcher of Saltoun', *Publications of the Edinburgh Bibliographical Society*, 4 (1901), pp. 117–48.

Macintyre, Alasdair, *After Virtue: a Study in Moral Theory* (London, 1981).

McLeod, W. R., and McLeod, V. B., *Anglo-Scottish Tracts 1701–1714: a Descriptive Checklist*, University of Kansas, Library Series 44 (Lawrence, Kan., 1979).

Macry, Paolo, *Mercato e società nel Regno di Napoli: Commercio del grano e politica economica nel Settecento* (Naples, 1974).

Maio, Romeo de, 'Il problema del Quietismo napoletano', *Rivista Storica Italiana*, 81, (1969), pp. 721–44.

Società e vita religiosa a Napoli nell'età moderna (Naples, 1971).

Pittura e controriforma a Napoli (Rome and Bari, 1983).

Makey, Walter, *The Church of the Covenant 1637–1651: Revolution and Social Change in Scotland* (Edinburgh, 1979).

Malcolm, Noel, *Aspects of Hobbes* (Oxford, 2002).

Malherbe, Michel, 'Hume's *Natural History of Religion*', *Hume Studies*, 21 (1995), pp. 255–74.

Marino, John A., 'Economic idylls and pastoral realities: the "trickster" economy in the kingdom of Naples', *Comparative Studies in Society and History*, 24 (1982), pp. 210–34.

Pastoral Economics in the Kingdom of Naples (Baltimore and London, 1988).

Marino, John A. (ed.), *Early Modern Italy* (Oxford, 2002).

Marshall, Gordon, *Presbyteries and Profits: Calvinism and the Development of Capitalism in Scotland 1560–1707* (Oxford, 1980).

Mason, Haydn T. (ed.), *The Darnton Debate: Books and Revolution in the Eighteenth Century* (Voltaire Foundation, Oxford, 1999).

Mason, Roger A., '*Rex Stoicus*: George Buchanan, James VI and the Scottish polity', in John Dwyer, Roger Mason and Alexander Murdoch (eds.), *New Perspectives on the Politics and Culture of Early Modern Scotland* (Edinburgh [1982]), pp. 9–33.

'The aristocracy, episcopacy, and the revolution of 1638', in Terry Brotherstone (ed.), *Covenant, Charter and Party: Traditions of Revolt and Protest in Modern Scottish History* (Aberdeen, 1989), pp. 7–24.

Kingship and Commonweal: Political Thought in Renaissance and Reformation Scotland (East Linton, 1998).

Mason, Roger A. (ed.), *Scots and Britons: Scottish Political Thought and the Union of 1603* (Cambridge, 1994).

Mastellone, Salvo, *Francesco d'Andrea politico e giurista 1648–1698. L'acesa del ceto civile* (Florence, 1969).

'La congiura di Macchia (1701)', in F. M. de Robertis and M. Spagnoletti (eds.), *Atti del congresso internazionale di studi sull'età del viceregno* (Bari, 1977), vol. II, pp. 39–48.

Matteo, Rodolfo de, *Il pensiero politico Italiano nell'età della controriforma* (Milan and Naples, 1982).

May, Henry F., *The Enlightenment in America* (New York, 1976).

Melchionda, Mario, 'La cultura inglese nei libri secenteschi della Biblioteca Oratoriana dei Girolamini a Napoli', *English Miscellany*, ed. Mario Praz, XXI (1970), pp. 265–341.

Melton, James van Horn, *The Rise of the Public in Enlightenment Europe* (Cambridge, 2001).

Meyer, Donald H., *The Democratic Enlightenment* (New York, 1976).

Mirri, Mario, 'Della storia dei "Lumi" e delle "riforme" alla storia degli "antichi stati italiani"', in M. Verga and A. Fratoianni (eds.), *Pompeo Neri* (Castelfiorentino, 1992), pp. 401–540.

Mitchison, Rosalind, 'The movements of Scottish corn prices in the seventeenth and eighteenth centuries', *Economic History Review*, Second Series 18 (1965), pp. 278–91.

Lordship to Patronage: Scotland 1603–1745 (London, 1983).

'North and South: the development of the gulf in Poor Law practice', in R. A. Houston and I. D. Whyte (eds.), *Scottish Society 1500–1800* (Cambridge, 1989), pp. 199–225.

Momigliano, Arnaldo, 'Vico's *Scienza Nuova*: Roman "Bestioni" and Roman "Eroi"', in his *Essays in Ancient and Modern Historiography* (Oxford, 1973), pp. 253–76.

'Gibbon from an Italian point of view', *Daedalus*, 105 (1976), pp. 125–35.

Montroni, Giovanni, 'The court: power relations and forms of social life', in Girolamo Imbruglia (ed.), *Naples in the Eighteenth Century: the Birth and Death of a Nation State* (Cambridge, 2000), pp. 22–43.

Moore, James, 'Hume's theory of justice and property', *Political Studies*, 24 (1976), pp. 103–19.

'Natural Law and the Pyrrhonian Controversy', in Peter Jones (ed.), *Philosophy and Science in the Scottish Enlightenment* (Edinburgh, 1988), pp. 20–38.

'The two systems of Francis Hutcheson: on the origins of the Scottish Enlightenment', in M. A. Stewart (ed.), *Studies in the Philosophy of the Scottish Enlightenment* (Oxford, 1990), pp. 37–59.

'Hume and Hutcheson', in M. A. Stewart and J. P. Wright (eds.), *Hume and Hume's Connexions* (Edinburgh, 1994), pp. 23–57.

'Hutcheson's theodicy: the argument and contexts of *A System of Moral Philosophy*', in Paul Wood (ed.), *The Scottish Enlightenment. Essays in Reinterpretation* (Rochester, N.Y., and Woodbridge, Suffolk, 2000), pp. 239–66.

'Natural rights in the Scottish Enlightenment', in M. Goldie and R. Wokler (eds.), *The Cambridge History of Eighteenth-Century Political Thought* (Cambridge, forthcoming).

Moore, James, and Silverthorne, Michael, 'Gershom Carmichael and the natural jurisprudence tradition in eighteenth-century Scotland', in Istvan Hont and Michael Ignatieff (eds.), *Wealth and Virtue: the Shaping of Political Economy in the Scottish Enlightenment* (Cambridge, 1983), pp. 73–87.

'Natural sociability and natural rights in the moral philosophy of Gershom Carmichael', in V. Hope (ed.), *Philosophers of the Scottish Enlightenment* (Edinburgh, 1984), pp. 1–12.

'Protestant theologies, limited sovereignties: natural law and the conditions of union in the German Empire, the Netherlands, and Great Britain', in John Robertson (ed.), *A Union for Empire: Political Thought and the British Union of 1707* (Cambridge, 1995), pp. 171–97.

Moran, Mary Catherine, '"The commerce of the sexes": gender and social sphere in Scottish Enlightenment accounts of civil society', in Frank Trentman (ed.), *Paradoxes of Civil Society: New Perspectives on Modern German and British history* (second rev. edn New York and Oxford, 2003), pp. 61–84.

Mornet, Daniel, *Les origines intellectuelles de la Révolution française* (Paris, 1933).

Morrill, John (ed.), *The Scottish National Covenant in its British Context 1638–1651* (Edinburgh, 1990).

Morrison, James C., 'Vico and Spinoza', *Journal of the History of Ideas*, 41 (1980), pp. 49–68.

Mossner, E. C., *The Life of David Hume* (second edn Oxford, 1980).

Munck, Thomas, *The Enlightenment: a Comparative Social History 1721–1794* (London, 2000).

Muramatsu, Shigemi, 'Some types of national interest in the Anglo-Scottish Union of 1707: Scotland's responses to England's political arithmetic', *Journal of Economics of Kumamoto Gakuen University*, 3 (1996), pp. 1–14.

'Andrew Fletcher's criticism of commercial civilisation and his plan for European federal union', in T. Sakamoto and H. Tanaka (eds.), *The Rise of Political Economy in the Scottish Enlightenment* (London, 2003), pp. 8–21.

Murphy, Antoine, *John Law: Economic Theorist and Policy Maker* (Oxford, 1997).

Musgrave, Peter, *Land and Economy in Baroque Italy: Valpolicella 1630–1797* (Leicester and London, 1992).

Musi, Aurelio, *La rivolta di Masaniello nella scena politica barocca* (Naples, 1989).

'*Non pigra quies*. Il linguaggio politico degli Accademici Oziosi e la rivolta napoletana del 1647–48', in Eluggero Pii (ed.), *I linguaggi politici delle rivoluzioni in Europa XVII–XIX secolo* (Florence, 1992), pp. 85–104.

Napoli, Maria Consiglia, 'Editoria clandestina e censura ecclesiastica a Napoli all'inizio del Settecento', in Anna Maria Rao (ed.), *Editoria e cultura a Napoli nel XVIII secolo* (Naples, 1998), pp. 333–51.

Norton, David F., *David Hume: Common Sense Moralist, Sceptical Metaphysician* (Princeton, 1982).

Nuzzo, Enrico, *Verso la Vita Civile. Antropologia e politica nelle Lezioni accademiche di Gregorio Caloprese e Paolo Mattia Doria* (Naples, 1984).

'Il congedo della "sagezza moderna" nella cultura napoletana tra '600 e '700. Vico e le tradizione dei "moralisti"', *Bollettino del Centro di Studi Vichiani*, 17–18 (1987–8), pp. 25–114.

'Antropologia e morale in Saint-Evrémond', in V. Dini and A. Taranto (eds.), *Individualismo Assolutismo Democrazia* (Salerno, 1992), pp. 211–73.

Tra ordine della storia e storicità. Saggi sui saperi della storia in Vico (Rome, 2001).

Osbat, Luciano, *L'Inquisizione a Napoli. Il processo agli ateisti 1688–97* (Rome, 1974).

Osler, Margaret J., 'Ancients, Moderns, and the history of philosophy: Gassendi's Epicurean project', in Tom Sorrell (ed.), *The Rise of Modern Philosophy: the Tension between the New and the Traditional Philosophies from Machiavelli to Leibniz* (Oxford, 1993), pp. 129–43.

Ouston, Hugh, 'York in Edinburgh: James VII and the patronage of learning in Scotland 1679–1688', in John Dwyer, Roger A. Mason, and Alexander Murdoch (eds.), *New Perspectives on the Politics and Culture of Early Modern Scotland* (Edinburgh [1982]), pp. 133–55.

Outram, Dorinda, *The Enlightenment* (Cambridge, 1995).

Oxford Dictionary of National Biography, ed. H. C. G. Matthew and B. H. Harrison (Oxford, 2004).

Oz-Salzberger, Fania, *Translating the Enlightenment: Scottish Civic Discourse in Eighteenth-century Germany* (Oxford, 1995).

'New approaches towards a history of the Enlightenment: can disparate perspectives make a general picture?', *Tel Aviver Jahrbuch für deutsche Geschichte*, 29 (2000), pp. 171–6.

'Cassirer's Enlightenment and its recent critics: is Reason out of season?', in Jeffrey Barash (ed.), *Ernst Cassirer: Symbol, Science, and Culture* (Madison, Wis.: forthcoming).

Ozouf, Mona, '"Public opinion" at the end of the Old Regime', *Journal of Modern History*, 60 (1988), supplement, pp. 1–21.

Paganini, Gianni, 'Vico et Gassendi. De la prudence à la politique', in Sylvia Murr (ed.), *Gassendi et l'Europe 1592–1792* (Paris, 1997), pp. 347–67.

Pagano de Divitiis, Gigliola (ed.), *Il commercio inglese nel Mediterraneo dal cinquecento al settecento* (Naples, 1984).

Pagano de Divitiis, Gigliola, *Mercanti inglesi nell'Italia del Seicento. Navi, traffici, egemonie* (Venice, 1990).

'Il porto di Livorno fra Inghilterra e Oriente', *Nuovi Studi Livornesi*, 1 (1993), pp. 43–87.

Pagden, Anthony, '*Fede pubblica* and *fede privata*: trust and honour in Spanish Naples', in his *Spanish Imperialism and the Political Imagination: Studies in European and Spanish-American Social and Political Theory 1513–1830* (New Haven and London, 1990), pp. 65–89.

Papini, Mario, 'Vicenda seicentesca di minimi e conati', *Bollettino del Centro di Studi Vichiani*, 22–28 (1992–3), pp. 131–69.

Parker, Geoffrey, 'David or Goliath? Philip II and his world in the 1580s', in Richard L. Kagan and Geoffrey Parker (eds.), *Spain, Europe and the Atlantic World: Essays in Honour of J. H. Elliott* (Cambridge, 1995), pp. 245–66.

Pattison, Mark, *Essays by the Late Mark Pattison*, ed. Henry Nettleship, 2 vols. (Oxford, 1889).

Perna, Maria Luisa, 'Giuseppe Galanti editore', in Aa. Vv., *Miscellanea Walter Maturi* (Turin, 1966), pp. 221–58.

Pesante, Maria Luisa, 'Il commercio nella repubblica', *Quaderni storici*, 105 (2000), pp. 655–95.

Petraccone, Claudia, *Napoli dal'500 all'800. Problemi di storia demografica e sociale* (Naples, 1974).

Petrusewicz, Marta, *Come il Meridione divenne una Questione. Rappresentazioni del Sud prima e dopo il Quarantotto* (Catanzaro, 1998).

Phillipson, Nicholas T., 'Culture and society in the eighteenth-century province: the case of Edinburgh and the Scottish Enlightenment', in Lawrence Stone (ed.), *The University in Society*, 2 vols. (Princeton, 1974), II, pp. 407–48.

'Lawyers, landowners, and the civic leadership of post-Union Scotland', *Juridical Review*, New Series 21 (1976), pp. 97–120.

'The Scottish Enlightenment', in R. Porter and M. Teich (eds.), *The Enlightenment in National Context* (Cambridge, 1981), pp. 19–40.

'Language, sociability, and history: some reflections on the foundations of Adam Smith's science of man', in S. Collini, R. Whatmore and B. Young (eds.),

Economy, Polity and Society: British Intellectual History 1750–1950 (Cambridge, 2000), pp. 70–84.

Pii, Eluggero, *Antonio Genovesi. Dalla politica economia alla 'politica civile'* (Florence, 1984).

Pincus, Steven, 'The English debate over universal monarchy', in John Robertson (ed.), *A Union for Empire: Political Thought and the British Union of 1707* (Cambridge, 1995), pp. 37–62.

Piro, Francesco, 'I presupposti teologici del giusnaturalismo moderno nella percezione di Vico', *Bollettino del Centro di Studi Vichiani*, 30 (2000), pp. 125–49.

Pittion, J. P., 'Hume's reading of Bayle: an enquiry into the source and role of the Memoranda', *Journal of the History of Philosophy*, 15 (1977), pp. 373–86.

Placanica, Augusto, 'Tra Spagnoli e Austriaci', in G. Galasso and R. Romeo, *Storia del Mezzogiorno*. IV: *Il Regno dagli Angioini ai Borboni* (Rome, 1986), pp. 285–366.

Pocock, John G. A., *The Machiavellian Moment: Florentine Political Thought and the Atlantic Republican Tradition* (Princeton, 1975).

Virtue, Commerce and History: Essays on Political Thought and History, chiefly in the Eighteenth Century (Cambridge, 1985).

'Clergy and commerce: the conservative Enlightenment in England', in Rafaelle Ajello and others (eds.), *L'età dei lumi. Studi storici sul Settecento europeo in onore di Franco Venturi*, 2 vols. (Naples, 1985), pp. 523–62.

The Ancient Constitution and the Feudal Law: a Study of English Historical Thought in the Seventeenth Century: a Reissue with a Retrospect (Cambridge, 1987).

'Settecento protestante? L'Illuminismo riconsiderato', *Quaderni storici*, 94 (1997), pp. 315–37.

Barbarism and Religion. I: *The Enlightenments of Edward Gibbon, 1737–1764*; II: *Narratives of Civil Government* (both Cambridge, 1999); III: *The First Decline and Fall* (Cambridge, 1999–2003).

'The re-description of Enlightenment', Isaiah Berlin Lecture, *Proceedings of the British Academy* (London: forthcoming).

Pompa, Leon, *Human Nature and Historical Knowledge: Hume, Hegel and Vico* (Cambridge, 1990).

Popkin, Richard H., *The History of Scepticism from Erasmus to Spinoza* (1960; Berkeley, Los Angeles, and London 1979).

The High Road to Pyrrhonism, R. E. Watson and J. E. Force (eds.), (1980, repr. Indianapolis, 1993).

Porter, Roy, 'The Enlightenment in England', in R. Porter and M. Teich (eds.), *The Enlightenment in National Context* (Cambridge, 1981), pp. 1–18.

The Enlightenment (London, 1990; second edn 2001).

Enlightenment: Britain and the Creation of the Modern World (London, 2000).

Porter, Roy, and Teich, Mikulas (eds.), *The Enlightenment in National Context* (Cambridge, 1981).

Preus, J. S., 'Spinoza, Vico and the imagination of religion', *Journal of the History of Ideas*, 50 (1989), pp. 71–93.

Rae, Thomas I., 'Historical scepticism in Scotland before David Hume', in R. F. Brissenden (ed.), *Studies in the Eighteenth century*, II (Canberra, 1973), pp. 205–21.

Rao, Anna Maria, 'The feudal question, judicial systems and the Enlightenment', in Girolamo Imbruglia (ed.), *Naples in the Eighteenth Century: the Birth and Death of a Nation State* (Cambridge, 2000), pp. 95–117.

'Enlightenment and reform', in John A. Marino (ed.), *Early Modern Italy* (Oxford 2002), pp. 229–52.

Rao, Anna Maria (ed.), *Editoria e cultura a Napoli nel XVIII secolo* (Naples, 1998).

Napoli 1799. Fra storia e storiografia (Naples, 2002).

Rao, Anna Maria, and Villani, Pasquale, *Napoli 1799–1815. Dalla repubblica alla monarchia amministrativa* (Naples [1995]).

Raphael, D. D., 'The impartial spectator', in A. S. Skinner and T. Wilson (eds.), *Essays on Adam Smith* (Oxford, 1975), pp. 83–99.

Reinhardt, Volker, *Überleben in der früneuzeitlichen Stadt. Annona und Getreideversorgung in Rom 1563–1797* (Tübingen, 1991).

Ricuperati, Giuseppe, 'La prima formazione di Pietro Giannone. L'Accademia Medina Coeli e Domenico Aulisio', in E. Sestan (ed.), *Saggi e ricerche sul Settecento* (Naples, 1968), pp. 94–171.

'Alessandro Ricciardi e le richieste del "ceto civile" all'Austria nel 1707', *Rivista Storica Italiana*, 81 (1969), pp. 745–77.

L'esperienza civile e religiosa di Pietro Giannone (Milan and Naples, 1970).

'A proposito dell'Accademia Medina Coeli', *Rivista Storica Italiana*, 84 (1972), pp. 57–79.

'Napoli e i Viceré austriaci 1707–1734', in Aa. Vv., *Storia di Napoli* vol. VII (Cava dei Tirreni, 1972), pp. 347–457.

'The historiographical legacy of Franco Venturi (1914–1994)', *Journal of Modern Italian Studies*, 2 (1997), pp. 67–88.

'In margine al *Radical Enlightenment* di Jonathan I. Israel', *Rivista Storica Italiana*, 115 (2003), pp. 285–329.

Rivers, Isabel, *Reason, Grace, and Sentiment: a Study of the Language of Religion and Ethics in England, 1660–1780*. Vol. II: *Shaftesbury to Hume* (Cambridge, 2000).

Robertson, John, 'The Scottish Enlightenment at the limits of the civic tradition', in Istvan Hont and Michael Ignatieff (eds.), *Wealth and Virtue: the Shaping of Political Economy in the Scottish Enlightenment* (Cambridge, 1983), pp. 137–78.

The Scottish Enlightenment and the Militia Issue (Edinburgh, 1985).

'Franco Venturi's Enlightenment', *Past and Present*, 137 (1992), pp. 183–206.

'Universal monarchy and the liberties of Europe; David Hume's critique of an English Whig doctrine', in Nicholas Phillipson and Quentin Skinner (eds.), *Political Discourse in Early Modern Britain* (Cambridge, 1993), pp. 321–48.

'The Enlightenment above national context: political economy in eighteenth-century Scotland and Naples', *The Historical Journal*, 40 (1997), pp. 667–97.

'Gibbon and Giannone', in David Womersley (ed.), with the assistance of John Burrow and John Pocock, *Edward Gibbon: Bicentenary Essays, Studies on Voltaire and the Eighteenth Century*, 355 (1997), pp. 3–19.

'The Scottish contribution to the Enlightenment', in Paul Wood (ed.), *The Scottish Enlightenment: Essays in Reinterpretation* (Rochester, N.Y., and Woodbridge, Suffolk, 2000), pp. 37–62.

'Enlightenment and Revolution: Naples 1799', *Transactions of the Royal Historical Society*, sixth Series 10 (2000), pp. 17–44.

'The Enlightenments of J. G. A. Pocock', *Storia della storiografia – History of Historiography*, 39 (2001), pp. 140–51.

'The case for the Enlightenment: a comparative approach', in Joseph Mali and Robert Wokler (eds.), *Isaiah Berlin's Counter-Enlightenment: Transactions of the American Philosophical Society*, vol. 93, part 5 (Philadelphia, 2003), pp. 73–90.

Robertson, John (ed.), *A Union for Empire: Political Thought and the British Union of 1707* (Cambridge, 1995).

Roche, Daniel, *Le siècle des lumières en province. Académies et académiciens provinciaux 1680–1789* (Paris and the Hague, 1978).

France in the Enlightenment (1993, English transl. Arthur Goldhammer, Cambridge, Mass., and London, 1998).

'Dell'Illuminismo. Per una storia sociale della cultura', *Rivista Storica Italiana*, 113 (2001), pp. 86–106.

Roche, Daniel, and others, *Livre et société dans la France du XVIII siècle*, 2 vols. (Paris and The Hague, 1965–70).

Romano, Ruggiero, *Napoli. Dal Viceregno al Regno. Storia economica* (Turin, 1976).

Rorty, Richard, 'The continuity between the Enlightenment and "Postmodernism"', in K. M. Baker and P. H. Reill (eds.), *What's Left of Enlightenment? A Postmodern Question* (Stanford, 2001), pp. 19–36.

Rosa, Luigi de, 'Land and sea transport and economic depression in the kingdom of Naples from the fourteenth to the eighteenth century', *Journal of European Economic History*, 25 (1996), pp. 339–68.

Rosa, Mario, 'Introduzione all' Aufklärung cattolica in Italia', in Mario Rosa (ed.), *Cattolicesimo e lumi nel Settecento italiano*, Italia Sacra, Studi e documenti di storia ecclesiastica, 33 (Rome, 1981), pp. 1–47.

Ross, Ian Simpson, *The Life of Adam Smith* (Oxford, 1995).

Rossi, Paolo, *I segni del tempo. Storia della terra e storia delle nazioni da Hooke a Vico* (Milan, 1979); English transl. L. G. Cochrane, *The Dark Abyss of Time: the History of the Earth and the History of Nations from Hooke to Vico* (Chicago and London, 1984).

'Chi sono i contemporanei di Vico?', *Rivista di Filosofia*, 62 (1981), pp. 51–82.

Le sterminate antichità e nuovi saggi vichiani (Florence, 1999).

Rothkrug, Lionel, *Opposition to Louis XIV: the Political and Social Origins of the French Enlightenment* (Princeton, 1965).

Rothschild, Emma, *Economic Sentiments: Adam Smith, Condorcet, and the Enlightenment* (Cambridge, Mass., 2001).

Rotta, Salvatore, 'Paolo Mattia Doria. Nota introduttiva', in R. Ajello and others (eds.), *Dal Muratori al Cesarotti*. v: *Politici ed economisti del primo Settecento* (Milan and Naples, 1978), pp. 837–72.

'Paolo Mattia Doria rivisitato', in Giovanni Papuli and others, *Paolo Mattia Doria fra rinnovamento e tradizione* (Galatina, 1985), pp. 389–431.

Rovito, Pier Luigi, *Respublica dei togati. Giuristi e società nella Napoli del Seicento.* 1: *Le garanzie giuridiche* (Naples, 1981).

'La rivoluzione costituzionale di Napoli 1647–48', *Rivista Storica Italiana*, 98 (1986), pp. 367–462.

Schmidt, James, *What is Enlightenment? Eighteenth-Century Answers and Twentieth-Century Questions* (Berkeley, Los Angeles and London, 1996).

'What Enlightenment project?', *Political Theory*, 28 (2000), pp. 734–57, 29 (2001), pp. 80–90.

'Inventing the Enlightenment: Anti-Jacobins, British Hegelians, and the *Oxford English Dictionary*', *Journal of the History of Ideas*, 64 (2003), pp. 421–43.

Schneiders, W. (ed.), *Lexicon der Aufklärung* (Munich, 1995).

Scott, H. M. (ed.), *Enlightened Absolutism: Reform and Reformers in Later Eighteenth-century Europe* (Basingstoke and London, 1990).

Sebastiani, Silvia, 'Race, women, and progress in the Scottish Enlightenment', in Barbara Taylor and Sarah Knott (eds.), *Women, Gender, and Enlightenment* (London, 2005), pp. 75–96.

Seki, Gentaro, 'Policy debate on economic development in Scotland: the 1720s to the 1730s', in T. Sakamoto and H. Tanaka (eds.), *The Rise of Political Economy in the Scottish Enlightenment* (London, 2003), pp. 22–38.

Sella, Domenico, *Crisis and Continuity: the Economy of Spanish Lombardy in the Seventeenth Century* (Cambridge, Mass., 1979).

Shaw, John Stuart, *The Political History of Eighteenth-Century Scotland* (Basingstoke, 1999).

Shepherd, Christine M., 'Newtonianism in Scottish universities in the seventeenth century', in R. H. Campbell and A. S. Skinner (eds.), *The Origins and Nature of the Scottish Enlightenment* (Edinburgh, 1982), pp. 65–85.

Sher, Richard B., *Church and University in the Scottish Enlightenment: the Moderate Literati of Edinburgh* (Edinburgh and Princeton, 1985).

'The book in the Scottish Enlightenment', in Roger Emerson and others, *The Culture of the Book in the Scottish Enlightenment* (Toronto: Thomas Fisher Rare Book Library Exhibition Catalogue, 2000), pp. 40–60.

Skoczylas, Anne, *Mr Simson's Knotty Case: Divinity, politics and due process in early eighteenth-century Scotland* (Montreal, 2001).

Smout, T. C., *Scottish Trade on the Eve of the Union 1660–1707* (Edinburgh and London, 1963).

'Where had the Scottish economy got to by the third quarter of the eighteenth century?', in Istvan Hont and Michael Ignatieff (eds.), *Wealth and Virtue: the Shaping of Political Economy in the Scottish Enlightenment* (Cambridge, 1983), pp. 45–72.

Sorkin, David, *'A wise, enlightened and reliable piety': The religious Enlightenment in Central and Western Europe 1689–1789*, University of Southampton, Parkes Institute Pamphlet 1 (2002).

Spink, J. S., *French Free-thought from Gassendi to Voltaire* (London, 1960).

Stein, Peter, 'Law and society in eighteenth-century Scottish thought', in N. T. Phillipson and Rosalind Mitchison (eds.), *Scotland in the Age of Improvement: Essays in Scottish History in the Eighteenth Century* (Edinburgh, 1970), pp. 148–68.

Stephens, Walter, *Giants in Those Days: Folklore, Ancient History, and Nationalism* (Lincoln, Nebr., 1989).

Stevenson, David, *The Scottish Revolution 1637–1644: the Triumph of the Covenanters* (Newton Abbot, 1973).

The Origins of Freemasonry: Scotland's Century 1590–1710 (Cambridge, 1988).

'Cromwell, Scotland and Ireland', in John Morrill (ed.), *Oliver Cromwell and the English Revolution* (London and New York, 1990), pp. 149–80.

Stewart, M. A., *The Kirk and the Infidel* (Lancaster, 1995).

'The Scottish Enlightenment', in Stuart Brown (ed.), *British Philosophy in the Age of Enlightenment* (London and New York, 1995), pp. 274–308.

'The dating of Hume's manuscripts', in Paul Wood (ed.), *The Scottish Enlightenment: Essays in Reinterpretation* (Rochester, N.Y., and Woodbridge, Suffolk, 2000), pp. 267–314.

'Two species of philosophy: the historical significance of the First *Enquiry*', in Peter Millican (ed.), *Reading Hume on Human Understanding* (Oxford, 2002), pp. 67–95.

'Religion and natural theology', in Alexander Broadie (ed.), *The Cambridge Companion to the Scottish Enlightenment* (Cambridge, 2003), pp. 31–59.

'Hume's intellectual development 1711–1752', in M. Frasca-Spada and P. J. E. Kail (eds.), *Impressions of Hume* (Oxford, 2005), pp. 11–58.

Stewart, M. A. (ed.), *Studies in the Philosophy of the Scottish Enlightenment* (Oxford, 1990).

Stewart, M. A., and Moore, James, 'William Smith (1698–1741) and the Dissenters' book trade', *Bulletin of the Presbyterian Historical Society of Ireland*, 22 (1993), pp. 20–7.

Stewart, M. A., and Wright, John P. (eds.), *Hume and Hume's Connexions* (Edinburgh, 1994).

Stone, Harold Samuel, *Vico's Cultural History: the Production and Transmission of Ideas in Naples 1685–1750* (Leiden, New York, and Cologne, 1997).

Suppa, Silvio, *L'Accademia di Medinacoeli. Fra tradizione Investigante e nuova scienza civile* (Naples, 1971).

Tagliacozzo, Giorgio, *The 'Arbor Scientiae' Reconceived and the History of Vico's Resurrection* (Atlantic Highlands, N.J., 1993).

Tagliacozzo, Giorgio, Mooney, Michael, and Verene, Donald Phillip (eds.), *Vico and Contemporary Thought* (Atlantic Highlands, N.J., 1976).

Tarzia, Fabio, 'Una supplica inedita di Giambattista Vico al papa Clemente XII del 20 novembre 1737', *Bollettino del Centro di Studi Vichiani*, 30 (2000), pp. 303–8.

Taylor, Barbara, 'Feminists versus gallants: manners and morals in Enlightenment Britain', in Barbara Taylor and Sarah Knott (eds.), *Women, Gender, and Enlightenment* (London, 2005), pp. 30–52.

Tortarolo, Edoardo, 'La rivolta e le riforme. Appunti per una biografia intellettuale di Franco Venturi (1914–1994)', *Studi Settecenteschi*, 15 (1995), pp. 9–42.

L'Illuminismo. Ragioni e dubbi della modernità (Rome, 1999).

Trevor-Roper, H. R., 'George Buchanan and the ancient Scottish constitution', *English Historical Review*, Supplement 3 (1966).

'The Scottish Enlightenment', *Studies on Voltaire and the Eighteenth Century*, 68 (1967), pp. 1635–58.

Religion, the Reformation and Social Change (London, 1967; second edn 1972).

'Queen Elizabeth's first historian: William Camden', in Trevor-Roper, *Renaissance Essays* (London, 1985), pp. 121–48.

'Pietro Giannone and Great Britain', *The Historical Journal*, 39 (1996), pp. 657–75.

Tuck, Richard, *Philosophy and Government 1572–1671* (Cambridge, 1993).

Turco, Luigi, 'Moral sense and the foundations of morals', in Alexander Broadie (ed.), *The Cambridge Companion to the Scottish Enlightenment* (Cambridge, 2003), pp. 136–56.

Ultee, Martin, 'The Republic of Letters: learned correspondence 1680–1720', *The Seventeenth Century*, 2 (1987), pp. 95–112.

van der Zande, Johan, 'Prussia and the Enlightenment', in Philip G. Dwyer (ed.), *The Rise of Prussia 1700–1830* (Harlow, London, 2000), pp. 89–107.

Vaughan, Frederick, '*La Scienza Nuova*: orthodoxy and the art of writing', *Forum Italicum*, 2 (1968), pp. 332–58.

Venturi, Franco, *Jeunesse de Diderot (1713 à 1753)* (Paris, 1939).

Dalmazzo Francesco Vasco (1732–1794) (Paris, 1940).

Saggi sull'Europa illuminista. I: *Alberto Radicati di Passerano* (Turin, 1954).

'La circolazione delle idee', *Rassegna storica del Risorgimento*, 41 (1954), pp. 203–22.

Roots of Revolution: a History of the Populist and Socialist Movements in Nineteenth-century Russia (1952, English transl. F. H. Haskell, London, 1960).

Illuministi italiani. III: *Riformatori lombardi, piemontesi e toscani* (Milan and Naples, 1958). V: *Riformatori napoletani* (Milan and Naples, 1962); VII: *Riformatori delle antiche repubbliche, dei ducati, dello Stato Pontificio e delle isole* (Milan and Naples, 1965).

'Alle origini dell'illuminismo napoletano. Dal carteggio di Bartolomeo Intieri', *Rivista Storica Italiana*, 71 (1959), pp. 416–56.

'Galiani tra Enciclopedisti e fisiocratici', *Rivista Storica Italiana*, 72 (1960), pp. 45–64.

Settecento riformatore (Turin, 1969–1990) I: *Da Muratori a Beccaria 1730–1764* (1969); II: *La chiesa e la repubblica dentro i loro limiti 1758–1774* (1976); III *La prima crisi dell'Antico Regime 1768–1776* (1979); IV: *La caduta dell'Antico Regime 1776–1789, 1. I grandi stati dell'Occidente, 2. Il patriottismo repubblicano e gli imperi dell'Est* (1984); V: *L'Italia dei lumi 1764–1790, 1. La rivoluzione di Corsica; le grande carestie degli anni sessanta; La Lombardia delle riforme* (1987), *2. La repubblica di Venezia 1761–1797* (1990).

English translations of vols. III and IV (both parts), by R. Burr Litchfield, *The End of the Old Regime in Europe 1768–1776: the First Crisis* (Princeton, 1989); *The End of the Old Regime in Europe 1776–1789*, 2 vols. (Princeton, 1991).

Saggi preparatori per Settecento riformatore. L'Italia dei lumi: la Repubblica di Genova (1761–1797) (Accademia Nazionale dei Lincei, Rome, 2002).

Utopia and Reform in the Enlightenment (Cambridge, 1971).

'Napoli Capitale nel pensiero dei riformatore illuministi', in Aa. Vv., *Storia di Napoli*, vol. VIII (Naples, 1971), pp. 1–73.

Italy and the Enlightenment: Studies in a Cosmopolitan Century, ed. S. J. Woolf (London, 1972).

'Scottish echoes in eighteenth-century Italy', in Istvan Hont and Michael Ignatieff (eds.), *Wealth and Virtue: the Shaping of Political Economy in the Scottish Enlightenment* (Cambridge, 1983), pp. 345–62.

Vidal, Enrico, *Il pensiero civile di Paolo Mattia Doria negli scritti inediti* (Milan, 1953).

Villani, Pasquale, 'Il dibattito sulla feudalità nel Regno di Napoli dal Genovesi al Canosa', in E. Sestan (ed.), *Saggi e ricerche sul Settecento* (Naples, 1968), pp. 252–331.

Villari, Rosario, *Mezzogiorno e contadini nell'età moderna* (Bari, 1961).

La rivolta antispagnola a Napoli. Le origini (Rome and Bari, 1967); English transl. James Newell, *The Revolt of Naples* (Cambridge, 1993).

'Masaniello: contemporary and recent interpretations', *Past and Present*, 108 (1985), pp. 117–32; repr. in *The Revolt of Naples*, Afterword One.

Visceglia, Maria Antonietta, 'Un groupe social ambigu. Organisation, stratégies et representations de la noblesse napolitaine xvie–xviiie siècles', *Annales ESC*, 48 (4) (1993), pp. 819–51.

Voitle, Robert, *The Third Earl of Shaftesbury 1671–1713* (Baton Rouge and London, 1984).

Vries, Jan de, *European Urbanization 1500–1800* (London, 1984).

Vries, Jan de, and Woude, Ad van der, *The First Modern Economy: Success, Failure and Perseverance of the Dutch economy 1500–1815* (Cambridge, 1997).

Wade, Ira O., *The Clandestine Organisation and Diffusion of Philosophic Ideas in France from 1700 to 1750* (Princeton, 1938).

Wahnbaeck, Till, *Luxury and Public Happiness: Political Economy in the Italian Enlightenment* (Oxford, 2004).

Waquet, Françoise, 'Qu'est-ce que la République des Lettres? Essai de sémantique historique', *Bibliothèque de l'Ecole des chartes*, 147 (1989), pp. 473–502.

Watkins, J. W. N., *Hobbes's System of Ideas* (London, 1973).

Westerman, Pauline C., 'Hume and the natural lawyers: a change of landscape', in M. A. Stewart and J. P. Wright (eds.), *Hume and Hume's Connexions* (Edinburgh, 1994), pp. 83–104.

Whatley, Christopher A., 'Economic causes and consequences of the Union of 1707', *Scottish Historical Review*, 68 (1989), pp. 150–81.

'The Union of 1707, integration and the Scottish burghs: the case of the 1720 food riots', *Scottish Historical Review*, 78 (1999), pp. 192–218.

Scottish Society 1707–1830: beyond Jacobitism, towards Industrialisation (Manchester, 2000).

Bought and Sold for English Gold? Explaining the Union of 1707 (second edn, East Linton, 2001).

Whyte, Ian, *Agriculture and Society in Seventeenth-Century Scotland* (Edinburgh, 1979).

'The emergence of the new estate structure', in M. L. Parry and T. R. Slater (eds.), *The Making of the Scottish Countryside* (London, 1980), pp. 117–35.

Williamson, Arthur H., *Scottish National Consciousness in the Age of James VI* (Edinburgh, 1979).

'Number and national consciousness: the Edinburgh mathematicians and Scottish political culture at the union of the crowns', in Roger A. Mason (ed.), *Scots and Britons: Scottish Political Thought and the Union of 1603* (Cambridge, 1994), pp. 187–212.

Winch, Donald, *Riches and Poverty: an Intellectual History of Political Economy in Britain, 1750–1834* (Cambridge, 1996).

Wood, Paul, 'Science in the Scottish Enlightenment', in A. Broadie (ed.), *The Cambridge Companion to the Scottish Enlightenment* (Cambridge, 2003), pp. 94–116.

Woodward, Donald, 'A comparative study of the Irish and Scottish livestock trades in the seventeenth century', in L. M. Cullen and T. C. Smout (eds.), *Comparative Aspects of Scottish and Irish Economic and Social History* (Edinburgh, 1977), pp. 147–64.

Wootton, David, 'Hume's "Of Miracles": probability and irreligion', in M. A. Stewart (ed.), *Studies in the Philosophy of the Scottish Enlightenment* (Oxford, 1990), pp. 191–229.

'Pierre Bayle, Libertine?', in M. A. Stewart (ed.), *Studies in Eighteenth-Century European Philosophy* (Oxford, 1997), pp. 197–226.

Wright, Johnson Kent, '"A bright clear mirror": Cassirer's *Philosophy of the Enlightenment*', in K. M. Baker and P. H. Reill (eds.), *What's Left of Enlightenment? A Postmodern Question* (Stanford, 2001), pp. 71–101.

Wrigley, E. A., *People, Cities and Wealth: the Transformation of Traditional Society* (Oxford, 1987).

Yolton, J. W. and others (eds.), *The Blackwell Companion to the Enlightenment* (Oxford, 1991).

Young, Brian W., *Religion and Enlightenment in Eighteenth-century England: Theological Debate from Locke to Burke* (Oxford, 1998).

Youngson, A. J., *After the 'Forty-Five: the Economic Impact on the Scottish Highlands* (Edinburgh, 1973).

Zambelli, Paola, *La formazione filosofica di Antonio Genovesi* (Naples, 1972).

DISSERTATIONS

Mijers, Esther, 'Scotland and the United Provinces c. 1680–1730: a study in intellectual and educational relations', University of St Andrews doctoral thesis (2002).

Rogers, Ben, 'In Praise of Vanity: the Augustinian analysis of the benefits of vice from Port-Royal to Mandeville', University of Oxford doctoral thesis (1994).

Stapelbroek, Koen, 'Moral philosophy in Ferdinando Galiani's early political economy', University of Cambridge doctoral thesis (2004).

Timperley, Loretta, 'Landownership in Scotland in the eighteenth century', University of Edinburgh doctoral thesis (1977).

Index

IDEAS IN CONTEXT

Edited by QUENTIN SKINNER,
and JAMES TULLY

Printed in the United Kingdom
by Lightning Source UK Ltd.
121118UK00001B/135